Maya Christians
and Their Churches
in Sixteenth-Century Belize

MAYA STUDIES

UNIVERSITY PRESS OF FLORIDA
Florida A&M University, Tallahassee
Florida Atlantic University, Boca Raton
Florida Gulf Coast University, Ft. Myers
Florida International University, Miami
Florida State University, Tallahassee
New College of Florida, Sarasota
University of Central Florida, Orlando
University of Florida, Gainesville
University of North Florida, Jacksonville
University of South Florida, Tampa
University of West Florida, Pensacola

Elizabeth Graham

MAYA CHRISTIANS
AND THEIR CHURCHES
IN SIXTEENTH-CENTURY BELIZE

UNIVERSITY PRESS OF FLORIDA

Gainesville · Tallahassee · Tampa · Boca Raton
Pensacola · Orlando · Miami · Jacksonville
Ft. Myers · Sarasota

Library of Congress Cataloging-in-Publication Data
Graham, Elizabeth A., 1949–
Maya Christians and their churches in sixteenth-century Belize / Elizabeth Graham.
p. cm.
Includes bibliographical references and index.
ISBN 978-0-8130-3666-3 (cloth : alk. paper)
ISBN 978-0-8130-6816-9 (pbk.)
1. Mayas—Belize—Religion. 2. Mayas—Missions—Belize. 3. Mayas—Belize—
Antiquities. 4. Indian Catholics—Belize—History—16th century. 5. Franciscans—
Missions—Belize—History—16th century. 6. Christianity and other cultures—
Belize—History—16th century. 7. Excavations (Archaeology)—Belize. 8. Social
archaeology—Belize. 9. Belize—Antiquities. I. Title.
F1435.3.R3G73 2011
282.'7282089974209031—dc22   2011011290

The University Press of Florida is the scholarly publishing agency for the State
University System of Florida, comprising Florida A&M University, Florida Atlantic
University, Florida Gulf Coast University, Florida International University, Florida
State University, New College of Florida, University of Central Florida, University of
Florida, University of North Florida, University of South Florida, and University of
West Florida.

University Press of Florida
2046 NE Waldo Road
Suite 2100
Gainesville, FL 32609
http://upress.ufl.edu

*This book is dedicated to the memory of
Elinor Melville, the best of friends
and the most supportive of colleagues.
It is my hope that her spirit is now
at peace in Tlayacapan, and that
I will always find her there.*

Contents

List of Figures *ix*

List of Maps *xiii*

Acknowledgments *xv*

Introduction *1*

Part I

1 · The View from Belize and the
Vision from St. Mike's *9*

2 · Yucatan and Belize on the Eve of Conquest *29*

3 · Cheese and Terms *59*

4 · Being Christian and the Doctrine of
the Church *86*

Part II

5 · The Environment of Early Contact *105*

6 · The Millennial Kingdom and the
Belize Missions *137*

Part III

7 · How to Tell a Church *167*

8 · The Churches at Tipu and Lamanai *189*

9 · Reductions and Upheaval in the
Seventeenth Century *239*

Part IV

10 · What Europe Did for Us *263*

11 · Being Pagan *285*

12 · Everyone Knows What a Dragon
Looks Like *307*

APPENDIX 1 · Friars in Belize *314*

APPENDIX 2 · Bishops of Yucatan to 1714 *323*

Notes *325*

Glossary of Terms *375*

References Cited *385*

Index *415*

Figures

0.1. Belize Maya chronology 2

1.1. Tipu, reconstruction of main plaza 19

1.2. Tipu, remains of Str. H12-18 20

1.3. Tipu, burials cut through Str. H12-18 20

1.4. Church of St. Michael the Archangel 21

1.5. Church of St. Michael the Archangel, main entrance 22

1.6. Tipu, glass bead bracelet 23

1.7. Tipu, glass bead necklace with jet 24

1.8. Tipu, Nueva Cadiz plain glass beads 24

1.9. Tipu, earrings from burials 24

1.10. Tipu, church burial 25

1.11. "Holy Picture" of San Martín de Porres 26

2.1. Kuuchkabal of Canul 31

2.2. Lamanai, glyphs from Stela 9 41

2.3. Chronology for Lamanai and Tipu 49

2.4. Lamanai, Yglesias-phase pottery 51

6.1. Aztec Templo Mayor, eighteenth-century print 146

6.2. Tipu, thurible (censer) from burial 154

6.3. Plan, single-nave Jeronymite church at Yuste, Spain 159

7.1. Tipu, reconstruction drawing church 169

7.2. Lamanai, stone chapel of YDL II 169

7.3. Ecab, perspective reconstruction drawing of the church 171

7.4. Schematic, open-air church 173

7.5. Dzibilchaltun, perspective reconstruction drawing of
     the church 174

7.6. Plan of St. Martin's church, Exeter, Devon 177

7.7. Traditional layout of Western church 177

7.8. Chapel components of Yucatecan churches 178

7.9. St. Andrew's Old Church, Upleatham, near Cleveland,
     North Yorkshire 179

8.1. Tipu, excavated remains of the church 191

8.2. Lamanai, YDL I looking southeast *193*

8.3. Lamanai, perspective reconstruction cutaway drawing of YDL I *205*

8.4. Lamanai, perspective reconstruction cutaway drawing of YDL II *206*

8.5. Lamanai, Str. N11-18 *206*

8.6. Lamanai, burials from YDL II cemetery *209*

8.7. Lamanai, Str. N12-12, rectory *209*

8.8. Lamanai, plan of church-zone buildings and features *210*

8.9. Lamanai, masonry chapel of YDL II with ruins of Str. N12-12, rectory *211*

8.10. Lamanai, nave area of YDL II *212*

8.11. Lamanai, censer fragments from centerline posthole *213*

8.12. Lamanai, effigy vessel from beneath Stela 4, YDL II *214*

8.13. Lamanai, effigy vessel from YDL II, north part of nave *214*

8.14. Lamanai, face cups and frog effigy vessels, YDL II *215*

8.15. Lamanai, animal effigy placed during construction of YDL I *215*

8.16. Lamanai, "shark" effigy cache and contents, found by Thomas Gann *216*

8.17. Lamanai, plan of YDL I *218*

8.18. Lamanai, centipede-lobster cache from YDL I, in situ *219*

8.19. Lamanai, centipede-lobster cache and contents *220*

8.20. Lamanai, atrio of YDL I during excavation *222*

8.21. Lamanai, YDL I and atrio after reconstruction *222*

8.22. Lamanai, effigy vessel from Str. N12-12, rectory *223*

8.23. Tipu, plan and section of the church, Str. H12-13 *225*

8.24. Tipu, perspective reconstruction cutaway drawing of the church *226*

8.25. Tipu, lock plate from a chest, Str. H12-7 *227*

8.26. Tipu, church nave feature *229*

8.27. Tipu, needles from church burials *234*

8.28. Tipu, thurible (censer) from church burial *234*

8.29. Lamanai, rosary of bone beads, YDL I *235*

8.30. Tipu, pottery maskette from Str. H12-7 *237*

9.1. Tipu, Yglesias-phase-style pottery vessel from Str. H12-14 *242*

9.2. Tipu, olive jar with stamped rim *242*

9.3. Tipu, examples of small side-notched points (arrowheads) from surface deposits *253*

9.4. Tipu, Lacandon-type censer fragment, Str. H12-18, the rectory *257*

10.1.a–e. The mouth of hell in European art *266*

10.2. Man emerging from a snail shell, from a sixteenth-century painting *268*

10.3. Late Classic Maya pottery vessel of a man emerging from a shell *268*

10.4. Lamanai, pottery vessel of a man (or deity) emerging from a shell *269*

10.5. a–e. Images of the Devil *270*

10.6. Image of an angel smoking, from a Delft tile *272*

10.7. Modern idols: Teddy bears *274*

10.8. "Idols of Campeche and Yucatan" *275*

11.1. St. Francis preaching to the birds *292*

11.2. St. Lazarus the beggar with dogs, from a votive candle *292*

11.3. St. Dominic, the founder of the Dominican order *293*

11.4. St. Martha and the dragon *293*

11.5. St. Michael the archangel, in medieval armor, defeating the Devil *302*

11.6. St. Michael the archangel, in Roman military garb, defeating the Devil *302*

11.7. Angel of the abyss and the infernal locusts, from the *Girona Beatus*, 10th century *303*

11.8. Guardian angel and children *304*

12.1. The mandarin of Wu and his court advisors *311*

12.2. Han and the great Cloud Dragon *312*

Maps

1.1. The Maya area showing modern boundaries and the locations of Tipu and Lamanai in Belize *13*

2.1a–d. Versions of pre-Conquest Maya provincial boundaries *32*

2.2. Roys's Chetumal province *48*

2.3. Major Spanish-period sites in northern Belize *53*

2.4. Peten lake communities and Tipu *54*

3.1. Two provinces called "Maya" in the sixteenth century *60*

5.1. Yucatan and the Bay of Honduras in the Conquest period *108*

5.2. The Caribbean Basin *110*

5.3. Map of the Kingdom of Guatemala between 1570 and 1650 *112*

5.4. Dudley's "Carta Prima Generale," 1646–47 *113*

5.5. Sanson map of Yucatan and the Gulf of Honduras, 1650, 1670 *114*

5.6. Blaeu map of Yucatan, 1665 *114*

5.7. Wytfliet map of Yucatan, 1597 *115*

5.8. Visscher map of Yucatan, the Gulf of Honduras, and the Kingdom of Guatemala, 1717 *115*

5.9. Belize and details of the coastal zone, cayes, atolls, rivers, and modern district boundaries *117*

8.1. Lamanai church zone, map square N12 *200*

8.2. Lamanai showing central and northern precincts *201*

8.3. Tipu town center during the Spanish colonial period *202*

9.1. Location of colonial-period communities in northern Belize, the upper Belize River, and adjacent Peten *241*

Acknowledgments

I am indebted to the Institute of Archaeology in Belize, formerly the Department of Archaeology, for permission to investigate the sites of Tipu and Lamanai and for allowing me to carry out archaeological investigations in the country. My deepest thanks go to the archaeological commissioners and acting commissioners who supported my work over the years: Joseph Palacio, the late Harriot Topsey, the late Winnel Branche, Allan Moore, George Thompson, John Morris, and Jaime Awe. In recent years, John Morris, as Associate Director of Research, and Jaime Awe, as Director of the Institute, have been especially helpful in encouraging cooperative projects at Lamanai that integrate archaeology, development, and local economic and educational initiatives. Without Brian Woodye and George Thompson the Lamanai Reserve would not be the productive setting it has become, in which park management, planning, archaeological investigation, tourism, and local involvement are so well integrated. Sherilyne Jones, Melissa Badillo, and the Institute staff have contributed in major ways to making all our efforts as productive as possible.

The making of this book would not have been possible without the award of a British Academy Readership that permitted me to carry out the research and writing from 2005 to 2007. I am eternally grateful to the academy for providing me with this opportunity.

I am also deeply thankful to the Dumbarton Oaks Research Library, in Washington, D.C., for awarding me a fellowship in 2007–8, which enabled me to devote attention to analysis and interpretation of recent archaeological data from Lamanai related to the church period, and to a range of data on community architecture and settlement. Some of the results are reported here, and some will be published in a succeeding volume. I benefited not only from the presence of Americanists but also from the work being carried out by Byzantine and landscape scholars. I thank the Director of Pre-Columbian Studies, Joanne Pillsbury, and the entire staff for their support. I wish also to express my appreciation to the staff of the Library of Congress, particularly

Anthony Mullan of the Geography and Map Division, for help in my research on early maps.

My excavations at Tipu were funded by the Social Sciences and Humanities Research Council of Canada (SSHRC) and the National Geographic Society while I held postdoctoral fellowships from the Tinker Foundation and SSHRC. SSHRC also provided funding for the analysis of Tipu and Lamanai faunal remains. York University, in North York, Ontario, Canada, provided an SSHRC grant through the university that enabled Sharon Bennett and me to produce the finished plans of the burials at Tipu. The Royal Ontario Museum kindly helped with field research through a grant from the Committee for Field Archaeology, and fully supported a range of laboratory and database research. I also thank my colleagues in the Department of Anthropology at York for their support and friendship over the years.

My excavations at Lamanai, which have focused on periods of transition, have been supported by the British Academy, SSHRC, the National Geographic Society, University College London, the Institute of Archaeology, and the Central Research Fund of the University of London. The discovery of new features of the church zone in 2008 was made possible by a contingency grant from the Foundation for the Advancement of Mesoamerican Studies, Inc. (FAMSI), in addition to major support from the U.S. embassy through the Institute of Archaeology in Belize, and through generous funding by Claude Belanger.

There are so many people who contributed to the success of the Tipu and Lamanai investigations that I fear I will be unable to name them all. First and foremost, I am deeply grateful to architect Claude Belanger and artist and illustrator Louise Belanger for being my friends and collaborators in both endeavors. It is no exaggeration to say that, without them, much of the excavation and what I have made of the excavation results would not have been possible. With regard to Tipu, I admit that I would not have excavated the site had I not been persuaded to do so by Grant Jones, who carried out documentary research on both Tipu and Lamanai, and by my husband David Pendergast, who began the excavations at Lamanai. David had originally been attracted to Lamanai owing to the presence of its "Indian church," and this stimulated Grant to consider trying to find other mission churches in Belize. Without Grant's findings and assistance, my research would not have proceeded, and I am grateful for his feedback over the years. David Pendergast gave me the opportunity to work at Lamanai, and without his insight, cooperation, and willingness to provide extensive feedback, including proofreading my manuscript, this book would not have come into being.

The research on the Tipu population owes its major findings to Mark Cohen and his team, under the aegis of the State University of New York at

Plattsburgh. Cohen and his associates have published and continue to publish extensively on the results of their studies of the Tipu burial population. Keith Jacobi has published his research on the genetic structure of the Tipu population, and Marie Danforth and her students continue their studies of the skeletal population. Prudence Rice, Leslie Cecil, and Jim Aimers spearheaded and continue to contribute to innovative ceramic studies, and Timothy Pugh to research on architecture. With regard to the excavations under my direction, I am indebted to site supervisors Sharon Bennett, Susan Reynolds Dermarkar, Juliette Gerhardt, Luis Godoy, Kitty Emery, Ruben Penados, Tino Penados, Stuart Speaker, Scott Simmons, and Sylviano Uck. Kevin Baxter and Tom Jamieson, who worked at Tipu with Bob Kautz, generously shared their findings. The team at Negroman-Tipu also included José Alfaro, Ann Bianco, Eduardo Cohuoj, Roberto Cohuoj, Venancio Chi, Oscar Chulín, Ventura Cocom, Leslie Cohen, Guadalupe Cunil, Reynaldo Cunil, Virgilio Godoy, Marcos Godoy, Francisco Gongora, Karla Heusner, the late Daniel Itza, Felicito Itza, Javier Itza, Luis Itza, Manuel Itza, Rudy Itza, Mark Jackson, Tom Jamison, Davíd Lobos, Ramiro Mai, Brian McIntosh, Marina Pinto Miller, Elfego Pantí, Lionel Pantí, Luis Pantí, Rosalio Penados, Filiberto Penados, Gliss Penados, Junior (Rosalio) Penados, Salvador Penados, Guadalupe Sánchez (Doña Lupa), Leslie Johannsen Simmons, the late Gilberto Uck, Féliz Uck, José Uck, Mónico Uck, Rene Uck, Felipe Valencia, Raul Valencia, Marta Vanegas, Orlando Vanegas, Andrea Vásquez, and Marta Vásquez. Carl Armstrong, Dan Bancroft, Marie Danforth, Keith Jacobi, and others worked with Mark Cohen on the burials, along with a range of individuals whose surnames I've lost track of: Jean, Phil, Carrie, Denton, Fred, and Margaret. The most interesting thing about the Tipu team is how many of the Maya names match the names of the sixteenth- and seventeenth-century Maya who appear in this book.

Lamanai investigations into the Late Postclassic and the Spanish and British colonial periods have received assistance from many quarters. My deep thanks go to Mark Howells and Lamanai Outpost Lodge for their continual help and support. Blanca Manzanilla and the hotel staff, among them Ruben Arévalo, Marvi Murillos, Marina Arévalo, Mirna Reyes, Mauricio Aguilar, Arturo Santos, and Doña Ophelia Zepeda and her staff, have been unfailing in their help. Thanks also go to the people of the villages of Indian Church and San Carlos: Oscar Ruano, Jorge Vásquez, Nazario Ku and family, Antonio and Blanca Esquivel and family, Dona Olivia Gonzales, the Las Orquideas women's cooperative, and all the others who help us every year to make the project a success.

As is the case with Tipu, digging at Lamanai was not my idea, but somehow I got started, with Laura Howard as my collaborator from the beginning. In addition to assisting in all aspects of the excavations and recording, she has acted as lab director; has designed the major elements of the field school; and has spearheaded public outreach, education, and community projects in the nearby village of Indian Church. Without the efforts of another member of the project, Karen Pierce, the Indian Church Village Artisans Cooperative and the present schools programs would not exist. Linda Howie is my right-hand person in all things Maya and is the individual with whom I exchange and generate ideas. Norbert Stanchley makes sure that Lamanai remains a top priority, and indeed the entire team at Lamanai have been terrific: co-Principal Investigator Scott Simmons, Jim Aimers, Kip Andres, Jenny John, Meredith Martinez, Tracie Mayfield, Richard Meadows, Terry Powis, Mark Shelby, Lorena Stanchley, Darcy Wiewall, and from the Institute of Archaeology in Belize, Jorge Kan and his team.

Support from the Institute of Archaeology, University College London, has never flagged. The late Peter Ucko and the present director, Stephen Shennan, have encouraged my research, as have my colleagues and students, who also make the Institute a great place in which to work. Special thanks to Stuart Laidlaw, who cooperated with Simon Martin and David Pendergast in making a photographic record of the Lamanai monuments, funded by the British Academy.

With regard to the completion of this book, I am indebted to a range of individuals. Three official reviewers read my manuscript and offered advice: Rani Alexander, Fernando Cervantes, and a third, anonymous, individual. There are also many who read the manuscript in its various stages, or read parts of it, or advised me on various topics, and others who helped with various editing or referencing tasks: David Pendergast, Grant Jones, Anthony Andrews, Elizabeth Baquedano, Oliver Boles, Leslie Cecil, Joyce Clements, Marie Danforth, Christophe Helmke, Keith Jacobi, Kitty Emery, Shirley Mock, Tsubasa Okoshi Harada, Conall Pendergast, Tessa Robinson, Kay Tarble, Lorraine Williams-Beck, and Claudia Zehrt.

As you see, this book rests on a foundation of help from many people in many places at many times. I am solely responsible for the volume's content, but I hope that all those I have named will feel that they have taken part in its gestation, and that they will be pleased with the result of our joint effort.

Maya Christians
and Their Churches
in Sixteenth-Century Belize

Introduction

When piety meets politics it can be a volatile mix.
—Christiane Amanpour, *The Observer Television*,
August 2007

The Christianity of sixteenth-century Europe came to the Maya of Belize in two major ways. The first, and better known, comprises the efforts of Spanish friars and clergy to convert the Maya to Christianity as part of a larger plan of imperial domination by Spain. The second is rarely considered significant, but must surely have figured in Maya deliberations about what it meant to be Christian. As Belize communities became more and more "frontier" relative to developing centers of power in Yucatan, Guatemala, and lower Central America, the Maya of these communities became more and more vulnerable to non-Spanish Christians: the British, French, Dutch, and other European seafarers, legal or otherwise, who plied the Caribbean, preyed on Spanish shipping, and carried on slaving well into the early eighteenth century. Historical sources tell us that British activity in Belize dates from the seventeenth century, but evidence suggests overwhelmingly (see chapter 5) that knowledge of Belize's fluctuating coastline—its shallow coastal shelf, barrier reef, and cayes—was built on many decades of sailing experience and ships pilots' detailed records. Thus, it is entirely reasonable to consider that non-Spanish activities, or at least activities unrelated to official Spanish imperial expansion, had repercussions for Belize as early as the sixteenth century (see fig. 0.1).

It is the Spanish encounter with which this book is concerned, owing to the fact that the ruined churches which we excavated at Lamanai and Tipu are the historical product of this encounter. Nonetheless, the nature of the challenges faced by the Maya of Belize extended beyond what the Spanish Christians alone would generate. Even if my proposal about sixteenth-century raids on the Belize coast is regarded with scepticism, there is no doubt that the kinds of Christianity that characterized Europe in the sixteenth century

BELIZE MAYA CHRONOLOGY

Period	Approximate calendar dates
Independence	1981 to present
Self-governing British Crown Colony	1964 to 1981
British Crown Colony	1862-1964
British colonial settlement	1660s to 1862
Spanish colonial	1544 to 1648/1708 (Spanish sovereignty claimed to 1798)
Terminal Postclassic/Contact	1450/1492 to 1544
Late Postclassic	1350 to 1450/1492
Middle Postclassic	1200/1250 to 1350
Early Postclassic	1000 to 1200/1250
Terminal Classic (Maya collapse)	800 to 1000
Late Classic	600 to 800
Middle Classic	450 to 600
Early Classic	250 to 450
Terminal Preclassic	100 B.C. to A.D. 250
Late Preclassic	400 B.C. to 100 B.C.
Middle Preclassic	900 B.C. to 400 B.C.
Early Preclassic	1500 B.C. to 900 B.C.
Archaic	pre-1500 B.C.

Figure 0.1. Belize Maya chronology.

deeply affected events in the Maya lowlands of Belize. This includes the late medieval Christianity of the mendicant friars, with its attendant energy, engagement, and optimism; the authoritarian Christianity that developed in response to the concerns of the Council of Trent; and the radical reform that led to what has come to be called Protestantism. All of these Christianities reached Belize, and to the extent that this book deals with them, it can be called a study of religion.

On the other hand, I devote considerable effort to describing the problems that arise in assuming that "religion" is a viable concept (see chapter 3). Perhaps it is safer to say that the book is about people in Maya communities in Belize who came to call themselves Christians in the sixteenth century, in particular the inhabitants of the towns of Tipu and Lamanai (see map 1.1).

These communities remained active in the seventeenth century, but it was during the pivotal years of the sixteenth century that the Maya encountered, learned about, weighed, wrestled with, and appropriated Christian thought and ideas. Even though historical conditions would change, in terms of diminishing Spanish activity, the encounter with Christianity was pervasive and its impact long-term. In fact, the impetus behind the writing of this book was the recovery of archaeological evidence which suggested that the Maya inhabitants of Tipu and Lamanai considered themselves Christians and remained Christian even in the absence of church or civil authority.

In the chapters that follow, I examine the evidence for how and why the Maya converted to Christianity in the region of Mesoamerica now known as Belize. The "when" we already know, at least in broad outline: the time of Spanish colonization of the New World in the sixteenth century. The "how" and "why" questions—about precisely what constituted conversion or what Spanish colonizers thought conversion would lead to—necessitate turning to the experience of the missionary encounter elsewhere in Mesoamerica, and even elsewhere in the world. This broadened spatial dimension is complemented by extension of the dimension of time, because the Christianization of Europe in Late Antiquity and the Early Middle Ages, from about the fourth to the tenth century A.D., turns out to be highly relevant to an understanding of how people "became Christian." The contemporary Western world and the history of its expansion are rooted in the process by which indigenous Europeans came to claim themselves as Christian. Although what constituted being Christian differed through time and in space, between interest groups, and especially among individuals, "claiming" Christianity in Mesoamerica and Late Antique Europe was a key process that affected reconfigurations of identity, kin, and tributary (economic) allegiances as well as landscape.

With regard to the towns in the land that became Belize, my thesis is that the Maya remained Christian in the absence of Spanish authority because they saw themselves as Christian. It has been argued that conversion was a matter of survival, or was incomplete (see chapter 11), but these arguments entail two faulty assumptions. The first is that Maya individuals were not interested or intelligent enough to separate the message from the medium; and the second is that the Christian belief of the time was readily apparent to an observer—to someone from Tipu, let's say—as qualitatively different from extant beliefs prior to the arrival of the Spaniards. In particular, I challenge the idea that Christianity was never properly assimilated by the Maya, mainly because what has been considered to be "proper" is problematic.

I first laid out some of these ideas on Maya encounters with the Christian world view in a paper presented to the Society for Historical Archaeology in 1992, when I was engaged in analyzing the results of the excavations at Tipu.

Since then, I have been able to add information derived from investigations at Lamanai, both my own and those of David Pendergast. For my arguments concerning the intensity and depth of Maya coastal interaction I have been able to draw on my excavations of coastal sites in Belize in the 1970s, and including work carried out in 1986 and between 1990 and 1993. The ideas and insights which are presented in this book are, however, not new to anthropology or in history; they have simply arisen in a new context in which archaeology adds another dimension. I like to think that, in the words of Clifford Geertz, I simply "plunge more deeply into the same things."[1] In doing so, I do not claim that archaeology is any better or more direct a tool than anthropology or history. My hope, rather, is to be seen to bring archaeological evidence to bear fruitfully not only on the topic of Maya-Spanish interaction in the colonial encounter but also on the processes of conversion in particular, and on what is often called "religious change."

Whatever the reception to my ideas, the descriptions of the archaeological remains of the churches and their associated finds at Tipu and Lamanai form a useful addition to our knowledge of Maya activities during the early years of Christianization. I am presently at work on a second volume, which presents architectural plans and sections as well as descriptions of the church zone excavations. In this first volume I have allowed my interest to stray beyond the bounds of description, to consider what the discoveries can tell us about changes in Maya beliefs in the early colonial period. At the same time, I have tried to present the material remains in a manner that will allow others to interpret the data independently.

The volume is divided into four parts. Part I consists of the chapters that cover the context of analysis: my approach to the data (chapter 1); the period before Contact (chapter 2); the terminology we use in describing religious behavior and its implications (chapter 3); and what it means to be Christian (chapter 4). Chapter 2, which discusses Yucatan and Belize on the eve of Conquest, draws heavily on the literature of archaeology and ethnohistory and will not always make sense to those outside the field of Maya studies. The chapter does not bear on discussions of the meaning of Christianity but is important in understanding the political and economic organization that provided the context for the colonial encounter and its aftermath, including the Christianization process. The colonial and modern Maya are commonly seen as divided by a deep chasm from the Maya widely known through towering ruins in tropical forests; chapter 2 attempts to bridge this gap, but also to lay to rest a number of myths about the pre-Columbian Maya which the Spaniards believed and called upon in order to legitimize their actions.

Part II comprises coverage of the critical dynamics that affected the Maya-European encounter in Belize. Chapter 5 focuses on the currents of change in Yucatan, Mexico, and Central America in the early sixteenth century and the implications for the Maya communities of Belize; the chapter also draws attention to the Belize Maya as part of a coastal band of interaction in which maritime travel, trade, and exchange had considerable time depth and generated a distinctive socio-cultural sphere. This, and the distinctive environmental setting represented by Belize's coast, cayes, and atolls, deeply affected the course of the Mayas' encounter with Europeans, in ways that have been overshadowed by scholars' concerns with what was happening in Guatemala, Yucatan, and Mexico. Chapter 6 provides background that is meant to help explain the drive and agendas of the Franciscans who were so instrumental in the dynamics of conversion in Belize. The mendicant orders in the New World have been intensively studied by historians, and I add no newly discovered documentary information. My contribution is to integrate the information gleaned from the documents with my knowledge derived from new archaeological discoveries, for the specific purpose of illuminating the history of the land that became Belize.

Part III consists of three chapters and turns from a concern with historical background to consider the material culture of conquest and conversion. Chapter 7 grapples with how churches have been described in colonial Mesoamerica, and with the problems that have arisen in emphasizing typologies. Chapter 8 and chapter 9 describe the discoveries from the perspectives of Tipu and Lamanai. I assume that not all readers are familiar with Grant Jones's seminal *Maya Resistance to Spanish Rule*,[2] which describes the colonial encounter in Belize on the basis of documentary research. I therefore take time in the two chapters to contextualize the archaeological discoveries by describing what we know from the documents about the arrival of the Spaniards in Belize, the establishment of *visita* churches, and the awarding to the Spaniards of *encomiendas*—grants to particular Spaniards of Maya labor and tribute. I have kept archaeological and ethnohistorical data separate, and I trust that referencing makes the sources of information clear.

Part IV introduces information beyond that presented in earlier chapters and uses the information as the basis for an assessment of the impact of Christianity. Chapter 10 examines aspects of the Christianization of Europe and draws from this to shed light on what happened in Belize. Chapter 11 considers what it means to be "pagan." Chapter 12 assesses scholarly and other debates about "religion" and archaeology's role in this process.

Terms which might not be known to all readers are defined in the glossary. These include Spanish terms for offices and people, archaeological terms, and terms used in anthropology which might differ from the dictionary definition or vary from practices in other disciplines. I normally use the term "colonial" to refer to the period following Columbian contact, although based on general practice I sometimes use the term "historic." I should note that Mayanists are moving away from using "historic" to distinguish the period after Columbian contact because the Maya have a long tradition of written history, a fact that makes Western, European-based distinctions, such as historic versus prehistoric, irrelevant. Where I refer to pre-Columbian Maya periods, such as the Classic or Postclassic, figure 0.1 provides details of chronology.

I sometimes use the term "Mayas" rather than "Maya" in cases in which I would like the reader to think in terms of individuals rather than of the group itself. This is admittedly an awkward term, but without knowing what the Maya from different towns or cities or areas called themselves, or without knowledge of individuals' names, it is an attempt to emphasize the individual over the group. In addition to using the term "Maya" (see chapter 3), I refer to other Mesoamerican cultural or language groups. I use "Aztec" to refer to the people who constituted the empire that the Spaniards faced upon their arrival in central Mexico, but I sometimes use "Nahuas" for the same people when I want to refer to Nahuatl-speakers as opposed to Maya speakers. See the glossary for details. None of these terms is adequate to express the diversity of languages and cultures that characterized Mesoamerica; they serve mainly to distinguish indigenous Americans from Europeans. Where I use "Indian," or "*indio*," it is normally with reference to the term as it appears in Spanish documents, although chroniclers sometimes also use "*naturales*."

Where I employ Spanish-language words or names, accents are used, but where I use Maya-language or Nahuatl words written in the Roman alphabet, I do not use the accents common in the Spanish-speaking world, because these words are not Spanish in origin. An exception is the word "Yucatán," but the accent here is used only when referring to the Mexican state. With regard to Maya names used in modern Belize, the situation is a bit more complicated, as can be seen in the acknowledgments. My use of accents there is based on knowledge of the individuals involved and whether it is their practice to use accents in their names. With regard to other non-English-language words, such as *encomienda, encomendero, visita,* or *cah,* among others, for those which I use frequently, I italicize the word at first usage but then cease italicizing in the remainder of the text. All translations not otherwise noted are mine. All photographs not otherwise acknowledged were taken by me or David Pendergast.

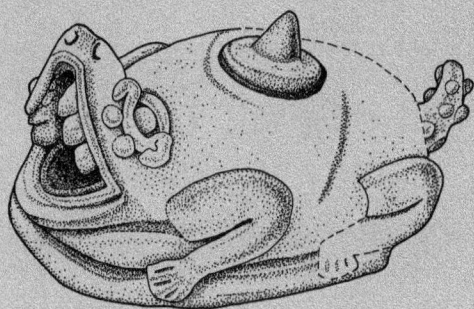

✛ ONE ✛

The View from
Belize and the Vision
from St. Mike's

As someone who was raised as a Roman Catholic, I found the exploration of early Christianity to be a process of self-discovery. Despite all my academic training, I never considered critically that what I had been taught to believe as a child had a history. In any intellectual discourse I would never have denied that ideas had histories, yet I had never applied this awareness to the very context in which I presumed to understand the Maya and the Spanish Conquest. On the surface of it, I had remained satisfied all these years that I was approaching archaeology and prehistory critically. I believed that, like the Franciscan friars, I knew what Christianity constituted, that there was such a thing as being pagan, that idols continued to be important to the Maya, and that "religion" was a real concept and not a product of culture and history.

In the following chapters I question these assumptions in the hope of contributing to alternative perspectives on what in our own times is described as "religious conflict." I also ask questions about pictures and images as forms of communication and misunderstanding, and why pictures can mean different things to different people. Pictures, images, or stylistic elements can be seen as means of aesthetic expression and therefore as art,[1] or they can be seen to tell a story, in which case the question of whether or not the images are art is secondary, or even a non-issue, depending on the viewer or the context. These different views or readings are sometimes difficult to distinguish or disentangle.[2]

Would things have been better or worse for the Maya if their images—their murals, wood carvings, and ceramic figurines—had been seen as art? When the Spanish friars preached in Mesoamerica, they did not see—or chose not to see—Maya or Aztec pictures, sculptures, books, carved monuments, or statuary as art. If they had, it is possible that a greater number of objects would have been saved. According to one sixteenth-century friar, destroying antiquities was justified, "porque cabe la supervivencia de la idolatría y consiguiente ruina de las almas, vale muy poco el monumento de piedra, de palo o de oro. A cristianizar, no a recoger materiales para museos" (because the survival of idolatry means the ruin of souls, monuments of stone or wood or gold are worth little. [We are here] to Christianize, not to collect materials for museums).[3]

On the other hand, "art" can also be described as a generalizing concept of modernity, the vocabulary of which has been used to justify the appropriation, and sometimes even theft, of the images, and hence the ideas of "the other,"[4] a factor which contributes to the other's powerlessness.[5]

As regards art telling stories, the Spanish Christians assumed they knew the stories that Maya objects were telling, and those in power used their readings as the justification for destroying the objects. They relied on their own cultural and personal frameworks to "explain" what Maya objects stood for. Similarly, the Maya were led to believe—and probably did indeed believe—that they understood what stories the Spanish pictures and images were telling, because the Spanish friars recounted the tales, reinforced with imagery, in the process of conversion. Like the Spaniards, and indeed like all of us, the Maya brought context, cultural or otherwise, to the reading of imagery.

How did the reading of imagery (and by this I mean representation in any medium) as stories affect interpretation on both sides? This question is an important one. What complicates matters is that despite the fact that conversion dynamics turned on the way stories were "read" or understood through imagery, scholars who discuss or describe Maya or European artifacts, particularly artifacts that display modification in the form of iconography or representation, commonly approach the material as "art";[6] or, in the case of archaeologists, artifacts become part of what we call "material culture."[7] Both these designations assign what people see (an image or a figurine) to a category that has nothing to do with the significance of what is represented.

In the Western scholarly tradition, classification of imagery or representation as art has generally provided the intellectual rationale for studying (and collecting) things. Archaeology characteristically embraces the study of imagery and representation as material culture. Does "material culture" bring us any closer than does "art" to the meaning of the objects? Do we know what generated the representations? Even if we devise ways—which we find satisfactory through our disciplinary approaches—to answer these questions regarding an ancient Maya object or image, should we not at the same time recognize explicitly that the level at which the concept of "material culture" operates or the level at which "art" operates has more to do with the object or image as part of *our* culture and history than as part of Maya culture and history?[8] Hans Belting has observed that "art history . . . simply declared everything to be art in order to bring everything within its domain,"[9] and we could say the same about archaeology and material culture.[10]

The recognition of limits to knowing can be interpreted as negative and self-defeating, but being critical about what we think we know—and by this I mean *how* we go about knowing—is as important as being critical about what we know. Archaeologists—and perhaps art historians and historians, too—remain more comfortable as critics of each other's readings or interpretations of the world than of the effects of our disciplinary standpoints as descriptions of the world. I hope to show that the practice of contextualizing—and thereby periodically undermining—our own standpoints[11] is not self-defeating but instead leads to new insights, to greater flexibility intellectually,[12] and even, for the scientifically minded, to a wider range of testable hypotheses.

An example of contextualizing that seems to undermine an approach to knowledge building can be seen through examination of the concept of "ethnicity" and its application. One could ask: Did the ancient Maya of Copan see themselves as ethnically different from the Maya of Tikal? Were Teotihuacanos an ethnic other? Did different ethnic groups live together at Lamanai? Closer examination of the concept of "ethnicity" reveals, however, that use of the term reflects social, political, and economic factors that arose at a relatively recent historical juncture in time and place. How valid, then, is writing about Maya ethnicity? How can I argue for the existence of ancient "ethnic" groups when "being ethnic" is a reflection of modern history? It would seem to follow that "ethnicity" as a term should be rejected; but an alternative is to turn to the historical circumstances that produced the modern idea of being ethnic and ask: Were there times in the Maya past—did socio-political or economic conditions ever exist—in which there might have been an "ethnicity" to know?[13]

Many of us engage in critical evaluation of interpretations of design motifs on ceramics or of events such as wars or alliances. It is less common to think critically about the categories with which we approach or capture such information about design or ceramics or wars through time, because "art," "material culture," "history," "ethnicity," or even "war" and "religion," are ingrained as part of our conceptual repertoire. We are not required by our disciplines or by the government or by the public, or even by research-funding institutions, to consider our approaches as culturally or historically bound. However, in addition to assuming that we are discussing Maya art by comparing murals or frescoes, should we not also ask if there is an "art" to know? Alongside examining lithics, ceramics, and ground stone tools as Maya material culture, should we not ask if there are "ceramics" or "lithics" or a "material culture" to know? Perhaps part of what motivated the painting of a mural also motivated the manufacture of a spear point. When we assume that we are studying the Maya past, should we not also ask if there is a "history" to know? Perhaps if this question had been asked by more scholars a hundred or so years ago, we would not have entertained the idea that Maya glyphs were solely calendric, or have viewed the Western European past as "historic" and the Maya past as "prehistoric." Among the Maya, as it turns out, there is indeed a history to know.[14] One of my concerns in this book, in addition to what would normally be understood as Maya-Spanish religious interaction, is whether there was, among the Maya or the Spaniards, a "religion" to know.

Framing the Questions

Considerations of Christianity and representation drive a number of questions in the chapters that follow: How did the Maya become Christian? In what ways did the Spanish Christians absorb Maya culture? What does it mean to be Christian? How did local cultural or religious expression in Spain affect the conversion process? Did individual agendas make a difference? And although we know that a picture may be worth a thousand words, how do we know what the words were?

What we know about the Maya in Belize during the time of the Spanish conquest of the Americas comes largely from ethnohistory,[15] although archaeology has played a part. In fact, it is the part played by archaeology that stimulated the writing of this book. When, following the discoveries of Robert Kautz and his team, I assumed directorship of the excavations focused on the Spanish colonial Maya town of Tipu at Negroman in west-central Belize (see map 1.1),[16] I naively expected the archaeological data to conform to the parameters set by the documents. Some information from the excavations added to what we knew from the documents, but other data, such as the details of local technological and subsistence changes, existed in a kind of parallel universe, presumably because they did not interest Spanish chroniclers. More important, some information appeared to conflict with what the documentary sources were claiming. As a result, I became aware of the existence of the occasional disjunction between archaeology and ethnohistory. Such disjunction exists owing to the nature of our sources—Spanish accounts in the case of ethnohistory, and material remains in the case of archaeology— but how does disciplinary disjunction affect our interpretations of what happened so long ago?

A primary thread that runs through the book is how we view "the other"

Map 1.1. The Maya area showing modern boundaries and the locations of Tipu and Lamanai in Belize. (Drawing by Debora Trein)

and how the character of the knowledge we gain depends upon whether we start out assuming sameness or difference.[17] I am not referring to the need to recognize the dilemma of Self versus Other in order, as Grant Jones has written, "to ask how the absence of an understanding of the Other was itself a factor in historical process."[18] I recognize, as Jones does, that we need some grasp of colonial ethnocentrism if we are to evaluate documentary sources, and that we cannot ignore the context of Spanish colonial culture in which the sources were written. However, given my background and what I consider to be my culture, I can find grounds for disagreeing with Jones's statement that the "essentially medieval Spaniard is as foreign to us as is the native."[19] As a Roman Catholic Italian-American,[20] I am closer to the medieval Spaniard than I am to the Maya man or woman who faced such an individual.

In support of this perceived bond between the medieval Christian and me, I refer to an observation made by Hans Belting, which, although it could be interpreted as prejudicial, brought a smile to my face. In discussing the relationship between popular practices and images, Belting comments that, "Only occasionally, in the Mediterranean Catholic area, do we now come across popular practices that had ceased to be universal customs by the end of the Middle Ages."[21] He goes on to mention a saint canonized in Naples in 1987 whose image, a larger than life-size photograph, was placed on an altar,[22] a practice well within my own religious traditions. Such continuity in veneration of images, and the observation that Spanish religion of the early sixteenth century was still essentially late medieval,[23] support my contention that there are similarities in outlook between me and the Spanish Christians of the time.

As the reader may already have guessed, *Maya Christians and Their Churches* is only partly about the Maya or Belize. I use my identification with the medieval Spaniard to make the volume as much about *us*—academics, Europeans, Euro-Americans, colonial inheritors—in the hope that new ideas, and old ideas that remain relevant, can be brought to bear on the role of what we single out as "religion" in violence, warfare, and politics in modern times. Where I assume difference, it is to illuminate the character of the knowledge gained as something that results from the conflict of us (the West) versus them (the Maya).

There are cases in the literature in which "difference" has not been clearly articulated or based on supportable data, but rather has been contrived, or simply assumed, and thus has stood as a barrier to seeing or observing.[24] I am not Maya, but to attempt to break through such barriers I include the Maya in my analysis and strive to understand Christianity in a Maya context. By what right do I assume this epistemic privilege? It can be argued that no such privilege is mine, because if I followed Deleuze and Foucault,[25] I would accept as fundamental the idea that speaking for others is an indignity. But even if one accepts that speaking for others is an indignity, the question remains: How can Deleuze and Foucault be so certain about who is "other"? Where or how are such lines drawn? Why do they position themselves as different from those they hold out as "others"?[26] Perhaps their stance can also be interpreted as a consummate effort to avoid criticism or error, which comes, "perhaps not from a desire to advance collective goals but a desire for personal mastery, to establish a privileged discursive position wherein one cannot be undermined or challenged and is thus master of the situation."[27] To this extent, then, my critique is not postmodern, because I bash on regardless.

Why? The first reason is that I do not expect to master the situation, and concomitantly, I am not averse to being wrong or to opening myself to criticism.[28] In all likelihood I will not prove to be completely wrong, and if being wrong will crystallize opposition, this process of helping to clarify thinking and intellectual advance will nevertheless proceed, albeit at my expense.[29] It follows that even if I sometimes err, I stand to contribute to the goal of a better understanding of the Maya-Christian encounter and its legacy.

My second reason for proceeding is that I use the common ground of learning the catechism to take a position in which I assume, whether in reality or simply for the sake of argument, that my experience was similar to and perhaps even like that of Maya children. The assumption is rooted in my belief that the way I was taught to view the world as a Roman Catholic is similar to the way Maya and Aztec children were taught to view the world: as Christians of the late Middle Ages.[30] I see the criteria I use in conceptualizing deities, images, or spirits—and the means by which I learned to internalize stories about the supernatural—as similar to those which affected Mayas and Spaniards. In this way, I undertake to speak about or for the Maya by positioning them as us.[31]

It is critical to note that positioning the Maya as us is not a truth claim. In other words, I am not arguing the truth of the statement that Maya children responded to the teaching of the catechism exactly as I responded. I am, however, positioning myself as if this were/was true, because assuming likeness or similarity provides me with a framework for asking questions that I would never have asked had I kept young Maya catechists at a distance and assumed that we could in no way think alike.[32] In the end, what is important and worth arguing about is not whether I can know what was in Maya children's minds, but whether my approach (that we thought alike, at least in some respects) leads to new knowledge or to inferences that can be strengthened (or not) as more evidence becomes available.[33] In other words, objectivity can be improved by certain kinds of non-neutrality.[34]

How am I to proceed, then, with subject matter that claims to address religion, art, imagery, archaeology, ethnohistory, and anthropology? I start by framing the context of the encounter between the Old and New Worlds, and then tell a tale derived from my initial research on the colonial Maya of Belize and from my experience excavating the Contact-period Maya town of Tipu. I proceed to describe how I became interested in the process of Christian conversion, and, in the recounting, I emphasize the process of discovery without relying on the details of Tipu Maya history. These details follow in later chapters, in which I summarize what we know about the Maya-Spanish encounter in Belize. My intention is to use the story presented here as a vehicle to explain the source of the questions I address in the chapters that follow.

Framing the Encounter

The accounts left by Spanish administrators and religious authorities who came to Mexico, Guatemala, and Belize in the sixteenth century are of inestimable value in providing us with a picture of an encounter that changed the face of the planet. Europeans did not arrive unaccompanied; they brought their plants, their animals, and their pathogens.[35] Although assessments of the full impact of European diseases on the Amerindian population have varied,[36] there is little doubt that thousands of Maya were affected; that many men, women, and children died; and that the Europeans began slowly but with great certainty to refashion the neotropical world in the image of temperate and Mediterranean Europe, a trend which continues to the present day.[37]

Europeans also brought with them different perspectives on ways of living and seeing the world. Perhaps the most powerful of these perspectives was Christianity. Conquest was often justified, as in Cortés's letters to the King of Spain, as a means of converting the Indians to a Christian way of life.[38] Yet willingness on the part of the Indians to convert, in any part of the Americas, rarely caused the colonizers to cease their relentless efforts at subjugation and control.[39] At least in Mesoamerica, the Maya were able to use Christianity as effectively to justify resistance as the Spaniards used Christianity to justify their own actions. In other words, Christianity did not make the Maya more-willing subjects, although it seems that the Spaniards thought it would. The Spanish colonizers, and the mendicant religious orders in particular, were initially buoyed by the idea of creating a Christian kingdom in the New World,[40] but subsequent resistance and rebellion on the part of indigenous peoples were generally interpreted as a religion-based rejection of the Christian god and adherence to idolatry.[41] This conflation of political resistance and rejection of Christianity also permeates scholarly thought, and has resulted in interpretations of events—such as the carrying out of pre-Columbian rituals in Christian churches, or the placement of Christian objects in pre-Columbian sacred places—as resistance and as rejection on the part of the Maya and other indigenous peoples of all things Spanish.

In the course of my narrative, I do not argue against the idea that resistance and rebellion occurred. I stress, as has Restall with regard to the Americas in general, that the Mayas' actions cannot be easily explained:

> In recent decades, scholars have painted a more complex picture of native reaction to Christianity. While some have argued that native religion survived behind a veneer of Christianity, and others have proposed that native and European religions blended into a set of unique regional American variants on Catholicism, the most sophisticated interpretations recognize that a combination of both processes occurred. With

variations right down to the level of the individual . . . natives accommodated and understood Christianity and its place in their world in ways that we are only beginning to grasp."[42]

I do not, however, weigh in on the side of complexity so much as I give serious reconsideration to the original claim of the Franciscans (one of Restall's seven myths of the conquest[43]), which was that native people had been converted in the early days of evangelization.[44] The basis for this statement will be seen to unfold in more detail in the chapters that follow, but to put it simply, the idea that the Maya were somehow less than true Christians—or the idea that superstition and what is often called recidivism, or a poor understanding of doctrine, or even the veneration of images unfamiliar to Europeans, makes one less Christian—is based both on an idealized notion of being Christian and on an assumption of difference between us and them held by conquering Spaniards and modern scholars alike. My claim is that the catechized Maya— with their supposed veneer of Christianity, their cultural contextualizing, their syncretic beliefs, their recidivism, *and* their so-called idolatry—were as full-fledged Christians as anyone, anywhere, would have been in similar circumstances.

The View from Belize

When I began to organize my approach to the excavations at Tipu, I tended to interpret the documentary evidence, brought to my attention by Jones's ethnohistoric research,[45] at face value. I assumed that what the Spanish priests and administrators said about Maya rejection of the Christian God was a matter of fact. This notion was reinforced by the Maya rebellions of 1638–41 in Belize, instigated in large part by the Peten Itza, in which Spanish economic and religious control was seriously weakened.[46] But the archaeology was to trigger ideas that ultimately led to my consideration of alternative interpretations.

Although the church at Tipu was discovered and its walls cleared in 1980 by Robert Kautz and his team, we continued to work in and around the structure from 1984 to 1987 for two reasons. The first was that church-period burials were found, during Mark Cohen's program of burial excavations in 1984, 1986, and 1987, to occur both within the nave and on the north, west, and south sides of the building. The second was our interest in where the church stood with respect to the community, as well as in the date of church construction.

Excavations from 1984 to 1987 recovered a range of colonial artifacts, and revealed other buildings that, along with the church, formed part of the town center (fig. 1.1). We also discovered that a courtyard, or perhaps more properly a churchyard or *atrio*, had existed on the church's north side, and that burials there had been repeatedly cut through the pavement stones. This suggested a greater time depth for the period of Christian adherence than was indicated by the tone of the documents.

To complicate the picture further, the foundation of the residence, or rectory, on the church's north side had itself been cut through by the Maya for burial placement (figs. 1.2, 1.3). The interred individuals were laid out in Christian fashion, with the head to the west, facing east, and the arms usually folded over the chest. This suggested that the period of Christian practice was not confined to the time when the church was a standing structure, but continued *after* the church and its associated buildings had collapsed. Because church collapse debris overlay the rectory and several additions to it, all indications were that the Maya continued to bury their dead according to Christian practice even when the church lay in ruin and the Spaniards were presumably no longer monitoring the community.

One could argue that the maintenance of Christian burial practices was due to cultural inertia, or to the loss of information on past practices, or to the fact that the Maya did not reflect critically on the relationship between burial practice and its meaning. But these arguments entail assumptions that the Europeans in cemeteries we accept as being Christian, either in the sixteenth century or in Late Antiquity, never followed practices as the result of cultural or social habit, never remained aware of past practices but consciously rejected them, or never reflected critically on the relationship between burial practice and its meaning. Archaeologists generally take burial position to represent cultural practice; therefore, if the Tipu Maya buried their dead according to Christian rules, there is no necessary reason to make them a special case and question their adherence to Christianity.

My failure to anticipate the persistence of Christian practice alongside rejection of Spanish rule was as much a product of my initial misconceptions about the nature of "pagan" belief as it was the result of a dependence on Spaniards' interpretations of the course of Maya conversion and religious practice. Like many archaeologists, I saw Christianity among the Maya as a thin veneer over a solid body of pre-Columbian belief. This metaphor seemed all the more appropriate for the time when those who had applied the veneer were the targets of considerable resistance and rebellion, particularly during the period from 1638 to 1641 but continuing to some extent until the seventeenth century drew to a close.[47] This surely seemed enough time for the thin application of Christianity to dry out and peel off, but if the Maya were continuing to bury their dead as Christians, the metaphor fails.

After considering the possibility that the Maya, or at least a good portion of them, remained Christian in the absence of Spanish authority, I realized that archaeologists' interpretation of the conquest experience in terms of oppressors and oppressed, or even in terms of subjugation and resistance, imposed

Figure 1.1. Artist's reconstruction of Tipu's main plaza.
(Watercolor original by Marianna Huston)

limits on our capability to envision the nature and breadth of change. I had neglected to consider that human beings, even under the worst of conditions, are capable of creating options and making decisions that cannot be explained or anticipated—and indeed can even be masked altogether—by a conqueror/conquered, oppressor/oppressed, or domination/resistance dichotomy. The maintenance of Christian practices accompanied by rejection of Spanish authority was one of these options.

The Vision from St. Mike's

At the time of the Tipu excavations, even though my eyes had been opened to the complexities of change, the awakening was peripheral to the bulk of my research, which instead was focused in good archaeological fashion on the material culture of the Spanish conquest. We had recovered hundreds of artifacts from burials, structures, and middens[48] that represented the period of Spanish incursion, and it was my responsibility to describe and eventually to make sense of the objects. One of the problems in this undertaking was that the writers of Spanish documents gave scant attention to their own material culture, let alone that of the Maya. The bulk of what archaeologists recover is of course material: objects, structures, and other things used by people in the course of everyday life. The gap between what mattered to the chroniclers and what matters to archaeologists was huge.

Figure 1.2. Archaeological remains of the residence associated with the church at Tipu, Str. H12-18. Photo looks southeast.

Figure 1.3. Burials cut through Str. H12-18, Tipu. Photo looks southeast.

It was by accident that I came to pursue the matter of perspective and change again with more intensity. I had the opportunity at Tulane University in 1988 to read sixteenth- and seventeenth-century manuals of Christian doctrine for the instruction of the Indians, which I was consulting, without success, for information on the material culture of Christian ritual in the New World. In the process, as I was reading the catechism written by Pedro de Córdoba, a Dominican friar who went to the island of Santo Domingo to preach to the Indians around 1510,[49] I realized that the descriptions I was reading matched what I had been taught as a child. This includes not only the sacraments and their ministration, but also detailed descriptions of the throne of God, the angels and archangels, the tiers of Heaven, and the flames of Hell. I felt myself pulled from a world of scholarly objectivity into one filled with angels and demons that I had long ago left behind, and thought I had forgot. This world took the form of a small room in an old building in the Italian parish of the Church of St. Michael, in Paterson, New Jersey, where I was taught what now seems to me to have been a wholly medieval brand of Catholicism (figs. 1.4, 1.5).

We children at St. Mike's were enraptured by our faith, but not by our devotion to Christian doctrine or to the catechism, although we certainly memorized our share of God-is-the-supreme-being-infinitely-perfect-who-made-all-things-and-keeps-them-in-existence. Our fascination was in large part attributable to the fact that the nuns and priests who taught us seemed to have innumerable, hidden, bottomless pockets in the folds of their robes from which they pulled the (mostly) sacred objects that were our rewards for

Figure 1.4. Church of St. Michael the Archangel, Paterson, New Jersey.

Figure 1.5. Church entrance, with St. Michael overpowering the Devil in relief over the doorway.

learning the catechism. There were holy pictures with gilt trim, medallions of saints, prayer books, and even the occasional baseball.

Thinking about the focus we had on pockets full of pretty or glittery things, my thoughts turned again to the cemetery at Tipu, where children were buried with the most elaborate adornments. Not many of the 585 burials contain individuals with jewelry—only 23—but of these, at least 16 are children.[50] Venetian glass bead necklaces are the most common, but there are also glass bead bracelets, silver earrings, and jet pendants (figs. 1.6–1.9), all European in origin. I suspected at first that these items were obtained through native trade networks, which we knew extended to Yucatan.[51] What struck me, however, was the absence of a pre-Columbian precedent for adorning children more elaborately than adults in death; burial goods generally reflect, or are assumed to reflect, social status and not age. Combined with documentary information that priests concentrated religious instruction on children,[52] the lack of pre-Columbian precedent led me to consider the possibility that the beads and other items were given to the children by the friars as rewards for learning the catechism, the practice that I had known so well.

Unfortunately, the documents enlighten us only regarding gifts, such as mirrors and needles, presented to converting adults. Many of the individuals at Tipu were interred with needles, usually found in the area of the lower chest (fig. 1.10) and probably used to fasten the shroud. However, glass beads seem to have been among a range of paraphernalia, including religious paintings, which the friars carried with them as gifts and as religious teaching aids for the Maya communities on the Belize frontier.[53] To date, glass beads have been found in burials associated with children only at Tipu and not at Lamanai, but glass beads have been found in middens at both sites. Beads were distributed and religious paintings utilized to encourage Christian belief and practice; like the Maya children in Belize, I too had been taught the catechism with colorful images as my teachers and with objects as rewards, although glass beads had been replaced by saints' medallions or pictures depicting saints, angels, Mary, or Jesus. As I studied the material and documentary record, the methods of Spanish colonial proselytization were suddenly brought home.

Could I use this experience to increase our understanding of the Maya-Spanish encounter? Perhaps it would permit me to add a dimension that has

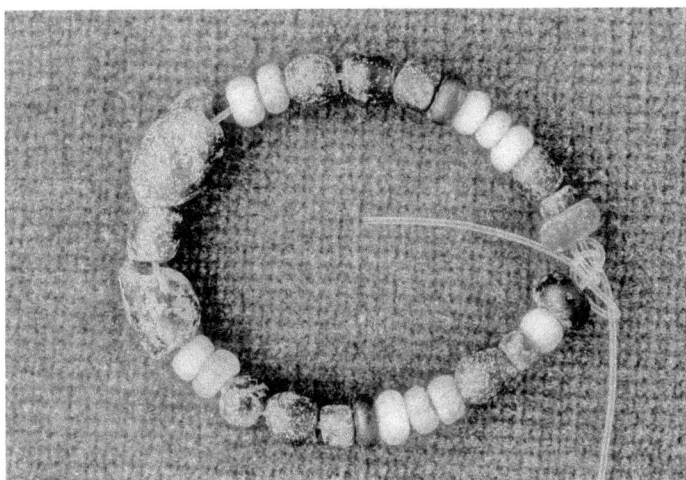

Figure 1.6. Tipu, glass beads from burial: B427, female, 25–35 years, T-891/1-28; D = 1.5–3.0 mm with maximum for 3 larger beads 7.0 mm; L/Th = 1.0–3.0 mm with 3 larger beads ca. 7.0 mm.

Figure 1.7. Tipu, glass bead necklace with jet from burial: B139, juvenile, 5–7 yrs, T-510/2-143; D = 2.5–3.0 mm for glass beads, 4.0–6.5 mm for jet beads; L/Th of glass beads 2.0–4.0 mm, jet beads 5.0–7.0 mm. (Photo by Brian Boyle)

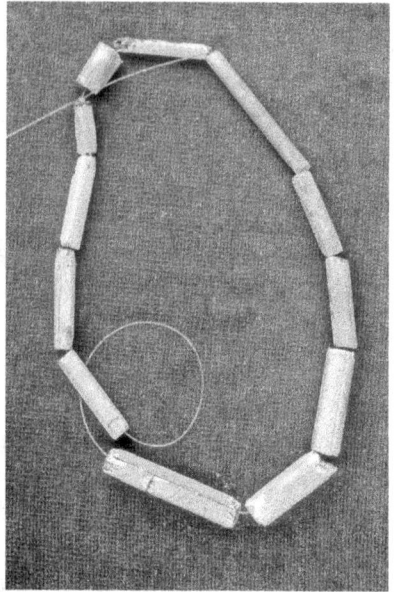

Figure 1.8. Tipu, Nueva Cadiz Plain glass beads from burial: B363, male, 18–22 years, T-882/10-21; D = 3.5–6.0 mm; L = 9.0–35.0 mm.

Figure 1.9. Tipu, earrings from burials: (a) silver and jet, B139, juvenile, 5–7 years, T-510/1; jet bead D = 1.2 cm, hoop 1.6 cm; D of wire = 1.0 mm. (b) silver, T-511/1, from area of mixed burials, B113, B114, B122, B124; D of hoop = 1.9 cm; D of wire = 1.0 mm.

Figure 1.10. Tipu, church burial showing needle
over midsection. (Photo by Robert Kautz)

thus far been absent from the literature. My view as a child of objects and images in the process of learning the catechism was very different from what would become the view held by my archaeological self, a self who catalogues Venetian glass beads as "Small Finds" and describes images as effigies or figurines. To us children at St. Mike's, the pictures and medallions were "holy," and the images helped us to remember stories about beloved angels or saints (fig. 1.11). How could two such disparate views exist side by side in the same mind—mine? Could I develop a strategy in the interpretation of imagery and representation that drew from this personal experience? Could I do this in a way that would help to develop ideas and interpretations to be tried out or tested, rather than use my beliefs to make a claim to have discovered truth?

Figure 1.11. A "Holy Picture" like those I received as a child. In this case, the saint is the Dominican, Martín de Porres, of Lima. Printed on glossy card, ca. 14 cm × 9 cm. San Martín's black-and-white robes are formed by raised stitching. (In possession of the author)

Whether or not the interpretations presented in the following chapters prove to be useful or applicable, or whether they endure, will be one basis for readers' assessment of what I have to say. Entailed in the process of interpretation will also be the weaving of an alternative understanding of cultural and religious interaction from the threads of archaeological data, critical reading of the information from the documents, comparative history, and personal experience.

Method and Theory

My method bridges archaeology, anthropology, art history, history, religion, and, to some extent, feminist epistemology. Although I do not focus on women in particular, situating oneself as author to further analysis and concomitantly integrating experience and perspective—whether personal, social, or cultural—are rigorously discussed and developed largely in feminist writings, particularly those on epistemology.[54] The implication for my method is that I insist on the importance of taking subjectivity into account, because I agree with Code that "objectivity *requires* taking subjectivity into account."[55] My intention is not to erode the status of empiricism and objectivity, but rather to emphasize the process of discovery in knowledge building.[56] Also, by taking the position that a part of my childhood experience was similar to the experience of Maya children, I invest my identity in a non-hierarchical relationship between me and those I study. This should go some way toward eliminating the differences in power that are implied in a dominant/compliant relationship between researcher and subject.[57]

At another level, it can probably be said that I combine what archaeologists have called processual and post-processual approaches,[58] although I do not employ these terms outside this chapter. One could say that post-processual insights have the potential to contribute to knowledge of the process of discovery—a concern with where and how ideas originate. The concern could encompass not only the ideas held by people in the past and what these ideas led to, but also the archaeologist's ideas and how his or her thinking stimulates particular lines of inquiry. Processual insights, on the other hand, emphasize the importance of a logic of proof: the rigor applied in validating particular lines of inquiry.[59]

How we arrive at knowledge also depends on what we wish to achieve, and in what practical context.[60] Being clear about what we wish to achieve enables us to select among methods rather than be driven by them.[61] In my case, I want to know as much as possible about the interaction between Mayas and Spaniards during the time in which Christianity was introduced to Mesoamerica, in a place which appears so often as a blank in the documentary record, and even as a blank in recent treatments of the colonial Christian encounter.[62] I am curious about how the Spaniards affected the Mayas' views of the world or the cosmos and their place in it, and how the Maya affected the Spaniards' views. I use the experience of learning the catechism as a lead to follow a number of avenues, based on how I think the ancient Maya might have been absorbing, reacting to, and appropriating imagery, belief, and doctrine.[63] I then explore these avenues more fully, and reach conclusions about social processes and cultural change during contact and Conquest. I articulate these conclusions, however, not as fact, but as possibilities, or even hypotheses, that need to be tested by future research.

Aims

My first aim in this volume is to evaluate scholarly interpretations of the conversion process with particular reference to the Maya of Belize. My second aim is to add depth and breadth to the ways in which images have traditionally been contextualized. I am particularly interested in the idea that the seeing or processing of imagery allows the viewer to personalize the experience of the representation, and thereby to appropriate the significance of the image. My third aim is to add another dimension of awareness to what is commonly called religious experience. In the process of attempting to achieve these goals, I consider how archaeology is positioned to contribute to knowledge.

My intention is not, however, to discredit other perspectives or other models. Approaches to interpreting pre- and post-Columbian beliefs or world views need not be thought of as mutually exclusive; one approach need not be deemed correct at the expense of another approach being wrong. Different models or approaches are incompatible only if they are understood to describe a single reality, but if each describes different objects or events, or highlights different sets of relationships, there can be room for what would otherwise appear to be competing models.[64]

Another way to express this view is to assert that approaches to understanding are operative or functional at different analytical levels, depending on the sort of information or insight one is seeking. What is it that changes people's minds about something as important as life, death, and the cosmos? From the perspective of time, more than five centuries after 1492, it is easy for us to talk about "conquest" as an explanation for change, but when and how does a person see himself or herself as conquered?[65] Is conquest a state of mind? To politicized archaeologists, domination and resistance seem to work as the terminology of explanation, but on an everyday level, what makes a person believe that he is dominating, and in turn, when do people see themselves as resisting? Are there spaces in between? This book is an exploration of just such spaces.

✠ TWO ✠

Yucatan and Belize
on the Eve of Conquest

The colonial and modern Maya are normally perceived as separated or different from the Maya known to tourists as the builders of temples and palaces in
the jungle. My first step, then, is to try to bridge this gap in perception in two
ways. I address Maya political and economic organization just prior to the
Conquest, because Maya dynamics provided the context for Maya-Spanish
interaction and affected the outcome. I also present new ideas on the stimulus
for Maya warfare and on the widely accepted concepts of slavery and "human sacrifice." What do these have to do with Christianity? Despite the fact
that commercial exchange and "elite visiting among polities" was intensive in
the centuries prior to the Conquest, few Postclassic cities and towns had defenses.[1] Yet modern scholars have rarely questioned the rationale provided by
the Spaniards on why the Maya carried out wars or why warriors were ultimately killed. Furthermore, the Spaniards used these judgments to justify the
decisions they made in converting the Maya and in administering Maya communities. Such judgments also contributed to Spanish perceptions of Maya
motivations.

Native Maya States

The first major attempt to elucidate the political geography of Yucatan was
made by Ralph Roys.[2] Although Roys expressed Maya domains of power
rather too strictly in terms of territorial boundaries (map 2.1.a),[3] his work is
foundational.[4] Geopolitical conditions across the Maya lowlands on the eve
of Conquest[5] are still not known with certainty, but ethnohistorians, historians, and archaeologists have proposed various scenarios as further documentary and archaeological information has come to light.[6] The most fruitful of

these have moved away from attempts at revising or detailing the boundaries originally proposed by Roys (maps 2.1.b–d show various proposed boundary revisions), and instead focus on how power was consolidated and changed hands over time among particular groups, and how this affected political and economic relationships among communities (fig. 2.1).[7] Thus, there remain territorial implications, but lines drawn on the ground are not a viable expression of the range of fluctuating economic, political, and administrative relationships.

Roys described the existence of native Maya states or territorial divisions, each known as a *cuchcabal*, or "jurisdiction."[8] The concept of "cuchcabal" (also rendered *kuchkabal, kuuchkabal* or *kúuchkabal*) has proved to operate on more levels than Roys originally envisioned, as we shall see. According to native traditions and archaeological evidence, two centers rose to prominence in the peninsula: Chichen Itza, formerly dated to the tenth and eleventh centuries, and Mayapan from about A.D. 1250 to A.D. 1450 (chap. 5, map 5.1). New evidence suggests that Mayapan may have been occupied earlier, and that Chichen Itza had declined by the 11th century.[9] With its demise in the fifteenth century, it is Mayapan that became known to the Spaniards as the last major Maya "capital" on the peninsula.

Roys noted that the Spaniards translated "cuchcabal" as "province" (*provincia*) and that, until recently, the term—or, by extension, the assumption that a province represented well-defined territorial limits—had permeated ideas concerning the nature of Maya geopolitical units at the time of the Conquest.[10] Most scholars, including Roys, seem to have used the term "province" with some hesitation, but the idea that territorial boundaries were at least expressed in some manner, if not as "provinces," by the Maya of Yucatan and Belize, became entrenched. By "territorial boundaries," I mean areas delimited on the ground in such a way that the delimitation itself provided the basis of the connection to a town. Whoever lived in the delimited space or derived produce from it was considered to be connected to the town (as a place) administratively and economically, probably through tribute.

Many researchers writing today now question the idea that provinces existed in the way the Spaniards seem to have envisaged them, which is as units around which meaningful boundary lines on the ground could be drawn, and which could therefore be equated with Spanish colonial units.[11] Caso Barrera, for example, recognizes the Spanish mindset but also refers to the various geopolitical units as *señoríos*, which can be translated as meaning the domain of a lord.[12] The word *señorío* carries the sense of a focus on a person and those obligated to a person, rather than a focus on a delimited space or place such that the lord had rights to whatever was produced or whoever lived in that space. This is a critical distinction which could be said to be matched

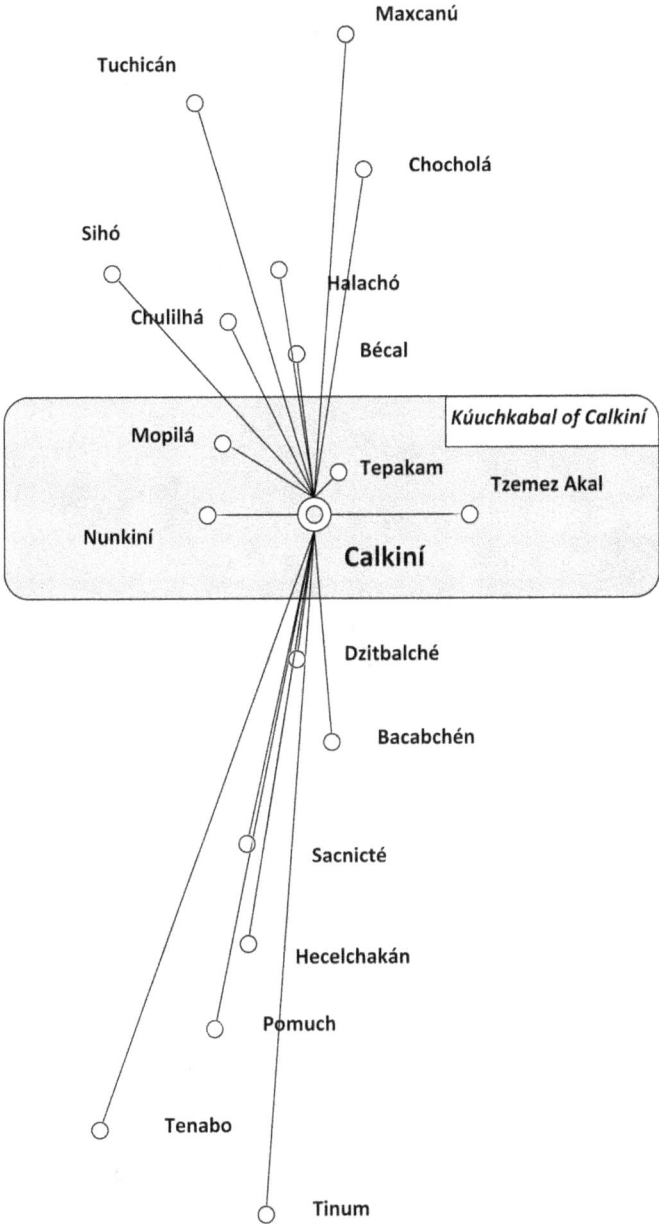

Maxcanú

Tuchicán

Chocholá

Sihó

Halachó

Chulilhá

Bécal

Kúuchkabal of Calkiní

Mopilá

Tepakam

Tzemez Akal

Nunkiní

Calkiní

Dzitbalché

Bacabchén

Sacnicté

Hecelchakán

Pomuch

Tenabo

Tinum

Figure 2.1. Kuuchkabal of Canul: a rendering by Okoshi (2006) of what Roys (1957) originally illustrated as the province of Ah Canul (see map 2.1.a). "Canul" is a Maya patronym, or lineage, name, and the towns shown each have a lord—likely but not necessarily a Canul—who serves as the batab (see text). The towns in the shaded quadrangle are dependents of the capital town of Calkini. The towns outside the gray quadrangle each have a batab and are semi-autonomous yet nonetheless recognize the authority of the Canul lord of Calkini without being dependents (Okoshi 2006, 43, fig. 3).

a

CHIKINCHEL

CEHPECH   AH KIN CHEL

TASES

CUPUL

CHAKAN   HOCABA

ECAB

AH CANUL

SOTUTA

MANI or TUTUL XIU

COCHUAH

CANPECH

CHANPUTUN

UAYMIL

CHETUMAL

ITZA

0   25   50   75   100 KM.

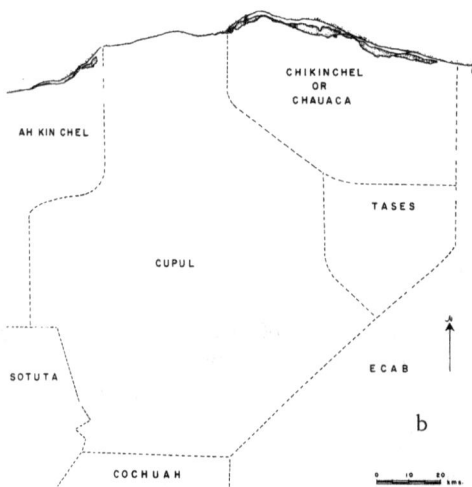

b

CHIKINCHEL
OR
CHAUACA

AH KIN CHEL

TASES

CUPUL

ECAB

SOTUTA

COCHUAH

0   10   20   kms.

c

CEHPECH

HOCABA

AH KIN
CHEL

SOTUTA

TUTUL XIU

COCHUAH

CANPECH

CHANPUTÚN

POTONCHAN   ACALANES

CHACTEMAL

TAH ITZÁ

N

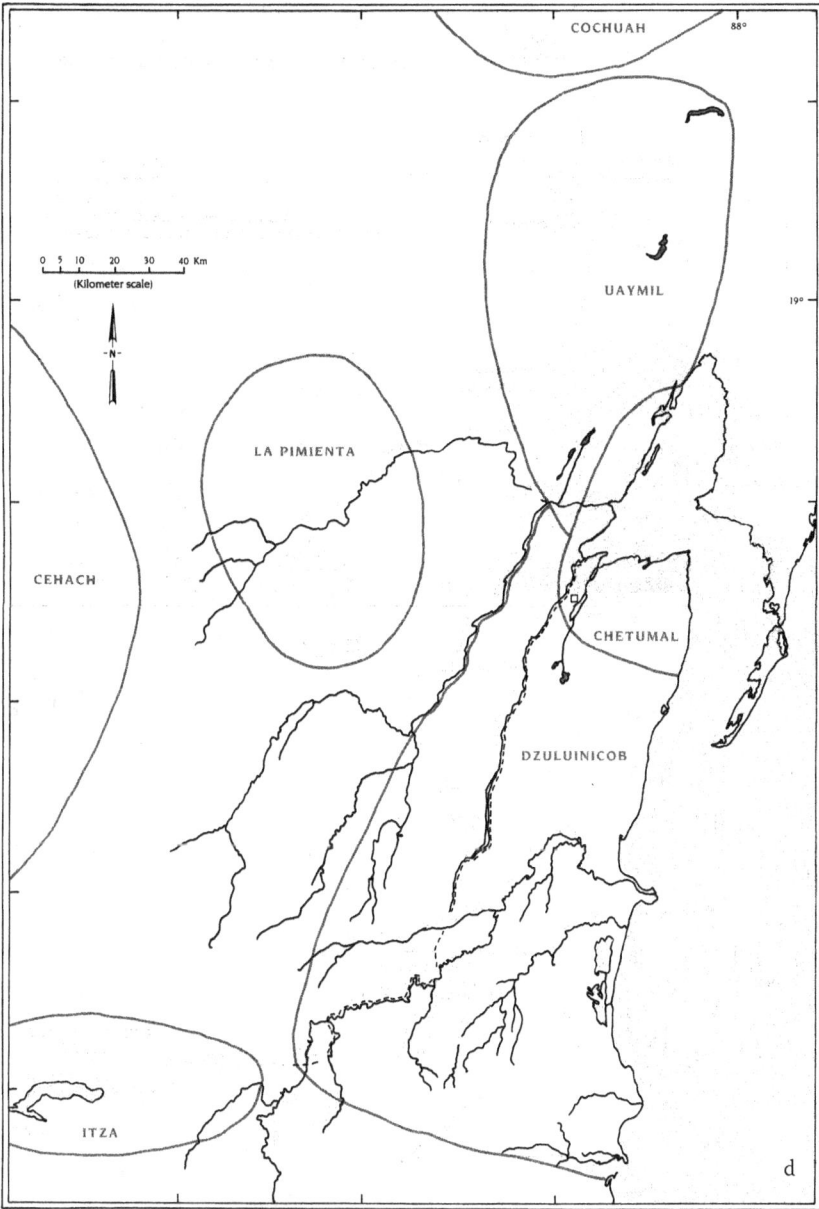

Map 2.1. Versions of pre-Conquest Maya provincial boundaries: (a) Maya provinces (from Roys 1957, 2, map 1). (b) revised map of provinces of Cupul, Chikinchel, and Tases (from Andrews 1984, 593, fig. 2). (c) *señorios indígenas* (indigenous domains), ca. 1517 (from Caso Barrera 2002, 18, map 1.1, based on Gerhard 1979, 5, map 1). (d) the southeastern frontier (according to Jones 1989, xvi–xvii, map 2). (All maps shown are adapted and redrawn from the originals by Oliver Boles)

conceptually in the term "cuchcabal," which is built around the concept of "cuch," a burden borne by a person, particularly an official (in the sense of governance or administration).[13]

A General Look at Relationships vs. Territory

Both "señorío" and "cuch" have spatial implications, in that relationships between a lord and those obligated to him or her were played out in space, and such spaces can become regularized through time. However, there is a substantial conceptual leap from defining one's world in terms of interpersonal relationships and whatever obligations these may bring, to defining one's world in terms of bounded space.[14] In medieval England, if a lord sold his land, his villeins and their families went with it.[15] The tie to a parcel or parcels of land owned by someone (even oneself) was one of the foundations of English medieval life. In modern times, our lands are divided into counties or states or boroughs, and it is in terms of space and place (size of our house or land, where we reside) that governing officials keep track of us, and of our obligations to the state.

Among the pre-Conquest Maya, the evidence indicates that relationships among people produced the patterning observed by the Spaniards in the landscape, not towns and their boundaries. In other words, Maya spheres of governance represented hierarchical tribute or administrative networks centered not on place per se but on a person or people who resided in a specific place or places.[16] Under these conditions, we can take the native Maya interpreter and historian Gaspar Antonio Chi[17] at face value when he said that there were no boundaries between towns.[18] Tozzer remarks, in fact, that the boundaries of the "provinces" varied from time to time and that it is almost impossible to define their exact limits at any given period,[19] which would be expected in a society in which tribute payments or social obligations or patron-client relationships[20] structured allegiances.

It is important to make clear that the foregoing discussion is not meant to imply that demarcation was unimportant to the Maya, although political boundaries as we understand them today, and as Giddens has pointed out, are a convention of modern nation-states,[21] and are not—owing to Mesoamerican cultural and historical conditions—applicable to the Maya of Yucatan and Belize. At the same time, I agree with McAnany, who suggests that the relatively dispersed pattern of lowland Maya settlement, as well as the expansive nature of aspects of the farming system,[22] led the Maya toward "hyper-boundary maintenance."[23]

How does one reconcile what seem to be contradictory statements (there are boundaries; there are no boundaries)? We must keep in mind that geopolitics—that is, the relationship between political power and landscape—operates on a number of levels. The fact that a cultivator had rights to land and that the land to which he had rights might be marked by stones or crosses or springs or wells or cenotes[24] need not have dictated that a ruler or governor, based historically in a particular town, would have marked *territory* on a scale that took into account all the produce and labor over which he had control, at least not in pre-Columbian times. Such a conceptual leap might well have become necessary after the Conquest, once the permanence of the Spanish presence was established and if pre-Columbian rulers wanted to keep some vestiges of the power they held over their subjects into colonial times.

During the early colonial period and in the wake of the establishment of *encomiendas*, the Spaniards staked out rights to tribute. According to Restall, it was in the Spaniards' interest that the Maya "take the opportunity to consolidate the territorial underpinnings of community and lineage."[25] Thus, the Maya were encouraged to express territorially what in pre-Columbian times need not have been expressed as such, owing to the existence of widely recognized practices concerning political and economic obligations.

Evidence that boundaries existed at the "provincial" level is often said to be provided by instances such as that of Nachi Cocom, a *halach uinic* of Sotuta, who "made a survey of the boundaries of his province" in 1545,[26] or by the conference held by Maya lords in 1537 at Mani, "in order to determine officially the boundaries of their provinces."[27] The lords themselves, and other lesser officials, made ritual circuits of the land which each lord was said to control. These actions seem on the surface to confirm the importance of land "boundedness" as a source of political power, but this may have depended on the eye of the beholder. The pre-Hispanic character of the accompanying feasting and gift giving; the participation by the halach uinic in the framing of the boundaries, accompanied by Maya officials "from allied towns"; and the fact that points along borders were not towns but natural features, particularly water sources,[28] all tell us that when the Maya determined "borders" it was not the equivalent of building fences. The process was a multilayered statement about relationships and obligations that had a territorial dimension.

On the Spanish side, there was frustration with what was seen as tremendous difficulty in determining matters of descent and relationship in connection with rulership, and in regulating boundaries.[29] The meeting of the lords at Mani in 1557 was, in fact, a response to Spanish policy aimed at establishing the boundaries of native states. The Spaniards assumed that what the lords controlled, or were arguing about controlling, were resources that were monitored in the only way they (the Spaniards) could conceive was possible: by keeping track of the land itself by drawing lines around it. The Conquest served to freeze the situation as it stood at the time of the establishment of the Yucatecan capital at Mérida, so that what was historically owed to the Xius in tribute and services, for example, suddenly became what was perpetually owed to the Xius on the basis of the way resource control was played out in the landscape *at that time*. To put this another way, although at any given time there may have been pre-Columbian macro-units which mirrored economic and political conditions that had a spatial dimension, such a spatial dimension, or "territory," *reflected* current relationships but *did not structure them*. Relationships based on tribute or other obligations may well have been the basis for conceptualizing boundaries, but these would not have reflected the dynamics of the system; they would have reflected a particular moment in time.

What we are seeing in the changes in the Maya lowlands at the time the Spaniards arrived are the kinds of changes that result when people who share a culture or are part of a group of related cultures (in this case, the states of Spain) conquer a people who share a culture or who are part of a group of related cultures (the Maya of the peninsular lowlands of Mesoamerica) with which the conquering culture is not historically entangled. The memories (in people's heads, or possibly recorded on paper or in books) that permitted the Maya of communities in Yucatan and Belize to keep track of who owed what to whom were part of a long culture history that seems not to have been disrupted, in terms of its structural dynamics, by pre-Spanish foreigners en masse (such as the Gulf Coast Maya, the Itza, or central Mexicans), although disruption occurred in terms of which rulers, local or non-local, had power at any given time. Indeed, the hegemonic empire of the Aztecs (who themselves comprised a number of "ethnic," or self-identifying, groups, such as the Culhua, Mexica, and Tepaneca) seems to have operated on similar structural dynamic principles of interpersonal relationships and tribute obligations.[30]

The Spanish invaders, unlike pre-Columbian "foreigners," lacked historical roots in Mesoamerica. They were ignorant of how the various tributary units had developed over time, and it would have required too much energy and commitment—and, most important, would have delayed economic return—to have attempted to learn the operating principles and the history of local governance. In such cases of conquest by cultural outsiders,[31] it is easiest simply to envision boundaries and divide up resources according to various territorial units.

It is sometimes said that the Spanish authorities did not attempt to restructure the indigenous hierarchical organization of production, and simply co-opted the existing structure.[32] Like my statements about boundaries, above, this is both true and false. Some aspects of the Maya tribute system were maintained under Spanish rule, in that indigenous elites were relied on to extract goods and services and to maintain order in their relative spheres, and some encomiendas, such as those in Belize, produced tribute products without resident Spaniards.[33] With the arrival of the Spaniards, however, and owing to their influence, we see a shift in the Maya world from an operative structure based on obligatory relationships which developed as the consequence of particular events and processes over time, to a structure based on obligations that arose from residence in a particular territory.[34] One question that arises when one recognizes this difference is whether conversion to Christianity was influenced by a Maya individual's pre-Conquest historical connections to a lord or lineage, as seems to have been the case in Ireland and northern Europe in Late Antiquity (chaps. 3, 10).

Geopolitical Units
in Yucatan and Belize

In addition to Western scholars' territorial mindset, a major difficulty in attempting to get a sense of Maya geopolitical units prior to the Conquest lies, as both Restall and Quezada have noted, in the nature of our dependence on Spanish sources.[35] Restall observes that Spanish sources are not only "vague and inconsistent" but also rooted in a poor understanding of Maya sociopolitical structures, and, just as critical, in blindness toward Maya sociopolitical systems and how they might have differed from Spanish expectations.[36] Quezada highlights how loosely the term "province" was used in the documents; it was applied to the entire territory of Yucatan as well as to a variety of Maya internal sociopolitical divisions.[37]

Recent research on Spanish colonial Maya-language documents indicates that the *cah* (plural *cahob*) was the fundamental unit of Maya society and culture.[38] It is difficult to convey the meaning of the concept of the cah in a few sentences,[39] but it is roughly equivalent to English-language concepts of "community" and "home" combined: "community" in the sense of the city or town or village where one lives, and "home" in the sense that the cah is also all the places within and around the community to which one has rights of access or use, such as one's place of residence, fields, orchards, roads, wells, or pathways. Restall suggests that the extension of the cah beyond the community itself was a consequence of the topography of the peninsula, which is characterized by thin soils and the necessity for long fallow periods, and hence access to larger areas of land. I suggest, however, that the cah's loose fit with Western notions of community went beyond northern Yucatan to reflect the pan-lowland demands of humid neotropical environmental conditions, and the frequency with which the Maya have always traveled long distances on foot, as well as a history of resource management based on cumulative tributary relationships rather than expansionist territorial acquisition.[40]

Besides the cah, another concept of cultural importance among the Maya, gleaned from Maya-language colonial documents, was the patronym group or *chibal*, which could also be called a lineage.[41] According to Restall, "The chibal . . . formed a partial basis for identity, economic organization, and sociopolitical faction within each cah."[42] The Maya rarely used the term "chibal" in the records, but instead would refer to their chibal by name, for example, Canul or Chel or Xiu. Within a cah, members of a chibal formed a kind of extended family.[43]

Although there is no evidence of post-Conquest chibal organization above the cah level, by the colonial period there was an established tradition of recognizing fellow chibal members from other cahob, possibly aiding them if they were in need, but definitely not marrying them. Furthermore, each "province" consisted of an area of cahob over which an extended ruling family or group of families within one chibal had achieved dominance; the cahob of the Ceh Pech area, for example, were linked by the fact that 90 percent of them were ruled by a Pech batab (cah governor).[44]

Some macro-units mapped as "provinces" in Roys's political geography, such as Ah Kin Chel or Ah Canul (map 2.1.a) were areas that were dominated by the Chel and Canul, respectively.[45] However, there is no evidence that chibalob controlled every cah within each "province," or that they ruled the area through a centralized government.[46] The existence of such features of sociopolitical power and influence that were not directly expressed in territorial claims led Restall to suggest that patronym groups may have been part of the basis for the supra-cah organization that existed in pre-Columbian times, particularly during the Late Classic period.[47]

A Model for Maya Governance

The argument I have constructed proposes that political power among the Maya at the time of the Conquest was not based on control of resources through acquisition of territory in which the actual resources lay or grew or were extracted, but rather, on control of resources through acquisition of rights to what was produced.[48] Under these conditions, the result would be a landscape that could not be interpreted on the basis of a simple correlation between people and territory, which is what the concept of "provinces" assumes. One could only interpret the pattern of cities, towns, and villages in the Maya landscape if one knew the histories of the people living in them and understood the complexities of tribute and other relationships.[49]

There are claims in Maya chronicles, written in the Maya language but in European script, that Yucatan had twice been united as a single empire,[50] although we should keep in mind that such claims were expressed in language that was influenced by Spanish concepts. If the model I have presented is correct, at least in broad outline, then the claim that the Itza ruled an "empire," or even a state, from Chichen Itza did not mean control of the territory, or even ownership (in terms of land) of the resources of other provinces. Instead, it meant success—through warfare or marriage alliances or negotiation—in appropriating a portion of the tribute historically owed to a wide range of Maya lords, or in increasing the load paid to these lords to include tribute payments to the Itza themselves. This would explain, more satisfactorily than the territorial state model, the complexities of Maya geopolitics, because the direction in which tribute flowed could change overnight and yet never threaten the survival of the system, or even necessarily the stability of production in communities.[51]

Where the communities of Belize fit into all this is a difficult question to answer, owing to our comparative lack of information on the area in the sixteenth century. It is nonetheless important to work through a model of Maya interaction as an alternative to the territorial assumptions that are common in the literature, because the process sensitizes us to information from both documents and archaeology that can contribute to a clearer and more nuanced understanding of Maya political dynamics. It is not likely that there existed a "province" of which all Belize communities were a part, but we can assume that Belize communities paid tribute to overlords at different levels. How the various communities may have been aligned under tributary lords, and what the regional hierarchy may have been, remains unknown, although the broad pattern of economic and political relationships has been ably described by Masson for northern Belize.[52] There are, in addition, some indications of general cultural orientation from the archaeological record that I will discuss shortly.

I distinguish three facets of Maya economy and organization about which we need to hypothesize in order to try to provide a framework for understanding Maya life in Belize before the Europeans arrived. I say this because present frameworks are inadequate to account for the complexity that is evident in both the documentary and the archaeological records. The first facet consists of the ways in which transfer of wealth and resources may have taken place. The second is the question of whether or not there were economic spheres of life that lay outside the tribute system.[53] The third is the complexity of the hierarchies that existed at the time of the Spanish encounter, to which we need to draw attention so that the Belize situation is not simplified owing only to lack of information.

Although it is common in the popular literature and in the media[54] to attribute Maya warfare to the desire to drag people into temples to extract their hearts for gods, it is hard to imagine any civilization surviving for long by adhering to a system in which men repeatedly risked their lives in war without economic gain. Because humans kill and are killed in wars, such killing must be justified, and this is where that part of culture we call religion serves a critical function. The idea that there is such a thing as "religion" that is the driving force in socially sanctioned killing is a myth, as is the concomitant notion that religion can be separated from other social forces. I deconstruct the myth in various parts of this book, beginning with the next chapter, although I am not the first to criticize the idea that religious proselytizing and the idea that saving people's souls under Christianity is somehow an issue that can be separated from territorial expansion, economic gain, and the spread of Castilian culture. Conversion, from the Spanish point of view, did not simply involve new ideas about supernaturals or an otherworld—it entailed economic and political transformations that could not be divorced from culture history or beliefs.

In the same way, religion was not a separate body of beliefs and action for the Maya, and the idea that religion motivated wars, or so-called "human sacrifice," is one of the most pervasive myths on record.[55] Socially sanctioned killing—institutionalized practices by which human beings can kill other human beings without punishment or penalty—is driven by a myriad of factors. Cross-culturally, there are actually rather few kinds of socially sanctioned killing: abortion, capital punishment, euthanasia, and war appear to represent the spectrum. Of these, the most widely accepted form that involves the greatest number of deaths without punishment is war. Just as warfare today mixes goals of economic gain with cosmic justification,[56] so it did among the Maya of pre-Columbian times.

The question that remains to be answered is how wealth or resource transfer took place. We know little about the details of warfare among the Maya, but we do know that rulers, nobles, and other elites made the decisions to go to war, that they captured rival rulers and nobles (as depicted on monuments), and that some captured rulers were subsequently killed in or near a temple or on an altar or perhaps on a ballcourt.[57] My points here are two: the first is that if death indeed occurred, it was part of warfare and we have no evidence to suggest that it was justified on the basis of gods' needs or desires to take away individual human lives. In other words, there is no justification for explaining death as a "sacrifice" if the Maya did not. In fact, there is no word in Yucatec (or Nahuatl) that is equivalent to the Latin-derived word "sacrifice"; it is the Spaniards who introduced the concept.[58]

The second point is that capture, or perhaps some other form of humiliation, rather than death seems to have been the pivotal action that contributed to "winning"—that is, it created the conditions for tribute transfer.[59] Martin and Grube's narrative of the lives and deaths of Classic-period rulers shows clearly that a number of defeated rulers lived on to pay tribute to new overlords.[60] Panel 12 from Piedras Negras, for example, shows Knot-eye Jaguar I, the ruler of Yaxchilan, as a bound prisoner of a Piedras Negras ruler in A.D. 518. Yet, a later stela erected at Yaxchilan indicates that Knot-eye Jaguar I survived to rule as a vassal of Piedras Negras.[61] Martin and Grube do not single this out as an exception, but link it to what is known in the hieroglyphic record about a number of other defeated kings.[62] This is surely the key to the transfer of wealth and resources among the Maya. Capturing a rival ruler, or perhaps capturing several nobles who were vassals of a rival ruler, must have given the captors negotiating leverage over the captives' tribute rights. Appropriation of tribute must surely have been the driving force behind warfare.

Few details that might have illuminated Maya power struggles prior to the Conquest have come down to us, because the Spaniards were not in the least interested in indigenous dynamics: the bloodier and more irrational they could make the Maya appear, the easier it was to excuse exploiting them. This makes it difficult to interpret warfare in any light other than through the language used by the Spaniards. Thus, the term "he died in battle," which is Roys's translation of a line from the *Crónica de Calkini*,[63] is assumed by us to mean that the individual was killed in the heat of the physical fighting, but it is just as likely that he died later in a temple, because this *was* an accepted manner of death "in battle." Even in our vocabulary, a "battle" refers to an overall struggle and its outcome, rather than simply to fighting. Among the Aztecs, the alleged champions of "human sacrifice," the aim of warriors was to engage and capture, but not to kill, a rival warrior in the fighting; arrows and darts were meant to weaken the enemy and to draw blood, not to kill, and whereas ambush was unthinkable to the Aztecs, it was a major tactic of the Spaniards.[64] In Clendinnen's words, "The psychological demoralization attending those sudden, trivializing deaths of great men painted for war, but not yet engaged in combat, must have been formidable."[65] Restall refers to the "tactical discrepancy between the Spaniards' willingness to kill large numbers of Mayas indiscriminately, and the Mayas' preference for person-to-person combat and the taking of captives."[66]

We do not know how decisions were made regarding the possibility of death in a temple, but death in warfare outside the physical engagements of combat would not have made the Maya any more committed to "human sacrifice" than we are in our wars. Their motives in risking their lives in war were almost certainly centered on significant economic gain. How negotiation proceeded once a rival was captured is unknown, but Classic-period cases indicate that a captive could return to his town following the transfer of tribute rights to the captor.[67] At other times, rulers or nobles were captured and killed subsequent to combat, nonetheless as the consequence of warfare. Killing the ruler or a noble in a temple was the Maya manner of death in war that was socially sanctioned, in the same way that we sanction killing on battlefields.

My narrative gives rise to questions that cannot be answered on the basis of present evidence. Such questions need to be asked, however, to replace the assumption that killing human beings in temples was solely an act of dedication to gods. Keeping in mind the model I have outlined, much can be explained when one reviews Roys's descriptions of Maya warfare in Yucatan on the eve of conquest.[68] For example, Roys states that slaves constituted a supply of labor recruited largely by means of warfare, yet he also says that the population lived scattered in hamlets, and that wars were fought when there was little agricultural activity. This suggests that warfare was ritualized, and that acquisition of "slaves" was not the motivation for wars. If it had been, it would be hard to imagine any group living scattered in the countryside. In addition, the idea that the most frequent motivation for war was to obtain slaves comes from *encomenderos*, not from Mayas;[69] if Maya elites could gain economically (in the form of tribute) from waging war, why would they pass this information on to their conquerors? I suggest that some commoners were recruited, or obliged at certain times, to protect their lords in wars. When such lords were captured, the commoners were obligated to provide services and labor to the captor or to his community as part of the tribute transfer.

The ritualized nature of warfare is also evident in the character of the Maya defenses that Roys describes. He attributes Spanish successes to the fact that they worked out how to go around the Maya-built palisades of timbers bound together by lianas. But do we really believe that the Maya themselves, when fighting against each other, could not have figured this out? It seems clear that such defenses were part of a pre-Hispanic style of fighting, the limits to which were agreed upon by all parties concerned—except, of course, Spanish soldiers.

Roys describes the possibility of a *nacom*, or war chief, being killed in an actual attack,[70] which may mean that the individual was a commoner or a lesser member of the elite whose capture would not have brought his captor economic gain. It is not clear in Roys's narrative just where people, other than the nacom, were killed. Researchers have assumed that the killing took place in battle, with "battle" interpreted in our terms, so no further questions have been asked. Yet Roys states that it was "most desired" to take prisoners who became the "property" of their captors, and that nobles were killed in temples ("sacrificed"), whereas commoners—the men who fought and the women and children who were the collateral damage of warfare—were "enslaved."[71] What this tells us, despite the confusion that comes from the use of Western terminology, is that appropriating tribute in the form of resources, labor, and services lay at the heart of waging war.

In Roys's discussion of the various details of the lords of particular communities who led their warriors against neighbors,[72] it is clear that economic gain is a factor, but except for the mention of "plunder," it is unclear exactly how resource transfer was achieved. I suspect that this is because most Spanish chroniclers and modern scholars have always accepted that "human sacrifice" was a motivation for Maya warfare. We ought to begin to consider seriously that capturing elite, tribute-receiving individuals must have been a major method by which the distribution of wealth and resources changed. Capturing people to cut out their hearts was an "explanation" only in the eyes of Spanish proselytizers and colonizers, used to justify their exploitation of the labor and services of the Maya and their suppression of Maya culture.

ECONOMIC SPHERES
OUTSIDE THE TRIBUTE SYSTEM

In addition to approaching Maya warfare from a new perspective, some expanded discussion of Maya economy is essential in order to make sense of what was happening in Belize just prior to the Conquest. With regard to Tipu, excavations were limited to finding evidence of historic occupation. At Lamanai, however, excavations over the years have been geared toward answering a number of questions that bear on pre-Columbian society and economy through time.[73]

Although many communities in the lowlands, and especially in Belize, weathered the Maya collapse, Lamanai is one of the communities for which the evidence reveals a transition from the Classic to the Postclassic period. The nature of the caches and tomb accompaniments from at least Middle Classic times suggests that Lamanai lords may not have been members of the dynasties that ruled the magnificent cities of the Peten, because elite material culture is so much more modest than that of sites such as Tikal, or even nearby Altun Ha. At the same time, the few inscriptions suggest that dynastic records were consonant with lowland hieroglyphic traditions,[74] although it remains unclear whether Lamanai was the seat of a *kaloomte'* (a ruler known

Figure 2.2. Lamanai, glyphs from Stela 9: the kaloomte' glyph is above, with "east" prefix, and the emblem glyph below. (Drawing by Christophe Helmke and Louise Belanger, based on original by H. S. Loten)

as a *batab*), as suggested by the presence of an "east kaloomte'" title on Lamanai Stela 9 (see fig. 2.2), or whether it fell under the aegis of a more powerful neighbor.

The evidence so far accumulated indicates that Lamanai continued to flourish well past the time of the decline of Chichen Itza in the eleventh century.[75] This is not to say that Lamanai "controlled" a vast territory, but rather that it remained a hive of activity throughout the Early and Late Postclassic; this is the period from about A.D. 1000 to A.D. 1500. Coastal communities in Belize also proved resilient against the forces of collapse, a matter which I discuss in more detail in chapter 5.

The evidence of persistent activity without concomitant dependence on dynastic strength, as in the Classic period, or control of large territories, as proposed for Chichen Itza in the Postclassic, suggests that Lamanai and the coastal sites east of it were part of a dynamic that operated alongside and complemented the tribute system. Kepecs, for example, posits the participation of commoners in production beyond the household level, and suggests that competitive entrepreneurs were particularly active in the Late Postclassic.[76] In a similar vein but in a more general sense, I argue that there were multiple levels of production and exchange even in Classic times. Inter- and intraregional trade and exchange always played a large part in Lamanai's economy, but whether or not this meant that merchants formed a significant element in the community is difficult to determine. It could be that no matter what elite machinations took place, Lamanai's position with regard to long-distance trade was too valuable to compromise or damage; hence the dynamics of commerce and trade proceeded uninterrupted, albeit within slightly different elite spheres.

The evidence from Lamanai and coastal sites also suggests that those involved in trade and exchange may have had rights to a kind of tax or subsidy or percentage that provided them with income and support, no matter how much of the remaining goods supplied elite demands. It may be that all of the

Maya whose families had been involved in coastal trade had for generations been part of interactions that could have bolstered, but were not dependent on, elite machinations and power plays. Certainly, the existence of the Aztec *pochteca*[77] suggests a long history of sophisticated commercial enterprise in Mesoamerica, and confirms the existence of a dynamic that, although it may have denied merchants and traders the high status of elites, may nevertheless have contributed to their resilience in the face of elite rivalries, as well as florescence and decline.

One could say that many, although certainly not all,[78] ancient communities in Belize never reached the heights of monumentality achieved by cities such as Tikal in Peten or Calakmul in Campeche. At the same time, occupation was characterized by longevity. Coastal sites, in particular, yield evidence of an intensive and continuous occupation and activity. It has been argued that Classic coastal interchange was qualitatively different in terms of the items exchanged and the intensity of community involvement,[79] but this does not alter the fact that the mechanisms of coastal exchange were in place in Belize from Preclassic times. The features that contributed to longevity of Maya communities may well, however, have sounded the knell for them at the time of the Conquest, a matter discussed in more detail in chapter 5. The orientation of communities in Belize toward trade, exchange, and commerce made them highly successful and resilient throughout the pre-Columbian period, but when the Spaniards arrived, coastal trade and exchange were among the first activities to be disrupted. Communities on the coast, cayes, and atolls would have been forced to deal early on with the effects of disease and slave raids. What sustained these communities for centuries—coastal activity, travel, and long-distance trade—would have made them the most vulnerable to initial European exploratory forays and interference.

THE NATURE OF HIERARCHY

Up to this point, I have presented a picture of pre-Columbian Maya communities in Belize acting to further their economic advantage in the same way that communities in Yucatan furthered theirs. I have also suggested that the coastal orientation of Belize's communities gave them an economic advantage and a resilience that stood them in good stead in times of political rivalry and upheaval. Nonetheless, Belize communities were clearly part of a network of domains of rulership that extended over the entire lowlands and were operative at the time of the colonial encounter.

Spanish colonists and administrators used the term *cacique* to apply to someone they recognized as a Maya lord—a title of Caribbean-language origin that was brought by the Spanish conquerors to Yucatan from the

Antilles.[80] In the Yucatec Mayan language, at least one lord in the hierarchy was the batab, a kind of governor.[81] Colonial evidence suggests that another lordly title, that of halach uinic, was given by the Maya to a batab of a cah that came to dominate a region—a kind of super-batab.

Quezada describes the cuchcabal (the basis, according to Roys, of the Spanish "province") as the territory that came under the jurisdiction of a lord (the halach uinic) who was resident in a particular town for which the name or toponym was known (e.g., Calkini, Mani, Chichen Itza). Therefore, it would seem that at least some of the geopolitical units which were called provinces by the Spaniards were the domains of the halach uinicob.[82] Other provinces were domains of batabob who were under no single territorial ruler but in large part belonged to a single chibal or lineage.[83] Still other provinces seem to have subsumed communities under batabob whose domains were not actually organized in any political sense, but were united in their focus on a particular economic resource, such as the salt beds along the coast of Chikinchel, to which, as some evidence suggests, each of the native communities held exploitation rights, perhaps even as property.[84]

I noted above that the term *cuchcabal*, as it appears in colonial dictionaries, embraces more levels of meaning than indicated in Roys's translation as "jurisdiction," or in the Spanish colonial translation as "province."[85] *Kuuchkabal*, according to Okoshi,[86] signifies the sphere of governors and officials who are obligated to a particular lord, whereas *kúuchkabal*, closer to the Spanish idea of "province," refers to territory governed by a seat of authority based in a particular place (i.e., capital?). In Okoshi's words, *kuuchkabal* refers to "los gobernantes y oficiales que el señor supremo tiene a su cargo en un espacio territorial," whereas a *kúuchkabal* is "un espacio territorial gobernado por un poder que reside en un lugar determinado."[87] Figure 2.1, for example, from Okoshi's analysis of a historic document written by the Maya in the Latin alphabet,[88] shows the kuuchkabal of the Canul, with only the shaded rectangle representing the kúuchkabal, with its capital at Calkini.

BELIZE ON THE EVE OF CONQUEST

This brings us to Belize and to what can be said about Maya communities there—which sadly is far less than we would like. Even the updated maps of Roys's original provinces (maps 2.1.b–c) show Belize largely as a blank. Jones has done the most to fill in the blank,[89] but what is known about Belize in the two centuries after Conquest has helped less in understanding the pre-Conquest landscape. The recent volume on Maya political geography edited by Okoshi and colleagues includes Soconusco, but not Belize.[90] With regard to northern Belize, however, Masson has synthesized a broad range of information from archaeology and ethnohistory on the economy and culture of northern Belize communities in Postclassic times, which is helping to build a picture of how communities in Belize were linked politically, both to each other and to changing centers of power in Yucatan.[91]

Nachan Kan is said to have been a halach uinic, or regional lord, of the Chetumal province of northeastern Belize and southwestern Quintana Roo at the time of Spanish contact, and at least some communities in northern Belize paid tribute to him.[92] Gerhard claims that "Chactemal was a large unified state ruled by a *halach uinic* [Nachan Kan] who directly controlled the territory between the east shore of Lake Bacalar (Bakhalal) and Tipú in the south."[93] Both the concept of a unified, controlling state and its extension to include Tipu are doubtful. It is possible, however, that many of the communities in this zone, including Lamanai, paid some form of tribute to Nachan Kan. Gerhard goes on to say that the area was a center for trade along the coast but that there was also probably an overland trade route that linked Chactemal with Acalan to the west.[94] That Lamanai's inhabitants were in contact with communities along the Gulf Coast is strongly suggested by aspects of its ceramic styles and possibly its architecture from Late Classic times.[95] We do not know, however, whether contact was rooted in coastal or overland connections, or both.

The period immediately preceding conquest in northern Belize is characterized by Masson, based on a study of ceramic styles, as having been marked by close relationships among the provinces of Chetumal, Uaymil, Ecab, and Mani.[96] Even if provinces per se were a fiction, the ceramics show strong connections among the communities of these regions. Hence, what we may be seeing, as described by Masson, are the vehicles by which tribute products were transported from place to place at the same time that tribute demands stimulated other avenues of trade and exchange. As outlined by Kepecs for the northeast coast of Yucatan, political decentralization following the fall of Chichen Itza was accompanied by economic competition;[97] and economic competition seems to have characterized the Belize region as well.[98]

The Chetumal province, as proposed by Roys, includes Lamanai and other settlements on the New River (maps 2.1.a, 2.2).[99] Jones's documentary research led him to propose a previously unknown provincial entity for the immediate pre-Hispanic period, called Dzuluinicob (map 2.1.d), which was noted as such in a *probanza*[100] of Melchor Pacheco (1570–71) who, as we shall see in chapter 5, was one of the conquerors who subdued the communities in Belize and brought them under Spanish control by 1544.[101] Jones's reading of the documents also led him to conclude that Tipu was the political center of the province, and that the province comprised the upper Belize River and extended northward as far as the New River Lagoon, thus including Lamanai.[102]

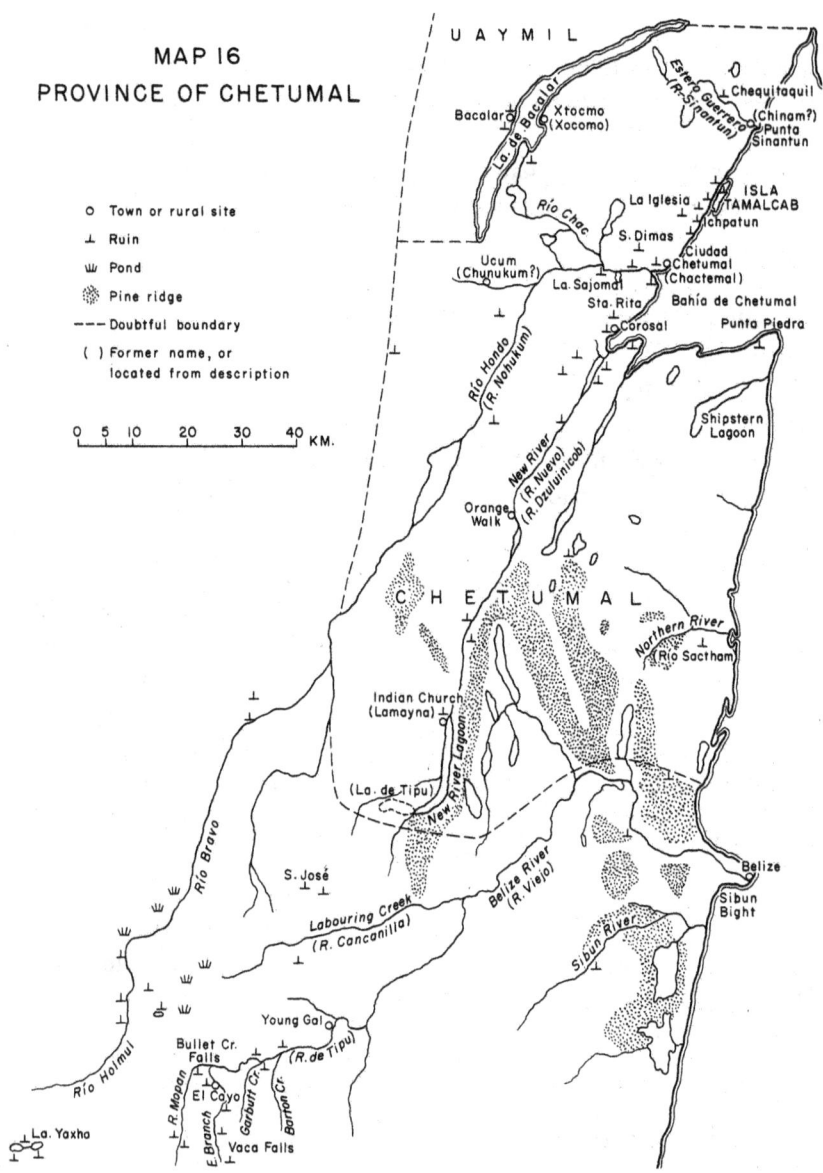

MAP 16
PROVINCE OF CHETUMAL

○ Town or rural site
⊥ Ruin
ɰ Pond
❀ Pine ridge
--- Doubtful boundary
( ) Former name, or
    located from description

0 5 10   20   30   40 KM.

UAYMIL

Chequitaquil
(Chinam?)
Punta Sinantun
Bacalar
Xtocmo (Xocoma)
La.de Bacala
Río Chac
La Iglesia
ISLA TAMALCAB
Ichpatun
S. Dimas
Ciudad Chetumal (Chactemal)
Ucum (Chunukum?)
La.Sajomal
Sta. Rita
Bahía de Chetumal
Corosal
Punta Piedra
Estero Guerrero (R. Sinantun)

Río Hondo (R. Nohukum)

Shipstern Lagoon

New River (R. Nuevo) (R. Dzuluinicob)

Orange Walk

C H E T U M A L

Northern River
Río Sactham

Indian Church (Lamayna)

New River Lagoon

(La. de Tipu)

Belize

Sibun Bight

Río Bravo

S. José

Labouring Creek (R. Cancanilla)

Belize River (R. Viejo)

Sibun River

Young Gal

Bullet Cr. Falls

(R. de Tipu)

El Cayo

Río Holmul

R. Mopan

E. Branch

Garbutt Cr.

Barton Cr.

Vaca Falls

La. Yaxha

Map 2.2. Roys's Chetumal province, which includes Lamanai (shown as "Indian Church" or "Lamayna") (Roys 1957, 160, map 16).

His claim is based on two lines of evidence. The first is that the New River is referred to as the Dzuluinicob (or variations of this name) throughout the seventeenth century, which suggests that the waterway represents an entry into the province of the same name. The second is that Tipu served as the principal force for the integration of the Maya throughout the region from the late 1560s until the end of the seventeenth century.[103]

The archaeological evidence adds some support to Jones's view but also suggests a different interpretation. The reason for the difference is that conditions in Belize were subject to change many times between 1400 and 1700. The idea that there was a pre-Conquest state of affairs that was characterized in terms of provincial relationships and was then altered by the Conquest into a state of affairs regularized by Spanish colonial administration is therefore probably wrong.

Archaeological evidence supports connections between Tipu and Lamanai during the period after establishment of encomiendas, which the records show took place in 1544 (fig. 2.3). Between 1544 and the end of the century, the mechanisms for closer connections between Tipu and Lamanai were provided by the evangelizing efforts of the Franciscans; the construction of churches and their related buildings and plazas; the remodeling of residences; the construction of specialized buildings such as the guest houses (*casas reales*); the training of young men as *maestros cantores*;[104] and the monitoring, however occasional, by religious and secular priests, probably because both

TIME SPANS	LAMANAI	TIPU
From 1981 to the present	Independence	
1964 to 1981	Self-governing British Crown Colony	
1800 to 1964	Late British colonial period	
1670 to 1800	Early British colonial period	
1648 to 1708	Late Spanish colonial period - Diminished activity	
1544 to 1648	Early Spanish colonial period - Major period of activity	
1492 to 1544	Coastal incursions - felt more at Lamanai but negligible at Tipu	
1350 to 1492	Late Postclassic	Late Postclassic
1200/1250 to 1350	Middle Postclassic	
960/1000 to 1200/1250	Early Postclassic	Early Postclassic
775 to 960/1000	Terminal Classic	Terminal Classic
735 to 775	Late Late Classic	Late Classic
625 to 735	Early Late Classic	
600 B.C. to A.D. 625	Preclassic to Middle Classic	Preclassic to Middle Classic

Figure 2.3. Chronology for Lamanai and Tipu.

communities were going through the same kinds of transformations. Thus, the conquerors may have helped to forge the very links between Tipu and Lamanai that became the ultimate undoing of the Spanish colonial enterprise in Belize.

The material culture inventory that was shared between the two sites at this time is European, not Maya: Venetian glass beads, copper needles, olive jars, and Spanish majolica pottery. Tipuans continued to use the kinds of Late Postclassic pottery that were in circulation prior to 1544, with no evidence of problems in obtaining slips or paints, and with no obvious change in the vessels' appearance, so that it is not possible to distinguish changes in ceramics at Tipu from the pre-Contact (Terminal Postclassic) to early colonial period.[105] This is not true at Lamanai, where changes took place even before encomiendas were established. What we have called Yglesias Phase ceramics, associated with the historic, or colonial, period, occur in contexts that predate activities of the encomienda period. The ceramics are distinctive, and show a decline in the quality of slips and in their application, as well as in the standardization of the ceramic body before 1544 (Figure 2.4). The possible reasons for such changes are discussed in chapter 5 on the environment of contact. Here, the important point to be made is that such evidence makes it difficult to think in terms of a line that divides Maya life across the board (i.e., to lump Tipu and Lamanai together) into one period before and another after the arrival of the Spaniards.

The appearance of Lamanai-style Yglesias pottery at Tipu, at a time when the community had probably been Christian for several decades, suggests that the ties between the two communities became even stronger in the seventeenth century. By this time, however, Spanish control and monitoring were weak, movement of people from north to south was on the increase, and resistance and rebellion were in the air. What drew Tipu and Lamanai together in the seventeenth century was resistance to Spanish rule.

The integration of the territory in which Tipu was a force was indeed a reality,[106] but it comprised two kinds of responses that changed over time. In the earlier stage, the communities were integrated by conditions that were brought about by Spanish colonial administrative and evangelizing efforts from 1544 to roughly the end of the sixteenth century. During this period, the Spaniards were successful at Christianization, and to a large extent were also reasonably successful at managing tributary communities.

By the opening years of the seventeenth century, things had changed. Tipu was still linked to Lamanai on the basis of colonial administrative and ecclesiastical conditions and contacts, but both communities became deeply affected by the centripetal forces generated by the Itza Maya of the Peten lakes area. The Itza remained resistant to Spanish colonial efforts and encouraged

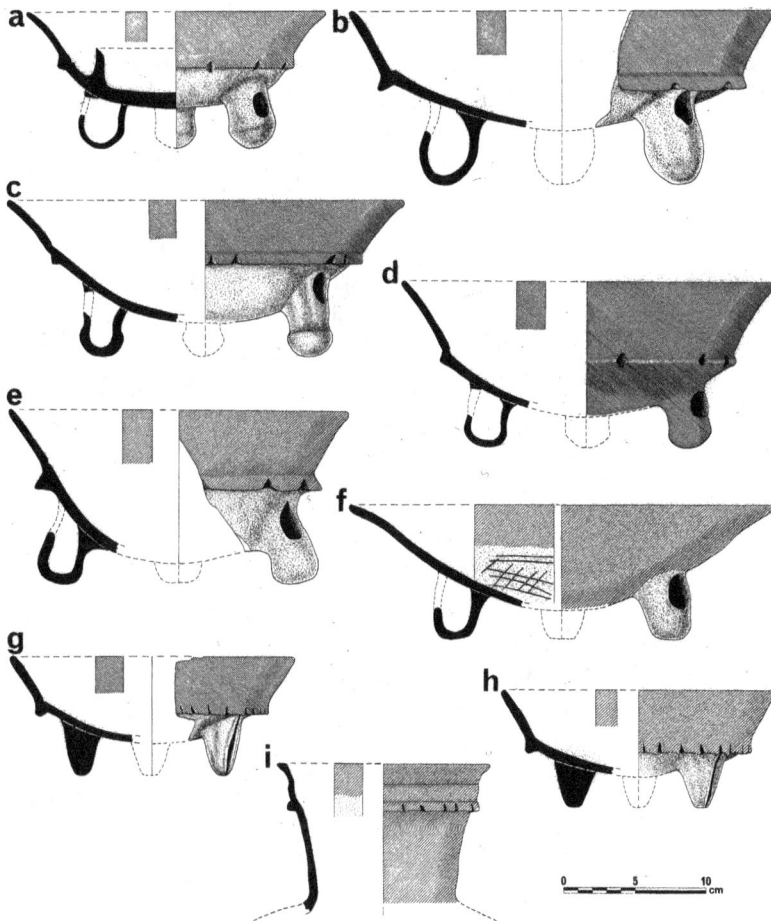

Figure 2.4. Lamanai, Yglesias-phase pottery. (Drawing by Louise Belanger)

flight, resistance, and rebellion wherever possible.[107] Mayas continued to flee from communities in the north, and Lamaneros themselves joined in the exodus (see chapters 8, 9).

Tipu's relationship with Lamanai prior to the time when encomiendas were established in 1544 remains enigmatic. From an archaeological point of view, the material culture inventory at Lamanai is without any doubt distinctive from that at Tipu, and it is hard to see them as part of a single "provincial" unit. Tipu shared material culture traditions with Peten and the Belize Valley, a pattern that continued throughout the Spanish colonial period. In the pre-Spanish colonial period, Tipu's sphere seems to have been more Peten-oriented than northern Belize–oriented.

Tipu and Peten on the Eve of Conquest

The site of Tipu is located on the Macal, or eastern, branch of the Belize River (map 2.3). In the immediate pre-Conquest period, ceramic styles and technology indicate that the residents of Tipu interacted fairly intensively with Maya groups living in the lakes region of central Peten to the west, in Guatemala (map 2.4).[108] In fact, Tipu is said to have been "virtually inseparable from [the] Petén cultural tradition."[109] There are also indications of interaction with communities in the Belize River Valley, downriver to the northeast (map 2.4).[110] Bones from marine fish recovered from colonial-period middens reflect ties to the coast, and it is not unlikely that communication with the coast was a feature of the period immediately prior to Spanish contact, as it was of Classic times.[111]

The Peten lakes region was occupied before, during, and after the Maya collapse, and may have served as a zone of refuge for elite lineages formerly associated with Classic hegemony.[112] The area was nonetheless in a state of demographic flux from about A.D. 800 to A.D. 1000, with some groups leaving the central Peten and others moving into the lakes region.[113] By the Late Postclassic period (fifteenth century), there was at least one major group settled along the shores of the Peten lakes: the Itza, whose communities occupied the region of the western lakes (most of the southern and western shores of Lake Peten Itza, and including the smaller surrounding lakes) (map 2.4). Their major town at the time of the Conquest, located on an arm of Lake Peten at its western extremity, was recorded in colonial sources as Tah Itza, now rendered more accurately in modern orthography as Nojpeten, or Nohpeten (map 2.4).[114] When the Itza arrived in Peten is a matter of debate; they were certainly there by 1450,[115] but may have arrived in the early 1200s or thereabouts, as a result of the decline of Chichen Itza in the north.[116] Although "Itza" appears commonly in the literature as a reference to a major Maya group, with the implication that members of the group self-identified as Itza, use of the term and to whom or to what it applies are often confusing. "Itza" seems sometimes to refer to a dialect of Yucatec Mayan, and hence to people who spoke this dialect; sometimes to refer to a place where people resided, as in Peten Itza or Lago Petén Itza; and/or sometimes to refer to people who had names that identified them as "Itza," independent of where they lived, with the implication that they belonged, or claimed to belong, to a kind of super-lineage or patronym group, although individual family names varied.[117]

A group called the Couoh, or Kowoj, who come across more strongly in the literature as people who self-identified as a group by the nature of their names or their lineage[118] (i.e., they were not associated with a place that bore the name Kowoj, and the language they spoke was the same as that of the Itza[119]),

Map 2.3. Major Spanish-period sites in northern Belize.
(Drawing by Debora Trein and Emil Huston)

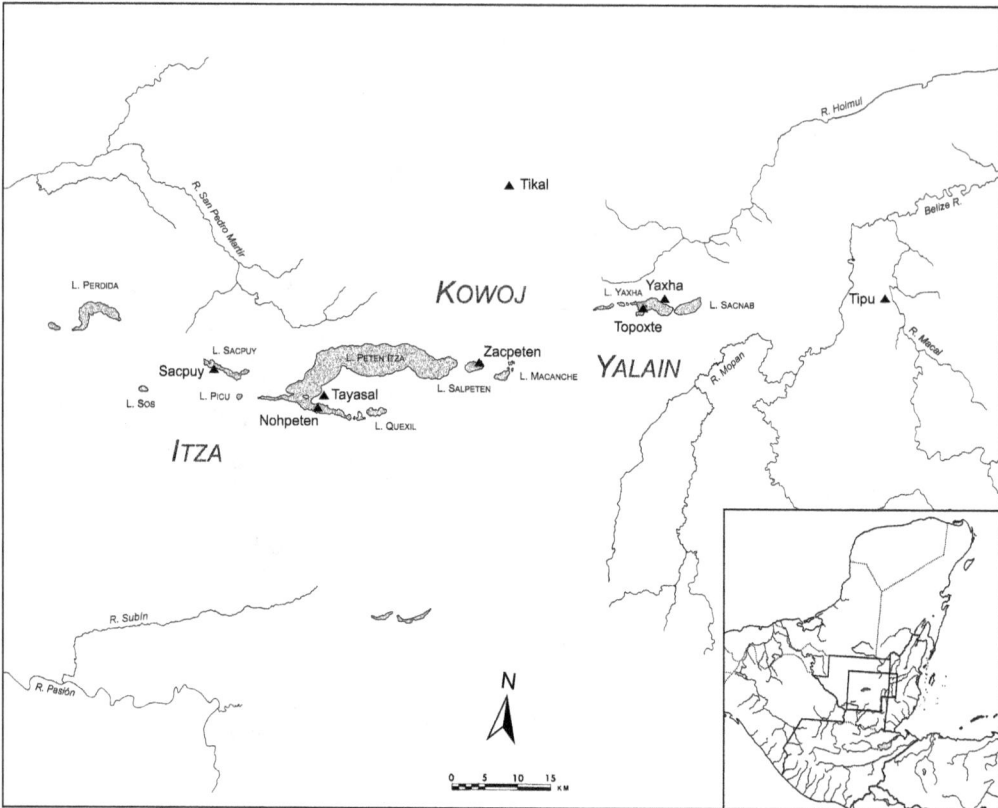

Map 2.4. Peten lakes showing the communities around the lakes and their relationship to Tipu. (Drawing by Christophe Helmke)

occupied the eastern lakes region. Their initial center of occupation, which archaeologists date to ca. 1450 at the latest, seems to have been the Topoxte Islands in Lake Yaxha, at the eastern end of the lakes chain (map 2.4).[120] The Kowoj then pushed westward and established communities around the smaller lakes, such as Lake Salpeten and Lake Macanche.[121] This scenario of arrival and subsequent expansion is derived from archaeological excavations in the eastern part of the lakes chain, which reveal a complex of decorated pottery, incense burners, and architecture and mortuary treatment that are interpreted as the expression of a distinct Kowoj identity.[122] In the documents there is a statement by a Spanish captain, who spent several months in Peten in 1699, that the Couoh (Kowoj) retreated from Tancab (Mayapan) to Peten at the time of the conquest of Yucatan,[123] which would have been in the 1540s.[124] The apparent discrepancy between an arrival dated to around 1450 as opposed to the 1540s can be explained by the fact that Maya groups who left one place for another often did so because they already had relatives (other members of the patronym group or lineage) at the place of destination.[125] Otherwise, such a long-distance migration would not have been possible without sustained violence or warfare; and it would have been difficult to plan war against Peten groups from a base at Mayapan. It is highly likely that there were already Kowoj connections in the eastern lakes at the time the Kowoj from Mayapan planned their move.

An architectural complex known as Complex I (see map 8.3, Strs. H12-1 to H12-4), considered to be a marker of Kowoj identity and ritual, was excavated at Tipu.[126] Cecil has also been able to identify decorated pottery groups that are common to a Kowoj sphere,[127] which includes the central Peten lake sites of Zacpeten, Lake Macanche, and Topoxte, and extends eastward to include Tipu (map 2.4). In most cases, pottery seems to have originated at Peten sites and to have been traded to Tipu,[128] although it is possible that some of the pottery was brought to Tipu as part of tribute payments. Individuals at Tipu almost certainly also had ties to the Peten Itza, as evidenced at Complex I by orange-paste pottery with black-painted reptilian motifs that may reflect the ruling lineage of the Peten Itza.[129] The lower frequencies of Itza pottery, compared to Kowoj pottery, suggests that during the time Complex I was in use, probably in the early sixteenth century, ties to the Kowoj were stronger than were ties to the Itza.[130]

A third group with whom Tipuans were associated before the Conquest period was the Mopan, who spoke a form of Yucatec. The origin of the designation "Mopan" is not known, although it is a name now applied to the western branch of the Belize River. The name appears in Spanish documents as a designator of a group of people who occupied a number of towns and villages in eastern Peten and Belize and who were probably resident in the region before the arrival of the Kowoj.[131] It is not clear that the group called "Mopan" self-identified as such; "Mopan" seems more likely to be a term adopted by Spanish chroniclers and modern researchers, although Jones has been able to identify lineage names that appear to be Mopan.[132]

Where does all this leave Tipu on the eve of conquest? Rather than suggest which ethnic group may have been in control, I propose the existence of a community in which a number of families looked on Tipu as their cah, but could also claim membership in more than one patronym group, or chibal. These groups gave them connections to Maya in communities in Peten, Campeche, northern Belize, and perhaps even Yucatan, even before the Conquest. Elites in the community received tribute and probably forged marriage alliances and waged wars in order to expand the resources which they controlled. The alliances almost certainly involved Itza and Kowoj, Kowoj and Itza, or Itza or Kowoj and Mopan, or any other individuals who happened to reside in the region. In other words, we have no basis for assuming that marriage alliances were forged or that wars were waged along what we think of as "ethnic" lines, because there is no evidence that the Maya thought in these terms. It is more likely that economic gain drove the elites at Tipu to seek a good marriage or wage a successful war prior to the arrival of the Spaniards. Hence, there is no reason to think that Kowoj or Itza did not wage war among themselves, or intermarry, or make deals. If they did, then Tipu as a community, or cah, is unlikely to have been ethnically Itza or Kowoj or Mopan, and instead was all of these and more.

Lamanai at the End of the Postclassic

Lamanai offers as complex a picture as Tipu. Beginning in Early Postclassic times, in the late tenth or eleventh century, it clearly generated a number of ceramic traditions of its own.[133] Yet from the Late Classic period (ca. A.D. 700 onward),[134] and possibly earlier, it never quite fit the mold of a southern lowlands Classic site. Its Late Classic architecture departs from practices previously shared among Belize sites and displays possible parallels with Champoton on the Gulf Coast of Campeche.[135] Ceramic analyses are ongoing and conclusions are provisional, but Lamanai seems overall to have been a community that maintained stability throughout its history by consistently being manageably unstable, which is my way of saying that Lamanai was open to ideas from outside the community throughout its history. Dzuluinicob[136] means "foreign people,"[137] and the New River may have borne this name because it connected the international routes of seafaring trade and communication with riverine communities that were the gateway to inland towns and villages. Thus, the river was always a force of integration, by bringing what was local into contact with what was non-local.

Were Lamanai and Tipu part of the same province in pre-Columbian times? The artifact inventory suggests that the two were not part of the same cultural sphere. Lamanai Yglesias-phase pottery, which was in use in the Terminal Postclassic (ca. 1492–1544; fig. 2.3)—judged in part by the fact that the contexts lacked Spanish artifacts—continued to be made in the Spanish colonial period; it shares features with the Late Postclassic Xabalxab Complex of Santa Rita Corozal, on Chetumal Bay.[138] The forms of Lamanai Yglesias jars and tripod bowls are broadly similar to examples from Santa Rita;[139] the Yglesias red slip is, however, more of a wash than the true slip of Rita Red. Although much of the Yglesias-phase pottery at Lamanai is from the period following the establishment of encomiendas in 1544, evidence suggests that the technology of slip and pottery manufacture may have declined at Lamanai before 1544, possibly beginning in the first half of the sixteenth century (hence the date span proposed in fig. 2.3). I discuss why this happened at La-manai and not at Tipu in more detail in chapter 5.

Another similarity between Lamanai and Santa Rita is the occurrence of effigy zoomorphs,[140] effigies of reptilians or felines or deer or fish, or, more commonly, combinations of traits from a variety of creatures. The mouth is open wide, with a human head protruding from it, and the effigy often takes the form of a container with a stopper.[141] At Lamanai, the zoomorphs appear to occur more commonly in the Spanish colonial period than earlier, although the zones of Terminal or even Late Postclassic settlement that have been ex-cavated at Lamanai are limited, in comparison to those that represent colo-nial settlement. Recent research on Terminal Postclassic and Spanish colonial households is, however, beginning to fill this gap in our knowledge.[142]

With regard to the period from 1250 or 1300 to 1500, large gaps also re-main. Cib Phase ceramics from this period[143] comprise vessels recovered largely from burials in a single structure near the lagoon, Str. N10-4, which post-dates the Early Postclassic and pre-dates the Terminal Postclassic.[144] This means that the pottery could fall anywhere from about 1250 to 1450/1500. The ceramics closely resemble what is known to archaeologists as the Red Payil Group of Tulum Red Ware, found at both Tulum, on the east coast, and May-apan, although Tulum Red Ware is generally considered to have been an east coast tradition.[145]

On the basis of the ceramics, Lamanai and Tipu seem to have belonged to different spheres of interaction, at least in the period immediately prior to Spanish contact. What such differences meant in terms of tribute rela-tionships remains unknown. Judging by material culture alone, Lamanai, just prior to the Spanish conquest, was part of a northward-looking sphere, whereas Tipu's sphere extended westward into the Peten, and to some de-gree northward and eastward along the upper reaches of the Belize Valley. During the Spanish period of encomienda, and perhaps even earlier, these distinctions would have become blurred, as Spanish tribute demands restruc-tured relationships throughout the peninsula. But the question remains as to whether or not material culture reflects the direction of tribute flow and hence some form of geopolitical orientation. The striking common elements in the architecture at Tipu and Lamanai can, as we shall see in chapters 8 and 9, be traced to Spanish colonial sources, as can the Spanish pottery and the burial practices, and hence, for this period, material culture can be taken to be an indicator that Tipu and Lamanai were part of territory that was tied to Spanish colonial seats of power farther north in Yucatan.

With regard to the pre-Columbian period, we need to know more about whether pottery and other artifacts were made locally or outside the commu-nity. It would also be helpful to isolate elite households and attempt to learn where their exotics originated. Even with this information in hand, identification of the exact direction of tribute flow may prove difficult, because tribute could have been paid in manufactured goods from afar rather than in raw materials. Lamanai, as a commercial center, may well have had access to many such materials. For the Postclassic, absence of the Classic-period glyphic record means that it will be some time before we are able to propose the spheres of geopolitics.

Tribute relationships—because they involve transporting goods from one place to another, and hence entail the frequent movement of people between one community (or cah) and another—entailed cultural or economic interchange and communication at several levels, including visits to markets and other sorts of social interaction. It is uncertain how regularly Lamaneros and Tipuans interacted in the pre-Conquest period; certainly their pottery inventories are distinctive, which suggests that they are not likely to have been part of the same tribute network, although there was likely some contact in the sphere of inter-regional trade and exchange. Lamanai and Santa Rita, on the other hand, are very likely to have interacted frequently, but we do not have enough information to be able to determine whether Santa Rita elites paid tribute to Lamanai, or vice versa, or if both paid tribute to a third, more powerful community farther north. If Santa Rita is indeed the site of the ancient capital of Chetumal, then Lamanai may have been part of a kúuchkabal of which the seat of power was based at Chetumal. At the same time, Lamanai lords may have been part of a different patronym group, and hence part of a kuuchkabal with a distinctive tribute network that overlapped with Santa Rita. There is also the possibility that communities such as Lamanai and Santa Rita, as well as smaller but commercially active communities such as Caye Coco (possibly ancient Chanlacan),[146] operated independently in commercial matters but exchanged tribute with some communities on the basis of family ties.

Suffice it to say that the communities in Belize on the eve of Conquest were, like the communities in northern Yucatan, in a state of flux. Entrepreneurship seems to have flourished at Lamanai, but it is possible that in time, and without Spanish interference, one community or communities in a region might have risen to prominence. This potential was curtailed by the arrival of Europeans and the development of the environment of early contact, which I discuss in chapter 5. In the next two chapters, I turn to the critical framework for discussion of Christianity and religion—terminology.

✠ THREE ✠

Cheese and Terms

Having attempted in chapter 2 to reconstruct conditions in Yucatan and Belize on the eve of Conquest, I turn in this chapter and the next to clarifying a range of terms commonly used in research on conquest and conversion. I intended originally to include issues of terminology in my conclusions, but the terms arise so frequently in literature that is meant to be solely "descriptive," it is not possible to proceed without highlighting problems in their usage and meaning. Rethinking problematic terms is not trivial, but essential, in order to find new ways to "read," or to "see" beyond, the accounts of Maya-Spanish interaction provided by the Spanish chroniclers. Accounts of Maya responses will always be colored by Spanish interpretation, but turning our attention to the Spanish colonial palette, in addition to our own, should afford insight into Maya conversion and the process of Christianization.

Spanish chroniclers used a common range of terms in explaining Maya actions and reactions during the colonial encounter. Some of the same terms were used by Christian chroniclers and missionaries in Late Antique and Early Medieval Europe. The result is that anyone interested in early conversion and Christianization cannot avoid forming a perception of the encounter framed, at least in part, by the labeling of practices as "idolatrous" or "pagan," or by the identification of forces as "devils" or "demons." These terms remain widely employed, as well as others about which there seems to be consensus through usage, such as "religion," "conversion," "Christianity," "cults," and "doctrine."

Before exploring these terms and their bearing on assessing the colonial experience in Belize, the practice I follow of using "Maya" and "Spaniard" to stand for the group should be explained. The name "Maya" originally appeared in Spanish records as a place name.[1] More than one source describes it

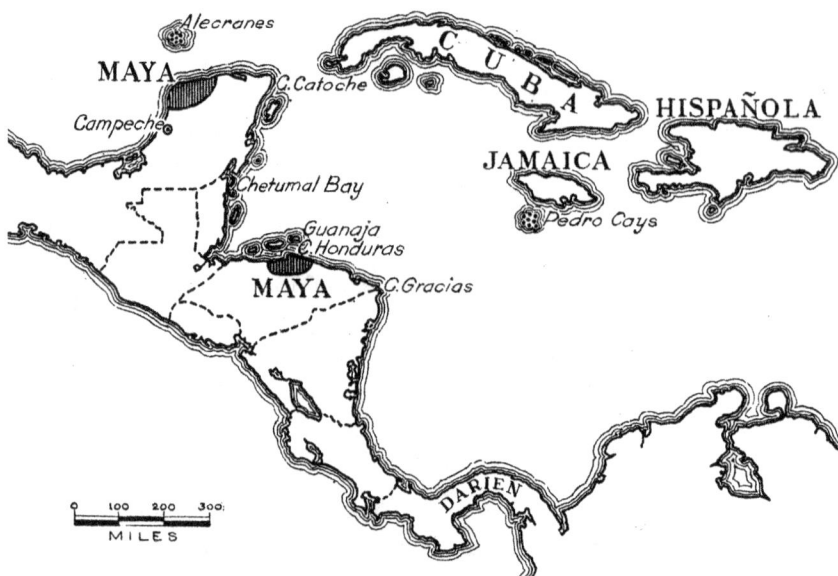

Map 3.1. Two provinces called "Maya" in the sixteenth century.
(Lothrop 1927, 352, fig. 136).

as the name of a province or part of the Yucatan Peninsula, and the Turin map of 1523 places "Maya" on the north coast of Yucatan.[2]

According to Diego López de Cogolludo, the Franciscan friar who wrote a history of Yucatan, the land known to the Spaniards as Yucatán was called "Maya" by the people who lived there. Cogolludo recounts that the land was governed for a long time by a supreme lord, whose seat was the city of Mayapan. By the time the Spaniards first arrived (in 1517), internal dissension had resulted in the breakdown of the rule of this particular lord, with many individuals ruling smaller areas and living in a state of constant warfare. In López de Cogolludo's opinion, "Maya" was probably derived from "Mayapan."[3] Lothrop assembled data—such as the appearance of "Maia" in print in 1516, a year before the discovery of what we now know as Yucatan—to suggest that the name "Maya," or "Maia," also applied to a native province on the north coast of Honduras (map 3.1).[4]

Although *indio* (or *naturales*, as is the case with López de Cogolludo[5]) was the common referent in Spanish-language documents, and "Maya" was used only infrequently and inconsistently in colonial Yucatec-language sources,[6] the name "Maya" came to be applied to the native people of the Yucatan Peninsula, and eventually to "a broad swathe of peoples" in southern

Mesoamerica,[7] all of whom speak a related but diverse range of languages and lay claim to a variety of customs and practices. Native individuals in Yucatan in colonial times identified themselves not as ethnically Maya but as members of a particular municipal community, the cah, as described in chapter 2, or as belonging to a patronym group, the chibal. They resisted any uniform ethnic identity until the twentieth century, when the seeds of forces that would lead to pan-Maya movements were sown.[8] Thus, with the exception, only very recently, of highland Guatemala,[9] "Maya" has served more as a term of ascription than of belonging.

With these data as caveats, I use the term "Maya" to describe the people living in the areas I cover in this book at the time of the Spanish conquest for two reasons. The first is that there are features of language and culture that distinguish the people we call "Maya" from others;[10] the second is that we simply do not know the range of identifiers (community or lineage names) that were used in the past, particularly in the communities of the region now known as Belize. Therefore even as a construction or invention[11] the use of "Maya" as a referent can advance discussion and debate about the processes of colonial expansion.

Similar caveats apply to use of the term "Spaniard," because Iberians of the time identified themselves as being from Castile or Navarre and not Spain.[12] The Franciscans who feature in later chapters on Spanish proselytization were predominantly from the Iberian peninsula, especially in the latter half of the sixteenth century when a kind of nationalism prevailed; but in the first half of the century, Franciscans were recruited not only from kingdoms in Spain and from Portugal,[13] but from Flanders, France, Italy, and even Denmark and Scotland.[14] All shared aspects of European culture and a point of view based on Christian missionary zeal that drew them to a new continent. Similarly, the people who inhabited the Yucatan Peninsula shared points of view and histories and origins distinct from those of the invading Europeans. It is with this dichotomy in mind that I employ the terms Spaniard and Maya; at the same time, I recognize that such a dichotomy can cloud awareness of the very agency that forms the core of my thesis. Until more research is carried out on the lives of individual Franciscans who journeyed to Yucatan and Belize, however, and until more archival information surfaces on individual Maya lives in sixteenth- and seventeenth-century Belize, these general terms must serve to provide the springboard for discussion. I will make every attempt to be clear about the various contexts of my discussion, however, and to be attentive to the way in which I apply terms.[15]

Archaeologists are among those who employ the collective term "Maya" to differentiate the native Americans of the Yucatan Peninsula from the invading

Spaniards. The practice facilitates discussion but we need repeatedly to remind ourselves that the collective is made up of individuals and that innovation, at least as we understand it,[16] is effected at the level of the individual.[17] It is important to accord each individual, whether at Tipu or Lamanai or Bacalar or Mérida or indeed in Seville or Plymouth, the power to assess and to analyze incoming information as well as the intelligence and capacity to refashion world view, globally or locally, on his or her own terms. I do not deny that an "individual's own terms" include socially derived values or ideas,[18] and I recognize that the concept of "culture" helps us as archaeologists to choose among likely options available to the group. Nonetheless, relationships between Mayas and Spaniards and their outcomes were potentially as varied as were individual Mayas or individual Spaniards.

Pinto's study of wills in fifteenth- and sixteenth-century Spain, for example, reveals the "amazing amount of creativity and range of choice displayed in an individual's interpretation of death and burial, even within the Christian cultural religious context."[19] The overwhelming drive represented in the wills that propelled choices about burial placement and ritual turned out to be the drive to preserve identity.[20] Obviously, such a discovery has implications for archaeological interpretations of burial placement, but it should also sensitize us to the fact that simply because a cultural pattern or a religious rule seems more knowable to archaeologists than a personality, we cannot assume that either culture or religion is more likely to be a driving force behind decision making.

Cheese and Worms

It is easy to say that change is catalyzed and configured at the level of the individual, but what information do we have from individual Mayas about their analyses of Christianity? We have nothing that has not been said within the hearing of the friars, but this does not mean that individuals were incapable of analysis. That the Maya were deeply concerned with the messages they were receiving from the Spanish Christians, and that they struggled proactively, and not just reactively, to accommodate as well as criticize the new ideas, is a major premise of this book.

The power of the individual to evaluate and criticize brings me to the "cheese" of the chapter title—a reference to the ideas of a sixteenth-century miller from a village in the hills of Friuli, Italy, who had read the Bible and felt that he was not only capable of arguing about the faith, but had the *right* to do so.[21] Sadly, records of a similar sort concerning Maya ideas about Christianity that were not expressed within the hearing of friars or church authorities, or by those concerned with church doctrine, are extremely rare. However, rarity in the historical record does not mean that individuals could not think for themselves. I intend the miller from Friuli to act as a model for the idea that Maya reactions to conquest, colonization, and Christianization involved complex adjustments and thinking on a number of levels, including the level at which individuals attempted to come to grips with the Christian cosmos that threatened to envelop their lives. One way to mitigate the threat was to take power over the message.

MILLERS AND THE MESSAGE

Carlo Ginzburg is the historian who discovered the Friulian miller's predicament, which he describes in a work entitled "Cheese and Worms."[22] The miller's name was Domenico Scandella, but he was known in his village by the nickname "Menocchio." He was born around 1532, and was tried for his ideas by the Holy Office of the Inquisition beginning in 1584. The cheese and worms of the title comes from one of Menocchio's expositions during his trial.

> I said that, in my thought and belief, everything was chaos, I mean earth, air, water, and fire all together; and that volume, revolving, formed a mass, just like cheese does in milk, and in that mass there appeared some worms, and those were angels; and the most holy Majesty decreed that those were God and the angels; and in that number of angels there was also God, he, too, created by that mass in the same time.[23]

The idea of order emerging from chaos is a creation theme common to many civilizations and cultures; nonetheless, Menocchio's graphic version did not endear him to the church establishment. Other heretical ideas of Menocchio's were that the clergy should have no particular authority in matters of faith; that when we are dead, we are nothing, only like worms and animals; and that Jesus Christ could not be born of a virgin. Menocchio owned a Bible that had been translated into Italian, which was considered a forbidden book.[24]

Ginzburg mentions the case of another miller, who was tried in 1570 by the Holy Office of Ferrara. This miller asserted that all sacraments, with the exception of baptism, had been established by the church and not by Christ, and he denied the validity of the intercession of saints, confession, and the fasts prescribed by the church. Unlike poor Menocchio, who was executed as 1599 drew to a close, the miller in the Ferrara case was simply exiled to another village.[25] According to Ginzburg, the Catholic authorities at that time were struggling to enforce the doctrines of the Council of Trent: "hence their pitiless persecution . . . against the aged miller."[26]

Although the Council of Trent (1545–47, 1551–52, 1561–63)[27] (see chap. 6) deeply affected church attitudes toward the Maya,[28] the case of the two millers is meant to show that deliberation and complexity of thought were not limited in Mediterranean Europe either to local elites or to educated men of the church. If the millers could think for themselves, so could Maya batabs or scribes, potters or stone masons, farmers or traders. Landa's trials of Maya "idolators" in 1562, to which we shall return in due course, do not give any of the accused Maya even the limited opportunity Menocchio had to explain the sources of their ideas in their own terms, because the good bishop made it clear that he already knew all the answers.

The documents on Landa's idolatry trials contain little direct testimony given by the Maya;[29] the stories were fashioned by their tellers rather than springing from events.[30] It is also true that when the accused Maya responded, they structured responses according to what they thought their accusers wanted to hear.[31] Like Carlo Ginzburg in his research on the attitudes and behavior of the lower classes in medieval Europe, those of us interested in the Maya-Spanish encounter face distortion of evidence. However, whereas Ginzburg faced a scarcity of sources, we cannot be sure that *any* documents exist in which the friars recorded the thinking behind Maya actions and beliefs in the way that the inquisitors recorded Menocchio's ideas.[32] There are hints of the nature of the distortion of evidence in the records of Landa's *auto de fé* and in Bishop Toral's investigation which followed,[33] but what the Maya thought about the Christian message in a critical sense remains hidden.

From Cheese to Terms

In an attempt to discover the ways in which Christianity may have appeared to Maya individuals and how Christian beliefs and ritual behaviors could have been interpreted, I have taken the step of assessing and deconstructing terms commonly used to categorize the presumed rationale behind Maya accommodations and reactions to Christianity. This is not the same as discovering documents on the critical thinking of sixteenth-century millers; however, updating our conceptual inventory is important in sensitizing us to the presence of depth of thought where we might otherwise see only acts of resistance or grudging accommodation or a pragmatic (or even deficient) cultural syncretism. Along with "religion," perhaps the most problematic term of all, I consider "cults," "idols," "devils," and "demons." In chapter 4, I turn to "conversion," "Christianization," "paganism," and "doctrine."

I cannot pretend to be even remotely comprehensive in discussing religion, and I do not wish to alienate readers by belaboring it, but I grapple with "religion" because it is very likely to be used to describe this book's focus, which is the Maya encounter with Christians and Christianity in early Belize. Indeed, I use "religion" myself. I also claim some analytical authority and identification with Spanish Christians on the basis of my Roman Catholic Mediterranean background. Christianity, or Roman Catholicism in my case, is commonly considered a religion; therefore I feel compelled to ask what religion is, and how both the word and the concept figure in our accounts of conversion, Conquest, and the aftermath.

Historians or archaeologists of the Spanish encounter in the New World (or, indeed, academics in their writing in general), of Catholic or Christian upbringing or affiliation, generally do not acknowledge such background in the text of their publications because they treat their works—as indeed their disciplines have treated their works—as part of the objective academic tradition. Others[34] openly identify with religious-affiliated institutions but adhere to scholarly criteria of objectivity. Chroniclers of the Franciscans among the Maya, such as Lopez de Cogolludo,[35] or more recent historians associated with a religious faith, such as Bayle or Lopetegui and Zubillaga,[36] have biases as members of religious orders, but they are clear in their narratives about their positioning. They can be critical—as in the case of Lopetegui and Zubillaga about the burning of Maya books by Landa and about López de Cogolludo's "professional indifference" toward the incident—but at the same time, they express admiration for what they see as spreading the word of God.[37] Given their commitment to their faith and its tenets, it is not to be expected that they will criticize evangelization as a process, because they are dedicated to spreading or teaching or upholding their faith. Anthropologists would say that "those . . . close to Christianity cannot always divorce themselves from the cultural and emotional associations that they entertain toward it."[38]

In the bulk of modern academic writing, if the author has a professed faith or religion, it generally remains hidden.[39] The academic stance comes across as a-theistic, or at least as a stance removed from any explicit identification with a religion. The irony is that, although scholars concerned with the Christianization of New Spain or Mesoamerica may not claim a religion, there is no hesitation in writing about it. To claim a religious identification, if one exists, would be seen as leading to a bias that would inevitably produce a prejudicial account. In fact, it has been suggested that analysts of religion should adopt a standpoint of "methodological atheism."[40] The implication is that not having a religion or not talking about one's religion or not talking about why one has no religion makes one better equipped to assess religion.

What Is Religion?

In literature that covers aspects of society that would be considered religious—for example, in ethnographies of the Maya of highland regions,[41] the lowland Maya,[42] the Maya more generally,[43] or in studies of groups in Mexico or Oaxaca,[44] use of the term "religion" varies, but it is notable that it is used sparingly, and rarely as a definitional or institutional category. Perhaps this is not surprising in the case of researchers who see the behavior that the term "religion" represents as integrated with other aspects of culture.[45] Contrary to Asad's contention that for twentieth-century anthropologists religion is "a distinctive space of human practice and belief which cannot be reduced to any other,"[46] one would be hard-pressed to define "religion" if one had to rely only on the way the word surfaces in ethnographies, which I think tells us something about the term.

Ethnographers of Maya and other native communities refer to "religious" activity to different degrees, but they actually organize or structure their studies in terms of the details of life, both daily or celebrated at regular intervals, which they have observed among the people they are studying, and headings and subjects vary: baptisms, ritual, souls, violence, gods, God, social existence, powers, prayer sayers, day-keepers, language, stories, synthesis, *cofradías*, community, politics, communications, and cosmology, to name but a few. Generally speaking, the term "religion" does not serve as a social institutional heading, as a line in the table of contents, or as an organizing principle, even when it occasionally serves as a subtitle; the result is that the various elements of social life come across as highly integrated and difficult to disentangle—or, to use Geertz's metaphor, as "knotted into one another."[47] Sometimes "religion" is referred to in studies of identity formation as a separate social institution or cultural context,[48] but these same studies make it evident that such identities are forged under conditions in which perceptions and beliefs cannot readily be divided into the religious vs. the non-religious.[49]

Monaghan,[50] in his discussion of "Theology and History in the Study of Mesoamerican Religions," notes a trend in recent years toward growing specialization and interest in "religion" as an organizing topic, not just among anthropologists, but among scholars of many disciplines. My question is: does this result from the fact that there is something called "religion" which has become a more important player as an "institution"? Or, is our increasing investment in "religion" as a topic, and thereby in the word as a category, an inevitable consequence of a global phenomenon of social fragmentation and the inadequacies of our conceptual repertoire, given its roots, to grapple with the process? In reflecting on the history of the anthropology of religion, Lambek explores the potential of certain aspects of Aristotle's thought for reconfiguring approaches to religion,[51] partly as a corrective for characterizing some societies as "traditional," and partly as a new way of thinking about "practice in the contemporary global dis/order."[52] Like me, he seems to be concerned with how the concept of religion as we have used it contributes to fragmentation. Perhaps the difficulties we have experienced historically in using "religion" as the name of something we like to think of as an institution, a system, or part of a cultural system,[53] makes it the concept whose failure will bring us to our senses.

What is religion, then? Lessa and Vogt's review of anthropological approaches to religion begins with nineteenth-century evolutionist theories.[54] For Tylor, religious beliefs derived from the concept of a soul, and then extended to worship of ancestors, spirits, deities, and eventually God. (Seeing gods and fearing death still reign as important identifying criteria for beliefs that are labeled "religious."[55]) For Durkheim, religion was rooted in the moral order of society and from people's obligations and experiences as social beings. Weber recognized the importance of meaning and the critical integration of religion with other forms of social institutions. Freud saw religion as a collective attempt to resolve anxieties that stemmed from conflicts in individual personality. Malinowsky and Radcliffe-Brown were interested in how religion functioned. In the 1960s the focus shifted to the meaning of religious symbols and beliefs.[56] Lessa and Vogt conclude that "the anthropological study of religion has moved from concern with the origins of religion to the elucidation of the sociological and psychological functions that religion fulfils to an inquiry into the way in which religious beliefs and thought are structured and expressed,"[57] which confirms Lambek's observation that the history of the anthropology of religion "is precisely what has constituted the substance of the subject."[58]

At the time they were writing, in the 1970s and 1980s, Lessa and Vogt lamented, as did Geertz,[59] the lack of progress in theoretical treatment of religion with respect to other aspects of culture, such as social structure or kinship or language. If our word "religion" does not really stand for a viable concept, or one about which consensus can be reached, then this might well explain the problems in theorizing about it. In other words, we have to ask whether there is a "religion" about which to theorize.[60]

In recent years, several new theories of religion have been proposed,[61] but the question "What is religion?" seems to be asked at one level only, which I will try to articulate. It is basically: "There is something called religion that is the source of religious representations or beliefs or ideas. Where do these ideas come from?" This quest for origins is different from earlier approaches because modern studies are not particularly interested in the diversity of representations or their social roots or function, but instead in their common cognitive foundations.[62]

In studies such as those of Eliade or, more recently, Smart,[63] the word "religion" appears more times than it would in an ethnography or cognitive study, because the concept is accepted as a valid description of the world and is used as the basis for investigation, although Smart equates religion with "worldview."[64] Such studies can be descriptive or analytical, but either way, the map is the territory.[65]

Why "religion" should be a category at all is less commonly considered. Boyer grapples partly with this question when he criticizes those who say that people who have no category of "the religious" have no religious representations or actions, because their culture has not constructed these categories.[66] The ancient and colonial-period Maya, for example, are among those whose languages have no category equivalent to our term "religion";[67] that is, there does not seem to be a term to designate what Western thinkers see as religious representations or religious behavior.[68] Boyer decides that an absence of the "religious" as a concept does not mean there are no representations or actions that *we* might categorize as religious. He argues that it would be simple-minded to claim that people who have no category of "the religious," and who do not distinguish between religious representations or actions and other sorts of actions, literally have no religious representations or actions because their culture has not constructed these categories.[69]

Boyer's reasoning is valid, first, if there is indeed consensus about the ideas whose foundations he is interested in exploring, and second, if prioritizing human unity takes precedence over diversity as a subject of study. Assuming consensus and prioritizing human unity solves his problem of legitimizing a search for a cognitive foundation for ideas that he has already subsumed under the category of religious ideas; but it does not solve *my* problem, which is the question of why he chooses to use the term "religious" to cover a group of ideas. Where did the notion originate that there is such a thing as religious ideas that are not something else? Boyer's interest is non-culturally specific and evolutionary—"that the variability of cultural ideas is not unbounded."[70] My interest lies in variability and is therefore culturally specific: why does western society put so much emphasis on the concept of religion as a reality?

Asad[71] answers this question by attributing the anthropological definition of religion—as an "autonomous essence" separate from science or politics, with the additional feature of being transhistorical and transcultural—to the history of Western knowledge and power from which the modern world is constructed.[72] In medieval Christianity, with which we are concerned in this book, the West was largely consonant with the Christian world and the church was the source of knowledge and of authenticating discourse. According to Smith, "religion" at that time was a concept akin to "ritual."[73] In the seventeenth century, religion became divorced from knowledge and reduced to beliefs—beliefs about a supreme being, about practices such as worship, and about ethics or codes of conduct. Knowledge, on the other hand, came to be associated with science, or with a secular perspective.[74] The right to individual belief was all that post-Enlightenment society would allow Christianity to appropriate.[75]

This is a powerful argument, but I suspect that the problem with "religion" goes even deeper than this. First of all, if we set aside the idea that belief is a mental state,[76] and see "it" instead as a dynamic phenomenon—the way in which we integrate (think about) what is going on in the world around us— then it is hard to visualize or internalize a separation between something secular that is the knowledge authority, from something religious that is not a knowledge authority, even if this is a viable way to describe a historical process from the point of view of an observer. Second, if we look at the "secular" world, we find that those who identify with it suffer a conceptual dearth when they attempt to describe beliefs that they say are not religious. After all, those who claim *not* to have a religion, because they do not believe in a deity, actually define themselves in terms of a deity: a-theists.[77] They are not believers *in something*, but "non-believers." This is not just a word game; it hints at something deep and important about the way we approach the world. I think it goes beyond even the history of how religion came to be conceptualized, or marginalized,[78] in Western discourse.

IS THERE RELIGION?

The etymology of the word "religion" is, interestingly enough, unknown.[79] According to the *Oxford English Dictionary*,[80] Cicero connected the word with *relegere*, "to read over again"; but later authors and modern writers have connected it with *religare*, "to bind." The anthropologist Bowie and the archaeologist Insoll provide other etymologies.[81] We certainly have come to think of the word "religion" as describing something that binds people together— usually, but not always, with the implication that the binding entails belief in an unseen higher power that can control human destiny and is entitled to obedience or reverence or worship. There are moral and mental attitudes that stem from this belief which are taken on by the individual or community as a standard of spiritual and practical life.[82] The concept of the sacred is normally associated with what we call "religion."[83]

Both Insoll and Bowie provide good discussions of definitions of "religion," and both agree that the term is problematic.[84] Both delve into origins, but whereas Bowie focuses on anthropologists' approaches to religion and its roots, Insoll considers evidence for the capacity for religious consciousness in early humans. Bowie stresses that "religion" is predominantly a Western categorization and that the concept seems not to have existed as such in Asia,[85] at least prior to modern times, when Asian languages have made allowances for Western terms.

Insoll asks whether "religion" is a concept that results only from a desire to classify what is unclassifiable and indivisible.[86] King carries this further by suggesting that "religion" is a theoretical construct that has its uses in examining an aspect of the human experience, but "should not be reified as if it could exist apart from that context."[87] Smith shares this attitude, which is that "religion" is a term created by scholars for their intellectual purposes and is theirs to define.[88] The humanist definition given by Firth is that religion and ideas of a deity are a human construct; indeed, he characterizes religion as a human art.[89] Except for the part about religion being art, both Dawkins and Lett would agree,[90] although both would undoubtedly add that religion is irrational. For our purposes, though, the observation that religion is either art or irrational has little explanatory value, because people who carry out the practices to which we apply the term "religion" do not see their beliefs or their practices in that way.

Perhaps the key concept in understanding "religion" is "experience," and what we call religion is our way of describing a range of expressions of experience[91] that may well be described differently both by other observers and especially by those doing the experiencing. If this is valid, then "religion" is not even explanatory.[92] I am going to pick up on the idea that what we subsume under the rubric of "religion" is not always definable or separable from experience in general. For example, if a Roman Catholic has a vision of a saint during a pilgrimage to a shrine, he would not describe such an experience as religious. He would wake the next day and run excitedly to his companions and say that the night before, St. Anthony had visited him. He might describe the vision as a transforming and deeply moving experience, and he might recognize that it affected his self-awareness, assuaged his fear of death, or helped him to regain self-mastery,[93] but he would not call it religious. Classifying oneself in terms of a "religion" is more likely to reflect the demands of filling out a government or census form than to represent how people choose to see themselves.

If I, as part of my analysis, use the term "religious" to classify experience, what does this mean? What does it mean when Boyer or Atran or Wilson uses the term "religion" to classify concepts or representations or ideas?[94] To some extent, all of these examples reinforce "religion" as a construct, except that the split between those who use the construct—anthropologists who study religion or evolution, members of departments of religious studies, journalists describing wars in the Middle East, or atheists criticizing those who hold beliefs that involve God—and those to whom the term "religion" is basically irrelevant but who define themselves by a set of beliefs and practices that *others* separate out and call "religion," militates against the idea that "religion" has explanatory value even as a construct, particularly if we are interested in social change. If "religion" has meaning largely from the perspective of an outsider using the term to refer to beliefs and practices that are not his or her own; or is used to describe phenomena accepted, but not challenged or criticized, as being definitionally and adequately represented by the term, how can "religion" be useful or meaningful, let alone be approached "scientifically"?[95]

Perhaps the term "religion" and its use reflect the user, and not, despite what its use implies, insight into the subject of study. It labels the user as someone who withdraws from or sits outside the faith(s) or belief(s) or culture(s) or world view(s) being studied or observed. The most useful thing that can be said in these circumstances is that investing in the term "religion" represents a fruitful node of interaction between the user—given his or her particular world view—and the experience of the other(s),[96] because the resulting conclusions or insights enhance self awareness of the user group. To push King's insight[97] one step further, "religion" does not exist apart from the context in which it is used by someone on the outside looking in. I can pick out "religious" ideas in someone else or in her group, but find it very difficult if not impossible to do so in myself, even as a lapsed Roman Catholic. In these circumstances, can "studying religion" lead to an insider perspective, or to anything that does not mask the very complexity we seek to understand? Taking our cue from Geertz, perhaps we need to think in terms of experience *and* meaning *and* identity *and* power[98]; the question of whether all these factors comprise "religion" to some people and not to others may not matter, or at least it is another question entirely. Perhaps tracing "religious change," as intimated by Geertz, is about writing "a social history of the imagination."[99]

Maya Religion

The foregoing discussion is geared to reexamine assumptions about an important term—"religion"—but also to contextualize my own study with respect to works on Maya religion. I recognize that both the terms "Maya" and "religion" are problematic. Together, they are even more problematic, although not everyone would agree.[100] Yet it holds true that the process of conversion assumed a homogeneous subject;[101] hence, conceptualizing "Maya religion" is not too far from reality in approaching the attitudes of the Spanish proselytizers, although the Spaniards did not always attribute a "religion" to the Indians.[102] It serves poorly, however, in approaching the attitudes of the proselytized, not least because there is no reason to assume that one "religion" was represented by all the Maya living in Yucatan and Belize in the sixteenth century.[103]

The Maya living in villages in Yucatan in modern times have been described as a folk culture.[104] The term is less common today, but Yucatec and highland Maya groups are commonly viewed as people with a religion that is traditional. Traditional practices have been described in early studies as the result of acculturation, which refers to the process of different cultures coming into contact, with changes occurring in the original patterns of one or both groups so that the result is distinctly new.[105] Another term devised to apply to change is "syncretism"—a generalization about elements from different religions or world views that are brought together, with a resultant product different from either of the originals.[106] "Syncretism" has been widely used to describe the consequences of Christian contact and conversion in the Maya region. Some reject it as a designation of a historical phenomenon because it can apply equally well to all expressions of religion; "syncretism" as a term is also problematic because it can imply that the syncretic result is devoid of coherence.[107] Most anthropologists and archaeologists, whether they emphasize strong continuity with pre-Columbian practices;[108] or describe the result of synthesis as neither purely indigenous nor purely Spanish;[109] or see the product as a reinvention or cultural production of Christianity, and the worshipers as Christianized Mayas or Nahuas[110]—all, at least in my judgment, see the beliefs that were engendered as the result of Christian proselytizing among the Maya and the Nahuas as coherent. An exception might be Early, who, like Wagley, sees the Mayas' Christianity, both past and present, as problematic.[111] Early has in mind criteria of "true conversion,"[112] and the Mayas' experiences seem to him to fall short of satisfying these criteria.

Although Early does not use "syncretism," his emphasis, like the emphasis of those who employ the term, is on the *outcome* of a process of interaction and integration. A focus on outcome—on combination and assimilation—can erase the agency of the actors, and thereby obscure process.[113] Early's conclusions that conversion was deficient are not meaningful to those whose beliefs he is assessing, just as "syncretism is irrelevant to those who are inside the faiths."[114] Like Early, my interest in the Maya and Christianity is personal, but we differ in the directions from which we come. He is highly educated in the doctrine of the church, whereas my background is about as close to a "folk religion"[115] as is it is possible to get in an urban setting in the modern era. Based on his descriptions, my Christianity, like the Christianity of Spain in the sixteenth century,[116] is one of traditional beliefs, focused on popular devotions and saints. Therefore, I now turn to the question of beliefs, how they are constructed, how they are labeled, and how they can influence behavior.

According to Firth, religious beliefs are related to "attempts of individuals to secure coherence in their universe of relations, both physical and social."[117] Horton, well known for his work on African religions, similarly supports an approach to what he calls "traditional religious belief," which sees religion as a theoretical system intended for the explanation, prediction, and control of space-time events.[118] Horton rejects the idea, at one time current in social anthropology, that spiritual beings—in this case associated with African cosmologies—should be understood as symbols.

Horton's rejection of the idea that African spiritual beings can be understood as symbols is noteworthy, because spiritual beings in early Western cosmology became symbols as a function of time and culture change, a transformation elegantly articulated by Seznec[119] for the Middle Ages. Seznec explains that pre-Christian supernaturals, such as the Greek gods, were unacceptable to Christians as objects of veneration, but that the gods remained alive as cosmic symbols, or their stories remained alive as allegories. Thus, it is possible that what seem to be contradictory definitions of "religion" (spiritual beings as symbols, or as controllers of events) become compatible if religious "systems" are seen as having histories.

With regard to the Maya, control of space-time events must have been a factor in their consideration of Christianity, because they were concerned with such control prior to contact. However, Maya society viewed prediction and control of space-time events as dependent upon human input, ingenuity, and rigorous observational methods, despite the fact that such control might involve supernatural events. I say this because the Maya practiced what we would call science, in their regular observation of the planetary bodies, in their reckoning of time, and in their application and use of mathematical concepts.[120] In fact, they were well ahead of most of Europe in terms of their knowledge of the movements of the heavenly bodies.[121]

The religions the Maya were practicing at the time of Conquest are not terribly illuminated by the terms "traditional" or "nature religions," although pre-Christian, or non-"world," religions have been categorized in this way.[122] Following Bowie,[123] I eschew these categories and refrain from applying them to the religions of the Maya-Spanish encounter for three reasons. The first is the fact, as I have noted, that the Maya applied observational methods to track the movements of the planetary bodies to an extent that was not matched in Europe at the time. Second, Maya civilization displayed some of the very same conditions under which Christianity originally developed and spread in the Mediterranean. It was not an empire in the sense of the Roman world, but its hierarchies, its elites, its tribute systems, and its commercial networks were urban.[124] Pre-Christian Maya religions could perhaps be called "pagan," but to call them "traditional" would be meaningless. The third reason has to do with the way Spanish Christianity has been depicted, a matter that will be revealed as my larger narrative unfolds.

Horton, in addressing the question of the causes of conversion from "traditional" to "world" religions, sketches a "typical traditional cosmology" and the spectrum of difference between traditional religious life and what he calls a "monolatric cult of a morally concerned supreme being," such as the God of Christianity or Islam.[125] What I find interesting is that his typical traditional cosmology, meant to cover the African religions with which he is concerned, in fact perfectly describes the Roman Catholicism with which I am familiar. Such a cosmology stresses the importance of the local community, as well as the association of lesser spirits (saints) with local concerns, and the supreme being (God) with the wider world; it also avows the approachability of the saints and the fact that neither God nor His Son (according to what I was taught) were to be bothered with people's mundane needs. To the extent that I can draw on my own experience, a dichotomy between "world" and "traditional" religions is unworkable. However, if we change Horton's "traditional religious thought" simply to "thought,"[126] which I will paraphrase as "how people think," his ideas provide insight into stimulus for change that can be applied to the New World.

Horton posits that how people think and experience is closely attuned to a particular set of social circumstances.[127] If these circumstances change and affect stability at the level of the microcosm (or local level), then people begin to feel that the lesser (their local) spirits are becoming weak or are failing them. If people are compelled to become involved in social or economic life beyond the confines of their microcosm, or beyond the boundaries of the familiar, a consequence can be that they develop a theory that involves the supreme being (God to the Christians, and perhaps a manifestation of the single divine [cosmic] principle[128] to the Maya) in a way that was not envisioned before. Horton has in mind the African religions with which he is familiar, and he ties the move to monolatry (or monotheism) to the degree with which people become involved in life beyond the boundaries of the microcosm. Thus, conversion to Christianity involves developmental change that is actually outside the evangelizing activities or influence of missionaries.[129]

In the case of the Maya in Belize, changes outside the evangelizing efforts of the missionaries would have included the demands of the new colonial economy and the consequences of its control by Spain, the disruption of previous tribute networks, and the raiding of coastal and island (caye) communities by pirates and privateers. What we do not know is how significant a conceptual change "monotheism" was for the Maya, or whether the term means anything in describing the process of conversion. Some argue for the existence prior to the arrival of Christianity of a Maya supernatural, or divine, essence, represented as a saurian and sometimes called Itzamna,[130] who was conceptualized as the totality, or essence, of life, and who subsumed all aspects of life, death, and rebirth, and all deities.[131] This divine essence, or vital force,[132] like the Christian God, permeated world view and could be expressed in different ways. Likewise, angels in Christianity, for example, are seen to represent the spirit of God. But if and when the Maya divine essence or vital force was given expression as an image, the image (like that of the Christian God) was not a widespread object of devotion. If these conditions applied, then monotheism as it was expressed by sixteenth-century Spanish Christians did not represent a significant change.

Another perspective to consider is to acknowledge that the Christianity of the Conquest claimed to be monotheistic but actually operated on the basis of a range of accessible supernaturals. The rapidity with which Christian saints took the place of or were conflated with local pre-Columbian lesser spirits suggests in fact that, operationally, the Maya cosmos and the Christian cosmos were similar.[133] Unlike Protestant Christianity, which was brought to Africa in the late nineteenth and early twentieth century, the Christianity which the Maya faced was the Christianity of the Late Middle Ages; God remained distant, but one's saints were always and everywhere accessible, even if the boundaries of the microcosm were transcended.

Despite some problematic assumptions, Horton's insight is invaluable, because it contextualizes conversion as more than a response to new ideas marketed by new people. The implication is that, however "religion" is ultimately defined, referring to religion cannot explain conversion on its own.

We also find that Horton's sketch of "typical traditional cosmology"[134] can be applied equally to medieval Christianity. This is owing not only to the characteristics of Christianity's supernaturals, but also to aspects of the religious behavior of Spanish Christians, such as their interaction with effigies in households and in shrines, as well as their belief in the concept of offerings to gain favor, all of which were familiar to the Maya.[135] Despite the claims of the heightened importance of a supreme being in Christianity, both Spanish and Maya world views evinced strikingly similar local behaviors.

What then is the relationship of behavior to belief? What is the effect of one on the other? Firth expresses interest in religious belief rather than ritual behavior. His statement that religion is an art grows out of his anthropological "outsider" point of view, which is that religion is a construct and (following Marx) a social product of the people under study.[136]

Religion as a *perceived* set of beliefs and rituals that binds people together is indeed a social product from the point of view of an outside observer such as Firth or Marx, and Firth consistently emphasizes the social or patterned aspects even of individual initiative.[137] But how or why individuals initiate, generate, act on, or configure beliefs is only partly social or cultural. During times of stability, it may well seem that patterned aspects of belief are ascendant, at least to an observer (although I would argue that change at the level of the individual ticks away quietly). But during times of social and cultural upheaval, such as the colonial encounter, individual configuration of belief is a powerful force that looms large and deeply affects the dynamics of change to govern the overall outcome. Thus, Firth's analysis, despite his view of religion as a social product, has, in the attention given to belief, provided us with a mechanism for understanding how individual behavior can change.

BELIEF AND THE HEISENBERG PRINCIPLE

Although archaeology as a discipline involves descriptions of past behavior—practices followed in house building or food processing or burial or exchange—how do archaeologists go beyond description to an interpretation of behavior? I am not referring only to interpretation on our part as researchers, but also to how we approach the way the Spaniards interpreted Maya behavior based on Spanish beliefs, of which we have some inkling via the documents, or the way in which the Maya interpreted Spanish behavior based on Maya beliefs, of which we have little evidence. Given the nature of archaeology, the claim is stronger that archaeological data are the result of patterns of behavior rather than patterns of belief.[138] In fact, although individual initiative in belief can be patterned upon religious forms,[139] the idea that there is any such thing as patterns of belief may be one of our myths—a social product of our history and experience.

How is it possible, then, to consider belief if we do not assume that it conforms to patterns? Despite all the limiting conditions I have outlined—the archaeological record, the academic stance as "outside," the bias of the Spanish documents, and the notion that beliefs do not conform to patterns—the key is to envision individuals as innovators or agents, particularly with reference to the evidence we have regarding the Maya, whose beliefs were of little interest to the Spaniards, except insofar as the study of such beliefs provided a means of thoroughly extirpating Maya "idolatries."[140]

A focus on individuals and on how individual thinking or belief may have influenced behavior, and ultimately the broader outcome of the Christianization process, has methodological consequences. One result here is that I give less emphasis to the concept of resistance as a mechanism of adjustment (and ultimately a cultural adaptation), and more to the concept of appropriation, in the sense of seizing for oneself one's right to ideas. In no small measure, I owe my inspiration to Grant Jones, who describes his agency-oriented efforts to "rewrite parts of an earlier model of indigenous resistance with one that . . . finds the actors, indigenous and Spanish alike, in significantly different relationships with one another."[141]

Unlike Jones, however, whose approach grows out of his extensive knowledge of the ethnohistorical accounts and their interpretation, I base my approach in large part on a subjective source: my own personal experience. One outcome of this experience is awareness of the inadequacy of the concept of oppression in illuminating people's options under conditions of subjugation. Out of my dissatisfaction with the dichotomy of oppressor vs. oppressed grew an interest in exploring the ways in which power can be effectively appropriated and dignity maintained in circumstances of subjugation and loss.[142]

I am aware of Asad's criticism that consciousness, in the sense of a person's everyday awareness, intent, and the way she gives meaning to experience, is not enough to account for agency.[143] Other factors, such as the unconscious mind and instinctive reaction, "work more pervasively than consciousness does," with the result that "an agent's act is more (and less) than her consciousness of it."[144] Asad goes on to say that to resort to consciousness as an explanation is a mistake, because it ignores "the politically more significant condition that has to do with the objective distribution of goods that allows or precludes certain options."[145] Thus, the actions that are possible, or impossible, are independent of the consciousness of actors.[146]

This makes sense at one level, but knowing what actions are possible or not possible often comes only in hindsight, after the passage of time. How limiting societal structures or options can be is information not often available until the operating effects of structures can be observed; and structures change continually. Perhaps more important is the fact that the observations made by Asad about the "structures" of possible actions—like the concepts of syncretism or religion—are, at most, analytical tools. They reveal knowledge to us on the outside, as historians or anthropologists or archaeologists, but can such knowledge inform decision making at the level of the subjects who choose to act? To make history or to effect change, analytical insight gained from the perspective of time or space is highly important, but how does such insight translate into action? Effective agents need knowledge that can inform choices at the level of individual decision making. For this reason, I try to focus in this book on factors or points of view or options that could have operated at the level of the consciousness of individuals in the sixteenth and seventeenth centuries, with the implication that agency (in Asad's terms) could potentially be effected.

In the case of the Maya of Belize, who became Christian in the sixteenth century and have largely remained Roman Catholic until the late twentieth century, when evangelical Protestantism became an option, it is counterproductive to characterize Christianization solely as a product of colonial power and control.[147] To do so is to equate the Mayas' identification of themselves as Catholic, or Christian, with Conquest. In effect, when archaeologists align themselves with arguments for syncretism or for the maintenance of pre-Columbian belief under a veneer of Christianity, there is the implication that any other situation, such as one in which aspects of Christianity were internalized, or one in which the Maya self-identified as Christian, qualifies as failure. Even the idea that Christianity was a veneer is risky, because it can be seen to buttress the validity of the assessment that the friars developed after their first flushes of success in Mesoamerica, which is that the Indians were conspiratorial, stubborn, and intractable under the cover of being Christian.[148] As Burkhart points out in the case of the Nahuas, both extremes of the friars' views—that the Indians were humble and devout and that the Indians were conspiratorial—were value judgments.[149]

There is also the view that the Indians were unorthodox Christians.[150] According to Burkhart, writing about central Mexico in the sixteenth century, the friars responded to their encounter with the Nahuas by remaking themselves.[151] They molded their Christianity to fit the Nahua context, and this "demanded a doctrinal flexibility which, though they rarely admitted it to non-Indian audiences, is clearly evident in their Nahuatl writings. On the whole, the friars managed to content themselves with an Indian Christianity that was hardly orthodox; the Nahuas, on the whole, were able to become just Christian enough to get by in the colonial social and political setting without compromising their basic ideological and moral orientation."[152]

I add to Burkhart's insight that the very process which she describes as having taken place in Mexico (and which likewise took place in Yucatan and Belize) is not an exception, but instead has been the rule of the Christianization process since the first century A.D. The idea that there exists an authentic or orthodox Christianity—a reference to the friars' Christianity before they molded it to suit the Nahuas or Mayas—is a relative mindset, not a reality. The very same statement about the unorthodox nature of Christianity could be made about the outcome of the Christianization of the German tribes in the early Middle Ages,[153] or about the survival of the pagan gods in European culture into the Renaissance,[154] or about the cult of saints in Latin Christianity,[155] all of which became part of European culture and hence provided the social and cultural context of the friars' own Christianity.

The European Christianity with which the Maya and the Nahuas were faced could be characterized as a veneer of orthodoxy—or claim to orthodoxy—over a body of beliefs that are the result of Europeans not compromising their pre-Christian ways of looking at the world. As Rabasa has observed, we should be talking about Catholicism as a history of religions.[156] The veneer metaphor, however, is as unsatisfactory here as it is in the case of Maya. The changes that conversion in Mesoamerica and in Europe entailed were both surficial and deep-rooted; they were also selective. They were effected in complicated ways that remain to be fully understood. Christian ideas and ideals were considered with full sincerity, but were altered in ways that reflected not only pre-Christian thought (as argued by many scholars) but also Christianity's empowerment of the individual and the interpretive leeway that this allowed. Internalizing aspects of Christianity, far from ensuring orthodoxy, could also have had the effect of encouraging personal mission, vision, and expression. As Geertz observes, "Religious faith, even when it is fed from a common source, is as much a particularizing force as a generalizing one."[157]

With regard to the effect of Christianity on Maya culture, being successful in retaining one's culture or basic ideology is clearly important, but the question is: what constitutes one's culture or ideology at any given time and in any given space? Is culture or are ideas ever basic or intact? Time is required for something to become cultural,[158] but what are the dynamics and how does culture change? What if ideas about the relationship between the natural and the supernatural world among the Maya did not fall neatly on one side or the other of a divide created by a date—the date of the arrival of Europeans?

In Belize, the date of European arrival could have been the Pacheco Conquest in 1544, or could even have been an encounter with the Franciscan friar Lorenzo de Bienvenida on his way from Guatemala to Mérida through Belize in 1543–44. Or it could have been as early as the first half of the sixteenth century, when seafarers (even buccaneers[159] hiding from Spanish ships) sought shelter in the Belize cayes or along the coast. What if there were Menocchios among the Maya, who, in learning about Christianity, appropriated ideas and felt they had the right to configure belief, not in spite of the friars but *because* of them? What if Christianity was consistently appropriated and used subversively? How would we know?

To consider the possibility, we must explore new ways to view the Maya-Spanish encounter, and I turn again to Firth's discourse on religious beliefs, because it lays the foundation for much of what follows in this book:

Religious beliefs appear less stable than ritual, more open to personal variation and modification. Their vagueness and lack of definition are seen in two respects. Different individuals in the same religious communion vary in their beliefs on a given topic, which makes it difficult to assign to any synoptic expression a truly representative value. Again, a single individual is often unable to formulate clearly his belief on even such fundamental concepts as God, Heaven or the soul. Variation in ritual is significant in the interpretation of the role which ritual has in the life of different individuals. Variation and lack of precision in belief, too, have analogous significance. Though they may complicate . . . analyses . . . , they are not fortuitous; they are characteristic and indeed essential to the functions which religious belief fulfils.[160]

In this view, religious beliefs would have been open to personal variation and modification among both Spaniards and Mayas. Individuals in the Spanish communion varied in their beliefs; individual Mayas varied in their assessments of Christianity. Variation complicates analysis, but in our case such variation is a key to characterizing the Maya-Spanish encounter in a different light. I could say that I am exploiting the weakness (or strength) of religion (or world view), which is that individual variations in beliefs exist and can be catalysts for reconfiguration. Such reconfiguration is neither a veneer nor syncretism, nor even resistance. It is what people do: they think. Ideas are appropriated in the first instance by individuals—not by societies or cultures—to secure coherence and power in an ever-changing universe of relations.[161]

In the preceding pages, we have journeyed from (almost) rejecting the term "religion" to discovering that its defects as a term or a concept can be exploited. On the one hand, the term "religion" has limited utility because its use reflects the positioning of an outsider. Hence, an understanding of the dynamics of whatever is of interest will be limited by the outside-inside nature of the subject-object relationship. On the other hand, if we can use what historians or anthropologists or archaeologists call "religion" as a way of getting at how individuals use ideas to empower themselves in a threatening world, then the term, as academics know it, becomes a means or a method, rather than an end or a reality. It is *our* construct (*pace* Firth), not the construct of those we study. As a method, it can connect the observers (us) to the observed (the Maya or the Spaniards) in potentially productive ways, because the human mind enters the inquiry as both object and subject.[162]

Cults and Idols

Although a Roman Catholic or a Muslim might not mind checking the appropriate box next to "Roman Catholic" or "Islam" under a category of "Religion" on a government form, few people would be likely to check a box identifying themselves as members of a "cult." The term "cult" is almost always used to describe the rituals or practices of the "other." Non-scientologists see scientology as a cult; non-Pentecostals see Pentecostal Christianity as a cult; non-lovers of Elvis Presley see Elvis fans as cult members. But none of these group members would be likely to choose the term "cult" to describe his or her group.

The use of "cult" to categorize practices of "the other" is why the term is sometimes said to have marginal, or "freakish," connotations.[163] The early Christians were characterized as members of a cult by non-Christian Romans, but they defined themselves as followers of Christ. This may seem a trivial point, but it is important to be aware that use of the term already reflects a judgment call. If we use it in a context in which we are attempting to understand people's beliefs, or to resolve conflict, then it contributes to misunderstanding rather than to clarifying points of view.

OUR SAINTS, YOUR IDOLS

The term "idol" is interesting because it, too, is an attribute of the "other." There is little question that the term is used to describe an effigy or image or statue venerated by a group to which we do not belong. No Catholic would describe a statue of St. Francis or a representation of an angel as an idol. At the same time, without Spanish prodding, no Maya would describe a representation of a Chac (a spiritual being associated with rain and agriculture) or Ek Chuah (associated with merchants), or a whistle made in the shape of a bird or a jaguar, as an idol, either. Yet the Spaniards considered all effigies or statues or images that did not have their origins in Spanish culture or Christian belief to be idols. The problem of idolatry will be discussed in more detail in chapter 10; at this juncture, because the term "idol" is commonly used in the literature and in the documents to which I shall later refer, it is important to flag the term and to contextualize it.

The imagery associated with one's own beliefs can tell stories or represent heroes or call to mind a particular supernatural or spirit. Some images or statues create sacred space in which individuals feel free to talk to supernaturals or to spirits (prayer), which can include ancestors or family members recently deceased. One's own images, however, are never idols. The Maya observed Spaniards with statues in their houses, carrying effigies, burning candles or kneeling in front of images, and wearing medallions of saints. It was clear that effigies or images of supernaturals, and human interaction with such effigies or images, was permitted, and indeed encouraged, in Christianity. Logically, the Maya must have thought, "How is this different from our own practices?" The answer is, of course, that it was not. The difference lay in the *identity* of the supernaturals and not in the practice of interacting with images.

The Spaniards must have seemed to the Maya to be full of contradictions. The Spaniards described themselves as worshiping one supreme deity, yet in practice they seemed to be worshiping many deities. The conditions in Yucatan and Belize were such that evangelization and catechization had been achieved in a comparatively short period of time. In addition, friars were in short supply and communities were often supervised in rituals and practices by resident Maya *maestros cantores* or sacristans who had been taught in Franciscan schools.[164] Under these conditions it is not difficult to fathom why veneration of effigies and images better known to the Maya than the Christian images would have continued, even alongside the veneration of saints. There is no reason to assume, as the friars did, that this constituted rejection of Christianity. Maya observation of Spanish Christian practices would have reinforced the legitimacy of using images as foci or loci of veneration.

It is also conceivable that Belize Maya, through their contact with English or Flemish or Dutch buccaneers who frequented the Belize coast, had come in contact with Protestant Christians, whose style of Christianity would have provided an example of the wide variation in Christian beliefs and behavior. As a result, in Maya eyes the reaction of the Spanish friars to Maya practices may well have seemed incomprehensible. The logic of the Mayas' assumptions is not likely, however, to have been acknowledged openly by the friars, for two reasons: in the first place, because such recognition would have meant that the Spaniards would have been forced to acknowledge their own practices as liable to different interpretation; and in the second, because the friars, and presumably most Spaniards, genuinely believed that Maya statues and effigies were inspired by the devil.

DEVILS AND DEMONS

In the ultimate irony, the friars gave tacit support to the Mayas' world of supernaturals by proposing not that the Indians' supernaturals did not exist, but that they were demons—a manifestation of "mankind's 'ancient enemy,' the Devil."[165] To some extent, this view reflects attitudes that permeated the late Middle Ages,[166] by which time demonology had become a "science."[167] However, this is not the whole story.

Some scholars claim that the devil in Christian belief arose out of Christian antagonism toward the deities of the people they were evangelizing. According to Silverblatt, "The nineteenth-century French historian Jules Michelet[168] interprets the devil in Western Europe as a figure who evolved from pagan beliefs, rooted in a pantheon of natural spirits, which were at the core of peasant folklore."[169] In other words, the Christians simply made the deities, or supernaturals, of "the other" into demons.

There is no question that pre-Christian beliefs in Europe must have influenced imagery of the devil. The devil of southern Europe—an image very familiar to me—often has bat-like characteristics, whereas the devil we read about in school, in American literature, sported horns and hooves, which suggests that local traditions affected the representation of supernaturals. It is also the case that individual artists had quite a free hand in depicting the devil and his influence through the ages, as long as the attributes could easily be recognized as associated with evil deeds, sex, or excess,[170] or with the grotesque.[171] Thus, almost any animal attribute could be used, as could particular colors, or forms that were not recognizable in nature (see chap. 10, figs. 10.1, 10.5).

On the other hand, the idea that demons exist has deep roots in Judeo-Christian supernaturalism.[172] In the Old Testament, the Judeo-Christian God despairs when his people spurn him for strange gods and idols:

> They offered sacrifice to demons, to "no-gods," to gods whom they had not known before, To newcomers just arrived, of whom their fathers had never stood in awe.[173]

Satan, who in Christian thought becomes conflated with demons, first appears in the Hebrew Bible, although he is not necessarily evil.[174] He is a messenger, or angel (the Greek word for messenger). The satan-as-messenger was sent by God to obstruct human activity, often because an individual was on the wrong path. In the Book of Job, Yahweh and the satan work together.[175] Through time, the satan took on a more adversarial role.[176] During the first century, groups marginal to mainstream Judaism, such as the Essenes or the followers of Jesus, began to use the satan to characterize their Jewish opponents; rival groups were said to be inspired by "Satan." They abandoned the traditional interpretation of the satan as a servant of God—although admittedly a servant who was asked to undertake unpleasant deeds—and transformed him into God's antagonist, enemy, and rival.[177]

Stories about the character of Satan proliferated, among them the tale that he was an angel who was once a trusted associate of God but turned against God and fell from Heaven.[178] Thus was born the Christian vision of the supernatural struggle between good and evil expressed in the Gospels, in which conflict was raised to cosmic proportions.[179] Mark, for example, describes Jesus's ministry as a continual struggle between God's spirit and the demons, who belong to Satan's kingdom; Jesus himself "drove out many demons."[180]

As Christianity spread to Gentile communities, different interpretations of Jesus's message circulated, and as attempts were made by bishops and others to institutionalize and control accepted practice (see "Doctrine and Dogma," below), some beliefs and practices, and even Gospels,[181] were labeled heretical and seen as inspired by Satan. Not surprisingly, pagan gods, such as the deities of Rome and Greece, became demonic forces. For the second-century convert Justin Martyr, "every god and spirit he had ever known . . . he now perceived as allies of Satan."[182]

Pagan (i.e., Greco-Roman) philosophers had characterized the universe as filled with spirit energies, or *daimones* in Greek; these would become the "demons" who Christians came to believe were responsible for creating false gods and for inspiring humans to commit evil acts.[183] In English, the words "devil" and "demon" are sometimes used interchangeably, but the derivation of "devil" can be traced through translations of the biblical Satan.[184] Even the sacrament of baptism, critical in Mesoamerica as an instrument of Christianization, was meant to wash away sins and expel evil spirits.[185] Exorcisms associated with baptism were only eliminated by the Catholic Church in 1969 for infants, and 1972 for adults, although prayers remain that petition God to avert satanic influence.[186]

There are two noteworthy concomitants to belief in a world of evil spirits and demons. As I have noted, belief in demons or the devil gives tacit support to the existence of the spirit world of "the other." The Christians did not claim that Maya supernaturals did not exist; they claimed instead that the Maya worshipped the *wrong* supernaturals. This may well have contributed positively to "an indigenous counter-memory,"[187] but perhaps more problematic, belief in the existence of demons and the devil challenges claims of monotheism. The Greek Platonic philosopher Celsus wrote in about A.D. 180 that Christians could not claim to be monotheist if they believed both in God and the Devil.[188] Surely this contradiction was not lost on the Maya, although it is worth noting that the dichotomy in the form in which it reached the Americas in the sixteenth century reflected a particular historical development in Christian thinking.[189]

Although historians, such as Hugh Trevor-Roper, place the origins of the development of demonology in the political culture of the Middle Ages and Renaissance,[190] this is simply a late flowering; the roots extend more deeply into the past, to Judaism's claim to comprise the chosen people, with the concomitant and thorny problems of: (1) how to safeguard the chosen against wrong behavior; and (2) how to deal with the unchosen. Among the fledgling Christians in the critical period of the first century A.D., "the other" had shifted from being culturally different and generally simply to be avoided (under mainstream Judaism), to being seen by one's group as an enemy of God. Under the master strokes of Late Antique Christianity, the forces of evil, and the battle against it, took on cosmic dimensions, and the mere existence of others became a threat to the group.

In Mesoamerica, the behavior of Bishop Landa and the friars who allied themselves with him becomes comprehensible only when we see Christianity in light of the cosmic struggle between good and evil, with otherness clearly identified as evil.[191] The friars saw the world in terms of the struggle of two hostile principles "warring for the mind,"[192] and they justified repression as part of the war against the evil principle.[193] As voiced by Burkhart with respect to central Mexico, "The authority of god, the Bible, and traditional Old World practice superseded whatever authority the native elders claimed to have, for they were ignorant of truth and deceived by the Devil."[194]

Although Bishop Landa spoke Yucatec, a Mayan language, and the Franciscans made every effort to recruit individuals who would learn the native language, there were only a handful of friars and the occasional secular priest who knew the language. As a result, few had the tools to accumulate Maya knowledge or gain insight into the complexities of Maya culture and society, and those who had the tools used their knowledge of the language to interpret Christian doctrine in terms that the Maya would understand.[195] Even when "the priest transformed himself into an ethnographer, responsible for systematizing the information gathered in contact 'on the ground,'" such information was placed at the disposal of agents of Christianization.[196] "The great challenge for the Catholic missionary, therefore, was to link in the narrowest possible fashion the canonical-doctrinal significance of the concepts and substance of their religion to the native concepts and to their concrete use in local reality."[197]

Otherness was something with which one had to come to terms in order to Christianize; it was not an opportunity to enrich one's understanding or to learn. Landa's *Relación de las cosas de Yucatán*[198] (whether partly written or partly assembled by him, or by others later on[199]) was neither written for a Spanish lay audience in order that Spaniards could know the Maya, nor created for a Maya audience so that the Spaniards could determine if what they wrote was correct or meaningful. It was written to aid in furthering proselytization, because the Spaniards were determined "to obliterate [the Mayas'] entire religious system."[200] Many of the friars, although not all, assumed they knew what Maya spiritual beliefs stood for and what they entailed; the result was that almost any material cultural expression which they did not understand, including the subjects of the codices, was seen either as the work of the devil or as potentially anti-Christian, and had to be destroyed.

✠ FOUR ✠

Being Christian and the Doctrine of the Church

Q. How shall we know the things which we are to believe?
A. We shall know the things which we are to believe from
the Catholic Church, through which God speaks to us.
Baltimore Catechism No. 1, Lesson First

Undermining the work of the devil is one thing, but turning people into Christians is another. Indeed, what in fact makes a Christian? The answers to this question—provided by the second-century author of the Gospel of Thomas;[1] by the third-century orthodox bishop Irenaeus of Lyons;[2] by Ulfilas the Goth in the fourth century;[3] by the Venerable Bede in the late seventh to early eighth century;[4] by St. Francis of Assisi in the late twelfth to early thirteenth century;[5] by the sixteenth-century Franciscan friars Toribio Motolinía[6] and Diego de Landa;[7] and by the sixteenth-century converted Maya noble, Francisco de Montejo Xiu[8]—would all have been different. All missionary orders in the New World seem to have agreed with St. Jerome, that "Christians are made, not born,"[9] but conversion meant different things to different people at different times, and what was required of the convert could change depending on circumstances,[10] and, I would add, on history. As described by Fletcher for early medieval Europe, "The study of . . . conversion can be bewildering; a game played in swirling mist on a far from level playing field in which unseen hands are constantly shifting the dimly glimpsed goalposts."[11]

Conversion and Christianization

William James, in *The Varieties of Religious Experience*, comments on the process of conversion: "To be converted, to be regenerated, to receive grace, to experience religion, to gain an assurance, are so many phrases which denote the process, gradual or sudden, by which a self hitherto divided, and consciously wrong inferior and unhappy, becomes unified and consciously right superior and happy, in consequence of its firmer hold upon religious realities."[12] Few would argue that the Maya adopted Christianity because it made them "happier," but the notion of individual engagement is worthy of attention, even in circumstances of conquest and colonization. The individual engagement that James describes is, as Geertz has argued so powerfully, "hopelessly entangled" with meaning, identity, and power.[13] Claiming Christianity is both personal *and* political,[14] but not, as it is often characterized in the literature, one or the other.

Conversion in Mesoamerica can also be seen as the ideological and behavioral modifications which resulted in the adoption of a new world view,[15] or at least this is what the religious orders and the Spanish secular authorities assumed. Sanmark, in her study of Christianization in Scandinavia, provides an overview of definitions of "conversion,"[16] some of which is drawn from Russell.[17] She acknowledges the adoption of a new world view, but she also includes conversion as turning from indifference; turning from one form of piety to another; change of belief; or accepting the reality and supreme power of God.

Some scholars use the term "conversion" to describe the first stage of the protracted societal changes resulting from the introduction of Christianity. In these cases—for example, when the royal and noble families of Ireland, who controlled Irish society, became Christian—conversion is conceptualized as a collective process rather than the process by which each individual undergoes a change in belief.[18] Somewhat similar cases may have arisen in Mesoamerica when native elites, such as Francisco de Montejo Xiu, converted, although we need to know more about the nature of lineage and tribute ties to be able to gauge the effects of his conversion on those—elites or commoners—with obligations to him.

Sanmark defines two stages of conversion with relevance to Scandinavia: the first comprises missionary efforts with little secular support; the second begins when a secular ruler takes charge of the spread of Christianity in an area, and eventually an organized ecclesiastical network emerges, a process that can take as long as 150 years.[19] These stages could be said to have applied to Yucatan or to highland Guatemala, but not to Belize, where Spaniards never settled and no ecclesiastical or Spanish governmental network ever developed. The situation in sixteenth-century Belize was somewhat like that in Europe in the early, patchy spread of Christianity to Ireland and to the Britons in Wales, Cornwall, and Cumbria. If these Christians had been left alone and had never been subjected to the later intensive missionizing of the fifth and sixth centuries,[20] one wonders what their sort of Christianity would have looked like and whether there would have been parallels with the communities of Belize, which, by 1700 or earlier, had been left to their own devices by the Spaniards.

Russell highlights the social transformations brought about by the introduction of Christianity, and uses the term "Christianization" to describe "the complexity of the interactive process which ensues when a non-Christian society and Christianity encounter each other."[21] He accepts a strict definition of conversion as "the reorientation of the soul of an individual"[22] and "adhesion" as religious change that involves less of a break with old cultural beliefs and practices.[23] He sees "Christianization" as a term that can encompass these two processes without necessarily implying radical religious reorientation.[24] This suits our purposes in Mesoamerica, to the extent that Christianization, as defined, implies a societal process that can follow any number of paths. Russell goes on to say that the core concept in Christianity is individual belief in redemption through the suffering and death of Jesus Christ, and that Christianization cannot be said to have occurred if a society's world view does not change to encompass this concept. Needless to say, this involves the assumption that one can read the minds of the ancient converts and judge their behavior and motives on rather minimal information. Furthermore, Russell does not accept that baptism alone may be equated with conversion.[25]

I find such a strict definition problematic, because assessment of the degree to which the concept of redemption has been properly understood can be highly subjective and fraught with difficulty, not least owing to cultural misunderstandings. I distance myself from Russell's strict renderings of Christianity and conversion,[26] and ally myself instead with what Russell refers to as a less stable, subjectivist definition of Christianity based on the self-identification of individuals as Christian.[27] The definition of conversion implicit in the chapters that follow, except as otherwise noted, is that a person who claims to be Christian has undergone conversion. He has thought deeply about the events and processes of change going on in the world around him, which entails consciousness at some level of where humans stand in the cosmos, and has decided to position himself as Christian. In this sense, conversion defines a process that operates solely at the level of the individual (in contrast with conversion as defined by Russell, who implicates society), because societies do not convert, people do. Our concept of society subsumes people, of course, but using a collective noun as a subject in a circumstance in which we would like to know how and why actions are taken obscures the very mechanics which we hope to elucidate. At the more abstract level of the discussion of societies or cultures, "Christianization," as suggested by Russell, is an apt term,[28] even if we cannot be sure that the individuals in the society understand the concept of redemption.

What It Means to be Pagan

It seems to be generally agreed that the English word "pagan" derives from the Latin *paganus*. The origin of the use of *paganus* to refer to non-Christians, however, or to those who do not worship the true God, remains a matter of debate. The *Oxford English Dictionary* tells us:

> The explanation of L. *paganus* in the sense "non-Christian, heathen," as arising out of that of "villager, rustic" (supposedly indicating the fact that the ancient idolatry lingered on in the rural villages and hamlets after Christianity had been generally accepted in the towns and cities of the Roman Empire) . . . has been shown to be chronologically and historically untenable, for this use of the word goes back to Tertullian c. 202, when paganism was still the public and dominant religion, and even appears . . . in an epitaph of the 2nd century.[29]

The *OED* suggests instead that the use of *paganus* to describe non-Christians can be traced to the custom of Roman soldiers, who applied *paganus* to those who were not in the army. *Paganus* did indeed mean "villager, rustic, civilian, non-militant," but as a term that stood in contrast to *miles*: "soldier," or "one of the army." Christians came to call themselves *milites*, or "enrolled soldiers" of Christ, members of his militant church, and they applied to non-Christians the name used by soldiers to refer to all who were not enrolled in the army. This is interesting, because it means that Christ's pacifist message was transformed by his followers very early in the history of Christianity.

The *American Heritage Dictionary*[30] seems to agree with the *OED* in treating the Latin *paganus* as "country-dweller, civilian," but adds that *paganus* derives from Latin *pagus*, which means "country, rural district." It also defines "pagan" as someone who is not a Christian, Muslim, or Jew. This reflects the use of "pagan" to refer to pantheistic or polytheistic religions, as opposed to monotheism. In the scholarly literature, pagans are those who did not adopt Christianity, and paganism refers to beliefs that were not considered Christian; thus, paganism almost always entails reference to religions or beliefs that were polytheistic, or that, as in dualism, recognized more than one god or supernatural force. The literature on barbarian Europe (outside the Mediterranean region) and on the New World is virtually silent concerning either the names of pre-Christian religions or the names ascribed to followers, and as a result, writers have little choice but to use the term "pagan" to describe pre-Christians.

In the Mediterranean world, the names of pre-Christian deities that attracted followers, such as Isis, Mithras, Cybele, or Serapis,[31] are well known, perhaps because practices associated with these deities were widespread and popular in an urban Greco-Roman environment at a time when Christianity was still a minor force. The gods of the Mediterranean world in general seem to have fared better, in terms of their survival, than the gods of barbarian Europe or Mesoamerica, although the reasoning that perpetuated their survival (see below) ultimately extended to barbarian Europe. At least their names and their associations—if not their followers' characterization of themselves—are still known. Seznec attributes survival of the pagan gods of the Greco-Roman and Mediterranean world to their transformation into forms—such as symbols or myths or subjects of fables—that were palatable to Christians, or at least to some Christians.[32] A notable exception was Gregory of Tours, who felt that deriving moral teaching from pagan fables was dangerous, because it simply perpetuated their memory.[33] Gregory of Tours and Diego de Landa seem to have had a great deal in common.

The palatable form in which the gods were accepted was a function of reasoning that long pre-dated Christianity.[34] This reasoning allowed knowledge of the gods and myths to be integrated with world history, natural science, and morals until the end of the sixteenth century and even through the Renaissance.[35] Gods survived as the incarnation of ideas;[36] stories about ancient deities could be seen as tales of living people who had been deified after death (euhemerism), and therefore as distortions of historical facts.[37] Although Seznec's discussion deals with the Greco-Roman and Mediterranean world, many of the Icelandic sagas about heroes would fit into this category.[38]

Deities also survived as metaphors for elementary powers that made up the universe, in which case gods become cosmic symbols. The success of this technique can be seen in the fact that Christianity, albeit not for lack of trying, was unable to dislodge the planetary week that we still use, although our English day-names, except for Saturday, derive from Germanic gods.[39] In other circumstances, stories about the gods became allegories—expressions of moral or philosophical ideas[40]—a technique in which the pagan past (or an event in the Old Testament) was understood to prefigure Christian truth.[41] The gods became palatable to the Christians in all these forms.

The extent to which the Maya "pagan" past may have undergone similar transformation has yet to be explored. It is not something easily studied, because each region or subregion was proselytized by Christian friars who came with their own cultural and individual baggage, and the baggage affected what was transmissible or acceptable and what was repressed. In a sense, the time of the Maya-Spanish colonial encounter held an advantage over the time of the original interface between the Mediterranean pagan world and the world of the early Christians, owing to the proliferation of saints that had occurred over the centuries. If the Maya communities appropriated saints rapidly enough, as the records indicate they did, then the saints provided a quick and ready cover for at least some pre-Christian ideas and forces, and even deities.[42]

There is, however, a down side to all this. To paraphrase Seznec, beneath the enthusiasm (ours) for recovering myths and deities lies a "stubborn disquiet."[43] This is because, as in the Mediterranean world, the gods survived but only under conditions in which there was a perceived need to bring them, or the forces associated with them, into line with the spiritual values of Christianity. Hence, to examine modern practices for pre-Columbian survivals or evidence of syncretism is to do exactly what the friars did: take things out of context. This also means that Conquest-period records, written or pictorial,[44] serve best not as windows onto native life but as sources of information on the Europeans' tools for the *management* of native ideas. If this caveat is ignored and the documents are examined as sources of information on pre-Columbian gods or practices, the context becomes one in which the gods, as Seznec would say, no longer arouse sentiments but exist as mere subjects of study.[45]

Seznec's subject is the Mediterranean world, but what he says has relevance for Mesoamerica as well. In the pre-Columbian world, the gods could not be excluded from their context, but by way of Christianization, this is exactly what happened. According to Seznec, as subjects of study, the gods are presented in the traditional compromise in which each is represented as a symbol (e.g., of corn or rain or fertility),[46] which is just how Greek or Roman or Aztec gods are presented in what we have come to accept as mythology. The next step belongs to New Agers, to whom "All mythology is nothing more—or pretends to be nothing more—than a system of ideas in disguise, a 'secret philosophy.'"[47]

Paganism, then, or what it seems to stand for, is nothing if not highly problematic. If we try to give life to the gods of the pre-Christian past, we set in motion their alienation from the context that gave them meaning. In the literature on conversion, all religions or beliefs that are not Christian are generally labeled paganism, and all people, no matter where they live or what language they speak or what world view they may have, are called pagans. The attribute of being simply "pagan" serves to demean pre-Christian or non-Christian beliefs by failing to delineate the details of the history or practice of local ritual or expression, and by promoting the deliberate rejection of a people's identification of themselves as belonging to a specific group.

There are powerful reasons why people associated with the official church—members of religious communities, bishops, or priests—gave scant attention to pre-Christian beliefs, a topic to which we shall return shortly, because the rationale was as strong in sixteenth-century Mesoamerica as it had been in Late Antiquity or Medieval Europe. In fact, given the history of Christianity in

Europe and the concessions to local beliefs in the Christianization process,[48] New World proselytizers may have felt greater pressure to remain inflexible in the face of local adaptations of Christianity—even before the Council of Trent.

Another danger in using the term "paganism" to refer categorically to all those who have not accepted Christianity is that it carries the implication that what it means to be Christian, that is, non-pagan, is crystal clear. But determining what is Christian can be as problematic as assuming what it is to be pagan.[49] Some take a relativist view and assert that there is a variety of Christianities, owing to the fact that cultures and aspirations change over time.[50] Russell prefers, as we have seen, to define the unique characteristics of being Christian as belief in individual redemption through the suffering and death of Jesus Christ.[51] These two views are probably at the opposite ends of the spectrum. In between is Jeffrey Burton Russell, who believes that the truth of Christianity is elucidated best by observing the way its traditions develop.[52] This is an interesting view, because Roman Catholic Church doctrine is based on the acceptance of some traditions and the exclusion of others.

Being Christian— ## The Role of Doctrine and Dogma

My approach takes the relativist view, which allows for the self-identification of the individual members of a society as Christian. Then and now, many Christians—including Roman Catholics—were and are not necessarily motivated by doctrine, or even by church tradition per se, but rather by what their belief means to them, something which can take many forms. As children, even though we memorized prayers and extracts from the catechism that constituted doctrine, such as carefully worded descriptions of the Holy Trinity, I cannot say that I understood what I memorized. We memorized as a way to gain a reward, such as an image on paper of the Virgin or of a favorite saint ("holy pictures"), which we slipped between the pages of our missals. According to Lindberg, "Doctrine makes no sense outside the worshipping community,"[53] but in fact doctrine may not make a great deal of sense even to those within the worshiping community.

The church has historically come to terms with this dilemma, at least to some extent. Augustine of Hippo did not consider insincere conversion to be an insurmountable problem, because the motives that brought people to Christianity were complex and could include fear or self-interest, but this would be a temporary stage on the road to the truth.[54] Church history shows that the reasons for prohibiting practices (that stemmed from particular beliefs) were not uniform; there were times when a range of practices was tolerated and other times when persecution was excessive.[55] Asad interprets Augustine's attitude as presaging what would become the power of the church. In this context, the Christian individual, once converted, would live out his life within a framework of powerful social, political, and economic institutions that would lend stability to his activities and to the quality of his experience, so that power was the key to creating the conditions for experiencing truth.[56]

Power certainly helped, but Augustine's reasoning seems to me to be based on his faith that the converted would, eventually, realize the truth of Christianity; thus, compelling people to convert was an option, and this brought with it a degree of tolerance. Even the medieval church was not obsessed with uniformity of practice, although there were limits. Ultimately, the church saw the need to subject "all practice to a unified authority, to a single authentic source that could tell truth from falsehood."[57] There had to be a single church that was the source of authenticating discourse, and church doctrine is the result.

Nock writes that because our views in the West are formed by the ideas we have of Christian and Muslim invasions, we expect that the conquered will accept the religion of the conquerors. He attributes this to the fact that Christianity and Islam are "prophetic and militant in origin and type," and that both are keenly attentive to dogma.[58] In contrast, he notes that in the ancient world, although conquerors did not generally accept the dogmas of the conquered ("for there were in general no dogmas to accept"), they nevertheless incorporated deities and rites or practices of the conquered.[59] This is a noteworthy insight, because it connects imperialist strategies to dogma in ways that began with Christianity and Islam and continue into the modern era.

In the process of writing this book, I explored various aspects of doctrine. Despite the fact that the *Catholic Encyclopedia*[60] and the *Catechism of the Catholic Church*[61] are geared to interested laymen, I found them both difficult to understand, and frequently impenetrable. Yet according to church fathers, it is an understanding of Church tradition through doctrine that makes the true Christian. Doctrine is described as a key to Christian memory and identity.[62] I do not know enough about late medieval church history to be able to say whether or not sixteenth-century missionaries saw doctrine as a key to Christian memory and identity, but if such a view was added to their cultural biases, it would help to explain much of their behavior.

"Doctrine" and "dogma" are related terms that are sometimes used synonymously. The difference between the two is that "doctrine" has its roots in a word for teaching and learning, whereas "dogma" has roots in a word meaning a philosophical tenet or opinion.[63] Both refer to principles, or to a body of principles, accepted as belief by a group. Because much of the criticism leveled at the Nahuas or Maya involved their failure to understand the true meaning of Christianity, mainly because (*pace* Augustine) sincere or meaningful conversion had not taken place,[64] it is important to examine what constitutes a sincere Christian. The answer is rather complicated.

Lindberg says that tradition is not just a mass of information, but "in its root sense means the action of handing on an understanding of that information, not just its rote repetition."[65] The key word here is "understanding," because it turns out that such understanding became a matter of "ecclesial consensus."[66] Not only did various individuals and groups disagree regarding an understanding of the tradition concerning Jesus, but also bishops and other church authorities failed to agree among themselves. Eventually, however, certain authorities and opinions won out over others.

Debates concerned a number of topics: whether God was transcendent and indivisible, in which case admitting that Jesus was God might lead to God's divisibility (the Arian controversy of the late third and early fourth century A.D.); whether salvation is received from God or can be achieved by humans (the Pelagian controversy, late fourth and early fifth century A.D.); whether Christ the Son is of the same substance as the father (Nicaea in A.D. 325); whether Mary was the Mother of God or the mother of a man (Ephesus in A.D. 431); whether the Holy Spirit proceeded *from* the Father and the Son, or from the father *through* the Son (the Great Schism in 1054 between East and West); and, not least, the issues raised by the Reformation in the early sixteenth century that led to the Council of Trent.[67]

The subjects of these critical debates are obscure and not something over which the average Christian loses a huge amount of sleep. Luther, Calvin, and Zwingli did, but they became the authoritative heads of new churches. What is significant is that the tradition concerning Jesus can be interpreted in so many ways by so many different people.[68] Despite the decision by church authorities to agree on one interpretation and reject others in order to maintain integrity as a church—a decision that has some merit in terms of practicality and survival—it is clear that reaching such a consensus could not put a stop to people thinking about the tradition concerning Jesus, because no decision was ever so overwhelmingly logical, or "true," that it appealed to all people's reasoning. Generally speaking, the decisions simply opted for one way of thinking over another.

With regard to what became the Roman Catholic tradition—the tradition that is relevant where the Maya are concerned—the decisions acted against those such as the second-century gnostic Valentinus, who argued for multiplicity of meaning and that individuals should be reading and thinking about scripture for themselves.[69] In fact, the teaching office of the church, called the

Magisterium, was established "to prevent the individual from being entirely left on his own" with regard to the "real substance of faith."[70] In other words, the church set out to discourage the Valentinuses and the Menocchios of the world. Although Menocchio may be taken to be emblematic of the "problems" of heresy, our miller posed no threat to his community or to their beliefs. In fact, his community maintained a rather flexible attitude toward him, and many seemed rather fond of him. As it turned out, it was the parish priest who denounced him.[71]

At the time of the Maya-Spanish encounter, Christianity was old in Europe but new to Mesoamerica, and one could therefore expect considerable variability in interpretations of Christianity, even within one Maya community, let alone among the Maya as a group. This is not to say that variability was any less in Europe. Marzal argues that the tension that had always existed between the universal church and local belief in Spain made its way to America;[72] but it can also be argued that by the Middle Ages, the church had become a familiar institution in Europe. It had, in effect, become part of European culture, and *still* produced Menocchios, which is to say that Christianity continued to engender contexts in which individuals felt that they could take control of the message. If this could happen in Mennochio's community, whose members were accustomed to the church and considered it (in our terms) part of their culture, how much more room was there for taking control of the message among the Maya, for whom both the church and its behavior were alien?

In the Mesoamerican context, the Maya were faced with friars who introduced them to Jesus's message—which in Europe had stimulated hundreds of years of fierce debate over its meaning and interpretation—at the same time that they told the Maya how they were to interpret the message (i.e., "doctrine"). Anyone with a working mind would have sensed contradictions inherent in such evangelization. That the native was perceived as a docile subject, ready to receive information and knowledge about what to believe, goes some way to explain the friars' approach.[73] Why the native was seen in this way is perhaps harder to explain. It had partly to do with the high hopes the religious had, particularly the Franciscans,[74] of establishing a Christian kingdom in a world that was new, at least to them; but there is also the kind of thinking, of which we are all sometimes guilty, in which we imagine how something might happen in a new place under new conditions, and this "imagining" somehow becomes transformed, on the basis of no data, into our expectations.

How did the church justify doctrine? According to Lindberg, the early church community's self-definition (read "doctrine") was necessary in the face of internal and external challenges, although he is not clear regarding how a challenge manifested itself.[75] Because early doctrines were acknowledged in imperial law, they were considered infallible, and this is also how "doctrine acquired the overtones of compulsion, as those who did not sub-scribe to the dogmatic decisions of the church were banished or worse by the state."[76] (The nature of "worse" is not spelled out.) He goes on to suggest that it is more helpful to consider doctrine as a "feed box, the purpose of which is to gather the herd by providing nourishment."[77] Thus, Lindberg links church tradition with the Lord's Supper, and doctrine is said to serve to nourish the "self-understanding and identity of the Christian community." "For the early church," Lindberg concludes, "the purpose of dogma was both to develop the community's reflection on salvation wrought by God through Jesus and *to im-part meaning to earlier reflections that was not originally perceived*" (empha-sis added).[78]

It is hard to know how to articulate a response to what seems to me to be a problematic justification for doctrine and its role, but then again, by com-menting in this way, I am standing outside the church. Were I to take my stance as a Roman Catholic, I could find a way for doctrine to come across as the voice of reason. I leave the reader to accept Lindberg's justification, or not, as the case may be; the important thing for present purposes is the matter of how the friars in the New World viewed doctrine.

The Franciscans and Dominicans were in fact part of the reform move-ments that began in the twelfth century, as we shall see in greater detail in the next chapter. Despite their reformist tradition, on the whole it seems that the Mendicants had firmly fixed in their heads an idea of what a sincere Christian should be, and this idea incorporated acceptance of church doctrine and its interpretation of tradition. Did they consider that such doctrine developed as a result of the suppression of alternative views of Christ's teaching over time? The Dominicans certainly did, because St. Dominic's early mission revolved around his hope of reconciling the Albigensian heretics to the church.[79] Dom-inic's mission never resorted to violence; nor did the Dominicans shy away from intellectual debate. They were an order dedicated to study, teaching, and preaching in the community, and knew well how important debate was to the learning process. They accepted the fact, however, that choices had to be made on the part of the church, and that these choices, once made, brought with them suppression of opposing modes of thought.

Did the friars and clergy consider that the general "acceptance" of doc-trine among the populace might have been due not to awareness of the logic or sense or justice of the church's argument, but to the fact that people had simply become accustomed to a climate in which debate about interpreta-tion of scripture or Jesus's message was discouraged and indeed considered threatening?

The internalization of church doctrine had become second nature to re-ligious (and secular) orders by the sixteenth century. Thus, the combination of the effects of this internalization with evangelization of Maya or other *indios*[80] exposed to scripture and prayers and teaching for the first time was not a happy one. The Articles of Faith,[81] for example, contained phrases that could not help but be received as enigmatic:

I believe in the Father;

I believe in the Son;

I believe in the Holy Spirit;

There is one God who made heaven and earth and all things visible and invisible;

Jesus for our love took human form, in the most sacred belly of Saint Mary, ever Virgin;

Jesus suffered and died on the cross for us and for our salvation;

After Jesus died on the cross, his soul descended into Limbo to take out the souls of the Holy Fathers that were waiting for him.

I believe in the Holy Church, the reunion of all the faithful of Jesus Christ, our lord, all the Christians, the communion of the faithful, the forgiveness of sins, the end of the world, the resurrection of the body and life everlasting.[82]

The Creed, the Our Father, the Holy Spirit, the Trinity, the concept of salvation, the concept of ascension; Limbo; judging the living and the dead, mortal and venial sins[83]—there are so many topics and hence many occasions in which the Maya might well have wanted to debate meaning in the way the early Christians did. Saying prayers, learning the articles, and confessing the faith—despite the fact that the church saw (and sees) these processes as explaining or resolving how to interpret the tradition of Jesus[84]—can stimulate as much debate as they are supposed to resolve, especially in a new community just exposed to the ideas for the first time.

The idea that doctrine serves as explanation or justification is deeply rooted in Western historical and cultural traditions, the development of which could not be "played back" to the Maya. In this light, it is not so difficult to understand why Maya practices and attitudes regarding Christianity embodied so much variation, and why such practices and attitudes need not have been deliberately part of a package of resistance.

The Doctrine of the Church

It is generally the case that in the literature on the Spanish conquest, doctrine is duly noted but not explained. If and when the Maya questioned doctrine, either openly or secretly, what were they up against? If this question seems speculative, I argue that to ignore it assumes that the Maya were neither intelligent nor perceptive enough to question what they were taught, or to sense contradiction, or to speak plainly or describe something as they saw it.

I turn to the *Catholic Encyclopedia*[85] as a source regarding the details of what doctrine was and is; despite the length of the passages, I quote them in full, because both language and length are important characteristics of the style of explanation:

> Broadly taken, the doctrine of the Catholic Church comprises all those teachings in faith and morals entrusted to the Church by Christ through the Apostles and given for the sake of our salvation. In this broad sense, the term "doctrine" is coterminous with the whole of revelation or the Deposit of the Faith [see below]. It may also refer to any particular teaching drawn from this body of doctrines. A narrow sense of the term refers to specific formulations of doctrines in the creeds (e.g., the doctrine of the Trinity), conciliar definitions confirmed by papal authority (e.g., the doctrine of infallibility), papal definitions (e.g., the doctrine of the Immaculate Conception), or other magisterial pronouncements. *These doctrines are "defined" and thus unoptional and authentic teachings of the Church* [italics mine]. They are also said to be *de fide*—as belonging to the very substance of the Faith—and thus calling for the assent of all Catholics. Normally, such definitions are formulated in response to heterodox challenges to a particular doctrine, or to give suitable expression to a universally held doctrine. In recent usage, the definition of doctrine in this narrower sense is said to represent an exercise of the "extraordinary Magisterium," while the main substance of Catholic doctrine—which has not been the subject of explicit dogmatic formulation—is taught by the Church in her "ordinary Magisterium."[86]

If one stands inside the Catholic Church and accepts its authority, then these words describe an existing situation and act to reinforce or to strengthen belief. In other words, the audience is already won over; details of substance or argumentation are unimportant to them. If one stands outside the Catholic Church and tries to analyze the text, it is almost as if it turns back on itself. What, exactly, is meant by, "the term 'doctrine' is coterminous with the whole of revelation or the Deposit of the Faith"? The intention seems to be: (1) revelation is truth; (2) doctrine is revelation (is "coterminous" or has the same range of meaning); (3) doctrine is truth. Logical in structure, perhaps, but, substantively, point 2 requires a leap of faith.

The *Catholic Encyclopedia* also describes the Deposit of Faith. Again, I quote the entire passage because its language and length help to make my points, which are: first, that the passage has meaning only from the point of view of an insider who has already accepted the righteousness of doctrine and the authority of the church; and second, that the explanation of doctrine, either inside or outside, exists on a plane that does not seem to connect with anything but itself.

> The Deposit of Faith is the body of saving truth entrusted by Christ to the Apostles and handed on by them to the Church to be preserved and proclaimed. In this sense, the term is very nearly coextensive with "objective revelation," in that it embraces the whole of Christ's teaching as embodied in Revelation and Tradition. But the metaphor of "deposit" highlights particular features of the apostolic teaching. It suggests that this teaching is like an inexhaustible treasure, one that consistently rewards reflection and study with new insights and deeper penetration into the mystery of the divine economy of salvation. Although our understanding of this teaching can develop, it can never be augmented in its substance. Thus, the teaching is a divine trust, something not to be tampered with, altered or, as it were, "devalued." This feature of the apostolic teaching has also been expressed in the traditional conviction that Revelation, properly so-called, was complete with the death of the last Apostle. The treasure of saving truth—in itself nothing other than Christ Himself—contains the definitive revelation of God's inner life and of His intentions in our regard. There can be no more complete revelation than that imparted by the very Word of God, the Son Who is the perfect image of the Father and Who sends the illuminating Spirit into the Church. *The position of the Church with respect to the Deposit of Faith is thus something similar to that of a trustee: charged to preserve a living tradition with fidelity, she must nonetheless proclaim it in new historical circumstances in such a way that its efficacy and richness are undiminished* [italics mine]. Although the term "Deposit of Faith" entered official Catholic teaching only with the Council of Trent, its substance is well-attested in the Scriptures and the Fathers.[87]

Complementary definitions come from the *Catechism of the Catholic Church*.[88]

> DOCTRINE/DOGMA: The revealed teachings of Christ which are proclaimed by the fullest extent of the exercise of the authority of the Church's Magisterium. The faithful are obliged to believe the truths or dogmas contained in divine Revelation and defined by the Magisterium.[89]
>
> MAGISTERIUM: The living, teaching office of the Church, whose task it is to give as authentic interpretation of the word of God, whether in its

written form (Sacred Scripture), or in the form of Tradition. The Magisterium ensures the Church's fidelity to the teaching of the Apostles in matters of faith and morals.[90]

TRADITION: The living transmission of the message of the Gospel in the Church. The oral preaching of the Apostles, and the written message of salvation under the inspiration of the Holy Spirit (Bible), are conserved and handed on as the deposit of faith through the apostolic succession in the Church. Both the living Tradition and the written Scriptures have their common source in the revelation of God in Jesus Christ. The theological, liturgical, disciplinary, and devotional traditions of the local churches both contain and can be distinguished from this apostolic Tradition.[91]

The Church and the Maya

All of the definitions in the excerpts above deal with the church's justification for making decisions about situations and subjects that are not clearly supported by Scripture. The need for justification does not mean that the Church went against Scripture, but only that the apostolic tradition and texts either are not clear or are not specific, or do not deal directly with the matter at hand. Therefore, the church made decisions; once made, the decisions were expected to be adhered to, even if powerful arguments were raised by Christians for alternatives also based on interpretation of Scripture.

As far as I can determine from the definitions I have quoted, the essence of justification for the church's authority in making doctrinal decisions is the following statement from the *Catechism of the Catholic Church*: "The first generation of Christians did not yet have a written New Testament, and the New Testament itself demonstrates the process of a living Tradition."[92] The implication is that the early Christians made decisions about what should be written down based on their knowledge of what the apostles preached. It follows from this that decisions about what it means to be Christian will have to be made in the lives of Christians down through the ages. Church authorities over time established rules and regulations, doctrines and dogmas, that are the results of decision making which the church frames as an aspect of what it calls the Living Tradition. How long did this take? It is still going on, although it has been argued that "the Church had developed its idea of orthodoxy and its conception of the providential economy of history" by A.D. 312, at the Battle of the Milvian Bridge, when Constantine's victory ensured the future of Christianity and the pattern of the "ruthless elimination of deviations" had been set.[93]

What I find interesting is the last part of Paragraph 83 of the *Catechism of the Catholic Church*, in which another sort of tradition is defined:

Tradition is to be distinguished from the various theological, disciplinary, liturgical, or *devotional traditions* [italics mine], born in the local churches over time. These are the particular forms, adapted to different places and times, in which the great Tradition [note the upper case "T"] is expressed. In the light of Tradition, these traditions can be retained, modified or even abandoned under the guidance of the Church's magisterium.[94]

This would seem to be the loophole for what William Christian[95] has called "local religion" and its idiosyncrasies, and indeed for the various devotional practices that developed in the early stages of Christianization. The problem is the phrase "In the light of Tradition," which means that church authorities, because they feel they are justified, based on reasons they themselves devised for justification, have the ultimate say in what practices will be allowed.

The passages quoted above present ideas about the role of doctrine that are part of the Roman Catholic tradition and were accepted by the Franciscan friars in Yucatan and Belize in the sixteenth and seventeenth centuries, both before and after the Council of Trent. Nonetheless, doctrine and dogma, and Tradition—however important they were and are to Church authorities and to archaeologists like me who use them to make a point—all held and hold far less interest for ordinary Christian believers (except perhaps for members of Opus Dei or other lay sects). This holds true whether our subjects are the sixteenth-century Maya, modern Maya, or modern anybody.

As children learning the catechism, we let doctrine, or whatever simplified forms of doctrine we were taught, float on the surfaces of our consciousness like oil on water. It was the saints and the statues and the pictures and the rituals that attracted us. And as far as "words" went, it was what Jesus said—or what the gospels told us he said—that held interest. Based on the stories we were told, Jesus seemed logical and straightforward in his words and his behavior to children, and more important, he practiced what he preached. Saints and ceremonies and rituals and prayers learned by rote were enough when combined with what we understood to be Jesus's words. They also seemed to be enough for my mother and aunts, uncles and cousins, grandparents and godparents and others around me who considered themselves Roman Catholic. Over the dinner table, or at the Feast of St. Michael the Archangel, in St. Michael's Grove in Paterson, we might have discussed the wisdom of turning the other cheek or the patron saint of shoemakers, but not the Nicene Creed or the Magisterium or the Council of Trent and its implications.

Some might argue that the opinions I express here are too implicated in contemporary issues, and therefore cannot be applied to arguments about the past. But my point is not that my personal experience should be considered scholarly proof of the unimportance of doctrine to the average Christian, or of its impenetrability, but rather that if I and my family and my extended family and my friends from St. Michael's Church, and later St. Theresa's Church, considered ourselves Christians without being weighed down too much by doctrine and dogma, and without worrying whether our offerings, set at the feet of the Virgin or St. Francis, were permissible or not, then how can I, as a scholar or a layman, possibly judge the Maya by criteria that I myself failed to meet? In the same vein, I see no reason to second-guess the Maya, as if they did not have the ability or the sense to know or to feel whether they were Christians or not. In view of the fact that very few individuals, except perhaps bishops or friars or popes, can agree on what it means to be a Christian, I suggest that we take the Mayas' word for it.

With the principle of doctrine or dogma as truth firmly established by the fourth century,[96] many doctrinal decisions, and decisions concerning ritual and practice, had been effected by the end of the Middle Ages. In addition, by the time the Maya were evangelized, the church had lost much of the flexibility that had characterized the evangelization of barbarian Europe (see later chapters). The irony was that this very flexibility had helped to create a Christianity permeated by pre-Christian traditions and attitudes, which existed alongside doctrine. The friars may have emphasized aspects of doctrine as essential to being Christian, but culture, behavior, and the acting out of personal belief told another story, one which was not lost on the Maya. Doctrine seems in principle to present strict criteria that cannot be waived, but in real life, considering doctrine requires the use of reasoning. As such, doctrine is just as liable to be reasoned away, especially in circumstances in which individuals are presented with the concept for the first time. For the Maya, evaluating the significance of doctrine could have begun by observing the behavior of European Christians. They would have come into contact with Spanish settlers from many backgrounds: friars of different orders; secular priests; and in Belize, English and other European Protestants. Such observations would have told them that Christianity had a life of its own independent of doctrine, but also that doctrine was a product of people's decisions and clearly not revealed identically to all Europeans by a shared God. This is critical, because it would have reinforced the idea that Christianity can be taken personally.

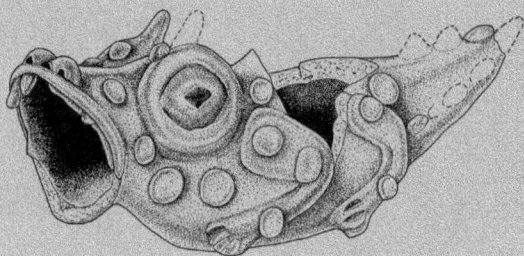

PART II

✠ FIVE ✠

The Environment of
Early Contact

I ended the previous chapter with the idea that Christianity can mean different things to different people. Among the Maya, variations in meaning were partly the consequence of Christianity's newness in a land with its own distinctive cultures, world views, and histories of growth and interaction, and partly a consequence of the process by which Christianity becomes molded according to personal experience. It follows that it is important to consider all the factors that might have affected the lives of Maya individuals in the towns and villages of Belize when Christians from Europe first appeared in the offing.[1]

Of the many factors to be considered, the choice made by Spanish Europeans *not* to settle the mainland, coast, and cayes that are now Belize is perhaps the most significant. There are no rivers whose mouths would have made good land-locked harbors, nor was there a single lagoon "in which all the ships of Spain could lie and be safe."[2] The consistent preference for places other than Belize meant that after the first flush of conquest and the establishment of the Belize missions, which was concentrated in a period from the mid-1540s to about 1570, the effectiveness of Spanish efforts to administer the region diminished considerably.[3] This could be said to be a reflection of the inability to marshal the necessary resources and the scant attention given to the matter.[4] Where Christianity took root in the land that became Belize, it was left veritably to its own devices. Such a situation was not uncommon in the early days of Christianity in a number of places in the world, one of which was Late Antique Britain.

Britons are thought to have converted rather early, probably in the second century, because Christians are recorded to have been living in Britain by the opening years of the third century.[5] St. Patrick, known for evangelizing

Ireland, was born into a Christian family, probably in the early fifth century, in what was then the Roman province of Britannia.[6] Christianity at that time was only one of a wide range of beliefs and practices on offer. Deities and spirits with a range of origins were worshiped: Romano-Greek, native British (Celtic), oriental (such as Mithra or Isis), and some that represented the blending of Romano-Celtic traditions.[7] The context of early Christianity in Mesoamerica was not dissimilar to the environment of Roman Britain, in that the many languages spoken, the several languages written, and the intensity and historical depth of interregional trade and communication imply the existence of a wide range of religious beliefs and practices.

There was some contact between Christian communities in Britain and Gaul,[8] but it is safe to say that British Christianity developed indigenously according to its own distinctive trajectory.[9] The Christianity that characterized the establishment and spread of monasticism in Britain in the sixth century,[10] and that came to be associated with the Anglo-Saxons by the seventh century, was almost another religion. The hostility expressed by the Britons toward anything Anglo-Saxon was rooted in the late fourth and fifth centuries, when Angles, Saxons and Jutes—some as invaders and some as mutinied militias employed by the Britons—had succeeded in displacing local rulers and their kingdoms, particularly in the east and southeast.[11] It is noteworthy that even when the Anglo-Saxons were persuaded by later missionaries (none of them Britons) to convert to Christianity, religion provided no bridge between them. The reaction of the Anglo-Saxons, such as Bede, was to denigrate British Christianity.

What was the nature of indigenous Christianity? Local ruling elites—Celtic rulers in the case of Britain, and Maya lords in the case of Belize—brought their own historical depth and sense of place to their encounters with Christianity, and to its course of development.[12] From the perspective of the later church, this kind of Christianity was "steeped in sin."[13] But in Roman and post-Roman Britain, the autocratic institution of the church as the dominant voice in interpreting Christianity had yet to appear on the horizon, and when it did appear, it slept with the enemy. In the case of the Belize Maya, the sixteenth-century church was a presence from the beginning, but was altogether too distant to dominate. In a sense, it, too, slept with the enemy.[14]

The church as an institution began in Britain with the first mission to convert the Anglo-Saxons, sent by Gregory the Great in 597.[15] Bede, a Benedictine monk from a monastery in Northumbria[16] who lived from about A.D. 672/673 to A.D. 735, wrote a Christian history of the *Gentis Angolorum*, the English people, in which he acknowledged the early conversion of the Britons but regarded their Christianity as heretical.[17] In fact, he characterized his homeland before the arrival of the Anglo-Saxons as "an island which always delights in hearing something new and holds firmly to no sure belief."[18] Like the Britons, the Maya were considered real Christians only when they adhered to beliefs and practices that were part of the institution of the church.

The Britons became "true" Christians as their island came to be settled increasingly by outsiders, a phenomenon that enabled the establishment and growth of a church institutional framework. Why was Belize not similarly chosen by European outsiders as a place to settle, and how did this affect the course of history? The answer is complicated, because Belize never crystallized as a place in European consciousness of the sixteenth century. If Belize was anything, it was a liminal, elusive, shifting, dangerous space, neither land nor sea, neither here nor there, betwixt and between an idea of a "Yucatan" and an idea of a "Kingdom of Guatemala."

> Such a manner of coast . . . has never been seen or heard of elsewhere, for it is all inundated by the sea for a great distance. Because of this, it is impossible to move by land. . . . [The Maya captives], who knew the coast, were set to rowing when necessary, and at the hour of vespers, or sometimes later, they landed, having gained . . . six or seven leagues. It was something to be marveled at how, just before sunset, they would find a stream or lagoon with a belt of sand, or beach, close to its entrance, where, with guards posted over the canoes, the men and horses could be put ashore.[19]

These comments reflect the seven months spent by Alonso Dávila and his party in 1533 traveling along the coast of Belize from Villa Real at Chetumal to Puerto de Caballos (map 1.1). Dávila was sent by Francisco Montejo to pacify the region of Uaymil-Chetumal (map 5.1) as part of the second stage of the conquest of Yucatan, but he and his men met fierce resistance from the Maya and were forced to flee. The journey convinced the Spaniards of the unsuitability of the territory that lay between Chetumal Bay and Honduras.[20] Thus, except for its "manner of coast," the land that became Belize never attained coherence as a place in Spanish consciousness during the colonial period. Neither the documentary sources nor the archaeology has produced indications or evidence of settlement by Spaniards.

Owing in part to neglect by Spain, this same coast attracted those bent on thwarting and capitalizing on Spanish activities associated with settlement elsewhere. Pirates and privateers from countries hostile to Spanish interests were attracted to Belize's inlets, estuaries, coastal lagoons, cayes, and atolls.[21] With no deep-water ports and a shallow-water coastal shelf protected by a barrier reef,[22] on which ships could easily be wrecked, Belize was not an immediately inviting prospect, despite the attraction these features have for tourists today. The impression made on Dávila and his compatriots became a

Map 5.1. Yucatan and the Bay of Honduras in the Conquest period, showing communities and language and culture areas. (Drawing by Debora Trein)

lasting one, but for those wishing to take advantage of Spain's relative inactivity in the waters of the barrier reef, it was worthwhile investing in learning to navigate cuts in the reef, in knowing where to drop anchor near the atolls or cayes to obtain fresh water, and in general in accumulating local knowledge—for example, learning which cayes gave easy access to the mainland to obtain food, water, and supplies, either owing to proximity or to local conditions such as currents or prevailing winds. Because the coastal zone was intensively utilized both by local Maya and by Maya traders engaged in long-distance commerce,[23] we must keep in mind that Europeans besides the Spaniards who established missions had an impact on Belize's Maya communities. The Maya resident in Belize and the Maya plying the Belize coasts came into contact not only with Spaniards but also with Europeans who were not Spanish Christians.

Such contact, in addition to providing a range of examples of what it meant to be Christian, did not serve the Maya well in the absence of the protection that went along with Spanish settlements. The records we have of English-Maya contact in the seventeenth century and very early eighteenth century, to which I return in chapter 9, tell of raids on Maya communities in Belize for supplies and slaves,[24] and we have no reason to believe that the first half of the sixteenth century, when enslavement of indigenous people was at its most intense and profitable, was a kinder era. If even a handful of pirates or privateers were active during this period, then the coastal Maya of Belize were vulnerable to attacks and slave raids, and hence to European diseases even before 1544, when the documentary records indicate that encomiendas, or tribute-paying obligations, were first introduced by the Spaniards to inland Maya communities such as Tipu and Lamanai. With reference to Yucatan, both Bricker and Restall comment on the impact of diseases the Spaniards unknowingly introduced even before the Montejo campaigns in 1527.[25] In the native literature, the coming of the Spaniards was closely associated with the onset of disease, but one wonders, from a Belize perspective at least, whether reference to "the mighty men from the East" included a wider range of Europeans than is generally acknowledged.[26]

An understanding of the larger context in which *visita* missions were established in towns such as Lamanai and Tipu is clearly important to our assessment of the ultimate fate of the missions and of the Maya who invested in them. In the sections that follow, I discuss the factors that framed the context of the early colonial encounter in Belize: the peripheral importance of the land that became Belize to Spanish colonizing efforts; the legacy of the dynamics of pre-Columbian Maya coastal trade and exchange; and the role that Belize's unique coastal environment played in attracting those who exploited Spain's colonizing activities. Keeping these factors in mind, I then turn to Yucatan and to the lands that comprised the Kingdom of Guatemala, the two major regions whose conquest activities affected Belize and the fate of Maya communities there. I recognize that these conquests have been detailed in more comprehensive works than mine. My purpose here is to draw on what is known to contribute to an understanding of how Spanish activities in core regions created conditions that have bearing on the colonial encounter in Belize in particular.

What's in a Name?

There is general awareness that the term for ancient and early colonial "Mexico" refers to a more restricted area than modern Mexico, and that the colonial Kingdom of Guatemala included more territory under its jurisdiction than the nation of Guatemala does today. Despite these differences, there is

Map 5.2. The Caribbean basin. (Drawing by Debora Trein)

generally little difficulty in finding terms to describe places that were once part of colonial Guatemala or Yucatan or Mexico but which are now separate countries. For example, the nations of Honduras, Nicaragua, and Costa Rica retain names by which their territories were known in colonial times; the Republic of Guatemala refers to the modern nation, the highland territory of which comprised the heart of a more extensive colonial kingdom. Tabasco and Chiapas, at one time part of Yucatan under Francisco Montejo, are now part of modern Mexico, but one can nevertheless refer to "Tabasco" or to "Chiapas" because both regions have retained their colonial names (map 5.2).

"Quintana Roo" is a modern name, but we know by the names of its communities that it was originally part of colonial Yucatan. In fact, "Yucatan" as a term today can refer to the northernmost state of the peninsula (Yucatán)(see Map 5.2) or in a more general sense to the geographic peninsula, in which case the modern states of Yucatán, Campeche, and Quintana Roo become subsumed under the name "Yucatan" or "Yucatan Peninsula." The northern part of Belize is sometimes included as part of Yucatan in this latter sense.

With regard to Belize, it is guesswork trying to discern how to refer to it, either whole or in part, by names that appear in the colonial records; it is even more difficult to know how Belize or its subregions stood in the consciousness of the early conquerors, colonizers, and religious. Spanish authorities based in Mérida or Valladolid or Bacalar seem to have seen the northern half of Belize as part of colonial Yucatan and their records do not differentiate it even with a subregional name (map 5.1). Colonial sources, if they refer to what we know as Belize at all, use names of towns and villages. When they identify the regional governing center that had jurisdiction over the towns in

Belize, they refer to the Villa de Salamanca de Bacalar,[27] which is in present-day Mexico in the state of Quintana Roo. We have no way of knowing what part Belize communities played in Spanish authorities' vision of the region, except perhaps for the comment appended to a set of Bacalar accounts, apparently required by the Crown in 1620, that the *villa* was inhabited by the most miserable people in all the Indies.[28]

The Franciscan friar Lorenzo de Bienvenida almost certainly passed through what is now Belize on his way from Guatemala to Mérida sometime between 1543 and the end of 1546. His route through Belize must, however, be inferred from documents that describe his journey as starting off in the regions of the Golfo Dulce (map 5.1) and then continuing as far as Salamanca de Bacalar before proceeding on to Mérida,[29] which meant that he had to pass through the land that is now Belize. Curiously, Bienvenida himself must not have considered the communities in Belize as part of Yucatan,[30] because in his letter to the Crown, written in 1548,[31] he described the province of Yucatan as having land that is level with no rivers, except for one river in Champotón (map 5.1). He also refers in his letter to Gaspar Pacheco's assignment of a captaincy to conquer provinces of the Golfo Dulce lying between Honduras and Guatemala and "this land" (Yucatan).[32] His wording suggests that he saw Belize communities not as part of Honduras or Guatemala, but as part of a larger region he called the Golfo Dulce. In this he would presage the Baymen by characterizing Belize in terms of its coast.[33]

The record is even more depauperate if one searches for cognizance of the land that became Belize in what is known from records of the Kingdom of Guatemala and Central America in the sixteenth and seventeenth centuries. Lists of names of Spanish or Indian towns, or of populations or products of towns, never include places in Belize.[34] Maps have lines drawn around what is now Belize territory, but the scant feature (such as a river) that sometimes shows up is either misidentified or the entire area within the lines is blank, in stark contrast with the flourish of dots and lines that represent towns, rivers, and boundaries in Chiapas, Guatemala, Honduras, Nicaragua, and Costa Rica (see, e.g., map 5.3).

On early maps, often only place names are shown, with no regional or subregional boundaries.[35] As time passed, boundaries began to appear. Because geopolitics changed many times during the early colonial era, boundaries changed, but patterns emerge. "Guatimala" comes to refer to a highland province on the Pacific coast, southeast of Soconusco, but also to a larger area that encompasses highland "Guatimala," Honduras, El Salvador, Nicaragua, Costa Rica, and Panama.[36] On other maps, "Guatimala" extends to include Soconusco, Chiapas, and Verapaz (map 5.8).[37] The one place "Guatimala" never includes on these maps is Belize.

Map 5.3. Map of the Kingdom of Guatemala between 1570 and 1650 showing absence of place names in the area of Belize and incorrect names of rivers. (Redrawn by Debora Trein from Villacorta Calderón 1942, 63)

The coastline of what is now Belize was considered part of the Gulf of Honduras, or Bay of Honduras, and what was to become the colony of British Honduras would derive its name from this usage, with its residents referred to as Baymen.[38] Therefore, when a colonial source refers to a ship that anchored off the coast of the "Gulf of Honduras," or "Bay of Honduras," the location could be anywhere from Trujillo or Puerto Caballos (map 5.3) to Ambergris Caye (map 5.1).

Francisco Montejo, who is credited with the conquest of Yucatan, had designs on Honduras-Higueras (map 5.1), and his plans almost certainly included Belize, if only because ships had to sail past the Belize coast in order to reach Honduras from Yucatan. In 1539, however, when Montejo was forced to relinquish the governorship of Honduras-Higueras to Pedro de Alvarado in exchange for Chiapas,[39] Belize does not seem to have been ceded to Alvarado, or at least was not foremost in negotiators' minds, because in the spring of 1543, Montejo appointed Gaspar Pacheco as Lieutenant Governor, Captain General, and Justicia Mayor of the province of Uaymil-Chetumal *as far south as the Golfo Dulce*.[40] It is therefore clear from Montejo's view of the matter—and from the fact that the Pachecos carried the conquest banner well into Belize—that Honduras-Higueras included modern Honduras and south coastal

Maya Christians and Their Churches in Sixteenth-Century Belize

Guatemala, but did not extend to the (unnamed) territory north of the Golfo Dulce.

If Belize had an identity among Europeans in the early conquest period, it is most likely to have reflected the perspectives of those who sailed past Belize in ships, or rowed or sailed boats through the waters of Belize's coastal shelf from caye to caye or from caye to coast, a notion which is supported by the features repeated in a number of early maps—namely, the Maya Mountains (the Cockscombs) and the multitude of offshore islands. For example, Dudley's Carta Primera General of 1646–47 (map 5.4) shows a veritable profusion of islands off the coast of Belize, a phenomenon which recurs in Sanson, Visscher, Vander Aa, Blaeu, and Loots (maps 5.4–5.6, 5.9).[41] Where mountains are shown (e.g., map 5.5), their placement suggests strongly that they represent the Maya Mountains, or Cockscombs, which can clearly be seen from coastal waters even from the deck of a ship outside the reef.[42] The Wytfliet map of 1597 depicts rivers draining the mountains in a way that is characteristic of the Cockscomb basin (map 5.7).[43] Although these maps are known to be stylized and speculative, because they were based on information gleaned by mapmakers from travelers to the New World, it is interesting that Yucatan is

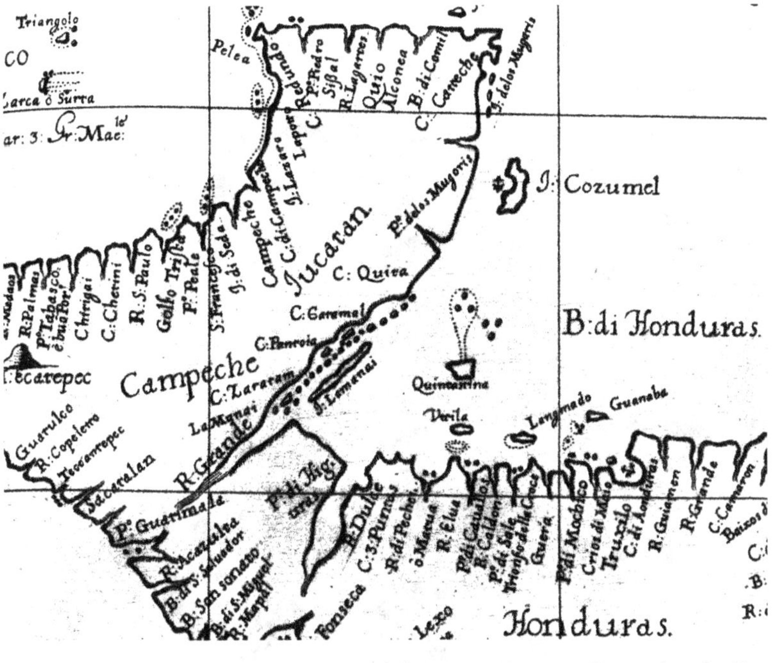

Map 5.4. Dudley's "Carta Prima Generale." Depicts Yucatan, Campeche, the Bay of Honduras, and Honduras. Shows Lamanai as an island with an additional bevy of small islands off the Belize coast (Dudley 1646–47). (Courtesy of the Library of Congress, Washington, D.C.)

Map 5.5. Sanson map of Yucatan and the Gulf of Honduras. "Lamanay" is an island with a chain of mountains on the mainland in the area of Belize (Sanson d'Abbeville 1650, 1670). (Courtesy of the Library of Congress, Washington, D.C.)

Map 5.6. Blaeu map of Yucatan showing "Lamanay" on the mainland (Blaeu 1665). (Courtesy of the Library of Congress, Washington, D.C.)

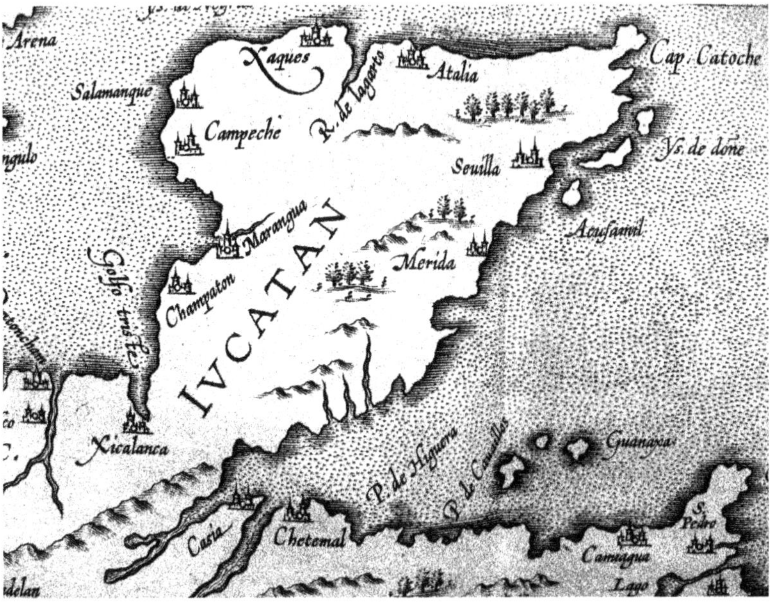

Map 5.7. Wytfliet map of Yucatan showing rivers and mountains in the area of Belize (Wytfliet 1597). (Courtesy of the Library of Congress, Washington, D.C.)

Map 5.8. Visscher map of Yucatan, the Gulf of Honduras, and the Kingdom of Guatemala, 1717 (copies a Montanus map of 1671). Belize is shown as part of Yucatan, with mountains near the coast and a string of islands, one of which is "Lamanay." The Kingdom of "Guatimala" seems to cover most of Central America, although on this map the status of Tabasco, Verapaz, and Soconusco is unclear (Visscher 1717). (Courtesy of the Library of Congress, Washington, D.C.)

shown, correctly, almost devoid of drainage. Of particular significance are the three large islands that appear consistently in early maps, which almost certainly represent Belize's atolls (e.g., maps 5.5, 5.6). These atolls, today known as Glover's Reef, Turneffe Island, and Lighthouse Reef were places where ships could anchor in deeper water yet gain access to land, fresh water, and supplies by fishing, foraging, barter, or stealth.

In the next section, I focus on Belize from a coastal perspective, in an attempt to evoke a picture of the land as it emerged in the minds of the Europeans who were intent on exploiting or colonizing the region of which Belize is a part. These Europeans' ideas, perceptions, and schemes provided the context in which conversion efforts were planned and carried out. At the same time, the ideas, perceptions, and schemes of the Maya of Belize coastal communities provided the initial context in which European advances into Maya territory were evaluated and assessed, and around which strategies were developed.

A Coastal Perspective

THE MAYA AND THE COAST

The Chontal Maya of the broad alluvial plain of Tabasco and southern Campeche (maps 5.1, 5.2) are generally considered to have been the masters of canoe-born commerce in the Maya lowlands.[44] Evidence from archaeological sites on the cayes and coast tells us that the Maya of Belize played an active part in this commerce. In the tenth century, for example, trade extended to Honduras and involved goods such as plumbate pottery, which was made along the Pacific coast in southwestern Guatemala.[45]

In the archaeological literature, this circum-peninsular seaborne trade is best known as a Postclassic phenomenon[46] that received impetus from the conditions following the Maya collapse in the ninth to eleventh centuries, and was in full swing when Columbus arrived in the New World. Smith and Berdan[47] observe that exchange and interaction were particularly intensive along coastal routes during the Postclassic period. Although they emphasize coastal interaction for its role in integrating the region as a whole, as do Scholes and Roys,[48] the existence of a coastal socioeconomic sphere that operated according to variables (and parameters) with deep roots in time almost certainly contributed to the viability of the Postclassic phenomenon.[49] Scholes and Roys cite an agent of Francisco Montejo the Elder, who observed:

> From the Ulua River to the River of Copilco-zacualco[50] it is all one language, and they all trade with one another and consider themselves to be the same; and all the Indians of those parts say that those are their boundaries. Beyond the River of Copilco-zacualco the language is that of New Spain [Nahuatl], and similarly beyond the said Ulua River it is another language [Jicaque?].[51]

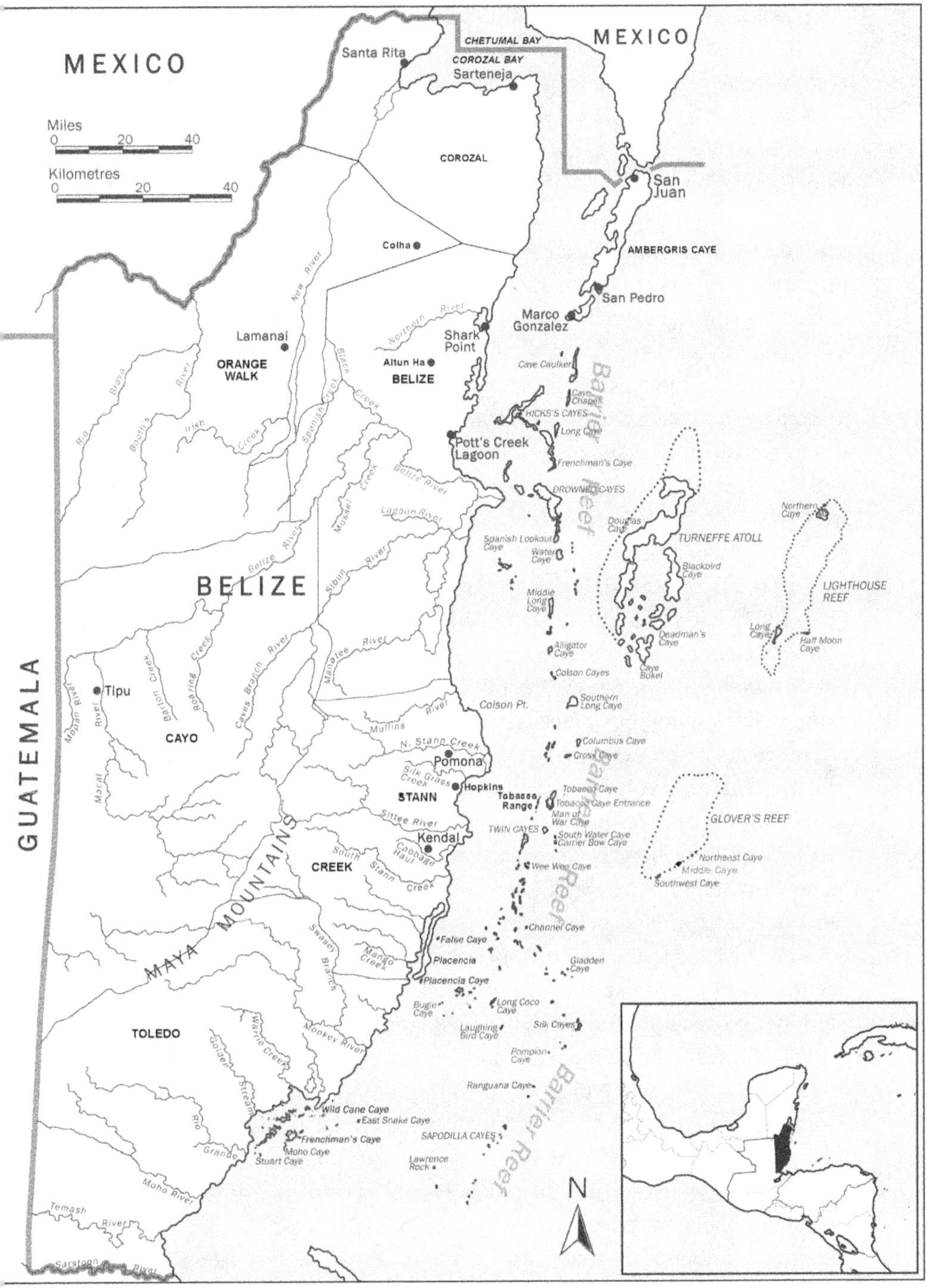

Map 5.9. Belize and details of the coastal zone, cayes, atolls, rivers, and modern district boundaries. (Drawing by Debora Trein)

Archaeological evidence from Belize adds layers of complexity to the coastal picture.[52] Ceramics and other artifacts from coastal sites reflect intensive coastal activity and seaborne trade from at least the Late Preclassic period (roughly about 300 B.C.),[53] without exhibiting the exponential change in the Postclassic that seems to characterize sites in the states of Quintana Roo, Campeche, or Yucatán.[54] The nature of activity and commerce changed through time, and in the Late Classic period in Belize, from about A.D. 550/600 to A.D. 750/800, salt processing was clearly the most profitable enterprise,[55] whereas at other times activities were more broadly based and included transport and trade of items such as ground stone, pottery, chert, obsidian, and salted fish.[56]

Most of the known sites, for all periods, that represent communities once located close to the sea in Belize would probably be classified as villages; some were extensions of mainland towns, whereas others were permanently settled.[57] The Salt Creek sites, for example (see Pott's Creek Lagoon, map 5.8), were probably coastal outposts of the Classic center of Altun Ha; the Northern River Lagoon activities were connected to Colha; and the Colson Point sites were almost certainly connected to centers in the Stann Creek Valley (map 5.8).[58] The predominance of villages rather than towns along the coast is largely attributable to the nature of Belize's seasonally inundated shores in combination with the availability of relatively stable dry areas for settlement along Belize's numerous creeks and rivers. Farther north, in Yucatan, there are no rivers or creeks, and the coastline, although rocky, has some stable beaches. There were, however, some towns in Belize positioned on the coast. Santa Rita on Corozal Bay was a town when the Spaniards arrived, as was San Pedro on Ambergris Caye (map 5.8).[59] Marco Gonzalez, San Juan, and Santa Cruz (all on Ambergris Caye) and Wild Cane Caye in southern Belize functioned as towns or permanently settled villages in earlier times (ca. A.D. 800–1200),[60] and there are a number of sites along the coast of northern Belize that were active in trade and exchange throughout the Postclassic, some until the arrival of the Spaniards (map 5.9, map 2.3).[61]

It is clear from the material remains that coastal villages were tied to towns that were situated on the mainland in more protected locations, often on the nearest river or creek.[62] The coastal villages themselves either looked out on lagoons or bays or were located on islands (cayes) both near- and off-shore. Rise in sea level and local aggradation complicate the task of reconstructing pre-Columbian conditions, but the critical factor in coastal settlement seems to have been the location of a stable, well drained area that stood above the level of periodic inundation and remained dry during the rainy season.

Belize's coast is characterized by mangrove. As Montejo's lieutenant Dávila discovered in his travels south along the Belize coast in 1533, towns were located in more stable settings up rivers. There are only a few places in which enough sand accumulates to form a stable beach; there is a beach at Sarteneja in the Corozal District, and at Hopkins and Placencia in the Stann Creek District (map 5.8), but most of the coastline is characterized by seasonally submerged mangrove communities, a factor which dictated that towns oriented toward coastal trade and commerce had to be situated inland in more protected and well-drained locales. The Belize cayes were the exception, because they were stable enough to support villages, and large enough in some cases to support towns. Ambergris Caye, as noted above, supported towns, although residents were sometimes forced to move, as coastal accretion triggered a variety of micro-environmental changes that impinged on access to the sea.[63]

With regard to the Spanish colonial period, two points can be made in light of the archaeological evidence. The first is that canoe-borne commerce was always a major part of Maya economy.[64] The way commerce was transacted, and who benefited, may have changed through time, but there is no question that coastal trade and travel, as well as the acquisition of coastal and marine resources, were always an integral part of Maya culture. The second point is that there were aspects of material culture, and culture in general, which coastal sites shared that were not shared with inland sites; and by "coastal sites" I include sheltered riverine settlements, such as those along the North Stann Creek River (map 5.8) or at Colha or Altun Ha, whose communities were connected to way stations or ports on the coast or cayes for the purposes of transacting commerce and loading and unloading goods transported via seaborne canoes.[65] Material culture would have included seagoing canoes; paraphernalia associated with building, crafts, and salt production; marine resource procurement tools; jars to store fresh water; and any other tools or facilities specific to marine resource procurement or trade or exchange. Aspects of non-material culture include knowledge of marine navigation (seasonal winds, currents, coastal and marine environments); expertise in the construction of canoes for marine travel; expertise in the waterborne transportation and storage of goods and equipment in both marine and riverine conditions; an emphasis on and knowledge of marine resource exploitation; frequent involvement in interaction beyond the boundaries of the local area; contact with people, languages, and material and non-material culture from a variety of places both near and far; and access to wide-ranging networks of communication.

Heaps of fragments of polychrome bowls, presumably the result of breakage during transport, are common at coastal sites in Belize, and date to the tail end of the Preclassic period and the bulk of the Early Classic (ca. A.D. 200 to A.D. 450–500), whereas such middens of polychromes are not a feature of inland sites. In the Late Classic (roughly A.D. 550/600 to A.D. 750/800), the debris of salt processing litters the coast from the Toledo district to Ambergris Caye. Polychrome vases were transported as part of a network of exchange along the coast in Late Classic times as well, although in far lower quantities than was the case with the earlier Classic polychromes.[66] By the time forces were set in motion that would lead ultimately to the collapse of sites in Peten (ca. A.D. 800), the orientation of coastal sites in Belize had changed again, from salt to hard goods such as pottery and obsidian, although salted fish, shellfish, and other marine items were probably always part of coastal trade and commerce.[67]

It is clear that coastal Maya were in close communication and contact with each other in ways that may not always have involved inland Maya, although inland communities produced goods passed on to coastal communities and received goods from them. Coastal sites have been characterized as outposts for an inland-based state,[68] but such relationships are not clear at coastal sites in Belize, at least not based on present evidence, unless riverine communities linked to coastal ports are interpreted in this way. Such an interpretation would be misleading, however, because the riverine communities (such as those in the North Stann Creek Valley) and the coastal ports or way stations (such as those at Colson Point) (map 5.8) were probably occupied by people who spent part of their time inland and part of their time on the coast, and were therefore part of a single community.[69] In the case of Marco Gonzalez and Lamanai,[70] details of community histories argue against Marco Gonzalez being any sort of "outpost" for Lamanai.[71] Marco Gonzalez was without doubt part of the coastal trading network that linked Honduras, southern Belize, and Chichen Itza, whereas Lamanai, although it clearly capitalized on its position as a node in networks of riverine and marine trade, displays a material culture assemblage distinct from that of the coast, which suggests that its relationship with Marco Gonzalez was not one of control.

The question of outposts aside, the groundwork was laid many years before the Postclassic period for intensive social contact and communication among coastal communities from Honduras to Belize to Yucatan to the Gulf Coast. Therefore, it should not be surprising that there were social, cultural, and economic ties among coastally oriented Maya that gave them a distinctiveness not shared by inland-based groups. The evidence from Belize indicates that coastal interaction was in place by Late Preclassic times, if not earlier, and networks of communication and contact were therefore long established by the time the Spaniards and other Europeans arrived.

Whether or not the same Maya cultural or language groups occupied the same sites through time is another matter. Coastal activity never skipped a beat,[72] but there are changes—in the tools used or in the way food was processed or in burial practices—that suggest concomitant changes in social or cultural identity over time.[73] Given the interregional (and in modern terms, international) scope of trade and exchange in Mesoamerica, the culture of coastal settlements must have been even more vulnerable to change than the culture of inland groups. At the same time, the occupational longevity of coastal sites in Belize suggests that the ability of coastal inhabitants to adjust to social, cultural, or economic fluctuations gave their communities stability not characteristic of many inland settlements, particularly during the Classic to Postclassic transition. One could hazard that as people involved in commerce, coastal Maya were accustomed to circumstances in which change was a way of life. As a consequence, a culture evolved among these communities that reflected coastal dynamics in particular.

Landa observes in his *Relación* that the Maya of Yucatan spoke one language, although he, along with others, also notes that there was some difference in words and in manner of speaking that separated people who lived along the coast from their inland counterparts.[74] According to Herrera, "The language is all the same although in the places along the sea coast they have prided themselves on speaking with greater refinement."[75] Kepecs, who carried out archaeological and documentary research on Maya communities of the territory of the Chikinchel, on the north coast of Yucatan, suggests that this polished dialect may have been Chontal.[76] Gerónimo de Aguilar, a shipwrecked Spaniard who had been held in captivity by a Maya lord in Yucatan, and whose release was negotiated by Cortés when the conquistador was on Cozumel Island in 1519, apparently spoke Chontal.[77] Indications are that both Chontal and Yucatec were spoken in coastal communities of Yucatan.

We cannot be sure (because the records do not mention places in Belize) that the comments on language extended to the Maya of coastal Belize, although Landa seems to have considered Bacalar and the area around it as falling under the jurisdiction of the ecclesiastical province of Yucatan. The quote from Scholes and Roys,[78] above, about the commonalities shared (including language) among people who lived around the Yucatan Peninsula from the Ulua River in Honduras to Copilco-Zacualco on the Gulf Coast (map 5.1), certainly includes coastal Belize. Scholes and Roys comment further that, "The area extending from Laguna Tupilco in western Tabasco to the Ulua River in northern Honduras emerges as an economic bloc, which, in spite of its political diversity, can be considered a single commercial empire."[79] The last note we could add to this discussion is that Dávila, on his journey south from the Villa Real at Chetumal in 1533, to which the passage quoted above refers, commented that the same interpreter (who must have been from coastal

Campeche)[80] served him as well on the Ulua as in Yucatan.[81] This suggests that Belize, apparently considered by Dávila as part of Yucatan, fell within the same coastal language sphere.

The concept of the existence of a Maya coastal band of interaction that was not just economic but also social and cultural is deserving of attention, particularly in view of the archaeological evidence on which I have just drawn.[82] It means that we need to keep at the forefront of our minds the idea that social relationships may have covered considerable distances, and that communication was well honed as the result of centuries of interaction. If coastal interaction extended beyond economics to spheres of social, cultural, and religious life, then the reaction to Spanish incursions—such as Montejo's east coast *entrada* in 1527–29, or even an event as early as the fourth voyage of Columbus in 1502–3—would have been structured by and channeled through this long-established coastal network.[83] It should be no surprise, then, that knowledge traveled rapidly and that the Maya reacted regionally or interregionally to events that to the Spaniards seemed local.

THE EUROPEANS AND THE COAST

Columbus reached Guanaja (maps 3.1, 5.1), the easternmost of the Bay Islands in the Gulf of Honduras, in 1502,[84] and news of his landfall almost certainly spread to Maya communities in Belize, since transport and trading activity by the Maya and between the Maya and other indigenous groups in far-flung regions was, as I have argued, intensive along this coast.[85]

Several navigators charted the Caribbean coastline of Central America in the first decade of the sixteenth century as an extension of their efforts to capture hundreds, or even thousands, of Indians, whom they carried to the mines of Hispaniola.[86] That ships' pilots had intimate knowledge of the Yucatan coast by 1519 is indicated by Cortés's experiences, when he was advised by his pilots against leaving Cozumel Island to sail his fleet along the coast of Yucatan to look for the Spaniards Gerónimo de Aguilar and Gonzalo Guerrero, who were reported to be living with the Maya. The pilots warned that the coast was too rocky and that the ships would be wrecked trying to approach the shore.[87]

There is some evidence to suggest that Spanish contact with Belize occurred in 1508.[88] At that time, Vicente Pinzón[89] and Juan de Solís were commanders of a small exploratory expedition of two vessels. They are known to have sailed along the Central American coast,[90] but historians are not in agreement about whether they headed north to Yucatan or south to Venezuela and Brazil. One interpretation is that they sailed along the Honduras coast and then northward along the coasts of Belize and Yucatan, and that they may have reached as far as Tampico. Pinzón, in a later testimony, described seeing mountains after passing a body of water that may have been Lake Izabal (Golfo Dulce) in Guatemala (map 5.1). If this was the case, the mountains must have been the Cockscombs, or Maya Mountains, which means that they sailed within sight of the Belize coast.[91] Winzerling, who wrote a highly intriguing history of British Honduras, unfortunately without citing his sources, commented that, "Every seaman is impressed by this isolated mountain group which is the colony's most conspicuous landmark from the sea."[92] Winzerling's observation is borne out, as I noted earlier in this chapter, by various early maps (see, e.g., maps 5.4–5.7).

McClymont's interpretation of the documents is that Pinzón and Solís sailed in 1508 along the coast of lower Central and South America.[93] He reviews other highly interesting documentary evidence, however, which suggests that Pinzón, possibly with Solís, explored the Bay of Honduras sometime between 1496 and 1499, and most likely 1498–99.[94] Outside these voyages, it is also clear from McClymont's account that many voyages were made to the Caribbean and Central America at this time for which no records are preserved.

Because such exploratory fleets had to replenish their food and water supplies regularly, it is highly likely that they came into contact with the Maya of Belize on the atolls or cayes or coast. Ships could have anchored off the barrier reef near the offshore cayes, or near atolls such as Glover's Reef (map 5.8), and taken boats to reach the mainland. The cayes off the coast of the Stann Creek District (map 5.8) are particularly strategic, not only because they are relatively close to the mainland,[95] but because the land in this region is characterized by a number of rivers and streams that drain the mountains and cross the narrow coastal plain to the sea.[96] (I noted above that the parallel rivers draining mountains shown on the Wytfliet map [map 5.7] are intriguing in this regard.[97]) Here fresh water was readily available, crops were grown not only on the fertile soil that bordered the rivers and creeks, but also very likely on the black soils in prominent zones along the coast itself, as well as on some of the cayes.[98] As Jones points out, the type of contact involving exploratory vessels anchored along the Belize coast could well have brought European diseases to the Maya of Belize at an early date.[99] It is also likely that Pinzón and Solís and other captains and crews of such fleets did what other Spanish explorers did, which was to capture Mayas as slaves, either to replenish the population in the Caribbean islands or to work on shipboard.

It is not too far-fetched to consider that the territory that is now Belize was included in more expeditions than that of Pinzón and Solís, leaving coastal Maya towns or fishing and shellfish-gathering outposts on the atolls and cayes open to attack and to slave raids. The fact that Maya seaborne traffic—related to both trade and resource extraction—was intensive at the time of contact meant that canoes regularly plied the waters both within the barrier reef and between the reef edge and the atolls. Particularly during the years of the first decades of the sixteenth century, the Maya living on the coasts and cayes, or traveling to and from the cayes and atolls, must have been sitting ducks as far as slave traders and buccaneers were concerned.

To summarize the implications of a coastal perspective, we can say that although European ships were not designed for navigation of the shallow waters of a coastal shelf rimmed by a barrier reef, and were therefore ill equipped to capitalize commercially on the resource extraction and trade so long enjoyed by the Maya, Belize's cayes and atolls would have been observed by Europeans as hubs of activity at the time of first contact. As a consequence of efforts to chart the coastal waters of the Caribbean Sea, ships' pilots would have become aware of the barrier reef and its string of cayes, as well as of the atolls, which lay in deeper waters outside the barrier reef. They would have recognized the perils of the reef for ships, although not for boats; at the same time, they would have recognized the advantages, in terms of supplying ships with water, food, information, and very probably slaves.

Mexico, Yucatan, Central America, and Belize

It is appropriate at this point to step back to consider how the early environment of contact in Belize was affected by the ways in which Yucatan and Central America were colonized. Among Mayanists, the conquest histories that are generally thought to be relevant comprise Cortés's conquest of Mexico, the conquest of Yucatan, the conquest of highland Guatemala, and the late conquest of the Itza of the Peten.[100] The implications of the conquest of Mexico for Belize communities were felt largely in the sphere of evangelization, discussed in the following chapter. With regard to the political wrangling that affected the context of evangelization in Belize, the conquests of Yucatan and Central America are equally relevant. This is not because Belize was ever effectively a part of colonial Guatemala or Central America, except as imagined lines on a map. But the combinations of circumstances, goals, and personalities that drove events in Central America and Yucatan were like two spiraling atmospheric storms. Both forces were felt in Belize, but the eyes of the storms were elsewhere.

BELIZE AND THE CONQUEST OF YUCATAN

The initial military effort to subdue Yucatan took place in 1527–28, but this was not the first time the Maya of the peninsula had come into contact with Europeans. In addition to the expeditions of Hernández de Córdoba in 1517, Grijalva in 1518, and the expedition led by Cortés, who made landfall on the east coast of Yucatan on his way to Mexico in 1519,[101] a few Spaniards had been living among the Mayas of the peninsula since 1511. Two of them, Gerónimo de Aguilar and Gonzalo Guerrero, remained the only long-term survivors of a ship that had been wrecked, possibly off the Yucatan coast, although exactly where the wreck occurred, and where the survivors ended up, remains a subject of debate.[102]

The consequences of such early contacts were in some ways as significant as those of later military efforts, in that they provided indications of what to expect from Europeans at the same time that they allowed the Maya a period in which to react and to strategize.[103] The early presence of Spaniards in Yucatan, together with the coastal orientation of many communities in Belize, would have made the Maya aware of, and perhaps even put them in contact with, Europeans from the time of Columbus's fourth voyage. This meant that the conquest of Yucatan did not take place in a vacuum, and that the lives of the Belize Maya had been altered long before the establishment of encomiendas in 1544.

Francisco de Montejo, made Adelantado as well as Gobernador, Capitán General, and Alguacil Mayor of Yucatan in December 1526,[104] began his efforts at conquering Yucatan in 1527–28 by focusing on the east coast. Jones attributes the Spaniards' interest in the east coast, which included Belize, to their desire to open up trade passages between Honduras and Guatemala.[105] I suggest, too, that the Spaniards were already armed at this time with information on the bustling trade that had been observed by early explorers along the east coast of Yucatan and Belize. Montejo sailed from Santo Domingo, and by late September the armada had anchored off the coast of Cozumel (maps 5.1, 5.2).[106] By late October, he and his company had established the settlement of Salamanca, near Xelha, on the mainland, probably located on the promontory of Punta Solimán, which is 2 kilometers south of the Maya town of Xelha (map 5.1).[107] It took three to four months for the men to adjust to the local conditions, and many sickened and died in the process. Relations with the Maya fluctuated, but by the end of 1527 or early in 1528 Montejo was ready to turn inland to begin his conquest.[108]

Montejo then spent about six months exploring the northeastern part of Yucatan.[109] It is impossible to summarize the complexities of the entrada; many communities greeted the Spaniards without hostility, whereas others attacked them. In Chamberlain's assessment,[110] Montejo had won the nominal allegiance of a considerable area, and it is indeed true that caciques and their representatives had, in Spanish eyes, acceded to Castilian domination.

Among Maya leaders, however, such diplomacy was the first step taken in a situation in which tribute relationships, and hence political power, were potentially to change. As was the case with the Aztecs, military action seems to have been considered a last resort, when other kinds of diplomacy or nego-tiation failed.[111] Although the Spaniards would later claim that the Maya were deceitful, the fact is that Maya actions and behavior were being judged on the basis of Castilian cultural practices. At least in this initial period, the Span-iards seemed to make no effort to learn anything about Maya governance or economics, except on Spanish terms. Hence, we have references in the docu-ments to the *cacicazgo* of Ecab, or to the "province" of Chikinchel,[112] when all ethnohistoric, glyphic, and archaeological evidence indicates that pre-Co-lumbian concepts of political and economic organization bore little resem-blance to such Spanish territorially rooted ideas.[113]

Montejo had three churchmen on his first entrada: Juan Rodríguez de Car-aveo was Montejo's chaplain; Pedro Fernández was chaplain of the armada; and Gregorio de San Martín was a Carmelite friar.[114] Of the three, the secular priest Caraveo is mentioned most for his efforts, first to learn to speak Maya, at which he was fairly successful, and second to bring the true faith to the Indians, although this may simply reflect the fact that Caraveo refers to his successes in his own *probanza*.[115] Given that the Spaniards spent many weeks in Maya towns, we can say with certainty that at least some Maya would have been evangelized and come into contact with Spanish rituals (baptism, mass, the lighting of candles, veneration of images), the material culture of Christi-anity (incense, oil, wine, rosary beads, portable altars, chalices, the concept of sacrifice), and the importance of saints and their effigies.

Once Montejo and his party had returned to Xelha, he sent his lieutenant Dávila southward by land and sailed south in a brigantine[116] that had recently arrived from Santo Domingo, mainly to find a location strategically superior to Salamanca at Xelha.[117] He reached the Maya coastal town of Chetumal, the location of which is still not certain, although Andrews and Jones place it on the west side of Chetumal Bay at the center of a zone that includes the Late Postclassic sites of Ichpaatun, Oxtancah, San Manuel, La Iglesia, and Isla Ta-malcab (maps 2.3, 5.1; see also map 2.2 for some of the sites mentioned).[118] Santa Rita, farther south in Belize, has also been proposed as ancient Che-tumal (map 5.8).[119] Montejo found that the shipwrecked Spaniard, Gonzalo Guerrero, whom Cortés had contacted in 1519 near Cozumel, was now liv-ing with his wife and three sons[120] at or near Chetumal. Despite entreaties from Montejo, Guerrero would not leave his family to join the Spaniards.[121] If this information is accurate,[122] Guerrero's move with his family from the Ecab region to Chetumal, and the attendant maintenance of his social posi-tion, could be highlighted as an example of the relationships, kin-based and otherwise, that would have developed among coastally oriented, culturally and economically interconnected communities. Such relationships facilitated residence shifts because they provided social networks that operated over long distances.[123]

Montejo continued his reconnaissance and sailed to within 30 leagues of Honduras,[124] which means that he clearly passed along the coast of Belize, but likely outside the reef. Although a brigantine is relatively maneuverable, we do not know whether he would have hazarded entering the relatively shallow waters inside the barrier reef. If he remained outside the reef, he could have ordered the use of boats to explore the cayes or coast. He and his men would have been able to observe the barrier reef and shelf that protected the Belize coast. They must have become aware of the problems to be overcome in reaching the Belize mainland, which included having to navigate dangerous cuts in the reef and then negotiate relatively shallow and unknown waters. In this light, it is easy to see why he, and later Dávila, who would gain some knowledge of the mangrove coast itself, would come to favor Honduras, with its deep coastal waters and potential ports. The custom among mapmakers, at least up to the early eighteenth century, of depicting the area we now know as Belize as virtually made up of islands (maps 5.4–5.6, 5.9)[125] may reflect the fact that information they received was consistently based almost entirely on coastal and seafaring perspectives such as those of Francisco Montejo and Dávila or on the experience of buccaneers, and not on accounts of individuals familiar with mainland travel.

Meanwhile, Dávila, who on his inland march had only reached a point about 30 leagues north of Chetumal, returned to the northern coast and was misled by the Maya into believing that Montejo and his party were dead, as Montejo at Chetumal had been led to believe regarding Dávila, a plan said to have been masterminded by Guerrero.[126] On the other hand, given the extent of Maya coastal interaction, networks were already in place, with or without Guerrero, to have enabled rapid communication and to have facilitated the initiation of effective responses to Spanish forces.

In the belief that Montejo had died, Dávila took it upon himself to move the small settlement at Salamanca from near Xelha to Xamanha in 1528 (map 5.1). Plans to establish a *villa* at Chetumal were postponed. Montejo returned to Mexico (New Spain), probably in the summer of 1528, and turned his attention, along with that of his son Francisco Montejo the Younger, to pacifying Tabasco and Xicalango (map 5.1).[127] He recalled Dávila from the east coast to reduce[128] the province of Acalan, a task undertaken in 1530–31 (map 5.1). The campaign was difficult, but it did not stop Dávila from moving on to Champotón (map 5.1).[129] The effect of the focus on pacifying the Gulf Coast in the three years from 1528 to 1531 was that Belize and the east coast received a short respite from Spanish incursions.

In the second phase of the conquest, in 1531, the Montejos, father and son, met Dávila in Champotón, where they planned another attempt to conquer Yucatan and Belize.[130] Dávila was sent overland to pacify various "provinces," including Uaymil-Chetumal (map 5.1).[131] He reached the Maya town of Chetumal, where he founded Villa Real in 1531–32. Lamanai and other towns on the New River must have been in frequent contact with Chetumal (fig. 2.7) and almost certainly traded there, and hence were surely aware of Montejo's actions. Dávila and his party found that native resistance in the region was considerable, which caused them to abandon Chetumal in 1532, and indeed to abandon the conquest of the area.

Dávila proceeded southward in canoes, past Belize to the Ulua River and then as far as Puerto Caballos[132] in Honduras (map 5.3), where he provided a detailed account of his seven-month journey before the members of the *cabildo* there in 1533.[133] Like Montejo the Elder, Dávila felt that Honduras held the attractions desirable for the establishment of a colony, which suggests, as does the passage quoted from his journey earlier in this chapter, that he was not tempted by any Belize location he passed in his journey. Of Belize, we learn from his account and that of Alonso Luján, a member of his party,[134] that there were no towns along the coast.[135] Dávila and his party had to travel for two or three days up the rivers to find towns from which to secure supplies, either by barter or by force. Owing to the reported absence of Maya towns, Jones suggests that the known colonial coastal communities of the sixteenth and seventeenth century in Belize, such as Zacatan and Manan (map 2.3), must have been reduction communities established by the Spaniards.

The archaeological evidence described earlier supports the contention that pre-Columbian Belize towns whose economies depended on seaborne trade and coastal resources were not situated on the mangrove coast. Villages and other small fishing and trading settlements were situated on protected coastal lagoons, on small islands or cayes near shore, on high ground in savannas where creeks drained into the Caribbean, on offshore cayes, and even on atolls.[136] Both Zacatan and Manan were situated on coastal lagoons,[137] which suggests, based on archaeological evidence from other coastal lagoons, that the Spaniards chose to congregate the Maya where a village or fishing settlement or way station already existed.

The question of why Dávila and his party would have missed the villages is interesting, because the Spaniards were aided by Indian captives from Chetumal who were familiar with the Belize coast.[138] Although the captives knowledgeably guided the Spaniards to river mouths and dry land for nightly camps, they are not likely to have been eager to point out places which the Spaniards could raid along the way. The Spaniards had intended to march by land whenever possible after leaving Chetumal, but the nature of the Belize coast, "almost unending swamps and lagoons," prevented this.[139] Many of the canoes were lashed together in pairs to carry the horses and heavier equipment. Canoes repeatedly overturned, weapons were made useless by salt water, and supplies were lost. One wonders how much of this was due to rough conditions and how much was due to manipulation by the Maya paddlers and guides.

It seems that the Dávila party found itself at times equipped with inappropriate technology, which must have slowed travel considerably. When party members raided communities on the rivers for food and supplies, they stole canoes that were suitable for river travel, but apparently tried to use them to travel along the coast. River canoes have no keels, which may explain why the Spaniards had problems dealing with coastal swells.[140] Many times they encountered native merchants along the coast in their large, well-built trading canoes, laden with merchandise.[141] When the Spaniards needed canoes, they took them from these coastal traders, although the traders were, so the Spaniards claimed, allowed to keep their merchandise.

We can assume that news of the presence of Dávila and his party traveled more rapidly than did the party itself, in which case communities near shore or on the cayes are very likely to have been abandoned immediately, although they were probably too small to have provided all the supplies the Spaniards needed. Only the towns would have had sufficient supplies, and a two- or three-day journey may well have been necessary to reach such communities, if Dávila and his men were traveling up the New River, the Belize River, or the Sibun (refer to map 5.8 for locations of rivers). North Stann Creek has three outlets, and considerable swells, as well as some rapids upstream, so it would have taken time to find one's way upriver, although the actual distance is not great.

South of North Stann Creek the rivers and creeks are not easily navigable for any great distance upstream, but there is a relatively short run from the Maya Mountains (Cockscombs) to the sea. It might have taken a day to travel to the nearest town on the Sittee River, but it was possible to walk along other waterways and creeks and in one or two days one would reach the foothills of the mountains.[142] However, the time taken to travel up the rivers would almost certainly have been increased both by Spanish deficiencies in knowledge and technology and by the fact that the Maya captives serving as guides, although they brought the Spaniards safely to shore, were not willing to assist their captors on their raids.

Can we assume that Maya coastal fishing and trading stations and ports were still in existence in 1532–33? Archaeological evidence provides us with something of an answer. Terminal Postclassic (late fifteenth- to early sixteenth-century pottery [fig. 0.1]), similar in style to the Yglesias-phase pottery from Lamanai, which is Terminal Postclassic to Spanish colonial in date (fig. 2.4), has been recovered from Ambergris Caye at Marco Gonzalez[143] and in the modern village of San Pedro (map 5.8), as well as from one or two sites along the coast north of the Belize River.[144] Santa Rita Corozal on Chetumal Bay was a major trading center in the Late Postclassic period and flourished until the Montejo entradas.[145] Farther south, however, along the coasts of the Stann Creek and Toledo Districts, although trade seems to have flourished in the Early Postclassic, there is little evidence (at least to date) for Late Postclassic or Spanish colonial-period activity.[146] Late Postclassic (probably late fourteenth or fifteenth century) effigy censers are reported from sites with ready access to the sea, such as Kendal, on the Sittee River, and Mayflower, on Silk Grass Creek in the Stann Creek District; and what archaeologists know as Tulum Red, a Late Postclassic ware, was found along the coast at Colson Point and on Wild Cane Caye. But how active these coastal sites were in the sixteenth century remains unknown (map 5.8).[147]

Maya pottery has been recovered from Middle Caye on Glover's Reef Atoll (map 5.8), as have a small amount of Spanish majolica and large quantities of British colonial ceramics, but the Maya pottery is so worn that dating is problematic. Pottery from Turneffe Atoll, however, has revealed some Classic and Postclassic activity.[148] Coastal sites and settlements south of Ambergris Caye must have been operative at the time of the European arrival in the Caribbean Basin in the early sixteenth century,[149] but it is also possible that slave raids originating from Central America had already had an impact, as we shall see in the next section. MacLeod[150] describes raiding for slaves on the coasts of Yucatan and among the Bay Islands and the north coast of Honduras before the area was conquered, as early as 1515. Under these conditions, it is possible that many villages and way stations, and even coastally oriented towns, had been abandoned in Belize by 1530. Spanish incursions into Belize, including the establishment of Christian missions in the mid- to late sixteenth century, may therefore already have met with a wary population and a hard-hit landscape.

While Dávila was traveling along the Belize coast, Montejo the Elder was fighting off attacks from the Maya in Campeche, and Montejo the Younger, who remained in Acalan until ca. 1531, moved in 1532 to focus on pacifying areas of Yucatan. After considerable difficulties with various groups,[151] the Spaniards moved in 1534 to a town called Dzilan, which was in the territory of the Chel Maya, who remained loyal to the Spaniards (map 5.1).[152] Montejo the Elder joined his son in the spring of 1534 and they continued to try to pacify the area, but unrest persisted and the father departed late in 1534 for Campeche, leaving his son behind to hold the fort at Dzilan, which had been established as a second Ciudad Real.[153] At this time, Dávila, recently returned from his coastal journey, joined Montejo the Elder in Campeche.[154] Continued unrest among the Maya forced Montejo the Younger finally to join his father in Campeche, and then both left for Mexico in 1535. The conquest of Yucatan was again halted.[155]

Some details of the foregoing paragraphs are worth highlighting at this stage because they affect interpretation of the course of events in Belize. One is that, according to Landa,[156] a young Chel lord was already Christian in 1534. If we can rely on Landa not to have compressed events here, this suggests that religious[157] other than the Franciscans had been proselytizing in the region even before Fray Jacobo de Testera [Tastera][158] arrived in Champotón in 1535 or 1537 (the sources differ) to convert Yucatan.[159] The secular clergy attached to the Montejos—Juan Rodríguez de Caraveo to Montejo the Elder, and Francisco Hernández to the forces of Montejo the Younger—had clearly been active[160]; Rodríguez de Caraveo describes his six years of hard work converting and baptizing large numbers of Indians in Yucatan, presumably from 1528 to 1534, and Hernández seems to have been equally dedicated.[161]

Clerical activity has to be inferred from the extremely rare references; in most of the documents concerning early entradas, no mention is made of whether clergy accompanied the soldiers or not, although their presence is often assumed. Even when clergy are listed, their activities are almost never described. The Chel lord's claim to Christianity suggests, however, that the seculars who accompanied entradas were more active in baptizing and preaching in the early years of conquest than it would seem based on Franciscan accounts, which tend to focus on Franciscan achievements. In any case, the implications are that evangelization took place of which we have no record; therefore, we can perhaps assume a parallel case in Belize at a later date. Evangelizing activity by seculars or regulars clearly paralleled the dividing up of Mayas into encomiendas or the assignment to the Mayas of other sorts of tribute or labor obligations that benefited Spaniards.

Another detail of interest that affected the human resources on which the Montejos could draw was that news had reached Yucatan of the conquest of Peru.[162] The lure of greater riches in South America caused many Spanish soldiers and colonists to leave Yucatan, and this crippled the effort of subjugating the Maya. The conquest of Peru would have the same effect in Central America, by drawing off those adventurers who were more interested in personal gain than in stable settlement.[163] Thus, not only did the Maya in Belize gain some respite, but individuals in more heavily administered areas, which were slowly being swallowed by encomienda, had the opportunity to flee to communities in Belize and gain time. The land that became Belize was beginning to emerge as a safe haven.

It is also significant that Montejo the Elder had, in Chamberlain's words, "early conceived the project of uniting under his authority as *Adelantado* the entire area from the western limits of Tabasco and Chiapas to and including Honduras-Higueras, with a corridor extending to the South Sea [the Pacific] at the Bahia de Fonseca" (maps 5.1, 5.2).[164] Montejo certainly had his eye on a huge swath of territory, but one wonders how he expected to be able to control it all.[165] It is perhaps no surprise that Belize somehow got lost in the grand design.

We left the Montejos, father and son, in Mexico in 1535, and it was at this time that Montejo the Elder was designated Governor and Captain General of Honduras-Higueras, which was then united with Yucatan for purposes of administration—a huge territory. Montejo the Younger, as Lieutenant Governor and Captain General of Tabasco, had more than the provinces of Yucatan and its recalcitrant east coast with which to contend. He returned to Tabasco from Mexico and appointed Lorenzo de Godoy as his lieutenant to reestablish Champotón as the base of operations for the final conquest of Yucatan. Also, sometime between 1534 and 1537 the Franciscan friar Jacobo de Testera arrived in Champotón from Mexico, with his brothers in Christ, to convert Yucatan. He had come with guarantees that Spanish laymen would be excluded from Yucatan, and he was meeting with success in converting the Maya, but he returned to Mexico at some point between 1537 and 1539, when trouble arose between him and the Spanish soldiery, most likely in the form of Godoy.[166]

Keeping it in the family, Montejo the Younger replaced Godoy in 1537 with his cousin, Montejo the Nephew, who was left with the task of maintaining a Spanish presence in Champotón. Late in 1540, Montejo the Younger, appointed by his father to conquer Yucatan, left Tabasco to join his cousin in Champotón. Thus, from a base first in Champotón, and then Campeche, the third phase of the conquest of Yucatan began under Montejo the Younger with the help of his cousin.[167]

Maya lords and their communities were required by Montejo the Younger to declare or to renew their declarations of allegiance to the Spanish Crown.[168] As might be expected, the response was mixed. Late in 1541 the two Montejos reached Tiho and established the city of Mérida, on January 6, 1542 (map 5.1). Although many communities received the Montejos without resistance, there were notable exceptions, particularly the Maya of the "eastern provinces."[169] Among the most resistant, as we shall see, was the region of Uaymil-Chetumal, which included towns in northern Belize and whose population resisted "till the end."[170]

After very considerable difficulties, Yucatan was finally caught in the Spanish net, although it was not until a series of revolts in 1546–47 were put down that Yucatan could be said to have been pacified. The provinces adjacent to and partly including Belize, Uaymil, and Chetumal, respectively, were left to their own devices until late 1543 or 1544, when a most cruel conquest of the area began.[171]

In the fateful spring of 1543, Montejo the Elder appointed Gaspar Pacheco as Lieutenant Governor, Captain General, and Justicia Mayor of the Province of Uaymil-Chetumal, which included territory as far south as the Golfo Dulce. Gaspar, his sons Melchor and Francisco, and his nephew Alonso already had a reputation for their use of trained greyhounds to kill and devour their Indian opponents, the Mixe, in Oaxaca.[172] Just prior to the conquest of Uaymil-Chetumal, Gaspar became ill and appointed his son, Melchor, to take his place.[173] Francisco seems not to have been involved in this venture, but Alonso acted as second-in-command.

The conquest, commanded by Melchor Pacheco and his cousin Alonso, has gone down in history as one of the most brutal on record. Their atrocities, including their use of dogs, are well known because they were reported in detail by the Franciscan Lorenzo de Bienvenida in 1548 in a letter to the Crown.[174] According to Bienvenida, Gaspar plundered the region of the Cochuah, employed women as bearers, and then starved them to death. Bienvenida then says that the captaincy was passed to Alonso, although other records say Melchor. In any case, when they both were in charge at Chetumal, individuals were tied to stakes; the hands, noses, and ears of the men and the breasts of the women were cut off; and women were weighted and drowned in lagoons.

The Maya of the area finally gave up hope of expelling the invaders, and many were said to have moved southward—which would have been deeper into Belize territory—to escape Spanish rule. Jones suggests that the Maya who survived the siege of their provincial capital at Chetumal reestablished a new capital at Chanlacan, on Progresso Lagoon in northern Belize.[175] The conquering Spaniards established their new Villa of Salamanca de Bacalar on Lake Bacalar, about 22 kilometers northwest of the mouth of the Rio Hondo and 20 kilometers northwest of the modern Belize border (maps 2.3, 5.1).[176] Apparently, no members of the clergy had accompanied the Pacheco expedition, and at the time of its founding Salamanca had neither a cleric nor a church.[177] It is this *villa* that was charged with the administration of the Christian Maya communities at Lamanai and Tipu.

CARIBBEAN CENTRAL AMERICA
AND THE KINGDOM OF GUATEMALA

Communities in Belize, such as Lamanai and Tipu, were impacted largely by Spanish goals for Yucatan, but early Spanish activity in Central America also had repercussions for those living along the Caribbean coasts. Exploration, entradas, and raiding for slaves were carried out in Central America almost as early as in Hispaniola and the Caribbean islands.[178]

In the first part of the sixteenth century, the areas that we now know as Guatemala, Honduras, Salvador, Nicaragua, Panama, and Costa Rica enjoyed considerable commercial activity based on precious metals, cacao, and the transport of slaves (map 5.2). Deposits of precious metals extended through central and southern Honduras to north-central Nicaragua, and also existed in Costa Rica, Chiapas, and Guatemala.[179] The lure of getting rich quickly by extracting gold or silver motivated the early rush of Spanish adventurers to these regions, whereas Belize had no metals and no readily exploitable resources that were attractive to Europeans. Mining was ultimately to prove less lucrative than expected, but up to the middle of the sixteenth century, mining was the beacon that attracted settlers[180] to Honduras, Panama, and other places in Central America—excluding Belize—and colonists arrived in considerable numbers.[181]

As exploration and conquest intensified in this region, attention focused on lower Central America, from Panama to Nicaragua, and on reaching the Pacific.[182] In 1523–24, the conquistador Pedro de Alvarado expanded colonial designs to include highland Guatemala, and interest in Honduras and El Salvador heightened. In contrast with Yucatan, however, the individuals involved in the conquest of this region were, so it is said, more concerned with amassing personal fortunes than in establishing themselves as colonists or in furthering development and administration.[183] Pedro de Alvarado, who fought with Cortés against the Aztecs in central Mexico, was made Governor and Captain General of Guatemala in 1527. The colonial Kingdom of Guatemala would, by the mid-sixteenth century, comprise what we now know as the nations of Guatemala, Costa Rica, Nicaragua, El Salvador, Honduras, and the province of Chiapas (maps 5.2, 5.9)[184]; only in Guatemalan maps, however, would Belize from somewhere south of the Belize River be included as part of the colonial territory of Guatemala (map 5.3).[185] In 1527, however, Honduras-Higueras—a term which covered Honduras plus the area around the Golfo Dulce—was still under Francisco Montejo the Elder's jurisdiction (see map 5.1).

At about the middle of the sixteenth century, colonists in Central America began to realize that the future lay in landholding, or, more accurately, in the control of labor to work the land.[186] The slave trade diminished in intensity, partly because encomiendas and, later, *repartimiento*, with their tribute and labor obligations, provided an alternative exploitative strategy to slavery, but also owing to the fact that many Indians had died from displacement and disease.[187]

Belize offered land which in theory could have been exploited. It was subject, however, to the same high humidity, heat, and rainfall that affected the low-lying coasts of southern Guatemala, Honduras, and Nicaragua, which, although they had better potential than Belize for the development of ports, were never high on the list of places attractive to Europeans for settlement or development. As for potential labor, as I suggested above, the Maya in Belize may already have abandoned settlements and way stations on the cayes and coasts and atolls, owing to pirates, privateers, slaving expeditions, and Spanish coastal traffic such as the Pinzón-Solís expedition of 1508 or Dávila's journey in 1532–33 between Yucatan and Honduras. The Maya living inland had tracts of territory yet unsettled and unexplored by Europeans into which to retreat; thus, the prospect of controlling indigenous labor by settling in Belize was even less likely than in the Caribbean coasts of Guatemala, Honduras, or Nicaragua.

After 1550, the Kingdom of Guatemala became a relative backwater in the Spanish commercial empire.[188] If, as a hypothetical part of the Caribbean coast of this region, Belize did not attract settlers before 1550, owing both to a dearth of resources of value to Europeans and to the challenges presented by its humid, tropical, and coastal conditions, such features were not going to increase its attractiveness after 1550.

The Environment of Early Contact

In the sixteenth and seventeenth centuries, the land now known as Belize seems not to have been named, or to have acquired a "handle," in the way that Yucatan, Peten, Guatemala, Honduras, Chiapas, Mexico, or Nicaragua had, at least in Spanish circles. In the world of the sixteenth-century Franciscans and the civil authorities in Mérida, Belize Maya communities were recorded and their individual names were known, but they generally were subsumed under the jurisdiction of the ecclesiastical province of Yucatán. There is an exception, in that in 1582 the Bacalar curacy, with its Belize towns, was included in the ecclesiastical province of Campeche.[189] It is difficult to know whether inclusion with towns of Campeche was an expedient measure (Belize communities were clearly *not* part of Yucatan, but otherwise difficult to place), or whether a Campeche orientation reflected a legitimate local perspective. In the Kingdom of Guatemala, what we know as Belize does not seem ever to have been referred to, or to have been called anything at all; the region was not included along with any place in particular, although the Dominicans were aware of the towns and villages in southern Belize as extensions of the Manche Chol region of Verapaz.[190]

I think we can safely say that in the context of the environment of early contact in the region we now call Mesoamerica or Central America or the

Caribbean Basin, the land that became Belize was unique. This is partly owing to its ambiguous place—and, in some cases, its almost total lack of identity—in Spanish consciousness; partly owing to the environmental conditions in Belize, which Europeans would never find inviting for settlement; and partly owing to Maya strategies, which made it difficult for the Spaniards to get a sense of what they could exploit in Belize, or how. This is the local context in which the first Christian communities would be founded in Belize. In the next chapter I describe what could be called the global, or even cosmological, context in which Christian communities were established. By this I mean the source of the inspiration which stimulated Europeans, and particularly the Mendicants, to envision Belize and its Maya communities as part of a larger cosmological enterprise.

✠ SIX ✠

The Millennial Kingdom and
the Belize Missions

That Belize Maya communities operated largely beyond or outside the focus of European colonial powers worked to their advantage in terms of Spanish colonial expansion,[1] but to their disadvantage in terms of the activities of buccaneers—pirates and privateers alike—who thrived in places where they had easy access to food, water, supplies, and people, and could elude capture and punishment by Spanish authorities. The pre-Columbian histories of communities in Belize—owing to the nature of coastal and riverine geography, the barrier reef, and the orientation of communities toward coastal exchange and commerce—left the Maya in Belize no choice but to follow a course distinctive from the Maya of the areas we now know as Peten or Yucatan or Guatemala. Centuries-old communication networks, maritime orientation, and local adaptive strategies—which in pre-Columbian times had fitted communities in Belize with the armor to weather collapse—set precedents that well equipped these same communities to be able to function and to communicate effectively over long distances in times of stress or change. What this means, as I sought to demonstrate in chapter 5, is that Belize must be viewed through a lens that attempts to adjust for local conditions and early European responses and reactions to these conditions.

In analyzing conversion and the spread and meaning of Christianity in Belize, in addition to framing the environment of contact, of equal importance is the question posed in chapter 4: what does it mean to be Christian? Being Christian meant (and means) different things to different people at different times. In this chapter, I describe the impetus behind the evangelization of Mesoamerica in the sixteenth century as it would have affected and helped to structure the Belize missions. Thus, we move from the local to the global. I draw attention to the friars and their ideals because their "apostolic intensity"[2] was an important force behind evangelization in Belize, where it was not until the relatively late date of 1544, over twenty years after the conquest of Mexico,[3] that Maya communities were forced to comply with the encomienda system and were converted in the process.[4] The outcome of events in Belize was contingent on both the kind of Christianity preached by the missionaries and the outlook of the evangelizers themselves.

Conditions in Belize, unlike Mexico or even Yucatan,[5] are hot and humid, with a long rainy season. Spanish Europeans would have discovered that crops with which they were familiar, such as wheat, could not be grown, food spoiled easily, travel was difficult, and beasts of burden were plagued by biting flies and worm infestations. Clearly, a Mediterranean background was not the best preparation for living and working in the humid tropics. Yet, the documents analyzed by Jones in bringing the Belize colonial experience to light depict the Franciscans as deeply dedicated to drawing Belize's Maya into the Christian fold.[6] Because Belize documentation is relatively sparse, such behavior would seem bizarre, if not unbelievable, without the knowledge of what happened in Mexico, and without knowledge of the European background that led to the apostolic fervor and humanist enterprises that characterized early colonial New Spain.

At least three factors combined to foster communities that fiercely valued independence from Spanish authority at the same time that they invested in Christian belief and practice: the zeal of the friars who originally brought Christianity to key communities in Belize, such as Tipu and Lamanai; the particular historical circumstances in which Belize communities, like those in east-coast Yucatan, were left "to their own devices";[7] and, finally, the wet tropical conditions avoided by Spanish settlers. I introduce the idea in this chapter, but expand upon it later, that Christian belief, particularly the Christianity described and transmitted to the Maya by the friars, rather than serving to support Spanish authority, was just as easily used to undermine Spanish authority.

Who Were the Mendicants?

Under the circumstances just described, both individual and social agendas acted forcefully as instigators of disruption and change. A critical factor—and perhaps *the* critical factor in the spiritual encounter between Europe and Mesoamerica—was the granting of privileges to the Mendicant orders to Christianize the Aztecs, the Maya, and other Mesoamerican cultural and language groups in the pivotal years of the sixteenth century.[8]

The Mendicant friars in Mesoamerica comprised a number of orders. After the first expeditions to the Antilles came the Franciscans, the largest religious order in Spain at the time,[9] and Dominicans, from about 1510, followed by the Mercedarians. A Mercedarian, Bartolomé de Olmedo, accompanied Cortés in his conquest of the Aztec empire.[10] The Augustinians began arriving in 1533.[11] Other orders that were active, although in smaller numbers, were the Carmelites, the Benedictines, the Hospitallers of San Juan de Dios, and the Bethlehemites.[12] The Capuchins came to the New World in the seventeenth century, starting in 1647, but worked mainly in South America and New France.[13] The Jesuits, considered both a Mendicant order and what are called "clerks regular," came to play a leading role in Belize in modern times.[14] Although they began preaching in 1566, with regard to the New World they were active mainly in Canada and in northern Mexico, and in South America in the seventeenth century. The Jesuit scholar José de Acosta spent a year in Mexico between 1586 and 1587 and included information he gathered there in his *Historia moral y natural de las Indias*, but the Jesuits as an order were not instrumental in conversion efforts in Mesoamerica during the contact period.[15] Caso Barrera tells us that one governor of Yucatan proposed in 1605 that the Jesuits take over the teaching and indoctrination of the Maya, but Franciscan power was too great for this to be effected.[16]

Dominican friars ventured into southern Belize from Verapaz in Guatemala, where they were active periodically.[17] But from as far south as the Sittee River, and at times as far south as the Monkey River (map 5.8), the religious province of Yucatán held sway, and the Mendicants known from the records to have traveled to Belize were Franciscans (appendix 1).[18] Of the nineteen bishops of Yucatan from roughly 1519 to the end of the seventeenth century (appendix 2), most (eleven) were Mendicants: five were Franciscan, three were Dominican, two were Augustinian, one was Benedictine, one Jeronymite,[19] and seven were secular priests.[20]

All those in the church who follow the religious life are termed "religious."[21] The Mendicant orders, however, also known as regular clergy, or regulars, are distinguished from secular clergy, because they take vows that sanctify poverty and that also forbid them to own property in common (although this has varied through time). In stark contrast to the older, monastic practices of rural retreat and hermetic solitude, the Mendicant vocation was an urban mission from the start.[22] Mendicant friars preached the Gospel and focused their efforts in towns.[23]

The expression of Christianity adopted by the Mendicant orders in Mesoamerica represented one of many efforts in the history of Christian belief and practice to return to the evangelizing mission and spiritual purity of the early church.[24] However, it was the particular nature of the reformist zeal widespread in Europe in the fifteenth century that was to affect Mesoamerica so deeply.

Who Were the Secular Clergy?

Before I proceed to discuss the role of the Mendicants, it is important to note that the secular clergy were involved in the Conquest from its inception,[25] although their activities were generally confined to towns with largely Spanish populations.[26] Both secular clergy and regular clergy were called to proselytize in the New World; Isabella herself called on "prelados y religiosos e Clérigos e otras personas doctas e temerosas de Dios" (prelates and religious and clerics and other learned and God-fearing people).[27]

Because sources differ, there is some doubt about whether only friars or both friars and seculars were represented on the first mission expedition in 1493.[28] With regard to Yucatan and Mexico, the Córdoba expedition had a secular priest, Alonso González, and the Grijalva expedition had a chaplain, Juan Díaz. Cortés was accompanied by at least one friar, a Mercedarian, Bartolomé de Olmedo, but a secular priest, Juan Díaz (presumably the same fellow who participated in the Grijalva expedition) is also mentioned, as is a Fray Pedro Melgarejo.[29] Two members of the secular clergy, along with a Carmelite friar, accompanied Francisco de Montejo the Elder, Adelantado, when he sailed to the coast of Cozumel at the end of September 1527; and the chaplain to Francisco de Montejo the Younger, Francisco Hernández, settled in Campeche in 1541 and was said to know the language of the Indians there.[30]

Entradas such as these, however, were platforms for conquest. The religious may not have had much time for anything but erecting crosses, leading an occasional procession, ministering to the soldiers and other Spanish members of the party, or standing by as representatives of the church as the *requerimiento* was read. That some clearly made the time, however, is suggested by the conversion of the Chel lord in 1534 during the conquest of Yucatan, as described in chapter 5.

By 1524, after Mexico had been conquered, Cortés requested in his Fourth Letter to the King not only that regular clergy exclusively should be sent to convert the Indians, but that bishops—normally drawn from secular clergy—be appointed from two of the religious orders: the Franciscans and Dominicans.[31] Many seculars had apparently responded to Cardinal Fray Garcia de Loaysa's call for appointments to parish churches in New Spain in 1541, but they came under heavy criticism.[32] Aversion to the seculars, in Cortés's words, rested on the following reasoning: "Because if we have bishops and other dignitaries, they will only follow the customs which, for our sins, they pursue these days, of squandering the goods of the Church on pomp and ceremony, and other vices, and leaving entailed estates to their sons or kinsmen."[33]

Cortés had the welfare of the conquerors and encomenderos in mind as much as the welfare of the church,[34] but it was indeed true that many of the seculars who first responded to the call "para adoctrinar a los indígenas y moradores dichos en la fe católica" (to indoctrinate the Indians and the said inhabitants in the Catholic faith)[35] were not well organized; the circumstances were new, they were isolated, and they were not well trained to withstand the rigors and challenges of penetration into unevangelized territory.[36] Even the historian who has done so much to put the record straight with regard to the contributions of the secular clergy, Constantino Bayle,[37] admits that the regular clergy were well suited in the early years of the Conquest to bring about the conversion of the Indians, whereas the secular clergy were better suited to attend to the life of the Spaniards in their parishes. As he put it, "Los unos, a plantar la fe; los otros, a conservarla y estimularla entre los cristianos viejos, como en España" (Some to plant the faith; others to keep and encourage it among the established Christians, as in Spain).[38] There is also the important point that missionary work, if it was expected to be enduring and stable, demanded institutional backing, so that evangelization necessitated more than the undertaking of a single individual.[39]

Training and education in both Spain and New Spain were to improve by the end of the sixteenth century. Seminaries were instituted, colleges were founded, and the universities in Spain turned out better-educated clerics. By the 1560s in Mexico, the numbers of seculars began to increase at Mendicant expense and relations between Mendicants and seculars were often strained. In 1574, the Mendicants began to feel the forces of viceregal and diocesan control, and a 1583 decree in Mexico ordered outright preferential treatment of secular clergy.[40]

Despite the initial problems, encomenderos and other colonists came to prefer the seculars; or, more accurately, the colonists withdrew support from the Mendicants. They insisted that rectifying what they saw as the Mendicant problem—that Mendicants put stumbling blocks in the way of extracting tribute and labor—was to bring in clergy of "higher cultivation" than had previously been available among the seculars.[41] According to Kubler, the Mendicants eventually lost the support of the encomenderos, at least in Mexico, partly because their efforts at compromise came too late.[42]

Not all Mendicants refused to ally themselves with encomenderos. The Augustinians seem to have been the most willing to work with the encomienda system, whereas the Franciscans vacillated but in general tried to keep Indian communities separate and protected from encomienda exploitation.[43] Mendieta represented this trend when he went so far as to say that the Indians could not be economically enslaved and spiritually free.[44] Although his was perhaps a minority opinion, the colonists nonetheless saw Mendicant support and attempts to protect the Indians as an obstruction to the colony's successful exploitation of Indian labor and production. Such a frame of mind is captured perfectly by Nancy Farriss when she relies on the voice of Bernal Díaz del Castillo to express the rationale for conquest: "To bring light to those in darkness, and also to get rich."[45]

During the first half of the sixteenth century, when fully supported by Charles V, who reigned from 1516 to 1556, and free from episcopal restrictions, the Mendicants were in a position of strength. Several factors then began to erode their power. Mexico attracted Spanish settlers, and the increasing number of colonists strengthened complaints against Mendicant activities; Philip II (1556–98) did not follow his father in supporting the Mendicants; the friars' status as priests outside the normal hierarchy increasingly irritated the non-Mendicant, or secular, bishops, who had no authority over them. In 1557, a year after Philip II came to power, the Crown took the first major step to restrict Mendicant activity by increasing the bureaucracy involved in founding new establishments, and in 1583 a decree actually ordered that preferential treatment be given to secular clergy.[46]

In Yucatan, because the religious were too few to attend properly to all the *doctrinas*, even in Landa's time, Landa himself entrusted to seculars and to other religious orders in the region the tasks of saying Mass and baptizing children during his tenure as provincial (prior to 1571).[47] However, from the time they began evangelization in Yucatan, sometime between 1535 and 1537, the Franciscans dominated religious affairs until 1582, when the height of their influence was reached.[48] At that time, in 1582, secular parishes existed only in the Spanish towns of Mérida, Campeche, Valladolid, and Bacalar, and in the Maya communities of Peto and Cozumel (map 5.1).[49] Officially, doctrinas, or parishes, under the administration of the Franciscans began to pass to the seculars in 1581–86, although the process did not intensify until the seventeenth century; for example, the doctrinas of Hocaba (map 5.1), Tixcocob, and Ichmul passed into the hands of the seculars in 1602.[50]

The remote Belize missions seem to have been caught between two forces: Mendicant dominance in evangelization, on the one hand, and on the other, growing secular hegemony as the result of pressure from colonists (in Mexico) and lack of resource personnel (in Yucatan). Belize, or at least all but its southern extremity, was made part of the province of Bacalar under the Spaniards in 1544, during the Pacheco Conquest (maps 1.1, 2.3),[51] but the religious administration of the province is a blank until 1565, when the first record appears of a resident secular priest based in the Villa of Salamanca de Bacalar.[52] The implication is that no religious personnel were present during the *villa's* early years, nor were reductions overseen by religious personnel.

Most of the documentary information on Belize pertains to the seventeenth century, when the seculars in Mesoamerica had increased their authority at the expense of the religious orders. As such, the early, critical years between 1544 and 1565 remain clouded. The archaeological evidence—such as the forms of the church at Tipu and the first of two churches at Lamanai (chaps. 8, 9), commonalities in Spanish-style residential structures between the communities, evidence for artifacts dating to the sixteenth century (e.g., fig. 1.8), and data that show that the communities experienced a significant amount of monitored but ordered changes in plan and organization—suggests that the changes that took place in these early years were not the result of supervision by encomenderos or their agents or unrecorded seculars, but of supervision by Mendicants, and Franciscans in particular.

The World and Otherworld of the Mendicants

The Mendicants' world view has two major implications that can help us to fathom the forces behind the missions in Belize. The first is that, if we consider the Mayas from a historical perspective as "pre-Christians," the conversion process in the New World is comparable to the conversion process in Europe in Late Antiquity (ca. A.D. 400 to A.D. 600) and in the early Medieval period (to about A.D. 900), when Franks, Celts, Anglo-Saxons, Vandals, and other European cultural and language groups were widely evangelized.[53] There are some parallels with the late Roman period, but Christianity was much more flexible in the second to fourth centuries than later on. The British historian Charles Thomas highlights post–A.D. 370 Gaul as the time and place in which Martin of Tours raised Christianity from a movement that was largely urban and aristocratic to one that was popular and militantly anti-pagan,[54] and it is this later form of Christianity that was brought to Mesoamerica.

For the Maya and other Mesoamericans, the Spanish conquest was a first encounter with Christian ideas and with people who called themselves Christian. Thus, a comparison with the early Europeans' first encounters with Christianity may help to make sense of behaviors among Maya converts that appeared enigmatic to Spanish civil and religious authorities, and which these same authorities characterized as opportunistic, hypocritical, confrontational, or particularly rebellious.[55] Although some of the Franciscans' spiritual leaders in Spain, such as Friar Juan de Guadalupe, had proselytized among the Muslims in Granada,[56] the friars in Mesoamerica, by and large, were making cultural contact with non-Christians for the first time. What they regarded as unique and enigmatic in Mesoamerica may turn out to conform to a pattern, and to have been at least partly predictable as the consequence of cultural and ideological encounters between those on a mission and those who did not ask to be evangelized.

At the same time, the ideals which essentially drove the Mendicant encounter in Mesoamerica—despite the Mendicant belief that such ideas simply reflected a return to the purity of Christianity's origins—were rooted and nourished in the experiences of the Middle Ages,[57] and thus were very much a product of history. Phelan goes so far as to say that "the Middle Ages sang its swan song in the New World in the sixteenth century."[58]

Periodically in the history of the church there have arisen movements to return to the Apostolic Age of Christianity—the period that fell within the lifetime of the original twelve apostles, when energy, optimism, devotion, and an otherworldly dedication often marked by poverty comprised the Christian way of life; or at least this is how later medieval civilization characterized the apostolic ideal.[59] Thus, the primitive apostolic church as envisioned by Mendicants in Mesoamerica, and particularly the Franciscans, was in fact a product of medieval civilization and medieval Christians who were reacting against the church's acquisition of temporal wealth and "worldly vices."[60] Phelan points to the thirteenth century in Europe as a period in which a profusion of movements sought to return to the ideal of the primitive church.[61] The same connection was made by Kubler, who traced the style of Mendicant evangelism that characterized the sixteenth century in Mesoamerica to roots in southwestern France in the thirteenth century.[62]

After 1229, first the Dominicans, but later the Franciscans and Augustinians, became dominant in the religious affairs of southwest France, as a reaction against the threat of heresy in the region.[63] As occurred later in Mesoamerica, under Charles V and *patronato real*,[64] the Mendicants in southwest France served as instruments of royal rule; they were authorized directly by the French king to found new towns, and came to exercise more power than the secular clergy, who were subject to episcopal authority. In both southwestern France and, later, Mexico and Yucatan, and to a lesser extent in Belize, the friars planned towns, built churches, and governed and educated communities.[65] Kubler argues forcefully that the particular kind of urban-oriented mission carried out in Mesoamerica was molded and developed in southwestern France. Kubler was particularly interested in the architectural and urban-planning significance of the French experience, which figures in chapter 7. Here, it is important to stress that a precedent had been set for a situation in which the Mendicants possessed an unchallenged authority that was otherwise unusual in the history of the church.

High Expectations

The standard set in Mexico was applied by the friars throughout Mesoamerica, and evidence indicates that this standard, along with the expectations of the Mendicants and other early religious in Mexico, was high. Kubler credits

Bataillon and Zavala with the research that demonstrates "that the intellectual leaders of the Mexican colonization were governed by the most novel religious and social ideas of their day in Spain, and that they formed a spiritual *avante garde* for the Late Renaissance in America."[66] In addition, the Mendicants saw the "agrarian collectivism"[67] of the Indians in Mexico and elsewhere in Mesoamerica as ideal material to realize the Christian community.

Although there are "successes" reported in the literature, such as Bishop Vasco de Quiroga's Utopian-patterned towns in Michoacán, for which he gained much fame,[68] a closer look reveals that such efforts, judged as achievements by Europeans, came at the expense of indigenous ways of life, and did not reflect indigenous choice but instead Spanish ideas of what was good for the Indians. Such high expectations in any context in which colonization was also expected to yield material rewards were bound to be problematic. It is also the peculiar case that these expectations were developed in Europe before any of the religious had become familiar with the culture or languages or people in Mesoamerica. It is a bit like the paintings and prints of the Aztecs made by artists who had never been to Mexico (fig. 6.1). These pictures were considered accurate simply because they fulfilled Europeans' expectations of what they thought should be true about the New World.[69] That the representations looked nothing like the Aztecs or their buildings or their cities parallels the dissonance between what the friars thought of as possible—in other words, what they imagined would happen—and the actual dynamics of interaction that followed.

Because the Culhua-Mexica, Tepaneca, Acolhua, Chalca, Xochimilca, Tlaxcalans,[70] and other groups of central Mexico brought to the conquest phenomenon their own cultural and historical trajectories, their reactions to Christianity are not directly, or uncritically, comparable to the reactions of the various Maya groups in Yucatan and Belize. What is important, however, is that the invading proselytizers from Europe shared critical experiences and goals, which makes some discussion of Mendicant and other religious and social activities in Mexico relevant.

The Mendicant evangelization in Mexico involved three major orders: the Franciscans arrived in 1524, led by Fray Martín de Valencia, and are known as the Apostolic Twelve; the Dominicans followed in 1526; and the Augustinians, as noted above, arrived in 1533.[71] The Franciscans established the widest network of foundations in Mexico, and to a great extent defined the pattern of evangelization.[72] This is important because it is the Franciscans who figure in the evangelization of Yucatan and the regions in which Tipu and Lamanai are located in Belize.

The source of Mendicant authority in Mexico was the Patronato Real, which was an agreement established in 1508 between the Papacy and the

Figure 6.1. Print of the Aztec Templo Mayor, dated 1719 (Chatelain 1705–1720).
(In possession of the author)

Spanish Crown that gave privileges to the Crown, which included the right to nominate candidates for all benefices—or ecclesiastical offices—in America. The Crown, influenced by Cortés, chose the Mendicant orders to fulfill the Christian mission in the New World. Under these conditions, Mendicants were permitted to be ordained as parish priests, and could even be bishops. The first Bishop of Mexico, Fray Juan de Zumárraga, was a Franciscan.[73] Thus, the Mendicants were positioned, as they had been in southwest France in the thirteenth century, to serve "as the instruments of royal rule over newly conquered territories."[74] Such temporal power was augmented by "spiritual imperatives of an apostolic intensity."[75]

What Happened
in Mexico and Its Implications

Comprehensive overviews of the spiritual encounter in Mexico have been provided by several scholars, and Mexico also figures in broad treatments of missionization.[76] Both the European roots of sixteenth-century religious zeal and the way this zeal was expressed in Mexico are essential to an understanding of the course Christianity followed elsewhere in Mesoamerica in early colonial times. Mexico was not just "core" in terms of production, distribution, consumption, and political administration;[77] spiritual imperatives elsewhere in Mesoamerica were partly structured by the Mexican experience.[78] In turn, the kind of Christianity that developed in the course of colonial exploitation also influenced subsequent historical trajectories. Assuming that interested readers will turn to sources such as those cited for details and more in-depth analyses, I will here isolate four critical trends:

First, Christianity was in no sense monolithic, although we archaeologists sometimes treat it as such.[79] It was consistently undergoing change based on individual perception, cultural interaction, and local experience within a framework that became increasingly institutionalized through time. In the case of Mesoamerica, the changes that took place in southern Europe in the fifteenth century are critical in understanding the nature of the Christianity that was brought to Yucatan and Belize.

Second, the humanist movement associated with Erasmus had significant effects both in Spain in the sixteenth century[80] and in Mexico. Thus, the extent to which humanism was adopted and the attitude of the church and its individual members toward humanist tendencies and other reformist ideals affected approaches to proselytization. With the Council of Trent, held in three sessions from 1545 to 1563,[81] came a significant change in attitude. That reforms had been important in the history of the church and should be ongoing was not denied;[82] in fact, "reform," in the sense of change introduced in order "to improve the functioning of ecclesiastical offices in view of the common good," was a major focus of the Council of Trent.[83] But reform means different things to different people,[84] and the Council of Trent was very much a part of the defense mounted by the Catholic Church against Protestantism,[85] which was rooted in reformation. The dissent and dissatisfaction that were to lead ultimately to Protestant separatism in Europe would not likely have been at the forefront of the minds of evangelizers in Mexico, but the separatism that had eventuated in Europe may well have affected the later evangelization of the Maya.

Third, individuals, as much as movements and trends, were critical in structuring the course of conversion and its social and religious outcome.

Fourth, interaction with the Aztecs (Culhua-Mexica or Tepaneca or Acolhua) or Maya (Chontal- or Chol-speakers, Itza, or Xiu) affected the form(s) Christianity took in the same way that the dynamics of interaction in Europe in late antique and early medieval times affected the form(s) of Christianity that emerged.

The Christianity Brought to Mesoamerica

APOSTOLIC REFORM

Giovanni di Bernardone (St. Francis, 1181/1182–1226), founder of the Order of Friars Minor, and Domingo Guzmán (St. Dominic, ca. 1170–1221), founder of the Order of Preachers,[86] are well known for their reformist efforts based on the ideal of Gospel simplicity and poverty in reaction to church excess and laxity. Both orders came to participate in the evangelization of Mexico, and both proselytized in Belize, the Franciscans in the north, central, and south-central parts of the country, reaching as far south as the Monkey River, and the Dominicans in the extreme south (map 5.8).[87] These orders were not alone in reacting to church excesses and accumulation of wealth, but they serve as examples of the currents and cross-currents of Christian thought and attitudes and, not least important, they are the orders that preached in Belize.

Both Franciscans and Dominicans faced challenges through time, partly because the ideal of corporate poverty was difficult to uphold, but also because the insistence on complete poverty could always potentially be interpreted as heretical by the established church.[88] For example, Pope John XXII in the early fourteenth century declared as heretical the Franciscans who held strictly to their vows.[89] In fact, the prohibition against holding revenue-producing properties was abolished for the Dominicans in 1475. The Franciscans, too, seem early on to have allowed for group ownership of convents and churches, even though the Rule of St. Francis prohibited corporate ownership.

Two factions thereby developed in the spread of the Franciscan Order. The Spirituals insisted on St. Francis's original rules; the majority preferred a more moderate approach. Pope John XXII, in addition to declaring the Spirituals heretics in 1317–18, allowed corporate ownership of property. The Franciscans who did not object to corporate ownership were named Conventuals, and dominated the order throughout the fourteenth century.[90]

It is in the late fourteenth and fifteenth century that we see the rise and spread of the reformatory zeal that was to characterize proselytization in Mesoamerica,[91] including Belize. Among the Franciscans, reaction against the Conventuals was manifested by many separate "Observant" movements, first in Italy in 1368, but shortly thereafter in France and Spain, all of which demanded a return to the true Order of St. Francis, with no relaxation of St. Francis's original strictures. "Observant" is in quotation marks because many of these radical reformers held that even the Observant orders were not strict enough, and rejected *any* sort of institutionalization. Not that the popes did not try to rein them in. Pope Julius II in 1506 ordered the many minor reform groups to ally themselves with either Observants or Conventuals and to discontinue separate existences,[92] but his efforts were not completely effective.

The Franciscan group which was later to send friars to Mexico was one of the strict, grassroots, reform movements that rejected institutional alliance. It was founded in 1487 by Fray Juan de la Puebla and came to be known as the Minorites of the Blessed John of Puebla.[93] When Blessed John died, his disciple and successor Juan de Guadalupe adopted an even stricter rule. Juan de Guadalupe introduced the pointed cape, short mantle, patched robe, and barefoot practice later adopted by the Discalced and Capuchin friars.[94] Guadalupe's reform movement took the name of the Minorites of the Holy Gospel.

Thus, with the passing of only one generation, we have the same order, two visionary men, and two reform movements with different names. Needless to say, ecclesiastical authorities in Rome were not happy with what they saw as a plethora of potentially uncontrollable movements, and in 1517 Pope Leo X gave the reforming branches in Spain and Portugal the choice of aligning either with the Conventuals or with the Observants; the reformers opted for the Observants.[95] Administratively, this resulted in three (ecclesiastical) provinces,[96] one in Portugal and two in Spain. But the fact is that, in reality, no province wished to be identified with *either* the Conventuals or the Observants.[97] Each wished "only to maintain the integrity of its preaching mission and austerity of retreat, independently of all institutional interference."[98]

All members of the Apostolic Twelve who arrived in Tenochtitlan in 1524, and many friars of the other missions in Mexico, Yucatan, and Belize, show connections with the strict reform movements described above: "They spent their lives as friars within the reform, before their departure to America."[99] Thus, in addition to apostolic intensity, particularly critical issues to the friars were autonomy and jurisdictional independence.

ADD THE HUMANIST FACTOR

Although the Apostolic Twelve who arrived in Tenochtitlan in 1524 had not been in direct contact with the political and religious movements of northern European humanism,[100] there was a strong northern influence in the Spanish reformist movements throughout the late fifteenth century.[101] The Franciscan lay brother, Pedro de Gante, who disembarked with two other Flemish friars in Veracruz in 1523 and was headed toward Mexico, was born and raised in the city of Gante, in Belgium.[102] The later Franciscan missionaries, under Juan de Zumárraga, who was made bishop by Charles V in 1527, were indeed steeped in Erasmian thought.[103] Zumárraga, who was influenced both by More's *Utopia* and by Erasmus's *Epigrammata*, used Erasmus's teachings in instructing the priests of the Mexican diocese.[104] He prepared a *Doctrina cristiana* as a catechism for Indian use. This catechism was based on the *Suma de doctrina cristiana*, by Dr. Constantino Ponce de la Fuente, the confessor to Charles V and at the forefront of the "Lutheran" movement in Seville.[105] This version of the catechism was widely distributed in Spain between 1543 and 1551, and insisted on the primacy of faith over works. What makes this interesting is that at least some of the Christianity that was brought to Mexico (although less likely to Belize or Yucatan, except prior to 1560) came from an intellectual environment that also gave rise to the Protestant reform movements of northern Europe.

The Council of Trent

As Lutheranism would come under suspicion by the church hierarchy in the latter part of the sixteenth century, so would the reform movements that gave rise to evangelization in Mesoamerica. The Council of Trent, which marked the Counter-Reformation, decided in favor of the papacy against the Catholics who wished for conciliation with the Protestants, and against the French and Spanish bishops who opposed papal claims.

In the latter half of the sixteenth century, the popes solidified discipline among the church hierarchy, and Spain under Philip II became the secular arm of what is known in academe as the Counter-Reformation.[106] Thus, the transfer of authority from the willful regular clergy to the secular clergy, well aware of their place in the hierarchy, makes sense in this atmosphere of discipline and authoritarianism. The question is whether and how Belize missions felt the effects of the decisions made in Europe.

Since the Council of Trent reaffirmed the sole right of the church to interpret the Bible, and affirmed the authority of the Vulgate rather than the Polyglot (multi-language) Bible, this eroded the support previously given to early friars in Mexico, such as Sahagún and Motolinía, who dedicated themselves to learning the Nahuatl language and recording Native traditions. According to Chuchiak, Philip II, intent on maintaining orthodoxy in the New World, refused the Mendicants permission to conduct ethnographic work in conjunction with Native assistants.[107] Thus, the cultural tolerance that marked evangelization in the first half of the sixteenth century did not remain a high priority once Council of Trent reforms took their toll.

How would these currents and cross-currents have affected the Maya in Yucatan and Belize? Chuchiak describes the bishopric of Yucatan as "post-Tridentine in nature,"[108] and he attributes the attitudes of the Franciscans in Yucatan to the post-Tridentine intellectual environment. A case can be made that Diego de Landa's severe reaction to Maya "idolatries," culminating in the *auto de fé* of 1562,[109] although certainly a reflection of the Franciscan provincial's particular psychology, is attributable to counter-reformatory zeal. This period of the 1560s was certainly a turning point in attitudes toward the nature of conversion.

The Council of Trent met for three periods between 1545 and 1563,[110] although it is said that the decrees of the council, confirmed in 1564 by Pope Pius IV, took many years to implement.[111] The Mexican church councils held in 1555, 1565, and 1585 gradually enforced the Trent decrees,[112] but the councils seem to have been more concerned with episcopal control of appointments than with what the Indians were taught. What we do detect at this time, however, is an increased obsession and anxiety with idolatry and heresy.[113]

Depending on who was preaching in Yucatan and Belize, what his background was, and how rapidly the papal reforms were felt, it seems reasonable to propose that the Christianity preached by friars who were active in Belize prior to the 1560s was influenced by humanist and reformist thought. Jones's research has demonstrated that by 1565 the Belize missions had been placed under the administration of secular clergy resident at Bacalar.[114] Even at that time, however, clerics were so few in the region, and so poorly prepared for the challenges that would face them, that the Franciscans were assigned, at least up until the mid–seventeenth century in northern Belize, the "active duty" of reduction and congregation in problem areas.[115]

In southern Belize, Campeche, and Peten, Mendicants continued to be active until the end of the century.[116] Mendicants had always been seen in Mesoamerica as best suited to bring the faith to non-Christians and to guard the faith in new converts,[117] but as Indian communities were pacified and conditions stabilized, religious authority was often passed to the seculars. The question remains in Belize whether the establishment of secular authority at Bacalar in 1565 reflected the perception that Christianization had been successful and that the pacified communities were therefore ready to be turned over to the seculars, or whether there were simply never enough friars to go around.

Individuals and Their Impact

Up to this point, individuals have been discussed largely as examples of larger social and religious patterns, but within these patterns, individuals did not act or think identically. Bishop Zumárraga has already been noted as instrumental in bringing humanism to Mexico through the instruction of the priests of the Mexican diocese.[118] Cardinal Jiménez de Cisneros, whose aim in Spain was to strengthen the preaching mission and austerity of the Mendicants, was hugely influential in the early sixteenth century in the Iberian peninsula.[119]

Cisneros had a string of titles which represented the scope of his position, among them Confessor to Queen Isabella (after 1492), Franciscan Provincial in Castile, and Archbishop of Toledo. He was also the instigator of the Polyglot Bible at the University of Alcalá, one of the most important reformist projects. As Elliott observes, Cisneros was not strictly a humanist, but he was an individual who "grasped the urgent need to harness the new humanistic studies to the service of religion."[120] Cisneros died in 1517 and had nothing to do with the choice of missionaries sent to the New World, but the head of the first Dominican mission to Mexico in 1526, Domingo de Betanzos, was deeply affected by Cisneros's ideas.[121] Betanzos in turn is said to have influenced Bartolomé de las Casas to enter the Dominican order. Cisneros also educated one of the most influential Augustinians in Mexico, Alonso de la Vera Cruz, who originally went to Mexico in 1535 as a secular priest, but took vows there in 1537.

Although all friars in Mesoamerica shared an apostolic zeal, each viewed his faith and his role as a missionary through his own life experiences, and this would have affected interaction and discussions with indigenous elites and others who were soon to adopt, appropriate, modify, or reject the Christian faith. In addition, the friars hailed not from what we would now consider nations, but from small states throughout Europe, each with its own identity, language, and cultural traditions; "Spain" itself comprised Navarre, Castile-León, Aragon, Portugal, and the kingdom of Granada.[122]

Phelan[123] discusses in detail some of the differences among the friars. Among the Franciscans who worked in Mexico, Gerónimo de Mendieta stressed that the Indians could achieve perfection on earth only if they remained under the exclusive supervision of the friars. According to Phelan, what Mendieta meant was that the Indians were more capable than the Spaniards of otherworldly superiority, as long as they did not come into earthly contact with the Spaniards who were evil and would destroy the Indians if they could.[124]

Mendieta, as noted above, also espoused the belief that the Indians could not be economically enslaved and spiritually free,[125] which is revolutionary in its implications. Although keeping the Indian communities spiritually focused and the Spaniards at bay became unworkable in a climate in which exploitation was the name of the game, certainly Mendieta reinforced rather than abated the Indians' dislike and distrust of Spanish colonists.

Pedro de Azuaga, on the other hand, saw the Indians' ready acceptance of Christianity as a manifestation of fear, and he characterized the Indians as hypocritical and opportunistic.[126] Azuaga thus supported the presence of Spanish military power, because he felt that without it, the Indians would repudiate Christianity and reject the friars.

Compared to the Franciscans and the Dominicans, the Augustinians, such as Alonso de la Vera Cruz, believed in the high moral capacity of the Indians, whether or not they had Mendicant protection. The Augustinians practiced a Christian humanism that reached far deeper than their Mendicant colleagues in assuming the spiritual readiness of the Indians to receive sacraments and to understand the meaning of various rituals and doctrine; in fact, the Augustinians had no objection to Indians entering the contemplative life.[127]

The Augustinians admitted the Indians to Communion and Extreme Unction, sacraments which the Franciscans were hesitant to administer without longer-term tutelage. The Franciscan Mendieta, for example, saw the Indians as exhibiting a childlike innocence—Christian noble savages.[128] They could be taught—and indeed he supported the Franciscan college of Santiago Tlatelolco, where Sahagún was an instructor—but they should not be ordained as priests.[129]

EXTRAPOLATING TO BELIZE

Although we do not have documents written by the individuals who first evangelized and administered communities in Belize, there are tantalizing bits and pieces of information. There must have been differences of opinion and approach, and none of this was lost on the Maya.

Jones's[130] pioneering research has produced a wide range of data to suggest what the effects of individual approaches might have been at Tipu or Lamanai, and clearly I have built on his work here. Without knowing more about the history of each community in the decades of the 1540s and 1550s, however, one can hypothesize about but not yet explain patterns and process. There is no question, however, that knowledge gained of local experience and local decision making by individuals can illuminate broader processes. At the same time, localized knowledge may also provide information that refutes expected patterns.

The conquest by Melchor and Alonso Pacheco of the Chetumal and Uaymil provinces in Yucatan, which included Belize, provides an example of individual acts of extreme cruelty.[131] These individuals' excesses may well have deeply affected any future reactions and responses to attempts by Spanish authorities to pacify and Christianize the region.

In trying to envision what it was like at Tipu and Lamanai when the evangelizing began, we have to keep in mind that each friar or preacher would have engendered different responses among individuals in the Native congregation, and ideas of what it meant to be Christian would have developed from this interaction. It is unlikely that doctrine was presented as any sort of a "package," but instead depended on how the individual friar internalized doctrinal implications. As important as the individual approaches of the friars were, so too were the attitudes, reasoning, and stances of individual Maya. Although we know less about Maya input into Christianity than we do about

Figure 6.2. Tipu thurible (censer) found in a burial, B96, under the floor of the church near the altar. (Photo by Brian Boyle)

Spanish Christian ideals, my assumption is that the Maya were as proactive as the Spaniards in the intellectual and spiritual development of the Christian faith.

MAYA AND SPANISH CHRISTIANS

We know very little about individual friars in Belize, but we know even less about individual Maya. Occasionally, details of individual lives are highlighted, such as the death of the cacique from Tipu, Don Cristóbal Na, who was killed along with Fray Diego Delgado at Nohpeten (Tah Itza) in 1623, or the bravery of Lazaro Pech, who protected Fray Bartolomé de Fuensalida on an ill-fated mission to Tipu in 1641.[132] The adolescent from Tipu who was buried with a locally made thurible (fig. 6.2) in an honored position near the altar in the church nave was clearly held in high esteem by the community.

On the whole, however, details of the lives of individuals at Tipu and Lamanai are scant. Nonetheless, the historical conditions I have described provide enough information to be able to reconstruct a context in Belize in which individuals who were evangelized would have had a good basis for thinking that Christianity accorded them a degree of decision-making power. By this I do not mean the kind of power granted to the office of a cacique or a batab, but the power of individual thought, experience, and imagination.

There is a level at which the reformist Christianity of the late fifteenth and sixteenth centuries encouraged individuals to value their faith and their individual relationship with the supernatural (Jesus Christ or the Blessed Mother or St. Peter or even St. Francis) over institutional mores. The Mendicant friars themselves were anti-institutionally inclined, and, in their vows of poverty, stood at odds, at least in principle, with the goals of colonists and encomenderos,[133] although they had to face the reality that their support was dependent on taxes and contributions from the community, both Spanish and Indian. Nonetheless, Mendicant zeal was rooted in a kind of Christianity that gave considerable credence and value to an individual's otherworldly, sometimes anti-establishment, relationship with the supernatural. St. Francis, after all, helped to change the course of Christianity by relying on what he personally experienced in his relationship with God. He then extrapolated from this experience to develop guidelines for religious conduct.

It is absolutely critical to emphasize that I am not arguing that "individualism"[134] had or has a role in Christian conversion. "Individualism" is another kettle of fish entirely and entails the primacy of the individual over the group. Nothing could be further from the Christian ideal. What I am emphasizing is the critical role of individual experience in St. Francis's encounter with God, in the Mendicants' interpretation of what it meant to be Christian, and in the Mayas' encounters with Christianity. Such experience is an internalization process and has nothing to do with acting against the primacy of any group, Spanish or Maya. In fact, the internalization process is inclusive and makes one part of a larger whole, in this case, the Christian community.[135] Although I argue strongly that what it meant to be Christian was used by the Maya of Belize just as easily to resist Spanish authority as it was used by both sides to justify conforming to Spanish authority, in no way am I saying that Christianity was individualistic. Christianity became meaningful to many of the Maya according to individual experiences; what they did with their lives as Christians is another story.

The importance of individual experience in becoming Christian harks back to the time of the apostles in the early years of the faith—a time when no church institutional framework yet existed to regulate Christian behavior or decision making to the extent that became manifested in the centuries to come. Paul's[136] contribution was particularly significant, because he encouraged a policy of evading the social and political demands of Roman society.[137] In addition, congregations and ritual were loosely organized; practical and business matters were administered by volunteers; and people generally met in whatever place suited the occasion.[138]

Perhaps most important, the reformist Christianity of the late fifteenth and sixteenth centuries valued apostolic Christianity's emphasis on the individual's relationship with the supernatural in faith and worship. Thus, as held true in Europe during the Christianization process, successful internalization of Christianity would be played out not only by individual holy men—*maestros cantores* or sacristans in Yucatan and Belize—who felt warranted and socially sanctioned to interpret relationships with the supernatural, particularly in the absence of resident friars or clergy, but in the veneration of saints and in the "localization" of the holy,[139] more of which will be discussed later on.

We need to compare how Aztec or Maya individuals affected the form Christianity took in various parts of Mesoamerica with the way that the pre-Christians in late antique and early medieval Europe dealt with Christian proselytizers and their ideas. In Europe, so-called pagan rituals, and even pagan beliefs, were made Christian through time (the use of candles, sacred water, sacred oil, kneeling, hands joined in supplication, deifying ancestors or holy men and women), partly because Christ's teachings involved behavior toward others and did not stipulate which rituals or doctrine to follow. This left Christianity vulnerable and absorptive. Thus, the Christianity presented to the Maya in communities in Belize was as much a product of history and syncretism and amalgamation and the ups and downs of local histories as were Mesoamerican or Maya religions.

This is not to say that Christianity had no significant message, but only that its packaging, at least from the Maya point of view, needed to be assessed and weighed and measured in the way all new ideas must be assessed and weighed and measured. What the Franciscan friars saw as an opportunity to achieve the Millennial Kingdom (because they favored the message over the medium) was the product of a long and cumulative European cultural history (i.e., the medium), the implications of which simply could not be transferred to the Indians. If one considers Marshall McLuhan's dictum, that the medium *is* the message,[140] then what the Spanish regular and secular clergy interpreted as misunderstanding, or even apostasy, was inevitable.

In the same way, the Aztec or Nahua or Maya experience and cultural histories could not be transferred to the friars. We can turn these obstacles to our advantage, however, by accepting that these barriers existed, and by asking ourselves how they served proactively, rather than passively, to structure both the medium and the message.

The Belize Missions

As laid out earlier in the chapter, Yucatan was first invaded in 1527–28. Although some contact was made at this time with populations in the Chetumal province (maps 2.2, 5.1), which probably included parts of northern Belize, the communities in Belize were not introduced programmatically to Christians and their agendas until 1544, when encomiendas were first established in the region by the Pachecos.[141] Some knowledge of Christians and Spaniards, however, is likely to have preceded the Pachecos' entrada.

Cortés's peaceful encounter with the Itzas at Nohpeten in 1525 probably had a ripple effect that reached Belize.[142] In this encounter, Franciscans who had accompanied Cortés preached to the Itzas through Cortés's interpreter, Doña Marina. The Itza ruler, Ajaw Kan Ek,' allowed a cross to be erected in his town, and even committed himself to destroying "idols," although he postponed actually becoming Christian. When Cortés left Ajaw Kan Ek' and the Itzas, he and his party traveled around the southern Maya Mountains and reached the Sarstoon River (map 1.1), and therefore likely traversed parts of what is now Belize. This region was Chol-speaking, but was apparently dominated by the Itzas;[143] communication between the Peten lakes and southern Belize was therefore frequent. Ajaw Kan Ek' commented, in fact, that he had "vassals" working in cacao orchards near the coast (in the region of Bahia de Amatique[144]), and that he was in contact with merchants who traveled daily between Nohpeten and the coast.[145] There is also the fact that six members of Cortés's expedition voluntarily remained behind at Nohpeten: a black man (Afro-Spaniard?), two Indians, and three Spaniards. Their fate is unknown, but as Jones[146] points out, surely they would have been important sources of information. Given the close ties—apparently largely through marriage, although some tribute relationships may have been involved—between the Maya living around the Peten lakes and Tipu, and given the nature of the coastal networks which I have argued tied Belize to the rest of the peninsula, there is little doubt that such information would have spread widely. One likes to hope, in any case, that the Belize Maya would have been aware of the existence of Spaniards other than the Pachecos.

Belize communities were to be administered from the Spanish colonial town of Salamanca de Bacalar, near modern Chetumal; as I noted above, Bacalar was established as a *villa* in 1544 by Alonso and Melchor Pacheco (maps 1.1, 5.1).[147] The Pachecos, as described, led a notoriously cruel conquest.[148] Unlike Cortés, who lived and interacted with the Aztecs, and who maintained a vision of a new empire consisting of Spaniards and Indians living and working together,[149] the Pachecos created an environment of fear. As individuals who saw the Maya solely as subjects to be exploited economically, they were highly unlikely to ask the king of Spain to "send religious persons of a goodly life and character"—specifically, representatives of the Order of St. Francis and the Order of St. Dominic—as Cortés had done,[150] to organize and minister to the Indians.

In addition, by this relatively late date in the history of the evangelization of Mesoamerica, the Crown had already begun to respond to the complaints of encomenderos in Mexico about the 1542 reform laws,[151] which were meant to protect the Indians from exploitation but which had resulted, according to the Spanish settlers, in crippling the major instruments of colonization.[152] It is hard to know whether the reaction to the New Laws had anything to do with the absence of missionaries from Bacalar itself during the community's first decade of existence,[153] or with the establishment of Bacalar as a secular mission.[154]

An important and influential Franciscan, Lorenzo de Bienvenida, who later sided with Bishop Toral against Landa's anti-idolatry activities,[155] is known to have stayed in Bacalar for an unknown period of time between the end of 1544 and 1547, on his way from Guatemala to Mérida (which he reached by 1 February 1547) to join the first group of Franciscan missionaries assigned to Yucatan.[156] Bienvenida unequivocally condemned the conquest techniques that had been applied in the region.[157] The fact that he was deeply concerned with conditions in Belize suggests strongly that he must have discussed the region's potential with other Franciscans. It is also true that from 1544 until 1557, Mendicant hegemony and Mendicant powers throughout Mesoamerica remained unchallenged;[158] thus, it is not beyond the bounds of belief to assume that Franciscans outside those who appear in the records were active in Belize at this time. The archaeological evidence from Tipu and Lamanai, such as the style of the early churches and the nature of community layout and planning, discussed in following chapters, suggests that the two communities were subjected to a common force of change. The simple, single-naved churches at Tipu and Lamanai, with apsidal ends and blind sanctuaries,[159] are excellent examples—in plan if not in materials—of the kinds of churches that were being built in Spain as a reflection of reformist traditions (fig. 6.3; see also figs. 7.1, 8.3). Documentary and archaeological evidence combined suggest further that Franciscan direction was responsible.

The Franciscans who chose to evangelize and to undergo what they saw as the hardships presented by conditions in Belize in the sixteenth century were, as I noted above, part of the reformist tradition. Surely, their attitudes were not lost on the Maya of Belize and Yucatan, who were evangelized in the years from 1544 to the 1560s. The children of elites who were educated in Franciscan schools in Yucatan must have absorbed this attitude even more strongly. Such dedication and zeal could have appealed to some Maya as individuals and may well have facilitated conversion.

Zeal and dedication have their perils, however, because like all heightened emotions they can be transmitted on their own steam, in advance of the opportunities to explain what originally generated them. It is unclear whether the proselytizers were aware of this danger, because they were absorbed with the importance of their message and, based on the documents left to us concerning Belize, did not attempt to view themselves and their message from

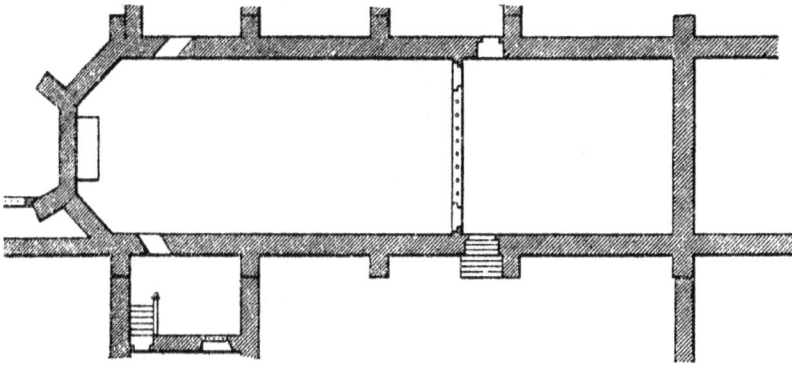

Figure 6.3. Plan of single-nave Jeronymite church at Yuste, Spain. Church was begun in 1408 and completed in 1525. (Adapted from Kubler 1948, 234–35, fig. 109)

the Maya point of view. They had already objectified the Maya as the targeted receivers of an essential message, the meaning and importance of which had already been established by God. There was no question of failure; nor was it considered seriously that the Maya had a choice, and hence ideological and cosmological cards to play of their own.

The friars' confidence in the significance of their message did not change the fact, however, that their Christianity was potentially dangerous and disruptive in the same way that early Christianity and later reformist Christianities were potentially dangerous and disruptive in western Asia, the Mediterranean, and Europe. At various junctures in history, ideas arose from individuals who believed that their experiences led to insights so powerful that they were meant to engender social change. Thus, what might be seen as an interesting juxtaposition in Belize—resistance to Spanish rule at the same time that Christian rituals were adopted and persisted—may reflect the irony that the Christian message in Belize, introduced by Franciscans, actually strengthened resistance to Spanish administrative and ecclesiastical authority.

THE FRIARS IN BELIZE

The only Franciscan who shows up in the records so far for the early period in Belize is Fray Lorenzo de Bienvenida, noted above, who was sent to evangelize in Yucatan with three other friars from Guatemala (please refer to appendix 1 for the following discussion of the friars in Belize).[160] Bienvenida had arrived from Spain either at the end of 1542 or early in 1543 and had immediately been sent to Guatemala, apparently to the region of the Golfo Dulce.[161] He then "entered Yucatan by way of the regions of the Golfo Dulce, going as far as the newly founded Spanish town of Salamanca de Bacalar, and from there he continued his journey northward. He devoted himself to learning the language and catechizing the natives."[162] Thus, it is conceivable that he proselytized in recently "pacified" communities in Belize as early as 1543–44.[163]

Three Franciscans—Francisco de Benavides, Martín de Barrientos, and Alonso Toral—visited Bacalar in 1568 and 1569, a visit that seems to be related to their participation in an important series of entradas and reductions in Belize in 1568.[164] By that time, the Belize communities had already been evangelized, and the authorities, both civil and religious, were dealing with what might be called maintenance and upkeep. The presence of the three Franciscans, however, suggests that an effort was being made to keep continuity with the initial evangelization, and that the secular clergy in Bacalar were not yet expected to take responsibility for the Belize missions.

Managing the congregation at Bacalar at this time, between about 1568 and the end of the century, was daunting enough without the challenges of maintaining Christian communities in what had by these times become "frontier."[165] Much energy was expended, for example, in the conflicts of interest that existed between the *vecinos* and the secular priests whom they had to support. Things do not seem to have been hugely improved in the seventeenth century, because the records show that secular authority at Bacalar had to be relinquished to Franciscans both in 1618–19 and again in 1641–42, not least because the Maya of Belize towns such as Tipu complained to Mérida about the behavior of secular priests.[166]

All the remaining friars in Belize—at least those of whom we are aware—were active in the seventeenth century: Bartolomé de Fuensalida and Juan de Orbita carried out reductions in Belize at Lamanai, Tipu, and Nohpeten in 1618.[167] Fray Diego Delgado traveled to Tah Itza (Nohpeten) through Tipu in 1623 and was killed there, along with Spanish soldiers and Tipuans.[168]

Fray Lopez de Cogolludo seems likely to have traveled through Belize on at least one occasion. In describing Fuensalida and Orbita's journey to Peten through Tekax and Pacha (map 5.1) in 1618,[169] he recalled an earlier journey of his in 1638, in which he passed through Pacha, which is north of Bacalar. At the time, he was returning from a celebration of a Guatemalan chapter (an ecclesiastical unit) with Fray Luis de Vivar, and both were on their way to Yucatan.[170] Lopez de Cogolludo returned to Guatemala once more in 1650, but does not mention how he got back to Yucatan.[171] It is tempting to suggest that he might again have come through Belize: he writes as if he has some knowledge of the New River Lagoon and the route to Tipu, but it is possible that this derived from his familiarity with the *relaciones* from which he drew his accounts of the region.

Fray Francisco de Moran, a Dominican, traveled from Verapaz to Salamanca de Bacalar in 1640, in search of runaway Maya from the Chol missions.[172] Fuensalida returned to Lamanai and to the upper Belize River in 1642 with Fray Juan de Estrada.[173]

The Franciscans Fray Bartolomé Becerril and Fray Martín Tejero pacified and reduced coastal towns in southern Belize in the same year, 1642.[174] In 1677, a Dominican, Fray Joseph Delgado, traveled from Guatemala through Christianized Manche Chol territory in southern Belize, and then through Tipu to Mérida.[175] In 1684, three Franciscan friars were reportedly killed at Paliac in southern Belize.[176] During the years in which the final subjugation of Nohpeten was being planned, from about 1695 until the end of the century, the secular clergy were by then clearly in charge of the Belize missions, with the Franciscans assigned to the entradas and reductions along the *camino real* to Nohpeten.[177]

All the Mendicants noted above, Franciscans and Dominicans, come across as highly dedicated evangelists who were fluent in Native languages.[178] These characteristics do not necessarily guarantee a reformist outlook; however, those active in Belize from the 1540s until the 1560s would have been trained during the period of the reformist movements. Thus, a humanist/reformist Christianity might well have slipped into Belize and permeated Maya Christian communities and fledgling Christian thinking before doors of tolerance were closed by the Council of Trent.

More important, Belize Maya may even have kept some doors ajar, especially if Franciscans, such as Bienvenida or others like him, were involved in the initial evangelization and community reorganization. I suggest that this was the case, partly because it took a particular brand of zeal, dedication, and cultural flexibility to attempt the Christianization of communities living in what to the Spaniards were remote and inaccessible forests; and partly because Council of Trent reforms were aimed first at central Mexico and the more highly populated regions of Mesoamerica, since these were considered economically important and stability of administration was essential, leaving (what became) the frontiers to drag behind.

Although the lives of the individual friars would have to be studied in detail, one could hazard that the differences in outlook between Fuensalida and Orbita reflect an early reformism, with a measure of cultural tolerance in Fuensalida's case, versus the orthodoxy that characterized Post-Tridentine Christianity and its obsession with idolatry, in Orbita's. Orbita, while experiencing Itza hospitality, rashly destroyed a statue of a horse which his hosts valued but which Orbita called an "idol."[179] He thus irrevocably endangered the chances of a peaceful conversion process. Fuensalida, on the other hand, later wrote that perhaps he and Orbita should have acted in the spirit of the advice of a Yucatecan theologian who, following St. Augustine, said to "first remove the idols from the hearts of the infidels and then the figures that adorned their altars."[180]

A NO-WIN SITUATION?
REGULARS, SECULARS, ENCOMENDEROS

Although Bacalar was responsible as a secular mission for ministering to Belize Christians, the Franciscans maintained an interest in Belize's mission communities throughout the late sixteenth and seventeenth centuries,[181] perhaps because, if colonization intensified and Spanish settlement took hold in Belize (it never did), there was always the possibility that residential Mendicant communities could be established as they had been farther north in Yucatan. Certainly the Franciscans had their eyes on the non-Christianized Maya of the Peten lakes.[182] This made stable Christian communities in Belize critical, if not to the spiritual conquest of Peten itself, then to the long-term survival of Christianity in the region. These special conditions argue that despite the transfer of power from the regular to the secular clergy in the Spanish colonies, the Franciscans in Yucatan seem generally to have been recognized, even as late as 1696, as the best equipped to accompany entradas, preach Christianity, and organize reductions.[183]

There are other reasons to argue for continuing Franciscan interest in Belize despite the context of increasing secular power. Two major elements thwarting the friars' plans in central Mexico, Oaxaca, and surrounding regions were the growing Spanish population attracted to the richness of Mexico and its resources, and the eagerness of Spanish colonists to exploit Indian labor. Thus, it is not unlikely that the low number of Spanish settlers in Yucatan and their virtual dearth in Belize, as well as the absence of easy routes to riches, may have served to keep Franciscan spiritual interest in Belize alive. As noted above, there were no mineral resources to exploit in Belize, and the humid tropical conditions were not conducive to the growth of crops with which the Spaniards were familiar. The scramble for wealth was inhibited by the fact that wealth, in European terms, was hard to generate.

On the other hand, the Franciscans could not operate without support. If, in the latter part of the sixteenth century, they were no longer favored by the Crown by being granted encomiendas of their own or by being given the time to build Indian Christian communities in which the Indians supported the friars and were exempt from tribute, then the friars needed the support of the encomenderos. Unfortunately, the situation in Belize was such that the region was too low in encomienda income to support both encomenderos and Mendicant residential communities. Belize communities were certainly as capable as those of Yucatan in producing the tropical products for which there developed a market in central Mexico,[184] but Spanish strategies did not succeed in building a framework that would make this possible.

The remoteness and poverty of the Villa of Salamanca de Bacalar, its role as the seat of the province, the attitude of the Pachecos, and the historical factors that led to the decline of the influence of the Mendicants, all may explain the commitment to secular rather than regular authority where the Belize missions were concerned. At the same time, Belize remained remote, difficult to administer, and replete with communities—Christian, quasi-Christian, or pagan—that went their own ways. This was not territory in which successful administration by seculars would have been predicted.

Proselytization and the Forces of Colonization

In Belize, as in the rest of Mesoamerica in the early colonial period, encomienda was considered by Spanish invaders as "an efficient instrument of colonization."[185] In Mexico it was superseded by other systems of economic exploitation by the end of the sixteenth century, whereas the encomienda lasted well over two centuries in Yucatan,[186] and for about a century and a half in Belize. The encomienda was not a land-grant institution,[187] but instead extracted agricultural or manufactured products from the Indians as well as labor; it was therefore loosely consonant with the pre-Columbian tribute system, in the sense that the basis of extraction comprised labor and products owed as tribute to particular individuals.[188] Where the tribute-extractors lived, either in pre-Columbian or Spanish colonial times, did not seem to have changed the basis of the extractive relationship.

With regard to those who paid tribute, however, the picture is less clear, and it is here that Spanish colonial practices are more likely to have differed from those of pre-Columbian times. Although the goods and services under both extractive systems (pre-Columbian Maya and Spanish colonial) were the products of the labor efforts of individuals who had access to land and resources, Spanish encomenderos and their accountants were not familiar with the dynamics of Maya agriculture, economy, labor, or social organization. Rather than trying to sort all this out, it was almost certainly easier for them to keep track of tribute obligations by capitalizing on an existing indigenous unit that linked residence and work with place. Restall suggests, in fact, that the Maya indigenous socio-geographical unit known as the cah formed the basis by which encomienda was organized.[189]

The cah in Yucatan was a basic indigenous geographical, political, and organizational entity that represented a fundamental unit of society and culture.[190] In regions such as Belize that remained virtually devoid of Spanish colonists, using cah organization as the basis of establishing encomiendas would have been a reasonably efficient first step in organizing resource extraction.[191] It may be that the cah made some sense to the Spaniards because its geographical implications were easy for them to grasp. Other pre-Hispanic divisions such as the *cuchteel*—represented or headed by an *ah cuch cab*—almost certainly had an important role in pre-Columbian tribute, particularly regarding labor requirements, but the *cuchteel* was not well understood by the Spaniards, and its coherence and structure suffered thereby under encomienda.[192]

How encomienda incomes were maintained during Belize's checkered history as a Christianized region is still not clearly understood, particularly given the recalcitrance of the communities and their relative proximity to the anti-Spanish machinations of the Itza.[193] The curious fact is that what we now know as Belize became a lacuna in Spanish colonization efforts by about 1700, yet its Maya communities, proselytized and then peripheralized by the Spaniards, remained Christian for the next three centuries. On the other hand, Maya populations within the boundaries of regions successfully appropriated by the Spaniards, such as Chiapas and Peten, include the Lacandon, many of whom remained staunchly non-Christian.[194] Clearly, colonization and proselytization, although linked as forces of economic and cultural change,[195] did not always produce the expected results.

Many archaeologists tend to emphasize a kind of categorical resistance to Spanish rule, and thereby focus on the way the Maya worked to undermine the Spaniards. Such resistance is certainly a key element in any colonial analysis. However, given that the modern Maya of Belize are Christian, and that the modern Maya of Belize are descendants of the ancient and colonial-period Maya, the assumption that the colonial Maya acted only to resist rather than to analyze, intellectualize, or appropriate religious ideas brought by the Spaniards would then lead logically to the conclusion that a spiritual conquest had occurred.[196]

Both the archaeological and documentary evidence suggest that a far more proactive intellectual and analytical process on the part of Maya individuals took place in the face of evangelization.[197] Archaeology cannot provide us with the details of the language or conversations that formed part of this analytical process, but it can provide us with the evidence for the existence of a framework in which such conversations were feasible or likely.

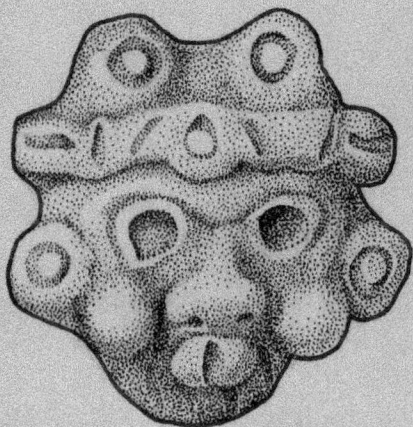

PART III

✠ SEVEN ✠

How to Tell a Church

In this chapter I remain within the remit of setting the Mendicant stage. As part of a discussion of the material culture of the mission experience, however, I consider the idea of a church. Because the excavated churches at Tipu and Lamanai served as the linchpins of our archaeological activity, it was important that I familiarized myself with church architectural terminology, with Spanish practice, and with what others before me had written about early churches in Yucatan and Mexico. I expected this process to be straightforward and to involve little more than a learning curve. The outcome, however, entailed a reevaluation of the implications of architectural typology. This chapter lays out my critical reassessment of the context and use of terms used to describe early colonial mission architecture.[1]

No term is more closely associated with the architecture of the mission experience in Mexico and Yucatan than the so-called open chapel, a term introduced by Toussaint for what was known in the sixteenth century as a *capilla de indios* (Indian chapel),[2] and no term has been more misused. Although *capilla de indios* makes sense from the perspective of sixteenth- and seventeenth-century liturgical practices, the term "open chapel" makes no sense at all.

The Existing Framework:
Terms and Typologies

No doubt we all think we know what a church is. Nevertheless, sorting through evidence of Maya and Spanish religious interaction at the time of early contact reveals a somewhat confusing picture of what have come to be called churches (*iglesias*) and chapels (*capillas*). Confusion arises in the terminology of both colonial Spaniards and modern architectural historians and archaeologists. The colonial Spaniards seem to be inconsistent when they call large edifices in towns *capillas* and small rural edifices *iglesias*.[3] However, if one considers function rather than form to be of primary importance, then this apparent inconsistency actually makes more sense than an architectural typology based on form.

The confusing picture of churches and chapels has multiple causes: existing typologies emphasize form rather than function; aspects of the history of use and the attendant implications for terminology have been overlooked; differences in environmental conditions (e.g., between central Mexico and Belize, or between central Mexico and Yucatan) have been minimized; the rationale behind researchers' approaches[4] is implicit rather than explicit; and analyses either have not detected or have chosen to gloss over Spanish colonial prejudices.

Why are church architectural typologies important? In large part because the focus of archaeologists on material remains includes the remains of churches. Andrews reflects this archaeological perspective in his description of the chapels and churches of early colonial Yucatan and Belize:

> Designed and administered by Spanish friars, and built and used by the Maya, [chapels and churches] lie at the core of the initial process of acculturation that resulted in . . . Spanish domination. . . . These structures, often built with stone from Maya pyramids, became the new focus of the cultural and social life of native communities. . . . The chapels and churches were also the social hub of the communities, the locale for baptisms, weddings, fiestas, civic gatherings, and funerals. And, to complete the life cycle, the members of the community were often buried underneath these structures.[5]

It is therefore not unexpected that archaeologists would have interest in the details of church architecture and in church plans and their variations, because these details reflect aspects of community history or identity that are not always recorded in the documents.[6] In places peripheral to the main economic thrust of Spanish colonialism, such as Yucatan and Belize, architectural detail may be all that is left to reflect the colonial experience. If I draw from typologies to describe the most important excavated building at Tipu as a ramada (thatched) church (fig. 7.1),[7] or refer to the central room of the masonry-walled portion of one of the Lamanai churches as a presbytery (fig. 7.2),[8] the terms help to provide the reader with an image of the building. They also have the potential to be adopted as standards in describing particular architectural elements.

On the other hand, the same typologies can be problematic when an

Figure 7.1. Tipu, reconstruction of church, looking east-northeast. (Drawing by Claude Belanger and Louise Belanger)

Figure 7.2. Lamanai, stone chapel of YDL II. Photo looks southeast.

attempt is made to compare structures on a broader geographic basis in order to gain insight into how the buildings were used, or to achieve insight into Maya and Spanish religious experiences. The problem is that sixteenth-century names or terms for buildings, spaces, or rooms derived from their function. They arose as a response to how people knew the buildings or spaces or rooms were used. They were not always formal categories, but they have come to be taken as such. The result is that the literature on churches and chapels in Mexico, Belize, and Yucatan takes terms for granted that warrant careful attention.

Problematic Definitions
and Elusive Evidence

Andrews has taken steps to standardize the typology of known church struc-tures for archaeology, and García and Gussinyer have added a historical de-velopmental dimension.[9] Earlier typologies upon which these later classifi-cations have drawn are informative as regards gaining a perspective on the spectrum of early churches in Mexico and Yucatan.[10] Difficulties and incon-sistencies nonetheless persist, owing to the fact that some of the terms basic to typologies, such as the "open chapel" (*capilla abierta*), or even "chapel" vs. "church," are not clearly defined and, as Andrews observes, remain problem-atic.[11] For example, the church at Xcaret in Quintano Roo, Mexico, is mistak-enly described as a "chapel," as are the churches at Lamanai and Tipu, and the mission churches in Yucatan in general.[12]

Other terms are applied selectively. For example, "ramada" is defined as "thatched,"[13] and yet the term is applied to structures such as those at Ta-malcab, Ecab (fig. 7.3), Xlacah, and the second church to be built at Lamanai (YDL II) (figs. 7.2, 8.4),[14] all of which had massive altar ends built of stone and either flat beam and mortar or barrel vault roofs.[15] Surely, if a category of "ra-mada" is to be used, it should refer to the early churches at Tipu and Lamanai, both of which were entirely thatch-roofed (figs. 7.1, 8.3, 8.24). Even the term "open-air," or "open," used so widely to describe early churches, is never ex-plicitly defined by McAndrew,[16] who was responsible for the foundational, if not the original, use of the term. One has to read his entire history of the early church in Mexico to be able to infer what he means, and even then one is left wondering whether what he describes as "open" was a church or a chapel by his own definition. What, exactly, is it that is open? Lara describes open cha-pels as "external chapels,"[17] which introduces yet another question: external to what?

The "Open Chapel"

What McAndrew broadly refers to as an open-air church subsumes the area that would functionally be classified as the nave (fig. 7.4). When he uses the term "open chapel,"[18] the picture is less clear. The chroniclers do not seem to have used the adjective "open" to apply to a chapel; the term "open" origi-nated, as I noted above, with Toussaint.[19] But the term *capilla* (chapel), which appears frequently in chroniclers' accounts, seems at first to be no less straightforward, although I hope to show that, within the context of Christian liturgical practices, it makes eminent sense. The case would seem to be that *in certain historical circumstances*, when the sanctuary or presbytery and other

Figure 7.3. Ecab, perspective reconstruction of the church (Andrews 2006, 25, fig. 2.17). (Reproduced courtesy of Anthony Andrews)

restricted-access space or spaces were enclosed fully or partly by masonry walls as an architectural entity distinct from the nave, the resulting structure was called a *capilla*, or chapel. In modern scholarship this has sometimes been referred to as a *presbiterio*, or presbytery,[20] although strictly speaking, the presbytery was (is) only the sanctuary area around the altar (I will elaborate on the historical circumstances below).[21] Such a *capilla* was usually built in a patio or plaza (as in fig. 7.4) to accommodate large numbers of people. The *capilla* was *not* termed "open" by its users, although an example in Mexico has been described as being "outside,"[22] which implies free-standing.

It is not unusual for such sacred spaces as a sanctuary (presbytery) and the area around it, which could even include a choir[23] and chancel, to *function* as a *capilla*, or chapel, but it is unusual for what is effectively the major functioning element for worship in a community to be called a chapel. The sixteenth-century Spaniards understood this, and when they used the term *capilla*, it referred only to the stone-built eastern end of churches in Yucatan and Belize, with their sanctuaries and adjacent rooms, whereas a number of modern scholars have used *capilla* to apply to the entire church. This rather unorthodox, and hence problematic, usage by scholars of the word "chapel" has been a source of confusion to those wishing to describe Maya religious structures in Yucatan and Belize, particularly with respect to the very earliest constructions—sometimes called Paleochristian architecture[24]—of the sixteenth century.

What is "Open"?

The adjective "open," rather than clarifying a phenomenon, weaves a web of confusion. When it was first used by architectural historians,[25] it seems to have been meant to reflect a practice, early in the history of the Christianization of central Mexico, in which native peoples stood to hear Mass in the open air in what was called an *atrio* (fig. 7.4).[26] The atrio was functionally equivalent to, and in some cases probably was in actuality, the pre-Columbian plaza or patio; only the Christian sanctuary/presbytery, with its altar and related ritual space(s), were enclosed by masonry walls. Even if one felt comfortable with the use of "open" as an adjective to describe architecture related to the phenomenon I have just described, the term has stuck like a limpet to such a wide variety of phenomena that it has become meaningless.[27]

"Open" is applied to the mosque-like "chapel" at San José de Naturales in Tenochtitlan, which in its finished, roofed form is estimated to have been 17,000 square feet and to have held 2,000–3,000 people.[28] McAndrew provides the following rationale for the "open," but not the "chapel," part:

> Since over 2,000 could attend Mass inside, as in a normal church, it might be claimed that the finished seven-aisled version of San José ought not to be called an *open* chapel, even though it was open all across its 200-foot front. . . . To those inside the chapel—whether 2,000, 3,000 or 300—its function would have been no different from that of an ordinary roofed church but, since its long front was open, and since the chapel could serve other thousands out in the atrio and usually did, most of the time its function was concurrently that of an open chapel."[29]

In the first place, if one is going to apply the term "open" in this case at all, it is the church that is open, not the chapel. Second, as reconstructed, three sides of the chapel were full-height walled and the fourth side was columned. If the columns make the edifice "open" then many mosques should be called "open mosques" instead of just mosques. There is also the fact that many chapels are walled on three sides, with the fourth side unwalled; in most cases, these form part of a larger architectural entity such as a cathedral or church, and yet they are not called "open chapels," but simply "chapels."

The fact that there were times when individuals in the Indian community had to stand in the open air, because only the sanctuary of their church was walled, is interesting in more ways than simply as a basis for architectural

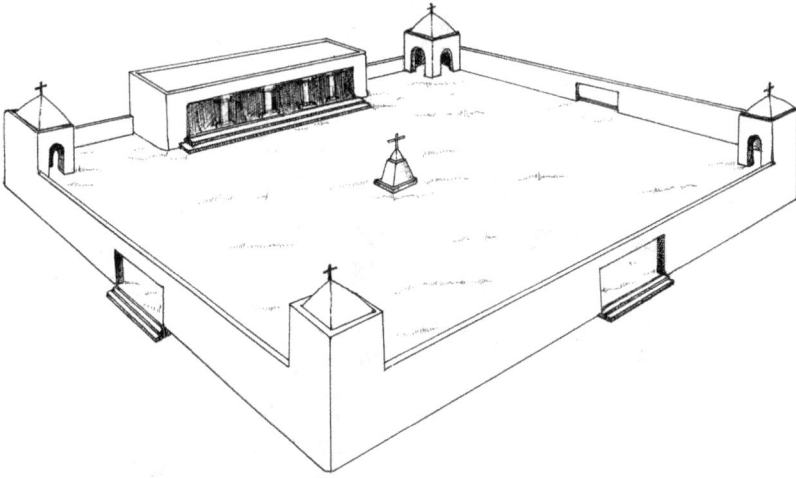

Figure 7.4. Schematic drawing of an open-air church showing stone-enclosed altar area (*capilla*, or chapel), the walls delimiting the *atrio*, and the corner *posas*. Based on information from McAndrew (1965, 279–339 on *posas*, and 374–86 on San José de Naturales) and Artigas (1983, 239, fig. 202). (Drawing by Louise Belanger)

terminology. When people stand in the open air to worship, is this phenomenon a function of colonial priorities, or does it represent practices and spatial organization that go back to pre-Columbian times, as suggested by both Lara and McAndrew?[30]

The term "open" also inexplicably continues to be applied to churches in Yucatan with substantial naves that were roofed with thatch and had altar ends that were masonry-walled and roofed with timber and mortar or vaulted. The "open chapel" at Dzibilchaltun,[31] classified as an "open ramada church,"[32] is shown in the perspective drawing (fig. 7.5) as having post supports for the roof frame, but no walls.[33] This is based on the presence of rectangular holes high in the masonry walls enclosing the sanctuary, which probably served as sockets for beams that supported the rafters. Excavations, however, did not reveal postholes for vertical supports. The presumed absence of walls, masonry or otherwise, seems to be the source of the adjective "open."[34] This presumption, in turn, may have been influenced by Father Ponce's description of a church complex at Tizimin in which a "big chapel" stood at the head of a ramada (nave) that was open-sided and served the Indian community.[35]

In a further complication, Andrews[36] cautions that the category of "open ramada church" does not preclude the possibility of a perishable wall around

Figure 7.5. Dzibilchaltun, perspective reconstruction of the "open chapel."
(Drawing by Gordon and Ann Ketterer, from Folan 1970, 182, fig. 1).
(Reproduced courtesy of William Folan)

the nave, although this would seem to remove the last vestige of openness. Even in the event that postholes for the large uprights shown in the reconstruction drawing were preserved, setting down a series of light, vertical wooden sticks or poles to rest on the floor between the posts to form a wall would be quite likely to leave no evidence. This is partly because the sticks or poles do not penetrate the floor plaster, but also because the drip water from the eaves can erode the floor edges considerably so that any marks made by the line of the poles are highly likely to be obliterated. Andrews acknowledges the problem of evidence for a perishable wall when he states: "However, the existence of these perishable walls may never be ascertained, even with the aid of archaeological excavation."[37]

The fact that evidence of perishable walls is elusive is no more proof that walls did not exist than that they did. Therefore, one major disadvantage of existing "open" classifications is that they seem to opt for the former—perishable walls did not exist. Any church with no walls that stood along the east coast of Yucatan, where winds drive the wet-season rains rather powerfully, could not have encouraged regular attendance.[38] Farther south in Belize, where the rainy season can last for nine months of the year, it is hard to imagine the utility of a thatched structure with upright posts and no walls.

Capilla de Indios

Sometimes *capilla de indios*, or "Indian chapel," is used as an architectural term, usually to apply to a form of "open chapel" if a large structure is involved,[39] but this label is also problematic. According to Kubler,[40] a non-architectural meaning of *capilla de indios* is suggested by a sixteenth-century document from Guatemala:

> The capilla was sometimes an administrative and fiscal institution for the maintenance of the cult assigned to the Indians, related in kind, very possibly, to the later cofradías of the seventeenth century. But the cofradías existed within individual communities, whereas the capilla de indios was maintained for a cluster of communities. With the increasing particularization of Indian communities the capilla de indios became obsolete, yielding to the cofradías in the individual communities. It would appear that the capilla de indios survived as long as there existed a shortage of personnel. When ministers became numerous enough to serve the many Indian parishes individually, there was no further need for the regional association implied in the capilla de indios.[41]

It is of course possible that the term *capilla de indios*, as applied to an institution, grew out of the fact that the Indians congregated on Sundays and feast days in groups,[42] in an area in which they once heard Mass before a more formal church was built. Bretos observes that in the sixteenth century, *capillas de indios* was not a reference to form but to the identity of the congregation.[43]

Chancel, Sanctuary, Presbytery, Choir?

There is also confusion in the use of terms employed to describe what might be called the business end of the church, which is generally restricted to celebrants such as the friars or secular priests, although those assisting, such as sacristans or *maestros cantores*,[44] were also admitted. As far as I can ascertain, this confusion arises partly from the fact that liturgical usage has changed through time, partly from the fact that sources vary, and partly from the fact that the positioning of the altar has also changed.

The earliest Christian altars in the Old World were free-standing tables in private houses,[45] which gave rise in early Roman churches to the celebrant standing on the far side of the altar facing westward toward the people. The custom of positioning altars near the east wall seems to have been established by the end of the fourth century.[46] The celebrant's position gradually changed to eastward-facing, with his back to the people in the nave.[47] This was the practice during the period of the Spanish conquest and is reflected in the churches in Belize and Yucatan; it was also the practice until recently, but since the late 1960s or early 1970s the westward-facing position of the altar has been restored in many Roman Catholic and some Anglican churches.

Most sources on church terminology agree that the sanctuary is the part of the church that contains the altar, and today it refers to the area around the altar, although the term "presbytery" is also used.[48] The history of "chancel" is more complicated, and not all sources are in agreement. One source states that "chancel" originally had the meaning that "sanctuary" has now, but came to refer more specifically to the area between the altar and the nave, which is restricted to the clergy and choir (figs. 7.6, 7.7).[49] Another defines the chancel as part of the choir near the altar of a church, where individuals stand to assist the priest.[50]

One thinks of "choir" as referring to a group of parishioners singing in chorus, but in the sixteenth century it referred to a place with restricted access where the friars recited the holy offices. In Belize and Yucatan, the choir was the area in which Maya with religious training helped to officiate Mass, or in which the liturgy was chanted. In this context, "choir" can refer to people who chant the liturgy or to the space designated for this purpose. "Chancel" is solely a spatial term, and came to be used to designate the space between the altar and nave, access to which was restricted to the clergy and/or the choir. In some churches, a screen separated the nave from this space, and the word "chancel" is said to derive from the Latin word for lattice, or screen.[51]

"Chancel" is now often used to designate the entire area east of the nave (and east of the transepts, where they exist).[52] This is a looser definition than the original meaning, and at one point I thought it could serve in the case of Yucatecan and Belize examples to designate the stone-built part of the church east of the nave, because it refers to the space designated for activities associated with the altar (sanctuary), as well as space devoted to other liturgical activities performed either by priests or, in the Maya case, by individuals from the community who were officiating at Mass. "Chancel" does not, however, encompass the rooms that in Yucatan were traditionally adjacent to the sanctuary, such as the baptistery and sacristy (fig. 7.8), although in the sixteenth century the baptistery, where the baptismal font was kept, could also serve as the choir (fig. 7.8).[53]

McAndrew, in translating a sixteenth-century source, uses the term "chancel" to refer to the body of the church east of the nave: "All the other churches of the parishes for Indians in these parts are of thatch except for the chancels where Mass is said, and those are of stone."[54] Unfortunately, he does not identify the source in this instance, so we have no way of knowing the original Spanish term. García y Granados uses *presbiterio*,[55] and "chancel" is a term used by others.[56] With reference to Tipu and Lamanai, we have used

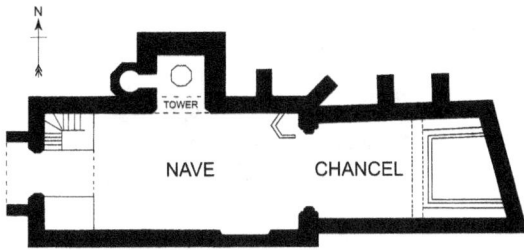

Figure 7.6. Plan of St. Martin's Church in Exeter, Devon, showing the chancel and its relationship to the nave and sanctuary. (Adapted from Scott 2004, 4)

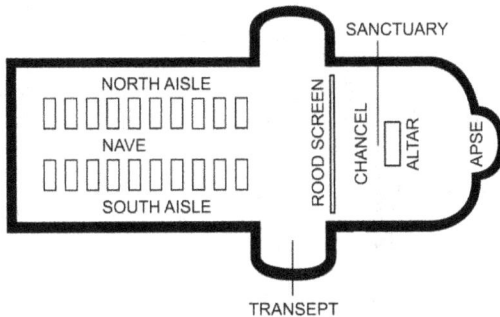

Figure 7.7. Traditional layout of the Western church shows the relationship of the chancel to other parts of the church. (Adapted from Taylor 2004, 28)

"sanctuary" in earlier publications.[57] "Chancel" seems at first to be a reasonable choice to designate the area east of the nave, but the term does not, as noted above, account for the rooms on either side of the sanctuary.

Where the sanctuary is supplemented by other spaces or rooms and is differentiated architecturally (type and design of construction) from the nave, no commonly accepted term exists. McAndrew refers to a "chancel-chapel,"[58] but this is awkward. Examples would be the "business ends" of the churches at Tamalcab,[59] Lamanai (fig. 8.4), Ecab (fig. 7.3), and Dzibilchaltun (fig. 7.5), all of which would fit Cárdenas Valencia's description:

Tienen iglesias muy grandes y muy capaces, que aunque de paja y de palmas silvestres, son de gran defensa y dura. . . . Las capillas son edificadas de cal y canto, cubiertas algunas de azotea y las más de bóvedas y en ésta están los altares y colaterales hechos todos los más de muy lindo pincel y molduras sobredoradas.[60]

(They have very large and spacious churches which, although of straw and wild palms [thatch], offer good protection and are lasting. . . . The chapels are built of masonry, some covered with a flat roof and the rest vaulted and in this are the altars and associated parts all painted artistically and with gilded mouldings.)

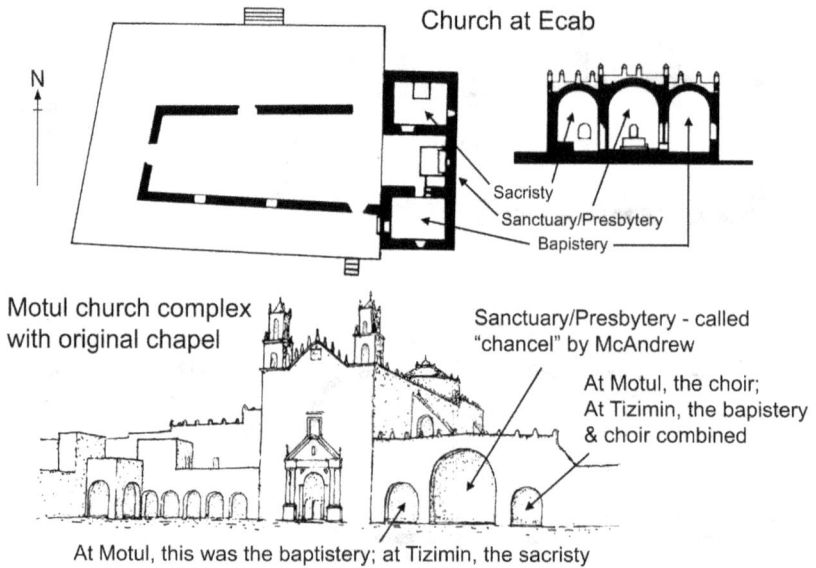

Figure 7.8. Chapel components of Yucatecan churches. (Ecab example adapted from Andrews 2006, 18, fig. 2.6; Motul example adapted from McAndrew 1965, 520, fig. 264)

Perhaps *capilla*, or "chapel," is in fact the most appropriate term for the stone portion east of the nave, because it was the term used in the sixteenth century. Although there is theoretically no difference between *capilla* in Spanish and "chapel" in English, the complexity implied in the sixteenth-century use of *capilla* can become lost in translation, as I shall explain below. An alternative might be a term that was also sometimes used in colonial times, *capilla mayor*, or large chapel, as long as one remembers that the *capilla* or *capilla mayor* was functionally part of a larger whole—a church.

The situation is somewhat more complicated in the cases of the first church at Lamanai (fig. 8.3) and the lone church at Tipu (fig. 8.24). Each church comprises a long, narrow space enclosed by part-stone, part-perishable walls with apsidal or half-hexagonal[61] or polygonal ends, and a roof of thatch. The altar area is separated from the nave in elevation by two lines of stones that served as the risers of steps. Both churches also had a room east of the sanctuary and separated from the sanctuary by a wall.

My inclination was at first to call the entire area east of the nave, and separated from the nave by steps, simply a sanctuary, because the space is relatively small. However, the sanctuary in both cases is clearly separated from the nave, creating in effect a "screen"; the areas around the altars (or around where the portable altars were placed) have features which suggest the existence of hierarchical or differentiated space for the priest and for Mayas who officiated at Mass; and a separate room was constructed behind (east of) the sanctuary and probably served as a sacristy. Hence, despite the small size of these early churches, the east ends are more than simply sanctuaries.

Church or Chapel?

The use of the term "church" versus "chapel" seems often to reflect the belief that size matters. A church is, however, the consecrated building where Mass is said and which serves the community; it can be any size. Taylor[62] displays a photograph of a lovely stone church in North Yorkshire that measures only 5 meters by 4 meters (fig. 7.9). As long as the structure or structural element serves the Christian community—which is also called the "church"[63]—by providing sacred space where Mass can be said, it is a church. A chapel, on the other hand, is sacred space that serves a smaller-scale function and serves a limited audience. It is described as being "less than a church"[64] in terms of its functions. If chapels are smaller than churches in size, it is because the smaller size serves the purpose.

Figure 7.9. St. Andrew's Old Church, Upleatham, near Cleveland, North Yorkshire. Measures 5 meters (17 feet, 3 inches) by 4 meters (13 feet), with space for about thirty (Taylor 2003, 29). (Reproduced with permission of the E&E Image Library)

Chapels can be parts of churches, as in the cases of chapels along the aisles of cathedrals, usually separated from the nave by a series of columns. Such chapels are places of private or family worship where prayers can be said and candles lit.[65] Chapels can be set in schools or hospitals or airports to serve people in these settings. Chapels can be separate buildings, as in the case of *posas*, which stood in the corners of the atrio (fig. 7.4), although Masses were not said in posas. A chapel can be a sacred building in a sacred place where people stop to pray or to chant during a religious procession. None of the identified sacred buildings at Tipu or Lamanai was a chapel, because all were constructed to serve the entire community; they were churches. In the case of the "open chapels" as described by McAndrew, these, too, were constructed to serve the community, and were therefore, properly speaking, parts of churches.

All of the examples of open-air sacred buildings described by McAndrew are churches according to standard ecclesiastical criteria—*if*, that is, one considers that native peoples formed the Christian community. McAndrew uses the term "chapel" in describing all his examples of the masonry portions of his open-air churches,[66] perhaps because he was focusing on the non-perishable architectural elements of the Indians' churches. As described by McAndrew, these "open chapels" were part of larger complexes, or monasteries,[67] that normally included: (1) a residence, or *convento*, for the clergy; (2) one or more walled open areas, or atrios, where the Indians, but not the Spaniards, stood to hear Mass[68] and onto which faced a stone building—the chapel, or *capilla*—in which the altar was sheltered and where the priest or celebrant stood (fig. 7.4); (3) posas, or "corner chapels," in the atrios,[69] which were tiny and distinct from the "open" chapel (fig. 7.4); and (4) what was called by the Spaniards an iglesia, or monastery church.[70]

One factor that explains the use of atrios was the sheer size of the indigenous communities, whose congregational demands, according to McAndrew, "could not be met with the ordinary repertory of church-building forms" because "Europe had had no need for anything like atrios."[71] He also argues that there were not enough friars to say Masses if the Indians were subdivided into groups to hear Mass in the monastery church.[72] This makes sense, at least as an early measure. In Mexico by the end of the century, and in many places by 1576, the use of atrios and open chapels was obsolete;[73] this does not, however, explain why Spanish residents were not expected to stand in the atrios.

As strongly as McAndrew argues for sheer numbers as the stimulus to open-air worship, he recognizes that Indians were still segregated outdoors in some places as late as the 1690s, while the Spaniards were inside the church, as in Cuautitlan.[74] Therefore, another factor must have been the prejudicial attitudes of the Spaniards, both clergy and lay people, toward the *indios*. A third factor was the history of use of religious structures, but this matter will be clearer once I have described the major components of church complexes in Mexico, which McAndrew says were in effect by 1540 and standardized by 1550,[75] and from which Yucatecan and Belizean types derived.

With regard to order of construction, it seems from McAndrew's comments that the first priority was a place in which the friars could celebrate Mass:

> What is most significant here is that when the friars were beginning a friary . . . they made some sort of chapel as soon as they could because it was the single most important integer in the monastery scheme. They could live in old Indian buildings, recite their offices in them, and even say their own conventual Masses in them; they could teach the Indians their Catechism in old buildings or old courtyards, and preach to them there: but in no building could they suitably celebrate Holy Mass for their Indian converts until they built it themselves. During both the Conquest and Conversion, many Masses must have been said entirely outdoors, or under a temporary shield of cloth, thatch, or wood, because there was no place else to say them, but Masses without a chapel must always have been recognized as a makeshift once the Conversion was well under way.[76]

The second priority was a residence for the friars, with the monastery church the last component to be built. The monastery church was a place of worship for clergy and Spanish or mestizo townspeople, but not Indians.[77]

> Once the monastery church was completed, or well along, the first temporary open chapel would often be replaced by an architecturally more respectable structure of masonry; or sometimes, if it had not been too flimsily improvised, the first chapel might be kept on as the regular Indian chapel after the monastery church was done.[78]

Here lie the roots of prejudice. In Europe, the church community was the community, although segregation almost certainly manifested itself with regard to where people sat in the nave. In the New World, the community was formally and functionally divided into Indians (*naturales*) and Spaniards. If anything, given that the Indians outnumbered the Spaniards, it was the Indians who formed the true church community. At the very least, *both* activity areas—the atrio, or nave, with its stone-sheltered altar (*capilla*, or chapel), which the Indians used, and the roofed nave and sanctuary that the Spaniards used—were churches. In fact, even McAndrew observes that sixteenth-century chroniclers sometimes referred, correctly in my opinion, to the atrio as an iglesia.[79]

The questions to be asked are: Why were Indians and Spaniards expected to worship separately? Why is *capilla* often used to describe the Indians' place of worship? Why is "open"(an adjective that seems relevant only in the earliest stages of church development in central Mexico[80]) so tenacious in architectural typologies? And how could "open" be expected to have any utility at all as a descriptive term when it covers so many different structural variations?

The situation in Yucatan was somewhat different from that in central Mexico. In many places in Yucatan, no church for exclusive use of Spaniards was built; the friars used rooms in the *convento* for their rites, and the chapel, or *capilla*, was the walled structure where the friars stood when Mass was recited for the Maya community, who gathered in a ramada in the atrio.[81] The implication is that because in Yucatan there were many Mayas and few to no Spaniards, depending on the community, it was not worthwhile to build a substantial stone structure within the monastery. Where churches were finally constructed, in places such as Mérida (and this is how the building is described in the literature, where "church" refers to roofed structures like the ones built in Europe, in which roofs are not made of thatch), they were built by the secular clergy, and the Maya were served by the monasteries.[82]

Although the open chapel and the atrio/patio with which it is associated have been described and praised as an architectural type distinctive to the New World, what is distinctive instead seems to be the origin of the practice of using the term "church," or "*iglesia*," to designate a place where Mass was said for Spaniards and from which *indios* were largely excluded.[83] What is also distinctive is the use of "chapel" to refer to the main place of worship of the Christian community.

In the case of the Spanish friars, use of the term *capilla* may have another explanation, which I am convinced has contributed to subsequent confusion. McAndrew noted that the friars' first priority in a new area was to establish a place to say Mass,[84] and given the importance of ministering to the Indians, they said Mass for the Indians as well as for themselves under whatever shelter for the altar they could devise. In Mexico, this sheltered altar area fronted the atrio and became the stone-built *capilla*. McAndrew claims that sixteenth-century writers commonly called this a *capilla de indios* because it had been created for the Indian congregation,[85] but reference simply to a *capilla* also occurs in the sources.

In monasteries, the place where friars say their own daily masses is called by them a "chapel" because it is not for the general use of parishioners and is a private place for the friars' use only. Hence, it is "less than a church,"[86] because it is part of the whole. It is possible that the early combined use of a roofed and walled sanctuary and altar area by friars for their private services *and* by Native parishioners as part of their church is responsible for the persistence of the term *capilla* (chapel), or *capilla mayor* in Yucatan, to describe what came to function as the "business end" of the local church. McAndrew defines the *capilla mayor* as "liturgically the principal part of the church, the space for officiating clergy and altar, usually the same as the chancel or presbytery."[87] It is conceivable that the circumstances of early church history in Mexico and Yucatan are partly responsible for the error made, not by those in the sixteenth century, who knew the function of a chapel, but by modern scholars in referring to indigenous places of worship as "chapels."

I say "partly" because, as the chapel and the space for the nave became incorporated into larger construction efforts, and as the Spanish or non-Indian population increased, the idea that the space established for worship by the Indians was "less than a church" may have been reinforced. If archaeologists' attention, however, is properly to be focused on the effects of contact and conquest, it is critical to recognize and acknowledge such prejudices—not perpetuate them.

Does Size Matter?

If size mattered, one could argue that the "open chapels" were correctly labeled, because they were smaller than the monastery churches, although they could on occasion, according to McAndrew, be more elaborate or even more spacious than the neighboring monastery churches.[88] But small size is a qualifier only if one considers the stone-built *capilla* or *capilla mayor* to stand for the whole, when in fact it is only a part. The Maya congregation stood in the atrio which the *capilla* bordered. A thatch-roofed structure almost certainly served to shelter the congregation in the atrio in tropical zones, and even in Mexico people were not expected to stand in the open under "endless local drizzle."[89] Where they stood, however, was nevertheless part of what should have been considered, but for the absence of stone, to be a church. Indeed, sixteenth-century chroniclers, as practicing Christians, applied the term *iglesia* (sometimes spelled *yglesia*) not only to atrios in Mexico, as noted above, but to open-air chapels in Yucatan.[90]

McAndrew realizes this predicament and attempts to explain it.[91] Part of the rationale seems to be cultural bias against considering the atrio space, even when it was covered by thatch, as an element of the actual structure of worship. Masses were traditionally celebrated indoors in Christian practice, at first in houses, later in structures built as community or meeting houses, and ultimately in formal churches;[92] there came to be agreement that the church should be a permanent or durable structure. Owing to the Christian bias toward structural durability, McAndrew surmises that Masses said in atrios could never be considered to have taken place in churches, in the traditional sense.

> It [the atrio] cannot have been formally consecrated or dedicated, instead it probably was merely blessed, as chapels or private oratories were, though possibly it was not formally sanctified at all, any more than would be the space where an outdoor Mass for an army or hunting party might be said. Even today Canon Law makes no provision for temporary churches, and when the first atrio began to serve for Masses it may well have been viewed as a temporary makeshift. Its unconsecrated status could have persisted after the atrio had become virtually a permanent church.[93]

McAndrew appears here to be building a case on the basis of no evidence. Given the dedication the religious had toward indigenous Christians, and the general liturgical rules of the church, it is highly unlikely that where Nahuas or Maya or Otomi worshipped would not have been at least blessed, and certainly consecrated, if worship utilizing atrios, with their "open chapels," or *capillas*, continued for any length of time. If in their early years of use, however, the stone-built altar ends of churches were blessed rather than consecrated, in the manner of private oratories or chapels,[94] this might have encouraged the later use of the terms *capilla* or *capilla mayor* to refer to them.

Given the definition of *capilla mayor* as "the space for officiating clergy and altar, usually the same as the chancel or presbytery,"[95] incorporation of the term "chapel" in the terminology makes sense, especially if one takes into account that in churches that were to serve a community of friars as well as Indians, there were days when Mass was said with no congregation. Therefore, the stone-built altar ends of churches in these cases—and perhaps wherever *capilla* was the term used by the friars—indeed served as a chapel for a small audience, in addition to being part of a church. The audience in this case would have comprised friars or other clergy, and they would have sat in the space between the nave and the altar.

McAndrew claims that beyond the earliest days when some sorts of temporary structures were needed to get started, neither in Mexico nor in Yucatan (he does not mention Belize) did the friars use the chapels associated with atrios (his "open chapels") for their conventual Masses or for the reciting and chanting of their prescribed offices.[96] In Mesoamerica, however, where Christianity was brand new, the earliest days may have structured all that followed, and a good argument can be made, I believe, that the terminology employed in the initial stages of Christianization remained in use.

If I have offered a reasonable hypothesis for the continued use of *capilla*, or chapel, in a situation where it refers to a structural element that is clearly part of a church, the problem remains that the term "open" covers a lot of territory. The larger open-air chapels in Mexico almost look like mosques in plan,[97] with three walled sides, leaving one columned side partly open.[98] No examples of this particular form are known in Yucatan or Belize. What McAndrew illustrates as the typical Yucatecan "open" chapel is the stone-built east end of a space that functioned as a church. (The elements of such an open chapel are similar to the stone-built chapel with sacristy and baptistery at Lamanai, and similar to a number of rural structures in northern Yucatán and Quintana Roo illustrated by Andrews.[99]) McAndrew's "typical open chapels" were parts of monasteries, and the stone chapels bordered atrios (see fig. 7.8). In rural Yucatan, what Andrews called "open and closed ramada churches" are freestanding and are not part of monasteries.[100]

Artigas has devised a five-part typology of a subgroup of open chapels (*capillas abiertas*) that includes the kinds of structures found in Yucatan and Belize (the stone-built *capillas* with their adjacent rooms), which he calls *capillas abiertas aisladas*, or open chapels that are isolated or free-standing.[101] He makes the point that *aisladas* is an appropriate term because the structures antedated *iglesias techadas*, or roofed churches.[102] However, the *capillas abiertas* are only *aisladas* if one focuses on form rather than function, or on material rather than purpose. Whether people stood or sat or knelt in a space that was covered or uncovered makes no difference in terms of the function of the overall structure, which served without any doubt as a church, or iglesia. That only one end of the church was built of stone does not make the chapel functionally isolated. Although the stone end could have been used by the friars for their own private use as a chapel, a church is a church is a church.

No Unifying Criterion

According to Andrews,[103] McAndrew's unifying criterion for the open chapel designation is the presence of a thatched roof over a nave. But this would be a criterion for an open *church*, not a chapel, and even then, usage is inconsistent. Based on my reading of McAndrew, if one tried to find a common thread among open churches, it would involve a situation in which a Mass was being said in, or at one side of, an atrio, or forecourt, where people could spill out into the atrio if the covered or protected sanctuary space (the chapel) was not large enough for the congregation. McAndrew also conceived of ramadas as being temporary or impromptu, hastily constructed to provide some protection from the sun; this does not, however, apply in the Maya area, where thatched structures were carefully constructed and were intended to last. Thus, although McAndrew's concept of an open-air church holds up for central Mexico in the early years of the Conquest period, his and others' use of the term "open chapel" has given rise to confusion because identifiers that originated in the past to reflect functions, such as "chapel" and "church," have been tethered to size and construction material.

Andrews recognizes that applying what has been taken to be McAndrew's definition of an "open chapel" to the religious structures at Mani, Calkini, and Ecab is problematic, owing partly to these structures' large size.[104] At Ecab there existed a thatch-roofed, walled, and enclosed space (fig. 7.3);[105] therefore the structure cannot be called "open." Clearly, the builders had some idea of the size of the community, and in the Ecab case people could not spill out of the nave without missing direct participation in the Mass. There is a large platform that could have served as an atrio in the structure's earliest manifestation, and in this sense it could have been "open" at one phase in its history, with the stone chapel and its sacristy and baptistery rooms being the first architectural element, where the friars would have carried out their own rites. This is another case in which the source of the structure's "chapel" (*capilla*) designation in the eyes of the Spaniards might reflect its history rather than an attempt to conform to an architectural type. Finally, if the religious structure served the community of Ecab, then it was, as Andrews clearly implies, a church and not a chapel.

The Spanish Sources Were Right

Andrews goes on to say that the Spaniards were inconsistent in labeling religious structures: "The massive ramada structures that abutted the sixteenth-century convents of Maní and Calkiní were known as *capillas de indios*, while many rural structures (such as those of Ecab, Polé [Xcaret], and Lamanai) were often referred to as '*yglesias*.'"[106] This labeling is perfectly in keeping with the Spanish world. The structures in which the Maya worshipped at Mani and Calkini were parts of monasteries of which convents were the residential portions. Therefore, the criteria would be much as I have described above for central Mexico, in which the native focus of worship is designated a *capilla* partly because it incorporates an element which could have served as a chapel for the friars in the early stages of the planned community, and partly because this element of stone is the (Indian) church's outstanding feature, but also because a real (stone) church was envisaged for the use of non-Maya as part of the ideal plan. Referring to the spaces in which the Maya worshipped at Mani and Calkini as "chapels" or *capillas de indios* is consistent with the practice established earlier in Mexico, despite the fact that a monastery or other church might never have been built. (There is also Kubler's option, which is that *capilla de indios* reflects a reference to an Indian organization rather than to something material.)

The Ecab, Xcaret, and Lamanai structures are indeed iglesias, or churches, from the Spanish point of view, because they were built to serve the entire community of Maya with no expectation of a Spanish population of any size. It therefore follows that Bretos's two formal categories[107] of *capillas de indios* and *capillas de visita* are inappropriate. The first has some validity because it was in use in colonial times,[108] but it was nonetheless rooted in prejudice; if *capilla* is to be used at all as a type, perhaps *capilla de atrio* is better. As for the second, the *visita* structures are by definition churches, because they were intended as places of worship for the entire community.

Putting Typologies Aside

This brings me to the remaining categories suggested by Andrews.[109] It is not in keeping with past or present church practice to label small structures "chapels" and larger ones "churches." Whether a building is a chapel or a church depends on its function rather than its size, even though size can sometimes reflect function.

The term "ramada" seems best applied to the type of structure described by Andrews[110] as one in which the sanctuary, chancel, and nave form a continuous space under a single thatched roof; if the space between the chancel and the nave is divided in some way by a wall or a rail, and the space is therefore not continuous, the fact that a single thatched roof covers everything seems in keeping with the definition. However, whether the structure is defined as a ramada church or a ramada chapel should reflect its known function. Ramada chapels were ephemeral, and likely built only in the very earliest days of contact for use of the friars during evangelization. In Belize, the first religious structures (of which we have evidence) built for community worship at both Tipu and Lamanai were ramada churches.

Churches such as the second church at Lamanai, the one Jones describes at Bacalar,[111] and the church at Ecab seem to be alike. They all have a stone-built element or *capilla*/chapel that comprises the sanctuary, with space for officiating clergy, a sacristy, and a baptistery, but unless they fit McAndrew's criterion of allowing the congregation to spill out into a walled atrio or forecourt with no thatched nave, they are not "open." There is also the problem I noted earlier of detecting archaeologically whether the nave had walls or not, which means that the standardized reconstruction of an open ramada church in Roys[112] cannot be confirmed archaeologically unless one takes negative evidence as unequivocally indicating absence. Also, only the nave is thatched in these cases; the *capillas*/chapels (sanctuary, sacristy, baptistery, chancel, choir) are either roofed with beams and mortar or vaulted. Calling these churches "ramada" implies that the entire interior space was roofed with thatch, which is misleading.

In the case of churches in Belize, and probably elsewhere where there is a long rainy season, it is highly unlikely that buildings would have been completely open-sided. If the second church at Lamanai had a thatched nave with open sides, as has been shown in the reconstruction of the Dzibilchaltun structure (fig. 7.5),[113] people could have attended Mass only in the dry season, or only when the daily winds off the lagoon abated. During the rainy season from May through January, the winds off the lagoon would have driven the rain right through the nave.

Given the problems outlined, I have not attempted in the chapters that follow to fit the excavated churches into an existing typology, although I describe their features. The original impetus behind my reassessment of terms and categories stemmed from an attempt to sort out what to call the Lamanai and Tipu churches, based on prior typologies. My conclusion is that the typologies as they stand are problematic; they do not aid in our understanding of building function or even form. The term "open" can perhaps be retained informally as an adjective in describing space, but it should not be used to designate a type. It is not even clear that Toussaint[114] intended "open" to constitute a type. Form is important to archaeologists because, as I have noted, it is often all that we have to go on, and we therefore operate on the assumption that form is an indicator of function. In the case of the "open chapel," however, we have allowed use of a formal typological designation to cloud critical issues, not least of which is how to tell a church. For those interested in the dynamics of the sixteenth-century colonial encounter, particularly in Yucatan and Belize, how to tell a church is a primary concern.

✤ **EIGHT** ✤

The Churches at Tipu
and Lamanai

The ruins of colonial Tipu lie on the west bank of the Macal River in central
Belize. Lamanai, in northern Belize, is on the north shore of the New River
Lagoon near the point where the lagoon narrows to form the upper reaches of
the New River (maps 2.3, 5.8). Both communities were a focus of conversion
and conquest activity in the early Spanish colonial period. In this chapter, I
present the results of the archaeological excavations of the churches at Tipu
and Lamanai, and I discuss these results against the backdrop provided by the
documentary record.

The Excavations

ARCHAEOLOGY AT TIPU

In 1983 I assumed the direction of archaeological excavations at a place called
Negroman, on the Macal River in the Cayo District of Belize, Central America. The upper reaches of the Macal drain the western flanks of the Maya
Mountains, but the river then flows northward to join the Belize River at San
Ignacio, the capital of the Cayo District. "Negroman" is the local name for an
area that lies on the west bank of the Macal at a bend where the river's direction changes slightly from north to northeast, about 10 kilometers south of
the confluence of the Macal with the Belize. The east side of the river, across
from Negroman, is called "Macaw Bank."

At the time of writing, Negroman is known in Belize as the site of one of
the Espat family farms. Although by the 1990s much of the area had been
planted in papaya, in the 1980s the farm had been cleared for cattle pasture.
In that period, pasture dominated the perennially dry second river terrace,

and as one descended to the river, where the ground was subjected to annual floods, pasture gave way to secondary bush and to river banks bordered by bullet trees (*Bucida buceras* L.). The river's waters, then and now, are clear and fast-moving. Crocodiles sun themselves in bends upriver, where the force of the water is slowed by sand bars or vegetation. Where we used to approach the river, there was a conveniently wide and shady spot for bathing or washing clothes. The river itself drains metamorphic and igneous rocks and then flows through limestone, with the result that its waters have a close to neutral pH and leave no detectable residues of lime or iron or any other minerals on skin or hair or clothes. From this vantage, Negroman is a choice spot in which to manage a household.[1]

"Tipu," or "Tipuj," is a rendering, based on the colonial documents, of the Maya name for a town that thrived at this locale in the sixteenth and seventeenth centuries, and probably for many years before.[2] We know that the town was called "Tipu" because Grant Jones had for many years explored archives of documents pertaining to the Spanish invasion of Mesoamerica. Although documents on Spanish activities in Mexico and Guatemala far outnumber those on Belize, Jones was particularly interested in the role of the wider area of which Belize was a part, what he has called the southern Maya frontier.[3] He followed the lead of Sir J. Eric S. Thompson,[4] the well known British Mayanist who, in addition to his research in epigraphy and archaeology, searched colonial documents for information on the Spanish presence in Belize. Thompson had used references in the documents to narrow down the location of an early Spanish-period church to a community once located at the bend in the Macal, but which side? Was it Negroman, or Macaw Bank? Thompson thought it was probably Macaw Bank, but in 1978 Jones and the archaeologist David Pendergast visited the area to see if they could provide an answer to the question. Apart from the more obvious mounds that represented pre-Columbian structures, they detected a zone of distinctive, undulating relief in one of the cattle pastures at Negroman that hinted at the presence of the ruins of a long-abandoned community that could be colonial Tipu.

The first investigations at Negroman-Tipu, from 1980 to 1982, were directed by Robert Kautz and Grant Jones with the assistance of Claude Belanger. Belanger was responsible for architectural recording and mapping at Tipu, and he also played a substantial role at Lamanai in the excavation and recording of historic buildings. His involvement at both sites, and indeed my involvement at both sites, and the nature of cooperation between Pendergast and Jones has facilitated the sharing of information, with the result that what we are able to say about the elusive Spanish colonial experience in Belize has, we hope, been enhanced.

Only pre-Columbian structures were encountered when Kautz, Jones, and

Belanger began work at Negroman. At the end of the season in 1980 Jones suggested they take a look at an innocuous low mound that was distinguished by a clear east-west orientation. Jones undertook a bit of troweling, and revealed what would turn out to be the steps leading to the sanctuary of a church. Test pits eventually exposed burials associated with the Christian mission church (fig. 8.1).[5] Mark Cohen of the State University of New York at Plattsburgh and his students undertook research and excavation focused specifically on these burials.

The second phase of investigations at Negroman-Tipu began under my direction in 1984;[6] no excavations were carried out in 1985, but fieldwork continued in 1986 and 1987. Cohen and his team directed the excavation of the burials in and around the church, which numbered 604; of these, 585 were colonial,[7] and 19 were Postclassic. I focused on the structures that we had identified as part of the historic-period community center, although we also carried out excavations of church standing walls, collapse debris, sacristy, altar area, and nave features. Publications and reporting include results of the excavations;[8] human skeletal indicators of health and genetics;[9] dietary studies from faunal remains;[10] analysis of various classes of artifacts;[11] and the methods of conjoining archaeology and ethnohistory.[12]

Figure 8.1. Tipu, excavated remains of the church. Photo looks northeast. The altar is at the east end, and the plaster floor of the sacristy can be seen just to the right of the tree. (Photo by Robert Kautz)

Known throughout Belize as "Indian Church," at least since the 1860s,[13] Lamanai is located in northern Belize, on the western shore of the New River Lagoon (maps 2.3, 5.8). It sits just at the point where the lagoon's north end narrows to form the headwaters of the New River, which wends its way slowly from the lagoon northward to Chetumal Bay. "Lamanay ó Lamayná" appears in Lopez de Cogolludo's history of Yucatan,[14] and "Lamanay" is the spelling used in most seventeenth-century and early eighteenth-century maps (maps 5.5, 5.6, 5.9).[15] In most cases, Lamanay is shown as an island. The exceptions of which I am aware are the Blaeu map (map 5.6),[16] in which Lamanay is on the mainland, and the map by van DeCust in Loots's *Sea-Mirrour*, in which Lamanay is both an island and a place on the mainland directly across from the island.[17]

Thompson[18] proposed "Laman/ai," based on his reading of the word as "drowned insect," and this is the spelling now enshrined in the literature. "Lamanai" does appear, however, in Dudley's "Carta Prima Generale" of 1646–47 (map 5.4). More recently, the various renditions of the site name have been suggested to reflect a corruption of what the Spaniards first heard as the Maya name for the site—Lama'an/ayin—which has been proposed as meaning "submerged crocodile."[19]

Excavations at Lamanai were initiated by David Pendergast in 1974 and continued until 1986, with the result that Maya occupation was demonstrated to have extended from as early as 1500 B.C. to the Spanish and British colonial periods.[20] In 1998, I initiated a second phase of investigation, which continues to build upon earlier work.[21] Like Tipu, Lamanai boasts a substantial colonial component; in fact, two Spanish colonial-period churches were excavated at Lamanai, designated YDL (Yglesia de Lamanai) I and YDL II (figs. 8.2, 7.2). The substantial size of YDL II suggests that Lamanai was of considerable importance as a center for Christianized Maya in Belize in the sixteenth and early seventeenth centuries.[22]

TIPU AND LAMANAI

Both Tipu and Lamanai periodically served as congregation or reduction centers—*congregación* or *reducción* in Spanish administrative parlance.[23] These centers were designated towns or villages into which the Maya from surrounding communities, each with its extended and scattered landholdings,[24] were brought, to facilitate both their monitoring as new Christians and their integration into the tribute system. It is probably owing to the fact that Tipu and Lamanai were reduction centers that we know anything about them at all,

Figure 8.2. Lamanai, YDL I, looking southeast. The altar and sanctuary are at the east end (top left of photo). The platform of the razed Tulum-like structure, just below the steps leading to the sanctuary, has been cleared, but it was originally buried beneath the floor of the nave during church construction.

because reduction centers would have generated documentation and record-keeping critical in the early years of Spanish colonial administration.

Archaeology at Tipu and Lamanai has contributed information on colonial conditions, particularly with regard to architecture, community layout, and material culture.[25] Pottery vessels, figurines, censers, stelae, caches,[26] burial accompaniments, and buildings all reflect a process by which community members were attempting to maintain control over their natural and spiritual lives at the same time that they were adjusting to rapidly changing conditions. In this light, the contexts of archaeological discoveries and the artifacts associated with the churches are particularly revealing. Because pictures were used by the friars to facilitate conversion, pre-Columbian imagery and its post-Columbian contexts are as important in understanding the conversion process as is Spanish catechizing.

The Spanish colonial encounter cannot always and everywhere be enriched by archaeology, however, and there are currents of change that affected the environment of conquest and conversion which are known only through the documents.[27] Because the colonial experience in Belize as seen through the documents has been detailed elsewhere by Jones,[28] I try in this context to bring together information that is relevant to Tipu and Lamanai in particular, with an eye to emphasizing events, people, and processes that illuminate the encounter with Christianity.

The Belize Missions

Jones has observed that the archaeological and historical records are so different that each requires its own reflections before complete integration can be achieved.[29] I would go so far as to say that integration will always be problematic and incomplete because, although we use the term "record" for both ethnohistory and archaeology, what constitutes the ethnohistorical record is not directly comparable to, or necessarily compatible with, what constitutes the archaeological record. What people say happened could turn out to be only one version of events, or may not have happened at all, and what we know from archaeological remains is based on inference.[30] Nonetheless, attempting to make sense of what we think we know from archaeology and ethnohistory is a critical exercise because it stimulates us to ask better questions, even if we do not always get answers. It can throw inconsistencies into high relief, suggest alternative explanations, and point to the direction in which research should be headed.

With regard to ethnohistory, Jones's work has entailed study of documents written in Spanish by Spanish colonial authorities, and to this extent he follows in the footsteps of scholars who have studied Spanish documents in an attempt to understand Maya-Spanish interaction in Yucatan, such as Scholes, Menéndez, Mañé, Adams, Chamberlain, J. Eric S. Thompson, Roys, García Bernal, Hunt, Clendinnen, and Farriss.[31] Restall[32] makes the point that another perspective is to be found in indigenous-language sources. He draws attention to a recently strengthening current of scholarship, traced back to Roys,[33] that takes into account Maya native-language documentation and the idea that there exist intellectual ties between the language of pre- and post-conquest texts (e.g., the work of Bricker, Burns, Christenson, Edmonson, Hanks, Okoshi, Philip Thompson, and Restall himself).[34] To date, no Maya-language documentation from the Belize missions has been discovered, although the requirement of yearly visits to Mérida to confirm administrative posts, and the fact that the Maya were clearly familiar and comfortable with a system in which written documentation figured importantly in socio-political affairs, both suggest strongly that such documentation was indeed generated.

Research such as Restall's,[35] although focused on northern Yucatan, has been instrumental in widening our perception of the possible range of activities in which the Belize Maya engaged, and in encouraging us to recognize the potential of the Maya in Belize for meeting the Spanish legal and administrative system head-on and using it to their advantage. Admittedly, flight-as-resistance, rather than use of the legal system as resistance, is the first thing that comes to mind when Belize villages and towns under Spanish rule are considered, simply because towns with any significant number of Spanish settlers did not exist in Belize,[36] and forested terrain provided safe haven. However, aspects of Jones's descriptions of villages and towns that were contacted more than once and then reduced with little outward resistance, at least in the decades before 1638 and after about 1650, suggest that the Maya, even in remote Belize, had a good understanding of Spanish administrative behavior, and used this knowledge to work with rather than always against Spanish dicta. How much of this hypothesized engagement made its way to Mérida as petitions to authority is not completely known, but Jones's analysis paints a picture of a highly dynamic, proactive region, and Restall emphasizes that population numbers in Yucatan were in the Mayas' favor.[37]

One extension of this dynamic is that we should be careful not to see the modern Belize national boundary as having been a boundary to the Maya in the past. Families and individuals in Yucatan used centuries-old paths, which crisscrossed the peninsula, to flee from tribute burdens in towns, and many of these paths led to Belize. Much of my interpretation of events rests on the assumption, detailed in chapter 5, that effective and even intensive communication along indigenous networks that connected Belize and Yucatan provided the Maya with information that became a good basis for action.

BELIZE THEN AND NOW

The Spanish colonial history of the Belize missions, including Tipu and Lamanai, can be said to extend from about 1543–44 to 1707, although mission towns were established, and apparently soon abandoned, in southern Belize as late as 1724.[38] The *villa* of Bacalar, little more than a hamlet, was the last outpost of Spanish settlers one would encounter en route from Mérida to Maya settlements such as Lamanai and Tipu in Belize. Bacalar's life as a thriving settlement during this period was short,[39] but it nonetheless remained in the Spanish sphere, whereas the lands to the south of it did not.

The northern part of the peninsula, north of Belize, grades to subtropical conditions and is drier than the humid lowlands of Belize or the Guatemalan Peten. Therefore, Yucatan (the modern Mexican states of Yucatán, Quintana Roo, and Campeche [see map 1.1]) attracted Spanish settlers, whereas Belize did not. No skeletons of Spanish individuals have been found in the excavated colonial cemeteries at Tipu and Lamanai (585 individuals at Tipu,[40] and about 243 at Lamanai); and Spanish artifacts, although important, form a very small percentage of the totals recovered.

Owing to the presence of Spanish settlers, Yucatan was administered more intensively than Belize. On the other hand, compared to highland regions, Mayas greatly outnumbered Spaniards in Yucatan (even without including Belize and the frontier) until as late as the late eighteenth century.[41] Maya-Spanish relations therefore took a distinctive turn in Yucatan that surely influenced the course of Maya-Spanish relations in Belize. Spanish settlers in Yucatan wanted a system that worked; their interest was profit, but at the same time, they recognized that they were outnumbered and were completely dependent on the people who outnumbered them as regards human resources. Hence, as long as the system functioned and they received tribute and taxes, they were not interested in interfering with Maya politics or with how the Maya ran their lives.[42]

Overall, we can probably say that such a situation allowed the Maya a degree of autonomy in Yucatan and Belize that did not exist in areas of denser Spanish populations and intensive Spanish economic interest. This autonomy, or semi-autonomy, probably contributed to the fact that the Maya in Belize were able to develop and to capitalize on new kinds of long-distance trade between the zones with minimal to no Spanish resident population (such as Belize, the Peten lakes, and southern Campeche, which nevertheless produced items in demand by the Spaniards) and the more populated towns of northern Yucatan.[43] Such trade in Belize centered on riverine towns which, like Lamanai and Tipu,[44] offered not only refuge from excessive tribute and taxation but also new economic opportunities.[45]

The Southern Maya Frontier

Jones includes Belize in a zone he calls the southern Maya frontier. By this he means land and people that lie beyond direct interaction with the dominant society,[46] and in this case, the dominant society was the colonial administration based in Yucatan. The quality of remoteness possessed by the frontier—or at least what was "remote" to the Spanish world—will be seen to have served the Maya well. Spanish authorities did not find it easy or pleasant to penetrate the southern forests. Only the Franciscans seem to have taken such hardships in their stride, but they simply lacked the numbers to maintain a significant presence in Belize. How many of the Maya fleeing Yucatan actually made their way to Belize is not known, but accounts suggest that economic oppression was the stimulus to flight.[47]

Paying tribute was not new to the Maya, nor were they unfamiliar with a world in which people worshiped in different ways. Providing tribute to Spanish overlords whose attention focused on a deity that was new to the Maya world replaced supplying tribute to the overlords of the past, who could have been either local or foreign.[48] Although attempts to obtain tribute-exempt or tax-exempt status perpetuated economic differences among elites,[49] one difference from the past was that the uppermost strata could no longer jockey for positions and power at the top by intermarriage or negotiation or warfare. The Maya were now excluded from the ruling stratum simply because they were non-Spaniards. The other difference—which in fact may not have been all that different—was that it often became difficult to meet Spanish tribute or other tax demands. In some cases, the Maya found that they could not feed themselves or their families,[50] and it was in these cases that individuals often chose simply to pick up and move to a place where it would be difficult for the authorities to find them.

Despite the increasing remoteness of communities in Belize, the Spaniards made efforts to maintain contact, even in the difficult years after a series of rebellions took place in 1638–41.[51] Belize communities had been subject to encomenderos since as early as 1544,[52] and even though the sizes and make-up of encomiendas changed, tribute had nonetheless to be collected. In addition, as part of the colonization effort, the Belize Christians had to be visited and ministered to. The archaeological remains—ordered communities, churches, buildings that incorporated non-Maya layouts, established cemeteries, practices consonant with Christian ritual, however superficial—suggest strongly that either Spanish priests and encomenderos (or their agents) visited Lamanai and Tipu regularly, or if they visited less than regularly, then the initial efforts expended in obtaining tribute commitments by encomenderos (or their agents, backed by soldiers?) and in proselytizing, almost certainly by Franciscans, must have been considerable.

For the Maya, paying tribute did not constitute a change from pre-Columbian practice; change instead took the form of paying different people different things in different amounts, and according to new rules. Cotton was high on tribute lists in both pre- and post-Columbian times, as were honey, salt, beeswax, maize and cacao.[53] Jade, shell, salted or dried fish, ground stone, chert, obsidian, slate-backed mirrors, pre-Columbian religious icons, and other items not valued by Europeans were not part of tribute payments, although some of these items continued to be exchanged among Maya communities.[54] Because the concept of regular tribute was not new, Maya communities adjusted by accepting a shift in overlords as part of a process rooted in their pre-Columbian experience. Christianity, however, is normally seen to be foreign to pre-Columbian experience, which makes the persistence of Christianity in the face of irregular visits by the religious harder to explain.

As I commented in early chapters, some have argued that Christianity was simply a veneer, but when preaching and participation are aimed at children, a practice to which the Franciscans directed their principal efforts,[55] the world changes for the children and there is no such thing as veneer, except to an outside analyst. Proselytization was highly successful because (1) the Maya were open to new ideas about the spiritual world because there was precedent for openness in their pre-Columbian past; and (2) the incorporation of pre-Christian practices did not make them less Christian, because this is what Christianity has always been about. If one looks closely at the history of Christianity elsewhere, syncretism *is* Christianity. Put another way, the new Christians saw nuances in Christianity because they were faced with choices; the old Christians could not look at what they believed as other than a complete, take-it-or-leave-it package.

Rethinking Christianity and syncretism is a topic taken up in other chapters; at this juncture, it is important simply to emphasize that Belize at this time was a region of contradiction. The greater or denser expanses of "bush," or forest,[56] than existed in Yucatan permitted the Maya relative freedom of movement. Yet given frontier conditions and the difficulties Europeans had (and still have) in adjusting to the heat, humidity, vegetation, and insects of the tropical lowlands, the Spaniards were surprisingly effective in maintaining any sorts of networks in these areas at all. Jones's account of various entradas presents a picture of people readily setting off from Bacalar to Tipu, a journey that even today would be arduous. Thus, the story of the frontier that became Belize remains an enigma. The archaeological data presented here do not simplify the story, but the phenomenon of growing complexity probably brings us closer to truth.

Dzuluinicob

Tipu and Lamanai were part of a region referred to by Jones as "Dzuluinicob."[57] Dzuluinicob was the pre-Columbian name for the New River (map 2.3), and translates as "foreign people."[58] Basing his interpretation on a reference in a document written between 1570 and 1571, Jones sees Dzuluinicob as a pre-Columbian provincial entity, and he includes in Dzuluinicob the territory from the Sittee River north to the lower New River (map 2.1.d), at the head of which Lamanai is situated. Thus, he sees both Lamanai and Tipu as part of this pre-Columbian province, with Tipu serving as its political center in Spanish colonial times.

Based on the archaeological evidence alone, it is difficult to envisage Tipu and Lamanai as belonging to the same geopolitical pre-Conquest unit, particularly one that was territorially defined. Following the arrival of Europeans in the New World in 1492, however, it is possible that the disruption caused by the Spaniards and other Europeans in Central America and central Mexico, and the flight from the coasts generated by the raids of buccaneers and other seafarers in the Caribbean Basin, may have combined to create conditions in which Tipu and Lamanai, and indeed many Belize communities, were drawn together and became more intimately connected than they had been in the past. Hence, the two communities may have become part of an effectively integrated region following the Uaymil-Chetumal-Belize conquest in 1544. In any case, I retain "Dzuluinicob" to refer to a region that subsumes Tipu and Lamanai in the colonial period, with the caveat that the existence of well-developed, supra-community, pre-Conquest units based on delimited territory is open to question.[59]

The year 1544 marked the first encomiendas, or tribute-paying regions, as inferred from Spanish records.[60] About twenty-five towns in Belize are named in colonial documents,[61] but the locations of only five are supported to varying degrees by archaeological evidence: Chanlacan,[62] Chetumal, Colmotz, Lamanai, and Tipu[63] (map 2.3).

Archaeologists at the site of Santa Rita Corozal uncovered remains that date to as late as A.D. 1532, and they have proposed Santa Rita as the site of ancient Chetumal.[64] Colmotz is described in the documents as being at the south end of the New River Lagoon. The east bank location suggested by Scholes and Thompson[65] is extremely unlikely because the land on the entire eastern side of the lagoon is characterized by poorly drained soils of the savanna, or, as savanna is known in Belize, "pine ridge." However the west bank, known as Hill Bank, once served as the headquarters for the Belize Estate and Produce Company. Construction operations in the late 1970s by the manager, Martin Meadows, yielded a sherd of Spanish pottery and several pieces of distinctive stonework which strongly suggested Spanish colonial origin.[66] I have therefore located Colmotz at Hill Bank on the map (map 2.3). This leaves us with Lamanai and Tipu as the only sites that have revealed the presence of mission churches and their associated communities.

The Towns of Tipu and Lamanai

The town of Tipu (fig. 1.1) was the last of a string of visita missions extending south-southwest from the *villa* of Bacalar.[67] Lamanai, at the north end of the New River Lagoon (map 2.3), is relatively close to Bacalar and was the first of the Belize missions to be identified archaeologically, owing to the presence of a stone *capilla*, or chapel (see chap. 6) that at one time formed part of a substantial church (fig. 7.2).[68] Lamanai's position at the headwaters of the New River probably made it a logical port for canoe traffic, and the documents confirm that Spanish authorities, both secular and religious, would often stop at Lamanai on the way southward to communities, such as Tipu, that lay along the upper Belize River. In getting to Tipu from Bacalar, a Franciscan friar would have to have covered about 200 kilometers, using river and overland routes.[69] Tipu, perhaps owing to the difficulties of such a journey, is distinguished by Jones[70] as never having been visited by anyone of importance in the Spanish colonial government.

Archaeologically, colonial Tipu seems smaller and less impressive than Lamanai—less impressive owing to the absence of a church with a stone chapel (fig. 8.1); smaller because historic-period ceramics occur in a number of scattered locales throughout the Lamanai settlement (maps 8.1, 8.2), whereas at Tipu, based on evidence to date, the historic ceramics are restricted to the

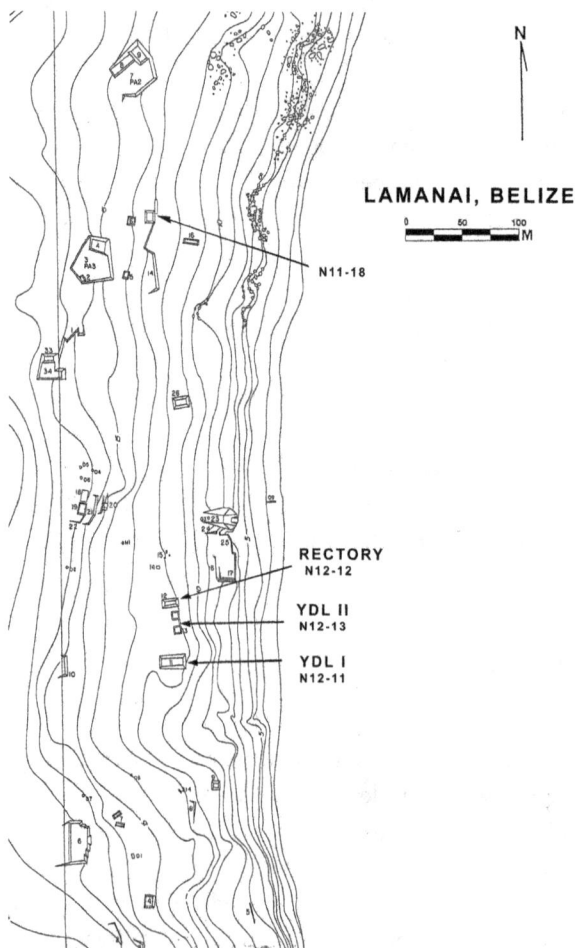

Map 8.1. Church zone, Lamanai, map square N12. Note that the platform at top left, PA3, is shown on the larger Lamanai map in the bottom right square, a continuation of map square N12. (Drawing by Claude Belanger and H. Stanley Loten)

Map 8.2. Map of Lamanai showing central and northern precincts.
(Drawing by H. Stanley Loten and Claude Belanger)

colonial site center. Only one historic-period plaza group was investigated at Tipu (map 8.3: Strs. H12-7, H12-8, H12-12, H12-13, H12-14, H12-18), albeit one that included the church (Str. H12-13), but it is likely that the remains of more structures surround or extend outward from the main plaza.[71] The burials that lay north of the church had been cut through cobblestone pavement, which suggests that Tipu's layout included more plazas than the one we excavated

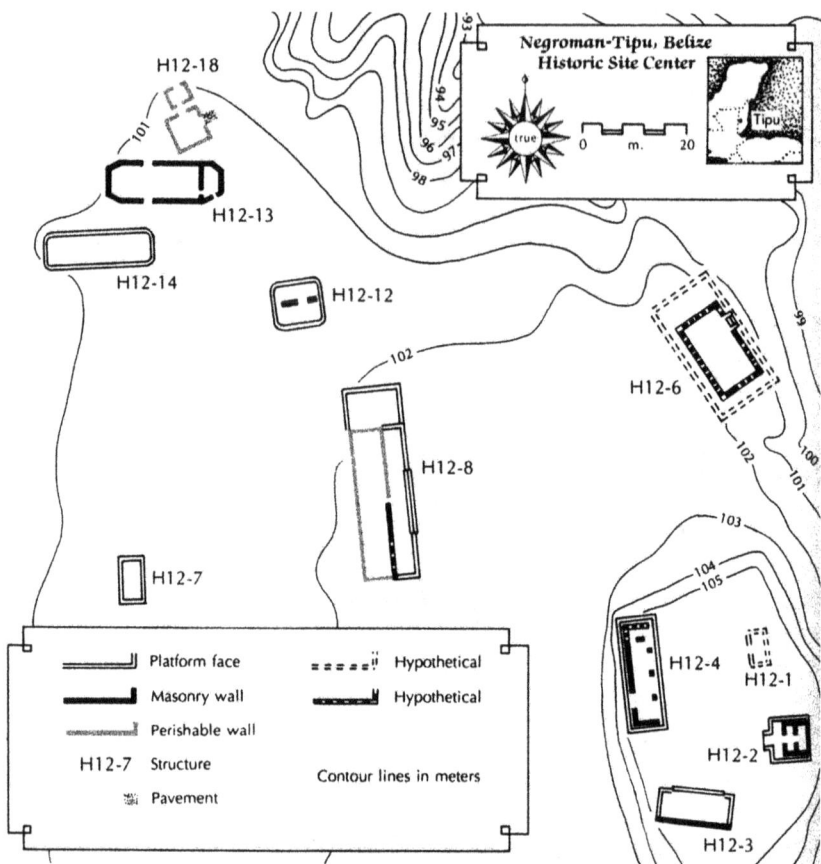

Map 8.3. Tipu town center during the Spanish colonial period (see also fig. 1.1.). Complex 1, the abandoned Postclassic ceremonial group, is represented by Strs. H12-1 to H12-4 in the lower right corner. (Map by Claude Belanger; drawing by Emil Huston)

on the south side of the church, and on which we focused the majority of our attention. At Lamanai, the impressive stone chapel of the second church (fig. 7.2), paralleled only at the *villa* of Bacalar,[72] suggests that the community boasted a population larger than that of Tipu.

Tipu's size apparently belies its former importance, because it is well documented in the ethnohistorical sources, whereas Lamanai is seldom mentioned.[73] However, the attention given to Tipu in the documents could simply reflect the vagaries of preservation. Or, as Jones argues, Tipu's position between the non-Christianized Maya communities of the Peten lakes and the successfully Christianized towns of Belize made it a strategic focus for Spanish authorities who were intent on extending Spanish rule and religion to Peten. As such, Tipu was as important strategically to the Itzas at Nohpeten (map 2.4) as it was to the Spaniards, and Tipuans adjusted their allegiances as the situation demanded.

Tipu's position also served to enhance its economic growth, owing in part to the freedom with which the Maya could control their own affairs, and in part to the success of what Jones has called its planter-traders.[74] Tipu was highly successful as a producer of fine-quality cacao, which was a major item of tribute in the colonial era, and its traders used well-established contacts with northern Yucatecan sources to acquire manufactured tools, such as machetes and knives, which were then sold to the Maya communities around the Peten lakes.[75] Lamanai's activities in colonial times are unclear from the documents, although the archaeological evidence suggests (as discussed below) that Lamanai interacted more intensively with the colonial realm than did Tipu, at least in the earlier years of contact and evangelization. The results of archaeological excavations, combined with the information described in chapter 6, also suggest that the main investment in evangelizing and ministering to communities in Belize took place at the early end of the colonial encounter, and probably primarily in the sixteenth century.

The Framework of Events

COMING TO TERMS WITH THE SPANISH PRESENCE

From 1544 until about 1553,[76] the Villa of Salamanca de Bacalar was home to Melchor and Alonso Pacheco, both of whom were listed as *alcaldes*. The records point to the existence of five encomiendas. By far the largest was held by Melchor Pacheco; four much smaller encomiendas seem to have been held by Alonso Pacheco and three *regidores* of the villa.[77] Of the encomiendas established in Belize at this time, only Chanlacan was identified by Jones with certainty, although Tipu and Lamanai are believed to have been among these early encomiendas, based on references in later documents. What is important is that the encomienda Maya towns of this early period were difficult to control. Those that were farther away from Bacalar, such as Tipu, could not be monitored, and those that were closer, such as Lamanai, were composed not only of local populations but also of those forcibly brought in as part of congregation efforts.[78]

Both flight and population loss characterized the years after 1544 in the Bacalar province, although the trend began as early as 1531, if not before. Most observations concerning population estimates before 1544 refer not to Belize (Dzuluinicob) specifically but more generally to Cochua, Uaymil, and Chetumal (map 5.1), which were described by Dávila (and his companion Alonso Luján in 1531 [see chap. 5]) as having many towns close to one another.[79] Bienvenida claimed that there had been towns of 500 to 1,000 houses, but that by 1548, a town of 100 houses would have been large. Jones estimates, based on information from the documents, that by 1582 the province of Salamanca de Bacalar had only about 856 Mayas, which seems incredibly low.[80] Although both Dávila and Bienvenida had traveled through Belize—Dávila southward along the coast and Bienvenida northward on his way from highland Guatemala to Bacalar—it is unclear whether their comments on dense populations included Belize towns, although there is no reason to think otherwise. It may also be true that the population was higher in 1582 than Jones's estimate, but that, given conditions in Belize, many Maya were living outside the tribute system.

What exactly was happening at Tipu in the years just after 1544 is unknown. Lamanai, being close to Bacalar and accessible via the New River from Chetumal Bay, may well have been accessed by encomenderos or their agents in Bacalar more frequently than Tipu; however, we simply do not know the details of Spanish-Maya interaction at Lamanai and Tipu at this time, other than that the two communities had probably become part of encomiendas and were supposed to be paying tribute to a Spaniard based in Bacalar. It is worth commenting that Jones's picture of Bacalar and its tributaries is so bleak[81] that it is hard to imagine as much went on at Lamanai and Tipu as is indicated by the archaeology.

The earlier church at Lamanai, YDL I (figs. 8.2, 8.3), which was identified originally as a pre-Columbian structure (see below),[82] may well have been built during or shortly after the 1544 Pacheco entrada.[83] The possibility exists that Bienvenida was responsible for its construction, as he is said to have evangelized on his journey from Guatemala through Belize to Mérida. This inference of an early construction date is based on two types of archaeological evidence: that the construction of YDL I reflects a learning process—trial and error between someone (a Franciscan?) overseeing the construction and the Maya doing the constructing[84]; and the fact that no sherds of Spanish pottery or any other European artifacts were recovered from the core of the church platform or its walls.[85]

Whether YDL I was built following the Pachecos' entrada or later, what we know from the documents is that rebellion broke out almost immediately in the eastern provinces of Yucatan in 1546, and in northern Belize in 1547 at Chanlacan (map 2.3), which had become a new gathering place for local Maya forces.[86] Despite the fact that the inhabitants of Chanlacan had killed their encomendero, the rebellion was said by Juan de Aguilar[87] in his *probanza* to have been peacefully quelled, with the help of people from Lamanai, in 1547.[88] Participation by the people of Lamanai leaves little doubt that the community had been among the earliest to be contacted, and was probably among the original encomiendas.

In 1568 Juan de Garzón led entradas into Cehach territory just north of Lake Peten Itza, through Belize to Tipu and its environs, and farther south into Manche Chol territory (map 5.1), after which the party returned to Bacalar via Lamanai.[89] In Cehach territory, a Maya priest was encountered who is described by Garzón as having led his people in returning to pre-Columbian religious practices; this same individual spoke Spanish and had been raised with friars[90] (probably in Mani[91]). From this we can infer that conversion efforts between 1544 and 1568, even in these remote regions, had been intensive, and that some boys had been taken either to Campeche or to Yucatan to be raised and taught by the Franciscans. At Tipu, Don Francisco Cumux, a *principal*, sent his sons to the schools run by the friars,[92] probably in Yucatan.[93]

Garzón apparently found many "idols" at Tipu. The reference to Tipu confirms that it was an established colonial town with existing *cabildos*, and it is the nature of this reference that led Jones to the conclusion that Tipu had been made part of an encomienda in 1544. In 1568, Mayas were congregated (reduced) by Garzón and his men at Tipu. The fact that Garzón chose Tipu as the reduction center suggests that the community was a place that had indeed been visited periodically by Spanish authorities and could therefore be monitored, despite its remoteness, more easily than other towns.

Franciscan friars accompanied Garzón's entradas,[94] and it may have been

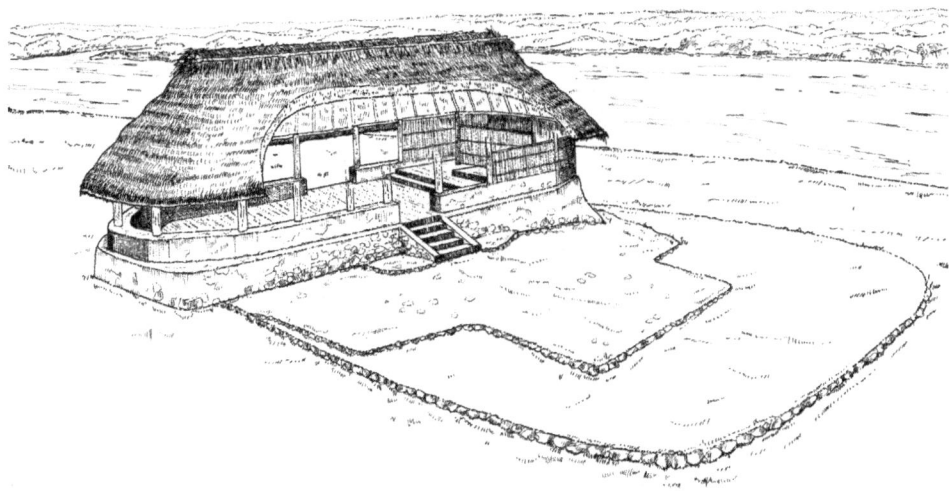

Figure 8.3. Lamanai, perspective reconstruction cutaway of YDL I, looking northeast. Shows church and atrio. Drawing by Claude Belanger and Louise Belanger.

on these occasions that major rebuilding and repair efforts took place. It is even possible that the second church at Lamanai (figs. 7.2, 8.4) was built at this time. In any case, the presence of Franciscans may explain the commonalities in construction techniques and plans of at least two of the houses—Str. H12-8 at Tipu (map 8.3) and Str. N11-18 at Lamanai (map 8.1, fig. 8.5)—as well as any work done on the churches. By this I mean that building efforts

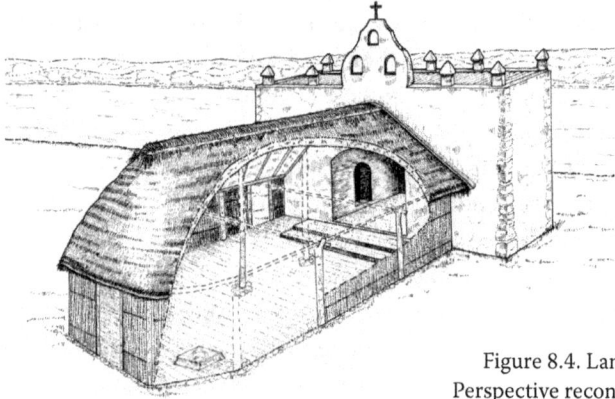

Figure 8.4. Lamanai, Perspective reconstruction cutaway of YDL II, looking northeast. (Drawing by Claude Belanger and Louise Belanger)

Figure 8.5. Lamanai, Str. N11-18, looking north.

are likely to have been monitored by Franciscans; it is not that the combination of European design and layout, local materials, and Maya construction practices and features[95] could not have occurred under seculars or Spanish civil authorities, but the similarities reflect a strategic and structural plan for the Maya communities, and generally it was the regular clergy who had these sorts of plans.[96]

One of the major tasks that occupied the Franciscans at Tipu and other Belize Maya towns in 1568 was the burning of books.[97] Chuchiak explains that this intolerance was a driving force in the proselytization of the Maya, whereas earlier, in central Mexico, preservation of aspects of native culture had been considered useful in understanding native thought.[98] The climate of the times, then, helps to explain the zeal with which the Franciscans working in Belize approached the extirpation of "idolatry."

GOOD CHRISTIANS: FROM 1568
UNTIL THE EARLY SEVENTEENTH CENTURY

Jones describes the period between 1568 and 1618 as a time when the Spaniards from Bacalar struggled to hold on to their encomienda villages and towns, which numbered only about twenty.[99] Because it took two months for a single priest to visit the communities in Belize, everyday religious care was placed in the hands of local Maya, who could be *maestros cantores* (choirmasters) or *maestros de capilla* (chapel masters) or simply *maestros*,[100] although the documents on Yucatan also mention the position of *sacristan mayor*. The *maestros* were individuals who taught catechism, acted as scribes, and could carry out rituals required for baptism and burial.[101] The sacristans looked after the vestments and ritual objects of the church. A *maestro de capilla* is mentioned at Tipu in 1618,[102] but it is likely that there were designated individuals who looked after the church and its contents as well.

Reductions centered on Tipu took place in 1608 and in 1615, with the result that encomienda restructuring had taken place by 1622.[103] No archaeological evidence can yet be tied to influxes of Spaniards in particular years, but the excavated evidence at Tipu argues for periodic construction of new houses as well as additions and alterations to previous ones, so that despite the intermittent Spanish attention, the community seems to have grown and to have maintained a colonial face. It is interesting that Jones[104] describes the period of the early seventeenth century as one in which Bacalar's control over its hinterland was nearing a state of collapse; by 1608, flight from the encomienda towns of the southern Bacalar province had increased, although this probably contributed to rather than detracted from Tipu's strength.

The Framework of Material Remains

Although we now know that YDL II (Str. N12-13) was the later church to have been built at Lamanai, it was the first to be discovered and excavated. The remains of YDL II and selected structures in or near the historic town center, most notably YDL I and the probable residence, Str. N11-18 (map 8.1, fig. 8.5), were excavated under Pendergast's direction at various times during the years from 1974 to 1986.[105] The ruins of the stone chapel of YDL II were well known throughout Belize and gave the site its name of "Indian Church."[106] It was this crumbling structure (fig. 7.2) that originally drew attention to the site, and on which excavations focused from 1974 to 1976.[107]

In 1985 a cemetery was discovered at Lamanai just east of YDL II.[108] (This was the second historic-period cemetery to be discovered, the first associated with YDL I, to be discussed below.) Only 13 burials were excavated, but the apparent limits of the cemetery suggest a large area—Pendergast estimates that there may be as many as 400 or more individuals (fig. 8.6).[109] The graves were dug into a platform that was situated in the gradually descending terrain between YDL II and the lagoon (see map 8.1).

Pendergast thinks that the graves may have been marked, because disturbance of earlier burials, in contrast with what we shall see was the case with the first church, was infrequent. When an earlier grave was disturbed, the bones were gathered together and set atop the newly interred body. Pendergast feels that a good case can be made for this second cemetery being contemporaneous with the use of YDL II.[110]

Beginning in 1998, I directed excavations in the hope of clarifying features of YDL II's plan and its relationship to the structure to its immediate north, Str. N12–12, which is believed to have served as the "rectory," or residence, for friars or secular clergy when they came to Lamanai to minister to the population (map 8.1, fig. 8.7). The results of the 1998 excavations suggested that a connection or passageway between YDL II and the rectory, which would have served the resident priest, lay just west of the northwest corner of the chapel (map 8.1, figs. 7.2, 8.8, 8.9). In 2007, clearing and excavation as part of the Belize Institute of Archaeology's program of consolidation of the churches at Lamanai resulted in clarification of further critical features of YDL II;[111] Claude Belanger and Jorge Kan discovered three postholes that defined the size of the nave (figs. 8.4, 8.8, 8.10).[112]

The nave of YDL II was almost certainly wood with a thatched roof; no nails were found to indicate European construction, so it is likely that the native Maya method of framing, with lianas, or vines, rather than nails, was used. As a result of the work carried out in 2007, we now know that the nave

Figure 8.6. Lamanai burials from YDL II cemetery. Photo looks north.

Figure 8.7. Lamanai, Str. N12-12, rectory. Photo looks southeast. Stone chapel of YDL II can be seen in the upper right corner of the photo; modern access road is in the lower right and overlies part of Str. N12-12.

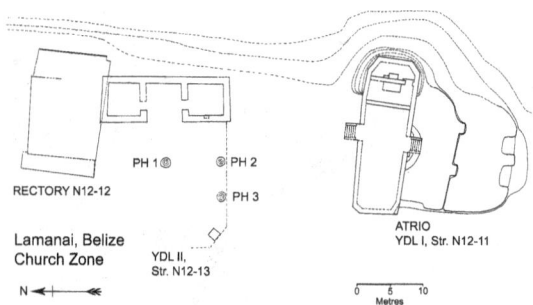

Figure 8.8. Lamanai, plan of church-zone buildings and features. (Drawing by Claude Belanger)

of YDL II was approximately 17 meters wide (east-west) and 19 meters long (north-south) (fig. 8.4).[113] Of the postholes discovered, one held a centerline post and two were supports for the south side (fig. 8.8). A small stone platform ca. 1 meter on a side, from which a majolica sherd was recovered, was excavated in what would have been the southwest corner of the nave interior (figs. 8.8, 8.10).[114] I say "corner," but the orientation of the platform is consonant with the expectation that the church had an apsidal/polygonal end. The platform is most likely to have supported a church feature—a holy-water font or saint's image—which would have been accessible from a western entrance. The doorway shown in figure 8.4 is, however, speculative; there is no evidence for it, except for the position of the small platform.

Fragments of a pre-Columbian-style censer were found associated with the centerline posthole, about 20 centimeters below the surface (fig. 8.11). We cannot be certain, but the depth and scatter suggested that the censer had been deposited after the church had fallen into disuse. There was a larger platform-like feature, ca. 2 meters on a side, about 22 meters west of the stone chapel of YDL II and 16 meters west of the centerline posthole. This feature, however, pre-dated the construction of the church and is likely to have been associated with the pre-Columbian structures that immediately antedate the church period.

The 2007 excavations provided enough evidence for a reconstruction of YDL II (fig. 8.4). Like all reconstructions, it is one of a number of possibilities. With regard to the chapel, the reconstruction of its dimensions, the nature of the stonework, the existence of three rooms with one major entranceway between the sanctuary and the nave, and the lack of access to the rectory through the north room of the chapel are all based on solid archaeological evidence. The roof and upper-zone ornamentation are conjectural, based on churches with chapels (*capillas*) in Yucatan and Mexico. The arch over the entranceway between the nave and the sanctuary is conjectural, although such a feature is consistent with other Yucatecan chapels, as are the steps leading up to the chapel. It is interesting that Thomas Gann,[115] who visited

Indian Church in 1919 or slightly earlier,[116] reports the presence of arches, although it is not clear where these stood. His exact words are: "By far the most interesting structure in this ancient settlement was the little building which had given it the name Indian Church. The walls and part of the roof were still in an excellent state of preservation, and the entries were surmounted by true arches."[117]

The doorway shown leading from the nave to the rectory (Str. N12-12) in figure 8.4 is based partly on archaeological excavations, but the evidence is far from certain. The rectory was built on a pre-Columbian platform (fig. 8.9 shows the south face of this platform), part of which was dismantled during the construction of the chapel. Figure 8.9 shows the line of the north wall of the chapel actually extending beyond (north of) the former face line of the N12-12 platform. The N12-12 facing stones here had been removed and the platform cut back during chapel construction. It is likely that the cut-back platform was re-faced in the past, but none of the facing stones remains. The rectory, Str. N12-12, was in fact in a considerable state of collapse and almost denuded of facing stones, which suggests that it was extensively mined for building material in the past. Nonetheless, based on the nature of the relationship between the chapel and the N12-12 platform, on the remaining stones

Figure 8.9. Lamanai, masonry chapel of YDL II with the ruins of Str. N12-12, the rectory, on the north side (viewer's left). The re-erected stela (Stela 4) stands in front of the chapel in what once was the church nave, possibly the chancel. Stones of the face of the pre-Columbian platform on which the rectory was built can be seen along Str. N12-12's south face. Photo looks east (slightly north).

of the south face of the N12-12 platform (fig. 8.9), on the orientation of the nave, and on the fact that some access would have been essential between the church and the rectory, I have proposed that access was provided by means of a doorway on the nave's north side just west of the chapel wall (fig. 8.4).

Pendergast[118] makes the important point that the form of the union between the chapel and the nave would have required a joint between masonry and thatch that would have posed significant engineering problems, not least of which would have been the difficulties evident when it rained. For this reason, in the reconstruction drawing (fig. 8.4) a stone drain is depicted at this juncture, mortised into the chapel wall.

Unfortunately, the British entrepreneurs who were engaged in sugar production at Indian Church in the nineteenth century used the church's chapel as a smithy[119] and destroyed any stratigraphy that might have been preserved from Spanish times. The colonial documents report that visiting friars found the church burned in 1641, apparently as a consequence of the rebellion that from 1638 had spread throughout the southern Maya frontier.[120] There were no archaeological remains that could be connected to a burning event, but pre-Columbian-style ritual activities, for which there is evidence, clearly post-dated the church's Christian phase, although by how many years is not known.

Figure 8.10. Lamanai, nave area of YDL II. Center posthole can be seen in upper left; stones from the holes supporting posts of the south wall of the nave can be seen in the upper right; in the lower right is the interior platform feature. Looks east. (Photo by Claude Belanger)

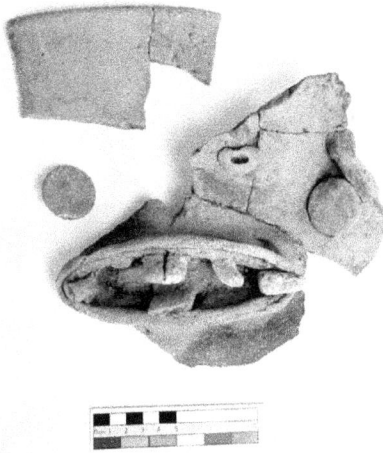

Figure 8.11. Lamanai, censer fragments from centerline posthole, YDL II. (Photo by Claude Belanger)

Two stelae were erected at an unknown point in time subsequent to the burning of the church.[121] One plain stela still stands in situ in the nave, near the chapel entry (fig. 8.9). The other stela, observed by Thomas Gann around 1919, was described in reports to him as a "big tombstone in the bush by the side of the church, all covered with curious devices, painted in different colours."[122] When Gann arrived at the site, he found that the stone was no longer covered with curious figures. "It was a solid slab of stone, standing some 5 ft. out of the ground, rather well sculptured to represent a gigantic snake's head." Gann proceeded to dig up the stone, and was surprised to find that "the lower foot or so of it, which had been buried in the ground, and so better preserved than the upper part, had been covered originally with three layers of white stucco, superimposed the one over the other, and that upon each of these layers were distinct traces of painted devices in various colours!"[123]

The decorated stela, like the first, stood in what was once the church nave.[124] It must then have been removed by Gann, because a description of it appears in the records of the National Museum of the American Indian.[125] The card in the museum's catalogue states: "Stela with serpent's head at one end and covered in places with two layers of stucco formerly painted. This was standing in situ near an ancient building in the vicinity of Indian Church, British Honduras."[126]

The plain stela excavated by Pendergast revealed a small fragmented ceramic figure of a crocodilian creature (LA 423/4, fig. 8.12) buried at the base, along with a reworked jade pendant (not pictured). At the same time or later, a larger, two-headed ceramic figure, a composite of creatures but at least part-crocodilian (Cache N12-13/5, LA 767/1, fig. 8.13), was buried in the northern area of the nave just outside the chapel wall.[127] Just south of the chapel entry

Figure 8.12. Lamanai, effigy vessel from beneath the stela (Stela 4) erected in the nave of YDL II. Found with a recut jade pendant in the form of a human face, and a fragmentary jade bead. LA 423/4, L = 9.7 cm. (Drawing by Louise Belanger)

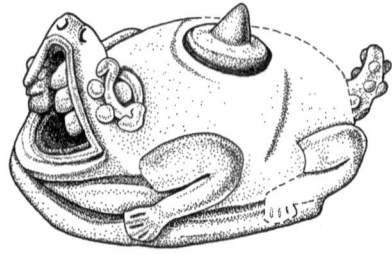

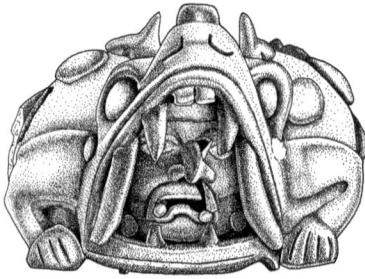

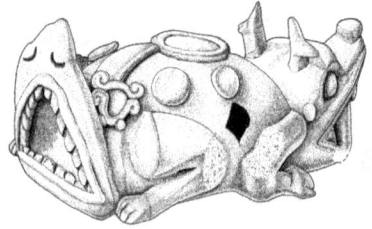

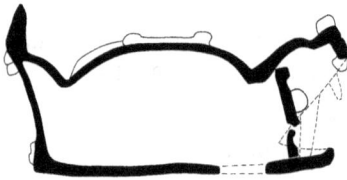

Figure 8.13. Lamanai, two-headed effigy with a human head emerging from one of the open mouths, from YDL II. Recovered from the northern part of the nave just outside the sanctuary wall. Cache N12-13/5, LA 767/1, L = 20.8 cm. (Drawing by Louise Belanger)

lay a cache of small pottery frog figurines and human-face cups (Cache N12-13/4, LA 766/1-5, fig. 8.14).

Gann got his hands on a cache from Indian Church at some point in his career (fig. 8.16). We do not know for certain where on site the cache came from because it does not seem to be reported in the literature; its existence is known because the cache and its contents are part of the National Museum of the American Indian collections. It is likely, however, that the cache came from the area of the churches because we know Gann observed the stelae and excavated in the church zone.[128] The main component is a ceramic effigy of a shark-like creature, which, like the cache associated with the plain

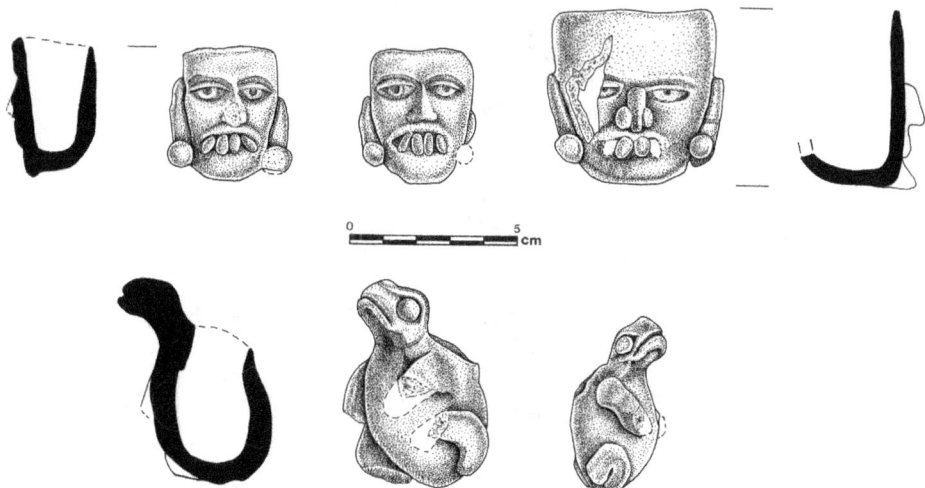

Figure 8.14. Lamanai, miniature human-head and frog-effigy vessels, YDL II. From a pit in bedrock at the corner of the south jamb of the sanctuary entrance. Cache N12-13/4, LA 766/1,2,3,5,4. Height of 766/3 is 5.2 cm. (Drawing by Louise Belanger)

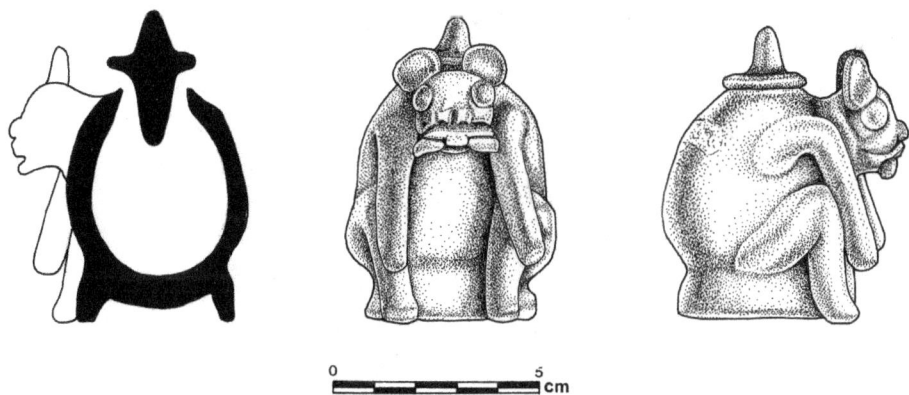

Figure 8.15. Lamanai, animal effigy (feline?) vessel, YDL I. From a small, unsealed pit cut into the surface of a raised unit, apparently a plinth for a statue, that flanked the stair of the razed pre-Columbian structure within YDL I. The effigy vessel contained charcoal and bone pin or needle tips; a chert blade pointing northeast lay beneath the vessel. Cache N12-11/2, LA 739/1, height 7.2 cm. (Drawing by Louise Belanger)

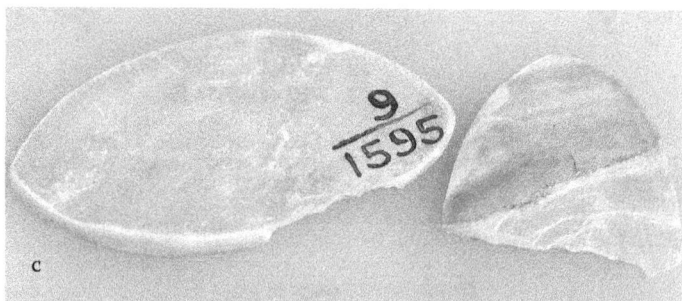

Figure 8.16. Lamanai, "shark" effigy cache and contents. Found by Thomas Gann at "Indian Church" and given to the Museum of the American Indian: (a) effigy, 9/1594; (b) stopper, 9/1600; (c) carved shell, 9/1595; (d) carved shell, 9/1596; (e) chert bifaces, probably points, 9/1597; (f) two perforated shell ornaments, 9/1598; (g) *Spondylus* shell bead, 9/1599; (h) jade bead, 9/1601; (i) copper bell, 9/1602. (Photos courtesy of the National Museum of the American Indian)

d

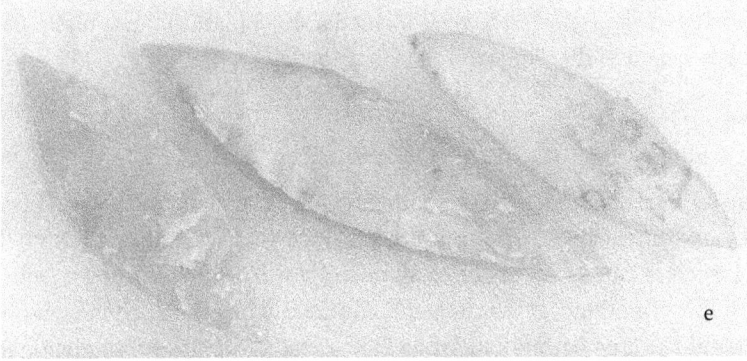

e

cm

f

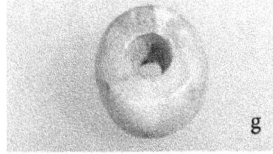

g

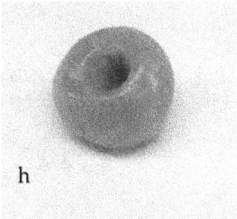

h

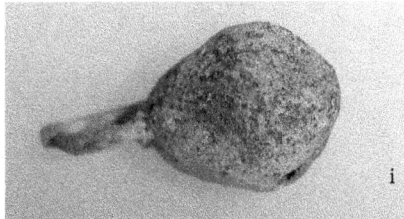

i

stela (see fig. 8.12), is hollow-bodied with a circular opening in its back, fitted with a stopper. Typically, the creature's mouth is wide open, with an anthropomorphic head emerging from it.[129] Found inside Gann's effigy were two shell inlays, probably conch; one perforated squared shell piece, also probably conch; three perforated beads—one cylindrical and two disc-shaped—probably *Spondylus*; three small bi-pointed chert points; one small jade bead; and one copper bell (fig. 8.16 a–i).[130]

In addition to the caches and stelae associated with YDL II and its environs, Pendergast reported the occurrence of a small altar built in the ruins of the nave;[131] the altar stood just west of what I have suggested served as the doorway between the nave and the rectory (fig. 8.4 shows the doorway). The stones were cleared in 1976 and do not appear in the photo (fig. 8.9) taken in 1998, but they are reported to have formed a small platform, not dissimilar to what was found in the Tipu church (see below).

YDL I

A "burial mound" 7–8 meters south of YDL II, which contained approximately 230 interments, was excavated in 1976 (map 8.1, figs. 8.2, 8.17).[132] A Late Postclassic building on a low platform, similar to those known from the site of Tulum in Quintana Roo,[133] and commonly termed a temple, had been razed and the area within and around the razed structure subsequently used as a burying-ground during the church period.[134] The mound was originally thought to have served solely as the cemetery for YDL II,[135] but in 1983 further investigation revealed it to be the remains of an earlier church, YDL I,

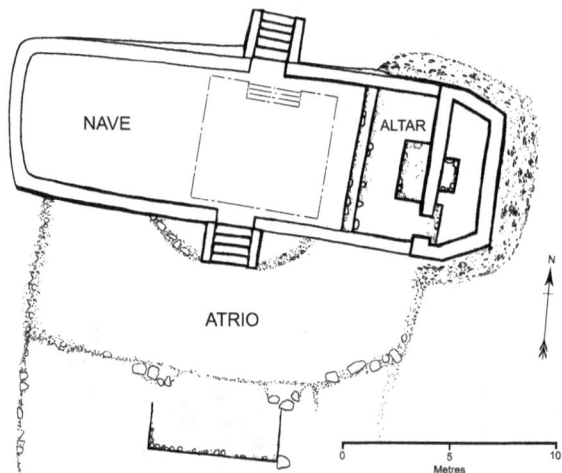

Figure 8.17. Lamanai, plan of YDL I. (Drawing by Claude Belanger)

Figure 8.18. Lamanai, centipede-lobster cache (N12-11/3) in situ in front of north stair of YDL I; the bifurcated tail of the effigy, visible in the photo, points south. Photo looks southeast. (Photo by Claude Belanger)

simpler in design and construction than YDL II.[136] Excavations delineated the masonry portion of what had been part-masonry, part-pole walls, as well as the features of a small sanctuary at the east end (figs. 8.3, 8.17), almost identical to the layout at Tipu (see below).

Two caches were associated with YDL I; one was deposited during the church's construction, and the other probably post-dates construction. In 1983, two apparent plinths (for statuary?) were cleared that flanked the north-side stair of the razed pre-Columbian structure (figs. 8.2, 8.17). A small animal-effigy (Cache N12-11/2, fig. 8.15; the plinth is visible in fig. 8.2), apparently feline, was found in a small unsealed pit cut into the western plinth; the pit and plinth had been overlain by core of the church platform. In 2007, another animal-effigy vessel was found buried just north of the north stair of YDL I (ca. 1 meter, 10 centimeters north and 60 centimeters west of what remains of the eastern balustrade) (figs. 8.17, 8.18). In this case, the animal appears to be a combination of a centipede and a lobster (Cache N12-11/3, fig. 8.19.a).[137] Like the effigies associated with YDL II, it is hollow and stoppered. The fired clay is reddish in color and has traces of grey-blue stucco paint. The vessel contained two small chert points with rounded bases, a stingray spine in two fragments, and three shark's teeth (fig. 8.19.b).

Perhaps the most significant feature of YDL I was discovered in 2007.[138] Clearing of the area south of the church revealed a series of low, broad,

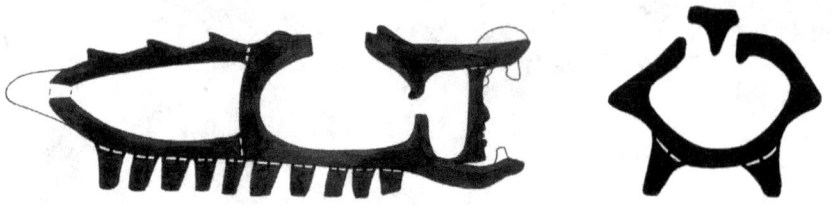

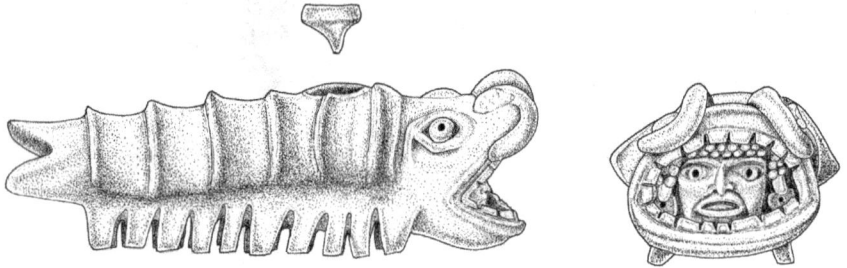

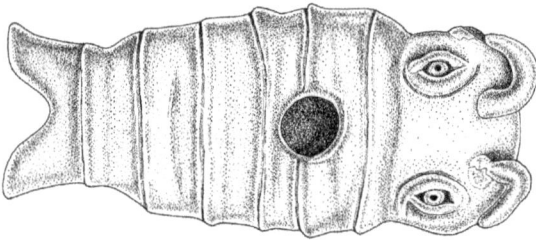

Figure 8.19. Lamanai, centipede-lobster effigy and contents: (*above*) various views of the effigy, Cache N12-11/3, LA 3035/1. (*left*) contents: chert bifaces, LA 3035/2,3; stingray spine, LA 3035/4,5; shark's teeth, LA 3035/5,6,7. Effigy L=21 cm; bifaces L=3.2 cm. (Drawing by Louise Belanger)

stone-bordered terraces that formed a patio or atrio, which was almost certainly the site for fiestas, masses, and other rituals and ceremonies related to the church (figs. 8.20, 8.21).[139] It would have been the setting for the teaching of Christian doctrine to the new congregation; such patios/atrios were sometimes set at different levels to facilitate teaching. In central Mexico, trees were planted to shade those who were assembled, usually groups of children.[140] In the case of our atrio, thatch was likely erected to provide shelter from the sun. The plan of YDL I and the atrio (fig. 8.8) and the reconstruction drawing (fig. 8.3) show only two stone-bordered terraces south of YDL I, but the ground contours indicate that a third, as yet unexcavated, terrace extends to the east. There was also a feature, akin to a small stone-bordered platform, that was situated at the junction of the first and second terraces along the axis of the YDL stair (see fig. 8.20). There is no evidence of its function, although it could have served to support a wooden cross. According to McAndrew, people would come to the patios/atrios to pray and would kneel there in front of the church door in rows.[141] One could imagine the friar or priest or *maestro* standing at YDL I on the highest level, perhaps at the base of the stair near the south door, preaching to the community.

A number of years earlier, in 1984, Claude Belanger and I had been involved in the planning and recording of Str. N11-18, a probable residence that was part of a zone of historic-period structures located about 200 meters north of YDL II (map 8.1, fig. 8.5). This zone had only just been discovered early in the 1984 season amidst thatched houses newly built by recent immigrants from Guatemala and El Salvador.[142] Recording Str. N11-18 afforded us the opportunity to become acquainted with the distinctive features of historic, non-ceremonial Maya buildings. This experience at Lamanai helped to prepare me for the work that lay ahead at Tipu later on in that year. Belanger, however, had been assisting Kautz at Tipu from 1980 to 1982, and it was his familiarity with the church at Tipu—a ramada church with modest sanctuary—that enabled Pendergast at Lamanai to reassess what he thought had been a cemetery or burial mound for YDL II as the remains of an earlier church.

In 1998 we focused broadly on late occupation at the site. This included the time of the Maya collapse, the years following the collapse, and the transition from the Late Postclassic period to Spanish colonial times. In addition to Scott Simmons's work on metallurgy in Postclassic and historic times,[143] we focused on Str. N12-12 (figs. 8.7, 8.8). Excavations of portions of the structure by Pendergast in 1976 yielded a ceramic animal effigy (Cache N12-12/1, LA 757/1, fig. 8.22) as well as the remains of Spanish olive jars in refuse. The phenomenon of Str. N12-12 will be seen below to be mirrored at Tipu by Str. H12-18, which abutted the north side of the church at its east end. In accordance with church-building practices of the time, these structures served as residences

Figure 8.20. Lamanai, atrio of YDL I during excavation. Looking east. (Photo by Claude Belanger)

Figure 8.21. Lamanai, YDL I and atrio after reconstruction by Jorge Can and team from Belize Institute of Archaeology. Looking northeast. (Photo by Claude Belanger)

for whoever was in charge of maintaining the church and its Christian flock. Remote communities such as Lamanai and Tipu did not have full-time resident Spanish priests or friars, and hence the rectory probably served to house the visita priests, whether it was the Spanish secular priest from Bacalar or the Mendicants who were supervising evangelizing and building activities.

From 1998 to 2002, expanded excavations of Str. N12-12, which we have dubbed "the rectory," revealed a complex history. The structure began its historic life cycle by incorporating an earlier (probably Late Postclassic) platform, to which additions were made unevenly through time that belie any strict adherence to traditional Maya building techniques or planning, although the

Maya practice of using stone to face platforms is in evidence. However, techniques seem to have been shoddy, quality of stone poor, and planning minimal. Some additions almost certainly post-date the Spanish period, and British colonial activity is indicated by the presence of an Irish soda bottle in the core of the Postclassic platform at its southwest corner.

A large part of the structure continues under the surface of the modern road constructed to facilitate tourist access, so we were not able to sort out its sequence or dating satisfactorily. We did, however, learn a good deal more about the nature of colonial-period construction and its oddities. In fact, one cannot help but see Str. N12-12, particularly in its later stages, as a reflection of the intermittent and ineffectual attention afforded Lamanai by the secular priest from Bacalar, Gregorio de Aguilar, who was in charge of all Bacalar-administered missions on his own from 1632 to 1641.[144]

In addition to various analyses, ongoing work at Lamanai includes Simmons's expanded excavations of buildings in the historic residential center, particularly Str. N11-18, where he is examining evidence for metallurgy in both the Postclassic and the historic period; and Darcy Wiewall has recently completed a study of colonial period households.[145] Wiewall's research, together with excavations sponsored by the Belize government's Tourism Development Project (2001–3) have revealed intensive Late Postclassic and colonial-period occupation in a band paralleling the lagoon. This adds support to Pendergast's earlier contention[146] that the strip form of settlement characteristic of Lamanai in Spanish colonial times, in which dwellings were scattered along the lagoon shore for at least 700 meters north and 1,000 meters south of the

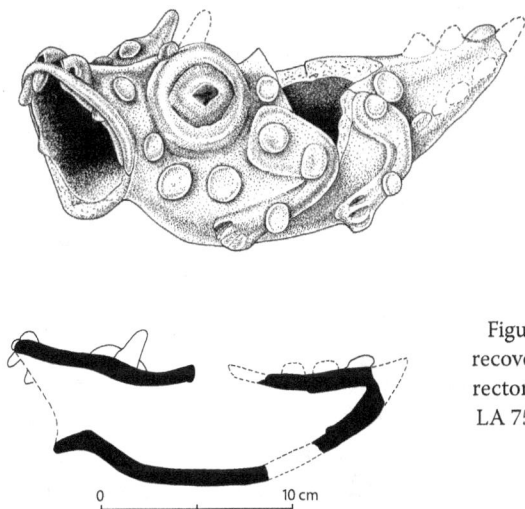

Figure 8.22. Lamanai, effigy vessel recovered from axial trenching of the rectory, Str. N12-12. Cache N12-12/1, LA 757/1, L = ca. 20.9 cm. (Drawing by Louise Belanger)

churches, simply continued a practice established in Postclassic times. Easy access to a source of water, to transport, and to goods and commerce must all have been factors in this settlement choice.

The Lamanai Town

At Lamanai, the fact that the colonial town underlay the modern residences and shops of the local village of Indian Church, at least in the village's first incarnation,[147] made excavation problematic. Therefore we know less about Lamanai's non-church-related structures than we know about those at Tipu. The largest structure excavated, Str. N11-18 (map 8.1, fig. 8.5), yielded copper artifacts, European glass beads, and Spanish majolica sherds.[148] Like Str. H12-8 at Tipu (see below) (map 8.3), it may also have served as a *casa real*. Its layout and its features are similar to those of Str. H12-8, and Spanish artifacts were found in refuse. Pendergast has suggested that it served as the residence of the town's cacique, or principal leader.

The difference is that in the case of Str. N11-18 at Lamanai, the refuse was primary. By this I mean that refuse had not been reused in platform construction, as was the case at Tipu, but instead represented tip off of the sides of the platform(s). The absence of Spanish artifacts reused in construction suggests also that Str. N11-18 almost certainly dates to an early period of contact in the sixteenth century, whereas Str. H12-8 could well have served the Tipu community until the end of the seventeenth century, at the time of the Itza conquest.

Tipu and Its Church(es)

As noted above, the nature of the records from the late 1560s indicates that Tipu was already part of an encomienda in 1543–44, and the focus of a major reduction effort in the 1560s.[149] I originally proposed that the church at Tipu was probably built during reduction efforts in the late 1560s.[150] My conclusion was based on our recovery of Spanish majolica pottery[151] from the core of the church's masonry walls. The sherds were not part of a cache, or offering, but had been swept up as part of construction. My thought was that imported ceramics were not likely to have been lying around in 1544, and that a later date was more probable.

Given the unfettered enthusiasm for conversion among the Mendicants that characterized the period prior to the 1560s (see chap. 4), it is possible that the first church at Tipu was built earlier than 1560, and perhaps as early as initial evangelization, sometime between 1543 and 1550. Unlike Lamanai, where the first church was a rather slapdash effort, with non-parallel walls

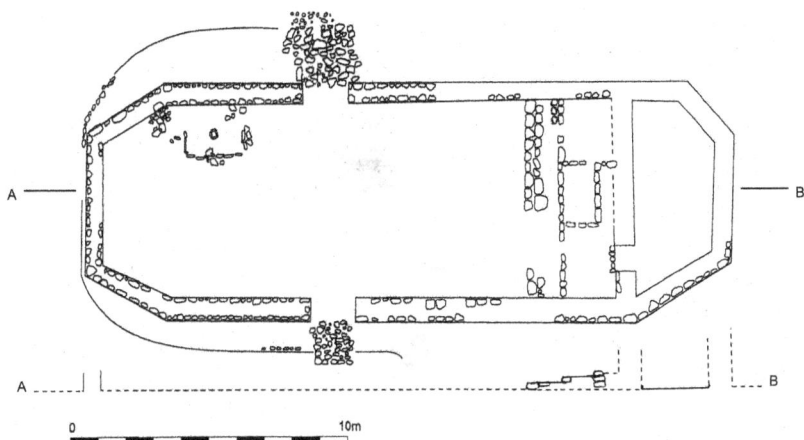

Figure 8.23. Tipu, plan and section of the Spanish colonial church, Str. H12-13. (Drawing by Claude Belanger)

and evidence of in-progress adjustments and corrections to alignment—and where the second church was a relatively elaborate affair—the situation at Tipu seems never to have called for anything beyond a simple but functional building. I now think that the ruined church discovered in 1980 at Tipu was the last of a series of buildings constructed, added to, and repaired on the same spot.

The excavations under Kautz's direction revealed that the church at Tipu was constructed in at least two phases. The first phase comprised the nave and a simple sanctuary; a later phase or phases involved elaborating the sanctuary by raising it, and providing access via three steps (figs. 8.1, 8.23). At one point, the rear room, which probably served as a sacristy, was also added to the original building.[152]

The form of the church as excavated included a masonry bench, 2 meters north-south by 1 meter east-west, set against the rear (east) wall of the sanctuary (figs. 8.23, 8.24). The bench, which at one time stood somewhere between 50 and 70 centimeters high, almost certainly served to support a portable wooden altar base, which the friars or clerics would have carried with them on visitas. On the altar base would have been set the portable altar, or *ara*, a "small, hard, rectangular stone slab, about 12 by 14 inches . . . which symbolically represented Christ, and was the holiest part of the altar."[153] Church rules in effect from the eighth century required that if a priest was on a journey or in a place where there was no permanent church, he had to use a stone table or slab consecrated by a bishop; this practice became embedded in what was emerging as Canon Law in the twelfth century.[154]

Normally, in permanent stone-built churches, the altar base would have

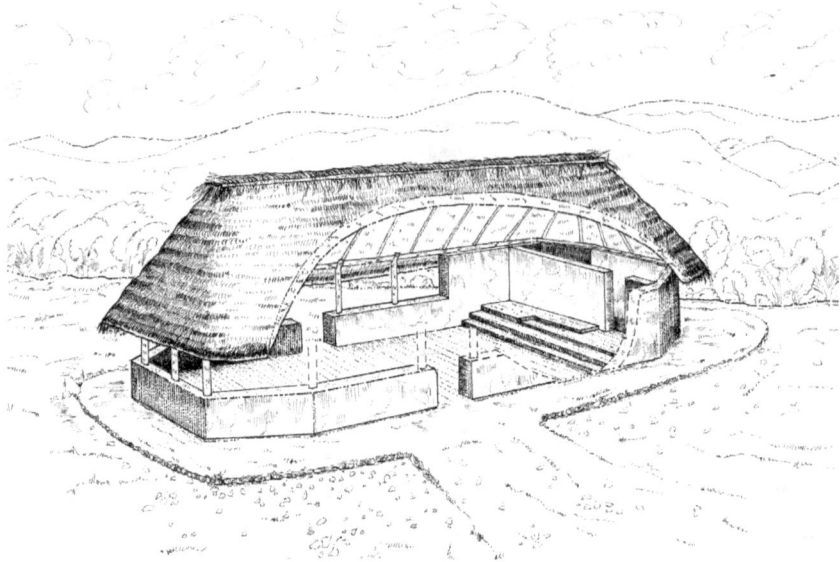

Figure 8.24. Tipu, perspective reconstruction cutaway of church, looking northeast. (Drawing by Claude Belanger and Louise Belanger)

supported a slab called a *mensa*, or table, and the ara would have been set on or in the mensa,[155] but in new territories undergoing evangelization, where there was no resident priest, a consecrated ara that could be carried in a locked chest was essential, whereas a consecrated mensa was not.[156] What we excavated at Tipu (and also at Lamanai in the case of YDL I), represented by lines of stone forming a rectangular platform, or base, abutting the wall between the sanctuary and the sacristy (fig. 8.23; for Lamanai YDL I, see fig. 8.17) is the *stipes*, which is the name for the fixed base, or pedestal, that supported the altar base.[157] In the case of Tipu, the reconstruction drawing shows the stipes as low, but it could well have been higher. Based on the archaeological evidence, it was at least as high as it has been reconstructed.

The stipes would have supported a wooden altar base. The ara would have been placed on this base, and the chalice and other liturgical paraphernalia on the ara. All these items, including the ara, would have been stored in a lockable wooden chest that could be carried by the visita priest or the assistants who accompanied him.[158] The Franciscan friars Fuensalida and Estrada brought boxes (small chests?), one of which contained a portable altar, on their attempt to reach Tipu in 1641 during a period of rebellion. The boxes were destroyed en route by Maya rebels, but the altar and other objects (chalice, missal, chrismatory) were returned to the friars.[159] Iron locks from small chests have been found at both Tipu and Lamanai—at Tipu in association with the church and with a residence (fig. 8.25), and at Lamanai in association with a residence, Str. N11-18.

The sanctuary of the Tipu church was further subdivided by slight changes in floor level, apparently to differentiate ritual space. Each change of level—or change in ritual space— was marked by a step. An individual mounting the two steps from the nave (fig. 8.24) would reach the first level, or landing, between the second and third step. The landing extends the full width of the church, and a person standing or kneeling on it would be about 25 to 30 centimeters above the nave floor.

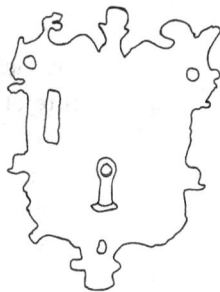

Figure 8.25. Tipu, lock plate from a chest, Str. H12-7, T-226/1.

The next higher level is the area around the stipes, which rose a minimum of 10 to 15 centimeters above the landing (ca. 35 to 40 centimeters above the level of the nave floor). The small area south of the stipes (see fig. 8.23) is separated from the area directly in front of the stipes by a line of stones, but no clear change in level was in evidence in excavation. This is why, in the reconstruction drawing (fig. 8.24), the space in front of the stipes and the area just bordering it on the south (which leads through a doorway to the probable sacristy) are shown as contiguous and at 10 to 15 centimeters above the landing. This makes sense, because the priest or servers would then have easy access (to administer sacraments or to receive the offerings during Mass) to communicants standing or kneeling on the landing; any difference greater than 15 centimeters would have made such access awkward.

There is a step up of about 10 to 15 centimeters, however, from the space in front of the stipes to the area north of it (see fig. 8.24), which is shown as contiguous with the surface of the stipes, whereas in real life the surface of the stipes could have been higher. In any case, the area north of the stipes stood 25 to 30 centimeters above the landing (ca. 55 to 60 centimeters above the level of the nave floor), which is a good-sized step up. Given the size restrictions on the reconstruction drawing for publication, it is difficult to show these subtle variances in level. The presence of a line of three stones forming a step from the landing to the area north of the stipes (see the plan, fig. 8.23) suggests that access from the nave was indeed intended, perhaps for a choir. Access to the altar (on the stipes) for the individuals saying or serving Mass was clearly from the south, because the doorway that leads from the sanctuary to the rear room is on the south side of the altar. The rear room almost certainly served as a sacristy; the floor was very well preserved and the room well built. The chest with liturgical paraphernalia is very likely to have been kept here, at least during the times when a priest was in residence. The little room may also have been used by the priest and servers for the donning of ritual clothing for Mass. A feature expected but not present is access via a doorway to the rectory, or residence, to the north; but there was no evidence for a doorway in the sacristy other than the one that led to the sanctuary.

One other feature of the Tipu church deserves to be noted. I mentioned above that Pendergast had reported the occurrence of a pre-Columbian-style altar or small platform in the nave of YDL II, which would have abutted the north wall of the nave just west of the access door to the rectory, Str. N12-12. A platform was also found at Tipu which abutted the north wall of the church about 2 meters west of the north door (figs. 8.23, 8.26).[160] In the Tipu case, however, although I had thought at first that the platform represented a return to pre-Columbian ritual within the church, it became clear that it marked an interior church feature of some kind. A pedestal for a font or for statuary is suggested by four stone slabs set on their sides forming a square support base (fig. 8.26). The presence of a perishable element of wood, possibly an altar or shrine, is also suggested by the dimensions of the platform and the gap between it and the church wall.

Although I have described the Tipu church as representing two phases of construction, it is almost certain that there were more, and that the church was modified and repaired through time in ways that destroyed evidence of earlier features. Compared to YDL I at Lamanai, more attention, care, and expertise are in evidence at Tipu, and the church was well maintained through time.

The Tipu Plaza

The reduction of the late 1560s must have been reasonably successful, if the ordered plan of buildings around the plaza is any indication (see fig. 1.1, map 8.3). The largest building, Str. H12-8, may have served as a *casa real*: a large, thatched building which housed important visitors. The reconstruction drawing of the buildings around the plaza shown in figure 1.1 reflects a late, probably seventeenth-century, manifestation of the building.

Because the reconstruction drawing (fig. 1.1) was made before the excavations were completed, there are some features that require correction. What look like broad steps on the plaza-facing side of Str. H12-8 probably extended the entire length of the structure, which is about 36 meters. They were not steps, but served as low terraces or platform extensions (see map 8.3).

In addition, Str. H12-18, just north of the church (in the lower-left corner of fig. 1.1), comprised two thatched buildings, the smaller of which stood just north of the one shown, and therefore outside the frame of the picture; stone paving connected their doorways (see Str. H12-18, map 8.3). Finally, excavations directed by Rhanju Song in 2006 revealed that another building, Str. H12-19, stood between Str. H12-7 and Str. H12-14.[161]

The variety in form and layout of Str. H12-8 (refer to both fig. 1.1 and map 8.3) suggests that although it started out as a pre-Columbian structure, it was altered, expanded, and added to repeatedly through time. Spanish pottery and other artifacts were found in refuse that had been reused in the construction of the main platform and the low terrace extensions. Given the layout of the building, it seems to have had a largely residential function, but the variety in pavements, extensions, patios, and what seems to have been roofed and unwalled space suggests that it served a multiplicity of purposes.

Residences around the main plaza varied in size. The two houses on either side of the church are relatively large; on the north side, Str. H12-18 served as the residence for the visiting priest. This could have been the *padre beneficiado*, which is Lopez de Cogolludo's term for a secular priest who, in the case of Tipu, served the town from his base in Bacalar. The friars Fuensalida and Orbita also resided in Str. H12-18 on their mission to Tipu in 1618.[162]

The house on the south side, Str. H12-14, and Str. H12-12 probably belonged

Figure 8.26. Tipu, church nave feature. Vertical stones formed the face of a platform that abutted a perishable church furnishing of some kind, possibly a wood altar or shrine. The stones of the north wall of the church can be seen at the top of the photo. Photo looks north.

to principales of Tipu. Str. H12-7, a house which was probably larger than the cobblestone-paved portion excavated in 1984 (and hence larger than the plan shown in map 8.3), produced olive jar sherds, a copper ring, a glass bead, and a lock plate for a chest (fig. 8.25).[163] Vestments and other church items are known to have been carried in chests, and it is tempting to speculate that Str. H12-7 was the home of a *maestro cantor* or sacristan.

Comparing Tipu and Lamanai

THE RAMADA CHURCHES

YDL I at Lamanai and the church at Tipu share many features. Both have been described as ramada chapels,[164] which reflects the fact that they were simple structures with thatched roofs, but I have already argued in chapter 7 that both structures at Tipu and Lamanai were, in fact, churches, because they were constructed to serve the entire Christian community at each site.

YDL I at Lamanai and the church at Tipu are both long and narrow with apsidal east ends and side entrances, and their naves were part masonry and part wood. Both churches have two steps leading up from the nave to a landing, which in the Lamanai case is broader than the one at Tipu (cf. fig. 8.3 with fig. 8.24). In both churches, the spot where the portable altar, or ara, was to be placed is delineated by a low masonry bench. Preservation is much poorer in the Lamanai case, so the details of the area around the altar are unknown; for example, we do not know if the sanctuary space was functionally subdivided. However, the doorway from the sanctuary to the sacristy is on the south side of the altar, as at Tipu.

Lamanai has a feature which Tipu lacks, which is a low, raised bench along the west wall of the sacristy (fig. 8.17). Paraphernalia used in the Mass probably rested or was stored in a chest here, and the dimensions of the Tipu sacristy suggest that there was room for an equivalent feature in perishable material, perhaps a wooden table. Thus, one could argue that the plans of the ramada churches at Lamanai and Tipu are almost identical.

As described by McAndrew: "The principal instrument for [the conversion of the American natives] was to be not the secular but the regular clergy: Mendicants sent across the sea expressly for this mission. . . . As a corollary, one finds that since the friars came first, they built first and fastest, and soon established the local church types."[165] McAndrew was speaking largely with central Mexico in mind, but it is interesting that he saw the local church types that developed as being distinctively Mexican products in design and execution, partly owing to the influence of local indigenous building traditions,[166] a theme richly developed in more recent years by Edgerton.[167]

There is no reason to believe that we are not seeing the same phenomenon in Belize. The Tipu and Lamanai ramada churches could be considered a distinctive type developed by Franciscans and Mayas for frontier missions in Yucatan and Belize. Arguments have been put forward that the simple construction of the first churches reflects the Mendicants' emphasis on apostolic poverty and simplicity,[168] but it may be more accurate to attribute the styles of the churches to a combination of Franciscan ideals, local circumstances, and local architectural traditions.[169]

SOME DIFFERENCES

Although Lamanai's YDL I (fig. 8.3) had roughly the same layout and construction as Tipu's (fig. 8.24), one difference is that the Tipu church was built on a very low platform (15–20 centimeters), whereas the Lamanai church had a more substantial platform that varied in height from approximately 50 centimeters to about a meter. The dimensions suggest that in both towns, builders were aiming at the same form, but YDL I at Lamanai comes across as an earlier effort. For one thing, the presence of a substantial platform is a pre-Columbian convention, one which was not maintained as the colonial period wore on. For another, the builders were clearly having problems keeping walls in alignment, possibly because they were responding to directions for a layout with which they were unfamiliar (note the north wall in fig. 8.17). According to Belanger, the evidence suggests that different construction teams were working on different parts of the church; those working on the south side maintained the desired east-west alignment, but those working on the north side constructed platform sections that were not in alignment. Eventually the problem with the north platform face was resolved by connecting the existing construction units. (Fig. 8.17 shows the platform out of alignment, just west of the north stair, and how the walls were then brought into alignment.) The end result at Lamanai is that the church, or at least its platform, is slightly narrower at the west end (ca. 6.5 meters), whereas the 22-meter-long building measures approximately 7.5 meters in width at the sanctuary.

Another difference between the two churches is that the Lamanai church building—the superstructure that stood on the platform—was probably part-masonry, part-wood in its entirety, whereas the Tipu church had full-height masonry walls at the east end (inferred from the collapse debris). Excavations revealed that although the bulk of YDL I had been constructed over limestone bedrock, the east end, from the sanctuary onward, was constructed over unstable *bajo* (swamp) mud, which caused considerable slumping. There was simply not enough support for full-height masonry walls.[170] If there was a blind sanctuary at this end, as I suggest (if only to shield the congregation from the strong winds off the lagoon), then the full-height walls were constructed of wood, as shown in the reconstruction drawing (fig. 8.3; note that the wall at the east end, south side, has been "cut away" by the illustrator to reveal the church interior, but the full-height wall is visible on the north side).

The core material of the platform of YDL I at Lamanai is interesting because it yielded largely Preclassic pottery, which dates to about 100 B.C. This in itself is not surprising, because the Maya perpetually reused material in construction, but it may partly explain why the church escaped detection initially as a piece of sixteenth-century construction.[171] The absence of Spanish pottery or other colonial material in the platform core provides further evidence to suggest that construction took place in 1544 or shortly thereafter.

The Tipu church was slightly larger than YDL I at ca. 23 meters in length (east-west) and a little over 8 meters in width (north-south). Although both churches had apsidal (polygonal, not semicircular) east ends, each church's expression had a distinctive local flavor. At Lamanai, there is evidence that both the church building (the superstructure) and the platform on the east end conformed to a polygonal shape, but the shapes of the west ends of the platform and the building are unclear.[172] The evidence is unequivocal, however, that walls of the Tipu church were polygonal on the west end (fig. 8.1). The preference for a polygonal/apsidal east end reflects conformation with the Franciscan ideal of the primitive, single-nave church (see chapter 7) and argues strongly for Franciscan influence in the case of both communities.

CHURCH BURIALS

Over 585 burials were recovered from the church cemetery at Tipu, which comprised the area under the floor of the church nave as well as a zone surrounding the church on its north, west, and south sides, but not on the east. Of the individuals interred, there were 176 males, 119 females, 249 juveniles, and 41 adults whose sex could not be determined.[173]

As observed by Cohen, O'Connor and colleagues,[174] it is difficult to know what portion of the community is represented by the population buried in the church cemetery. If, as I have proposed, the site of the church remained constant, with only its structural features modified or changed, then the church was conceivably in use from first contact until at least the 1638–41 rebellion. Both the history of contact in the post-rebellion period, which will be described in the next chapter, and the stratigraphic evidence (that some individuals on the north side were interred after the church collapsed) suggest that the cemetery was used by at least some Tipuans throughout the seventeenth century, and possibly until the community was moved in the first decade of the eighteenth century.

Approximately 230 individuals were buried beneath the floor of the nave of YDL I at Lamanai,[175] in what Pendergast has characterized as "a jumble that defies description."[176] Below-floor burials in the nave were obviously not marked, because earlier interments were repeatedly disturbed and the bones reburied. Bedrock at Lamanai is so close to the surface that it was not possible to bury people in the zone surrounding the church walls. Burial within the nave was made feasible by the fact that pre-Columbian and colonial-period platform-construction efforts had involved a considerable build-up of earth and stones that served as a matrix for interments. Individuals at Lamanai were buried, as they were at Tipu, with head to the west "facing" east, a common Christian pattern.[177]

Burial accompaniments at Tipu comprised needles, found usually in the area of the chest and believed to have fastened shrouds (figs. 1.10, 8.27); rings; lacetags;[178] pendants;[179] silver earrings[180] (fig. 1.9); glass bead necklaces and bracelets[181] (figs. 1.6–1.8); a thurible[182] (figs. 6.2, 8.28) which was locally made but European in form; some objects of jet (figs. 1.7, 1.9.a) and amber;[183] and local jewelry made from *Spondylus* shells or dog's teeth.[184] A few individuals were buried in coffins, as evidenced by the placement of iron nails. A chest buried with another individual is represented by a lock plate (similar to fig. 8.25).[185] European manufactured goods were clearly reaching Tipu, and influencing design there.

Burials at Lamanai yielded fewer, although no less interesting, artifacts: an iron lock; a ring; what was probably a needle fragment; and bone beads that are believed to be from a rosary not dissimilar to one found on the *Mary Rose* (fig. 8.29). All came from mixed and disturbed burial contexts and hence none could be tied to an individual.[186] No bracelets or necklaces or earrings adorned individuals in death; in fact, at Lamanai approximately 90 percent of the 46 glass beads recovered were encountered within and around the residential Str. N11-18,[187] and the rest came from two other colonial-period structures at the site.[188] At Tipu, only 7 beads, one of them amber, came from various redeposited middens associated with buildings. The remaining 816 beads came from only eighteen burials, and most of the beads accompanied children.[189]

DIET AND HEALTH

Although Lamanai and Tipu are often viewed as two communities in the same region, diet and health of the populations differed during the early colonial period. Lamanai's population shows mixing that reflects either Spanish-Maya intermarriage or relationships between individuals of different native Maya groups, perhaps between local Maya and those from northern Yucatan,

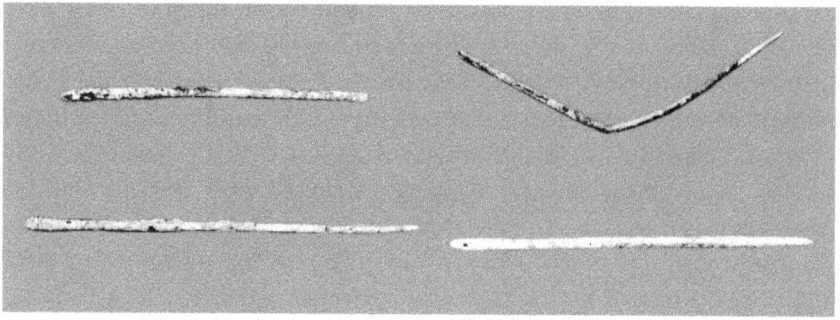

Figure 8.27. Tipu, needles from church burials: T-893/1 (*upper left*), T-908/1 (*upper right*), T-906/1 (*lower left*), T910/1 (*lower right*).

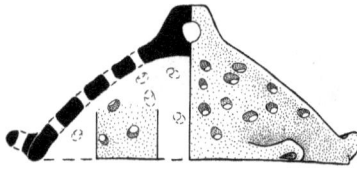

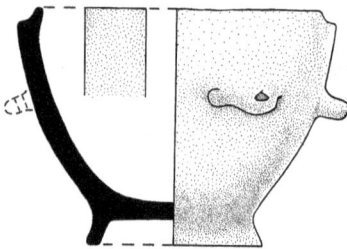

Figure 8.28. Tipu, thurible (censer) from church burial, B96, T-522/1. See also figure 6.2. (Drawing by Louise Belanger)

whereas Tipu's population comes across as homogeneous and appears to reflect a single, regional indigenous population.[190] With regard to general health of the population, there is no evidence at Tipu of hasty or mass burial that might be expected to occur under epidemic conditions.[191] Trauma is rare, evidence of infection is infrequent or minor, and symptoms of anemia are low or in keeping with Classic populations. Generally, skeletal and dental indicators do not suggest high levels of stress associated with epidemic or enzootic infections with severe nutritional deprivation. Instead, the pattern is consistent with the image of a healthy population.[192] The Lamanai skeletal population, on the other hand, exhibits a higher occurrence of anemia than is evident in the pre-Columbian sample, and enamel defects were almost three times more common in historic-period teeth than in the pre-Columbian sample.[193]

Dietary practices during the colonial period in both communities show continuity with pre-Columbian times. The indications are that none of the basic patterns of existence at Lamanai or Tipu was significantly affected by Spanish presence.[194] However, trends in patterns of animal use over time indicate that diversity of utilized faunal species at Tipu remained high over time, whereas diversity at Lamanai dropped significantly, although the decrease in diversity began at Lamanai before the conquest, in Late Postclassic times. In colonial times at Lamanai, riverine resources were overwhelmingly abundant, whereas animal use at Tipu reflects a pre-Columbian pattern of generalized resource use in which a wide range of ecosystems was represented.

Skeletons at Lamanai show high lesion frequencies attributable to heavy physiological stress, which seems to be attributable to changing epidemiologic conditions.[195] This suggests that individuals from Lamanai interacted with Spaniards and with northern Maya more frequently than did individuals from Tipu, and that Lamanai was visited more frequently by Spaniards and perhaps other Europeans.

Comparatively speaking, Tipuans engaged in strategies that, despite periodic reductions and visits by Spanish authorities, allowed them a degree of stability that was denied to individuals at Lamanai. The paths followed by

Figure 8.29. Lamanai, rosary of bone beads, YDL I. From a burial, but area was disturbed and beads too dispersed to determine which burial.

people from Lamanai and Tipu were clearly not the same, despite pressures from colonial conditions. Some of the differences may have been due to the advantages that accrued from Tipu's greater distance from colonial authorities, but we must keep in mind the likelihood that individual Mayas and their organizational capabilities also played a part.

Lamanai and Tipu
as Christian Communities

Lamanai must have been established as a Christian community with tribute obligations about 1544, judging by the role of Lamanai inhabitants in the 1547 Chanlacan uprising (map 2.3).[196] Archaeologically, the investment in two churches, as well as the size of the second church, gives Lamanai an importance that is simply not reflected in the documents. A possible parallel situation is known in the case of the Awatovi mission in the U.S. Southwest, where the size and design of the mission buildings imply the existence of a substantial population, yet no such buildings are mentioned in the documents.[197] The impression from archaeology is that the population of Lamanai must have been quite large, although it is also possible that the second church simply reflects the grandiose vision of a particular friar or cleric concerning the community's potential,[198] which in Spanish colonial terms it never reached. The second church is like the one described by Jones[199] as having been built at Bacalar, with a stone chapel and a nave roofed with thatch. I think Pendergast is correct in his observation about YDL II, which is that "the building should be seen as part of the construction pattern established in more settled areas to the north, rather than as a frontier response to the need for an imposing religious edifice."[200]

The presence of two cemeteries and a church with a stone chapel reflects a community of significant size, and one which the Spanish authorities, both civil and religious, seem to have seen as having the potential to grow and possibly, ultimately, to have attracted Spanish settlers. Yet it is Lamanai's church that was found desecrated in 1641, with its population no longer in residence (see chap. 9). It is possible that flight was short-term and generated by word of an imminent visit by the friars, but it seems unlikely that a community of large size could have been so rapidly abandoned, unless flight had already become a pattern. Whereas Tipu seems to have been attracting Maya, Lamanai had perhaps become too close to Bacalar for comfort. Jones's research has led him to conclude that Lamanai was abandoned under pressure from the Peten Itza.[201]

In the second church at Lamanai we see an architectural style—the stone chapel as a discrete architectural element—that was first developed by Men-

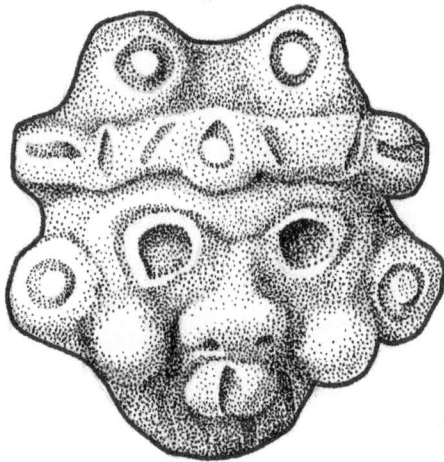

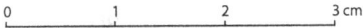

Figure 8.30. Tipu, pottery maskette. From axial cache, Str. H12-7, T-247/1. (Drawing by Louise Belanger)

dicants in Mexico. By the time it reached Yucatan and Belize, it had become part of a standardized "Indian church." Not only the churches but also Strs. N11-18 and H12-8 reflect colonial standards or ideas. Admittedly, Strs. N11-18 at Lamanai and H12-8 at Tipu served secular (residential) purposes, so that their design was not necessarily a reflection of a Franciscan New World ideal, but given that both Tipu and Lamanai were vulnerable as new Christian communities in 1567–68, it is highly likely that the Franciscans continued to handle the direct interactions with the Mayas. They were more likely than Garzón and his men to have worked with the Mayas in laying out and constructing either new buildings or modifications to existing buildings.

At Tipu, Spanish pottery and glass beads from the cores of various house platforms suggest also that other structures were either added to or built anew in the 1567–68 period. One house platform, Str. H12-7 (map 8.3), contained a pre-Columbian-style offering of a bivalve shell and a maskette (fig. 8.30),[202] but we do not know on the basis of the artifacts if the residence was built in 1567–68 or possibly as late as 1618.

An important question is whether YDL II was constructed under the aegis of Franciscans or secular clergy. If Franciscans built it in 1568, as I have suggested, the construction of a stone chapel opens up the possibility that the friars built YDL II as part of never-to-be-realized plans for a monastery complex, which might explain why the colonial-period site center turned out to be farther from YDL II than anticipated, some 200 meters north of the church zone (map 8.1).[203] If YDL II was built by seculars, the implication would be that tribute from Lamanai was reaching the community's encomendero, and that the settlement seemed securely Christian enough to allow it to be turned over to secular administration from Bacalar. It is difficult to say, without knowing who built the church at Bacalar,[204] but given Spanish Christian practices in New Spain and Yucatan, it is more likely that seculars assumed responsibility for ministering to communities but did not supervise construction associated with evangelization or community reorganization in newly Christianized or frontier zones.

The relationship between what we have called the rectory and YDL II reflects an effort less well planned than the monumental chapel, and could be the result of the seculars' stamp on Lamanai, no matter who supervised the construction of YDL II. We know that Lamanai was under secular authority prior to the seventeenth century, and a church official, however infrequently present, required appropriate quarters in the requisite spot north of the church. Spanish settlers in Bacalar could extend their monitoring of tribute-payers in Belize through the secular cleric and his visita rounds, and Lamanai was well positioned to exploit canoe traffic, which brought cacao, cotton, honey, and wax. The dearth of Spanish artifacts that followed Lamaneros to their graves suggests, however, community dynamics different from those of Tipu. It is hard to say whether the dynamics are attributable to restricted access to Spanish goods at Lamanai; to disinterest on the part of the Lamanai community in Spanish goods; to a different sort of religious education and administration; or simply to different conditions under which conversion was effected, for example, the personalities of individual friars and what they carried with them.

✠ NINE ✠

Reductions and Upheaval in the
Seventeenth Century

Ironically, the community of Lamanai—closer to Bacalar, more susceptible to monitoring, and the site of two churches—comes across as more rebellious than Tipu, the distant community. Then again, detecting irony reflects a point of view that assumes a direct relationship between Spanish energy investment and Maya compliance.

As described in chapter 8, Tipu was the focus of at least two reduction efforts in the early seventeenth century, in 1608 and in 1615, with concomitant changes to encomienda restructuring effected by 1622.[1] This was also the period marked by Bacalar's weakening control and by flight from a number of its encomienda towns.[2] The state of affairs for Bacalar and communities to its south stands in contrast to communities north and northwest of Belize, in which the period from about 1602 to 1615 was a time in which Franciscans were reasonably successful in gathering apostate and pagan Maya into mission communities at places such as Champoton and Tixchel (map 5.1), and even the east coast.[3] These successes were, however, dependent on keeping Spanish soldiers and settlers at bay, and the only reason for holding back seems to have been that military expeditions were repeatedly failing. Once some success in establishing reduction communities had been achieved by the friars, the Spaniards stood poised to expand economic exploitation.[4] Overall, the small-scale reductions of the first decade or so of the seventeenth century seem not to have satisfied the Spaniards in terms of bringing their idea of order to the frontier, and such a climate simply intensified concerns about the influence of the non-Christian Maya of the Peten lakes.

Two major undertakings reflected the "problem-solving" of this period. First, the colonial government based in Mérida sought to isolate the alcaldes and secular priests of Bacalar from control over territory they had sought to exploit, which included the Belize missions.[5] The encomienda restructuring of 1622 represented this first effort, and the absentee encomenderos of Bacalar, already resident in Valladolid, had control of their encomiendas wrested from them and assigned to people in Mérida. This was certainly bad for Bacalar, but could have gone either way for the Maya of Tipu or Lamanai, depending on the economic contribution of their tribute and the regularity with which it was collected.

Second, and in this case bad for the Mayas of Tipu, a new entrada was conceived in 1618 that deeply affected the town. Beginning in 1614–15, problems began emerging in the recently reduced communities in Campeche and along the east coast, apparently the result of incursion by Spanish colonists and soldiers.[6] The entrada into Tipu at that time is a well-known venture, undertaken by the Franciscan friars Bartolomé de Fuensalida and Juan de Orbita. It was originally described by Lopez de Cogolludo,[7] but is richly contextualized by Jones on the basis of further documentation.[8]

Several factors are important to highlight here. First, the friars Fuensalida and Orbita were happy to make the journey without military escort. Several Spanish officials had been trying to obtain permission from the Council of the Indies to lead an armed entrada to the Peten, but they had so far been denied and the Franciscans hoped to persuade the Itzas to convert without armed conflict.[9] This emphasizes the competing agendas that existed in the colonial period, of which the Maya were aware, and which almost certainly factored in their decision making.[10] It is also interesting that the friars needed a special commission from the bishop to administer the sacraments at Tipu and other towns. In 1618, and probably since the 1568 reductions, the secular priest based in Bacalar had jurisdiction over Tipu and presumably other Belize and New River mission towns.[11] That the order from the bishop forbade the secular priest to visit Tipu while the Franciscans were there says something about the strained relationships between Mendicants and seculars, and perhaps also about the quality of ministration by seculars.

Also of interest is the description of the items the Franciscans carried with them as gifts for the Mayas:[12] crosses, knives, needles, rosary and glass beads, a chalice, vestments, white raiments, other ritual items for the Mass, a crucifix, and religious paintings for the church.[13] The friars left Mérida in mid-April of 1618, recruited Maya maestros from towns around Tekax (map 5.1), stopped in Bacalar, and then made their way to Tipu via Lamanai and other towns on the New River (map 9.1). At Tipu, which at the time had a population of about 340,[14] they were met with ceremonies of prayers in the church, and we learn that the church's patron was San Pedro. (One of the possible functions of the feature excavated on the north side of the Tipu nave, just west of the north doorway [figs. 8.23, 8.26], was to support the requisite statue of the church's patron saint.) The friars were lodged in what Jones describes as "the house of the secular priest, located next to the church."[15] This is almost certainly Str. H12-18.

The alcalde of Bacalar accompanied the friars, and he was put up in the house of Doña Isabel Pech, who was one of the principales of the town and the widow of a former cacique, a post also known as a batab, or governor.[16] Her house is described as being adjacent to the church,[17] and is most likely to have been Str. H12-14, just south of the church (fig. 1.1, map 8.3), where

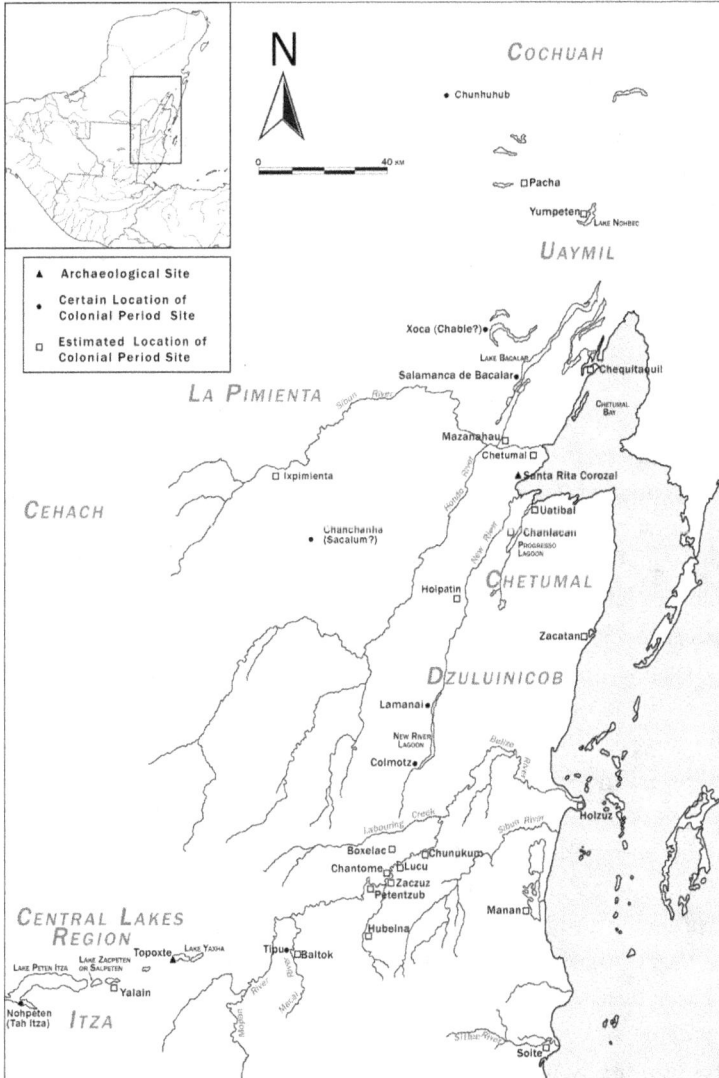

Map 9.1. Location of colonial-period communities in northern Belize on the upper Belize River and in adjacent Peten. (Drawing by Debora Trein)

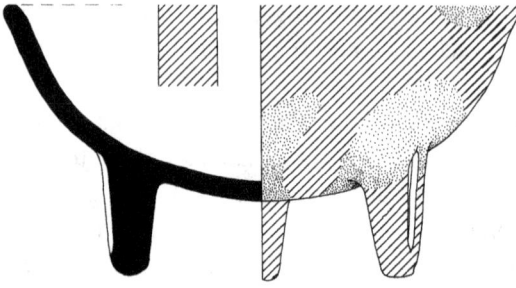

Figure 9.1. Tipu, Yglesias-phase-style pottery vessel from Str. H12-14, T-779/1. D= 16 cm.(Drawing by Louise Belanger)

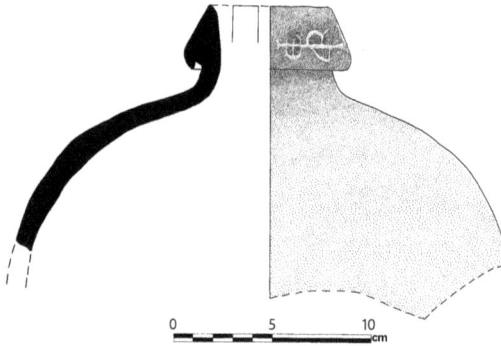

Figure 9.2. Tipu, upper portion of olive jar with stamped rim, from area of Str. H12-14, T-695/1. (Drawing by Louise Belanger)

we recovered a broken and discarded pottery vessel with tapered tripod feet and slender vertical perforations, similar to a number of Yglesias-phase vessels from Lamanai (fig. 9.1; see also fig. 2.4).[18] A fragment of a stamped olive jar was found on the pavement near the house (fig. 9.2).

The Pech chibalob allied themselves with the Spaniards early on in Yucatan; in the Ceh Pech area, 90 percent of cahob were ruled by a Pech batab (cah governor).[19] Doña Isabel's presence at Tipu exemplifies the close ties Tipu must have had with Yucatan. The fact that Doña Isabel's husband had died imprisoned in Mérida—Jones[20] thinks that idolatry figured in the accusations—suggests that effigies other than Christian might have been kept in the house, but no such "idols," even in fragmentary form, turned up in the excavations of Str. H12-14.

I noted above that a pre-Columbian-style cache was found in the core of Str. H12-7 (map 8.3), along what appeared to be the transverse axis. The cache, probably an offering, comprised a small pottery maskette of a supernatural (fig. 8.30), whose pursed lips suggest association with breath or the wind, and a bivalve (*Antigona listerei* Grey). Spanish artifacts, such as olive-jar fragments recovered from the core of the platform, anchor Str. H12-7's construction firmly to the historic period, but as noted in chapter 8, we do not know whether this could have been as early as the later sixteenth century or during the 1618 reduction.

The context of the maskette is reminiscent of the contexts of the saurian, shark, and centipede effigies reported from Lamanai, except that the effigies at Lamanai date either to construction of the first church or to after the rebellion of 1638–41. The Tipu cache—typically pre-Columbian on the primary (transverse) axis of the residence—seems to have been deposited during a time when Tipu was expanding as a Christian community, at least in Spanish eyes. It suggests that Fuensalida was right to worry about "what was going on in their hearts."[21]

While the friars were there, the Mayas of Tipu attended Mass and sent their children every day for catechism.[22] Such instruction would have gone on normally in any case, under the direction of the *maestro de capilla* or *sacristan mayor*, although the adult community would have been expected to attend Mass just on Sundays and feast days.[23]

After seeing to the regularization of daily Christian rituals and activities, the friars then organized a delegation of Tipuans to send to Nohpeten in Peten (map 9.1) to announce the friars' intention to visit the Maya ruler there, Can Ek, and extract a commitment to Christianity. After receiving an invitation from the Itzas, and after minor setbacks, a delegation left Tipu for Nohpeten on 28th of September 1618. Orbita had recently visited Nohpeten in 1616 or 1617,[24] and Jones believes that the friar must have received some encouragement from Can Ek, because his expectations were high on the return visit in 1618; other factions at Nohpeten seem, however, to have won out.[25]

The Itza respectfully received the friars in 1618; they were just not prepared to convert. They were hospitable, but they made it clear that they were not yet ready to become Christians. Things might have succeeded in passing uneventfully, but the story is that the friars saw an "idol" of a horse in one of the temples along the lake. Cortés had passed through this area on his way to Honduras and left a horse with the Itzas. The horse died, and the Itzas apparently created an effigy of it, which would in any circumstance have been a logical step, because horses were not an animal familiar to the Itzas and an effigy would have served as a mnemonic device, or at least a reminder of what a horse looked like. Had this been nineteenth-century Europe, the effort would have been seen as good science. The friars, however, claimed the statue of the horse was an object of worship. Orbita could not contain himself, and destroyed the effigy, which did not please his hosts. Although the friars and the delegation from Tipu were still treated civilly, they left in a few days without achieving their goal. It is notable, however, that Can Ek never said "no"; he simply said it was not the time. A cross left by Cortés was still standing in the town,[26] which is somewhat difficult to explain unless it was believed to have some importance or efficacy. In any case, the visit was a failure, and the Itzas remained non-Christian.

Jones relates that Fuensalida and Orbita, with the unwelcome "help" of Gregorio de Aguilar at one point, found a resurgence of idolatry at Tipu in 1619.[27] Mounting fears that an alliance was developing between Tipu and the Itzas were to prove correct.[28] The friars made another trip to Nohpeten in 1619, the success of which was apparently foiled by Can Ek's wife.[29]

In the meantime, Bacalareños continued their excessive demands for cacao from the southern Maya towns, and the restructured encomienda that included Tipu in 1622 (noted above) probably reflected the encomenderos' efforts to keep the supply of cacao flowing in the face of flight and shifting allegiances among the Maya. Tipu leaders sent complaints to Mérida, but apparently to no avail.[30]

Tipuans Join the Ranks
of Christian Martyrs in 1623

An ill-fated visit to Nohpeten (Tah Itza) was organized from Tipu by another Franciscan, Fray Diego Delgado, in 1623. Delgado originally worked in La Florida, and then served in Franciscan administrative posts in Yucatan before turning to the saving of new or recalcitrant souls by "reducing" fugitives.[31] In 1621 he was assigned by Governor Diego de Cárdenas, who by Jones's account was both ambitious and ill-informed, to accompany a military entrada, with aims to conquer the Itzas, under Captain Francisco de Mirones y Lezcano. Such an entrada was strictly forbidden by the Crown, but this did not seem to faze either Mirones or Cárdenas, and Delgado had his own agenda based on religious zeal.[32]

Delgado reported to his Franciscan superiors in Mérida on Mirones's cruelty and exploitation of the Mayas at Sacalum and Ixpimienta in early 1623 (map 9.1). The response was that Mirones's expedition—despite the fact that it had gone ahead—was officially prohibited, with the implication that Delgado need not follow Mirones's orders, so the friar left shortly for the land of the Itzas. Delgado, along with the cacique from Tipu, Don Cristobal Na, plus eighty Tipuans, reached Nohpeten in July of 1623. All were promptly killed. One of the reasons given by the Itzas was the insult they had received from Orbita's destructive acts in their temple.

More Martyrs at Sacalum
in 1624 and Emerging Resistance

Mirones and his men were subsequently massacred at Sacalum in January of 1624. They had settled themselves at Ixpimienta and then Sacalum the previous year, and had been treating the Mayas badly. Mirones had difficulties, in fact, in replacing Delgado once he had left Mirones's party for the Peten region, because news of the conditions at Sacalum had reached the Franciscan provincial in Mérida. A friar was finally sent to Sacalum, but he left after only fifteen days, disillusioned by the behavior of Mirones and his men. Mirones's fall-back position was to ask the governor for a secular priest, but even this was refused. Eventually, a friar volunteered, but he was killed along with Mirones and his men at Sacalum.

The leader of the Maya attackers, described as a non-Christian Maya priest named Ah Kin Pol,[33] allowed the Spanish soldiers to confess to the friar before their death. The Maya under Pol apparently pleaded for the life of the friar, but he was nonetheless killed by Ah Kin Pol himself.[34] In Franciscan terms, this manner of death granted martyrdom to the friar. Given pre-Columbian religious beliefs, Ah Kin Pol's action was also in keeping with an honorable death. In war in pre-Columbian times, elites put their lives on the line in hand-to-hand combat with the intention of capturing the enemy and bringing him back to the community to be killed in the temple by a priest. Ah Kin Pol may therefore have reckoned that by allowing the Christian soldiers to confess, and then killing them and the friar himself, he was acting within the strictures of both Maya and Christian faiths. He cut out the hearts of Mirones and the friar, but not those of the soldiers. Jones's recent reinterpretation[35] suggests that Ah Kin Pol (now rendered AjK'in P'ol) was the Itza territorial ruler, priest, and military leader (also known as AjChata P'ol and Nakom P'ol) who fairly treated Fuensalida and Orbita in 1618 and 1619. If so, then this strengthens my suggestion that Ah Kin Pol, as a Maya leader, was acting within the boundaries of the rules of elite warfare at the same time that he granted Christians an honorable death.

Not long afterward, the Maya governor of Oxkutzcab (map 5.1), Don Fernando Camal, and 150 men from the town, were commissioned to kill Pol and his followers.[36] Thus, Maya were recruited by Spaniards to kill Maya. After Camal's success, he was rewarded with an inherited (Spanish) title as well as exemption from labor and taxes.

The question remains as to the extent of cooperation among the Maya of Tipu, Nohpeten, and the Sacalum region. Jones observes that "the massacres of 1623–1624 at Tah Itza (Nohpeten) and Sacalum" were "a major departure from previous Maya strategies of rebellion,"[37] and he suggests the unusual violence reflects a katun prophecy: the time had come to deny the right of Spaniards to impose control. The character of the violence, however, in which the enemy was captured and beheaded, is consonant with pre-Columbian Maya warfare. This supports what Jones later argues, which is that the uprising reflected the tactics and regional influence of the Itza.[38] An argument could be made, based on the evidence, that if Mirones had acted differently at Ixpimienta and Sacalum, or had been held back, and if Orbita had not destroyed the effigy of the horse in the Itzas' temple, things might have been different. Even so, this chapter in frontier history, from about 1600 to 1624, exemplifies the conflicting and competing agendas of both Spaniards and Mayas, and the complexities of what so often is simply called conquest and resistance.[39]

Flight from the North to Belize,
1628–1638

Governor Cárdenas was replaced in 1628 by Juan de Vargas, who was as self-serving and exploitative as his predecessor,[40] and clearly the wrong man to solve the problems of the times. Reports began to trickle in of non-Christian Mayas killing Christian Mayas in Cehach (map 5.1). Even though Franciscan efforts continued in the frontier at this time, greater numbers of Spanish colonists and soldiers began penetrating the remote regions.[41]

To add to excesses perpetrated by Spanish officials, the peninsula was struck by four shortfall harvests, and famine resulted. This alone stimulated many people to flee to the forests of Belize, southern Campeche, and Peten. At the same time, the depredations of pirates along the eastern coasts increased, and many Mayas from coastal villages in Belize fled inland to the area around Tipu.[42]

The 1630s come across at first glance as a period of confusion, and yet as Jones points out, what caused confusion to Spanish authorities—the restricted pool of labor owing to flight—strengthened communities in Belize and elsewhere on the southern Maya frontier.[43] The documents pertaining to communities along the Sibun River (map 9.1) are illustrative of this period.

In 1630–31, Mayas fled the towns of Xibun and Soite. The position of Soite is known to have been near the mouth of the Sittee River (map 9.1); Xibun was on the Sibun River, but its exact location is not yet known. Those who fled were persuaded to return through Spanish intervention, with the help of Mayas from the nearby town of Zacatan (map 9.1), but their flight is believed by Jones to have been a response to a call from a center of resistance, and that the call was legitimized by religious or prophetic claims.[44] According to the Spaniards, the Maya were found in the forest with many idols; but they had also, in the case of Xibun, brought their church bells and church ornaments with them.[45] They returned to their towns, but this acquiescence turned out to be the calm before the storm.

The year 1638 ushered in a new katun, and with it, resistance to Spanish control in the Belize Maya communities intensified, influenced no doubt by powerful pressure from the Itzas.[46] Despite the deaths of the Tipuans at the hands of the Itzas in 1618, Tipu seems to have thrown its lot in with the anti-Spanish movement. A contributing factor seems to have been Bacalar and its abuses.[47] When the Yucatan governor sent investigators to Bacalar, the local Spanish inhabitants prepared to hang them. The same governor reported in a letter to the king of Spain on the 10th of July, 1638, that the lone secular priest based in Bacalar, Gregorio Marín de Aguilar, was too old to do his rounds any more. The priest who was sent to assist Aguilar behaved so tyrannically that he had to be sent back.[48]

Just days after the governor had written this letter, Bacalar advised the governor that the inhabitants of Tipu had rebelled and had disclaimed their obedience to the Crown. A Tipuan then in Mérida was sent back to Tipu with a "friendly letter" from the governor in order to report back to Mérida on what had happened. He returned with Tipu's cacique and others, who brought with them the results of their elections for confirmation (as was annually required of Maya towns).

All this behaviour certainly argued for normalcy. The cacique reported that Tipuans had indeed fled, but it was owing to fear of the Bacalareños and their cruelties. On the strength of the governor's friendly letter, the cacique said that he would attempt to bring everyone back who had run away.[49] This blend of adhering to Spanish bureaucratic demands (having results of elections confirmed in Mérida), and resorting to unauthorized behaviour (such as flight) with placement of blame on cruel local officials, conforms to a pattern in Yucatan,[50] and in retrospect can be seen as highly effective.

Later on, in September 1638, Mayas from Manan claimed that they received threats from the Tipuans to abandon their town, as did those from Holpatin, which was just north of Lamanai (map 9.1). Some of Lamanai's inhabitants had apparently been moved to San Juan Extramuros, which was the Maya town just outside Bacalar. Similar reports of threats and flight were emerging from throughout Belize, and there were repeats of the Soite and Xibun incidents of flight.[51]

From 1639 to 1642 the situation would worsen. So few towns and villages remained loyal that congregation of those who did not flee was limited. Apparently, some people were resettled at both Tipu and Lamanai during this time, but most had fled.[52]

Fuensalida Returns to Tipu, 1639–1641

By 1639, Maya passive resistance had turned to open rebellion. The governor in Mérida decided to send a secular priest to Bacalar to encourage the rebels to return to their towns. The rebels, however, sent him packing, although they indicated that they would meet with Franciscan representatives if the despised secular priest, Gregorio de Aguilar, who had been based at Bacalar since 1632, was replaced by members of the Franciscan order.[53] Chuchiak, in fact, places some of the blame for the Maya rebellion on the harsh treatment of the Maya by local secular priests.[54]

Plans were then made in Mérida to recruit Franciscans, and Fray Fuensalida, in recognition of his prior experience at both Tipu and Nohpeten, was appointed to return with three other Franciscans. One, Fray Juan de Estrada, had godchildren in Tipu. All were fluent Maya speakers.[55]

When the friars reached Bacalar, Father Gregorio was sent back to Valladolid, apparently not unwillingly. Fuensalida and one of the other friars, Estrada, went on to Belize with a party of Mayas. (Fray Becerril went to reduce the coastal towns, and Fray Tejero stayed behind at Bacalar.) When they reached Lamanai, Fuensalida and Estrada found the houses and church burned[56] and the inhabitants gone; apparently, the approach of the friars had been closely watched by "spies" sent by Tipuans.[57] It is also possible that Lamaneros abandoned the community of their own accord. No standing stela was reported in the ashes of the nave, which supports the contention that the stela erection associated with YDL II probably occurred after the period of rebellion.

The party then traveled south for the length of the lagoon until they reached the community of Colmotz, which was on the western shore at the lagoon's southernmost point (known today as Hill Bank) (map 9.1). Here they left their river transport, a *falca*, and began the walk overland to the Belize River. When they reached the banks of the river, they encountered some of the inhabitants of Holpatin, the village situated north of Lamanai on the New River. Holpatin had also been abandoned and burned.[58]

The group from Holpatin, including the cacique, then took the friars and their companions in canoes upstream to Zaczuz (map 9.1), where the houses and church had also been burned and the church bell thrown into the bush. Here, some of the Maya accompanying the friars fled out of fear. Zaczuz had been abandoned (for another location called Hubelna [map 9.1] three leagues into the mountains), so the cacique of Zaczuz let the friars stay in his cacao orchard. Eventually, the friars' party was met by Tipuans, who warned them not to proceed to Tipu. One of the Tipuans, who appeared to be moved by the friars' pleas, promised to come back with canoes, but this never materialized.[59]

The rainy season began, and the party tried to seek shelter at Hubelna. There was an emotional scene in which Fuensalida assembled a throng to read letters from the governor, but one by one the audience disappeared until the friars and their servant were left alone with the cacique. It was not long before the house where the friars were staying was surrounded, and the friars and their Maya servant, Lázaro Pech, were thrown to the ground and their hands were tied behind them. The attackers then tore open the boxes with church ornaments and clothing and broke the images. Itzas seem to have been present, because shouts from the attackers reminded Fuensalida of Orbita's attack on the horse effigy at Nohpeten.[60]

Surprisingly, the friars and their servant were set free, although they were thrown out of Hubelna. The other Mayas who had travelled with the friars from Bacalar had been hiding in the bush, but they joined the friars and the entire party went first to the Zaczuz orchard to retrieve a canoe left for them, and then journeyed as quickly as possible down the Belize River, overland to Colmotz, where they found their *falca* and supplies destroyed. They discovered old, abandoned canoes, which the Mayas from Bacalar repaired, and they set out toward Lamanai.[61]

Fears of being attacked kept them wary, however, and they paddled through the night at one point in order to reach the mouth of the New River. Eventually, they reached what is now modern Chetumal (map 1.1). Estrada carried the news to the governor in Mérida that only a military solution was now feasible.[62]

The Rebellion and Its Aftermath

By 1641 it was clear that Tipu leaders, or at least the most powerful of them, had joined the Itzas in a full-scale effort to establish hegemony over central and western Belize.[63] Along the coast of Belize, things could conceivably have turned out better for the Spaniards, because the coastal towns of Manan, Soite (map 9.1), and Campin (map 5.1) seemed less influenced by Tipu's aggression. Campin was in Manche Chol territory; Soite (Sittee) had both Yucatec and Manche Chol speakers. Fray Becerril and Fray Tejero, who had set out when Fuensalida and Estrada started their journey to Tipu, had some success in converting and reducing the Mayas of coastal towns. Jones provides a fascinating description of Tejero's experience in first-time conversions of Manche Chol.[64]

Unfortunately for the Spaniards, and in this case for Mayas as well, all this came to nothing, owing to the activities of pirates, who attacked towns along the Belize coast and forced the inhabitants to flee. In November 1642 the pirates attacked Bacalar, and by 1643 Bacalar seems to have been severely decimated.[65] It received a final blow in 1648, when the few people left were attacked again.[66] The *villa* of Bacalar was then moved to a town called Pacha (map 9.1), on the road to Valladolid.

The Pérez Entradas into Belize,
1654–1656

One would think that at this point the Spaniards might have given up, but between 1652 and 1654 a captain based at the new *villa* location in Pacha,

Captain Francisco Pérez, attempted to regain what had been lost in Belize, partly because he held several towns, such as Uatibal and Chanlacan (map 9.1), in encomienda. Pérez was serving as alcalde at Bacalar/Pacha and thus was interim governor of the Bacalar province. His reports were first analyzed by Scholes and Thompson,[67] but Jones was able to place Pérez's efforts in context, and he details the Pérez entradas, which took the captain on one trip to Holzuz (apparently near the Belize River mouth) and on another to the upper Belize River, to Holpachay and Chunukum but never to Tipu itself, between 1654 and 1656.[68] (The proposed locations of Holzuz and Chunukum are shown in map 9.1, but the location of Holpachay is not known.)

Basically, the entradas produced records of population counts as well as individuals' names. People traveled to a location on the Belize River and reported to Pérez there. Most individuals claimed to be from Tipu; one was from Lamanai; nine other towns were represented,[69] as were "indios del monte" (forest Indians, who were not Christianized and who retained pre-Conquest naming practices). According to Jones,[70] the non-Christian Maya were elite Itza residents of Tipu, some of whom were members of a royal Itza lineage. As representatives of Nohpeten, these non-Christian elites were simply allowing their subject population to be counted to keep Pérez at bay.

Although no Spanish official returned from Bacalar/Pacha after 1656 to administer the region, it is significant that Tipuans and others cooperated in completing the census, in partaking of the sacraments, and in having town officers named, even if the action was a ploy of Itza masters. Also interesting is that the names recorded revealed that the population of Tipu was heavily Yucatecan in origin, and the diversity in names that existed was consistent with what would be expected for a mobile population with a high rate of immigration and emigration.[71] Despite being subject to the Itza, as Jones claims, we do not know that Tipuans had no decision-making power, and their alliance with the Itzas was clearly undergoing some adjustment.

From 1678 to 1707

In 1678 there is evidence that Tipu was contacted via an entrada that originated at Sahcabchen, near Champoton on the Gulf Coast (map 5.1). Six hundred persons were said to have been baptized, but this did not change the fact that Tipu remained beyond the Spanish orbit.[72] Although an effort was made in 1687, via an entrada to Chanchanha (map 9.1), to open a route to Nohpeten that would pass through Tipu,[73] it was at this juncture that Tipu became peripheral to the Itza conquest. In 1696, Governor Ursua began the *camino real* that was to connect Mérida directly with the Peten region along a north-south axis that bypassed Tipu.[74]

In 1695 an important event occurred. Tipu was contacted by an alcalde of Bacalar, Captain Francisco de Hariza y Arruyo. Upon reaching the town, Hariza sent seven Tipuans to Mérida to render their obedience and to request that their elections be confirmed. The Tipuans also requested that priests be provided to the community.[75] Thus, with Hariza's visit, Tipu's rebellion can be said to have ended, and Tipuans quietly changed strategy to one of cooperation with colonial demands.

Of Lamanai during these years, we know little. The town is not mentioned in the documents, but this does not mean that it had been abandoned. The archaeological evidence from YDL II—the animal effigy caches and the use of the stone chapel as a residence—and from scattered locations around the site, suggests that the Maya returned after 1641, but they seem to have lost all contact with Bacalar/Pacha. Further excavation aimed specifically at illuminating the late sixteenth- and seventeenth-century occupation is called for, but we need to know more about what to expect of the material culture of this period.

In the meantime, pressures on Nohpeten steadily increased.[76] As Governor Ursua continued his road, a Spanish party set out from Guatemala to conquer the Cholti-speaking Lacandones in western Peten (map 5.1). This party had encountered some Mayas near the lake, and fighting broke out in which Mayas lost their lives. The Guatemalans had other agendas, however,[77] and did not wish to pursue the Itza conquest; it was thus left in Ursua's hands. In June 1695 Ursua sent the Franciscan Fray Andres de Avendaño y Loyola to Nohpeten, but the behavior of the friar's military escort disturbed him, so he returned to Mérida and started out again in December, carrying a letter to Can Ek from Ursua. Despite initial positive overtures, Avendaño was forced out of town by those hostile to Can Ek. An Itza delegation had apparently gone to Mérida in December of 1695, but Jones observes that such a delegation was in fact probably staged by Ursua as a means of legitimizing his planned conquest.[78]

With regard to Tipu, the governor had promised the Tipu delegation that priests would be newly assigned to their community. The Franciscans tried to gain control of this mission, but they were restricted by the Crown to the entradas and reductions along Ursua's new *camino real*. The Tipu mission remained in the hands of secular clergy because, it was argued, Tipu had been part of Bacalar. As a result, nine secular priests were sent to Tipu in 1696. The priests had hoped to go on to Nohpeten, but news reached them about Avendaño y Loyola's expulsion, with the result that they decided to stay on at Tipu. Apparently, Captain Hariza had twenty-one soldiers stationed at Tipu at this time.[79] They are reported to have constructed a fortification; we did not find evidence of a fortification archaeologically, but there is a strong possibility that Str. H12-8 in its final phase of construction served to house the soldiers (map 8.3).

After a couple of months at Tipu, the mission leader and seven other priests became ill and returned to Mérida, leaving two priests behind. By this time, the road to Nohpeten was almost completed, and a skirmish ensued between Spanish soldiers and the Itzas. The Francisan friar who had come with the Spaniards, Fray Juan de San Buenaventura, was last seen being carried off, along with his lay brother, by the Itzas.[80]

As described by Jones,[81] Nohpeten was attacked early on the morning of the 13th of March in 1697. In effect, the Maya of Nohpeten were dispersed rather than beaten, and the Spaniards took possession of the island.

What Happened to Tipu and Lamanai

The establishment of a *presidio* at Nohpeten in 1697 (Nuestra Señora de los Remedios y San Pablo, Laguna del Itzá) comprised a formal, if small, impoverished and embattled Spanish settlement.[82] Such Spanish presence in Peten was, however, the source of intermittent missionary and military activity which stimulated the flight of Mayas into the Belize forests.[83] The date of 1707 marks the year when Tipuans were forcibly removed to Lake Peten Itza,[84] presumably to facilitate being administered by the small number of Spaniards then based in Peten. There were several reasons for the move: the administration of Tipu was difficult, given its location; Tipuans were being carried off by Spaniards from Yucatan as forced laborers, despite Tipu's cooperation in pacifying Lake Peten and also in attacking English logwood cutters who had settled lower down on the Belize River at Zacatan; and, finally, the British had raided Tipu for slaves. By early 1708, there was reportedly a settlement near the *presidio* known as the town of the Tipuans.[85]

Even with this move, the record reflects the fact that Mayas who had been moved to Peten were repeatedly forced to relocate, because they continued to flee eastward to Belize and to forested regions. How large the population was in Belize, however, is unknown, and it is clear that the British in Belize continued to present a threat, first in the form of slave raiding and later in the extraction of timber.[86]

Archaeologically, there is evidence that a battle took place at Tipu very late in the community's history. Unusually large numbers of small side-notched points (arrowheads) and small, bipointed bifaces (spearheads?) were found in surface deposits (fig. 9.3).[87] Jones reports that Tipu had indeed been attacked by "Musuls" (Mopan Maya) in 1708.[88] They killed Tipu's cacique, his lieutenant, and as many as fifteen principales. Why this happened remains

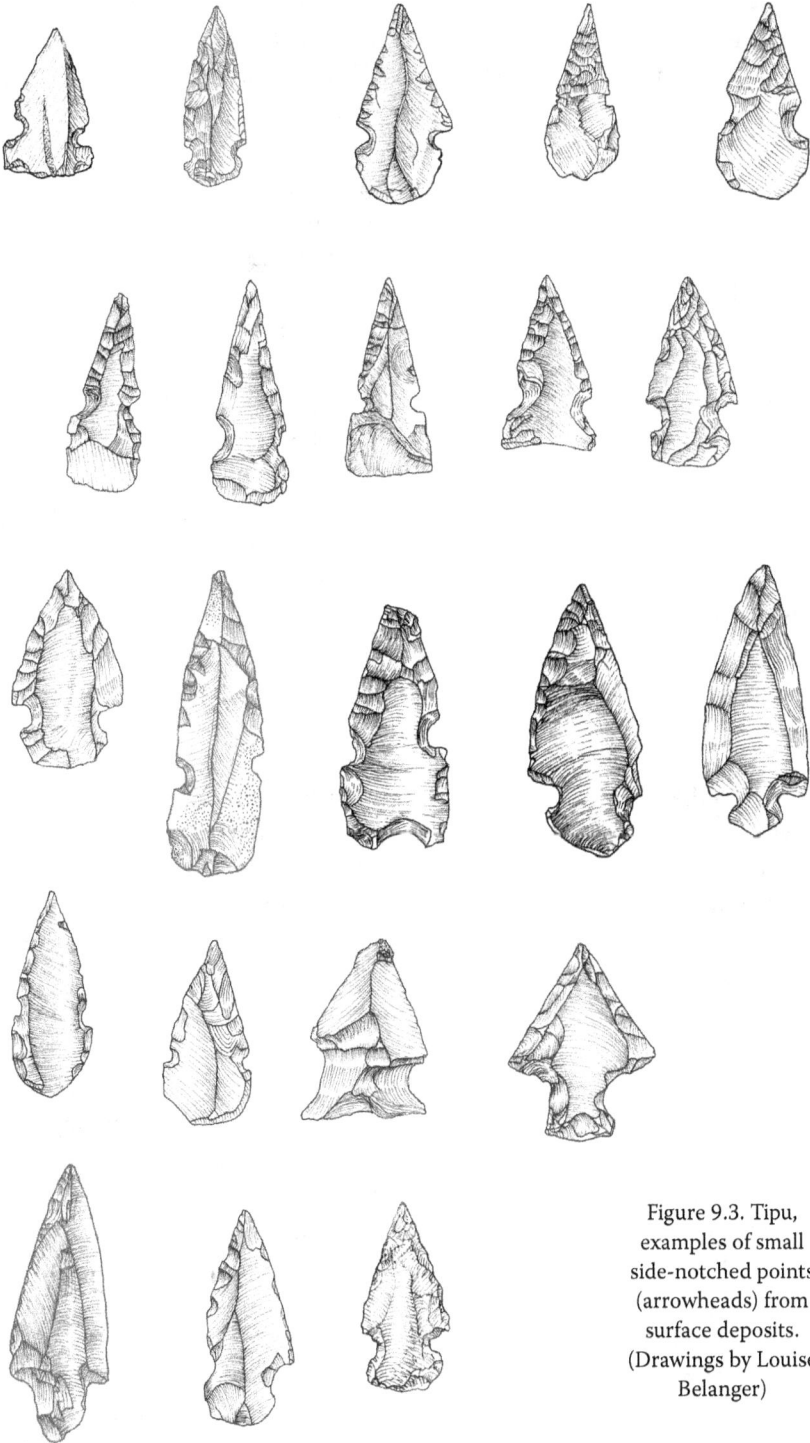

Figure 9.3. Tipu, examples of small side-notched points (arrowheads) from surface deposits. (Drawings by Louise Belanger)

unknown, but given the challenges that the Maya were to face in the next centuries, it is sad to see the century begin with Mayas fighting Mayas.

As for Lamanai, it seems simply to fade into obscurity in the documents, although the archaeological record points to occupation and use after church abandonment. The residence I have referred to as the rectory, Str. H12-12, exhibits modifications and additions that suggest, although do not yet prove, that occupation in the area continued on into the eighteenth century.[89] The stelae described in chapter 8 had to have been erected after the rebellion of 1638–41. Before that time is unlikely, because stelae cannot be easily removed to please visiting clerics, and Fuensalida made no mention of their presence in 1641. Except for the offering at the base of one of the stelae, which is associated with the stela in time, it is hard to date stelae erection or the other cache deposits found within and outside of the chapel with any security, except to say that they are likely to post-date 1641 and may even be much later.[90]

Other evidence for continued activity and apparent occupation takes the form of an individual who was interred in a sitting position in the south part of the sanctuary,[91] the center room of the three that formed the chapel. This subfloor burial, as well as the occurrence of midden material around and outside the walls, suggests that the chapel was used as a residence.[92] The ceramics from the midden are interesting in that they are indistinguishable from pre-Columbian pottery; for example, fragmented censers were found that are very similar to those found both at Mayapan and at Lamanai that normally would be dated to the fifteenth century.[93] Taken together, these occupational, caching, and burial activities must certainly have contributed to the obliteration of evidence of the burning of YDL II in 1641. If any evidence or church-period stratigraphy remained after these events, it was destroyed in the nineteenth century when the chapel was used as a smithy by those associated with the British sugar mill operation.[94]

Pendergast also reports small structures on a low escarpment at the lagoon edge: "From some of the mounds close to the churches we recovered pottery and other evidence of sixteenth-century (or later) occupation, but a good many that were clearly built by the Maya yielded almost nothing but 19th-century English crockery and ironmongery."[95] It is hard to know whether the nineteenth-century structures represent reoccupation of Maya structures by British (or Chinese) residents,[96] or whether Maya in the area were using British pottery, a phenomenon that characterizes the British colonial period in Belize.[97] Pendergast's view, however, is that "there was no link between the 19th century British sugar producing community and the settlement of three hundred years earlier, save for use of the same territory, including the second church."[98] Stone platforms that appear to have supported houses or other buildings can be found south of the church, on a line stretching almost to the boundary of Lamanai Outpost Lodge, which is about one kilometer from the church zone. These are post-Columbian, but the style of construction differs from the domestic architecture of the Spanish colonial period. They are almost certainly post–Spanish colonial in date.[99]

The End of Spanish Colonial Influence

Spanish records of the encounter reflect either Mendicant zeal in spreading Christianity or settlers' justifications for exploiting the Maya economically. Under Spanish colonialism, the Maya were subjects (or objects) of inclusion, but a problematic inclusion. The British invaders, on the other hand, viewed the Maya as interlopers in a land that was exclusively British to exploit. The British colonial record is thus one of exclusion. Jones characterizes the Maya of the post-Spanish period in Belize as "only refugees . . . fighting helplessly as they witnessed a new invasion of British colonists whose interests were single-mindedly focused upon the extraction of timber."[100]

With timber extraction, one would think that the Maya would be given respite, because logwood grew along rivers near the coasts and British logwood extraction would not have extended too far upriver, or inland. In addition, the suppression of privateering after the Treaty of Madrid in 1667 encouraged a shift from slave-raiding to logwood cutting and settlement.[101] However, as described above, the British raided Tipu for slaves sometime around 1707, which is why the Spaniards sought to move the town to the shores of Lake Peten.[102] In fact, during the decade following the routing of the Itza in 1697, Tipuans remained cooperative with Spanish forces in Peten. According to Jones,[103] this had less to do with sympathy for the Spaniards than with a desire to seek protection from the British and their allies, the Miskitos of the Nicaraguan coast. As I described above, Jones reports that in 1701 Spaniards from Yucatan attacked British logwood cutters in northern Belize, and heard reports that buccaneer slavers were plying the Belize River in search of Maya captives. Thus, the English raid at Tipu for slaves in 1707 may have been an extension of this activity.

Jones[104] recounts a horrid tale told by an *alcalde mayor* of Tabasco in 1733. The individual, Francisco López Marchán, had been traveling in a Spanish fleet from Cádiz when his ship had been attacked by a British war frigate near Campeche. He was taken to the port town of Hampton, in Virginia, where he encountered Yucatec-speaking Maya held as slaves. The same individual was then taken to Jamaica, where he encountered another fifteen Mayas. One was a nine-year-old boy who, "upon seeing him and realizing that he was a Spaniard, began to cry; at this point an Englishman grabbed the boy and took him away."[105] At an inn, López Marchán spoke with two Maya women from the town of Tenosique on the Usumacinta River, but he never saw them again because they were kept hidden. In the countryside, he met another Maya woman, who reacted as the boy had reacted when she found out López Marchán was a Spaniard, and she asked him to rescue her and her sister. They had been enslaved six years earlier when Miskitos attacked their town and apparently carried everyone off. She said that in Jamaica an infinity of Mayas had been sold to work in the plantations.

López Marchán was released and reached Campeche, where he told his story to the Bishop of Yucatan, who instructed him to write to the king. Given the attitudes of the Spaniards toward the British, and vice versa, we have to approach such accounts with caution, but the news of illegal traffic in Maya slaves apparently caused a huge reaction in the Council of the Indies. Many other instances of Miskito attacks on the Maya had been documented, most outside of Belize itself. Jones suggests that because relatively few Spaniards ventured into Belize during the eighteenth century, British attacks on Maya villages were seldom recorded.[106]

Colonial History in Perspective

Although recent documentary and archaeological research is beginning to add flesh to our skeletal picture of Spanish-Maya contact in Belize in the sixteenth and seventeenth centuries, no material evidence has been recovered at Lamanai or Tipu, or elsewhere in Belize, of settlement by Spanish colonists. By 1700, active Spanish interest in colonization had evaporated, although *re*-active interest was maintained, owing to the perceived threat of the expanding British presence.[107]

We learn about Spanish responses to what was seen as British incursion into Spanish territory through the documents,[108] but there is nothing in the way of archaeological remains to argue for continued Spanish presence. In fact, one reason it is difficult to date eighteenth-century Maya occupation in Belize is that artifacts associated with Spanish occupation—such as olive jars or locks from chests manufactured in Spain, or Venetian glass beads or jet or amber jewelry transported to the New World—disappear from the record. As indicated by the evidence of activities associated with reuse of the YDL II chapel, the Maya continued to use and to circulate locally produced goods.

Archaeological evidence from Tipu and Lamanai suggests that the Maya continued, if intermittently—which is completely in keeping with Maya residence patterns—to live in Belize after 1700[109] when Spanish interests focused elsewhere. As we have seen, the Itza and other Maya groups of the area around Lake Peten were routed and resettled by the Spaniards in 1697,

Figure 9.4. Tipu,
Lacandon-type
censer fragment
from surface
deposits of Str.
H12-18, the
rectory.

and Tipuans were resettled on the Peten lakeshore a little more than a decade later.[110] Nevertheless, there are indications that Tipu was revisited after abandonment. The Christian cemetery continued to be used after the church had collapsed and after the residence north of the church (Str. H12-18) had fallen into disuse (figs. 1.2, 1.3). There is also evidence of ritual activity atop the ruins of the abandoned historic community. We excavated what is known as a Lacandon-type censer (fig. 9.4)[111] from soil that had accumulated over the collapse debris of Str. H12-18, the building that served as the residence for the church priest or guardian.

Based on stratigraphy and relative dating alone, the censer is no earlier than the beginning of the eighteenth century, and could be later. Thompson, who builds a strong case for continuity of Maya settlements in western Belize,[112] also classifies the style as post-Columbian, and observes that it was a type of censer still used by modern Lacandon, hence its name. He reported in 1977 that two other Lacandon-type censers had been recovered many years earlier from "Negroman."[113] Taken together, the evidence indicates that the upper Belize Valley was at least intermittently a region of Maya activity, and very possibly a locus of settlement after 1700. At minimum, Tipu lived on in Maya memory, and both Christian and non-Christian Maya considered the location to be sacred space, not just in the colonial period, but for some time thereafter.

Sacred Space, Christianity, and Landscape

The idea that sacred space can be both Christian and pre-Christian is consonant with my emphasis in this book on Maya appropriation and internalization of Christian ideas and beliefs. At one time, the Maya of Belize were accustomed to conditions in which cities, towns, villages, forests, and the complexities of the marine environment—mangrove coast, coral reef, deep sea, and atolls—formed a highly integrated peninsular urban system (see chap. 5).[114] The arrival of Europeans changed all this, and Belize became a frontier to Spanish colonists and a frontier of frontiers to the British. The Maya from Ambergris Caye to the Toledo District (fig. 5.8) were forced inland relatively early in the colonial sequence, and throughout the eighteenth and part of the nineteenth century the Mayas' main option in Belize was to settle and manage forested landscapes, away from Spanish and British villages and towns. Much of their territory before the arrival of Europeans had been cleared, was densely inhabited, and had been well traveled, but it was rapidly becoming forested. These forests provided, among other factors, both a physical and a psychological environment critical to Maya survival. Other factors contributing to survival were the humid lowland setting, which was generally shunned by Spanish settlers; the fact that the British in the region did not encourage farming or the spread of extensive agriculture and cattle-raising;[115] and the fact that the forests could serve as havens, if sometimes only temporarily, for Mayas fleeing Spanish colonial activity or British raids. Inadvertently on the part of the colonials, conditions were created which may well have facilitated the persistence of indigenous ideas of landscape, and this is a possibility which archaeologists, anthropologists, and historians need to consider.

What does this have to do with Christianity? Of all the areas that the Spaniards attempted to control, the land that became Belize was home to communities that became Christian, remained elusive, and yet persisted in the absence of Spanish religious or secular control. Even Lake Peten, the center of Maya resistance, had a *presidio* plunked down on its shore. We therefore need to consider the possibility that the Christianity practiced by the Maya in Belize may have been a key to their survival strategies. In the first instance, as Christians, the Belize Maya were not seen to be as dangerous as the pagan Itza. If the Maya of Belize had openly refused Christianity, Spanish colonial authorities would have found a way to bring troops to the region and declare open war. As it was, because the Maya became Christian at an early date, and because they were so far from centers of control, they were at greater liberty than the Maya of Yucatan or Guatemala to integrate Christian beliefs with a range of pre-Columbian views of the world, not least important of which were sacred landscapes. This is not the old argument for the existence of pristine pre-Columbian thought; it is instead an argument that the Maya of Belize should be considered on their own terms. From the very beginning, the Mayas' adoption of Christianity involved investing it with local traditions, rituals, and supernaturals. Although the core of Christian belief is said to be the concept of Jesus Christ as redeemer and savior of mankind, there is no barrier to holding this as an article of faith at the same time that rituals are celebrated and new supernaturals are interpreted with local traditions, histories, and landscapes in mind.

One Last Tale to Tell

There is one last tale to tell which bears on the post-Spanish colonial occupation of Lamanai. I have stated that YDL I was viewed simply as a cemetery before it was recognized as the remains of a church. In Pendergast's words:

> In the course of work on the church and burials within its platform in 1983, the presence of the interments came to the attention of Pastor Mesh, a Maya from the northern Orange Walk District who had settled near the northern end of the site in 1973. In establishing a small farm at Lamanai, Don Pastor was simply returning to the place of his birth; his parents were part of a group . . . who settled on the land, which was then owned by the Belize Estate and Produce Company Limited, some time prior to 1909, the year of his birth. In 1917, the company drove [them] from the spot and destroyed their settlement. Fifty-five years later, Don Pastor and his sons returned to what he regarded as his land. . . .
>
> Upon being told that we were excavating burials from what we subsequently determined was the first church, Don Pastor informed us that his grandfather, together with others who died in the eight- to ten-year life of his village, was buried in the building. He also stated that the choice of the burial spot was dictated by the fact that the villagers knew the featureless mound to be consecrated ground that had been used as a cemetery in times past. It is apparent that this knowledge led the villagers to transport their dead almost two kilometers south for burial. . . . The knowledge on which their choice rested cannot have come to them by any means other than oral transmission, for it was to be another seventy years before the identity of the church became known through archaeological research.[116]

This story adds weight to the argument that further work at Lamanai will yield information on greater continuity of occupation in Belize than has heretofore been acknowledged. It is curious, however, that the cemetery of YDL I became part of collective memory, and not the cemetery associated with YDL

II.[117] We have always assumed, because of its proximity to YDL II, that use of the cemetery discovered in 1985 replaced the use of YDL I. Don Pastor's story suggests, however, that the practice of burial in YDL I may have continued long beyond the building's life as a church, in preference to use of the YDL II cemetery. Alternatively, the burning of YDL II and the fact that it was used as a setting for pre-Columbian-style rituals may have changed the nature of its sacred space in the eyes of some Christianized Maya in the community; we simply do not know. We can say, however, on the basis of Don Pastor's story and the presence of the two cemeteries, that social and cultural changes in the sixteenth and seventeenth centuries were nothing if not complex, and it is clear that we must never underestimate the variety of responses to colonial conditions.

The churches and the features associated with them seem to have lived on in Maya memory, both at Lamanai and at Tipu. This tells us that the appropriation of sacred space—by both converters and converted—is a key part of the process of what, for lack of a better term, can be called culture contact. Hence, a key anthropological inference that can be drawn from the colonial experience in Belize is that sacred spaces long outlive, and serve beyond, the particular beliefs that generate them.

✛ **PART IV** ✛

TEN

What Europe Did for Us

In the foregoing chapters I examine the conversion process with reference to the Maya of Belize, and I focus in particular on the towns of Tipu and Lamanai, where we have archaeological evidence of church complexes that served as modest but pivotal "theaters of conversion."[1] In this chapter, which forms the first part of my synthesis and conclusions, I examine particular aspects of the context of conversion. The chapter title is taken from the name of a British television program that examined the contributions made by earlier societies to modern Britain, such as "What the Romans Did for Us" or "What the Victorians Did for Us."[2] My interest, however, is not in the legacy of sixteenth-century Spain per se, but instead in what about Europe's past led to the sixteenth-century attitudes, behaviors, and beliefs that were exported to Mesoamerica.

First I examine the roots of the obsession with idolatry and hence the justification for its extirpation. I then examine Christianity's links to imperial strategies. Finally, I isolate particular phenomena in the Christianization of Europe that I believe help to explain what happened in Mesoamerica.

Idolatry

The claim made by Spanish authorities, and particularly religious officials, that the Maya practiced idolatry provided the primary justification for suppression of time-honored cultural practices and for the destruction of material culture that reflected vibrant pre-Columbian traditions: buildings, records, books, paintings, reliefs, and representational imagery. Some religious were not hostile to the Maya past, but these were not the individuals whose wisdom prevailed. Even Las Casas believed that the devil controlled the Indians' imaginations, because they had not been exposed to doctrine and grace.[3]

The triumph of conversion under these conditions should be examined both for the effects on the Christianity that ensued, and perhaps for the implications of the legacy for the modern world.

In the medieval West, Christian proselytizers explained the origin of pagan gods in two ways: they were either demons who had deluded humans, or they were historic individuals who had been mistakenly or falsely deified by their people after they died.[4] The second alternative was the option exercised predominantly during the Christianization of Europe, a process which was completed by about A.D. 1000 with the conversion of the peoples of Scandinavia and eastern Europe.[5] By the time of contact with the Maya of Yucatan and Belize, the gods of "the other" were viewed as demons.[6]

The question might arise as to why the gods of the Maya were not just written off as the products of ignorance; the answer is that, given the tenor of Christianity in the sixteenth century, the devil loomed too large. In chapter 3 I have provided some background on the origins of the devil, who had changed from a creature completely subordinate to the will of God to a force to be reckoned with in his own right. Attitudes fluctuated over time, with claims of the devil's influence dismissed with skepticism by church authorities in Mexico by the closing years of the seventeenth century.[7] In the sixteenth and early seventeenth centuries, however, devil-worship and idolatry were real threats and constituted crimes against God and the church.[8]

The particular conjunction between the sixteenth- and early seventeenth-century fear of the devil and the spiritual conquest of the New World is admirably described by Cervantes.[9] He traces some of the significant developments that would affect sixteenth-century religious thought to the monastic reform movements—or perhaps, more accurately, to the context that produced these movements—of the twelfth and early thirteenth centuries,[10] such as those associated with Francis of Assisi and Dominic Guzman, which I have touched on in chapter 6. From as early as the late eleventh century, those seeking spirituality within religious orders began to leave the shelter of monasteries to operate in the secular world, a move that paralleled a more widespread trend toward spirituality, introspection, and lay piety. A concomitant development was that the devil assumed a more insidious character than had been the case in monasteries (where the devil could be controlled) or in the pre-twelfth-century secular world (where the devil was doomed to defeat by the bearers of a militant faith). The devil came to be seen as having the power to penetrate individuals' souls or consciousness without their knowledge, hence laying the groundwork for a demonology in which idolatry—the worship of false gods—was the great fear.[11]

Attendant changes, culminating in Franciscan nominalism, entailed rejection of the moral system of Thomas Aquinas, which was based on the idea that humans can only construct an intelligible order through sense experience systematized by reason.[12] Part of the problem giving rise to these conflicting theologies or philosophies seems to have been misrepresentation of Thomist ideas in the thirteenth and fourteenth centuries;[13] but however unfounded anti-Thomist tendencies may have been, Cervantes traces the foundations of early modern demonology to their influence.[14]

The Devil in Disguise

The Spanish Christians' fear of the devil's power was almost certainly fed by imagery encountered in Mesoamerica, and perhaps particularly by the saurian imagery of the Maya region, which the Spaniards proceeded to "read" and interpret on the basis of their own cultural norms. It is important to gain some understanding of these norms to help to explain the behavior of the religious in suppressing Maya rituals and destroying Maya artistic expression. I do not pretend to be comprehensive in my discussion, but I draw attention to Maya symbolism that was highly likely to have been misinterpreted by Spanish friars and clergy, and thus to have reinforced their belief that the Mayas' religion was the religion of the devil.

THE OPEN MOUTH

A common theme or symbol in Mesoamerican representation from the Classic period to Spanish colonial times is a composite creature (part-saurian, mammalian, and/or fish), often with an anthropomorphic head emerging from the creature's mouth (figs. 8.13, 8.16.a, 8.19). The symbol of an open mouth is also an important theme in European art (fig. 10.1.a–e). In European art, however, the open mouth is more accurately a maw, and symbolizes the gates of hell. In some examples, individuals are seen entering hell (fig. 10.1.a); in others, they are simply biding their time (figs. 10.1.c,d); and in others, Jesus is shown rescuing souls from a gaping maw that is probably Limbo (fig. 10.1.e). A twelfth-century relief from a church in France shows an unusual version: a devil or demon with a huge open mouth about to devour a human, head first (fig. 10.1.b).

ANTHROPOMORPH EMERGING FROM A SHELL

An anthropomorphic figure emerging from a shell (fig. 10.2 is a European example) is a well-known image in Maya representation (fig. 10.3). An example from Lamanai dates to just before the Conquest (fig. 10.4.a,b). The figure, particularly when it shows signs of age, is interpreted as a specific deity, God N.[15]

Figure 10.1. The mouth of hell in European art: (a) woodcut showing the mouth of hell guarded by the devil and his demons (adapted from Wilson 2002, 12). (b) The devil with open maw devouring a human, from an archstone in the church of Saint-Brice, Saint-Mandé-sur-Brédoire (Charente-Maritime), 12th century (adapted from Muchembled 2002, 20). (c) Jesus leading St. Patrick to a cave that is the entrance to hell, from a fourteenth-century miniature (adapted from Cantor 1999, 341). (d) a detail from *The Mouth of Hell*, an illumination from the *Hours of Catherine de Clèves*, 1440, from the Pierpont Morgan Library, New York (adapted from Muchembled 2002, 36–37) (e) taken from a polychromed wood sculpture entitled *Descent into the Netherworld*, ca. 1460, attributed to the Lower Netherlands or Cologne Master; in this case, the Netherworld is Limbo and Christ is actually freeing those from Limbo who led a worthy life (adapted from Giorgi 2003, 46). (All drawings by Louise Belanger)

Shells were associated with the earth, the afterlife, and death, but also with life, birth, and water. They were linked with the feminine, and in form are said to resemble the uterus. In Mesoamerica, a mollusk emerging from a shell was seen as a symbol of humans emerging from the womb.[16] Generally speaking, a human emerging from a shell symbolized a state of transition between the natural and supernatural worlds and not something inherently evil.

Images of a human-like figure emerging from a shell also occurred in Europe. The detail (fig. 10.2) from a painting, *The Inferno*, dated to the first half of the sixteenth century, by Herri met de Bles, depicts a half-man, half-snail. According to Muchembled,[17] the shell-creature was sometimes depicted as a monster or demon in the Gothic period. Pieter Bruegel the Elder also painted a demon emerging from a shell, in the *Descent into Limbo*. In the tradition of artists of northern Europe, sins of the flesh were symbolized by a scatter of mussels or oysters. The small demon depicted by de Bles pulls on the feet of a damned soul.[18] There is a clear association in Europe between hell and the human-like figure emerging from the shell; if the interpretation of European symbolism was applied to Maya representation, the devil could be seen to lurk in many corners of Yucatan and Belize.

THE PRESENCE OF DEVILS AND DEMONS

Depictions of the devil and demons in European art vary widely.[19] Although it is often claimed that there is a set of symbols associated with the devil, it is context that tells us how to interpret the image rather than the symbol or depiction alone. My impression is that there was also tremendous artistic license where devils and demons were concerned.

In early Christian and medieval art, the devil or demon commonly displays traits of an animal—and by this I mean any non-human creature, such as a bird or fish or reptile or mammal or insect (figs. 10.5.a,b,e; see also fig. 11.7). Traits can vary, however, from simple feathery wings on a human-like creature, as in a representation of Jesus driving out an unclean spirit, in which the demon looks like an angel,[20] to creatures with one or some (never all) of the following: bat-like wings, claws, horns, hooves, tails, feathers, scales, beaks, chicken-like legs, insect eyes, fangs, fur, long ears, or scales. The devil can be hideous and bestial, but is not always depicted in such a form. He can be symbolized by something as cute as a rabbit, as in an early thirteenth-century scene from an illuminated manuscript in which the rabbit creature is said to represent a fallen angel.[21] In fact, in thirteenth-century and earlier representations, the devil can appear unthreateningly human, with a calm visage and only selected animal traits (feathers, hooves, or abundant hair).[22]

Satan (the devil) in biblical literature can be referred to as a dragon, and

Figure 10.2. Man emerging from a snail shell, detail from *The Inferno* (oil on canvas), Bles, Herri met de (Civetta) (c. 1510– p. 1550) / Palazzo Ducale, Venice, Italy / Cameraphoto Arte Venezia / Bridgeman Images.

Figure 10.3. Pottery vessel of man emerging from a shell, Late Classic period, 18 centimeters, in the Museo Nacional de Antropología, Mexico City, Inv. no. 10-076519. (Courtesy of the Museo Nacional de Antropología; photograph by Michel Zabé)

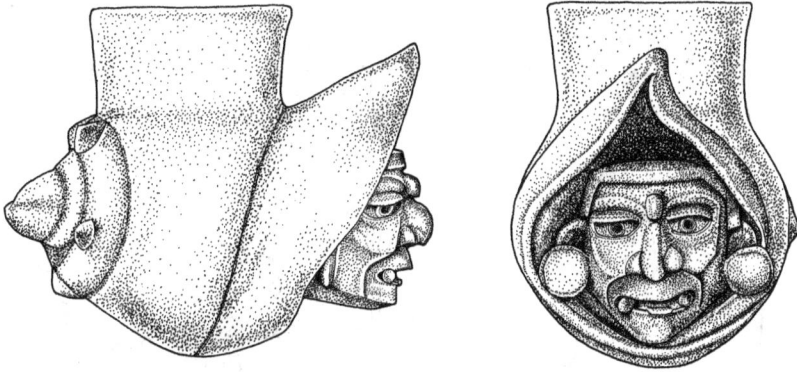

Figure 10.4. Lamanai, pottery vessel of a man (or deity) emerging from a shell. Cache P8-26/1, LA 411/1; lone object from the core of the platform of a structure built in the 7th century but cached (intruded) ca. 700–800 years later. (Drawing by Louise Belanger)

in the eleventh century, artistic representations of Satan change from being serpent- or snake-like (with no legs) to having legs and feathers and bird wings[23]—that is, to what we would call a "dragon" (fig. 10.5.e, dated to the 9th century,[24] seems to represent the transition from snake to dragon). Hence, following the European representational tradition known to the friars, the presence of a feathered saurian associated with the devil provided a basis for misinterpretation of the saurian and feathered saurian imagery so ubiquitous in the Maya world.

The devil and his demons continued to be depicted with various and sundry animal traits, but representations became truly bizarre by the fourteenth and fifteenth centuries, and persisted in this mode into the early seventeenth century. Giorgi[25] observes that such images have medieval bestiaries as their source, but I have no doubt that individual imagination was also operative. After all, were monks not plagued by dreams in which the devil appeared in various forms? In earlier centuries, monks were the inventors of visual conventions for the representation of demons in ecclesiastical sculpture and manuscript illumination;[26] this set the precedent for the devil to be a product of the imagination.

Devil and demon representations in the fourteenth through early seventeenth centuries can have an additional face with a huge mouth in the anal or vaginal region, or on the buttocks (fig. 10.5.a,b). Features can be grotesque, such as distended bellies or skeletal bodies, or the devil can incorporate vegetal or insect traits. Sometimes the devil (or a demon) is depicted devouring humans (figs. 10.1.b, 10.5.a). In the hands of someone such as Hieronymus

Figure 10.5. Images of the Devil: (a) detail from *Heaven and Hell* from the Church of St. Petronius, in Bologna, Italy, 15th century, in which the devil is both eating and excreting a human (adapted from Wilson 2002, 34). (b) Detail from *Fall of the Rebel Angels* by Guillermo Talarn, dated to the 15th century (adapted from Wilson 2002, 70–71). (c) taken from a relief of the Egyptian deity Bes, 205–31 B.C., from the Museo Barracco in Rome (adapted from Giorgi 2003, 233); (d) from an engraving in London, Central Saint Martins College of Art and Design, by François de Ligny after Gustave Doré, *Night Her Course Began . . .* , plate 26, book VI, line 406 from Milton's *Paradise Lost*, 1882 edition (adapted from Muchembled 2002, 147). (e) the devil as a dragon, from the Trier Apocalypse, ca. 800–820, in the Stadtbibliotek (MS 31, fol. 38*r*), Trier (adapted from Link 1995, 166, illus. 71). (All drawings by Louise Belanger)

Bosch, who painted in the early sixteenth century, just about anything was possible, although he was not alone. Demons could be bat-like; bird-like; snail-like; lizard-like; fish-like; skeletal; goat-like; could possess exaggerated features of any kind, but often genitalia; or could be an amalgam of bizarre shapes, organs, and limbs, as in the Hell panel of Bosch's triptych, *The Garden of Earthly Delights*.

Although this variety in depictions at first seems to have no common denominator, an argument can be made that it is the grotesque or the monstrous that serves to communicate what is not holy and hence is associated with sickness, punishment, suffering,[27] and, ultimately, in late medieval Christianity, with the work of the devil. The idea of the grotesque is discussed by Constantinou in the case of Byzantine miracle stories from the early centuries of Christianity (the fifth to tenth centuries), in which gravely ill and suffering individuals are healed by a saint.[28] Sickness was often depicted in these miracle stories in terms of the grotesque body, which Constantinou (after Bakhtin) describes as a body in which the genital organs, belly, buttocks, or any lower parts are emphasized; orifices, where the body opens out into the world, are important (mouth, anus, nose, ears, phallus, vagina); the grotesque body is a devouring body; bodily products are exalted; and, finally, the grotesque body is in a state of flux, with its power expressed through eating, defecating, dying, or giving birth.[29] Therefore, it is possible that ideas of the grotesque and the monstrous associated in early Christianity with illness and punishment persisted and ultimately worked their way—sometimes as a conflation of human-animal forms—into imagery of the devil and demons of later periods.

Sometimes the actions depicted give a demon away, such as pushing an object up a human's anus or, in the seventeenth century, smoking tobacco.[30] In contrast, by the eighteenth century it was angels who were smoking (fig. 10.6). In the nineteenth century, the devil became mostly human-looking again, with human proportions but with some animal traits, such as bat wings and horns (fig. 10.5.d). The devil of my childhood, in fact, was very like the individual in figure 10.5.d.

Animals on their own can symbolize demonic forces, although this is more characteristic of the Middle Ages than of the early Christian period.[31] According to Giorgi,[32] the monkey alluded to evil but was not considered a symbol of the devil, whereas a scorpion was a demonic symbol. In early representations, bears, wolves, and lions could function as images of the devil, but they later gave way to the cat, the frog, and the snake. The snake, sometimes rendered as a dragon, personified evil (fig. 10.5.e). It is likely that in the Christianization of pagans, if particular animals were sacred in a pagan pantheon they were certain to become demonic symbols to the Christians. Bes, for example, a be-

Figure 10.6. Angel smoking. From Delft tile, 18th century. (In collection of the author)

nevolent Egyptian divinity, came to represent the devil in Christian eyes (fig. 10.5.c).[33]

I expected to find proof that associating the devil with reptilian or amphibian imagery would have contributed to the Spanish friars' belief that Maya imagery was demonic, but demonic imagery in Europe is so eclectic that, although reptiles and amphibians do seem to be popular as demonic imagery in some circles, as far as I can tell, they do not dominate the imagery to which the friars would have been exposed before they set out for the New World. In fact, it may be that the experience of proselytization in tropical regions in the Maya and Gulf Coast lowlands influenced European artists in their choice of reptiles and amphibians as demonic.

Admittedly, the account of the snake tempting Eve occurs in the Old Testament, which proves that there is considerable time-depth to the association of snakes or serpents with evil. Snakes or dragons also represented the devil hidden in the idol,[34] and a profusion of saurian imagery in Maya representation may well have fed the fires of the friars' zeal. Nonetheless, the driving force was the idea that the devil existed, that demons existed, and that their existence inspired fear and loathing.

As we have seen, it was not the individual traits per se that identified the devil in European painting or sculpture, but the context of the painting or composition. When Europeans viewed the painting or the sculpture or the manuscript pages, they already knew the stories. They joined the images to the narratives in their heads. When individuals did not know the stories and approached imagery literally and ahistorically, as the friars and clergy approached Maya (and Mesoamerican) imagery, they would expectably have been baffled and perhaps confused. What could not be read or interpreted within the European representational tradition would have been in danger of becoming the devil in the idol.

Idols and False Gods

Seeing evidence of the influence of the devil in Mesoamerican imagery was not the whole picture, however. The devil was not just a feature of the Maya/Mesoamerican environment, but was also seen to be an active, anti-Christian force responsible for *setting up* false idols. Maya imagery was not perceived as an artistic expression of cultural beliefs that were the product of the development of Maya civilization; missionaries denied any recognition of the native religion as a distinctive imaginative universe.[35] Maya images were idols—false gods deliberately set in place by the devil.

How did such a concept as idolatry develop? The reasoning derives ultimately from the Decalogue, or Ten Commandments, in which the Judeo-Christian God requires that no other gods be worshiped. The fashioning of "idols" or effigies or images serves as evidence that people might be worshiping other gods, and the mere existence of an effigy or an image is taken to identify the place or process of worship of a false or strange god.

Such a stricture seems clear enough, yet there are problems with the Old Testament emphasis on images as intrinsically dangerous. For one thing, humans are supposed to have been made in God's image or likeness. If the mere presence of an image or likeness carries with it the potential to stand for a false god, then the creation of humankind is in itself problematic. For another, does the association of a false god with an image mean that it is acceptable to worship another supernatural besides the Judeo-Christian God as long as one just *thinks* about a force of some kind but has no material representation of this force? According to Megged,[36] the friars were taught in Spain that idolatry could only be practiced in the presence of idols.

Are all images or effigies to which attention is devoted representations of false gods? This is the view of Judaism and many Protestant sects as regards the images and effigies venerated by Catholics. My childhood Jewish and Protestant friends claimed, based on their observations of our behavior in the presence of images, that we Catholics were idolators. Based on patterns of behavior, this conclusion makes sense. Roman Catholics would rebut the accusation of idolatry by saying that the images are not worshiped; but this is an insiders' point of view, and was no doubt held by those associated in the Bible with the golden calf. Outsiders see people interacting with an image and "read" the interaction as "worship."

Statues or images play no role in Jewish or most Protestant places of worship. Yet members of Jewish and Protestant faiths do not seem to hesitate to buy stuffed animals (fig. 10.7) or action figures for their children, or to go to the cinema, or perhaps even to buy Staffordshire figures for their mantelpieces. If behavioral interaction with images is the criterion for idolatry, then

Figure 10.7. Modern idols: Teddy bears in Shoppers' Drug Mart, Toronto.
(Photo by E. Graham)

one would be hard-pressed to find an idolatry-free universe anywhere on earth. It must therefore follow that only *some* images or effigies are false gods.

How, then, are false gods identified? Who does the identifying? The Anabaptists, in a revolution in Münster in 1534, went so far as to regard money as an idol and hence a false god.[37] Money indeed often displays images, but the coin or paper bill is not itself a figurative representation, although money is certainly worshiped for what it represents. Most religions of the world accept the use of money, however, or accept the use of an exchange item, such as (among the Maya) cacao beans or copper bells.

For everyone besides the Anabaptists of the mid-sixteenth century, the defining criterion of a false god was inevitably that it was a representation that was part of the culture or society of the Other (fig. 10.8).[38] In fact, the choice of the serpent in the story of the temptation of Eve in the book of Genesis is said to reflect Judaic denunciation of an ancient cult, practiced until it was suppressed by King Hezekiah (ca. 716–687 B.C.), in which snakes were worshiped.[39] What better example could there be of the image of the other as the motivating force behind the representation of evil?

The key factor in identifying false gods in Mesoamerica was the difference or divide perceived by the Spaniards between themselves (as a self-defined group) and the Indians—rather than a careful assessment of the characteristics of a supernatural or the practices surrounding its worship or veneration. In fact, comparisons reveal close parallels between Maya beliefs and practices and Christianity: ritual purity; fasting; continence; forms of baptism and confession; the use of "virgin" or holy water; belief in more than one abode for the dead; a hierarchy corresponding in some ways to bishops, priests, deacons, and acolytes; the use of pageantry; incense; the importance of blood as an offering; the conflation of socially sanctioned killing and war; and the veneration of the cross as a symbol.[40] In addition, an argument could be made that Itzamna was an all-pervasive power, both natural and supernatural, not dissimilar to the Christian God, in that both were ever present and held in awe, yet neither (unlike Ix Chel in the case of the Maya, or the Virgin of Guadalupe in the case of Spanish Christians) was an object of devotion or pilgrimage.

Taking all of this into account—including the information outlined in

Figure 10.8. "Idols of Campeche and Yucatan." The upper image on a page of two engravings. Vol. 7, no. 24, facing p. 165 of Picart 1723. (In collection of the author)

chapter 3—three powerful forces, plus a fourth, which will be discussed below, combined in Mesoamerica to provide justification for acts of suppression and, in some cases, terror: (1) the perception of a cosmic struggle between good and evil with the supernaturals of "the other" pre-identified (if you will) as evil; (2) the perception that the devil, and hence evil, lurked in every corner which, although not a feature of the conquest of central Mexico, surfaced in religious thought among a number of Franciscans at the time of the conversion of the Maya; and (3) the fear of idolatry, an ancient offence in the eyes of the Judeo-Christian God, identified by the presence among "the others" of effigies or images which were assumed to be inspired by the devil or demons.

All three ideas were alien to Mesoamerican thought. As far as we can ascertain, Maya and Nahua (Aztec) deities represented the forces of both good and evil, both creativity and destructiveness.[41] Therefore, a cosmic struggle between two discrete forces did not make sense in the frame of Mesoamerican belief. It would have been difficult if not impossible to imagine a purely evil supernatural; hence, the devil must have been an enigmatic figure.[42] With regard to "idolatry," it must have been difficult, as I noted in chapter 3, for the Maya to get a handle on which effigies were "idols" when they observed the numerous effigies of saints and other objects that formed the paraphernalia of Christian worship among the Spaniards. From a behavioral point of view— that is, the observation of Spaniards by Mayas and of Mayas by Spaniards— both sides were idol-rich.

The Idol Rich

The extirpation of idolatry consumed the Franciscans in sixteenth-century Yucatan, especially during the years when Fray Diego de Landa—first as provincial, and later as bishop from 1573 to his death in 1579—was the motivating force.[43] Chuchiak gives an extraordinarily detailed account of these years in which hundreds of Mayas, from Yucatan to the Campeche-Tabasco region, were persecuted and even suffered severe corporal punishment, all accused of idolatry.[44] According to Chuchiak,[45] Landa would, in his tenure as bishop, prosecute more Maya for idolatry than he had prosecuted during his infamous 1562 *auto de fé*.[46] Even the chief ecclesiastical judge of the Archbishopric of Mexico condemned Landa and his Franciscan commissary judges' methods and their excessive punishments.[47]

Although the situation would become regularized and the Franciscan commissary judges' power restricted after Landa's death in 1579, mainly through the secularization of Franciscan doctrinas, such zealotry almost certainly had a unique influence on the course of Christianity in the Maya lowlands. For one thing, it inspired many Mayas to flee to the shelter of the southern forests,[48] which almost certainly resulted in increases in population in villages and towns in Belize. Although Landa's and his Franciscan brothers' campaigns in the 1560s and 1570s seem brief in historical terms,[49] such upsets in peninsular population dynamics were never righted.

Furthermore, we gloss too easily over the term "idolatry," as if it were a definable phenomenon that is clear to everyone. The term is often used uncritically in literature on the historic period. Admittedly, use of the term "idolatry" is understandable when one reads Franciscan documents and attempts to explain Franciscans' motives. But scholars' use of "idolatry" or "idols" to describe Maya actions or Maya material culture is incomprehensible. What, exactly, is an idol? A figurine? A statue? An effigy? A toy? Household objects and tools? Private offerings? A container for burning incense? A piece of decorated crockery? Ornaments to decorate the house for a feast?

There is no word in a Maya language for "idol." In Yucatec, *lak* is a ceramic censer; *sak lak tun* is a stone censer; *k'oh* is a mask or carved wooden image; *lakam tun* is a stela; *b'ah* is an image of the face or head; *kulche'* or *k'ohob* or *k'awil* is a statue; *läkil k'uh* or *u lakil k'ul* is a Lacandon censer with a modeled face on one side.[50] I have not exhausted the inventory, but the point is that there is no concept which embraces "idol" in Maya belief.

In addition, the contexts of Maya images or objects called "idols" by the Spaniards do not unequivocally indicate an intention to worship a false god. Within my experience at Lamanai and Tipu, few post-Conquest effigies or figurines or representations have been recovered from contexts that are not Christian sacred space. Where they are recovered from axial residential caches, the Maya seem to be hedging their bets rather than engaging in apostasy. All the post-Conquest Lamanai effigies that appear in this volume have been found in Christian sacred space. A number of options are possible:

The Maya were honoring the Christian god by caching items that had meaning for them in Christian sacred space.

The Maya were honoring the Christian god by caching images of supernaturals that they saw as simply adding to the panoply of Christian saints.

The Maya cached effigies that they saw as other versions of saints.

The Maya cached effigies and other items as part of calendrical or other rituals they had long practiced, but they appropriated Christian sacred space in the process.

These are only a few options, none of which places the Maya in a category in which they were necessarily denying the power of the Christian god. At least their behavior was no different from that of Spanish Christians whose effigies of saints took up considerable room in both sacred public and private residential space. Unless early Maya-Spanish liaisons produced individuals who were able genetically to inherit (like Jean Auel's Neanderthals[51]) the "memories" of what had happened in Europe since Christ's birth, it is hard to imagine how the Maya could have acted differently.

Judgments about Maya idolatry were riddled with unanswered questions and assumptions. No questions were asked about where the effigies were found, in what ritual context they were used, what prayers were said in front of them, how Maya representation compared to Christian representation, or how the Maya interpreted Christian behavior. The failure of the regular orders and secular clergy to pose such questions did not automatically leave open the possibility that there was idolatry among the Maya. There might have been some argument for persecution if the Anabaptists had been present in Yucatan, because they do not accept imagery of any kind, and they might therefore have been justified in claiming that the use of imagery by the Maya was idolatry. The Anabaptists were strict pacifists, however, so they would have been highly unlikely to have subjected the Maya to torture or to have imprisoned them.

From the Maya point of view, having the friars call them idolators must have been the pot calling the kettle black. Christian practitioners with enough effigies and statues to sink a ship were condemning the Maya categorically as idolators because they continued to use imagery that was familiar to them in their worship—as, I might add, did the Christians in Europe. Some worship might have been strictly pre-Hispanic, but this is doubtful. Given the way Christianity proceeded in the early years of evangelization, complex patterns of religious practice may already have been infused with Christian concepts. The Maya certainly appropriated Christian sacred space early on, and adopted saints readily.

In the next chapter I argue for the idea that Christian practice and ritual are themselves largely "pagan"—that is, that a number of Christian practices grew out of pre-Christian ritual and religion. As ideas of Christianity became accepted, people tended to celebrate their faith in ways that were culturally familiar to them, and out of this grew the customs and paraphernalia now identified as Christian (Roman Catholic) ritual: lighting candles, kneeling, using water and oil in ritual, using certain foods in offerings, praying and leaving offerings in front of images, using knotted interlace symbolism to decorate crosses and reliquaries,[52] placing shrines in sacred spaces, venerating the spirits of people who died. Even the sacraments were defined in accord with the medieval number seven, in complete disregard for the exegetical, historical, and theological objections raised at the time.[53] What happened in the Maya area was simply parallel evolution.

The Christianization of Europe

How can we explain the apparent ease with which the Maya accepted and appropriated Christianity? The Mendicants were frequently at odds with Spanish authorities both in Europe and the New World, and often sided with the Maya of Yucatan against encomenderos and soldiers;[54] despite this, why was the divide deepest between Spaniard and Maya, and not, say, between Spanish settlers on the one side and Mayas and Franciscans on the other, particularly given the similarities in religious practices and Franciscan sympathies? The Franciscan belief in the existence of idolatry among the Maya goes far to explain aspects of their allegiance to things Spanish, but Spanish colonial behavior was inexcusable by any stretch of the Christian imagination.

Why were Mendicants and secular clergy complicit in this behavior? The primary justification in religious terms was without doubt the extirpation of idolatry. I suggest, however, that another explanation stems from how effective church-state integration had become by the sixteenth century, from the legacy of the historical trajectory of the Christianization of western Europe, and from the centralization of jurisdiction of church government in Rome.[55] No one has better expressed how tightly these factors were integrated than Muchembled, who observes: "The Devil is the hidden face of an astonishing unifying dynamic that melds together the imperialist dreams inherited from classical Rome and those of the dominant proselytizing Christianity."[56]

In the following paragraphs, I examine aspects of the processes of conversion and Christianization in Europe in Late Antiquity and the Middle Ages.[57] The inferences I draw are meant specifically as an attempt to understand the behavior of those who justified evangelization of the Maya in Yucatan and Belize. Armed with some idea of what was driving the religious orders and the secular clergy in Mesoamerica, as well as some understanding of the social and political context of the encounter, I turn in the chapter that follows to the Maya perspective.

THE IMPERIAL MACHINE

The span covered by Late Antiquity, A.D. 400 to A.D. 600,[58] overlaps with the more familiar term "Middle Ages" and covers the early years of that period. In chapter 6 I focused on the contribution of the Late Middle Ages to the New World encounter by describing the reform movements, beginning in the thirteenth century and continuing through the fifteenth century, which produced the ideas that were to structure expectations. Distinguishing Late Antiquity, however, is also useful for those with interests in the conversion process in

Mesoamerica, because the period sheds light on the kind of Christianity that would be passed on to the Mendicant friars who proselytized the Maya.

By as early as the sixth century, asceticism and monasticism had become established as important paths for Christians, but it is also true that by this time, as Herrin observes, Christian unity had taken the place of the unity of the Roman Empire.[59] "There is a sense in which the Christian faith, rather than the barbarian kingdoms, constituted the successor of the Roman Empire in the West. As a universal and fundamentally extra-territorial system, it could and did unite the various imperial remnants and non-Roman governments of the mid-sixth century."[60] Herrin also notes that although Christianity "could not claim the exclusive political allegiance" of those converted, it was nonetheless able to extend control effectively to areas beyond the old Roman Empire because it had developed the structure and rationale required for the task.

In the seventh century, unity would break down into a Christian West and East,[61] but the fundamental structure of integration developed by and for Western Christianity in Late Antiquity persisted. By the ninth century, a separate medieval Christendom existed in the West, which continued under the Holy Roman Emperor until 1804.[62] Rome, the focus of spiritual loyalty in the West, "became transformed into a supranational authority independent of any secular power."[63] Christianity was a catalyst in the amalgamation of ancient Roman and barbarian authority structures, which resulted, along with changes in economic relations, in a unique and powerful political system called feudalism.[64] "Without the special role and function of the church, it is doubtful whether feudal relations would have spread so extensively through western societies."[65] The result, it could be said, was that church and state were two sides of the same coin.

A perspective on the course of church development in Late Antiquity makes it easier to fathom how church and state worked so effectively in Mesoamerica, despite the apparently vehement disagreements between Mendicants and secular authorities. Although the Mendicants' beliefs were rooted in an attempt to return to a primitive apostolic Christianity, and although they often railed against military and political forces, the church of which they were a part was a political animal with a thick skin.

The Germans and Franks in the seventh and eighth centuries had weapons to combat domination because they could still claim political authority through the allegiance of their people. They had more bargaining power than did the Maya rulers, who were politically dominated, although not initially displaced, by European settlers, soldiers, and adventurers. As we have seen in previous chapters, however, this did not mean that the Maya were not proactive in their confrontation with Christianity, and in fact I will eventually draw upon other aspects of European resistance to illuminate Maya initiatives. Here I wish only to suggest that the events of Late Antiquity are of interest to us because they help to explain the origins and effectiveness of what functioned as the Christian imperial machine.

<h2 style="text-align:center">FROM "CHURCH" TO "CHURCH"</h2>

The concept of church authority—that particular individuals within the church, rather than everyone, had the power to think about and evaluate Jesus's message and the proper relationship with the supernatural—had passed the point of no return by Late Antiquity.[66] Claims had been made as early as A.D. 90 by Clement, the second or third bishop of Rome, that people were refusing to accept the superior authority of priests.[67] In the second century, the church leader Tertullian of Carthage and Bishop Irenaeus of Lyons concurred in the view that what should characterize the true church was that all should agree on doctrine, morals, and leadership.[68]

Remedies for controlling behavior took the form of institutionalization. The justifications that would come to frame future decision making regarding who was practicing the true Christianity, or more important, who was not, had been planted deeply enough by this time that no one could uproot them. Various forms of Christianity would continue to arise and develop—even the scriptural canon continued to be interpreted in different ways—but the idea that there should exist a correct Christianity and that there were people within the church who had the authority to decide what was correct was fully developed by Late Antiquity. Basically, such authority rested with bishops, and by the sixth century, primacy was accorded to the bishop of Rome; the sixth century also saw doctrinal consolidation of the church.[69] In Peter Brown's words, "The tranquil ease of access to the supernatural . . . now seemed to belong to a distant, more turbulent age of equal spiritual opportunities. . . . In the Christian church, the spiritual dominance of the few was made ever firmer and more explicit by a denial of ease of access to the supernatural that would have put 'heavenly' power in the hands of the average sinful believer."[70]

As I noted in chapter 3, however, this spiritual dominance was never left long unchallenged.[71] Generations came and went, and the idea that true authority lay with priests and bishops and others of the church hierarchy became part of European culture. This is extremely important, because such authority is not self-evident in Jesus's message or in scripture. It is the result of a hard-won battle, the details of which lie in European history and culture. Because the Maya were neither part of European history nor were they heirs to European culture, we have another severe and serious disjunction which proselytizers failed to recognize, and another explanation (in addition to resistance) for what could be called the idiosyncrasies of the Mayas' reaction to evangelization and, in some cases, their refusal to recognize—or their tendency to ignore—ecclesiastical authority.

HOW LONG DOES IT TAKE TO BECOME CHRISTIAN?

The Middle Ages traditionally embody the rather long stretch of time from the fall of the Roman Empire in the fifth century, when the city was sacked first by Visigoths and later Vandals (and which I have subsumed under Late Antiquity), to the beginning of the Italian Renaissance in the first half of the fourteenth century. From the seventh to the tenth or eleventh century, Christian missionaries ventured into new territory, or perhaps more accurately into old but only weakly or spottily Christian territories, and consolidated their spiritual gains.[72] A start had been made between the third and sixth centuries, but as Fletcher describes it,

> "The challenge of converting the countryside to Christianity . . . would continue to tax the energies of bishops for centuries to come. . . . More than a few generations of episcopal exhortation or lordly harassment would be needed to alter habits inherited from time out of mind. Ways of doing things, ways that . . . people living at subsistence level had devised for managing their visible and invisible environments, were not going to yield easily, perhaps were not going to yield at all, to ecclesiastical injunction. But even granite will be dented by water that never ceases to drip."[73]

Perhaps it is already evident why these centuries in Europe are so significant. Yet the religious in Mesoamerica despaired of the habits of those they proselytized after only a few years. In the case of the Maya towns of Tipu and Lamanai, as we have seen, initial evangelization probably took place around 1544, with renewed and expanded efforts in the 1550s and 1560s. In the case of Yucatan, the introduction of Christianity began a bit earlier, with the Montejos' conquest attempts in 1527–28 and 1535–37, but intensified in the 1540s. Yet Fray Diego de Landa was almost beside himself with rage at what he interpreted as apostasy in 1561! If it took so many centuries to spread and to consolidate Christianity in western Europe, why did the religious expect change to be effected in such a short period in Mesoamerica? Not all did, of course, and Lorenzo de Bienvenida and Bishop Toral immediately come to mind, but they were not the individuals whose attitudes triumphed. The implication is that even though some people learn from history, their opinions hold little weight in the face of more powerful considerations.

Urban and Rural, Local and Global

Although I have been proposing similarities between the evangelization of Mesoamericans and Europeans, I do not mean to discount differences. One significant difference is that conversion and Christianization in Europe involved not just new beliefs and loyalties, but also the spread of Roman urban and Mediterranean customs and values to "barbarians." The Germanic states, the Burgundians, and the Anglo-Saxon kingdoms had not theretofore been urbanized, and it was through Christianity that they were introduced to literacy, books, notions of law, authority, property, and government, as well as to the habits of living in towns and using coins for exchange, and to new architectural and artistic conventions.[74]

The people of Mesoamerica, however, had been urbanized for many centuries, and this surely contributed in part to the facility with which Christianity, its hierarchies, its textual validation, and the complexity of its organization could be "read" by the Maya. Despite this fact, scholars as well known as Kubler write in terms of the "urbanizing work of the Mendicants."[75] But what Kubler refers to as "urbanization" seems to be the process of reduction, or *reducción*, whereby the friars forced the *indios* to leave their communities and settle in towns or villages that were restructured and sometimes entirely planned by the friars, rather than true processes of urbanization.

Another difference is that the Christianity preached by the friars in Mesoamerica was imbued with regional European customs, many of which were the product of the process whereby local "pagan" or pre-Christian worldviews and practices had been absorbed into Christianity. Such absorption tends, however, not to be observed by historians who are writing within the church. Hellenic pagan thought is seen to affect what the church had to say about doctrinal issues—that is, it is recognized as something that elicited doctrinal response from the church[76]—but no church writer, and perhaps even no practicing Christian historian, seems to acknowledge any debt to local or regional barbarian paganism in the development of Christianity as a faith. Where historians seriously consider the influence of local groups on Christianity,[77] such influence is presented as a cultural phenomenon.

There are in fact good reasons for this, which I will discuss below. In the meantime, I too will turn to culture and say that the friars' Christianity in the Mesoamerican encounter was culturally (locally or regionally) influenced;[78] but they did not see this as a barrier, or as a potential source of confusion, in the acceptance of their Christianity by the Maya. That the Maya contextualized their Christianity locally—and by this I mean that they internalized understanding based on their own experiences with individual friars or other religious in the context of their local villages, towns, and landscapes—suggests that such "cultural packaging" of Christianity was as critically important to the Maya as it was to the proselytizers.

Therefore, despite the fact that Christianity served in Europe as an instrument of urbanization and, in a sense, globalization, it is also true that local or regional contextualization—as in, for example, the Germanization of early Medieval Christianity[79]—was nonetheless a critical feature. The result was that missionaries in Northumbria or Ireland had to contend with the issue of where the limits were to be drawn between what was tolerable in traditional belief and local practice and what was not.[80] The Mendicant friars were faced with the same challenges among the Mesoamericans, but on the whole—an exception might be Motolinía—they seem to have greeted such challenges not as something to be expected, given the historical circumstances, but instead with expressions of surprise, dismay, or consternation, which in turn affected how they viewed various groups in Mesoamerica and the cultures and societies they encountered.

To some extent—and I am aware that this is a generalization—we could say that the friars and other evangelizers among the Maya saw the world as they saw the world, whereas earlier, in Europe of Late Antiquity, evangelizers had to try to see the world as others saw it, not least because Christians started out as a minority and proceeded accordingly. By the time Christianity came to Mesoamerica, learning from history, it seems, had less to do with maintaining flexibility and more to do with positioning and power. There was strength, but perhaps not wisdom, in time and numbers.

✠ ELEVEN ✠

Being Pagan

In this chapter I draw together different threads in order to construct a hypothetical Maya perspective on conversion. I do not position myself as Maya so much as I seek to envisage what it might have been like had the Franciscans or other religious attempted to see themselves as the Maya saw them. If my view is even close to being correct, there is an explanation beyond spiritual conquest for the persistence of Christianity among the remote communities in Belize through the seventeenth and eighteenth centuries, despite their distance from Spanish centers of authority.

There is also an explanation for the courses followed by Christianity in Yucatan and Belize, and "apostasy" and "idolatry" are not appropriate to describe them. Although the Franciscans argued that the baptized Maya were not being Christian, evidence can just as easily be marshaled to show that the Franciscans, along with other Spanish Christians, were seen by the Maya as "pagan."

There are several themes that have arisen in preceding chapters and which I bring together here. These are the trans-local (or global) versus the local; the influence of individuals; internalizing the Christian message; imagery and its interpretation; Christian thought and its impact; and sacred landscapes. First, I distill what is important about these themes, and then I bring them to bear on the process of envisioning the evangelizers as the Maya might have seen them.

The trans-local versus the local. Although Clendinnen has argued that the friars who proselytized had traveled widely and were preoccupied with doctrine, and thus were trans-local in their perspectives,[1] there is still no such thing as escaping the local. By this I mean that although a group of people might decide to internalize a particular approach, this does not mean that the approach did not originate with an individual and a perspective which were locally rooted and culturally mediated.

The influence of individuals. Although I write about "Christianity" and "the Maya" and "the Franciscans," my emphasis in chapter 3 on the importance of thinking in terms of the individual is paramount. In Belize, where relatively few friars and clergy seem to have been responsible for spreading and maintaining the faith, individual interpretations of Christianity and Christ's teachings would have had considerable influence on Maya thought. Chuchiak enlightens us in this regard when he emphasizes how great Landa's influence was in Yucatan:

> What could explain the Franciscans' excessive measures in dealing with Maya idolaters? To answer this specific question, we must remember that in scholastic training and practical influences, almost all of the Franciscan friars conducting these extirpation campaigns had been students, protégés, or colleagues of Landa. His earlier role in the initial linguistic and missionary instruction of all newly arrived Franciscan friars likely influenced new missionary friars' mindsets and their attitudes toward the Maya.[2]

In addition, Landa surrounded himself with Franciscans who proved themselves to be his most loyal supporters in 1562; and, when he was bishop, he selected his commissary judges from those who had consistently stood by him.[3] Lorenzo de Bienvenida, who passed through Belize in 1543–44 and may well have introduced Belize Maya communities to Christianity, was not one of Landa's supporters. It is tempting to entertain the idea that Bienvenida's more flexible approaches to evangelization may have affected the kind of Christianity developed among at least some Maya communities in Belize.

In the same vein, the *maestros* and sacristans who, in the absence of resident priests, assumed local authority in a number of Belize mission communities, would also have had considerable influence on the courses taken by Christianity, particularly in light of the fact that Belize communities were left to their own devices.

Internalizing the Christian message. I have emphasized the idea that the individuals to whom the friars preached, including children, would have assessed what they were being taught. They would have detected nuances of difference and even contradiction, not only if they were exposed to passages from the Old and New Testaments but even in the words of the catechism. The evangelizers may have thought that the Christian message was straightforward, but they had heard it all their lives and devoted themselves to refining it and discussing options. The message itself never was clear—nor is it now—to those who hear it for the first time. But even if this were not true, nothing that was said to the Maya could be internalized without the involvement of thought processes and feelings, and such thought processes and feelings reflected individual personalities, family histories, community politics, and previous cultural and ritual knowledge. This was as true of the Maya as it was of the Anglo-Saxons in the early seventh century,[4] or of the Castilians who took vows of poverty in the fifteenth and sixteenth centuries.

Imagery and interpretation. Late medieval representation was rich in its variety, both topically and materially. Paintings, woodcuts, statues, and figurines all appeared on the scene in Yucatan and Belize. Churches and convent walls in major towns were painted; saints' statues were housed in churches, chapels, and convents; and missals, breviaries, books of scripture, books of saints, crosses, crucifixes, decorated cloths, chalices, and almost certainly saints' images, were used in proselytization.[5] We know from Jones that the church at Tipu was dedicated to San Pedro.[6] The world of Christianity introduced to the Maya was as rich as their pre-Hispanic world, and filled with images of spirits and supernaturals who, in the right circumstances, could help humans. It is this commonality, strengthened and not weakened by Christian images, that loomed largest in the spiritual encounter—not any immediate change in outlook or philosophy.

Christian thought. Major changes in thought and outlook among the Maya were of course possible, but if European history is any guide, such transformations would have taken generations to effect; the pragmatic Jesuits counted on at least three.[7] Raising the sons of Maya elite families in monasteries solved some of the cultural problems, although it almost certainly added psychological ones, but the physical and cultural environment in Yucatan and Belize was Maya, not Spanish. Thus, despite considerable conflict and repression by the invaders, the Maya cosmos stood to be influenced by and even invigorated by Christian thought; from the Maya point of view, the Christian cosmos posed no threat. Where Christian thought involved change, as we shall see, it involved behavioral change that was compatible with Maya patterns.

Landscape. It is important to keep in mind that the Spaniards entered the Maya world; they could not bring to Mesoamerica their local springs around Cordoba or their rocky outcrops on the plains of La Mancha. Whatever stories they knew and recounted about where they grew up would have features that were alien to the landscape of the humid tropics. In addition, they almost certainly found that the local landscape had already been "mythologized."[8] Under these conditions, it is unlikely that places believed by the Maya to have accumulated power would have lost their force. Instead, new spirits or supernaturals were likely to have become associated with traditional places of power, perhaps at first sharing the company of traditional deities. Local springs, cenotes, caves, creeks, orchards, or clearings in the forest would have become places where saints and spirits took up their abode.[9]

In relatively heavily forested areas such as Belize, which was not settled by Spaniards and came to lie beyond the reach of Spanish administration, the Maya ritual landscape would have been far less influenced by Spanish urbanization and Spanish settlement patterns. The English are known to have attacked Maya communities and to have raided communities for slaves, but they did not attempt, at least until the nineteenth century, to administer them. Therefore, Maya communities in Belize may well have preserved ritual landscapes least influenced by European spiritual agendas.

Seeing Ourselves as Others See Us

To continue with the experimental process of envisioning the Maya perspective on Christian conversion by envisioning the proselytizers as others might have seen them, I will build on the themes just discussed and take a look at several issues: what scholars make of the sources of the encounter; the "uniqueness" of the problems the clerics faced in Mesoamerica; how conversion was facilitated; what Christianity might have had to offer the Maya; and ritual practice and belief versus doctrine.

WHAT SCHOLARS MAKE OF THE SOURCES

The categories that follow are to some extent arbitrary. Most of us fit into more than one category, and there may be categories for which I have not accounted. It is important to consider agendas or standpoints because they can affect conclusions. An agenda or a standpoint is not necessarily a bad thing, and cannot really be avoided; neither does it invalidate results. However, it may make results relative or conditional rather than absolute. We all write out of genuine interest, but we are all goal-directed, too.

The literature on Christian conversion, perhaps more than other subjects, reveals aspects of the standpoint of the writer. Even without knowing the identity of the writer, one can often detect who has a Christian background, who considers himself or herself outside the fold, who is still a practicing Christian, who is writing to justify the church, who is sympathetic to the church, or who is carrying the flag for the pagan underdogs. Who we are affects what we make of the sources on the encounter.

I have cautiously identified five types of scholarly approaches to the conversion process:

1. Accepting the church's assessments of Indian behavior as true

There are scholars who accept the Spanish religious' assessments of Indian behavior as valid, at least in broad outline. Robert Ricard is a good example, regarding assessments of idolatry and pagan practices.[10] Ricard does suggest a European, and not a native, origin for many of the problematic beliefs of the Indians. However, he accepts the claims of the religious, that the Indians hid their "idols" beneath the crosses or in the altars of the churches solely as a mark of willful and conscious resistance, and not because they had come to regard these Christian places as sources of spiritual power. Anthropologists and ethnohistorians who have written after the Columbian Quincentennial tend to be more critical of Spanish sources than Ricard, but have continued to use the term "idolatry" to describe Indian behavior, and the persistent reference to Maya effigies and statues as "idols" displays a lack of critical judgment.

2. Using the documents to uncover pre-Conquest ways of life

Many scholars, archaeologists among them, use the documents in the hope of obtaining information on pre-Conquest ways of life. Landa's *Relación* is a primary source in this regard. Yet Landa was so opinionated about idolatry, and often careless about his reporting of colonial-period events, that one wonders how much of his information on the pre-Columbian Maya is reliable. Landa aside, the Conquest-period literature cannot be ignored. The caveat is that we have to keep in mind that the ethnography was done with a purpose—to enable proselytizers to undermine local beliefs and make people good Christians.

3. Taking apostasy at face value and interpreting all Indian post-Conquest practices as resistance to Spanish authority

It is common among archaeologists to interpret Maya post-Conquest actions as resistance, not least because this seems to serve as a good explanation for a range of behaviors. There is little doubt that if the Spaniards had left the peninsula, the Maya would have been happy campers. On the other hand, once new ideas had been introduced, it is possible that some cultural features might have interested the Maya. The problem is that an exchange between equals was not the rule; the Maya were instead faced with economic subjugation.

Although "resistance" is a viable model, as Jones has shown[11] it can hide the extent to which decision making was proactive rather than reactive. In the case of religious change, we need to be even more careful in using "resistance," because it prevents us from examining details of particular situations that might reveal far more complex and effective behaviors and processes.[12]

Morrison, for example, argues that the Canadian Montagnais came to view baptism by the Jesuits as a way of coping with historical crisis,[13] and many of the Maya might well have held the same view. On the other hand, baptism was interpreted by some groups in Mesoamerica as a commitment to a tribute relationship,[14] a subtlety which is likely to have escaped Spanish notice. Among the Maya of Yucatan and Belize, baptism could have been seen as a perfectly acceptable ritual that nonetheless did not preclude biding one's time. Of course, the full range of possibilities could be true, with the implication that "resistance," although it functions as an explanation at one level, can mask such subtleties of response.

4. Seeing Christian conversion as superficial only, with maintenance of a core of indigenous belief

My criticism, elaborated in an earlier chapter, is that the veneer/core metaphor is suspect. The Maya were prepared to listen to what the religious had to say, and it is probable that selective aspects of Christianity made inroads, particularly given the impact of the imagery (books with pictures, colorful saints' statues) used in proselytization. Children were targeted and would have grown to adulthood as Christians, at both Tipu and Lamanai. It is difficult to imagine how one could claim that they absorbed what they were taught simply as a veneer. That their ideas as adults may have had roots in both Christian and Maya culture is true, but the idea of a "veneer" of Christianity over a "core" of indigenous belief is too simplistic a description of the complexities of ongoing thought processes and resultant changes in ideas.

5. Interpreting Indian response to conversion as a reflection of the religious' ineffectiveness in presenting Christianity in its total and meaningful context

Scholars who hold this view suggest that a "sincere" or "meaningful" acceptance of Christianity did not take place, owing to problems in communication and cultural conflict between the religious and the Indians. They characterize what took place in Mesoamerica as an example of "incomplete" conversion.[15]

The point of view I express in this book cross-cuts the types listed above, but also adds the dimension in which I take the Maya to be Christian because they said they were Christian. The Maya were not dissembling or lying; where pre-Columbian traditions were continued and where elements of pre-Hispanic religion persisted, I attribute this to the fact that such traditions and rituals "express rather than contradict the Catholic worldview."[16] I question whether there exists a sincere and legitimate Christianity that all Christians know about and adhere to,[17] and against the measure of which the Conquest-period Maya or the Nahuas fell short. I also challenge the idea that Christian churchgoers (Roman Catholics) are all familiar and comfortable with church doctrine and see it as the center of their faith.

In the paragraphs that follow, I add evidence to the above discussion, which I hope will strengthen the idea that the Maya who identified with Christianity were indeed good and true Christians.

HOW CONVERSION WAS FACILITATED

I have already explained in chapter 1 how personal experience led me to examine the conversion process. Based on insights gained from that personal experience, I now consider how conversion may have been facilitated. The question that provides the framework for discussion is: What basis existed for the ready exchange of information between Maya and friar?

I consider three categories of phenomena that can shed light on the exchange process: (1) accommodations to the spirit world, (2) the mechanics of proselytization, and (3) the liberation of the cult of the ancestors.

A World of Spirits

A critically important facilitator of conversion was the fact that both Spanish Christians and Mayas accommodated to and called upon a world of spirits and supernaturals in their everyday lives. Maintaining a range of potentially helpful supernaturals was a practice rejected categorically by Protestant reformers, prohibited by Jews, and obviously does not exist even as a twinkle in the eye of atheists, unless they believe in alien abduction. Modern scholars might only go so far as to recognize the occasional muse. But the colonial-period Maya and the Spanish Christians had (and the Roman Catholics still do, of course) a rich spirit world at their disposal. This spirit world can be broken down in a number of ways, almost all of which can be shown to have been shared by Maya and Spaniard.

The Animal World of Christians and Mayas

One shared aspect of the spirit world of Mayas and Christians was that both domains were populated by supernaturals that combine human and animal characteristics. For the Christians, this included the three hierarchies of angels: seraphim, cherubim, and thrones; dominations, virtues, and powers; principalities, archangels, and angels.[18] "Roman Catholic doctrine, as set forth by Saint Thomas Aquinas, argues for the necessity of angels."[19] How do Christians know about angels? According to Giorgi, the visual image has its roots in preexisting spiritual creatures that were part of Syrian myth of the first millennium B.C., or possibly in Assyrian-Babylonian iconography from which the first representations of angels are likely to have migrated to the Judaic-Christian world.[20] The concept of angels as messengers of God has Judaic roots, but as supernatural beings arranged in a hierarchy in Zoroastrianism.[21]

In the first known image of the Annunciation from the Catacombs, and dated to the second and third centuries, the angel has no wings. At a certain point in the history of art, angels with wings made their appearance.[22] Giorgi states that their wings made them flying creatures,[23] an idea reinforced in the film *Dogma* by the angel Bartleby, played by Ben Affleck, who bleeds once shorn of his wings.[24] I suspect that wings were originally a symbol, meant to communicate spirituality and the idea that angels could be wherever God wanted them to be. Because humans were incapable of moving in such a way, artists borrowed wings from birds and gave them to humans. Seraphim were portrayed with six red-colored wings, whereas the wings of cherubim have eyes like a peacock's feathers, although such distinctions seem to have been lost over time.[25] The spirit with the greatest variety of human-animal

Figure 11.1. St. Francis preaching to the birds. Picture in author's possession.

Figure 11.2. St. Lazarus the beggar with dogs, from a votive candle purchased in Belize. (Votive candle in author's possession)

Figure 11.3. St. Dominic, the founder of the Dominican order. (Original print in collection of the author)

Figure 11.4. St. Martha and the dragon. (Print in collection of the author)

characteristics in art is none other than Satan himself—the devil and his demons, meant to represent the forces of evil, as we have seen in detail in the previous chapter.

Animals and animal symbolism have always played an important role in Christian tradition. Many saints were said to live with or to have been visited by animals. Being part of and communicating with the natural world was considered a mark of holiness and saintliness. Among the early Irish saints, St. Gall shared a cave and life's necessities with a bear, and St. Ciaran lived in the wilderness and was attended by wild animals.[26] Francis of Assisi's relationship with the natural world is well known, and the saint is often depicted surrounded by attentive birds (fig. 11.1).[27] Saints are commonly portrayed with animals; in fact, it is hard to find a saint who does not share the limelight with an animal of some kind, real or mythical (figs. 11.1–11.4). St. Lazarus—not the Lazarus whom Christ raised from the dead—is known from a parable,[28] as the archetypal beggar at the gate of the rich man; the military order named after Lazarus in the Middle Ages took care of lepers.[29] St. Lazarus's popular image is that of a leprous beggar with dogs for companions (fig. 11.2).

St. Dominic is commonly shown accompanied by a dog with a torch in its mouth (fig. 11.3). This is said to be a play on the name, *Domini canis*, and the torch a herald of truth,[30] but another version traces the dog to a dream that Dominic's mother had before he was born.[31] The Peruvian Dominican, San Martín de Porres, was also known for having special relationships with animals (fig. 1.11).[32] Animals shown with saints are not always realistic; both Margaret of Antioch and Martha, the sister of Lazarus and Mary, faced dragons.[33] The woman depicted in figure 11.4 is more likely St. Martha, who subdued a dragon by sprinkling it with holy water and tying her sash around its neck.

Some colonial sources claim that the Indians brought offerings to the animals that were part of saints' statues, and not to the saints themselves.[34] Offerings then and now are placed at the feet of saints' statues, where the animals are normally represented, and it is not the custom in Christianity to pray aloud in these particular circumstances. Therefore, it would be useful to know how the Spanish observers ascertained that the animal was in fact the object of veneration. In any case, if one were not long initiated into the Catholic faith and observed Spaniards praying at saints' altars, one would be hard-pressed to know whether animals or people were the objects of reverence.

Christian stories are filled with details that blur distinctions between humans and animals: Christ as the sacrificial lamb; saintly kings with the hearts of lions; a doe nourishing St. Giles with her milk; a stag bearing a crucifix that spoke to St. Eustace; ravens nourishing saints in their isolation; two lions who, using their paws, helped St. Anthony dig a grave for St. Paul the Hermit.[35]

Aside from the inability or refusal of many friars, although certainly not all, to see themselves as sharing practices with the idolatrous Maya, the religious, as I noted earlier, read their own imagery, including animal imagery, metaphorically, or as symbols or mnemonic devices that helped tell a story. In contrast, they read Maya imagery literally, and interpreted Mayas' actions literally. If questions were asked, they were structured to reflect the fact that the questioner already knew the response.

Spanish friars and laymen also leveled the accusation that the Maya worshiped jaguars or bats or other animals represented in Maya statuary. As above, they were guilty of reading Maya imagery literally, and of assuming that Maya imagery was not as metaphorically complex as Christian imagery. If Christians could see angels' wings as symbols of the ability to travel between heaven and earth as God's messengers, or see gold rings around people's heads as an indication of holiness and not as metal bands affixed to people's skulls, then why did they assume that Maya imagery was meant to be read literally and simplistically? To many Spaniards, religious or secular, a Maya carving of a monkey was a monkey god; a figurine depicting a half-man, half-animal was a god that was half-man, half-animal. Yet such images were just as likely to represent symbols or stories with complex levels of meaning, or to be mnemonic devices. They could be *about* gods and not necessarily *were* gods in themselves.

In 1223, Francis of Assisi built, or so it is said, the first crèche at Grecchio.[36] It thereafter became customary at Christmas in the Roman Catholic world for churches to display crèche scenes, which included statuettes of the infant Christ, Mary, Joseph, the Wise Men, and farm animals such as oxen, sheep, and a donkey. A dove is often shown above the stable entrance, and the wise men can be accompanied by a camel. If one applies the same approach to the crèche as the Conquest clergy and religious orders applied to figurines and statues made by the Maya, then the oxen, sheep, donkey, camel, and dove are all gods.

Offerings

Another practice shared by Mayas and Christians in conceptualizing the spirit world was the use of offerings. In the Catholic church, it is possible to bring all manner of things to rest before saints' statues. Such practices were common in the late medieval Christianity of the Conquest period, and indeed persist to this day. The meaning or symbolism of the offering can be known to the entire community, or can be understood only by the individual making the offering. Offerings need not mimic the appearance of the supernatural to whom the request is made. The forms taken by offerings, whether human, animal, vegetable, mineral, or abstract, reflect the nature of the request or the nature of the message, not the nature of the supernatural.

William Christian, in his book on *Local Religion in Sixteenth-Century Spain*, has a wonderful photo of the votive offerings in the modern regional shrine of Our Lady of Cortes.[37] There are miniature wax members of parts of the body, representing areas that had been healed by the saint's intercession; photos of people who were cured; and effigy heads, presumably of those who were cured. Crutches and the occasional coffin are also known. In the sixteenth century, babies painted on boards were common.[38] The shrine of Our Lady of Cortes serves as an example of the kind of situation in the past in which complexity on the Spanish side was not projected onto the Maya side.

Saints

The veneration of saints was hugely popular in the Old World and quickly became so in Mesoamerica. Much of the inspiration for veneration of saints and martyrs was almost certainly pre-Christian,[39] but it became eminently acceptable Christian practice. "Wherever Christianity went in the early Middle Ages, it brought with it the presence of saints. . . . Late-antique Christianity, as it impinged on the outside world, *was* shrines and relics."[40]

Although the veneration of saints was readily adopted by the Maya, Geary[41] maintains that the same reverence in Europe for corporeal remains as seen in relics failed to develop in Mesoamerica. He states that major pilgrimages, in Mexico, for example, were not inspired by the physical remains of a saint. Instead, the figurines and images that became the focus of pilgrimages represented pre-Columbian traditions rather than European traditions of "body cults."

This is interesting, because I suspect he has relied on the fact that New World scholars have not yet divested themselves of the habit of assuming that "idolatry" and "idols" are anything but Spanish terms for aspects of material culture they did not take more time to explore or inquire about. If one reads the literature, as I noted earlier, the term "idolatry" as used in Spanish sources is almost never questioned or analyzed.[42] Certainly, archaeologists, when consulting ethnohistoric documents, seem to accept "idol" as if it were a term that meant something with regard to pre-Columbian traditions or thought. Spanish descriptions and treatments of "idols" are of little use in gaining insight into pre-Columbian representation. We simply do not know enough about what Geary calls "pre-Columbian traditions" to be able to assess the role of the images in pilgrimages on that basis.

In the Classic period (A.D. 250–800), there certainly was reverence for corporeal remains. Maya rulers' remains are incorporated into major structures at the very centers of cities. The fact that burials throughout Maya pre-Columbian history are found within platforms and below building floors, including houses, also reflects reverence for corporeal remains. One would have thought that in addition to the reverence for saints, a focus on relics would have found ready acceptance among the Maya.

Further research is definitely needed on this subject, but I suspect that veneration of relics may have been discouraged in Mesoamerica, perhaps owing to what the religious saw as precariously close ties with pre-Christian practice. It is doubtful that relics of European saints would have been considered particularly holy by the Maya, unless perhaps there had been a local manifestation or vision.

Relics of Europeans are all that we ever had at St. Bonaventure's, a Franciscan church and monastery in Paterson, New Jersey, where I attended novenas with my grandmother.[43] We never had a local, home-grown saint; but we were strangers in a strange land, and the cultural affinities of my parish community in Paterson lay with the Old World and southern Italy. The Maya landscape, on the other hand, had great ritual time-depth. If there were going to be meaningful relics at some point, it would have made sense that the relics came from canonized Maya holy men and women. This did not happen.

On the other hand, the just-past-pagan Europeans got away with the immediate sanctification of the local because Christianity was relatively young when saints were named and when their relics became important. Even so, the urban, non-Christian Romans protested, because they found the Christians' obsession with relics and the bodies of the dead abhorrent.[44] It may be that the Germanic tribes, such as the Franks and the Frisians, to whom proximity to ancestors' graves was critical, contributed much to the importance with which relics were regarded in Christian thought.[45] According to Geary, there are indications in Germanic beliefs of the idea that the personality of the dead persevered and was centered on the grave.[46]

In western Europe, the placement of Christian churches over the graves of ancestors acted to Christianize the ancestors.[47] Geary provides an apposite example of a parish church at Flonheim which was destroyed by fire.[48] During its reconstruction, from 1883 to 1885, earlier phases were discovered. The oldest portion of the church that had burned was its Romanesque tower, dated to about 1100. The tower overlay burials, some of which dated to the fifth century, although the church is not mentioned in the literature until 764–67. One of the fifth-century graves was especially rich and seems to have been the burial of a family founder in pre-Christian times. The implication is that when the first chapel was built in Merovingian times (fifth to early eighth century), the pre-Christian burial site was known and the church was built atop it.

Such reverence for ancestors and the need to be within proximity of their remains could easily have been transferred to Christian saints and hence to their relics. To the Franks in the eighth and ninth centuries, images were not important; relics alone could share in the resurrection at the end of the world.[49] By the early part of the ninth century, it was assumed that all churches had relics.[50]

Evidence from the two Maya mission communities, Lamanai and Tipu, suggests that Christian proselytizers were as ready as they had been in Flonheim to appropriate pre-Christian holy ground. At Lamanai, as we saw in early chapters, the first church was built over the razed remains of a pre-Columbian structure that almost certainly served as a temple. Whether the friars knew there were burials in the temple's platform is not known. At Tipu, both Late and Early Postclassic burials underlie the area where the church was built, although we have no evidence of a pre-church structure directly associated with the interments. However, there are scant remains of a pre-Columbian structure underlying the church sanctuary. The evidence strongly suggests that the practice in Europe in which Christians appropriated pre-Christian sacred spaces was brought to the New World.

There is contrary evidence in the 1560s, during the notorious *auto de fé* of 1562, when Landa ordered disinterred the bodies of Maya who had died during the previous year but who were said to have been guilty of idolatrous practices; the bodies were then burned.[51] This sort of event makes it hard to comment on what, if anything, the Spanish policy was toward pre-Christian Maya corporeal remains. Thanks to Landa, the technique of appropriating pre-Columbian sacred space may ultimately have given way to fear of pre-Christian corporeal remains as demonic. As a result I reiterate that Geary's statement that reverence for corporeal remains in Mexico failed to develop is problematic.[52] With regard to central Mexico (and not the Maya), there is also the thought that, given the way in which the devil or demons were conceptualized,[53] the Day of the Dead provides an excellent example of reverence for corporeal remains.

With or without relics, saints became important to the Maya. In Nancy Farriss's words, "The clergy could be confident that although the Indians' grasp of Christian dogma might be feeble, their devotion to the saints was unshakable."[54] Farriss provides a rich and detailed description of the role of saints in maintaining the Maya cosmos.[55] From the archaeological excavations, we know that there existed internal church features at both Lamanai and Tipu that may have functioned as supports for saints' images, although we have found no images or image fragments in the excavations. In any case, my interest here is the close parallels in behavior between Mayas and Spaniards in venerating saints, and in their use of imagery in prayer and veneration.

WHAT THE CLERGY FACED

Although the regular and secular clergy in Yucatan reacted with shock to what they saw as widespread apostasy among those whom they thought they had Christianized, I suggest that their reaction was the result of naive and ill-informed expectations rather than any correctness of their perception that they were faced with unusually virulent forms of intransigence and deception. Brown argues that mass conversions presented more of a challenge to the church hierarchy in the New World than in the early conversions in Europe.[56] But the "challenges" as we know them were described for us by those in the church. In the Old World and in the New, the sources we have on apostasy and heresy are the writings of the religious, who talk about what they see as good or bad in popular practice. Practices are condemned not because they have been weighed carefully against expectations of spiritual fulfillment, but because they developed outside the official framework of the church.[57] We have seen in earlier chapters that such a framework developed very early in the church's history.

Unfortunately, direct evidence from those who were condemned, both in Mesoamerica and in Europe, is lacking. This book is an effort to find the voices of those who were not given an opportunity to speak. In the meantime, we must keep in mind that the reports of the Franciscans and the seculars are often polemical, and do not necessarily provide accurate information on the phenomena.

What Did Christianity Have to Offer?

In reviewing the exchange of information and ideas between Mayas and Spaniards, I have a proposal that I think is worth considering, but I admit that it stands as speculative. In the Old World, the development of the veneration, or "cult," of saints has a complex history.[58] Saints were those who were believed by Christians to be close to God because of their holiness but were nonetheless accessible to humans because they shared a human nature. Martyrs, those who suffered or died for the faith, were considered saintly, but a life of renunciation and holiness also gave an individual the makings of a saint.[59] The graves of saints became charged and powerful locales because they were places where heaven and earth could be said to meet through the body of the individual.[60] As in the Maya world, where the dead were incorporated into the living structures of the city or town or village, the place of the dead was a liminal zone, part otherworld, part this world. It is interesting that Brown distinguishes the Christian view of the places for the dead (which could be argued is also the Maya view) from that of the pagan Mediterranean world, where the soul or spirit separated completely from the body and became part of another, separate, celestial sphere, and where, on earth, cemeteries lay outside the walls of cities.

In Christianity, although the saint was indeed in heaven, he was also believed to be present at his tomb on earth.[61] Gradually, graves of saints which lay in cemeteries outside city walls became centers of religious worship of the Christian communities. If the saint or even a part of his body was moved, his saintliness moved with him. Any part of the body, such as a finger bone, was seen as a powerful means of communication with the divine. According to Brown,[62] the boundary between the city of the living and the realm of the dead came to be breached by the entry of relics and their housing within the walls of towns; graves clustered in towns in the vicinity of relics soon followed. As relics became incorporated into altars,[63] and altars into permanent churches,[64] the Christian community could remain close to its saints. In fact, according to Belting,[65] whatever reservations the church hierarchy may have had at one time about the venerated image, they were dropped once the relic came on the scene.

In the clustering of the dead around churches we can see the origins of the medieval pattern that would be transferred to Tipu and Lamanai. Unlike Mediterranean Europe of Roman times, the Maya world did not find this mixing of the dead with the living incompatible with its practices. At Tipu, there is some evidence—such as dental modification—which suggests that burials inside the church represent the first converts.[66] If this was the case, it is hard to know whether the preference for burial within the church nave, rather than in the churchyard, represents a transfer by the religious to the Maya of the Christian practice accorded to elites (burial inside the church), or the Maya practice of interring individuals within the foundations of houses and temples, or, fortuitously, both. I suggest tentatively that we may be seeing an unexpected conjunction of beliefs between the Old World and the New concerning the dead and access to supernatural power.

The other possibility—and this is more tenuous—has to do with kinship links to the deceased. Brown calls the early church in Europe an artificial kin group.[67] The custom in Roman times, and indeed through the fourth century, was that the family celebrated at the grave of the deceased. Saints and martyrs seemed, however, to "belong" to more than just their kin group. Among the non-Christian German and Frankish tribes, being related to the dead was critical in accessing power that the dead might have. The example I mentioned previously of early Christian churches being situated in barbarian Europe over ancestors' graves must have been an accommodation to this belief. The view of ancestors as links to spiritual or supernatural aid existed in the Maya world as well, at least among elites but almost certainly more broadly.[68] Classic-period rulers identified with the supernatural world, and claimed to have descended from gods.[69]

There was clearly more than one way to tap into the power of the supernatural. Elites, more than commoners, could conceive of and market themselves as having descended from gods, because, conveniently, they had the power and the position to deify their own ancestors. Like the German elites of Europe, the Maya elites of Classic times were in such a position. In the Postclassic world, Maya elites used lineage ties to claim access to rituals that were critical to community long-term survival.[70] Where lineage ties were weak or limited, or where powerful kin were few or nonexistent, another way to access supernatural power was to appropriate a powerful ancestor. This may be why saints became so popular cross-culturally. By making the power of the saints accessible to anyone, Christianity in the Old World broadened the nature of access that the living had to the world and power of the dead. No kinship relationship was necessary except the fictive kin of the church. The veneration of saints and their relics almost certainly fed this phenomenon, because power was so clearly tied to a locus: a shrine, altar, or other holy place. Power abiding in places is easier to access than power abiding in an otherworld spirit.

Could Christianity have been seen by the Maya as providing increased access to supernatural powers through the institution of fictive ancestors in the form of the saints? Saints and archangels are said to replace pre-Columbian supernaturals, such as the chaakob (or chacob), who bring rain, or the Pauah-tuns, who guard the cardinal directions.[71] If this was indeed the case, then my suggestion is groundless, because there were plenty of Maya gods and spirits to go around. Yet, as Farriss argues, the friars ensured "that the parochial level of religion would eventually be expressed exclusively within the framework of Christianity,"[72] which, as she points out, changed the relationship forever between the community and those who had, in pre-Christian times, medi-ated with the supernatural on behalf of the community. It may be that in pre-Christian times, as was true in many parts of Europe, the style of mediation, if you will, was qualitatively different from what it would become under Chris-tianity, with its non-local priests as mediators and its saints as intercessors for individuals. Although *cofradías* would arise which performed civil and reli-gious functions for the community,[73] individual access to saints in Christian-ity could be seen to have fostered and legitimized a self-serving trend that was as divisive to a community as it was attractive to individuals. Unfortunately, we do not know enough about pre-Columbian religions to be able to specu-late in any detail about the character of the spirits or deities whose power an individual could or could not access, or how such access was effected.

Christianity as an Opening
into Maya Religion and Representation

In the Christian world, spirits such as angels exist and have different degrees of power, but angels are generally not intercessors for humans. They repre-sent the power of the Christian God and they can pass on messages from God. A tradition inherited from Judaism, although only expressed in imag-ery in Christianity, has an angel guarding the body and soul of each human (fig. 11.8);[74] but angels are not generally beseeched by humans to provide aid. Saints, on the other hand—people with a history, who died after a lifetime of holiness—are special in the eyes of God and can intercede in any meaningful way for humans.

I am not saying that angels were not prayed to in the past and that only saints were supplicated, but only that there were supernaturals in the past who tended to fulfill particular niches: that is, some supernaturals were more likely to be asked for things than others. I make no assumptions that the Maya spirit world was identical to the Christian spirit world, but I have often won-dered if there might be a way to analyze the Maya spirit world more deeply by exploring the relationships between art and representation of the Chris-tian supernaturals to see if there are patterns that can be sought in the Maya experience.

Figure 11.5. St. Michael the archangel in the armour of a medieval king defeating the Devil. (Original print in collection of the author)

Figure 11.6. St. Michael the archangel in Roman military garb defeating the Devil.

Figure 11.7. The angel of the abyss and the infernal locusts. (Copyright M. Moleiro, editor, *Beatus of Liébana, Codex of Gerona*, f. 156v)

Michael, for example, the patron saint of my neighborhood church in Paterson, New Jersey, is an archangel (figs. 11.5, 11.6). His origins lie in myth, not in history as we know it. His representations display patterning that is very different from the representation of historical saints. His story—that he overcame Lucifer, the devil, and sent Lucifer and his rebel angels to hell—is so powerful that it is played over and over again in representation and in art. St. Michael is consistently depicted in military garb, with weapons, subduing the devil. Because he is an angel, he is almost always depicted with wings; but

Figure 11.8. Guardian angel and children.

the style of his military garb has changed through time. He can be dressed as a Roman or medieval or modern man, but he invariably is suited up for battle. Even a humanoid from outer space could, I think, after seeing enough images, discern that an important cosmic myth was being represented and that the figure transcends time and is an essential part of the myth (see also fig. 11.7).

Saints, on the other hand, are historical figures. Their iconography is filled with symbols that represent phenomena in their lives. Such symbolism is not always accurate, of course; some saints, such as St. Margaret of Antioch, apparently never existed. Even so, saints' iconography reflects a repertoire of material culture that is limited and potentially identifiable as regards time. Unlike normal humans, saints always have circular bands (haloes) drawn around their heads to represent their holiness. An outside observer may not realize this right away, but eventually, after seeing enough images, it should be possible to ascertain that the image focuses on a historical figure who became exalted or deified. Depending on *where* such images are found—as part of a household, or in a communal setting, or in a restricted setting such as a shrine or cave—one would get some hints as to how the image functioned and whether elites or non-elites had access to the power represented by the image.

Imagery and Sacred Space

One of the ways in which Christian images can potentially teach us about the context and significance of Maya images is through examination of saints' statues and their functions. The word "worship" is often tossed around liberally in the archaeological literature. The Maya are sometimes said to worship ancestors, or to worship effigies that seem to us to represent deities.

Having been raised, so to speak, as an idolator, in that imagery was always part of my religious ritual, I doubt that representations figured so simply in Maya ritual life. What, indeed, goes on when a person situates himself or herself in proximity to an image, or in a shrine with pictorial imagery in the form of painting or stucco relief? Is the person thinking, communicating, praying? An observer might say that the person is praying *to* or communicating with the image, and this would be an understandable inference, since the person is facing or surrounded by the imagery and is apparently devoting a considerable degree of concentration or energy to it. The person might even assume a subservient pose, either kneeling or with hands clasped or arms across the chest or head down.

Insight into this situation came from an unexpected source. I was reading *Touch*, by Elmore Leonard, in which a character named Lynn Marie Faulkner, an ex-baton twirler for the Uni-Faith church, falls in love with a young man called Juvenal, an ex-Franciscan brother who works and lives at an alcohol rehabilitation center and has the stigmata and the power to heal. At one point, Lynn is talking to Juvenal in his room about the stigmata and its effects. She asks:

"Do you, like pray and think about being holy all the time?"

"I pray, yeah, but not the way I used to, or for anything in particular. It's more like talking to God."

"Do you think he hears you?"

"Sure, or I wouldn't pray."

"How do you know He does?"

"I don't *know* it, I believe it."

"Do you ever pray to a crucifix?"

"Not *to*. You pray before a crucifix," Juvenal said.[75]

Ah. Those of us who are accustomed to ritual and prayer involving images pray *before* them. Now, in the terms of an observer who has had nothing to do with images or religion, what's the difference? What possible difference could a preposition make?

The plot thickens. For one thing, praying before an image is not something the insider or penitent or devotee, Maya or Christian, would ever choose to put into words, or try to explain. Ritual is not to be explained. It is to be experienced—colors, silence, sounds, scent, and even touch, but not words.[76] The very attempt to explain interaction with an image makes the experience something that it is not.

It is sometimes said that the Lacandon Maya of Chiapas see their "god pots," which are censers decorated with applied, human-like faces and sometimes other human features (see fig. 9.4), as being the actual deity. But according to Jon McGee,[77] although each pot has unique characteristics and each is dedicated to a particular god, they are not effigies of a god. They act as a portal through which the gods can take their offerings, which are burned in the vessel. The same was said of saints' images in the early Middle Ages: that saints could take up their abode in the image or speak through it.[78] In this way, they mark the *place* where the god can interact with the human world.

In all of this, place, or perhaps space, is the key. As explained by Juvenal, the crucifix (or a cross or icon or image, which could be a painting or a statue or a figurine) marks out sacred space. If one prayed "to" an image, one would not have to be positioned in front of it. The image could remain at the far end of the church or temple, or indeed anywhere. But prayer or interaction involving an image is rarely so distant, except perhaps in a procession, and even then people wait until the image is nearby to speak or to pray. Thus, it is more productive to think of religious images (and sometimes symbols) in terms of their relationship to the space they occupy, rather than as simple objects of veneration. The role of the image is then, in part, to create sacred or charged space. The place of the image, and not just its symbolism, marks out (liminal or transitional?) territory (a portal?) in which a human can interact with the supernatural world, and where the human can transcend what we like to call the natural world, at least for a time. The Postclassic world that preceded the Conquest period was rich in imagery: effigies, figurines, statues, wall paintings, and ceramics. So much of this imagery, no matter how diverse or complex, was classified and demeaned as idolatry by the invaders.

Perhaps the best subversive weapon we have in our inventory to fight the prejudices of the conquerors and their legacy is the use of Christianity—its practices, world views, beliefs, and imagery—to put life back into the ancient Maya world of spirits and supernaturals.

✠ TWELVE ✠

Everyone Knows
What a Dragon Looks Like

The title of this chapter is taken from a children's book written by Jay Williams and beautifully illustrated by Mercer Mayer.[1] I return to the book shortly as a device to resolve—or, more accurately, as a device to dissolve—issues that arise in claims by different agents to know what an authentic Christianity should "look like." First, however, I reconsider what it meant to be Christian among the colonial-period Maya of Belize and how we would know what Christianity meant—to the Maya or to the Spaniards. How do archaeology and ethnohistory fit in?

Maya Christians in Belize

What it meant to be Christian is especially interesting for the area we now know as Belize because, as I have observed in earlier chapters, the Maya in the region remained Christian after 1700 under circumstances in which Spanish authorities were no longer in control. Admittedly, after two hundred years of Spanish interference it might have been difficult to maintain a corpus of beliefs and images that were not influenced by Christian imagery and thought, but it is worth noting that the Maya in Belize did not resort to rejection of all things Spanish, despite their relationships and alliances with the Itza and Kowoj of the Peten lakes region.

The Mayas' choices were probably affected by the fact that they could benefit to some extent from the colonial economy.[2] They were far enough away from Spanish religious authorities to be able to lead their own lives for considerable periods at the same time that they could act as intermediaries in transactions with frontier communities in acquiring cacao, honey, annatto and other products, which they could then exchange and profit from in more heavily administered regions to the north. Although Lamanai suffered more than Tipu as regards community members' health,[3] the material culture does not reflect settlements deprived of material goods, and some European goods reached both communities. The Belize Maya could not have achieved this strategic position had they maintained the "pagan" profile that characterized the Maya of Peten.

Both Classic- and Postclassic-period history suggest that this straddling of different worlds was not new to Maya communities in Belize. Their proximity to the sea and to coastal and coral islands served them well as regards access to a wealth of marine resources and to goods made available through coastal trade.[4] Rivers and streams fostered inland travel and communication overland with Peten, which was important for the cities, towns, and villages in Belize in Classic times, and with Campeche and Yucatan where centers rose to prominence in Postclassic times. Many sites in Belize may not reflect the wealth of architecture and material culture of a Tikal or Calakmul, but neither do they give evidence of collapse or of a radical fluctuation in fortunes, at least until the Spanish colonial period.

Such generalization is not meant to imply environmental determinism, but simply to assert that Belize Maya communities made good use of a good situation—one that offered diversity in resources and a range of choices in routes of communication. Even in the early colonial period, it would not be Spaniards, but rather British and Continental privateers and pirates who drove the Maya from the coast. Nonetheless, the long history of involvement of Belize Maya communities in trade and exchange from Honduras to Tabasco must have given many individuals substantial knowledge of overland, coastal, and maritime travel that would have served them well in times of upheaval.

Despite the claims in Spanish sources that there was widespread apostasy, the stratigraphic sequence at Tipu provided evidence that the Maya continued to bury their dead in the churchyard long after the church and adjacent buildings had fallen into disuse. This, in addition to placement of caches in churches at Lamanai after the 1638–41 revolts, suggests strongly that Christianity made deeper inroads into Maya life than was recognized by the Spanish ecclesiastical authorities who were responsible for the administration of Belize in the sixteenth and seventeenth centuries. It may have been that only some individuals at Tipu continued to use the churchyard, whereas others reverted to pre-Columbian practice. Yet the question is why any individuals at all would have continued to practice what we usually describe as the religion of the colonizers when the colonizers were no longer powerful or even proximate, and when Itza machinations against the Spaniards intensified, as seems to have been the case as the seventeenth century wore on? As I noted in an earlier chapter, no matter how one evaluates what the friars might call the

Christian message, it had a life of its own unrelated to that foreseen by the religious and hence not mirrored in the documents.

Archaeology, Religion, and Magic

Shall I dichotomize archaeology and ethnohistory then, and make ethnohistory the voice of an authentic Christianity and archaeology the voice of popular practice? I could do so, but the result would be misleading and somewhat manipulative. Critical reading of the documents can lead to insights into Maya behavior that do not reveal deceit or apostasy but instead bespeak efforts to cope with historical crisis.[5] Even without archaeology, being sensitive to the layers of meaning in the documents can lead to the inference that the Maya saw themselves as Christian. In turn, I have argued that the style of the early churches at Tipu and Lamanai reflects Franciscan presence and hence significant Franciscan input into church construction and community organization. The archaeological evidence reinforces the idea that Mendicants were responsible for evangelization, and also that the Franciscan world view has to be taken into account when one considers the conversion process. Tipu and Lamanai have shown us that the excavation of a church can add to what the documents tell us about the Franciscan ideal of an authentic Christianity.

There is one way, however, in which ethnohistory and archaeology can be seen to represent, respectively, an elite and a popular Christianity. If we knew more about Maya religions and religious practices, we might also find that the codices embodied elite ideals and that popular practices were therefore largely accessible only through archaeology.

Ethnohistory focuses on texts and the written word. Partly as the result of Christianity's Jewish roots, textual sources are imbued with sacredness. In fact, the term "scripture," from the Latin for "writing," is applied both in Judaism and in Christianity to the textual sources that are seen as canonical and embodiments of divine communication.[6] The Church is said to venerate the Scriptures as she venerates the Lord's body.[7]

With regard to tangible objects, Christian iconography "expresses in images the same Gospel message that Scripture communicates by words."[8] Church history tells us, however, that venerated objects have not been as well received as scripture in the hierarchy of holiness. Rejection of images was a major issue in the Protestant Reformation, and images, relics, and "holy" objects of various sorts invariably lie at the heart of problematic popular practices, whether Spanish or Maya. The careful way in which the modern church tiptoes around the issue of images is instructive. It takes quite a bit of ferreting in the *Catechism of the Catholic Church* to find a passage that deals squarely with imagery. There is a glossary entry only for "icon" (the religious painting tradition of the Eastern church), and the passage from the Council of Nicaea II in A.D. 787 which confirms the veneration of images is secreted in the section on "How is the liturgy celebrated?"[9]

Just as the pagan Romans turned their noses up at the burial customs and rituals of Christians, in which bones could be handled and people gathered to celebrate at the graves of martyrs,[10] bishops and clergy often saw a focus on objects and the tangible interaction they stimulated—such as kissing the feet of saints, or touching Christ's wounds—as legitimate but misplaced expressions of piety. Objects, however holy, are not equal to the power of Scripture. Interaction with images also had to be watched carefully, because it could easily lead Christians to backslide into paganism or fall prey to magic. Magic was defined as wonders wrought by demons, whereas wonders wrought by Christians were miracles.[11]

Archaeology, with its digging in the earth, its obsession with objects, and its quest for the tangible could be equated both with popular practice and perhaps, at times, with the magical arts.[12] By this I mean, drawing from Tambiah's definition of magic, that excavation can be viewed as a ritual act focused on objects and their properties. The objects we excavate have desirable properties that become transferred to us, and our elaborate cataloguing and object manipulation are performative acts.[13]

Documentary sources, on the other hand, are meant to be read and are venerated as such. The veneration of text is so powerful a force in academe that post-processual archaeologists have encouraged reading the archaeological record as text.

Excavation relies on *touch*, and it is the sensation of touch that produces the archaeological record: finding pottery, feeling glass beads or chert scrapers, brushing bone, nicking a finger on obsidian, describing the patterns and colors of things, or even catching the scent of a remnant of copal resin. Why is this relevant? First, our obsession as archaeologists with things, and indeed with actually *digging up* things, in some ways makes us almost "childlike,"[14] and hence close to the Christians, both Spaniard and Maya, who venerated objects in ways that the religious hierarchy sometimes found naive, if not idolatrous. Second, there is a level at which being able to feel, touch, and even catch the scent of things that were handled by people hundreds or thousands of years ago is a kind of magic, at the same time that it reinforces, perhaps in an unexpected way, the importance of the senses in knowledge.[15]

I stated in chapter 1 that I hoped to identify ways in which archaeology could contribute to our understanding of religious experience. My answer to the question of archaeology's contribution is that it is effected through our use of the five senses, and not solely through seeing or reading. We may also be encouraged to read the archaeological record as text, and to learn enough through our excavations to be able to contribute to the formation of a new approach or a new theory that will help us to understand religion. But even if we never reach such intellectual heights, our practices—popular, religious, or magical—involve a sensual array and hence are deeply experiential and informative.

Gods and Dragons

The tale told in *Everyone Knows What a Dragon Looks Like*[16] has multiple meanings, but at one level it is about people's perceptions of the natural and supernatural forces at work around them and how decisions are made on the basis of these perceptions. It is also about belief and action and about how people think and interpret the world.

The story focuses on Han, a young orphaned boy who is the gatekeeper for the walled city of Wu in northern China. It comes to pass that the Wild Horsemen of the North are on the move, and messengers warn the people of Wu that attack is imminent. The city's leaders cannot think of what to do against such indomitable forces, except to call on the Great Cloud Dragon for help. "So the gongs were beaten, and the smoke of sweet incense rose up while everyone in the city prayed." There is, unfortunately, no immediate and recognizable reaction from a dragon of any kind, and the city prepares for the worst.

The next morning, an old, corpulent traveler appears at the city gates and introduces himself to Han as a dragon. Han takes the old man to the mandarin and his advisors, who, despite the threat from the Wild Horsemen, are just finishing a sumptuous breakfast. The only interest they take in the old man is that he is tracking dirt on the carpet. However, his arrival stimulates lengthy

Figure 12.1. The mandarin of Wu and his court advisors debating dragon-ness, with Han and the old man looking on. Illustration from *Everyone Knows What a Dragon Looks Like* copyright © 1976 by Mercer Mayer.

Figure 12.2. Han and the great Cloud Dragon. Illustration from *Everyone Knows What a Dragon Looks Like* copyright © 1976 by Mercer Mayer.

discussion and debate about what dragons really look like and how the people of Wu will recognize the Cloud Dragon when he arrives (fig. 12.1). The ruler and his advisors cannot reach a consensus; each is convinced that his idea, and his image alone, is the correct one. They all laugh at the old fat man and refuse to treat him with courtesy. Soon, screams are heard, because the Wild Horsemen are galloping toward the city gates. Everyone, including the mandarin and his advisors, takes cover.

Han takes pity on the traveler because the old man is hungry and tired. Although there is not much time before the horsemen arrive, Han gives the old man all that he has: his daily ration of a bowl of rice and a cup of wine. The old man eats and drinks, and then tells Han that he does not think much of Wu, but for Han's sake, he will save the city.

The old man causes the winds of the northern plain to blow with great force, and they scatter the Wild Horsemen far and wide. Han then witnesses the transfiguration of the small, fat, bald old traveler into a shimmering Dragon, "the color of sunset shining through rain," who disappears into the sky (fig. 12.2). In the end, everyone celebrates and honors Han as the savior of the city of Wu. The story ends with the mandarin grinning and claiming, "Best of all, we now know what a dragon looks like. He looks like a small, fat, bald old man."

The Religious Experience

This story and its characters help me bring this book to a close. In the process, I hope to leave the reader with some thoughts on spiritual beliefs and the role of religion in violence and war. For the Dragon of the tale let us read "religion" or "god."

It is interesting that the kind of decision making which ultimately brought about results was Han's wish to help the old man, an action that bore no relationship to the ability to recognize a Dragon. In the debates that dragged on between the ruler and his three advisors—the head of the army, the head of public works, and the court sage—each saw the dragon as an image of himself, or as mirroring characteristics that each man believed to be important. Each of the four was convinced that he knew what Dragons looked like, how they were represented, and what they were supposed to do—knowledge based on scholarly books, stories, or traditions. Han operated on a completely different plane, one that made use of his feelings, senses, resources, and judgment. Perhaps he was treating the old man as he himself would have liked to be treated.

When we archaeologists or historians study "religion," we are not *experiencing* in a phenomenological sense, but instead we are accumulating information about what others have experienced. We are very concerned about what religion looks like. The Spanish friars, not dissimilarly, were very concerned with what God "looked like." Ironically, drawing from our story, when one interacts with what turns out to be a Dragon, the basis for that interaction has nothing to do with debates about Dragon-ness. So concerned were the mandarin and his advisors with identifying an authentic Dragon that they put the city at risk. So concerned were the Spanish friars and secular clergy with spreading an authentic faith among the Maya that they all too often used their preoccupation to justify cruelty, exploitation, and even deaths.

Does this mean that study and debate are irrelevant? Not necessarily. If study and debate are what lead me to the recognition that such endeavors are not what is important in life, then they take on importance for that reason alone. To claim that this volume is about religion would be to relegate it to the sphere of study and debate and to exclude it from the sphere of action and interaction. But this is why, at various points, I have thought about interacting with Dragons based on my childhood experiences with saints, guardian angels, and the devil himself. It was Han rather than the mandarin and his councillors who saved the city of Wu and who ultimately gained insight into the beauty of the cosmos and the significance of dragons. As much as I admire the methods of academe, I remain unconvinced that debates about Dragon-ness empower us to act. As much as I admire people of faith, I remain unconvinced that the authenticity of one's faith should be the basis for debate, or worse, the basis for action. In the end, it is saving the city that counts.

Appendix 1

Friars in Belize

Name of Friar(s)	Actions	Pages in Jones 1989	Dates	Order
Fr. Lorenzo de Bienvenida	• 1545 or 1546, in Bacalar. • 1548: writes to Crown about Pachecos. • Comes to Yucatan in what is known as the Third Company of friars, sent from Guatemala by Fray Toribio de Montolinía; other friars in the Company were Luis de Villalpando, Melchor de Benavente, and Juan de Herrera (Tozzer 1941, 68n306). • First sailed from Spain in August 1542; travelled to Yucatan from the Golfo Dulce region and was in Bacalar early in 1547 (Canedo 1952, 499–500). • Allied with Toral against Landa (Tozzer 1941, 82n345).	42 86, 60	1545 1546 1548	Franciscan
Fr. Francisco de Benavides	• Visited Bacalar in 1568, 1569.	86	1568	Franciscan
Fr. Martín de Barrientos	• Probably participated in entradas and reductions of Juan Garzón in 1568.		1569	
Fr. Alonso Toral	• Fr. Toral was the brother of the Bishop in Yucatan.			
Fr. Juan de Orbita	• Native of Arcila; grew up in the villa of Torrijos in the kingdom of Toledo. • Came to Yucatan in 1615 in the company of Fr. Francisco Fernández and Fr. Diego Porras. • Applied himself to learning Maya "scientifically." • Visited Tah Itza, probably in 1617.	133–34	1615 1617	Franciscan

Fr. Bartolomé de Fuensalida	Franciscan	1618	135–52	• Visited Tah Itza twice, in 1618 and 1619.
Fr. Juan de Orbita	Franciscan	1619		• Chosen at Franciscan provincial chapter meeting, Merida, 25 March 1618. • Took over authority temporarily from Gregorio Marín de Aguilar, the secular. • Stayed in Casa Real at Bacalar. • 1618 visit was when Orbita destroyed horse effigy; Orbita then stayed in Tipu while Fuensalida reported to Merida in December of 1618. • Then Fuensalida returned to join Orbita at Tipu in 1619. • In early October, they headed again for Tah Itza. • This is when Can Ek's wife (persuaded by Maya priests?) influenced him to throw the friars off the island; Orbita was knocked unconscious. • They went back to Tipu, where Fuensalida noted that the Tipuans were "happy . . . to be left alone to live as they wanted", and then back to Merida.
Meanwhile	Franciscan	1622 1623	157–58, 163	Fr. Delgado was killed with Don Cristobal Na and others at Tah Itza in 1623 during the Mirones expedition.
Fr. Juan de Estrada	Franciscan lay brother	1626 1627	215; 322n6	• Creole lay friar (could not say Mass). • Had been alcalde and military captain in Bacalar for many years. • Was comisario or procurador of Bacalar in 1626–27. • Apparently was also an encomendero of Chanlacan and Yumpeten, 1626 (when encomienda was granted?), and "defensor de naturales" in 1627, which Grant says was the title of the encomienda. • Was a native of Mérida.

Appendix 1 (continued)

Name of Friar(s)	Actions	Pages in Jones 1989	Dates	Order
	• Died in 1646 of an illness contracted on the trip with Fuensalida to the Bacalar province. • Had many godchildren at Tipu.			
Fr. Lopez de Cogolludo	• According to Jones, went to Bacalar province on two separate trips from Guatemala and was familiar with the area around the New River Lagoon. • Some of this familiarity must have come from his gleaning of information from *relaciones*, which he duly refers to in his writing. • It is highly probable however that he traveled through Belize on at least one occasion. In describing Fuensalida and Orbita's journey to Peten through Tekax and Pacha in 1618, he recalls an earlier visit of his to Pacha, located not too far north of Bacalar. It was 1638, and he was returning from Guatemala with Fr. Luis de Vivar, heading for Yucatan, and it seems reasonable to consider that he and Vivar came through Belize (Lopez de Cogolludo [1688] 1971, bk. 9, chap. 5; see also bk. 12, chap. 16). • He returned to Guatemala in 1650, but makes no mention of how he got back to Yucatán (Lopez de Cogolludo [1688] 1971, bk 12, chap. 16).	311–12n31	1630s	Franciscan
Fr. Francisco de Moran	• Traveled from Verapaz to Salmanca de Bacalar in search of runaway Maya of the Chol missions (Sapper 1985, 28–30).		1640	Dominican
Fr. Bartolomé de Fuensalida	• Fuensalida returned to Bacalar in 1641 with the intention of going to Tipu.	215, 216	1641	Franciscan
Fr. Juan de Estrada	• Took with him to Bacalar: Fr. Juan de Estrada, Fr. Bartolomé de			Franciscan

Becerril, and Fr. Martín Tejero.

- Fuensalida and Estrada went on to Tipu.
- Becerril was to attempt to reduce the coastal towns.
- Tejero stayed behind but then joined Becerril.
- This is the trip where they found Lamanai burned.
- Never got to Tipu; got to Zaczuz.

Fr. Bartolomé de Becerril	Franciscan	1641	224	• Traveled down Belize coast to Manche Chol area.
			215	• He was in the area of Soite (Zoité, in Cogolludo) and Cehaké, near the mouth of the Sittee (Soite) River, when he encountered unconverted fugitives from Campin (Monkey River?). He taught them the catechism, baptized them, and settled them in Soite and Cehaké (Lopez de Cogolludo [1688] 1971, vol. 2, bk. 9, chap. 16).
				• Spanish, but fluent Maya speaker.
Fr. Francisco de Triana	Dominican	1641	225	• From Verapaz.
				• Had carried out conversions in Campin, on the Monkey River.
				• Wrote to Tejero (below) from Campin encouraging him to come to Campin.
Fr. Martín Tejero	Franciscan	later in 1641	215	• Spanish, but fluent Maya speaker.
		1642	224–25	• Travelled to Manan (Manatee), which was involved in the rebellion; "Manan" is called "Maná" in Lopez de Cogolludo ([1688] 1971).
			224, 226	• Reduced Manan and moved the inhabitants to an island called (by Lopez de Cogolludo) Zulá; encountered no resistance; baptized children older than two years and administered sacraments to the rest.
			224–25	• Returned to Bacalar, then back to Manan with a Spaniard, Lucas de San Miguel (Lopez de Cogolludo [1683] 1971, vol. 2, bk. 9, chap. 16).
				• Dutch pirates later captured Tejero and San Miguel and held them prisoner.
				• Pirates raided Soite and Cehake taking food, etc.

Appendix 1 (*continued*)

Name of Friar(s)	Actions	Pages in Jones 1989	Dates	Order
	• Tejero and San Miguel eventually returned to Bacalar and sent food down to the raided towns of Soite and Cehake.			
	• He then learned that uncovered Manche Chol at Campin (Monkey River) wanted him to go there and baptize them.			
	• That Campin was on the Monkey River is from Scholes and Thompson, "The Francisco Pérez *Probanza*," 67.	See also 323n26		
	• Campin had been visited by Dominican Fr. Francisco de Triana from Verapaz, and inhabitants of Campin wanted him replaced by Tejero, who received a letter from Triana at Soite encouraging Tejero to accept the invitation.			
	• Soite and Cehake were mixed Yucatec and Manche Chol, whereas Campin was Manche Chol.			
	• There was an *alcalde* at Soite, Don Diego Canche, who knew both languages.			
	• Canche took Tejero's message to Campin.			
	• Tejero went to the mouth of the Monkey River and travelled three days upstream to a small village of ten men, two of whom had been Christianized many years before. The villagers told Tejero that no priest had visited them for twenty-five years, yet other evidence indicated that the Dominican Fr. Francisco Triana, from Verapaz, had visited the community.			
	• While he was in the village, people from another Manche Chol settlement (beyond the nearest mountain) came and met him in the village (seventy-three men, women, and children in all), and he baptized and performed marriage ceremonies.			

Name	Details	Page	Date	Order
	• He had brought images of St. Michael the Archangel, St. Jeronimo, and St. Francis with him; St. Francis was chosen as patron saint; they then cut one another's hair, symbolizing conversion. • Returned to Bacalar with intent to go back, but pirates then raided the coast and Maya had to run away again to the mountains. • Same pirates then captured Bacalar. • This put an end to all effective missionary efforts in the province south of the Rio Hondo.		1642	Franciscan
Fr. Bartolomé de Becerril	• Was in Bacalar in late 1642 when the pirate Diego Lucifer de los Reyes el Mulato sacked Campeche and then raided the coast from Bacalar to Golfo Dulce.	323–24n28		
	• Kidnapped Maya from Soite to Honduras and took them to an island in Honduras.	226–27	1643	
	• The town that had been visited by Tejero (near Campin) also raided.	229–30		
	• Pirates attacked Bacalar.			
	• Becerril was in Bacalar and was fired upon.	227		
	• The pirates carried away what they could, including gold and silver from the church.			
	• Early in 1643 Bacalareños were still hiding out along the shore of Lake Bacalar.			
	• This attack damaged Spanish efforts at reduction and maintenance, because the area was clearly unstable and neither the Indians nor Spaniards could be protected from the pirates.			
	• ". . spelled the end of Spanish hopes to recapture the souls of the Bacalar-province Mayas." Beginning of the end of colonial domination.	229–30		
	• Becerril and Tejero were withdrawn from the province sometime in 1643 and replaced by a secular priest.			
Fr. Joseph Delgado	• Was sent from Guatemala to find alternative land routes from the Christianized settlements of the Manche Chol, via Mopan to Tipu, and then to Bacalar and on to Mérida.	248–49[a]	1677	Dominican

Name of Friar(s)	Actions	Pages in Jones 1989	Dates	Order
	• Set out from Cajabon and reached Merida after a difficult trip.			
	• Fell into hands of English corsairs under Bartholomew Sharpe.			
	• Describes the southern part of Belize at this time: Spaniards from Bacalar or Tihosuco were there doing business; said they knew the area well already, as did other Spaniards from where they were from; Spaniards were buying cacao from villagers; apparently, Spaniards at this time could not do business on the upper Belize River (Tipu area).	249		
	• So Delgado reported no local opposition at this time to Spanish trading.			
Fr. Marcos de Muros, plus two other friars	• Franciscans killed at Paliac, on the Rio Grande in southern Belize.	248–50	1684	Franciscan
	• Had been accompanied by a man from Bacalar, Diego Martín, and other Bacalareños; they went off for a week to get food in Yaxal and in the interim the missionaries were killed.	328n16		
	• Apparently, a Joseph Delgado from Bacalar was there extorting cacao from the natives, and had whipped one of the caciques; he was killed too.			
Fr. Agustín Cano	• Accompanied Captain Juan Díaz de Velasco from Cahabon in Verapaz through Manche Chol and Mopan territory.	260	1695	Dominican
	• Part of an exploratory Guatemalan entrada to Tah Itza led by Velasco.			
	• Designated by the president of the Audiencia of Guatemala, Jacinto Barrios Leal.			
	• Main purpose was to conquer Cholti-speaking Lacandones around Sac Balam in western Peten.			

	• They were supposed to limit their activities to the Lacandon regions, but they went as far as Lake Peten and engaged Mayas there, and twenty Mayas lost their lives. One wounded Maya made it back to Tah Itza and distressed Can Ek. • I think all this took place around mid-year, 1695.			
Fr. Andrés Avendaño y Loyola	• June 1695 Ursúa sent Avendaño y Loyola along the *camino real* accompanied by Spanish soldiers; goal was to reach Tah Itza to convince Can Ek to submit peacefully. • Returned to Mérida though, because of distress caused by behavior of military escort. • Set out again in December of 1695; was convinced that Can Ek could be persuaded by the Mayas' own prophecies; but despite initial positive overtures by Can Ek, the friar was forced out of town. • Jones says that the friar who was martyred (see below) was with a group that had arrived just after Avendaño y Loyola's forced removal from Tah Itza.	261–62 267	1695	Franciscan
Fr. Juan de Buenaventura	• Martyred at Tah Itza. • Party sent by Captain Alonso García de Paredes. • Party consisted of the friar, a lay companion, sixty Spanish soldiers, some armed Mayas, and Maya bearers, and was headed by Captain Pedro de Zubiaur Isasi. • They had opened the road to within 3 or so leagues of Tah Itza. • When they arrived at the lake, they were met by hostile Mayas in canoes; around ten Spaniards and thirty Itzas were killed in the fighting. Fray Juan and some Maya carriers and the cacique of Sacabchen were carried off by the enemy.	266–67	1695	Franciscan

Assembled from Jones 1989; sources other than Jones are shown in second column.

a. (Jones is quoting Thompson 1972, 22; Jones gives his own documentation at 327n3; facts of trip are mainly from Thompson 1972, 24–27

Appendix 2

Bishops of Yucatan to 1714

	Years in Office	Name	Order or Affiliation
1st	1519	Dr. D. Fr. Julián Garcés	*Dominican* Governed from Puebla, where he resided.[a]
2nd	1542	D. Fray Juan de San Francisco	*Franciscan* Never took office in Yucatan.[b]
3rd	1552 1555–57[c]	D. Fr. Juan de la Puerta	*Franciscan* Never took office.[d]
4th	1561–71 1560–71[e]	D. Fr. Francisco Toral	*Franciscan* First to take office and to reside in Yucatan.[f]
5th	1572–79 1571–79[g]	D. Fr. Diego de Landa	*Franciscan*
6th	1580–87 1581–86[h]	D. Fr. Gregorio Montalvo	*Dominican*
7th	1587–1602 1590–1602[i]	D. Fr. Juan Izquierdo (Fr. Diego de Izquierdo)[j]	*Franciscan*
8th	1603–8	D. Diego Vásquez de Mercado	*Secular*
9th	1608–36	D. Fr. Gonzalo de Salazar	*Augustinian*
10th	1638–42	D. Juan Alonso de Ocón	*Secular*
11th	1643	D. Andrés Fernández de Ipenza	*Secular* Never took office.

Years in Office		Name	Order or Affiliation
12th	1644–49	D. Marcos Torres de Rueda	*Secular*
13th	1651–52	D. Fr. Domingo Villa-Escusa Ramírez de Arellano[k]	*Jeronymite*
14th	1656	Lorenzo de Horta	*Secular* Never took office.
15th	1657–76	D. Luis de Cifuentes y Sotomayor	Dominican
16th	1677–81	D. Juan Escalante Turcios y Mendoza	*Secular*
17th	1682–95	D. Juan Cano Sandoval	*Secular* Archbishop and Bishop
18th	1696–98	D. Fr. Antonio Arriaga	*Augustinian*
19th	1700–14	D. Fr. Pedro Reyes Ríos de la Madrid	*Benedictine*

Source: From Carillo y Ancona [1967] 1982, 56–59, except where otherwise noted.

Notes: a. Garcés arrived as the Tlaxcala bishop in 1527; his jurisdiction included Yucatan, although he never went there; he died in Central Mexico in 1542 (see Cuevas 1921–28, vol. 1, 238–333).

b. Juan de San Francisco was appointed by royal order in 1552, while he was resident in New Spain; he renounced the office in 1553 (Lopetegui and Zubillaga 1965, 500; Scholes et al. 1938, 1).

c. Scholes et al. (1938, 1) note that Juan de la Puerta was named bishop in 1555. Lopetegui and Zubillaga (1965, 501) say that various royal orders (*cédulas reales*) drawn up between 1555 and 1557 refer to a voyage of Juan de la Puerta from Spain to his new diocese in Yucatán, but he is known to have died in Seville in 1557, before taking office.

d. Ibid.

e. Scholes et al. (1938, 1) have Toral appointed by Phillip II in Spain in 1560.

f. Ibid.

g. Lopetegui and Zubillaga 1965, 500–9.

h. Ibid.

i. Ibid.

j. Lopetegui and Zubillaga (1965, 509) name the seventh bishop as Diego de Izquierdo; they write that he accepted the bishopric in 1590, took office in Yucatán in 1591, and governed until he died in 1602.

k. This is the last bishop mentioned by Lopez de Cogolludo ([1688] 1971) in his account (bk. 12, chap. 22).

Notes

Introduction

1. Geertz 1973b, 25.
2. G. D. Jones 1989.

Chapter 1. The View from Belize and the Vision from St. Mike's

1. This is not to say, however, that art is defined solely on the basis of aesthetics; Gell (1998, 2–3) argues strongly for the importance of social processes.

2. Freedberg 1989 is concerned with relations between people and images in history. He recognizes that not all images are considered art, but in any case is concerned primarily with the complexity of people's responses to images, artistic or not. This is a provocative approach from an art historian who suggests that art historians have avoided giving attention to the range of emotional responses to images, owing to some extent to embarrassment, because "we fear the strength of the effects of images on ourselves" (1989, 429). He goes on to say that "much of our sophisticated talk about art is simply an evasion. We take refuge in such talk when, say, we discourse about formal qualities, or when we rigorously historicize the work, because we are afraid to come to terms with our responses" (429–30). This is interesting, although it may well be that "discourse" is not the evasion, but rather "art" itself.

3. Bayle 1950, 270n378. The words are those of Fray Francisco Ruiz, who features in a *cédula* of the sixteenth century.

4. Here and throughout the text, when I refer to "the other," I mean "other" in the anthropological sense of the construction of (usually cultural) others—persons who are part of a group that is not one's own. This sense of otherness has roots in Emmanuel Lévinas's articulation of the other as different and not knowable (Wyschogrod 1998, 380), but in anthropology the emphasis is not so much on an encounter with an "other" individual or self in a philosophical or psychological sense. The term has instead been deployed widely in anthropology to refer to the idea of a cultural other, or the other as part of a group whose individuals share the perspective of that group. With regard to anthropology and the exploration of the globe, see J. Z. Smith 1985.

5. M'Closkey (2002) documents an example of such a phenomenon in the case of Navajo blanket designs when transferred to colorfield painting.

6. de la Garza (1998, 25–27) provides the introduction to a volume published on the occasion of a major exhibition on the art of the ancient Maya at the Palazzo Grassi, in Venice, which took place from 6 September 1998 to 16 May 1999; Lowden's (1997) book

is an example of a focus on early Christian and Byzantine art; Matos Moctezuma and Solís Holguín (2002) wrote the volume that accompanied the Royal Academy's exhibition in London dedicated to the art and culture of the Aztecs, 16 November 2002 to 11 April 2003.

7. Evans 2008, 28.

8. Belting 1994; see also Gell 1998, 3.

9. Belting 1994, 9.

10. See, e.g., Rodríguez-Alegría 2005, 552. This excellent paper, stimulated by archaeological finds, is full of insights on the negotiation of social relations in the Spanish colonies, but I am not entirely comfortable with the idea that food is material culture.

11. Here, I use "standpoint" in the looser, dictionary sense of a "position from which things are considered or judged; a point of view" (*American Heritage Dictionary of the English Language*, 3rd ed., 1992), rather than in the stricter sense used in feminist writings to refer to the "standpoint" of those who are subject to structures of domination and marginalization and are thereby epistemically privileged to analyze such structures (see Wylie 2003, 26).

12. Wylie (1994, 620–21) emphasizes the importance of critical inquiry, which includes a willingness to accept criticism from others and the necessity for investigating the context of our personal experience. I have extended this context to include the disciplines we embrace; although our disciplines are not of our own invention, we tend to take them personally. The term "undermining" is my own. Wylie (2003, 31–32) notes the importance of developing a critical consciousness about standpoint, and the difference this can make in how we conceptualize knowledge building.

13. See more extensive discussion in Graham 2006a.

14. E.g., Houston 1993; Martin and Grube 2008; Stuart and Houston 1993.

15. G. D. Jones 1989; J. E. S. Thompson 1972, 1977. J. Eric S. Thompson, the archaeologist and epigrapher, was the first to seek out documentary evidence that applied specifically to Belize. Grant Jones greatly expanded our knowledge in this realm and has published major works on both Belize (1989) and Peten (1998).

16. A number of publications have resulted from the archaeological excavations at Tipu and/or Lamanai, and they are cited in the text. For overviews, see Graham 1991 (on Tipu); Graham, Pendergast, and Jones 1989 (on Tipu and Lamanai); and Pendergast 1993 (on the Spanish encounter in Belize). The results of Robert Kautz's initial work are published in Jones, Kautz, and Graham 1986, and early work at Tipu under my direction is published in Graham, Jones, and Kautz 1985.

17. Graham 2009.

18. G. D. Jones 1989, 8.

19. G. D. Jones 1989, 8.

20. My grandmother's family is from Avellino, near Naples; my grandfather was born in Sonnino, in the Lazio region, which also includes Rome.

21. Belting 1994, 11.

22. Belting 1994, 11.

23. Kamen 2005, 190; Marzal 1993, 142–54.

24. See Graham 2009 for discussion in more detail.

25. Deleuze and Foucault 1977, 209.

26. In this context, they refer to prisoners and schoolchildren (Deleuze and Foucault 1977, 205–17).

27. Alcoff 1991–92, 22.

28. Alcoff 1991–92; Wylie 1994.

29. Kitcher 2001, 111. Here Kitcher notes that benefits to the growth of knowledge can accrue when members of the academic community disagree.

30. Kamen 2005, 190; Phelan 1970, 1.

31. Alcoff 1991–92.

32. Graham 2009.

33. Harding (1987, 23) discusses the disadvantages in a preoccupation with method (the technique for gathering evidence) over how the method is used or what the research can achieve.

34. Wylie 2003, 38.

35. Crosby 1986; Melville 1994.

36. E.g., Cook and Borah 1971; McCaa 1995; MacLeod 1982; Newson 1981; Sanders 1970.

37. At Lamanai, in Belize, Mennonite farmers who own the land around the archaeological reserve have turned acre upon acre of tropical forest into grassland. The two most visible crops are sorghum and maize (grown as animal feed), and the animals dominating the landscape are cattle.

38. Pagden 1986, 11:418–19. See also Restall 2003, 133n9.

39. G. D. Jones 1989; Clements 2005. Jones focuses on the consequences for the Maya of Belize; Clements documents the inevitable failure of the "praying towns" in the northeast U.S.

40. Phelan 1970, 5–16; Rubial García 1978–79.

41. Clendinnen 1987a, 114; Ricard 1966, 268–72. It is important to note that the claim that the Indians were idolatrous was often used as vehicle of control on the part of both religious and secular authorities (see Caso Barrera 1999); in this passage I mean to say that the religious nonetheless believed in the claim.

42. Restall 2003, 74.

43. Restall 2003, 74.

44. Ricard 1966.

45. G. D. Jones 1989.

46. G. D. Jones 1989 describes the resistance and rebellion that characterized the 1630s and 1640s in Maya towns in Belize (213–41); but see G. D. Jones 1998 for the role of the Peten Itza in these rebellions (49, 52–55).

47. See chap. 8, and pp. 241–48 of chap. 9, in G. D. Jones 1989.

48. A term used in archaeology for refuse dumps.

49. Stoudemire 1970.

50. One burial, B247 (T-883), contained three mixed and fragmentary individuals; two were determined to be juveniles, but the third is too fragmentary to be classifiable. Its association suggests a juvenile burial, which would bring the total of juveniles with jewelry to 17. The children range in age from 3–5 years to 12–14 years. Among the adults are two females, 25–35 years; two males, one 17–20 years and one 18–22 years; and one male, 20–30 years. The Tipu burial population and its genetic structuring are reported in Jacobi 2000. The European beads from both Tipu and Lamanai are reported in M. T. Smith, Graham, and Pendergast 1994 (27–29, table 3).

51. G. D. Jones 1982.

52. G. D. Jones 1989, 139; Mendieta 1945, 2:64, 3:72–73.

53. G. D. Jones 1989, 136. See Chuchiak 2003, 226–27, for a list of the church-related and ritual items carried by the friars.

54. Alcoff and Potter 1993; Code 1993, 1995; Harding 1993; Wylie 2003.

55. Code 1993, 32. Lara (2004, 2) comments on developing a "hermeneutic of suspicion" regarding the objectivity of the Mendicants, but I am suspicious of my own objectivity.

56. Attention to the process of discovery fell out of favor under the influence of positivism, but interest is reviving (see Longino 1990; N. R. Hanson 1971; Harding 1987, 31; Kitcher 2001, 110).

57. Oakley 1981, 41; Wylie 1994, 613.

58. Matthew Johnson's book on archaeological theory (1999) explains and contextualizes these approaches clearly.

59. For an original exploration of the logic of discovery, see N. R. Hanson 1971. For arguments on the importance of a logic of proof, see Popper 1972.

60. Kitcher 2001, 199–200.

61. Harding 1987.

62. John Early's (2006, 9) treatment of the introduction of Christianity to the Maya region avoids reference to Belize or its towns, and the area appears as a blank on his map.

63. The Dominican Pedro de Córdoba's *Doctrina Cristiana* (ca. 1510) is believed to be the first catechism produced in the New World; it was published in 1544 for use in Mexico. The Franciscan Fray Alonso de Molina produced *doctrinas* and *confessionarios*, in Spanish and Nahuatl, for the instruction of the Indians (Molina [1546] 1941, 1565a, 1565b, 1744). A version of Molina's catechism, as well as other instructions to the religious concerning doctrine and practice to be taught to the Indians, was compiled in the latter part of the sixteenth century, to be made available to all four of the Franciscan provinces of New Spain: (1) central Mexico (province of Santo Evangelio); (2) Michoacan and Jalisco (province of the Apostles St. Peter and St. Paul); (3) Guatemala (province of Nombre de Jesús); and (4) Yucatan and Campeche (province of St. Joseph), which included the land that became Belize (*Códice Franciscano* 1941).

64. Alcoff and Potter 1993, 9; Longino 1990.

65. Restall 2003.

Chapter 2. Yucatan and Belize on the Eve of Conquest

1. M. E. Smith 2003b, 38.

2. Roys 1957.

3. Roys 1957, 6.

4. See Izquierdo 2006, 159–61.

5. A period known to archaeologists as the Late, or Terminal, Postclassic.

6. A. P. Andrews 1984; A. P. Andrews and Jones 2001; Caso Barrera 2002; Farris 1984; Gerhard 1979; G. D. Jones 1989; Kepecs 1997, 2003; Okoshi 1994, 2009; Quezada 1993; Restall 1997.

7. See papers in Okoshi, Williams-Beck, and Izquierdo 2006. But see also Okoshi 1994; Quezada 1993; and, for a cogent summary, Kepecs and Masson 2003, 42.

8. Roys 1957, 3. In modern orthography this is sometimes rendered *kuchkabal* in the singular, *kuchkabaloob* in the plural (A. P. Andrews 1984, 589).

9. Occupation at Chichen Itza is traditionally seen to end at about A.D. 1200, but some scholars now date Chichen's fall to the eleventh century, with monumental construction ceasing at around 1000 (A. P. Andrews, E. W. Andrews, and Robles Castellanos 2003). Milbrath and Peraza (2003) propose a significant occupation at Mayapan in

the eleventh century. A. P. Andrews, E. W. Andrews, and Robles Castellanos (2003, 153) state that the native chronicles place the date of the founding of Mayapan at A.D. 1283, in a Katun 13 Ahau, but some chronicles have Mayapan in existence early in a Katun 8 Ahau (A.D. 1185–1204) (Okoshi 2006, 30).

10. Roys (1957, 3) discusses the idea of provinces as territorial divisions. For use of the term "province," see, e.g., A. P. Andrews 1984; G. D. Jones 1989; and Farriss 1984, 12. Gerhard (1979, 4) describes "a great many autonomous native states, most of them with diminutive and well-defined territorial limits."

11. Farriss (1984, 149–51), e.g., attempts to match parishes to Maya provinces as delineated by Roys (1957), and Quezada (1993) attempts to map *batabil* (which he interprets as Maya governorships) to the *cabecera* system. The *cabecera* was the head town of a Spanish administrative district. Rethinking of the concept of "province" can be seen in the works of Kepecs (1997); Quezada (1993); and Okoshi (1994, 2006, 2009).

12. Caso Barrera 2002, map I.1.

13. Bolles 2001. See also Quezada 1993, 34–36. For *kuuchkabal*, see Okoshi 2006. Kepecs and Masson (2003, 42) state that "the term 'cuchcabal' applies only to hierarchical polities consisting of multiple batabils centralized under halach uinics."

14. Emblem glyphs, e.g., are commonly used by Mayanists as if they were meant to represent a bounded polity or place with borders, but recent evidence suggests that emblem glyphs were perceived by the Maya to symbolize or refer to a unique place of origin (Tokovinine 2006).

15. Mortimer 2008, 48.

16. Okoshi 1994.

17. Gaspar Antonio Chi was born in Mani (see map 2.1.a) and lived from about 1531 to 1610. He became a Christian when he was fifteen years old, was educated by the Franciscans, and added fluency in Spanish and Latin to knowledge of Maya and Nahuatl. He served as an interpreter for Spanish authorities and authored a number of documents, some of which were his translations into Mayan of Spanish legal and administrative documents, others of which were written in Spanish about Maya affairs and traditions (e.g., Gaspar Antonio Chi, *Relación* [1582], in Tozzer 1941, 230–32). As an official interpreter in Yucatan, he also helped to prepare and write answers to government questionnaires, such as those that surveyed *encomenderos*. It is believed that much of the information Bishop Landa provided about the Maya in his *Relación de las Cosas de Yucatán* was from Gaspar Antonio Chi (Tozzer 1941, 44–46n219.)

18. "The lands were in common and (so between the towns there were no boundaries or landmarks to divide them)" (Roys 1962, 65). Chi states that boundaries or landmarks could divide one "province" from another. But, by that time, the Spanish word for "province" was in general use by the Maya, and it is difficult to discern why such a division would be dependent on a war rather than a result of a war, unless it reflected, as I propose, fluid tribute relationships.

19. Tozzer 1941, 17n96.

20. See R. Alexander in Kepecs and Masson 2003, 42.

21. Giddens 1995, 91–93.

22. Swidden farming, in addition to other farming systems, was practiced by the pre-Columbian Maya. Swidden farming in particular involved clearing growth, usually forest, to create fields, or *milpas*, which were cultivated for two years or more and then allowed to lie fallow (anywhere from two to ten years), during which time regrowth and regeneration occurred. This type of farming is usually called "extensive," because it

entails access to relatively large areas and often involves walking a good distance from the place of residence (see Sharer 2006, 81, 639–41).

23. McAnany 1995, 86–87.

24. McAnany 1995, 87; Restall 1997, 196; Roys 1943, 181.

25. Restall 1998, 49.

26. Roys 1939, 424–27, cited in Tozzer 1941, 43n216.

27. Tozzer 1941, 43n216.

28. McAnany 1995, 87.

29. Roys 1943, 161, 178.

30. M. E. Smith 1986.

31. "Cultural outsider" might not be the best term, but the Maya of particular towns or cities, in Postclassic and Classic times, saw the inhabitants of other towns and cities (although perhaps only those of other patronym groups) as outsiders, even though they shared cultural values.

32. McAnany 1995, 135.

33. Farriss 1984, 89. There were few resident encomenderos even in the *villa* of Bacalar, which had authority over the communities in Belize (Gerhard 1979, 69; G. D. Jones 1989, 55–91).

34. Such a shift could be described as a cultural evolutionary one.

35. Quezada 1993, 62–63; Restall 1997, 25.

36. Restall 1997, 25.

37. Quezada 1993, 62.

38. Restall 1997, 13; 1998, 47.

39. See Restall (1997, 14–40) for an in-depth discussion.

40. See Farriss (1984, 157) for instances of long-distance foot travel by the Maya between coast and interior, and for various reasons, including changes of residence, waxhunting expeditions, and visits to other communities. Graham (1996) discusses urbanism in neotropical environments and the kinds of relationships that develop under these conditions between humans and the land and resources around them. Graham (2006a) focuses on how cumulative tribute relationships, rather than land appropriation per se, formed the basis of the Maya landscape.

41. Restall 1997, 17–18, 28–29; 1998, 46, 235. According to Roys (1957, 4), the Maya thought of the chibal as a lineage. Restall describes the chibal as an extended family lineage, but also says that chibalob were closer to exogamous clans than to lineages, and bore similarities to both (1997, 2, 17).

42. Restall 1997, 28.

43. Restall 1997, 17.

44. Restall 1997, 28.

45. See Roys 1957, 2, map 1.

46. See Okoshi (2006, 2009) on the Canul and Canche of northwestern Yucatan.

47. Restall 1997, 28.

48. Graham 2006a, 2008b; Okoshi 1994.

49. See also Williams-Beck 2006, 330.

50. Roys 1957, 3; Edmonson 1982, 1986; Roys 1967. According to Roys (1967, 5–6), none of the books that has come down to us was compiled earlier than the last part of the seventeenth century. However, many portions are transcriptions of the old hieroglyphic manuscripts into European script, and comparison of the language used in the Books of Chilam Balam with the language of legal documents that date from 1557 shows that

many passages were copied verbatim from sixteenth- and early seventeenth-century originals.

51. See Graham 2004 and Howie 2006 for evidence of continuity in the complex use of local resources in the production of ceramics (perhaps suggesting some time depth to local expertise) despite changes in ceramic designs and use-sets.

52. Masson 2000, 2003.

53. Kepecs (e.g., 2003) has contributed in a major way to re-envisioning the Maya commercial landscape.

54. A recent example is the film *Apocalypto* (2006), directed by Mel Gibson and written by Mel Gibson and Farhad Safinia (information about the film is available at http://www.imdb.com/title/tt0472043/).

55. Graham 2008b.

56. E.g., control of oil fields in Iraq with a "war on terror" against an "axis of evil."

57. Martin and Grube 2008. I say "some" because we know from the Aztec case that the Spaniards greatly exaggerated the number of warriors who were killed in temples (see M. E. Smith 1986), and because the Maya hieroglyphic record also shows that captured rulers lived on to pay tribute or to fight other battles (see also McAnany 1995, 135n32).

58. Graham 2008b.

59. Tribute transfer is the key here, and it need not have been connected to "loyalty." As Clendinnen observes regarding Aztec-Spanish relations, "We cannot know at what point the shift from the Indian notion of 'he who pays tribute,' usually under duress so carrying no sense of obligation, to the Spanish one of 'vassal,' with its connotations of loyalty, was made, but we know the shift to be momentous" (1991, 71).

60. Martin and Grube 2008.

61. Martin and Grube 2008, 120–21.

62. Defeated in war, Bajlaj Chan K'awil of Dos Pilas and Nuun Ujol Chaak of Tikal both became subject to the Calakmul ruler Yuknoon the Great (Martin and Grube 2008, 56–57); Yich'aak Bahlam of Seibal survived his defeat to serve as a subject lord to K'awiil Chan K'inich of Dos Pilas (Martin and Grube 2008, 62–63).

63. Roys 1943, 66n2.

64. Clendinnen 1991, 79–80; Hassig 1988, 114–15.

65. Clendinnen 1991, 80.

66. Restall 1998, 13.

67. Martin and Grube 2008.

68. Roys 1943, 65–70.

69. Roys 1943, 68.

70. Roys 1943, 67.

71. Roys 1943, 67.

72. Roys 1943, 68–70.

73. E.g., Graham 2004; Pendergast 1986a, 1991.

74. Pendergast 1988c.

75. A. P. Andrews, E. W. Andrews, and Robles Castellanos 2003; Graham 2004, 2007.

76. Kepecs 1997, 323–24.

77. The *pochteca* were a class of merchants and traders in the Aztec empire (M. E. Smith 2003a).

78. Caracol is well known for its monuments and inscriptions (e.g, A. F. Chase and D. Z. Chase 2001a, 2001b; A. F. Chase et al. 2008).

79. Kepecs 2003; Masson 2003.

80. Pagden 1986, 455n30. According to Oliver (2009, 25), the term *cacique* (ka-sikua-ri [-li]) among the Lokono, who are Arawak speakers in Guyana-Surinam, translates as a male or female head of the house, and can refer to the head of a family, a lineage, a co-residential group, or "an apical leader of an entire polity." The islanders of the Greater Antilles, from whom the Spaniards derived the term *cacique*, are sometimes referred to as "Taino," or even "Arawak," by archaeologists. In linguistics, Taino and Arawak are the names of two of the five Caribbean languages grouped under Northern Maipuran, and are part of the Arawakan superfamily (Lewis 2009).

81. Restall 1997, 61–64; Quezada 1993, 36.

82. Quezada 1993, 33–34, table 1; Roys 1957, 6.

83. Quezada 1993, 62–63; Roys 1957, 6.

84. See Quezada (1993, 61–63) for analysis of the Spaniards' application of the term "province" to a variety of Maya geopolitical or sociopolitical units. See Kepecs (1997, 312) for the suggestion, drawn from the documents, that each native community in the Chikinchel region had in effect owned, or had rights to, a salt bed. Roys (1957, 104) also states that, "in preconquest times the beds belonged to certain towns." See Roys (1957, 6) for a description of the loose alliances that could characterize these sorts of "provinces" at the same time that individual communities could engage in war against each other.

85. Roys 1957, 3.

86. Okoshi 2006, 35n8.

87. "The rulers and officials whom the supreme lord has in his charge in a territorial space," and "a territorial space governed by a power which resides in a specified location" (from Okoshi 2006, 35n8, in which Okoshi cites two of his earlier publications: see Okoshi 2006, References Cited).

88. This is from Okoshi 2006 on the *Códice de Calkiní*.

89. G. D. Jones 1989.

90. Okoshi, Williams-Beck, and Izquierdo 2006.

91. Masson 2000, 2003.

92. Masson 2000, 2.

93. Gerhard 1979, 68.

94. Gerhard 1979, 68–69.

95. Graham 2004.

96. Masson 2000, 21.

97. Kepecs, 1997, 320.

98. Masson 2003.

99. Roys 1957, map 1.

100. Literally, "proof": an official record of merits and services; can also be a documentary proof of the nobility of a native family.

101. G. D. Jones 1989, 98, 306n13.

102. G. D. Jones 1989, 9.

103. G. D. Jones 1989, 98.

104. Choirmasters, or the persons (Maya) in charge of liturgy and catechism (Farriss 1984, 541).

105. Graham 1991, 323.

106. See G. D. Jones 1989, 98.

107. G. D. Jones 1998.

108. Cecil 2001, 2004; Cecil and Pugh 2004; P. M. Rice and D. S. Rice 2009a, 15n2.

109. P. M. Rice and D. S. Rice 2005, 153.

110. This statement reflects my assessment of pottery of the Augustine ceramic group, with its distinctive orange-red slip color and paste, which I think of as typical of Belize Valley clays. Cecil (2009a) thinks that some of the Augustine ceramic group pottery may be a local product of Tipu.

111. In earlier times, during the Classic period, Belize Valley communities maintained contact with the coast via routes that passed through the Hummingbird Gap and the North Stann Creek Valley (Graham 1994).

112. D. S. Rice, P. M. Rice, and Pugh 1998; D. S. Rice 1986; P. M. Rice 1987, 235; P. M. Rice 1996b, 293–316; P. M. Rice and D. S. Rice 2004.

113. P. M. Rice and D. S. Rice 2005, 153.

114. G. D. Jones 1989, 6, map 3; P. M. Rice and D. S. Rice 2009a, 11.

115. G. D. Jones 1998, 11, 12; see also 430n24.

116. P. M. Rice and D. S. Rice 2005, 156.

117. See G. D. Jones 1998, 24–27, table 1.1.

118. Cecil 2009a. G. D. Jones (2009, 55) states that the name Kowoj comes from their principal patrilineage, or *chibal* (ch'ib'al). See also papers in P. M. Rice and D. S. Rice 2009b.

119. G. D. Jones 1998, 18.

120. P. M. Rice and D. S. Rice 2005, 156.

121. Pugh 2001; P. M. Rice and D. S. Rice 2005, 157.

122. Cecil 2004; P. M. Rice and D. S. Rice 2005, 168; P. M. Rice and D. S. Rice 2009b.

123. G. D. Jones 1998, 17–19; P. M. Rice and D. S. Rice 2005, 156. Also G. D. Jones (1998, 11, 430n24) for the statement of Capitán don Marcos Abalos y Fuentes about the Couoh and Itza migrations.

124. Although G. D. Jones (2009) suggests that it could be as early as 1511, or possibly following the Xiu (Xiw) massacre by the Cocom in 1536.

125. See Restall (1997, 174–77) for the idea that mobility is nothing new to the Maya; the idea of movement as tempered by allegiance; Maya perceptions of boundaries as, by definition, permitting osmosis; and the importance of the *chibal*, whose members resided in more than one *cah*. Farriss (1984, 452n63) refers to the wide distribution of patronymics in early colonial censuses as probably characteristic of pre-Conquest times.

126. Cecil and Pugh 2004; Pugh 2001; P. M. Rice and D. S. Rice 2005, 164; and see also P. M. Rice and D. S. Rice 2005, 165, fig. 5.6. D. S. Rice, P. M. Rice, and Pugh (1998, 227–33) describe the architectural complex at Zacpeten and its relationship to Mayapan; see also Graham 1991, 322, fig. 15-1, Strs. H12-1 to H12-4.

127. Cecil 2004; Cecil 2009a, 2009b.

128. Cecil 2009a, 534–38.

129. Cecil 2009a, 538.

130. Cecil (2009a, 538) reports the lower frequency and the connection to Peten. The estimate of the date of use of Complex I is mine. It was in reasonably good shape during the early Spanish colonial period, which suggests that it was in use at the time of the Spaniards' arrival.

131. G. D. Jones 1998, 19–22; 2005, 305.

132. G. D. Jones 1998, 23.

133. Pendergast 1982a.

134. Graham 2007.

135. Graham 2004.

136. Tz'ulwinikob' in the new orthography.

137. G. D. Jones 1989, 10.

138. D. Z. Chase 1984, 1985; D. Z. Chase and A. F. Chase 1988.

139. Graham 1987; D. Z. Chase 1984, fig. 4-34 a–c, e–g, j, l–o.

140. John 2008.

141. D. Z. Chase 1984, 443, fig. 4-33.

142. Wiewall 2009.

143. Graham 1987.

144. Pendergast 1981, 1982a.

145. Aimers 2008; Sanders 1960; R. E. Smith 1971, 30. The types within the Red Payil Group would be Payil Red and Palmul Incised.

146. Masson 2003, 275.

Chapter 3. Cheese and Terms

1. Lothrop 1927.

2. Lothrop 1927, 356–57.

3. López de Cogolludo [1688] 1971, vol. 1, bk. 4, chap. 3, p. 233; see also Restall 2004, 67. In López de Cogolludo's words: "Esta tierra de Yucatan, á quien los naturales de ella llaman *Máya* fué gobernada muchos tiempos por un señor supremo. . . . Tenia este rey por cabecera de su monarquia una ciudad muy populosa, llamada *Mayapán* (de quien debia de derivarse llamar á este tierra *Máya*) que por guerras, y discordias entre él, y sus vasallos . . . acabó este gobierno, revelándosele muchos señores y caciques, dominando cada uno la parte que podia conservar, y estando siempre en continuas guerras." (This land of Yucatan, which the indigenous people call Maya was at many times governed by a supreme lord. . . . This king had as the principal town of his kingdom a very populous city, called *Mayapan* [from which the calling of this land *Maya* must be derived] which through wars, and disagreements between him, and his vassals . . . brought an end to this government, giving rise to many lords and caciques, each one dominating the part that he could retain, and being always in continuous wars.)

4. Lothrop 1927, 350–55.

5. See n. 3.

6. Restall 2004, 65–67.

7. Restall 2004, 64.

8. Eiss 2008, 503–8; Restall 2004, 73–74, 82.

9. Fischer 1996; 1999, 474–75; Hostettler 2004, 193; R. Wilson 1995.

10. Carlsen 1997, 49–51; Fischer 1999; Restall and Hostettler 2001; Sharer 2006, 23–28.

11. Schackt 2001, 10.

12. Elliott 2002, 77–86; Poole 1992, 4. See also Canedo (1952, 498–99) for documentary references to the Spanish Franciscan provinces of Santiago, San Gabriel, Murcia, and Andalucía.

13. Castile, Aragon, and Portugal were individual kingdoms at the time of the conquest (Elliott 2002, 29, 42; see also 16–17, map 2).

14. Canedo 1977, 24, 60. Canedo (1952, 507–8) mentions the General Chapter of the Franciscan Order held at Aquila, in Italy, in 1559, at which the princess then governing Spain, in the absence of Philip II, called for more Franciscan friars, across the Order, to spread the faith in Yucatan. Lara (2004, 207n2, 1) also makes the point that sixteenth-

century missionaries were not all Spaniards, and that neither Indians nor Spaniards were a homogeneous or unidimensional group.

15. Pharo (2007, 59) provides an excellent discussion of why it is important to be attentive to how we apply concepts.

16. By this I mean that "innovation," understood to mean an individual's ideas, has the most meaning for us as academics; otherwise we would not write books or papers that we hope will influence the way people think and act.

17. Darwin 1968, 102. There are alternative theories; see, e.g., Bateson 1972, 456–57.

18. Harries-Jones 1995, 35–39, 274–75n2, in discussion of Ruesch and Bateson 1951.

19. Pinto 1998, 113.

20. Pinto 1998.

21. Ginzburg 1979, 87.

22. Ginzburg 1979, 87–167.

23. Ginzburg 1979, 92.

24. Ginzburg 1979, 90–91. Vernacular translations of Holy Scripture were permitted only under circumstances in which both the text and the person having access to the text were approved by the bishop or an inquisitor. Even if Menocchio's Bible translation was one which the authorities had agreed was permitted, his particular possession of it was clearly not (see Schroeder 1978, 18–20, 274–75).

25. Ginzburg 1979, 162–63, 167.

26. Ginzburg 1979, 167.

27. Lindberg 2006, 122.

28. Chuchiak, essay in author's possession. This information is in the original manuscript Chuchiak wrote for Cecil and Pugh's (2009) *Maya Worldviews at Conquest* volume, but this portion was left out of the published chapter, ultimately entitled "De descriptio idolorum" (Chuchiak 2009).

29. Scholes and Roys 1938, 593–94.

30. D. Tedlock 1993, 147.

31. Klor de Alva 1989, 22–23.

32. An exception in central Mexico might be the interest the authorities showed in diabolism among the Indians (Cervantes 1994), or the early encounters with indigenous elites in Oaxaca (Terraciano 2007).

33. Scholes and Adams 1938; Scholes and Roys 1938.

34. Canedo 1952 would be an example.

35. Lopez de Cogolludo [1688] 1971.

36. Bayle 1950; Lopetegui and Zubillaga 1965.

37. Lopetegui and Zubillaga 1965, 498–99; López de Cogolludo [1688] 1971, vol. I, bk. 6, chap. 1, p. 411.

38. Lessa and Vogt 1979b, 4.

39. Although there are exceptions; see, e.g., Early 2006; Scotchmer 1993.

40. Pinney 2001, 157.

41. Annis 1987; Blaffer 1972; Bunzel 1952; Cancian 1965; Carlsen 1997; Christenson 2001, 2007; Colby and van den Berghe 1969; Deuss 2007; Hill and Monaghan 1987; LaFarge 1947; Maurer Avalos 1993; Nash 1958; Oakes 1969; Reina 1966; Siegel 1941; B. Tedlock 1982; Vogt 1976; Wagley 1949 (who uses "religion" as a classifier); Wasserstrom 1983; Watanabe 1989, 1992.

42. Boremanse 1998; Cruz 1934; Redfield 1941; Redfield and Villa Rojas 1934.

43. Bricker 1989; Early 2006.

44. Burkhart 1993; Ingham 1986; Monaghan 1995; Sandstrom 1991.

45. Geertz (1973a) sees religion as a cultural system; Foucault placed religious discourse as "part of the 'complex' and 'restrictive' exchange and communication in a particular system or culture" (Carrette 2000, 145), although it is not clear whether he took "religion" seriously as a limiting category. Kroeber (1944), in writing about cultural growth and change, takes religion seriously, and with some distaste, as a limiting category of the sacred as opposed to the profane (see, e.g., 802), and sidelines it.

46. Asad 1993, 27.

47. Geertz 1973b, 10.

48. K. Warren 1978, 55; R. Wilson 1995, 13.

49. E.g., one of Wasserstrom's chapters is subtitled "Domestic Life and Religious Change in Zinacantan, 1910–1975," but in it he concludes about Zinacantecos that "they have utilized religious ritual not . . . as a means of enforcing municipal solidarity [but] as a symbolic means of expressing their hard-won economic independence and their increased political autonomy" (1983, 235). In fact, meaning would not be lost if the word "religious" were removed, to leave simply "ritual."

50. Monaghan 2000, 24–25.

51. Lambek 2000.

52. Lambek 2000, 309.

53. Geertz (1973a) describes religion as a cultural system; Gutiérrez Estévez (1993) describes the European-Maya encounter as an encounter of two religious systems.

54. Lessa and Vogt 1979a.

55. Guthrie 1993; Richardson 2003.

56. Lessa and Vogt 1979a, 1–6; 1979b.

57. Lessa and Vogt 1979a, 3.

58. Lambek 2000, 309.

59. Geertz 1973a, 87.

60. See Smith (1998) for a superb discussion of the history of "religion" as a concept.

61. Atran 2002; Boyer 2004; Guthrie 1993; Richardson 2003; D. S. Wilson 2002.

62. Boyer 2004.

63. Eliade 1987; Smart 1997a, 1997b, 1999.

64. Smart 1983; J. Z. Smith 1998, 281.

65. The expression "the map is not the territory" is from Korzybski 1994, 58–61, 498, 747–51.

66. Boyer 1994, 30–31.

67. Pharo 2007.

68. Monaghan 2000, 25. It is interesting, though, that so many of us who write about indigenous ancient Mesoamericans nonetheless feel free to talk about Maya or Aztec or, even more perplexing, Mesoamerican "religion" (singular) (see Lara 2004, 3–7).

69. Boyer 1994, 30. He observes that doubt about whether it is possible to define "religious" representations at all is often based on the argument that the distinction (that there is a sphere of religion) is grounded in a set of criteria, such as sacred vs. profane, or supernatural vs. natural, which may be particular to Western intellectual traditions. This is a good point, but only with reference to those who equate the sacred with the religious, and not with the profane, in our own society and culture; and I think there is a case for dissolving this argument.

70. Boyer 1994, 5.

71. Asad 1993.

72. Asad 1993, 54.

73. J. Z. Smith 1998, 271.

74. Asad 1993, 38–42.

75. Asad 1993, 38–44.

76. Asad 1993, 49.

77. Hitchens 2007.

78. Asad 1993, 45–46.

79. J. Z. Smith 1998, 269.

80. *Oxford English Dictionary Online*, http://dictionary.oed.com/.

81. Bowie (2000, 22), drawing from Pieris (1988), notes that the word "religion" in Western European languages probably derives from the Vulgate, which is the Latin edition of the Bible translated by St. Jerome (ca. 345–420) from Hebrew and Greek; the Greek word *threskeia* was translated as the Latin *religio*. Insoll (2004, 6), citing Saliba (1976), adds that "religion" is an explicitly Christian term, widely used only from the time of the Reformation.

82. *Oxford English Dictionary Online*, s.v. "religion."

83. Insoll 2004, 7.

84. Bowie 2000, 1–37; Insoll 2004, 5–9.

85. Bowie 2000, 22n23, citing Pieris 1988, 90.

86. Insoll 2004, 6.

87. King 1999, 210, quoted in Carrette 2000, 144.

88. J. Z. Smith 1998, 281–82.

89. Firth 1996, 10.

90. Dawkins 2006; Lett 1997 in Bowie 2000, 6.

91. Turner 1986.

92. King 1999, 210.

93. Geertz 2000, 182.

94. Boyer 2001; Atran 2002; D. S. Wilson 2002.

95. Boyer (2004, 432) writes in terms of a science of religion.

96. See chap. 1, n. 4, on "the other."

97. King 1999, 210.

98. Geertz 2000, 182–84.

99. Geertz 1968, 19.

100. Edmonson (1993) writes about the "Mayan Faith."

101. Rabasa 1993, 70; see also Lara 2004, 2.

102. Delgado-Gomez (1993, 6) discusses first contact with the peoples of the Caribbean, whom Columbus described either as having "no religious beliefs" (with reference to Cuba), or as having "no false religion" (with reference to Hispaniola). Asad (1993, 27–28) makes the case that until the nineteenth century, religion was not considered an "autonomous essence" and hence a transhistorical or transcultural concept; therefore, we might not expect the Spanish Christians in the fifteenth and sixteenth centuries to conceptualize "religion" outside of Christianity. An exception to the nineteenth-century innovation might be Vico's *New Science* (Vico 1968), e.g., sec. 3, chap. 1.

103. Would the Nahuas have admitted the existence of a "Mesoamerican religion"? See Lara (2004, 3–7), in which he discusses Mesoamerican religion.

104. Foster 1953; Redfield 1941; Redfield and Villa Rojas 1934.

105. Siegel 1941, 62.

106. Leopold and Sinding Jensen 2004; see also Beatty (2006, 325, 333n2) for a comprehensive list of references on syncretism.

107. Baird 2004, 52–53.

108. E.g., Bunzel 1952; Carlsen 1997; Sandstrom 1991; Vogt 1976.

109. Redfield and Villa Rojas 1934; Reina 1966; Watanabe 1992.

110. Rabasa 1993; Burkhart 1993; Maurer Avalos 1993; Ingham 1986.

111. Early 2006; Wagley 1949.

112. Early 2006, 147–48.

113. Beatty 2006, 325.

114. Baird 2004, 56.

115. Early 2006, 100.

116. Marzal 1993, 140–69.

117. Firth 1996, 14–15.

118. Horton 1971, 94.

119. Seznec 1981.

120. Discussed in Graham, n.d.

121. It is worth noting that in terms of health and medicine, the Aztecs were likewise in advance of European health and medicine in the sixteenth century (Ortiz de Montellano 1990).

122. See discussion in Bowie 2000, 25–28. "World," or "universal," as opposed to "natural religions," were taxons introduced by Cornelius Petrus Tiele in his *Outline of the History of Religion to the Spread of Universal Religions* (1876), discussed in J. Z. Smith 1998, 278–79.

123. Bowie 2000, 28.

124. See discussions in Graham 1996 and Graham 1999.

125. Horton 1971, 101–3.

126. Horton 1971, 102–3.

127. Horton 1971, 102–3.

128. Monaghan 2000, 26–28; Sotelo Santos 1988, 11, 19.

129. Horton 1971, 102–3.

130. Sotelo Santos 1988, 11, 19; Taube 1992, 32; J. E. S. Thompson 1966, 263.

131. John (2008) discusses the Postclassic and early historic iconography of the cosmic dragon.

132. The concept of spirit is believed to extend as far back as Preclassic times (see Ringle 1999, 200–2).

133. "Rapidity" here is a relative term. According to Chuchiak, "The Maya believed that the earliest images of the Catholic saints were evil and brought bad luck to their owners. Even two generations after the Spanish conquest, some Maya rejected the cult of saints" (2000, 445).

134. Horton 1971, 101.

135. Christian (1981) discusses local religion in Spain; D. E. Thompson (1960) discusses commonalities between Christian and Maya beliefs.

136. Firth 1996, 12.

137. Firth 1996, 15, 168–69.

138. Walker (1995) argues strongly that ritual behavior in particular can be productively analyzed archaeologically.

139. Firth 1996, 169.

140. Durán 1967; Todorov 1984, 202–41.

141. G. D. Jones 2005, 288; see also G. D. Jones 1998.

142. Carlsen 1997; K. Warren 1978.

143. Asad 1993, 15.

144. Asad 1993, 15.

145. Asad 1993, 15.

146. Asad 1993, 15–16.

147. See also Edgerton 2001.

148. Burkhart 1989, 18; Caso Barrera 1999, 158.

149. Burkhart 1989, 18.

150. Early 2006.

151. Burkhart 1989, 184.

152. Burkhart 1989, 184.

153. J. C. Russell 1994.

154. Seznec 1981.

155. Brown 1981.

156. Rabasa 1993, 62–63.

157. Geertz 1968, 14. This insight clarifies much about what is happening today with regard to terrorism.

158. Discussed in Graham 2006b.

159. I will use the term "buccaneers" to mean both pirates and privateers when we cannot be sure who was licensed to plunder, and who was not.

160. Firth 1996, 15.

161. Firth 1996, 14–15.

162. Heisenberg 1958, 106.

163. Insoll 2004, 5.

164. Collins 1977; Farriss 1984, 233, 335–36.

165. Duffy 2005, 268.

166. Duffy 2005.

167. Silverblatt 1987, 161.

168. Michelet 1973.

169. Silverblatt 1987, 163.

170. Giorgi 2005; Link 1995; Muchembled 2004; A. Wilson 2002.

171. Constantinou 2007.

172. Case 1971.

173. Deut. 32:17.

174. Kelly 2006; Pagels [1995] 1996, 39.

175. J. B. Russell 1977, 199.

176. Bloom 1996, 63; Pagels [1995] 1996, 41.

177. Pagels [1995] 1996, 47.

178. Pagels [1995] 1996, 39–49; Bloom 1996, 62–70.

179. Pagels [1995] 1996, xix.

180. Mark 1:34; 3:23–27; Pagels [1995] 1996, xvii, 17.

181. Pagels [1979] 2006; [1995] 1996, 66–74.

182. Pagels [1995] 1996, 120.

183. Pagels [1995] 1996, 66–74, 112–48.

184. "Devil" as a modern English term has a wide variety of forms in Middle and Old English and the old dialects of England and Scotland (e.g., devel, dioul, deofel), but is said to derive from the Greek διοβολο⊠ through the Latin *diábolus*, meaning "accuser"

or "slanderer." The Greek διοβολο⊠ and the Latin version *diabolus* were the words used to render the Hebrew śātān of the Old Testament. Thus, it is understandable that through various translations (e.g., Jerome) and versions of the Bible, that Satan and the Devil would come to be synonymous (*Oxford English Dictionary*, 2nd ed., 1991).

185. Duffy 2005, 280; Pagels [1995] 1996, 149.

186. Kelly 2006, 319.

187. Rabasa 1993, 77.

188. Pagels [1995] 1996, 138–43.

189. See Cervantes 1994.

190. Trevor-Roper 1970; Silverblatt 1987, 162. Trevor-Roper was in fact concerned with the witch craze of the sixteenth and seventeenth centuries, which he describes as the product not of Christianity, but of the Catholic Church in particular. He recognizes, however, that elements were pre-Christian (Trevor-Roper 1970, 141).

191. Pagels [1995] 1996, 184.

192. The quotation is from a discussion of dualism in J. B. Russell 1977, 100.

193. Rabasa 1993, 74–77; J. B. Russell 1977, 99–101.

194. Burkhart 1989, 25.

195. Valenzuela Márquez 2004.

196. Valenzuela Márquez 2004, 176.

197. Valenzuela Márquez 2004, 177.

198. Tozzer 1941.

199. Restall and Chuchiak 2002.

200. Farris 1984, 286.

Chapter 4. Being Christian and the Doctrine of the Church

1. Koester 1990, 75–128.

2. Pagels [1995] 1996, 69.

3. Wood 2001, 7–8.

4. Bede 1969.

5. Farmer 1997.

6. Foster 1973.

7. Tozzer 1941.

8. Tozzer 1941, 58n279, 64n292, 76n338.

9. Goddard 2004, 57.

10. Fletcher 1997, 9.

11. Fletcher 1997, 9.

12. W. James [1902] 1982, 189.

13. Geertz 2000, 184.

14. Geertz 2000, 179–84.

15. Sanmark 2004, 13.

16. Sanmark 2004, 13–15.

17. J. C. Russell 1994, 26–35.

18. Sanmark 2004, 13–15; Brown 2003, 325.

19. Sanmark 2004, 13–15.

20. Wood 2001, 8–9.

21. J. C. Russell 1994, 30–31.

22. J. C. Russell 1994, 30 (citing Nock [1933] 1998, 7).

23. J. C. Russell 1994 (citing Nock [1933] 1998, 5–7).

24. J. C. Russell 1994, 30–31.

25. J. C. Russell 1994, 35–36.

26. J. C. Russell 1994, 26–38.

27. J. C. Russell 1994, 34.

28. J. C. Russell 1994, 31.

29. *Oxford English Dictionary*, 2nd ed., 1991.

30. *American Heritage Dictionary of the English Language*, 3rd ed., 1992.

31. LeGoff 1988, 199; Mathews 1993, 173; J. C. Russell 1994, 46.

32. Seznec 1981.

33. Seznec 1981, 89.

34. E.g., see Cicero's *De natura deorum*, written in 45 B.C., in Seznec (1981, 4). "It was thanks to these interpretations, which were proposed by the ancients themselves . . . , that the gods were to survive" (Seznec 1981, 4).

35. Seznec 1981, 4–5.

36. Seznec 1981, 5.

37. Seznec 1981, 4.

38. Sawyer and Sawyer 1993, 228–29.

39. Seznac 1981, 40, 43; J. C. Russell 1994, 188.

40. Seznec 1981, 4–5, 11–12.

41. Seznec 1981, 90n32, 94–95.

42. Farriss 1984, 320–51.

43. Seznec 1981, 320.

44. E.g., Durán 1994 or Landa (Tozzer 1941).

45. Seznec 1981, 321.

46. Seznec 1981, 321.

47. Seznec 1981, 321.

48. E.g., J. C. Russell 1994; Sanmark 2004.

49. J. C. Russell 1994, 33–38; Geary 1988, 84–85.

50. Clebsch 1978, v–vi.

51. J. C. Russell 1994, 35.

52. J. B. Russell 1977, 49–50.

53. Lindberg 2006, 20.

54. Chadwick 1993, 223.

55. Even the Donatists and Pelagians were tolerated, until issues were brought to a head in the early fifth century by what seem often to have been personal battles rather than the impossibility of reconciliation; at other times, such as the execution of Priscillian, the Bishop of Avila, in the late fourth century, the motivation was suppression of Manicheism (Chadwick 1993, 169–70, 219–35).

56. Asad 1993, 35.

57. Asad 1993, 33–38.

58. Nock 1998, 5–6.

59. Nock 1998, 5–6.

60. Stravinskas 1998.

61. *Catechism of the Catholic Church* 1997.

62. Lindberg 2006, 19.

63. *Oxford English Dictionary*, 2nd ed., 1991.

64. Early 2006; Klor de Alva 1982.

65. Lindberg 2006, 4.

66. Lindberg 2006, 18.

67. Lindberg 2006, 24–26, 30–32, 34, 122.

68. Pagels [1979] 2006.

69. Pagels [1995] 1996, 166–67.

70. Stravinskas 1998, 642–43.

71. Ginzburg 1979, 90.

72. Marzal 1993, 146.

73. Rabasa 1993, 70.

74. Phelan 1970.

75. Lindberg 2006, 20.

76. Lindberg 2006, 19.

77. Lindberg 2006, 20.

78. Lindberg 2006, 20.

79. Farmer 1997, 138.

80. *"Indios,"* not "Maya," is the term used in Spanish-language written sources (Restall 2004, 65–67.)

81. *Códice Franciscano* 1941.

82. *Códice Franciscano* 1941, 36–37 (translation mine).

83. *Códice Franciscano* 1941, 30–43.

84. Lindberg 2006.

85. Stravinskas 1998.

86. Stravinskas 1998, 342–43.

87. Stravinskas 1998, 320–21.

88. *Catechism of the Catholic Church* 1997. In the originals, there are numbers that refer to paragraphs in the body of the Catechism, but I do not include the numbers here.

89. *Catechism of the Catholic Church* 1997, 875.

90. *Catechism of the Catholic Church* 1997, 887.

91. *Catechism of the Catholic Church* 1997, 901.

92. *Catechism of the Catholic Church* 1997, para. 83, p. 26.

93. Momigliano 1963, 82.

94. *Catechism of the Catholic Church* 1997, 26–27.

95. Christian 1981.

96. Momigliano 1963.

Chapter 5. The Environment of Early Contact

1. Here I refer specifically to the nautical sense of "offing," as "the part of the visible sea distant from the shore" (*Oxford English Dictionary*, 2nd ed., 1991).

2. See Morison (1978, 411), where he quotes Columbus on Cuba.

3. This is my interpretation of the events as described by G. D. Jones (1989, 1998), but it also takes into account the history of Franciscan efforts in Yucatan. Attempts to administer Belize continued into the mid-seventeenth century, but with diminishing effectiveness.

4. G. D. Jones 1989, 12: "From the sixteenth century onwards, Spaniards demonstrated little sustained motivation or ability to bring their troublesome frontier under permanent control, due both to the perceived unhealthy, remote, unproductive, and

ungovernable characteristics of the region and to the lack of economic and human resources to carry out major conquests in such territory."

5. As recounted by Bede in bk. 1, chap. 4 of his *Historia ecclesiastica gentis Anglorum*4 (Bede 1969, 14); see also Thomas 1981, 43; Watts 1998, 11–12.

6. Wood 2001, 26.

7. Thomas 1981, 26–28, 354; Watts 1998, 7–8.

8. Thomas 1981, 198; Watts 1998.

9. Thomas 1981, 242, 354. The change came in the seventh century, when Christianity was institutionalized.

10. The monastic system reached Britain in about the last quarter of the fifth century, and spread widely in the sixth and early seventh centuries (see Thomas 1981, 347).

11. Thomas 1981, 241–42.

12. See Thomas 1981.

13. Thomas 1981, 242. I draw here from Thomas's comment on early British Christians being seen as "lapsed, steeped in sin, rarely devout, but Christian nonetheless."

14. By this I mean that the Mendicants who proselytized cooperated, on the whole, with colonial authorities.

15. Wood 2001, 9.

16. The monastery of Wearmouth was founded in 674, and that at Jarrow in 680 or 681. Bede seems to have been admitted to Wearmouth in 679/680 and probably remained based there, but because the two houses were combined under a single abbacy in 688, Bede's monastic connections are usually referred to as Wearmouth-Jarrow (McClure and Collins 1969, x–xiii).

17. Wood 2001, 9–10; Bede 1969, 20–21 (bk. 1, chaps. 8, 11).

18. Bede 1969, 20 (bk. 1, chap. 8).

19. Oviedo (1851–55, 32–38) on Alonso Dávila's journey along the Belize coast in 1533, from Chamberlain 1948, 121–22n30.

20. Chamberlain 1948, 99–127.

21. Woodward 1999, 26. Although much of the documentary evidence for increasing piracy in Belize in particular dates to the seventeenth century (G. D. Jones 1989, 23, 62), indirect evidence, both documentary and archaeological, argues for early activity in the Belize zone by seafarers.

22. N. P. James and Ginsburg 1979, 1–23.

23. See, e.g., Lothrop 1927 on Columbus's fourth voyage. For evidence from archaeology, see D. Z. Chase (1982), and D. Z. Chase and A. F. Chase (1988) for information on Santa Rita Corozal during the Late Postclassic and at the time of the Spanish conquest. A. P. Andrews (1990) discusses the role of trading ports in Maya civilization in general. Masson (2002, 356–59) describes the rise of affluent Postclassic mercantile society and the importance of coastal trade in northeastern Belize. Mock's investigations of several sites along the northern Belize coast have yielded evidence of Postclassic activity; see sources in A. P. Andrews and Mock (2002). Pendergast (1990) discusses Lamanai's occupation longevity and its long history of involvement in waterborne trade. Graham and Pendergast (1989, 13–14) discuss the evidence for Late Postclassic occupation and activity on Ambergris Caye.

24. G. D. Jones 1989, 224–30; 1998, 408–13.

25. Bricker (1981, 15); Restall (1998, 6–7). G. D. Jones (1989, 25) also recognizes the impact of disease, although he thinks that the region which included Belize remained viable during the early decades of colonization.

26. See Bricker 1981, 15, where passages of Roys's translation of the Chilam Balam of Chumayel are quoted.

27. G. D. Jones 1989, 5–6; Scholes et al. 1938, 51–65.

28. G. D. Jones 1989, 55, 302n1. Jones notes that the statement is from an AGI document, Contaduría 913, and was made by Julio Sarmiento Palacio and royal accountant Gil Carrillo, appended to Bacalar accounts, dated 4 March 1620.

29. Canedo 1952.

30. Or I am wrong and he never passed through Belize.

31. See Chamberlain 1948, 344–45, and Chamberlain's reference to "Fray Lorenzo de Bienvenida to the Crown, Merida, February 10, 1548, Spain, D1877, pp. 70–80" (345n24).

32. "Your Highness should know that the Adelantado about three years and a half ago assigned a captaincy to Gaspar Pacheco, a citizen of this municipality [of Mérida], to conquer certain provinces of the Golfo Dulce, which lie between Honduras and Guatemala and this land" (Chamberlain 1948, 235).

33. See Murray 2006, 19–25.

34. O. L. Jones 1994; MacLeod 1973; Rodriguez Becerra 1977; Woodward 1999.

35. E.g., Wytfliet 1597; Bertius 1602, 1612; Dudley 1646–47; van Keulen 1681–96.

36. Vander Aa [1761?]; Visscher 1717.

37. Sanson 1650, 1670; Covens and Mortier 1761 [no mapmaker's name was given, but the map strongly resembles a Visscher].

38. Bolland 1977; Dobson 1973; Thomson 2004.

39. Tozzer 1941, 53n261.

40. Tozzer 1941, 60–61n289.

41. Blaeu 1665; Loots 1717; Montanus 1671; Sanson 1650, 1670; Vander Aa [1761?]; Visscher 1717 (probably a copy of Montanus 1671).

42. See Montanus 1671; Sanson 1650, 1670; Vander Aa [1761?]; Visscher 1717; Wytfliet 1597.

43. Wytfliet 1597.

44. Izquierdo 2006, 161; Scholes and Roys 1948; Sharer 2006, 46.

45. Neff 2001, fig. 1.

46. A. P. Andrews 1990, 166; A. P. Andrews and Mock 2002; Kepecs 1997; Lothrop 1927; Masson 2000, 2002; Sabloff and Rathje 1975; Scholes and Roys 1948; J. E. S. Thompson 1970.

47. M. E. Smith and Berdan 2003, 30.

48. Scholes and Roys 1948, 3, 317.

49. A. P. Andrews and Mock 2002, 310; Kepecs 1997; Masson 2002.

50. The Rio Copilco flowed into the west end of Laguna Tupilco, which is about 150 kilometers west of the Laguna de Terminos (see Scholes and Roys 1948, 96 and map 3 [facing 108]).

51. Cited in Scholes and Roys 1948, 17. According to Scholes and Roys (17n5), the quotation is from a petition of an agent of Montejo the Adelantado, filed before the Council of the Indies in 1533. The petition is among documents in the Archivo General de Indias in Seville that record a dispute between Montejo the Adelantado and Pedro de Alvarado over the right to an encomienda (details are in Scholes and Roys 1948, 516; notes in brackets are Scholes and Roys's).

52. A. P. Andrews and Mock 2002; D. Z. Chase 1982; Freidel 1978; Graham 1989, 1994; Graham and Pendergast 1989; Guderjan 1993; Guderjan and Garber 1995; Masson 2000, 2002; McKillop 1996, 2002, 2005; Mock 1994.

53. A. P. Andrews 1990; McKillop 2002, 11–12.

54. A. P. Andrews 1990.

55. A. P. Andrews and Mock 2002; Graham 1989, 150; McKillop 2002.

56. Graham 1994.

57. Graham 1989; McKillop 2005, 155.

58. Graham 1989.

59. For Santa Rita, see D. Z. Chase 1982, and D. Z. Chase and A. F. Chase 1988. For San Pedro, see Pendergast and Graham 1991.

60. Guderjan 1993; McKillop 2005, 155.

61. A. P. Andrews and Mock 2002; McKillop 2002, 13–14, map 1.5; Mock 1994; Mock, personal communication, 2007.

62. Graham 1994; McKillop 2002, 2005.

63. Dunn and Mazzullo 1993; Guderjan and Garber 1995.

64. A. P. Andrews 1990, 167; Freidel 1978.

65. A. P. Andrews 1990; Hammond 1976.

66. Graham 1989, 1994; Graham and Pendergast 1989.

67. McKillop (2002) and Mock (1994) both deal with the changes that took place from the Late Classic to Postclassic period, including sea-level rise. A. P. Andrews and Mock (2002, 325) date the end of Belize salt production along the coast to A.D. 900–1000, whereas Graham (1989; 2002, 412–13) argues that salt processing was strongly associated with Late Classic florescence, and declined with the Classic political collapse of Peten and other southern lowlands communities in the late eighth and early ninth century.

68. A. P. Andrews 1978, 1990; A. P. Andrews and Robles 1985.

69. Graham 1989, 1994.

70. Guderjan 1993.

71. Pendergast 1990, 176–77.

72. Graham 1989.

73. Coe 1957; Graham 1989, 1994.

74. Tozzer 1941, 17n95, esp. Herrera.

75. Tozzer 1941, 17n95; see also appendix A, 214.

76. Kepecs 1997, 323.

77. Díaz del Castillo 1956, 68; Pagden 1986, 13, 17–19, 453n24. According to Díaz, as translated by Maudslay, "Doña Marina knew the language of Coatzacoalcos, which is that common to Mexico, and she knew the language of Tabasco, as did also Jerónimo de Aguilar, who spoke the language of Yucatan and Tabasco, which is one and the same. So that these two could understand one another clearly" (Díaz del Castillo 1956, 68).

78. Scholes and Roys 1948, 17.

79. Scholes and Roys 1948, 316–17. Laguna Tupilco is seaward of Copilco-Zacualco in map 5.1. See Izquierdo (2006, 161, 172–76) for discussion of the diversity of the Copilco *payolel* (jurisdiction).

80. Chamberlain 1948, 100.

81. Scholes and Roys 1948, 18.

82. See also A. P. Andrews 1990.

83. Chamberlain 1948, 35–66; Lothrop 1927.

84. Lothrop 1927.

85. Scholes and Roys 1948. See the discussion of the "Putun" and "Chontal" Maya in Sharer 2006, 528–29.

86. Woodward 1999, 26.

87. Pagden 1986, 13. The ships were probably caravels. What was later to be called the Bay of Honduras is also said to have been made known to the world by Spanish, French, Dutch, and English pilots (Bernstein 1947, 392).

88. G. D. Jones 1994, 5 n. xv. In this note, Jones lists the principal secondary sources pertaining to the 1508 Pinzón Solís voyage as: Henry Harisse 1892, 453–64; McClymont 1916; Morison 1974, 230–33; and Sauer 1966, 165–68. He also states: "For the initial royal orders for the expedition, preserved in the AGI, see *Colección de documentos inéditos relativos al descubrimiento, conquista y organización de las antiguas posesiones españolas de América y Oceanía* . . . , tomo 22 (Madrid, Manuel G. Hernández, 1874), pp. 5–13. See also *Colección de documentos inéditos relativos al descubrimiento, conquista y organización de las antiguas posesiones españolas de ultramar*, Segunda Serie, tomo 7, I de los pleitos de Colón (Madrid, Real Academia de la Historia, 1892), pp. 191–321. For reference to testimony on the 1508 expedition see *pregunta 9*."

89. Vicente Pinzón sailed with Columbus on his first voyage (McClymont 1916, 1–2). McClymont's spelling is Vicente Añes Pinçon.

90. Jones draws from Morison (1974, 230) to say that the two vessels were the caravel *Isabeleta* and the ship *Magdalena*. Reference to "ship" is most likely to a carrack (Gibbons 2001, 28). Pinzón was a highly experienced pilot and is not likely to have ventured through the reef with a carrack, but it is possible that some channels through the reef were hazarded by the caravel under oars. If they were in Belize waters, they almost certainly explored the waters around Glover's Reef, since it is surrounded by deep water (200+ meters) and the coastal shelf is both relatively deep (15–30 meters) at this latitude, without patch reefs, and at its narrowest in this region (N. P. James and Ginsburg 1979, 2–3, fig. 1-1, 1-2). This would have brought the explorers close enough to have viewed the coastline and the Maya Mountains on a clear day.

91. G. D. Jones 1984, 5.

92. Winzerling 1946, 5.

93. McClymont 1916, 23–25.

94. McClymont 1916, 8–9.

95. See N. P. James and Ginsburg 1979, 3, fig. 1-2.

96. Graham 1994.

97. Wytfliet 1597.

98. Evidence strongly suggests that these black soils are the product, at least in part, of anthropogenic processes, and that they were in place by the Postclassic period and certainly by the historic period (Graham 1998b, 2006b).

99. G. D. Jones 1994.

100. See, e.g., Sharer 2006, 757–78.

101. Chamberlain 1948, 11–15; Diaz del Castillo 1956, chaps. 1–9; Maudslay 1956, 3–28.

102. Lothrop 1927, 357–63. Lothrop says that Gómara's account (*Cronica de la Nueva-España*, chap. 11) is generally accepted, which is that the ship was wrecked on the reefs known as Las Vivoras, which he says is probably the Pedro Cays, near Jamaica, and that the survivors reached a province called "Maia," which is assumed to be Yucatan. Bernal Díaz (Díaz del Castillo 1956, chap. 18) placed the wreck on the Alacranes, which seem to be reefs, but Díaz does not specify a location; however, he does recount that the survivors ended up in Yucatan (see also Maudslay 1956, 45–46). Lothrop (1927, 359–61) says these reefs lie north of what is now the state of Yucatán, but he provides a rather convoluted argument that the survivors reached land in Honduras, where there was a province called "Maia"; he also mentions Sánchez de Aguilar's version, which has the

surviving Spaniards in Zama, or Tulum. Cortés placed the wreck off the shallows of Jamaica, with the survivors reaching Yucatan (Pagden 1986, 13, 17 ["The First Letter"]). Cortés's account, unlike those of Bernal Díaz and Gómara, makes no mention of the survivors being killed. He says only that the survivors, according to Gerónimo de Aguilar, were "scattered throughout the land."

103. See also Bricker 1981, 15.

104. Chamberlain 1948, 20. The information that follows on the conquest of Yucatan is drawn largely from Chamberlain 1948; G. D. Jones 1989; and Tozzer 1941, 47–61nn234–89.

105. G. D. Jones 1989, 26.

106. Where Cortés had landed in 1519, and Grijalva in 1518 (Díaz del Castillo 1956, 17, 18, 44; Chamberlain 1948, 13, 35).

107. Chamberlain 1989, 36. See E. W. Andrews and A. P. Andrews 1975, fig. 1, 90–97 (esp. 95–97).

108. Chamberlain 1948, 36–41.

109. According to Chamberlain (1948, 46–57), he visited Belma, Conil, and Cachi in the *cacicazgo* of Ecab; Chauaca in the *cacicazgo* of Chikinchel; and the large towns of Ake, Zizha, and Loche; and then marched through the heavily populated interior back to Salamanca at Xelha, probably gaining information about the *cacicazgos* of Sotuta and Cupul, and the great center of Chichen Itza, along the way (map 5.1 shows Conil, Ecab, Chauaca, Chikinchel, Ake, Loche, Xelha, Sotuta, Cupul).

110. Chamberlain 1948, 57.

111. M. E. Smith 1986.

112. Chamberlain 1948, 48, 49.

113. Kepecs 1997; Okoshi 1994; Quezada 1993; Restall 1997.

114. Chamberlain 1948, 33.

115. Chamberlain 1948, 38, 41n17.

116. The brigantine used in the sixteenth century was a small galleass (a galley being a ship designed for speed and maneuverability provided by rowers). The galleass was a sailing galley, which means that it could travel under sail. The brigantine, as a small galleass, is said to have been much favored by pirates in the Mediterranean for its speed under both oars and sail. It was fitted for shorter sea voyages, which fits with Montejo's decision to sail a brigantine from Santo Domingo to Yucatan. That is, he was probably planning on exploring, and opted for a ship that afforded maximum maneuverability. The caravel had a depth of only 3 meters, but it was well fitted for long ocean voyages and must therefore have been a heavier ship than a brigantine, and probably not as maneuverable. A carrack was also built for long distances, but had a depth of over 5 meters and seems the least maneuverable of the three. From the literature, it would seem that a brigantine was reasonably well suited to sailing along the barrier reef and negotiating the sea around the atolls (Gibbons 2001, 28–29, 40–41; Kemp 1980, 18–19, 22–23, 45). Its depth (3 meters) suggests that it could navigate the shallower waters of parts of the coastal shelf. The shelf off the coast of northern Belize is rarely deeper than 8 meters, whereas farther south, in the region of the Maya Mountains, it deepens considerably, apparently a reflection of the mainland topography. From a depth of 20–25 meters off Belize City, the shelf deepens to over 200 meters in the Gulf of Honduras. However, the main problem in negotiating the coastal shelf is that the barrier reef—that is, the coral reef that forms a rim at the margin of the coastal shelf—is 3–10 meters wide and rarely deeper than 3 meters. Therefore, no matter how maneuverable a ship was,

its pilot had to find a cut in the reef, and then hope that there were no patch reefs or other shallow waters within the coastal shelf itself. As it turns out, there are no patch reefs in the north but there are many off the southern coast of Belize in the region of the Toledo and southern Stann Creek Districts. The main cut, or channel, through the reef lies north of Lighthouse Reef and Turneffe and is used today by ships heading to Belize City. There are other options suggested by the isometric diagrams, however (see N. P. James and Ginsburgh 1979, 2, 12, fig. 1-1, fig. 1-8): south of Lighthouse Reef; around the southern part of Glovers Reef; or even passing between the north-south ridge that forms the basement of Lighthouse and Glovers Reef and the ridge that forms the basement of Turneffe Island (N. P. James and Ginsburg 1979, 1–13).

117. G. D. Jones 1989, 26.

118. A. P. Andrews and Jones 2001, 27–28; G. D. Jones 1989, map 2, 337nn20–22.

119. D. Z. Chase and A. F. Chase 1988.

120. Díaz del Castillo 1956, 45–46.

121. Tozzer 1941, 49–50n240.

122. It is not clear to me, in Tozzer's note, which documentary source the information is from.

123. I have repeatedly emphasized the importance of social links as a reflection of coastal Maya networks, but Jones has argued equally powerfully for networks extending inland: "The Mayas of Belize during the sixteenth and seventeenth centuries were well organized in extensive but ever-changing geographic and political networks that tied them not only to each other but also to Maya communities in the Yucatán peninsula and in Petén and Verapaz in Guatemala. These linkages among Maya towns and villages helped make possible a series of resistance movements and open rebellions that resulted in long periods of indigenous independence from colonial rule" (G. D. Jones 1994, 5).

124. G. D. Jones 1989, 26.

125. See Pendergast 1988b.

126. Chamberlain 1948, 60–65.

127. Tozzer, 50n242.

128. See the glossary for an explanation of "reduction."

129. Here the Couoh (or Kowoj) received him cordially. This seemed odd at first because it was the Couoh who had so violently repulsed the Córdoba expedition in 1517. Chamberlain attributes the friendliness of the Couoh in part to Montejo the Elder's efforts in sending emissaries to the town to win its allegiance (1948, 91–92). This may be true, but it could also have been that the Couoh were biding their time. (Chamberlain 1948, 69–93).

130. Chamberlain 1948, 99; Tozzer 1941, 50n242.

131. Chamberlain 1948, 99–127.

132. This is today called Puerto Cortes.

133. G. D. Jones 1989, 39; Tozzer, 50n242.

134. G. D. Jones 1989, 29, 39.

135. See also Chamberlain 1948, 99–127.

136. Graham 1989; McKillop 2002.

137. G. D. Jones 1989, map 2.

138. Chamberlain 1948, 120.

139. Chamberlain 1948, 121.

140. G. D. Jones 1989, 39.

141. Chamberlain 1948, 124.

142. Graham 1994.

143. Graham 1987; Graham and Pendergast 1989, 13–15.

144. Shirley Mock, personal communication, 2007.

145. A. F. Chase and D. Z. Chase 1987; D. Z. Chase 1982, 1984, 1985, 1986, 1989, 1990, 1991; D. Z. Chase and A. F. Chase 1986, 1988, 1994, 2001.

146. McKillop 2002, 13–14.

147. Graham 1994; McKillop 2005, fig. 6.28.

148. MacKie 1963. This is my assessment of the pottery illustrated by MacKie.

149. See A. P. Andrews and Mock 2002, esp. fig. 11.2.

150. MacLeod 1973, 50.

151. The Cupul, in the area of Chichen Itza, first acknowledged the Spaniards when they established the Ciudad Real there in 1532 (Chamberlain 1948, 135), but then rebelled against the demands of encomienda, in 1533, by refusing to pay tribute or render services. Assisted by other communities (Ecab, Sotuta, Cochuah) (map 5.1), they blockaded Chichen. The Spaniards held on but could not overcome their adversaries. They escaped and moved to Dzilan (Chamberlain 1948, 75–148; see also Tozzer 1941, nn. 244, 245.)

152. Chamberlain 1948, 75–148; Tozzer 1941, 50–52nn242, 244–47, 251, 253, 254, 256.

153. Tozzer 1941, 52nn256–57.

154. Tozzer 1941, 53n259.

155. Tozzer 1941, 53nn259–60.

156. Tozzer 1941, 52.

157. See the glossary for use of the term "religious" as a noun.

158. Canedo 1952, 494.

159. Mendieta states that Testera/Tastera went to Yucatán, accompanied by other friars, in 1534. Cogolludo says Testera and companions arrived at Champoton on 18 March 1535, and Canedo (1952, 494–95nn3–4) concludes that both Mendieta and Cogolludo are wrong and that Testera was sent to Tabasco and Yucatan in 1537 by the Provincial of the Province of the Holy Gospel of New Spain, Fray Antonio de Ciudad Rodrigo.

160. Chamberlain 1948, 33, 206.

161. Chamberlain 1948, 153, 206.

162. Chamberlain 1948, 160–64.

163. MacLeod 1973, 43, 47; Restall 1998, 10–11.

164. Tozzer 1941, 53n261. The Gulf of Fonseca is on the Pacific coast, at Honduras's southern limit (map 5.2), with El Salvador to the west and Nicaragua to the south and east. All three countries border the Gulf.

165. In 1537, Montejo went to Honduras to put down a rebellion, but his rivalry with Pedro de Alvarado eventually resulted in his being forced to relinquish the governorship of Honduras to Alvarado in 1539, in exchange for Chiapas (Chamberlain 1948, 179–81, 196).

166. Canedo (1952) says Testera's return to Mexico was in 1537. See Canedo (1952) for various dates given in the documents (Torquemada, Lopez de Cogolludo, Mendieta).

167. Chamberlain 1948, 186–202; Tozzer 1941, 67n303.

168. The Xius of Mani, for example, had declared submission to the Crown in 1532 (Chamberlain 1948, 202).

169. Montejo the Nephew was appointed Lieutenant Governor for the conquest of these eastern provinces (Chamberlain 1948, 219; Tozzer, 58n289(1).

170. Tozzer 1941, 58n280.

171. Chamberlain 1948, 232–34; G. D. Jones 1989, 410; Restall 1998, 15.

172. Varner and Varner 1983, 83–85. The Montejos (Younger and Nephew) used mastiffs in Campeche in 1541 (Varner and Varner 1983, 86).

173. Lopez de Cogolludo [1688] 1971, vol. 1, bk. 3, chap. 15.

174. See Chamberlain 1948, 235; G. D. Jones 1989, 42–43.

175. G. D. Jones 1989, 46.

176. Measured on large-scale INEGI sheets (Anthony Andrews, personal communication, 2008).

177. Chamberlain 1948, 234–35.

178. Later on in the sixteenth century, around the 1570s, Dominicans would proselytize among communities in southern Belize as an extension of their missions in Verapaz (Sapper 1985; G. D. Jones 1989, 50, 100). The Dominican efforts, however, do not ever seem to have been integrated into a broader program of conquest and colonization, in the manner of the conquest of Yucatan and its subsequent administration by both colonial and church authorities.

179. MacLeod 1973, 56–57.

180. MacLeod 1973, 58–61; Woodward 1999, 42.

181. Woodward 1999, 47.

182. Woodward 1999, 26–29.

183. MacLeod 1973, 43–44.

184. In addition to the Visscher 1717 map (map 5.9), see also Sanson 1650 and Sanson 1670, among others.

185. Rodríguez Becérra 1977, 45 (map 2), 67 (map 3); Woodward 1999, 53.

186. Woodward 1999, 42.

187. MacLeod 1973, 110–11; Woodward 1999, 43.

188. Woodward 1999, 42, 47.

189. Scholes et al. 1938, chap. 29, pp. 51–65.

190. Sapper 1985.

Chapter 6. The Millennial Kingdom and the Belize Missions

1. See G. D. Jones 1989, 12: "It was in part Spanish disavowal of the habitability of the southern forests that kept the southern frontier open to seditious enterprises that continuously undermined colonial governance."

2. Kubler 1948, 3.

3. Please see the glossary for the definition of "Mexico," but essentially, here as in the rest of the text, I refer to what would now be called central Mexico, or the heartland of the Mexica/Aztec/Nahuatl–speaking peoples.

4. G. D. Jones 1989.

5. Hunt 1976.

6. G. D. Jones 1989.

7. Farriss 1984, 302.

8. Kubler 1948, 2–4.

9. Canedo 1977, 23.

10. Díaz del Castillo 1956, 40.

11. Kubler 1948, 3–4.

12. G. D. Jones 1994, 25; Lopetegui and Zubillaga 1965, 196–97.

13. Lippy, Choquette, and Poole 1992, 101, 137, 155. For detailed information on the

Mendicants, see the *Original Catholic Encyclopedia*, s.v. both "Religious Life" and "Mendicant Friars." The encyclopedia is available online at http://oce.catholic.com/.

14. For more on the Jesuits as Mendicants and clerks regular, see *the Original Catholic Encyclopedia*, s.v. "Religious Life," "Cleric," and "Society of Jesus." The first Jesuits were British and came to Belize from Jamaica in 1851, joined not long after by Jesuits from Italy and elsewhere in Europe. Fray Salvatore Di Pietro, S.J. became the first Bishop of Belize, in 1893, and in 1894 the Missouri Province (U.S.) assumed, and continues to assume, responsibility for the pastoral and educational needs of Belize. A school for boys was established in 1887 that became St. John's College. According to a Jesuit website (Oulvey 2004), the Jesuits founded nearly all the parishes and most of the Catholic primary and secondary schools in Belize; the site also states that the Catholic educational system is the largest in the nation. See also a history of Holy Redeemer Cathedral, at http://www.holyredeemerbelize.org/history.html.

15. Lopetegui and Zubillaga 1965, 197; Pagden 1982, 147–48; Phelan 1970, 25, 109.

16. See Caso Barrera 1999, 157. She refers to an AGI document in which Carlos de Luna y Arellano proposes that the Jesuits come to Yucatan to found seminaries and instruct the Maya ("*naturales*").

17. Sapper 1985.

18. Canedo 1952; G. D. Jones 1989; Lopez de Cogolludo [1688] 1971, passim.

19. Jeronymites traditionally were hermits. Since Mendicants were active in communities, I am unsure where to place the Jeronymite in this case.

20. Carrillo y Ancona [1967] 1982, 56–59; Lopetegui and Zubillaga 1965; Tozzer 1941.

21. Refer to the glossary for definitions of "religious," "secular," "regular," "clergy," and other church terminology.

22. Kubler 1948, 96. The Mendicants were therefore not "monks."

23. Kubler 1948, 2–4; Livingstone 2000, 373.

24. Phelan 1970.

25. Bayle 1950, 3–4; Schwaller 1987.

26. Collins 1977, 239.

27. Bayle 1950, 4 (translation mine).

28. Bayle 1950, 4.

29. For Alonso Gonzalez on the Cordoba expedition, see Díaz del Castillo 1956, 5; for Grijalva's chaplain Juan Díaz, see Maudslay 1956, 458; for the Mercederian friar, Bartolomé de Olmedo, who was with Cortés, see Díaz del Castillo 1956, 40, 65; for the secular priest Juan Díaz, who was with Cortés, see Díaz del Castillo 1956, 65; and for Fray Pedro Melgarejo, who was with Cortés, see Díaz del Castillo 1956, 375.

30. Tozzer 1941, 304n234.

31. Pagden 1986, 332–34. See Elliott (2002, 99–102) for a description of why decisions concerning which clerics were to be involved in Mexico lay with the Spanish Crown and not the Pope.

32. Lopetegui and Zubillaga 1965, 188, 665.

33. Pagden 1986, 333 (translation is Pagden's).

34. Zavala 1973, 40–47.

35. Bull of Pope Alexander VI, cited in Bayle 1950, 4 (translation mine).

36. Lopetegui and Zubillaga 1965, 188, 665.

37. Bayle 1950.

38. Bayle 1950, 6 (translation mine).

39. Lopetegui and Zubillaga 1965, 666.

40. Kubler 1948, 20; Lopetegui and Zubillaga 1965, 665. Elliott (2002, 104) notes, however, that efforts to raise the standards of both the episcopate and the secular clergy actually began under Isabella in the late fifteenth century.

41. Kubler 1948, 20.

42. Kubler 1948, 18–21.

43. Kubler 1948, 19–20.

44. Phelan 1970, 77.

45. Farris 1984, 29n2.

46. Kubler 1970, 20.

47. Lopetegui and Zubillaga 1965, 511; Lopez de Cogolludo [1688] 1971, vol. 2, bk. 8, chap. 5, pp. 16–17.

48. Collins 1977, 237–38. Chuchiak (2000, 78) flags the year 1562: "After Landa's Inquisition, the Franciscans never again enjoyed the unlimited power they had enjoyed up until 1562."

49. Collins 1977, 239.

50. Lopetegui and Zubillaga 1965, 508, 511.

51. G. D. Jones 1989.

52. G. D. Jones 1989, 85.

53. Brown 1981; Cameron 1993; Fletcher 1997.

54. Thomas 1981, 353.

55. Eguíluz 1964; Phelan 1970, 61. See also Caso Barrera 1999, 158n14, who cites a document in the AGI in which the Franciscans, frustrated by occurrences of idolatry ("más indios idólatras") accuse the Maya of being incapable people without honor ("gente tan incapaz y sin honra").

56. Kubler 1948, 6.

57. Phelan 1970, 44.

58. Phelan 1970, 1.

59. Phelan 1970, 44.

60. Phelan 1970, 44.

61. Phelan 1970, 4–5.

62. Kubler 1948, 96, 232–38.

63. Livingstone 2000, 103.

64. Kubler 1948, 2.

65. Kubler 1948, 2; Lopetegui and Zubillaga 1965, 491–97.

66. The quote is from Kubler 1948, 15; Bataillon [1937] 1991; Zavala 1955.

67. Kubler 1948, 3.

68. Kubler 1948, 12–13; J. B. Warren 1985, 87 (merely refers to Quiroga's fame).

69. On the original, the full caption for this print reads, "Description, Situation & Vue De La Ville De Mexique, Des Deux Lacs Sur Lesquels Elle Est Batie, Du Grand Temple De Cette Ville, Des Sacrifices D'Hommes Qu'on Y Faisout, De L'Idole Des Mexicans, De Leurs Jeux, Divertis Semens, Costumes, Superstitions & Autres Usages Pratiquez Parmi eux."

70. These are but a few of the major Nahuatl-speaking ethnic divisions, all associated with different city-states, in the Valley of Mexico at the time of the Conquest. Sometimes the word "Nahua" is used, as a convenience, to apply to all peoples who speak Nahuatl. As one moves out of the Valley, however, languages other than Nahuatl were and are spoken, such as Otomí in the north. The Tarascans of modern Michoacan to the west, the second largest empire in Mesoamerica, also speak their own language,

Purépecha (Helen Pollard, personal communication, 2009; J. B. Warren 1985, 7). The term "Aztec" is most commonly used to refer to the people of the Valley of Mexico who fought against the conquistadors, but "Aztec" is not, properly speaking, an ethnic group. Like "Maya," it is an invention drawn from Spanish accounts, and relatively modern in usage. The Nahuatl-speaking group at the top of the hierarchy at the time of the Conquest was mixed, but largely Culhua-Mexica and Acolhua (Pollard 2005, 66; M. E. Smith 2003a, 4, 36, 164–65, 294n2).

71. Kubler 1948, 3–4; Foster 1973, 187.

72. Kubler 1948, 3–4.

73. Kubler 1948, 2–4.

74. Kubler 1948, 96.

75. Kubler 1948, 3; Phelan 1970.

76. Focused on Mexico are Kubler (1948), Phelan (1970), and Ricard (1966). For broader treatments, see Borges (1940), Canedo (1977), Lopetegui and Zubillaga (1965), and Sierra (1944).

77. Alexander and Kepecs 2005, 6–7.

78. Lara (2004, 1) describes New Spain as "the first theater of operations on the American continent for the event of the Contact."

79. I discuss the analytical tendency to treat Christianity as a monolith in Graham 1998a.

80. Bataillon 1991.

81. Livingstone 2000, 586–87; Stravinskas 1998, 287.

82. O'Malley (2000, 42) refers to Jedin (1946), who makes clear that reform of the church began in the late Middle Ages and continued into the eighteenth century. Jedin also affirmed the importance of the Council of Trent in church history (O'Malley 2000, 13).

83. See O'Malley 2000, 131–34 (quote at 134).

84. O'Malley 2000, 16–45.

85. O'Malley 2000, 42.

86. Cohn-Sherbok 1998; Farmer 1997; Hinnebusch 1973; Vicaire 1964.

87. G. D. Jones 1989; Sapper 1985.

88. Religious orders were not uncommonly in conflict with bishops and parochial clergy (O'Malley 2000, 124).

89. Phelan 1970, 45.

90. Livingstone 2000; Stravinskas 1998. A Conventual branch of the Friars Minor is still in existence (Stravinskas 1998, 437). They wear black tunic, white string around the waist, black cape and cowl, shoes, and hats. The Friars Minor wear a chestnut-colored habit with white rope around the waist and the cowl hanging from a short cape, sandals, but no hats. The modern Capuchins have beards, chestnut-colored habits, long and pointed cowl, sandals, no hats (Ghilardi 1969, 75).

91. Kubler 1948, 4–6.

92. Kubler 1948, 4–9.

93. Kubler 1948, 5–6.

94. The pointed cowl continues to be worn by modern Capuchin friars (Ghilardi 1969, 75).

95. According to Elliott (2006, 104), by 1517, "not a single Franciscan 'conventual' house remained in Spain," apparently owing to the reformist zeal of Archbishop Cisneros, a Franciscan and former confessor to Queen Isabella.

96. "Province" is probably one of the most confusing words in use in the contact-period literature, because it means different things in different contexts. In this case, it is an ecclesiastical term—an administrative district under the jurisdiction of an archbishop—but it can also refer to a civil/administrative territorial unit (see the glossary). It is associated with divisions of religious orders, and although these divisions are to a certain extent geographical, the jurisdiction over the religious is personal rather than territorial (see *the Original Catholic Encyclopedia*, s.v. "Provincial" and "Ecclesiastical Province").

97. Kubler 1948, 5–9.

98. Kubler 1948, 9.

99. Kubler 1948, 9.

100. Kubler 1948, 9.

101. Fernando Cervantes, personal communication, 2007.

102. Morales 1991, 75–81; Ricard 1966, 2.

103. Bataillon 1991.

104. Kubler 1948, 10; Phelan 1970, 46; Zavala 1955.

105. Kubler 1948, 10 (quotes in original).

106. Livingstone 2000, 147; see also O'Malley 2000.

107. Chuchiak, essay in author's possession. This information is in the original manuscript Chuchiak wrote for Cecil and Pugh's (2009) *Maya Worldviews at Conquest* volume, but a portion was left out of the published chapter, which was ultimately entitled "*De Descriptio Idolorum*" (Chuchiak 2009).

108. Chuchiak, essay in author's possession (see n. 107).

109. Tozzer 1941, 77n340; Scholes and Adams 1938.

110. Livingstone 2000.

111. Stravinskas 1998, 974.

112. Phelan 1979, 54; Ricard 1966, 57.

113. Ricard 1966, 57–58.

114. G. D. Jones 1989, 85, 266.

115. G. D. Jones 1989, 135–52, 214–24.

116. G. D. Jones 1989, 248–53, 266–67.

117. Bayle 1950, 6, 16, 103; Kubler 1948, 19; Ricard 1966.

118. Kubler 1948, 10.

119. Kubler 1948, 4.

120. Elliott 2002, 105.

121. Kubler 1948, 13.

122. Lippy, Choquette, and Poole 1992, 4.

123. Phelan 1970.

124. García Icazbalceta (1941, 38–39); Mendieta (1945, 152–57), in Phelan 1970, 61, 147n9.

125. Phelan 1970, 77.

126. Eguíluz 1964; Phelan 1970, 46–47.

127. Kubler 1948, 14–15; Lopetegui and Zubillaga 1965, 405.

128. Phelan 1970, 59–68.

129. Phelan 1970, 61.

130. G. D. Jones 1989.

131. Jones 1989, 42.

132. Jones 1989, 176–77, 221–23.

133. In Guatemala, the church sometimes held encomiendas. Ecclesiastics could be encomenderos on a personal basis or as a result of their duties, although there are few cases of encomiendas by ecclesiastical persons individually. Religious who had control of encomienda Indians are said to be exceptional, and only spanned the first few years of the Conquest (Rodríguez Becerra 1977, 142–43). They also seem generally to have been seculars rather than regular clergy.

134. "Individualism" is defined in the *Oxford English Dictionary* as, "Self-centred feeling or conduct as a principle; a mode of life in which the individual pursues his own ends or follows out his own ideas; free and independent individual action or thought; egoism," and in the *American Heritage Dictionary* as, "Belief in the primary importance of the individual . . . ; Acts or an act based on this belief; A doctrine advocating freedom from . . . regulation in the pursuit of a person's . . . goals; . . . that the interests of the individual should take precedence over the interests of the state or social group."

135. It does happen, however, that the way an individual experiences Christianity can be believed by the individual to represent the way the group should be behaving. Thus, St. Francis used his experience to reform Christianity, so that his behavior became the Rule of the group. Still, this is not an argument for individualism, because experiencing being Christian is what allows the individual to share in something from which he would otherwise be excluded. It does not in any way bolster separatism or the primacy of the individual.

136. Paul was an apostle in the sense that he was a missionary of the early church, but he was not an Apostle, one of the twelve disciples of Jesus.

137. Krautheimer 1986, 23.

138. Krautheimer 1986, 24–25.

139. Brown 2003, 173–74, 200, 388, 422.

140. McLuhan and Fiore 1967.

141. G. D. Jones 1989, 28, 41–44.

142. G. D. Jones 1998, 32 39.

143. G. D. Jones 1998, 38.

144. G. D. Jones 1998, 30.

145. G. D. Jones 1998, 35.

146. G. D. Jones 1998, 37.

147. G. D. Jones 1998, 55, 59.

148. G. D. Jones 1998, 59.

149. Lippy, Choquette, and Poole 1992, 31.

150. Pagden 1986, 332, 334.

151. Hanke 1935.

152. Kubler 1948, 15–16; Zavala 1973.

153. G. D. Jones 1989, 60.

154. G. D. Jones 1998, 266, 321n30.

155. Canedo 1952, 508; Tozzer 1941, 82n345.

156. Canedo 1952, 497–98.

157. G. D. Jones 1989, 60, chap. 1.

158. See Kubler 1948, 20.

159. We have archaeological evidence of the blind sanctuary at Tipu; the blind sanctuary at Lamanai is inferred from less conclusive evidence.

160. Luís de Villalpando, Melchor de Benavente, and Juan de Herrera (Canedo 1952, 496; Tozzer 1941, n. 306).

161. Canedo 1952, 496–500.

162. Canedo 1952, 500.

163. G. D. Jones 1989, 42, 60, 85.

164. G. D. Jones 1989, 85.

165. G. D. Jones 1989, 86–91; Rodseth and Parker 2005.

166. G. D. Jones 1989, 85, 214–15.

167. G. D. Jones 1989, 135–52.

168. G. D. Jones 1989, 176–77.

169. Lopez de Cogolludo [1688] 1971, vol. 2, bk. 9, chap. 5.

170. Lopez de Cogolludo [1688] 1971, vol. 2, bk. 9, chap. 5 and bk. 12, chap. 16.

171. Lopez de Cogolludo [1688] 1971, vol. 2, bk. 12, chap. 16.

172. Sapper 1985, 28–30.

173. G. D. Jones 1989, 214–24; see also Bracamonte y Sosa 2001, esp. 102–28, 196–204, 213–19.

174. G. D. Jones 1989, 224–26.

175. G. D. Jones 1989, 248–49.

176. G. D. Jones 1989, 249, 328n16.

177. G. D. Jones 1989, 265–66.

178. G. D. Jones 1989—e.g., 134, 215, 264–67.

179. G. D. Jones 1989, 144.

180. G. D. Jones 1989, 153.

181. G. D. Jones 1989; 1998.

182. G. D. Jones 1998.

183. G. D. Jones 1989, 265–66.

184. Altman and Lockhart 1976, 29.

185. Kubler 1948, 15–16.

186. Hunt 1976, 34; Restall 1997, 313.

187. Restall 1997, 224.

188. See Graham 2006a, Graham 2008b, and Graham and Golson 2006 for discussions of the nature and implications of pre-Columbian tribute systems.

189. Restall 1997, 312–13.

190. Lockhart 1992, 13–14; Restall 1997, 13.

191. In some circumstances, more than one *cah* (pl. *cahob*) became part of an encomienda (Restall 1997, 313).

192. Quezada 1993, 38–41, 59–60, 157; see also Farris 1984, 163.

193. G. D. Jones 1989, 1998.

194. Palka 2005.

195. Alexander and Kepecs 2005, 6.

196. Ricard 1966.

197. Bracamonte y Sosa 2001; G. D. Jones 1998, 2005.

Chapter 7. How to Tell a Church

1. Sources and definitions for terms under discussion can be found in the glossary. The main sources I have used for church terminology are A. P. Andrews 1991; Livingstone 2000; the glossary in McAndrew 1965 (653–64); and Taylor 2004.

2. The term "open chapel," or *capilla abierta*, was first used by Manuel Toussaint (McAndrew 1965, 340; Toussaint 1927). It has since become standard in the literature (e.g., Bretos 1987; García Granados 1935; Lara 2004, 17–39; McAndrew 1965, 340–524). McAndrew (1965, 340, 718–20nn) provides examples of the early sources for use of *capilla de indios*. Kubler (1948, 326–27), like me, finds the term problematic.

3. A. P. Andrews 1991, 366.

4. E.g., McAndrew 1965.

5. A. P. Andrews 1991, 355.

6. García and Gussinyer 2004, 98.

7. E.g., A. P. Andrews 1991; Artigas 1983; Bretos 1987; García Granados 1935; García y Gussinyer 2004; McAndrew 1965.

8. See A. P. Andrews, Benavides C., and Jones 2006 for a description of the presbytery at Ecab.

9. A. P. Andrews 1991; García and Gussinyer 2004.

10. E.g., Artigas 1983; Bretos 1987; and especially García Granados 1935.

11. A. P. Andrews 1991, 365–66.

12. C. A. Hanson 1990, 1995; Gallareta, Andrews, and Schmidt 1990, 35.

13. A. P. Andrews 1991, 360.

14. YDL (Yglesia de Lamanai) I and YDL II refer to the first (earlier) and second (later) churches at Lamanai.

15. For the "ramada church" at Tamalcab, see A. P. Andrews 1991, 360–61, fig. 17-2; for Ecab, see A. P. Andrews, Benavides C., and Jones 2006, 26, and fig. 2-17. For Xlacah, see Gallareta, Andrews, and Schmidt 1990, 35. Cárdenas Valencia (1937, 111) describes both flat and vaulted roofs.

16. McAndrew 1965.

17. Lara 2004, 21.

18. McAndrew 1965, 340.

19. Toussaint 1927.

20. Bretos 1987, 2; García Granados 1935.

21. See A. P. Andrews, Benavides C., and Jones 2006, 19.

22. See quote from Motolinía in McAndrew 1965, 340.

23. But only if the choir occupies the east end of the nave or a space near the altar; I use "chancel" here in the old sense of a screen that delimits the choir.

24. García and Gussinyer 2004; Gussinyer 1999.

25. See Toussaint 1927; García Granados 1935; and McAndrew 1965.

26. McAndrew 1965, 202–3, 205, 375, 204 (fig. 89).

27. See Kubler 1948, 325.

28. McAndrew 1965, 368, 388.

29. McAndrew 1965, 387–88.

30. Lara 2004, 21–23; McAndrew 1965, 236–46.

31. Folan 1970.

32. A. P. Andrews 1991, 364.

33. Folan 1970, 182.

34. A. P. Andrews 1991, 368; Folan 1970.

35. McAndrew 1965, 520.

36. A. P. Andrews 1991, 368.

37. A. P. Andrews 1991, 368.

38. Although the climate in Yucatan has been described as "rarely intemperate, and rain almost never fell before noon even during the wet seasons" (E. Wyllys Andrews in Folan 1970, 183).

39. A. P. Andrews 1991, 366; Bretos 1987; García Granados 1935. See also Lara 2004, 21.

40. Kubler 1948, 326–27.

41. Kubler 1948, 327.

42. Kubler 1948, 326.

43. Bretos 1987, 1.

44. The sacristan was in charge of the paraphernalia of the Mass, and the *maestro cantor* was the choirmaster. See "sacristan" and "maestro de capilla" in the glossary.

45. Krautheimer 1986, 24, 26, 40.

46. Krautheimer 1986, 29.

47. Livingstone 2000.

48. See A. P. Andrews, Benavides C., and Jones 2006, 19. Etymology suggests that "sanctuary" developed to refer to the space, and "presbytery" to refer to the users of the space.

49. Livingstone 2000.

50. See the *Original Catholic Encyclopedia*, s.v. "chancel," online at http://oce.catholic .com/.

51. Livingstone 2000; Taylor 2004, 28. See also *Encyclopaedia Britannica*, s.v. "chancel," online at http://search.eb.com/eb/article-9022373.

52. Livingstone 2000.

53. McAndrew 1965, 520, where he quotes from vol. 2, pp. 397–98 of Father Ponce.

54. McAndrew 1965, 519.

55. García Granados 1935, 9–11.

56. A. P. Andrews 1991, 360; A. P. Andrews, Benavides C., and Jones 2006, 19; McAndrew 1965, 141.

57. E.g., Graham, Pendergast, and Jones 1989.

58. McAndrew 1965, 598.

59. A. P. Andrews 1991, 361, fig. 17-2.

60. Cardenas y Valencia 1937, 110–11.

61. McAndrew 1965, 533.

62. Taylor 2004, 20.

63. See discussion in Livingstone 2000, 118–19.

64. Livingstone 2000, 110.

65. McAndrew 1965, 134–35.

66. McAndrew 1965, 340–597.

67. McAndrew 1965, 131.

68. McAndrew 1965, 203–9.

69. McAndrew 1965, 281.

70. See also Breto (1987, 1) for a description of the missionary assemblage in New Spain in the sixteenth century.

71. McAndrew 1965, 205.

72. McAndrew 1965, 206.

73. McAndrew 1965, 348.

74. McAndrew 1965, 348.

75. McAndrew 1965, 131.

76. McAndrew 1965, 342.

77. McAndrew 1965, 133.

78. McAndrew 1965, 342.

79. McAndrew 1965, 207.

80. McAndrew 1965, 342.

81. McAndrew 1965, 519–20.

82. McAndrew 1965, 520.

83. McAndrew 1965, 519.

84. McAndrew 1965, 342.

85. McAndrew 1965, 340, although McAndrew does not provide an example of a sixteenth-century source in which *capilla de indios* is used. He notes, however, that Kubler disagrees with his interpretation of the origin of the term *capilla de indios*, as I have described earlier in this chapter.

86. Livingstone 2000, 110.

87. McAndrew 1965, 655.

88. McAndrew 1965, 340.

89. McAndrew 1965, 346.

90. McAndrew 1965, 207; Cárdenas y Valencia, in McAndrew 1965, 519; Cárdenas y Valencia 1937, 110–11, 114.

91. McAndrew 1965, 205–9.

92. Krautheimer 1986, 23–43.

93. McAndrew 1965, 206.

94. McAndrew 1965, 206.

95. McAndrew 1965, 655.

96. McAndrew 1965, 133, 520.

97. McAndrew 1965, 235–36.

98. McAndrew 1965, 385, 404.

99. A. P. Andrews 1991, 365.

100. A. P. Andrews 1991, 365.

101. Artigas 1983.

102. Artigas 1983, 245.

103. A. P. Andrews 1991, 365.

104. A. P. Andrews 1991, 365–66.

105. A. P. Andrews 1991, 366, fig. 17-7.

106. A. P. Andrews 1991, 366.

107. Bretos (1987a), in A. P. Andrews 1991, 366.

108. McAndrew 1965, 340.

109. A. P. Andrews 1991, 364–69.

110. A. P. Andrews 1991, 366–67.

111. G. D. Jones 1989, 67.

112. Roys 1952, 149, in A. P. Andrews 1991, 368–69, fig. 17-9.

113. Benavides Castillo and Andrews 1979, 37, in A. P. Andrews 1991, 366.

114. Toussaint 1927.

Chapter 8. The Churches at Tipu and Lamanai

1. The time it takes to wash clothes is almost halved at Negroman as compared to Lamanai.

2. "Tipu" is rendered as "Tipuj" in the orthography for the writing of Mayan languages

approved by the Academy of Mayan Languages of Guatemala (AMLG) (G. D. Jones 1998, xiii). However, the name first appeared in the literature as "Tipu," and because so much of what I write about is concerned with sixteenth-century thought and events, I have adhered to the orthography developed in the sixteenth century.

3. G. D. Jones 1989, 6, 9.

4. J. E. S. Thompson 1972, 1977.

5. Jones, Kautz, and Graham 1986.

6. Graham, Jones, and Kautz 1985.

7. Jacobi 2000, 86.

8. Graham 1991, 2008a; Graham and Bennett 1989; Reynolds 1985.

9. Cohen et al. 1994, 1997; Danforth 1993; Danforth et al. 1985; Danforth, Jacobi, and Cohen 1997; Jacobi 2000; Wrobel, Danforth, and Armstrong 2002.

10. Emery 1990, 1999.

11. Aimers 2004, 2008; Cecil 2001, 2004; Foor 1994; Lambert et al. 1994; Simmons 1991, 1995; Simmons, Pendergast, and Graham 2009; M. T. Smith, Graham, and Pendergast 1994; E. W. Wilson 1991.

12. Graham, Pendergast, and Jones 1989; Pendergast, Jones, and Graham 1993.

13. Castells 1904; Pendergast 1981, 31; Pendergast 1982b, 62, 64.

14. Lopez de Cogolludo [1688] 1971, vol. 2, bk. 9, chap. 6, p. 213.

15. Blaeu 1665; Montanus 1671; Sanson 1650, 1670; Visscher 1717 (probably copy of Montanus).

16. See also Pendergast 1988b for a Blaeu map of 1640 with Lamanay on the mainland.

17. Loots 1717, map by van DeCust.

18. J. E. S. Thompson 1972, 10.

19. In the way Maya languages are written, the single apostrophe represents a glottal stop. Barbara MacLeod first suggested this reading (see Pendergast 1981, 32 and n. 9).

20. Pendergast 1981, 1982a, 1982b, 1986a, 1986b, 1991, 1993.

21. In 2004, Scott Simmons of the University of North Carolina at Wilmington became co-Principal Investigator at Lamanai.

22. Graham 2008a; Pendergast 1991, 1993.

23. G. D. Jones 1989.

24. Restall 1997, 20–21, 172.

25. E.g., Graham 1991; Graham, Pendergast, and Jones 1989; Pendergast 1993.

26. "Cache" is a term used in archaeology to refer to a special deposit of some kind, usually hidden from view; see the glossary for details.

27. G. D. Jones 1989; Scholes and Thompson 1977; J. E. S. Thompson 1972, 1977.

28. G. D. Jones 1989.

29. G. D. Jones 1989, 4.

30. See Thomas 1981, 17–24, for an excellent discussion of the problems in integrating approaches from history and archaeology.

31. Scholes et al. 1936–38; Chamberlain 1948; J. E. S. Thompson 1977; Roys 1943; García Bernal 1972; Hunt 1976; Clendinnen 1987a; Farriss 1984.

32. Restall 1997, 8–9.

33. E.g., Roys 1939.

34. Burns 1983; Christenson 2007; Hanks 1990; Bricker 1981; Edmonson 1986; Okoshi 2009; Restall 1997; P. C. Thompson 1999.

35. Restall 1997.

36. Spaniards resident in Belize occasionally turn up in the documentation. E.g., a

Spanish "servant" and a "mulatto" appear to have been living at Soite (on what is now called the Sittee River) in 1630 (G. D. Jones 1989, 202).

37. G. D. Jones 1989; Restall 1997.

38. G. D. Jones 1998, 420.

39. G. D. Jones 1989, 55–91.

40. Jacobi 2000, 86.

41. Restall 1997, 18, 217.

42. Restall 1997, 83.

43. G. D. Jones 1982; G. D. Jones 1989, 101–6.

44. G. D. Jones 1989, 103.

45. G. D. Jones 1989, 106; Restall 1997, 173, 186–87.

46. G. D. Jones 1989, 6. See also Rodseth and Parker 2005 on the study of frontiers.

47. Caso Barrera 1999, 156; G. D. Jones 1989; Restall 1997.

48. Our term "Maya" for the native people of Yucatan was not an identity they recognized. Individuals identified with their community and with family or kinship groups that cross-cut communities (Restall 1997, 2, 13–50). Therefore, in pre-Columbian times, two Maya groups who spoke the same language could conceivably have seen each other as foreign. Nahuatl speakers or Maya groups from outside the lowlands might also have been seen as foreigners by communities in the Belize region, depending on the nature and time-depth of interregional ties and kin relationships.

49. Restall 1997, 288.

50. Restall 1997, 173, 259.

51. G. D. Jones 1989.

52. G. D. Jones 1989, 44.

53. Restall 1997, 52, 104, 181.

54. Graham 1991, 323–24, 328.

55. Peñalosa 1969, 70; Ricard 1966, 98.

56. The term "bush" is used today to refer to forested landscapes outside towns and villages; the Spanish term is *monte*.

57. In the new orthography, this is Tz'ul Winikob' (G. D. Jones 1998, 3).

58. For Dzuluinicob as a "province," see G. D. Jones 1989, 5, 10, and esp. 98; as the name of the New River, see G. D. Jones 1989, 95; as "foreign people," see G. D. Jones 1998, 3, 427n2.

59. Restall 1997, 24–26.

60. Tipu does not appear on a tribute list for 1544, but it is recorded as an already established encomienda town in 1568, which indicates that it had functioned as part of an encomienda for some time. This, plus what is now known about the extent of the Pacheco conquest, suggests strongly that Tipu was brought into the encomienda system not long after the Pacheco conquest (G. D. Jones 1989, 17, 44, and esp. 51).

61. G. D. Jones 1989, 277–91.

62. Oland and Masson 2005.

63. Pendergast, Jones, and Graham 1993, 62.

64. D. Z. Chase and A. F. Chase 1988; 2001, 41.

65. Scholes and Thompson 1977, 44–45, map 2-1.

66. Pendergast, personal communication, 1980.

67. G. D. Jones 1989, 13.

68. G. D. Jones 1983, 13; Pendergast 1975.

69. G. D. Jones 1989, 13.

70. G. D. Jones 1989, 14.

71. In 2006 Rhan-ju Song discovered the remains of another building, Str. H12-19, that lies on the west side of the plaza, more or less opposite Str. H12-12.

72. G. D. Jones 1989, 67.

73. G. D. Jones 1989, 286.

74. G. D. Jones 1982, 284; 1983, 85–87.

75. G. D. Jones 1989, 104.

76. Melchor Pacheco's encomienda was reassigned to the Crown in 1553 (G. D. Jones 1989, 45).

77. G. D. Jones 1989, 44–45.

78. G. D. Jones 1989, 44–45.

79. G. D. Jones 1989, 45.

80. G. D. Jones 1989, 45, discusses Bienvenida's observations and data on population loss in the province of Salamanca de Bacalar.

81. G. D. Jones 1989, 45.

82. Pendergast 1986b, 1.

83. Pendergast 1993, 120.

84. Graham 2008a.

85. Pendergast, personal communication, 2008.

86. G. D. Jones 1989, 45–46; Restall 1997, 3.

87. Juan de Aguilar was sent to Chanlacan by Francisco de Montejo the Nephew to quell the rebellion. His *probanza* is dated 1566 (see G. D. Jones 1989, 46, 302n37).

88. G. D. Jones 1989, 46, 302n7.

89. G. D. Jones 1989, 47–53.

90. G. D. Jones 1989, 49.

91. G. D. Jones, personal communication, 2006.

92. Lopez de Cogolludo [1688] 1971, vol. 2, bk. 9, chap. 7.

93. G. D. Jones, personal communication, 2006.

94. G. D. Jones 1989, 51.

95. Pendergast 1993, 119–23.

96. McAndrew 1965, 25–29.

97. G. D. Jones 1989, 51.

98. Chuchiak 2009.

99. G. D. Jones 1989, 18.

100. G. D. Jones 1989, 107. According to Farriss (1984, 233), *ahcambezah* or *ahcamzah* (chief teacher) were also used.

101. Farriss 1984, 335–36, 341.

102. G. D. Jones 1989, 140.

103. G. D. Jones 1989, 18, 132.

104. G. D. Jones 1989, 132.

105. YDL II was excavated in 1974–76; YDL I in 1976, 1983, 1985; the "rectory," Str. N12-12, in 1975–76, 1983; the historic residential community in 1984; the second cemetery in 1985.

106. As Archaeological Commissioner for the Government of Belize in 1977, I attempted to convince Pendergast to keep "Indian Church" as the name of the site, because that is what everyone called it. At that time, if one referred to "Lamanai," people thought the reference was to "Limonal," another place entirely.

107. See Pendergast 1975.

108. Pendergast 1985; 1986b, 4; 1993.

109. Pendergast 1986b, 4.

110. Pendergast 1986b, 4.

111. Funding was provided by a grant from the U.S. State Department's Ambassador's Fund for Cultural Preservation to the National Institute for Culture and History in Belize, through the Belize Institute of Archaeology and under the direction of Jaime Awe and John Morris as part of the Lamanai Historic Monuments Conservation Project (LHMCP), and by a grant from FAMSI (Foundation for the Advancement of Mesoamerican Studies, Inc.) to Elizabeth Graham (see Awe 2007; Graham 2008a).

112. Graham 2008a.

113. Graham 2008a.

114. See also Graham 2008a, fig. 24c.

115. Thomas Gann was a medical doctor-turned-archaeologist who worked in Belize in the early part of the twentieth century and spent his leisure hours excavating Maya ruins. He published a number of books on his excavations. Hamilton Anderson, Belize's first Archaeological Commissioner, knew Gann and recounted to David Pendergast that Gann had the habit of leaving his assistant in charge of excavating, for sometimes as much as month, and would return only periodically to examine the finds (Pendergast, personal communication, 2009). This may well explain the vague contextual information for the artifacts recovered through Gann's activity.

116. This date is based on the catalogue entry for the collections of the National Museum of the American Indian in Washington D.C., which states that a stela from Indian Church was presented by Gann to the museum when it was in New York City.

117. Gann 1926, 64.

118. Pendergast 1986b, 4.

119. Pendergast 1986b, 6.

120. Lopez de Cogolludo [1688] 1971, vol. 2, bk. 11, chap. 13; G. D. Jones 1989, 214–44.

121. Gann 1926, 64–65; Pendergast 1986b, 5.

122. Gann 1926, 64.

123. Passages describing the decorated stela are from Gann 1926, 65.

124. Gann 1926, 64–65; Pendergast 1986b, 5.

125. The stela Gann reported seems to have been removed by him and ultimately found its way to the Museum of the American Indian—the Heye Foundation, when the museum was still in New York City. When the MAI collections were transferred to the Smithsonian Institution in Washington, D.C., however, between 1999 and 2004, the stela was found to be missing (Patricia Nietfield, personal communication, 2008).

126. The card also says: "Collected by Thomas Gann. Presented by James B. Ford" (National Museum of the American Indian, Smithsonian Institution, Santa Rita and Lamanai, Belize Collections, Cat. No. 9/1818, barcode: 091818.000, object ID: Stela Representing Serpent Head; the date of acquisition is 1 January 1919).

127. Pendergast 1986b, 5.

128. Gann 1926, 64–65.

129. John 2008 discusses the iconography of the Postclassic and early colonial period.

130. The catalogue card from the National Museum of the American Indian reads: "Pottery Jar Representing Fish with Mouth Open and human head inside. Traces of red and blue painted decoration. In this jar were found specimens 9/1595–9/1602. Indian

Church, British Honduras. Collected by Thomas Gann, Presented by James B. Ford." The square-shaped shell artifact, Cat. No. 9/1594, may have been reworked after it was excavated.

131. Pendergast 1986b, 5.

132. Pendergast 1986b, 4.

133. Lothrop 1924; Sanders 1960; Vargas 1997.

134. Pendergast 1981, 52.

135. Pendergast 1981, 52.

136. Pendergast 1993.

137. Graham 2008a.

138. Graham 2008a.

139. See McAndrew 1965, 202–31.

140. McAndrew 1965, 211.

141. McAndrew 1965, 209–10, from Mendieta, 3:156–57.

142. Pendergast 1986b.

143. Simmons, Pendergast, and Graham 2009.

144. G. D. Jones 1989, 214–15, 321n30.

145. Wiewall 2009.

146. Pendergast 1986b, 2.

147. The village has since moved to a new location outside the reserve.

148. Pendergast 1991, 1993.

149. G. D. Jones 1989, 43–53.

150. Graham, Pendergast, and Jones 1989, 1256.

151. Columbia Plain is the type of pottery recovered (Deagan 1987, 56–57).

152. My description of the excavation of the sanctuary is based on the field notes of Kevin Baxter, 1980. Baxter suggests in his notes that the area in front of the altar was probably raised above the area south of the altar, but he also states that the line of stones dividing the two areas was no higher than the third step of the landing. This, as well as the fact that the area north of the altar was accessed from the landing, led me to err on the side of caution and suggest that the area in front of the altar was at the same floor level as the area to the south. There isn't all that much room in front of the altar, and given that the priest needed to interact with those who served Mass, both giving and receiving various objects, it is likely that the servers, probably boys from the community, stood in the area to the south of the altar, and if so, a change in floor level here would have been awkward. On the other hand, the evidence does not totally rule out such a change in level, and if excavations of other churches provide such evidence, it is unlikely that Tipu is the exception.

153. McAndrew 1965, 353; Paine 2008.

154. Paine 2008, 6; Welsh 1951. The oldest portable altar known was found on the chest of St. Cuthbert when his coffin was opened in 1827 in Durham Cathedral. In that case, the portable altar was a seventh-century oak tablet, but by the Middle Ages the portable altar was normally stone (Paine 2008, 4, 6).

155. McAndrew 1965, 353.

156. McAndrew 1965, 354.

157. McAndrew 1965, 353.

158. McAndrew 1965, 355.

159. G. D. Jones 1989, 220–21. Jones refers to "boxes containing the friars' ornaments and clothing," and I assume these can also be described as small chests.

160. The feature is not shown in the reconstruction drawing, owing to the difficulties of depicting it at the small scale required for publication.

161. These excavations were directed by Rhan-ju Song.

162. G. D. Jones 1989, 139; Lopez de Cogolludo [1688] 1971, vol. 2, bk. 9, chap. 6, p. 217.

163. Reynolds 1985.

164. A. P. Andrews 1991, 366–67.

165. McAndrew 1965, 25.

166. McAndrew 1965, 130.

167. Edgerton 2001.

168. Phelan 1970, 49.

169. Edgerton 2001, 1–4; McAndrew 1965, 130.

170. See Graham 2008a, figs. 14, 15.

171. Pendergast 1981.

172. The YDL I platform appeared to have rounded corners, and there are too few stones left from the wall to indicate the original form the wall took at the west end. The reconstruction as apsidal is speculation.

173. Jacobi 2000, 86.

174. Cohen et al. 1994, 123.

175. Pendergast 1986b, 4.

176. Pendergast 1981, 52.

177. Taylor 2003, 35.

178. A lacetag is a short, hollow rod with tapered ends and, often, cotton fibers attached, to wrap loose ends of clothing (Martinón-Torres et al. 2007).

179. M. T. Smith, Graham, and Pendergast 1994, 34, fig. 6 and plate IIIA.

180. M. T. Smith, Graham, and Pendergast 1994, plate IVC.

181. M. T. Smith, Graham, and Pendergast 1994, plates IIC, IIIB, IVA–B.

182. A thurible is a censer or incense burner of the type shown in figs. 6.2 and 8.28.

183. Lambert et al. 1994.

184. With regard to the metal artifacts from Tipu, which have been recovered from both burials and middens, Michael Wayman from the University of Alberta performed an initial study in the 1980s. Analysis has since been resumed by Bryan Cockrell (2009) and is ongoing at the time of writing. Preliminary results as reported by Cockrell, Martiñon-Torres, and Graham (2010) indicate that, despite technological consistencies, the objects exhibit variety. Of the objects so far analyzed, e.g., some needles (4 out of 9) and all bells (13) reflect indigenous practices, whereas other needles (5 out of 9) as well as the lacetags reflect European technology. What have been termed "rings" for the purposes of analysis subsume different kinds of ornaments, including earrings, but so far suggest a largely European origin, although one ring form has indigenous American parallels.

185. The figure shows a lock plate from Str. H12-7, but it is very similar to the lock plate found in the grave context; see also examples in Pendergast 1993 (131, fig. 8), and Burr 1964 (figs. 129, 185).

186. Pendergast 1981, 52; 1993, 129–31, fig. 8.

187. Pendergast 1993, 128; M. T. Smith, Graham, and Pendergast 1994, 33.

188. M. T. Smith, Graham, and Pendergast 1994, 25.

189. M. T. Smith, Graham, and Pendergast 1994, 33, 43–44. See also Hancock and Graham 2004.

190. Jacobi 2000, 186–88.

191. Cohen et al. 1994, 125.

192. Cohen et al. 1994.

193. White, Wright, and Pendergast 1994.

194. Emery 1999, 76; White and Schwarcz 1989; White, Wright, and Pendergast 1994.

195. White, Wright, and Pendergast 1994.

196. G. D. Jones 1989, 46.

197. Brew 1994, 31, 45–56; Graham 1998, 35.

198. Pendergast 1993, 110.

199. G. D. Jones 1989, 67.

200. Pendergast 1986b, 4.

201. G. D. Jones 1998.

202. Reynolds 1985.

203. Pendergast 1986b, 2.

204. G. D. Jones 1989, 67.

Chapter 9. Reductions and Upheaval in the Seventeenth Century

1. G. D. Jones 1989, 18, 132.

2. G. D. Jones 1989, 132.

3. Chuchiak 2003, 221–33.

4. Chuchiak 2003.

5. G. D. Jones 1989, 196.

6. Chuchiak 2003, 232–33.

7. Lopez de Cogolludo [1688] 1971, vol. 2, bk. 9, chaps. 5–10.

8. G. D. Jones 1989, 135–54.

9. G. D. Jones 1989, 135.

10. See Caso Barrera 1999.

11. G. D. Jones 1989, 137.

12. See G. D. Jones 1989, 136, for details.

13. An expedition under Fray Juan de Santa María in the region of Champoton and Tixchel in 1604 carried several silver chalices decorated with jewels; two wooden tables to serve as altars; two silk cloths to adorn the front of the altars; two larger silk *corporales* to cover the altar stops; two small iron bells; two crosses, one fixed on an iron pole and another, smaller one to rest on the altar; two new missals; two breviaries; one book of Scriptures; a Book of Saints; a book to aid in the taking of confessions and administering penance; and a book on the rule of St. Francis (Chuchiak 2003, 226–27). One wonders if the "two wooden tables" included an ara, or portable altar, or whether the tables were supports for consecrated portable altars, which would be kept only by the friars and would not constitute gifts.

14. G. D. Jones 1989, 139.

15. G. D. Jones 1989.

16. Restall 1997, 62–64; G. D. Jones 1989, 139.

17. G. D. Jones 1983, 77.

18. Graham 1987.

19. Restall 1997, 28; Roys 1957, 40–53.

20. G. D. Jones 1983, 77.

21. G. D. Jones 1989, 139.

22. G. D. Jones 1989.

23. Scholes et al. 1938, 25–34. See also Lopetegui and Zubillaga 1965, 398–400.

24. G. D. Jones 1989, 134, 152.

25. G. D. Jones 1989, 152.

26. G. D. Jones 1989, 145–46.

27. G. D. Jones 1989, 18, 148–49.

28. G. D. Jones 1998.

29. G. D. Jones 1989, 149.

30. G. D. Jones 1989, 18–19.

31. G. D. Jones 1989, 159.

32. G. D. Jones 1989, 159–63.

33. In G. D. Jones 1989, 180.

34. G. D. Jones 1989, 159–80.

35. G. D. Jones 1998, 48–49.

36. G. D. Jones 1989, 185–86.

37. G. D. Jones 1989, 187.

38. G. D. Jones 1998, 51.

39. Restall 2003 explores the complexities of the Spanish conquest.

40. G. D. Jones 1989, 197.

41. Chuchiak 2003, 238.

42. G. D. Jones 1989, 17–18, 197–98.

43. G. D. Jones 1989, 199.

44. G. D. Jones 1989, 203; G. D. Jones 1998.

45. G. D. Jones 1989, 201.

46. G. D. Jones 1998.

47. G. D. Jones 1989, 205.

48. G. D. Jones 1989, 205.

49. G. D. Jones 1989, 206.

50. See Restall 1997.

51. G. D. Jones 1989, 207 8.

52. G. D. Jones 1989, 210.

53. G. D. Jones 1989, 214–15.

54. Chuchiak 2003, 239. This is consistent with what has been said about Gregorio de Aguilar, but it is not clear in Chuchiak whether the criticism of the seculars comes from Franciscan or government sources.

55. G. D. Jones 1989, 215.

56. This was YDL II.

57. G. D. Jones 1989, 216.

58. G. D. Jones 1989, 216–17.

59. G. D. Jones 1989, 217–18.

60. G. D. Jones 1989, 219–220.

61. G. D. Jones 1989, 221–22.

62. G. D. Jones 1989, 222–23.

63. G. D. Jones 1998, 49, 52–54.

64. G. D. Jones 1989, 225. In this case, the Manche Chols asked to become Christian. They were given the choice of a patron saint from among the three "images" Tejero brought with him, St. Michael the Archangel, St. Jerome, and St. Francis. The word "image" is in Jones's translation; presumably these were pictures, although I wondered if they could have been small statues.

65. G. D. Jones 1989, 226–27.

66. G. D. Jones 1989, 230.

67. Scholes and Thompson 1977.

68. G. D. Jones 1989, 230–40.

69. Zacatan, Zaczuz, Mayapan, Holpatin, Lucu, Chanlacan, Chinam, Xibun, Soite (G. D. Jones 1989, 236). For Zacatan, Zaczuz, Holpatin, Lucu, Chanlacan, and Soite, see map 9.1. Xibun is not marked, but was situated somewhere along the Sibun (Xibun) River (map 9.1). Chinam is believed to have been located where the Rio Hondo empties into Chetumal Bay (G. D. Jones 1989, 66). Mayapan (other than the one in Yucatán) was among the Belize encomiendas, but its location is not known (G. D. Jones 1989, 194).

70. G. D. Jones 1998, 54–55.

71. G. D. Jones 1989, 235.

72. G. D. Jones 1989, 245–48.

73. G. D. Jones 1989, 250–59.

74. See G. D. Jones 1989, xiv–v, map 1.

75. G. D. Jones 1989, 259.

76. G. D. Jones 1989, 259–68.

77. G. D. Jones 1998, 112–13.

78. G. D. Jones 1989, 265.

79. G. D. Jones 1989, 259–67.

80. G. D. Jones 1998, 228–29.

81. G. D. Jones 1989, 269; G. D. Jones 1998.

82. It took many years for the Spaniards to adjust to Peten and to establish a presence there, but that they persisted, if in small numbers, is attested by the fact that some *cofradias* in Yucatan supplied beef to military posts (*presidios*) in Bacalar and Peten in the eighteenth century (Restall 1997, 186).

83. G. D. Jones 1998, 419.

84. G. D. Jones 1989, 14.

85. G. D. Jones 1989, 270–72; G. D. Jones 1998, 408–12.

86. G. D. Jones 1989, 272–73; 1998, 408, 411, 417, 418–21.

87. Simmons 1991, 1995.

88. G. D. Jones 1998, 408.

89. Graham 2004.

90. Pendergast 1986b, 5.

91. Pendergast 1988a, 322.

92. Pendergast 1986b, 5–6.

93. Pendergast 1986a, 243–44. Archaeologists know these censers as Chen Mul Modeled.

94. Pendergast 1982b.

95. Pendergast 1985, 2.

96. Pendergast 1982b.

97. Yaeger et al. 2005.

98. Pendergast 1988a, 322.

99. Wiewall 2009. Work on the material culture of the British period can be found in Mayfield 2009.

100. G. D. Jones 1989, 273.

101. Bolland 1977, 25–26; Shoman 2000, 16–17.

102. G. D. Jones 1989, 271.

103. G. D. Jones 1994.

104. G. D. Jones 1994.

105. G. D. Jones 1994, 14.

106. G. D. Jones 1994, 14.

107. E.g., Dobson 1973, 68–70.

108. Dobson 1973, 68–70.

109. Graham 2004; Pendergast 1986b.

110. G. D. Jones 1989, 271–72; G. D. Jones 1998.

111. J. E. S. Thompson 1977, 30–33.

112. J. E. S. Thompson 1977, 9–10.

113. J. E. S. Thompson 1977, 32, plate 1-9.

114. See Graham 1996. See Whitehouse and Wilkins 1986 for the concept of urbanism as a set of relationships; and Graham 1996 for application to the humid tropics.

115. Bolland 1977, 7.

116. Pendergast 1988a, 322.

117. Pendergast 1986, 4.

Chapter 10. What Europe Did for Us

1. The term "theaters of conversion" is from Edgerton 2001.

2. Hart-Davis 2000. The name of the TV program was taken from the Monty Python film *Life of Brian*, specifically from the scene in which the People's Front of Judaea ask, "What did the Romans ever do for us?"

3. Cervantes 1994, 32–33.

4. Hamilton 1990, 96; Sawyer and Sawyer 1993, 229.

5. Brown 2003, 467.

6. Not all explorers or religious in Mesoamerica took this view; on Columbus, Cortés, and the Spanish Jesuit José de Acosta, e.g., see Cervantes 1994, 10–11, 25–26.

7. Cervantes 1994, 126.

8. Cervantes 1994, 21.

9. Cervantes 1994.

10. Cervantes 1994, 20–21.

11. Cervantes 1994, 19–21.

12. Thomist philosophy is clearly much more complex than this, but St. Thomas's belief that the natural and supernatural realms were joined by God's being, and that humans participated in God's being through reason and faith (Cervantes 1994, 22), can be seen to be at odds with the Franciscans' emphasis on spirituality. As Cervantes observes, "The nominalist tendency to separate nature and grace made the realm of 'the supernatural' much less accessible to reason, thereby enhancing the attributes of both the divine and the demonic" (Cervantes 1994, 24-25).

13. Cervantes 1994, 24.

14. Cervantes 1994, 20–25. Cervantes also discusses a change of emphasis over time from a moral system based on the seven deadly sins throughout most of the medieval period, to the authority of the Decalogue, or Ten Commandments, beginning in the late medieval period (20, 24).

15. See Reents-Budet 1994, 278–79, fig. 6.50.

16. Cardós de Méndez 1998, 593.

17. Muchembled 2004, 40.

18. Muchembled 2004, 40.

19. See Battistini 2005, 156–65; Giorgi 2003, 2005; Link 1995; Muchembled 2004; A. Wilson 2002.

20. Muchembled 2004, 23.

21. Muchembled 2004, 18.

22. See Muchembled 2004, 18–19, 22–23.

23. Kelly 2006, 148–49, 238.

24. Link 1995, 166, fig. 71.

25. Giorgi 2005, 75.

26. Muchembled 2004, 18.

27. Constantinou 2007.

28. Constantinou 2007.

29. Constantinou 2007, 4.

30. Muchembled 2004, 76–78; as in *A Scene of Sorcery*, by David Teniers the Younger, 1633, in Douai, *Musée de la Chartreuse*.

31. Giorgi 2005, 89.

32. Giorgi 2005, 89.

33. Giorgi 2005, 233.

34. Giorgi 2005, 97, as in *Saint Philip before the Idol*, ca. 1385, by Giusto de' Menabuoi, a fresco in Padua, Basilica del Santo.

35. Clendinnen 1987b, 230–31.

36. Megged 1995, 66.

37. Belting 1994, 460.

38. As elucidated in chapter 1, "Other" is used here in the anthropological sense of the construction of (usually cultural) others, persons who are part of a group that is not one's own.

39. Giorgi 2005, 241.

40. D. E. Thompson 1960.

41. Burkhart 1989; Cervantes 1994, 40–41.

42. The concept of sin, too, which is often associated in Christianity with influence of the devil, did not exist in Maya belief (see Chuchiak 2000, 451–54).

43. Chuchiak 2005; Clendinnen 1987a; Scholes and Roys 1938.

44. Chuchiak 2005.

45. Chuchiak 2005, 620.

46. Scholes and Roys 1938.

47. Chuchiak 2005, 626n1.

48. Chuchiak 2005, 628.

49. Chuchiak 2005, 628.

50. My thanks to Joel Palka and Jon McGee for their help in suggesting various words for objects that might have been considered "idols." See also P. M. Rice 1996a, 130.

51. Auel 1980.

52. Alcock 2003, 319, 327, 329; Nees 1978, 3–8. Tessa Robinson, who is carrying out research on knot symbolism among the Classic Maya, steered me to these sources.

53. Küng 2001, 136.

54. Chuchiak 2005, 613; G. D. Jones 1989, 176, 265–66.

55. Mayr-Harting 2001, 45.

56. Muchembled 2004, 12. Muchembled here refers specifically to the Fourth Lateran Council in 1215, which is said to provide the doctrinal basis for belief in the devil. But see also Kelly 2006, 316.

57. I refer the reader also to chapter 3, where I base my arguments on information from the first centuries of Christianity and earlier Judaic beliefs.

58. Cameron 1993; Brown 1993.

59. Herrin 1987, 90–127.

60. Herrin 1987, 126.

61. Herrin 1987, 250–90.

62. Herrin 1987, 476.

63. Herrin 1987, 477.

64. Herrin 1987, 477.

65. Herrin 1987, 477–78.

66. See, e.g., Brown 1993; Freeman 2002; Pelikan 1971.

67. Pagels [1979] 2006, 152.

68. Pagels [1979] 2006, 69, 163.

69. Pelikan 1971, 349–57.

70. Brown 1993, 98–99.

71. Küng 2001, xviii. Küng notes that authority is still challenged, even within the church.

72. Fletcher 1977.

73. Fletcher 1977, 64.

74. Fletcher 1977, 2.

75. Kubler 1948, 66.

76. Pelikan 1971, 11.

77. E.g., J. C. Russell 1994.

78. *Pace* Clendinnen 1987b.

79. J. C. Russell 1994.

80. Fletcher 1997, 9.

Chapter 11. Being Pagan

1. Clendinnen 1987b, 238.

2. Chuchiak 2005, 627.

3. Chuchiak 2005, 627.

4. Fletcher 1997, 3–4.

5. See Chuchiak 2005, 226–27.

6. G. D. Jones 1989, 139.

7. Vega [1744] 1974. This reference was kindly provided by Kay Tarble and Franz Scaramelli.

8. Reff 2004, 17–18.

9. Chuchiak's extensive documentary research tells us that caves retained their significance (2000, 424), and that the Maya "adapted images of saints to their own sacred geography by placing the legends and stories of the saints into the context of their own sacred landscape" (Chuchiak 2000, 448).

10. Ricard 1966.

11. G. D. Jones 1998, 2005.

12. Wilk 2006, 6–7.

13. Morrison 1990, 416.

14. Weeks and Black 1991, 251.

15. Early 2006; Klor de Alva 1982.

16. Ingham 1989, 1.

17. Graham 1998a.

18. Bloom 1980, 59; Giorgi 2005, 294.

19. Bloom 1980, 54.

20. Giorgi 2005, 301.

21. Bloom 1996, 37–53; Browning 2004, 16; Livingstone 2000, 22.

22. Giorgi 2005, 282.

23. Giorgi 2005, 282.

24. *Dogma* 1999.

25. Giorgi 2005, 301–3.

26. Marnell 1978.

27. St. Francis is said to have preached to the birds (Farmer 1997, 193).

28. Luke 16:19–31.

29. Browning 2004, 226–27; Delaney 1980, 351.

30. Farmer 1997, 138.

31. Giorgi 2003, 107.

32. Farmer 1997, 416.

33. Delaney 1980, 381; de Voragine 1993, 23–26; Farmer 1997, 327, 333; Giorgi 2003, 236, 246.

34. Weeks and Black 1991, 251.

35. Fletcher 1997, 11–12; Giorgi 2003, 36, 119, 121, 149.

36. Delaney 1980, 235; Farmer 1997, 193.

37. Christian 1981, 96, fig. 4.

38. Christian 1981, 95–96.

39. See J. C. Russell 1994; or Brown 1981, 27.

40. Brown 1981, 12.

41. Geary 1994a, 41.

42. For an exception, see Chuchiak 2009.

43. A novena is a nine-day period of devotion. It can comprise nine consecutive days or devotion once a week for nine weeks, the latter of which is more familiar to me. Novenas are generally undertaken for a favor, and are often dedicated to a particular saint. The practice originates in the seventeenth century, but the number, nine, is said to come from the time Mary and the Apostles waited for the coming of the Holy Spirit, between Ascension and Pentecost (Farmer 1997, 407; Stravinskas 1998, 715).

44. Brown 1981, 7.

45. Geary 1994a, 36; J. C. Russell 1994, 36.

46. Geary 1994a, 42–43.

47. Geary 1994a, 37–38.

48. Geary 1994a, 37.

49. Geary 1994b, 184.

50. Geary 1994b, 184–85.

51. Scholes and Roys 1938, 595.

52. Geary 1994a, 41.

53. See Cervantes 1994.

54. Farriss 1984, 336.

55. Farriss 1984, 320–51.

56. Brown 1981, 29.

57. See Geary 1994b, 177.

58. Brown 1981.

59. Livingstone 2000, 512.

60. Brown 1981, 3.

61. Brown 1981, 3.

62. Brown 1981, 5.

63. Geary 1994b, 184–85.

64. Krautheimer 1986.

65. Belting 1994, 298.

66. Danforth et al. 1985.

67. Brown 1981, 31.

68. McAnany 1995.

69. Martin and Grube 2008.

70. See Farriss 1984, 334.

71. Farriss 1984, 310; Sharer 2006, 726.

72. Farriss 1984, 309.

73. Farriss 1984, 265.

74. Livingstone 2000, 251.

75. Leonard 1987, 135.

76. Classen 1998. According to Geary (1994a, 44), medieval religion "was not believed but danced."

77. McGee, personal communication, 2008. See also McGee 1990, 1998.

78. Belting 1994, 6.

Chapter 12. Everyone Knows What a Dragon Looks Like

1. Williams 1976.

2. G. D. Jones 1982.

3. White, Wright, and Pendergast 1994.

4. Species of reef-dwelling fish show up at Tipu in historic middens.

5. Morrison 1990.

6. Browning 2004, 57, 342; *Catechism of the Catholic Church* 1997, 30–31.

7. *Catechism of the Catholic Church* 1997, 30.

8. *Catechism of the Catholic Church*, 300–301, 882.

9. *Catechism of the Catholic Church*, 299–301.

10. Brown 1981, 2–7.

11. Ward 1987, 9.

12. "Magic" is difficult to define. Scholars interested in religion have engaged in many attempts to distinguish between magic and religion. See, e.g., Cunningham's (1999) survey of the development of the study of the sacred in modern disciplines, in which he describes a number of approaches (by sociologists, historians, and anthropologists, among others) in which the term "magic" is distinguished with respect to "religion." As I see it, "magic" as a concept is rooted in attempts to label the prayers or supplications or rituals of an "other." Use of the word "magic" gained in status and frequency with the rise of Christianity because it was used to describe practices that were not Christian. Tambiah (1990) suggests that "magic" as an analytical category is tendentious and historically embedded, although he originally put quotation marks around these two descriptors, which I have omitted. The quote from Tambiah is: "When we have acquired some appreciation of these historical and contextual circumstances, we shall not only

better understand the epistemological and philosophical debates of the past, but also comprehend why we have to confront today the question whether or not the categories of magic, science and religion may be 'tendentious' and their analytical value rendered suspect by their historical 'embeddedness'" (Tambiah 1990, 2).

13. Tambiah, as described in Cunningham 1999, 68.

14. I have been criticized for using this term, but it should not be seen to detract from being effective in scholarly research. Being childish is undesirable, but being childlike can be an advantage in adulthood, particularly with regard to recognizing the importance of sensory experience.

15. Classen 1998.

16. Williams 1976.

Glossary of Terms

The sources for church terminology are the *Original Catholic Encyclopedia* (*OCE*), Livingstone (2000), and Stravinskas (1998). Other sources used: the *American Heritage Dictionary* (*AHD*), the *Oxford English Dictionary* (*OED*), Andrews (1991), Taylor (2004), and glossaries in Farris (1984), Jones (1989), McAndrew (1965), Ramirez (1989), Restall (1997, 1998, 2004), and Thompson (1999).

alcalde (Sp.): Justice, magistrate, or judge in Indian town government; the administrator of a *cabildo*, or town council.

alcalde mayor (Sp.): A provincial governor; Spaniard.

alguacil (Sp.): Constable or bailiff; the word may be derived from a Mayan term.

altar: In its most general sense, an altar is an elevated feature that serves as a ritual focus in religious ceremonies. The Hebrew word for "altar" in the Bible comes from a word that means "to slaughter" for sacrifice. In the early church, the Eucharist was celebrated in homes on a table, a practice that persisted when churches first became permanent and altar tables, often of wood, were put in place for the liturgy and then removed. (We find that portable altars were the practice at Tipu and Lamanai and presumably in all the Belize missions. This must partly reflect convenience, but can also be seen as part of the return to the primitive church.) As Christian communities grew in size, the meal dimension of the Eucharist diminished in importance, and the sacrificial dimension took on greater importance in the fourth century. At that time, fixed stone or metal altars came into use. This is ascribed to the decline of paganism, in that it became possible to use permanent altars without "having pagan associations confuse the faithful. Thus, the danger no longer existed that the unique Sacrifice of Christ would be perceived as the same as the many animal sacrifices of the Temple in Jerusalem or those of the pagans" (Stravinskas 1998, 57). In the Maya lowlands, of course, fixed altars of the Christians would bear strong resemblance to altars used in pre-Columbian rituals. Even the later practice in the Christian world of associating relics with altars would have parallels in Maya practices, in which rulers' tombs lay in the cores of platforms on which altars were placed, and ceremonies held.

In the early church, the altar was free-standing, and in Rome, churches were built with the doors facing east. From the fifth century onward, the custom was to have the apse and the altar face east, and the altar was placed against the apse wall. This held true until Vatican II (1965–68), when the practice reverted to that of the early church, with the altar free-standing to serve as a table around which the clergy and people can gather.

If altars are attached to the floor and are immovable, they must be consecrated by a bishop. Movable altars are simply blessed. Today, movable altars no longer need to enclose relics, and although since 1977 relics are no longer required to be part of fixed altars, the practice of enclosing relics in or under the altar is nonetheless recommended (Stravinskas 1998, 57). Placing relics in altars was an important part of late medieval practice, but we do not know if the movable altars used at Tipu and Lamanai included relics, although I expect this would have been important to the friars. On the other hand, having relics in altars would have increased the parallels with pre-Columbian practices, which the friars would have wanted to avoid.

The sources differ in one important point on why relics became important to the church and associated with altars. They agree that it probably derived from the fact that early Christians often celebrated the Eucharist at martyrs' gravesites. But Stravinskas (1998, 57) states that although the celebration involved the gravesite, it did not take place on the tomb, whereas Livingstone (2000, 17) asserts that the custom of celebrating the Eucharist on the tombs of martyrs led to the introduction of stone altars. This is an important point which is discussed in more detail in the text, but the association of inhumations of honored individuals with an elevated feature (altar) that served as an important focus of ritual is a common feature of both Maya and Christian religious practice.

ara (Latin): A portable altar stone or slab symbolically representing Christ.

artifact: An object or material modified in some way by humans.

audiencia (Sp.): High court.

auto de fé (Sp.): Act of ecclesiastical sentencing, or the resulting punishment.

Aztec: A term applied by the Spaniards to one of the Nahuatl-speaking groups, the Mexica-Culhua, who were the most powerful of the rulers of the empire that dominated Mesoamerica at the time of Spanish contact. "Aztec" is often used, however, to describe all the Nahuatl-speaking ethnic groups that comprised the empire. *See also* Nahua.

batab (Yucatec Mayan): Head of a *batabil*, a Maya political unit of governance; in the colonial period, Spaniards used the term *cacique* to refer to the head of a pueblo, and later, *gobernador*.

batabil (Yucatec Mayan): A political unit of governance, headed by the *batab*; comprised several *cuchteelob*.

benefice, or beneficio (Sp.): An ecclesiastical office, no longer in existence as a Catholic institution, which carried certain obligations and was also a source of income for the office holder. The most common example was a parish. (Stravinskas 1998, 138).

brigantine: According to the *AHD*, a two-masted sailing ship, square-rigged on the foremast and having a fore-and-aft mainsail with square main topsails.

cabecera (Sp.): Head town of a Spanish administrative district.

cabildo (Sp.): Town or village council.

cache: "Cache" is a term used in archaeology to refer to a special deposit of some kind, usually hidden from view. Caches are common at Maya sites of all periods, under floors or surfaces (of patios, plazas, houses, civic buildings, palaces, temples) or in benches, under altar stones, stelae, beneath stairs, or within doorways, and often lie along the primary or transverse axis of structures. A cache could have been an offering, and sometimes this interpretation is proposed, but there are just as many cases in which we cannot be certain.

cacique: Derived from one of the Caribbean languages, the term was adopted by the Spaniards to refer to a hereditary lord or chief throughout New Spain. In Yucatan, it referred to the principal leader of an Indian community, who could be a batab or other community leader.

cah (Yucatec Mayan): Town, community, pueblo, place of residence. *Ah cahnal* means *cah* member or resident.

canon: A member of a chapter of priests serving a cathedral; or, a member of a religious community living under a rule that serves a cathedral. All canons have taken Holy Orders—that is, all are priests and can say Mass. Not all friars are priests, and it appears that not even all clerics are priests. So what distinguished a canon in Yucatan would have been that he could say Mass and was part of a chapter of priests serving a cathedral.

capitulación (Sp.): An agreement or pact.

Carmelite order: This is the Order of the Brothers of Our Lady of Mount Carmel (near the port of Haifa, in Israel) and dates from the late twelfth century. Their original Rule established ca. 1208 was austere. By the mid-thirteenth century, some had migrated to Europe and founded the order there in 1247. Communities of women were formally incorporated in 1432. Like the Franciscans and Dominicans, the Carmelites effected reforms in the fifteenth century in reaction to the decline in religious observance of the later Middle Ages. Today, there are several branches of Carmelite orders, including Carmelite Friars of the Ancient Observance, and Discalced Carmelite Friars, who were inspired by St. Theresa of Avila (1515–82). The records do not state the affiliation of the Carmelite friar who accompanied Montejo I in 1528, but he probably pre-dated the Teresian reforms.

caye (cay): Pronounced as the English "key." Refers to a small coral island. The *AHD* says from the Spanish "cayo," probably from the Taino language of the Caribbean.

cédula (Sp.): Certificate or document. A royal cédula (Real Cédula) is a Royal Decree.

chalice: The cup used to contain the wine consecrated in the Eucharist.

chancel: Like many church terms, the meaning of chancel has changed through time. It has come to refer to the space around the altar which is reserved for those who officiate at Mass, a space now generally called the sanctuary. This space around the altar has also been called the presbyterium, or presbytery, because it refers to the part of the church reserved for the higher clergy (presbyters). In the past, chancel referred to the part of the choir (the stalls or the space where the clergy were positioned who sang or chanted during Mass) that was near the altar, and not to the whole area around the altar as it does now. The English word chancel comes from the Latin *cancellus*, Old French *chancel*, which refers to latticework, because a lattice or railing was used to separate the chancel from the rest of the church.

chantre (Fr.): In English, a precentor, who is either the cleric responsible for the direction of the choral services in the cathedral, or he is a minor canon or chaplain.

chapter: A chapter is a corporate ecclesiastical body. The term originally applied only to a conventual or monastic assembly—that is, a group living under a rule, and in Yucatan this would have been the chapters of the Franciscan order. However, through time it eventually came to be applied to analogous assemblies of other ecclesiastics, such as the secular clergy.

chibal (Yucatec Mayan): Members of a chibal share the same patronym. Restall has this to say about the chibal (plural *chibalob*):

Within a given cah, members of a chibal . . . formed a kind of extended family, most of whose members seem to have pursued their common interests wherever possible through political factionalism, the acquisition and safeguarding of land, and the creation of marriage-based alliances with other chibalob of similar or higher socioeconomic status. Such marriages were in part necessary because chibalob were exogamous, a principle that seems to have been applied across cah lines, although after the conquest there was no formal organization of chibal members beyond the cah level (Restall 1997, 17).

choir: Strictly speaking, the part of the church where the stalls of the clergy are. The choir can occupy a position in the east nave; it can be behind or in front of the altar; or it can be in the center of the nave. In the earliest churches there was no architectural choir (that is, stalls); the sanctuary was joined to the nave and the choir was simply the east part of the nave, where it was fenced off by *cancelli* (refer to "chancel"). I believe that this was the case with the second church at Lamanai.

chrismatory: A small vessel for keeping the three kinds of holy oil used in Christian rituals: oil of the catechumens; oil of the sick; and chrism, which is a mixture of olive oil and balsam.

cleric (or member of the clergy): *Clergy* refers to the body of people ordained for religious service; a *cleric* is a person who has been received into the ranks of the clergy or ecclesiastical hierarchy, and to whom clerical privileges have been extended. As part of the ecclesiastical hierarchy, clerics must receive the *tonsure* and wear clerical dress. Clerics can be regular or secular clergy.

cofradía (Sp.): Parish confraternity dedicated to the veneration of one or more saints.

congregation or congregación (Sp.): Policy of resettlement of scattered, small communities; or gathering individuals together who have fled communities into larger village or town units. Also known as reduction/*reducción*. Both processes were at work, in that many communities were reduced to one community in which the previously scattered population was congregated.

consecration: This term refers to the setting aside of a person or an object exclusively for the service of God.

convent or convento (Sp.): The building in which a body of religious live together. It can also refer to the religious community itself. In the sixteenth- and seventeenth-century documents, it is the common term used to refer to the building built by the friars for their residence in Mexico and Yucatan (we have no evidence yet of convents in Belize). In English modern usage, "convent" has come to refer to the domicile of women.

core: The body of material, usually stones and earth, which forms the heart of a platform or other construction unit.

curate: A cleric, especially one who has charge of a parish; its roots lie in the Latin word for *care*; a curate can also be someone who assists a rector or vicar.

diezmo (Sp.): A tithe paid to the church of 10 percent.

Divine Office: The name of the official, public, daily liturgical prayer (worship) by which the church sanctifies the hours of the day. It is recited at stated times, which differentiates it from other liturgical services. In the Catholic church this prayer is now called the *Liturgy of the Hours*. In the Church of England the traditional Offices were combined into Morning and Evening prayer (Mattins and Evensong). Monastic Offices were more complex, with recitation at least seven different times during the day and night—for example, Vespers in the evening and Compline as the last Office before retiring for the night. The friars in Mexico, Yucatan, and Belize would have recited a shorter version of the Divine Office, developed in the twelfth century. Where a conventual church was not present, as in the Belize missions, it is assumed that the Divine Office would have been recited in the church.

doctrina (Sp.): There is no good English equivalent for this Spanish term. A doctrina seems to be the same as a parish or a curate, except that the term "doctrina" subsumes a group of people, all of whom know or need to be taught Christian doctrine, whereas "parish" comes from a word meaning "neighbor" or "neighboring," and "curate" comes from the root "to heal." All of these—doctrina, curate, and parish—can apply to the same church subdivision, but each seems to have derived from one of the functions the church was supposed to serve: "doctrina" from teaching, "curate" from healing, and "parish" reflects a term for those who live near one another.

doctrine: A principle or body of principles presented for acceptance or belief by a group. From Latin *doctrina*, from *doctor*, teacher, from *docere*, to teach.

dogma: A doctrine or corpus of doctrines set forth by a church; an authoritative principle, belief, or statement of ideas especially considered to be true. From the Greek, opinion, belief, from *dokein*, to seem or to think.

encomienda (Sp.): In Belize (as part of Yucatan), encomiendas entailed grants of Indian labor, service, and tribute. After the Maya revolts of 1546–47, however, the Crown removed labor and service from the encomienda. In Yucatan, it appears that only service was prohibited, as the result of the efforts of the oidor of the Audiencia of Guatemala, Tómas López, in 1552. We therefore assume that encomiendas in Belize continued to entail both tribute and labor obligations.

encomendero (Sp.): The Spanish overlord who was entitled to tribute or labor from his encomienda(s).

entrada (Sp.): The Spaniards' first entry into an area; usually dominated by the military component.

episcopal, episcopacy: The system of church governance by bishops is known as the "episcopacy." Therefore, reference to episcopal authority is a reference to the authority of the bishops. It is from this authority that the Mendicant orders were exempt at particular junctures in history (Livingstone 2000, 193; Stravinskas 1998, 382).

Eucharist: The word means "thanksgiving." Other names are Holy Communion, the Lord's Supper, or the Mass. The Eucharist conveys to the worshiper the Body and Blood of Christ. The *OCE* defines Eucharist as "the name given to the Blessed Sacrament of the Altar under its twofold aspect of sacrament and Sacrifice of the Mass, and in which, whether as sacrament or sacrifice, Jesus Christ is truly present under the appearances of bread and wine."

Extreme Unction: A rite or ritual that in modern times is also called the "Anointing of the Sick" and is intended for those who are seriously ill or dying. It can include rites of penance as well as a special rite of Communion for those who are about to die. The definitions provided by Stravinskas (1998, 757–58) for this rite are confusing more than enlightening. Livingstone (2000, 594) is more helpful in telling us that "unction" is the anointing with oil as part of a religious ritual, usually by a bishop or priest. The word is most commonly applied to the sacrament of the Unction, or Anointing of the Sick, in which case the illness is serious enough that death might ensue, hence the adjective "Extreme."

falca (Sp.): As used in the contact period, the term for a small boat of a type that often served as a river ferry.

friar: A member of one of the Mendicant orders founded in the Middle Ages. Derived from the Latin *frater*, "brother," via Old French *frere* and Middle English *fryer*. A friar is not tied to a particular monastic community that is secluded from the world, as is a monk, although friars share many of the religious observances associated with monasticism, such as prayer and ascetisim (renunciation of marriage, home, personal property; fasting and deprivation). Friars lead a more itinerant life and are active in communities, and of course are bound by the distinctive commitments of the Mendicant Rule.

friary: The term "friary" usually refers to a house or residence of one of the branches of the Franciscan orders. The Dominicans use the term "priory" for their residence. In the evangelization of Mesoamerica, we do not see either of these terms used. Instead, "convent" is employed to refer to the building in which the religious live.

governor: *see* batab

halach uinic (Yucatec Mayan): Translates into English as "true man"; regional or chief ruler; it was the highest Maya office in Yucatan at the time of the Conquest, and after the Conquest was used to refer to the Spanish provincial governor.

indios (Sp.): A term sometimes used in colonial sources to refer to the Maya or other indigenous inhabitants.

Late Antiquity: Refers to a period of time that bridges Classical Antiquity (ca. the fifth century A.D.) and the Early Middle Ages (A.D. 500 to A.D. 1000). The term "late antiquity" has been used by German historians since the late nineteenth century but is also known through the work of Peter Brown (1981, 20).

maestro de capilla (Sp.): Master of the chapel; also known as *maestro cantor,* choirmaster, or *maestro de escuela,* and in Yucatec Mayan as *Ah cambesah.*

Mazdaism: A reference to religions of dualism that can be traced back to Zarathustra, or Zoroaster, a Persian prophet who lived from about 628 to 551 B.C. Ahura Mazda was the one true God, although spirits were said to exist who were inferior to the One (Russell 1977, 104–5; *Encyclopedia Britannica,* s.v. "Zoroaster," http://search .eb.com/eb/article-9078456).

Mendicant orders: The term is based on the Latin *mendicare,* which means "to beg." Those who join these orders give up the right to own possessions, and "depend completely upon God's providence and the alms of the faithful" (Stravinskas 1998, 665). The Franciscans (founded by St. Francis of Assisi, 1181–1216) and Dominicans (founded by Domingo Guzmán, 1170–1221) are Mendicant orders, as are the Augustinians (founded in 1256) and Carmelites (late twelfth century). As shown by the founding dates of these orders, the late twelfth to early thirteenth centuries were a critical period in the life of the church, when many rebelled against the church's opulence and accumulation of wealth. Through time, the Mendicant prohibition against holding revenue-producing properties, and indeed against all corporate ownership of property, weakened. In fact, it was rebellion against this laxity in the fifteenth century that produced the Orders whose members evangelized Mexico, Yucatan, and Belize.

Mesoamerica: The regions of Middle America in which urban civilizations developed. This includes central Mexico (Valley of Mexico) southward and eastward to Yucatan, all of Guatemala and Belize, and the western portions of Honduras and El Salvador.

Mexico: In the text, the term "Mexico" almost always refers to central Mexico and excludes Yucatan, Oaxaca, Tabasco, and Chiapas.

midden: A word commonly used in archaeology to mean the accumulation of refuse, rubbish, or garbage.

missal: In the Roman Catholic Church a missal is a book that contains the prayers said by the priest at the altar and the responses necessary for participating in the Mass throughout the year. The word seems to derive from the Late Latin word *missa,* for "Mass."

mission: In its most basic meaning, the propagation of the faith among non-Christian peoples; the term has also been applied to the physical establishments involved in such propagation.

monolater: A worshipper of one god.

monastery/monasticism/monks: "Monastery" was originally the term for the cell or cluster of cells in which a hermit lived. It has come to refer to the dwelling place of a community of men or women who live in seclusion. Those who live in monasteries lead a life of contemplation and recite the Divine Office in common. "Monasticism" is meant to refer to those who withdraw from society to devote themselves totally to God through prayer, penance, and solitude. In one kind of monasticism, the monk or nun lives by himself/herself as a hermit; in the other, monks or nuns live in a community. Although the Mendicant friars who proselytized the New World borrowed practices from monasticism, such as personal poverty and devotion to God and prayer, they were not monks and, strictly speaking, they did not live in monasteries, because they did not maintain seclusion and instead preached and worked actively in the community. However, monasticism was very important in the conversion process in Late Antiquity in Europe because monks were largely responsible for conversion of the Celts, Germans, and other cultural groups in Europe. The Benedictines, established in the early sixth century by Benedict of Nursia, are an example of a monastic community that spread widely in Europe.

monte (Sp.): Forest and other vegetation in unoccupied or lightly occupied territory.

Nahua: A term sometimes used to describe all the people who spoke and still speak the Nahuatl language. It can be applied to the ethnic groups that composed the Aztec empire as well as to those who outlived the empire.

naturales (Sp.): A term sometimes used in colonial sources to refer to the Maya or indigenous inhabitants.

neotropical: New World tropics.

New Spain: In the literature of concern in this book, New Spain usually refers to central Mexico, and is therefore differentiated from Yucatan or Honduras or Guatemala. Later on, it came to include all land north of the Isthmus of Panama under Spanish control as well as the Caribbean possessions, and even later, what are now parts of the United States and the Philippines.

-ob (Yucatec Mayan): Makes terms plural.

Observants: Those members of the Franciscan Order who choose to observe the Rule of St. Francis with no relaxation.

parroquia (Sp.): Clergy of a parish; parish church.

payolel (Chontal Mayan): Refers to a political entity, translated as "jurisdiction" (Izquierdo 2006, 161).

Polyglot Bible: Contains text in several languages. Issued especially in the sixteenth and seventeenth centuries.

prebendary: A member of the clergy who is the holder of a portion of a cathedral benefice, or endowment.

presbytery: Stravinskas (1998, 807) defines "presbytery" as the part of the church set aside for the exclusive use of the clergy. Livingstone (2000, 465) holds that it refers to the sanctuary or eastern part of the chancel of a church, beyond the choir. Both say that "presbytery" can also refer to the residence for the priest or clergy, although this is apparently a Roman Catholic practice. (For reasons explained below under "rectory," I have chosen to use "rectory" for the priest's residence.) Because "presbytery" derives from a reference to people and their authority (presbyter, or elder) rather than to a designated space, I largely refrain from using it except in circumstances where the meaning is clear.

presidio (Sp.): A fortified settlement, generally including a permanent military garrison.

priest: The priest or presbyter is an ordained minister of the church. His role is to offer sacrifice—that is, the priest acts in the person of Christ in the sacrifice of the Mass, where he joins the offerings of the faithful to Christ's sacrifice. Priests are consecrated to preach the Gospel, instruct and attend to the faithful, and to celebrate the Mass. Not all friars were ordained as priests. However, it seems clear that among the friars who evangelized the Maya communities in Belize, many if not most were priests.

principal (Sp.): A member of the native elite.

probanza (Sp.): A record of merits and services made by an individual.

province: A group of dioceses, normally territorially contiguous, which forms an ecclesiastical unit. According to one source, the term arises because such groups of dioceses were originally coincident with the provinces of the Roman Empire (Livingstone 2000, 472). The term can also refer to a territorial division of the houses of religious institutions, such as the Franciscan and Dominican Orders. The "provincial" in this case refers to the official in charge of the province. He would exercise authority over all houses of the Order within a particular area.

The term "province" is used very loosely in the literature on the Spanish colonial period, and it is often difficult to know what it is meant to delineate. For example, it is applied to what were thought by the Spaniards to be pre-Columbian political units, but there is no equivalent concept in Yucatec. It is also used in referring to Spanish territories governed as administrative or political units, as in the case of the Bacalar province, but it is not used consistently to apply to territorial entities across New Spain or Yucatan.

ramada (Sp.): A thatch-roofed structure.

rectory: Strictly speaking, this is the residence of a priest, or "rector," who is entrusted with the care of a church that is neither a parish church nor a church attached to a religious community. Nonetheless, because it is the term we all used for our parish priest's residence where I grew up, it was the first term to come to mind for the structures that abutted the north side of the churches when we excavated Tipu and Lamanai. Therefore, the term "rectory" is used in the archaeological reports. The house where the clergy of a parish live can also be called a "presbytery," although I have avoided this term for a particular reason (*see* presbytery). According to Stravinskas (1998), the common term for the priest's residence in the United States is "rectory."

reduction (*see* congregation)

regidor (Sp.): Councillor or member of a *cabildo*.

regular clergy: A general term for members of the clergy who take religious vows, live in a community, and follow a rule. Strictly speaking, regulars are those who take solemn vows (or who have made solemn profession) as opposed to simple vows, but there are exceptions. The term comes from the fact that regulars follow a particular Rule, such as the Rule of St. Benedict or the Rule of St. Francis. Regulars stand in contrast with the secular clergy, who comprise priests living in the world. The Mendicants are classed as regular clergy, whereas parish priests, such as the individuals assigned to Salamanca de Bacalar, were secular clergy.

religious: As a noun, it refers to any member of what are now, since Vatican II, called Religious Institutes, in which individuals live consecrated lives. Religious Institutes, or "religious," comprise any religious order, society, or congregation in which members take public vows of poverty, chastity, and obedience, and live the common life. A detailed description of the "Religious Life" can be found in the *OCE*, where religious and seculars are clearly distinguished (see sec. C on "Religious Life and the Sacred Ministry"). Secular Institutes of consecrated life also exist. Opus Dei is a good example of a modern Secular Institute in which members dedicate themselves to the sanctification of the world while living in it (Stravinskas 1998, 730; Livingstone 2000, 414–15).

repartimiento (Sp.): A form of advance payment made by Spaniards to the Maya, usually in the form of money, raw materials, or European imports, in the expectation of delivery of a specified local product, such as wax, honey, cotton cloth, or maize. The payment had to be made within a specified time period. This was an exploitative system, and technically illegal. It peaked in the latter half of the seventeenth century, when it was controlled primarily by colonial governors and their employees (Jones 1989, 296n26).

requerimiento (Sp.): A legal formula summoning the Indians to allegiance to the Crown of Castile and acceptance of Christianity. It was to be read to the Indians by interpreters before warfare began. No Indians were to be enslaved unless they refused to heed this requerimiento, because enslavement was contingent on "just, legal and necessary war" (Chamberlain 1948, 23).

residencia (Sp.): Judicial process applied to former colonials. If someone stands residencia, it appears that he checks to see that the person formerly in the office did not embezzle funds or use them illegally.

sacristan: The person who has charge of the contents of a church, including the vestments and sacred vessels.

sacristy: A room that is annexed to a church, in which sacred vessels and vestments are kept for use in the Mass.

sambenito (Sp.): A garment worn by a penitent convicted by the Inquisition.

secular clergy: The seculars make no profession—that is, they do not take the kinds of vows which the regular clergy take—and do not follow a Rule, but instead live in the world. The secular cleric can possess his own property, and practices celibacy. He owes obedience to the bishop, and as a cleric (member of the clergy), he is part of the ecclesiastical hierarchy. He is not a member of a religious order.

templo (Sp.): The term can refer to a Catholic church as well as to a place of worship that is associated with a religion other than Christianity.

thurible: A metal vessel for the ritual burning of incense, or what archaeologists would call a censer. It is usually suspended on chains and is swung to spread the smoke. The Tipu "thurible" is not metal, but it has the form of a thurible and is blackened on its interior.

tonsure: The rite by which an individual is received into the clerical order. It involves shearing the hair (not always practiced) and investment with the surplice, which is the tunic worn by all clergy and the official priestly dress of the lower clergy.

Tridentine: Having reference to the Council of Trent.

vargueño (Sp.): A portable wooden chest, usually fitted to serve as a desk.

vecino (Sp.): As used in the documents, a householder or citizen and usually, but not always, referring to a Spanish inhabitant.

vestry: Another word for "sacristy."

villa (Sp.): A town that serves as a local seat of government.

visita (Sp.): A town or village that is part of a *doctrina*, or parish. The term comes from the fact that the town had no resident priest and had to be visited by the parish priest or priests. "Visita" can also refer to a tour of towns by a church or civil official who is specially appointed to check on the accounts, records, and activities of other officials.

References Cited

Acosta, José de. 1962. *Historia natural y moral de las Indias.* Mexico City: Edmundo O'Gorman. First published 1590.

Aimers, James J. 2004. *Cultural Change on a Temporal and Spatial Frontier: Ceramics of the Terminal Classic to Postclassic Transition in the Upper Belize River Valley.* BAR International Series, no. 1325. Oxford: Archaeopress.

———. 2008. "Snakes on Planes: Sinuous Motifs in the Art of Lamanai." In *Archaeological Investigations in the Eastern Maya Lowlands: Papers of the 2007 Belize Archaeology Symposium,* edited by John Morris, Sherilyne Jones, Jaime Awe, and Christophe Helmke. Research Reports in Belizean Archaeology, vol. 5. Belmopan, Belize: Institute of Archaeology, National Institute of Culture and History.

Alcock, Leslie. 2003. *Kings and Warriors, Craftsmen and Priests in Northern Britain, AD 550–850.* Monograph Series/Society of Antiquaries of Scotland, no. 24. Edinburgh: Society of Antiquaries of Scotland.

Alcoff, Linda. 1991–92. "The Problem of Speaking for Others." *Cultural Critique,* no. 20: 5–32.

Alcoff, Linda, and Elizabeth Potter, eds. 1993. *Feminist Epistemologies.* London: Routledge.

Alexander, Rani T., and Susan Kepecs. 2005. "The Postclassic to Spanish-Era Transition in Mesoamerica: An Introduction." In *The Postclassic to Spanish-Era Transition to Mesoamerica: An Archaeological Perspective,* edited by Susan Kepecs and Rani T. Alexander, 1–12. Albuquerque: University of New Mexico Press.

Altman, Ida, and James Lockhart. 1976. "The South." In *Provinces of Early Mexico,* edited by Ida Altman and James Lockhart, 29. UCLA Latin American Studies, no. 36. Los Angeles: UCLA Latin American Center Publications, University of California.

Andrews, Anthony P. 1978. "Puertos costeros del Postclásico Temprano en el norte de Yucatán." *Estudios de Cultura Maya,* no. 11: 75–93.

———. 1984. "The Political Geography of the Sixteenth Century Yucatán Maya: Comments and Revisions." *Journal of Anthropological Research* 40(4): 589–96.

———. 1990. "The Role of Trading Ports in Maya Civilization." In *Vision and Revision in Maya Studies,* edited by Flora S. Clancy and Peter D. Harrison, 159–67. Albuquerque: University of New Mexico Press.

———. 1991. "The Rural Chapels and Churches of Early Colonial Yucatán and Belize: An Archaeological Perspective." In *The Spanish Borderlands in Pan-American Perspective,* edited by David Hurst Thomas, 355–74. Columbian Consequences, vol. 3. Washington, D.C.: Smithsonian Institution.

Andrews, Anthony P., and Grant D. Jones. 2001. "Asentamientos coloniales en la costa de Quintana Roo." *Temas Antropológicos* 23(1): 20–35.

Andrews, Anthony P., and Shirley B. Mock. 2002. "New Perspectives on the Prehispanic Maya Salt Trade." In *Ancient Maya Political Economies*, edited by Marilyn A. Masson and David A. Freidel, 307–34. Walnut Creek, Calif.: Altamira Press.

Andrews, Anthony P., and Fernando Robles C. 1985. "Chichen Itza and Coba: An Itza-Maya Standoff in Early Postclassic Yucatán." In *The Lowland Maya Postclassic*, edited by Arlen F. Chase and Prudence M. Rice, 62–72. Austin: University of Texas Press.

Andrews, Anthony P., E. Wyllys Andrews, and Fernando Robles Castellanos. 2003. "The Northern Maya Collapse and Its Aftermath. *Ancient Mesoamerica*, no. 14: 151–56.

Andrews, Anthony P., Antonio Benavides C., and Grant D. Jones. 2006. "Ecab: A Remote Encomienda of Early Colonial Yucatán." In *Reconstructing the Past: Studies in Mesoamerican and Central American Prehistory*, edited by David M. Pendergast and Anthony P. Andrews, 5–32. BAR International Series, no. 1529. Oxford: British Archaeological Reports.

Andrews, E. Wyllys, IV, and Anthony P. Andrews. 1975. *A Preliminary Study of the Ruins of Xcaret, Quintana Roo, Mexico*. Middle American Research Institute, no. 40. New Orleans: Middle American Research Institute, Tulane University.

Annis, Sheldon. 1987. *God and Production in a Guatemalan Town*. Austin: University of Texas Press.

Artigas, Juan B. 1983. *Capillas abiertas aisladas de México*. Mexico City: Universidad Nacional Autónoma de México.

Asad, Talal. 1993. *Genealogies of Religion: Disciplines of Power in Christianity and Islam*. Baltimore: Johns Hopkins University Press.

Atran, Scott. 2002. *In Gods We Trust: The Evolutionary Landscape of Religion*. Oxford: Oxford University Press.

Auel, Jean M. 1980. *The Clan of the Cave Bear*. London: Hodder and Stoughton.

Awe, Jaime. 2007. "Of Burnt Churches and a Buried Sugar Mill: The Lamanai Historic Monuments Conservation Project." *Belize Today.org* 3(17): 24–28.

Baird, Robert D. 2004. "Syncretism and the History of Religions." In *Syncretism in Religion: A Reader*, edited by Anita Maria Leopold and Jeppe Sinding Jensen, 48–58. London: Equinox.

Baltimore Catechism No. 1. 1977. Originally issued as *A Catechism of Christian Doctrine* by the Third Plenary Council of Baltimore, 1885. This edition reprinted from the 1933 edition of Benziger Brothers by arrangement with Benziger, Bruce and Glencoe. Rockford, Illinois: Tan Books and Publishers.

Bataillon, Marcel. 1991. *Erasme et l'Espagne: Recherches sur l'histoire spirituelle du XVIe siècle*. Travaux d'humanisme et Renaissance, no. 250. Geneva: Droz. First published 1937.

Bateson, Gregory. 1972. *Steps to an Ecology of Mind*. Chicago: University of Chicago Press.

Battistini, Matilde. 2005. *Symbols and Allegories in Art*. Translated by Stephen Sartarelli. Los Angeles: J. Paul Getty Museum.

Bayle, Constantino. 1950. *El clero secular y la evangelización de América*. Biblioteca "Missionalia Hispánica," no 6. Madrid: Consejo Superior de Investigaciones Científicas, Instituto Santo Toribio de Mogrovejo.

Beatty, Andrew. 2006. "The Pope in Mexico: Syncretism in Public Ritual." *American Anthropologist* 108(2): 324–35.

Bede, the Venerable, Saint. 1969. *The Ecclesiastical History of the English People*. Edited with an introduction by Judith McClure and Roger Collins. Oxford: Oxford University Press.

Belting, Hans. 1994. *Likeness and Presence: A History of the Image before the Era of Art.* Translated by Edmund Jephcott. Chicago: University of Chicago Press.

Bernstein, Harry. 1947. Review of *The Beginning of British Honduras, 1506–1765*, by E. O. Winzerling. *William and Mary Quarterly* 4(3): 392–93.

Bertius, Petrus. 1602. *Tabularum geographicarum contractarum libri quinque, cum luculentis singularum tabularum explicationibus.* 2nd ed. Amsterdam.

———. 1612. *Bertius Geographischer Tabeln.* Frankfurt: Heinrich Lorenzen.

Blaeu, Joan. 1665. *Achtste Stuck der Aerdrycks-Beschryving, Welck Vervat Spaenjen, Africa, en America.* Amsterdam: In de Druckery van Joan Blaeu.

Blaffer, Sarah C. 1972. *The Black-man of Zinacantan: A Central American Legend.* Austin: University of Texas Press.

Bloom, Harold. 1996. *Omens of Millennium.* New York: Riverhead Books.

Bolland, O. Nigel. 1977. *The Formation of a Colonial Society: Belize, from Conquest to Crown Colony.* Baltimore: Johns Hopkins University Press.

Bolles, David. 2001. *Combined Dictionary–Concordance of the Yucatecan Mayan Language.* FAMSI (Foundation for the Advancement of Mesoamerican Studies, Inc.). http://www.famsi.org/reports/96072/index.html.

Boremanse, Didier. 1998. *Hach Winik: The Lacandon Maya of Southern Chiapas, Mexico.* Albany, N.Y.: Institute for Mesoamerican Studies, University at Albany, State University of New York.

Borges, Pedro. 1940. *Métodos misionales en la cristianización de América, siglo XVI.* Madrid: Consejo Superior de Investigaciones Científicas, Departamento de Misionología Española.

Bowie, Fiona. 2000. *The Anthropology of Religion.* Oxford: Blackwell.

Boyer, Pascal. 1994. *The Naturalness of Religious Ideas: A Cognitive Theory of Religion.* Berkeley: University of California Press.

———. 2001. *Religion Explained: Evolutionary Origins of Religious Thought.* New York: Basic Books.

———. 2004. "Religion, Evolution, and Cognition." *Current Anthropology* 45(3): 430–32.

Bracamonte y Sosa, Pedro. 2001. *La conquista inconclusa de Yucatán: Los Mayas de la montaña, 1560–1580.* Mexico City: Centro de Investigaciones y Estudios Superiores en Antropología Social: Porrúa; [Chetumal]: Universidad de Quintana Roo.

Bretos, Miguel A. 1987. "Capillas de Indios yucatecas del siglo XVI: Notas sobre un complejo formal." *Cuadernos de Arquitectura de Yucatán*, no. 1: 1–12. [Published by the Facultad de Arquitectura, Universidad Autónoma de Yucatán, Mérida]

Brew, J. O. 1994. "St. Francis at Awatovi." In *Pioneers in Historical Archaeology: Breaking New Ground*, edited by Stanley South, 27–47. New York: Plenum.

Bricker, Victoria R. 1981. *The Indian Christ, The Indian King: The Historical Substrate of Maya Myth and Ritual.* Austin: University of Texas Press.

———. 1989. "The Calendrical Meaning of Ritual among the Maya." In *Ethnographic Encounters in Southern Mesoamerica: Essays in Honor of Evon Zartman Vogt, Jr.*, edited by Victoria R. Bricker and Gary H. Gossen, 231–49. Studies on Culture and Society, vol. 3. Albany, New York: Institute for Mesoamerican Studies, University at Albany, State University of New York.

Brown, Peter. 1981. *The Cult of the Saints.* Chicago: University of Chicago Press.

————. 1993. *The Making of Late Antiquity*. Cambridge, Mass.: Harvard University Press.

————. 2003. *The Rise of Western Christendom*. 2nd ed. Oxford: Blackwell.

Browning, W. R. F. 2004. *Oxford Dictionary of The Bible*. Oxford: Oxford University Press.

Bunzel, Ruth. 1952. *Chichicastenango: A Guatemalan Village*. Publications of the American Ethnological Society, vol. 22. Locust Valley, N.Y.: J. J. Augustine.

Burkhart, Louise M. 1989. *The Slippery Earth: Nahua Christian Moral Dialogue in Sixteenth-Century Mexico*. Tucson: University of Arizona Press.

————. 1993. "The Cult of the Virgin of Guadalupe in Mexico." In *Southern and Meso-American Native Spirituality: From the Cult of the Feathered Serpent to the Theology of Liberation*, edited by Gary H. Gossen, 198–227. London: SCM Press.

Burns, Allan F. 1983. *An Epoch of Miracles*. Austin: University of Texas Press.

Burr, G. H. 1964. *Hispanic Furniture from the Fifteenth through the Eighteenth Century*. New York: Archive Press.

Cameron, Averil. 1993. *The Mediterranean World in Late Antiquity, AD 395–600*. London: Routledge.

Cancian, Frank. 1965. *Economics and Prestige in a Maya Community: The Religious Cargo System in Zinacantan*. Stanford, Calif.: Stanford University Press.

Canedo, Lino Gomez. 1952. "Fray Lorenzo de Bienvenida, O.F.M., and the Origins of the Franciscan Order in Yucatán: A Reconsideration of the Problem on the Basis of Unpublished Documents." *The Americas* 8(4): 493–510.

————. 1977. *Evangelización y conquista: Experiencia franciscana en hispanoamerica*. Mexico City: Editorial Porrúa.

Cárdenas y Valencia, Francisco de. 1937. *Relación historial eclesiástica de la Provincia de Yucatán de Nueva España escrita el año de 1639*. Mexico City: Robredo.

Cardós de Méndez, Amalia. 1998. "301, Effigy Vessel, Late Classic period, Inv. no. 10–1076519." In *Maya*, edited by Peter Schmidt, Mercedes de la Garza, and Enrique Nalda, 593. Milan: RCS Libri–CNCA INAH.

Carlsen, Robert S. 1997. *The War for the Heart and Soul of a Highland Maya Town*. Austin: University of Texas Press.

Carrette, Jeremy R. 2000. *Foucault and Religion*. London: Routledge.

Carrillo y Ancona, Crescencio. (1967) 1982. *Compendio de la historia de Yucatán*. Mérida, Yucatán: Talleres Gráficos "Guerra".

Case, Shirley Jackson. 1971. *Experience with the Supernatural in Early Christian Times*. New York: Benjamin Blom.

Caso Barrera, Laura. 1999. "Religión y resistencia indígena en Yucatán, siglos XVI–XIX." *Colonial Latin American Historical Review* 8(2): 153–84.

————. 2002. *Caminos de la selva: Migración, comercio y resistencia, Mayas Yucatecos e Itzaes, siglos XVII–XIX*. Mexico City: El Colegio de México y Fondo de Cultura Económica.

Castells, F. de P. 1904. "The Ruins of Indian Church in British Honduras." *American Antiquarian and Oriental Journal* 26(1): 32–37.

Catechism of the Catholic Church. 1997. 2nd ed. Città de Vaticano: Libreria Editrice Vaticana.

Cecil, Leslie. 2001. "The Technological Styles of Late Postclassic Slipped Pottery Groups in the Petén Lakes Region, El Petén, Guatemala." Ph.D. diss., Department of Anthropology, Southern Illinois University, Carbondale.

————. 2004. "Inductively Coupled Plasma Emission Spectroscopy and Postclassic Peten

Slipped Pottery: An Examination of Pottery Wares, Social Identity, and Trade." *Archaeometry* 46(3): 385–404.

———. 2009a. "Kowoj Worldview: A View from Tipuj." In *Maya Worldviews at Conquest*, edited by Leslie G. Cecil and Timothy W. Pugh, 239–60. Boulder: University of Colorado Press.

———. 2009b. "Technological Styles of Slipped Pottery and Kowoj Identity." In *The Kowoj: Identity, Migration, and Geopolitics in Late Postclassic Petén, Guatemala*, edited by Prudence M. Rice and Don S. Rice, 221–37. Boulder: University Press of Colorado.

Cecil, Leslie G., and Timothy W. Pugh. 2004. "Kowoj Symbolism and Technology at Late Postclassic Tipuj." Paper presented at the 69th Annual Meeting of the Society for American Archaeology, Montreal, Quebec.

Cervantes, Fernando. 1994. *The Devil in the New World: The Impact of Diabolism in New Spain*. New Haven, Conn.: Yale University Press.

Chadwick, Henry. 1993. *The Early Church*. Harmondsworth, U.K.: Penguin.

Chamberlain, Robert S. 1948. *The Conquest and Colonization of Yucatán, 1517–1550*. Washington, D.C.: Carnegie Institution.

Chase, Arlen F., and Diane Z. Chase. 1987. "Putting Together the Pieces: Maya Pottery of Northern Belize and Central Peten, Guatemala." In *Maya Ceramics*, edited by Prudence M. Rice and Robert J. Sharer, 47–72. BAR International Series, no. 345. Oxford: BAR.

———. 2001a. "The Royal Court of Caracol, Belize: Its Palaces and People." In *Royal Courts of the Ancient Maya*, vol. 2, *Data and Case Studies*, edited by Takeshi Inomata and Stephen D. Houston, 102–37. Boulder, Colo.: Westview Press.

———. 2001b. "Ancient Maya Causeways and Site Organization at Caracol, Belize." *Ancient Mesoamerica* 12(2): 273–81.

Chase, Arlen F., Diane Z. Chase, Elayne Zorn, and Wendy Teeter. 2008. "Textiles and the Maya Archaeological Record: Gender, Power, and Status in Classic Period Caracol, Belize." *Ancient Mesoamerica* 19(1): 127–42.

Chase, Diane Z. 1982. "Spatial and Temporal Variability in Postclassic Northern Belize." Ph.D. diss., Department of Anthropology, University of Pennsylvania, Philadelphia.

———. 1984. "The Late Postclassic Pottery of Santa Rita Corozal, Belize: The Xabalxab Ceramic Complex." *Ceramica de Cultura Maya*, no. 13: 18–26.

———. 1985. "Ganned but not Forgotten: Late Postclassic Archaeology and Ritual at Santa Rita Corozal, Belize." In *The Lowland Maya Postclassic*, edited by Arlen F. Chase and Prudence M. Rice, 104–25. Austin: University of Texas Press.

———. 1986. "Social and Political Organization in the Land of Cacao and Honey: Correlating the Archaeology and Ethnohistory of the Postclassic Lowland Maya." In *Late Lowland Maya Civilization: Classic to Postclassic*, edited by Jeremy A. Sabloff and E. Wyllys Andrews V, 347–77. Albuquerque: University of New Mexico Press.

———. 1989. "Routes of Trade and Communication and the Integration of Maya Society: The Vista from Santa Rita Corozal." In *Coastal Maya Trade and Exchange*, edited by Heather McKillop and Paul Healy, 19–32. Peterborough, Ontario: Trent University.

———. 1990. "The Invisible Maya: Population History and Archaeology at Santa Rita Corozal." In *Prehistoric Population History in the Maya Lowlands*, edited by T. Patrick Culbert and Don S. Rice, 199–213. Albuquerque: University of New Mexico Press.

———. 1991. "Lifeline to the Gods: Ritual Bloodletting at Santa Rita Corozal." In *Sixth Palenque Round Table, 1986*, edited by Merle G. Robertson and Virginia M. Fields, 89–96. Norman: University of Oklahoma Press.

Chase, Diane Z., and Arlen F. Chase. 1986. *Offerings to the Gods: Maya Archaeology at Santa Rita Corozal*. Orlando: University of Central Florida. http://www.caracol.org/include/files/chase/offerings.pdf. Prepared in conjunction with an exhibit at Loch Haven Art Center, Orlando, 11 January.

——. 1988. *A Postclassic Perspective: Excavations at the Maya Site of Santa Rita Corozal, Belize*. Pre-Columbian Art Research Institute, monograph no. 4. San Francisco: Pre-Columbian Art Research Institute.

——, eds. 1994. *Studies in the Archaeology of Caracol, Belize*. Monograph/Pre-Columbian Art Research Institute, monograph no. 7. San Francisco: Pre-Columbian Art Research Institute.

——. 2001. "Underlying Structure in Maya Persistence: An Archaeological Perspective." In *Maya Survivalism*, edited by Ueli Hostettler and Matthew Restall, 37–50. Acta MesoAmericana, vol. 12. Markt Schwaben, Germany: Verlag Anton Saurwein.

Christenson, Allen J. 2001. *Art and Society in a Highland Maya Community: The Altarpiece of Santiago Atitlán*. Austin: University of Texas Press.

——. 2007. *Popul Vuh: Sacred Book of the Ancient Maya*. Austin: University of Texas Press.

Christian, William A., Jr. 1981. *Local Religion in Sixteenth-Century Spain*. Princeton, N.J.: Princeton University Press.

Chuchiak, John F., IV. 2000. "The Indian Inquisition and the Extirpation of Idolatry: The Process of Punishment in the Provisorato de Indios of the Diocese of Yucatán, 1563–1812." Ph.D. diss., Department of Latin American Studies, Tulane University, New Orleans.

——. 2003. "'By Faith, Not Arms': The Role of Franciscan *Reducciones* and the Frontier Mission Experience in the Subjugation of the Maya Hinterland of Colonial Yucatán, 1602–1672." *SMT: Swedish Missiological Themes/Svensk MissionTidskrift* 91(2): 215–48.

——. 2005. "*In Servitio Dei*: Fray Diego de Landa, the Franciscan Order, and the Return of the Extirpation of Idolatry in the Colonial Diocese of Yucatán, 1573–1579." *The Americas* 61(4): 611–45.

——. 2009. "*De Descriptio Idolorum*: An Ethnohistorical Examination of the Production, Imagery, and Functions of Colonial Yucatec Maya Idols and Effigy Censers, 1540–1700." In *Maya Worldviews at Conquest*, edited by Leslie G. Cecil and Timothy W. Pugh, 135–58. Boulder: University Press of Colorado.

Classen, Constance. 1998. *The Color of Angels*. London: Routledge.

Clebsch, William A. 1978. *Christianity in European History*. Oxford: Oxford University Press.

Clements, Joyce. 2005. "'A Winding Sheet for Deborah George': Searching for the Women of Ponkapoag." Ph.D. diss., Department of Women's Studies, York University, North York, Ontario.

Clendinnen, Inga. 1987a. *Ambivalent Conquests: Maya and Spaniard in Yucatán, 1517–1570*. Cambridge: Cambridge University Press.

——. 1987b. "Franciscan Missionaries in Sixteenth-Century Mexico." In *Disciplines of Faith: Studies in Religion, Politics, and Patriarchy*, edited by Jim Obelkevich, Lyndal Roper, and Raphael Samuel, 229–45. London: Routledge and Kegan Paul.

——. 1991. "'Fierce and Unnatural Cruelty': Cortés and the Conquest of Mexico." *Representations* 33: 65–100.

Cockrell, Bryan. 2009. "Negotiating a Colonial Maya Identity: Metal Ornaments from the Church Cemetery at Tipu, Belize." Master's thesis, Institute of Archaeology, University College London.

Cockrell, Bryan, Marcos Martinón-Torres, and Elizabeth Graham. 2010. "Negotiating a Colonial Maya Identity: Metal Ornaments from Tipu, Belize." Poster presented at the 38th International Symposium on Archaeometry, May 10–14, University of South Florida, Tampa.

Code, Lorraine. 1993. "Taking Subjectivity into Account." In *Feminist Epistemologies*, edited by Linda Alcoff and Elizabeth Potter, 15–48. London: Routledge.

———. 1995. "How Do We Know? Questions of Method in Feminist Practice." In *Changing Methods: Feminists Transforming Practice*, edited by Sandra Burt and Lorraine Code, 13–44. Peterborough, Ontario: Broadview Press.

Códice Franciscano. Siglo XVI. Informe de la Provincia del Santo Evangelio al Visitador Lic. Juan de Ovando. Informe de la Provincia de Guadalajara al Mismo. Cartas de Religiosos, 1533–1569. 1941. Mexico City: Editorial Salvador Chávez Hayhoe.

Coe, William R. 1957. "A Distinctive Artifact Common to Haiti and Central America." *American Antiquity*, no. 22: 280–82.

Cohen, Mark N., K. O'Connor, Marie Danforth, Keith Jacobi, and C. Armstrong. 1994. "Health and Death at Tipu." In *In the Wake of Contact: Biological Responses to Conquest*, edited by Clark Spencer Larsen and George R. Milner, 121–33. New York: Wiley-Liss.

———. 1997. "Archaeology and Osteology of the Tipu Site." In *Bones of the Maya: Studies of Ancient Skeletons*, edited by S. L. Whittington and D. M. Reed, 78–86. Washington, D.C.: Smithsonian Institution.

Cohn-Sherbok, Lavinia. 1998. *Who's Who in Christianity*. London: Routledge.

Colby, Benjamin N., and Pierre L. van den Berghe. 1969. *Ixil Country: A Plural Society in Highland Guatemala*. Berkeley: University of California Press.

Collins, Anne C. 1977. "The *Maestros Cantores* in Yucatán." In *Anthropology and History in Yucatán*, edited by Grant D. Jones, 233–47. Austin: University of Texas Press.

Constantinou, Stavroula. 2007. "Grotesque Bodies in Edifying Tales: The Monstrous and the Uncanny in Byzantine Miracle Stories." Paper presented at the Dumbarton Oaks Fall Colloquium, "Symposium on Byzantine Literature: New Voices and Current Approaches," November 9–10, Washington, D.C.

Cook, Sherburn F., and William Borah. 1971. *Essays in Population History: Mexico and the Caribbean*, vol. 1. Berkeley: University of California Press.

Covens, Jean, and Corneille Mortier. 1761. *Atlas Nouveau, Contenant Toutes le Parties du Monde. . . .* 9 vols. Amsterdam: Jean Covens and Corneille Mortier.

Crosby, Alfred W. 1986. *Ecological Imperialism: The Biological Expansion of Europe, 900–1900*. Cambridge: Cambridge University Press.

Cruz, Pacheco. 1934. *Estudio etnográfico de los mayas del ex Territorio Quintana Roo*. Mérida, Yucatán: Imprenta Oriente.

Cuevas, Mariano. 1921–28. *Historia de la iglesia en México*. 5 vols. Tlalpam, Mexico.

Cunningham, Graham. 1999. *Religion and Magic*. Edinburgh: Edinburgh University Press.

Danforth, Marie E. 1993. "Marriage and Childbirth at Colonial Tipu." In *Texts of the Pre-Columbian/Spanish Encounters, 1492–1650*, edited by J. H. Seabrook, 36–44. Philadelphia: Community Colleges Humanities Association.

Danforth, Marie E., Keith P. Jacobi, and Mark N. Cohen. 1997. "Gender and Health among the Colonial Maya of Tipu, Belize." *Ancient Mesoamerica* 8(1): 13–22.

Danforth, Marie E., C. W. Armstrong, D. Light, and Mark N. Cohen. 1985. "Measures of Genetic Distance among Subgroups of the Maya Population at Tipu." Paper presented at the 1985 Northeastern Anthropological Association Meetings, Lake Placid, N.Y.

Darwin, Charles. 1968. *The Origin of Species by Means of Natural Selection*. London: Penguin Books. First published by John Murray, 1859.

Dawkins, Richard. 2006. *The God Delusion*. London: Bantam Press.

Deagan, Kathleen. 1987. *Artifacts of the Spanish Colonies of Florida and the Caribbean, 1500–1800*, vol. 1, *Ceramics, Glassware, and Beads*. Washington, D.C.: Smithsonian Institution.

de la Garza, Mercedes. 1998. "The Rediscovery of a Civilization." In *Maya*, edited by Peter Schmidt, Mercedes de la Garza, and Enrique Nalda, 19–27. Milan: RCS Libri-Bompiani.

Delaney, John J. 1980. *Dictionary of Saints*. New York: Doubleday.

Delgado-Gomez, Angel. 1993. "The Earliest European Views of the New World Natives." In *Early Images of the Americas: Transfer and Invention*, edited by Jerry M. Williams and Robert E. Lewis, 3–20. Tucson: University of Arizona Press.

Deuss, Krystyna. 2007. *Shamans, Witches, and Maya Priests: Native Religion and Ritual in Highland Guatemala*. London: Guatemala Maya Centre.

Díaz del Castillo, Bernal. 1956. *The Discovery and Conquest of Mexico, 1517–1521*. Translated by Alfred P. Maudslay. New York: Farrar, Straus and Cudahy.

Dobson, Narda. 1973. *A History of Belize*. Trinidad: Longman Caribbean.

Dogma. 1999. Film directed and written by Kevin Smith. View Askew Productions.

Dudley. 1646–47. *Dell'Arcano del Mare, 1646–1647* (Concerning the Secret of the Sea). 3 vols. Firenze.

Duffy, Eamon. 2005. *The Stripping of the Altars: Traditional Religion in England, 1400–1580*. New Haven, Conn.: Yale University Press.

Dumond, Don E. 1997. *The Machete and the Cross*. Lincoln: University of Nebraska Press.

Dunn, Richard K., and S. J. Mazzullo. 1993. "Holocene Paleocoastal Reconstuction and Its Relationship to Marco Gonzalez, Ambergris, Caye, Belize." *Journal of Field Archaeology* 20(2): 121–31.

Durán, Diego. 1967. *Historia de las Indias de Nueva España e Islas de la Tierra Firme*. 2 vols. Mexico City: Porrúa.

———. 1994. *The History of the Indies of New Spain*. Translated, annotated, and with an Introduction by Doris Heyden. Norman: University of Oklahoma Press.

Early, John D. 2006. *The Maya and Catholicism: An Encounter of Worldviews*. Gainesville: University Press of Florida.

Edgerton, Samuel Y. 2001. *Theaters of Conversion: Religious Architecture and Indian Artisans in Colonial Mexico*. Albuquerque: University of New Mexico Press.

Edmonson, Munro S. 1982. *The Ancient Future of the Itzá: The Book of Chilam Balam of Tizimin*. Austin: University of Texas Press.

———. 1986. *Heaven Born Merida and Its Destiny: The Book of Chilam Balam of Chumayel*. Austin: University of Texas Press.

———. 1993. "The Mayan Faith." In *Southern and Meso-American Native Spirituality: From the Cult of the Feathered Serpent to the Theology of Liberation*, edited by Gary H. Gossen, 65–85. London: SCM Press.

Eguíluz, Antonio. 1964. "Fr. Pedro de Azuaga, O.F.M., Nuevo teorizante sobre Indias." *Missionalia Hispanica*, no. 20: 173–223.

Eiss, Paul K. 2008. "Constructing the Maya." *Ethnohistory* 55(4): 503–8.

Eliade, Mircea. 1987. *The Sacred and the Profane: The Nature of Religion.* Orlando, Fla.: Harcourt.

Elliott, J. H. 2002. *Imperial Spain, 1469–1716.* London: Penguin.

Emery, Kitty F. 1990. "Postclassic and Colonial Period Subsistence Strategies in the Southern Maya Lowlands: Faunal Analyses from Lamanai and Tipu, Belize." Master's thesis, Department of Anthropology, University of Toronto.

———. 1999. "Continuity and Variability in Postclassic and Colonial Animal Use at Lamanai and Tipu, Belize." In *Reconstructing Ancient Maya Diet,* edited by Christine D. White, 61–81. Salt Lake City: University of Utah Press.

Evans, Susan Toby. 2008. *Ancient Mexico and Central America.* London: Thames and Hudson.

Farmer, David. 1997. *Oxford Dictionary of Saints.* 4th ed. Oxford: Oxford University Press.

Farriss, Nancy M. 1984. *Maya Society under Colonial Rule: The Collective Enterprise of Survival.* Princeton, N.J.: Princeton University Press.

Firth, Raymond. 1996. *Religion, A Humanist Interpretation.* London: Routledge.

Fischer, Edward F. 1996. "Induced Culture Change as a Strategy for Socioeconomic Development: The Pan-Maya Movement in Guatemala." In *Maya Cultural Activism in Guatemala,* edited by Edward F. Fischer and R. McKenna Brown, 51–73. Austin: University of Texas Press.

———. 1999. "Cultural Logic and Maya Identity." *Current Anthropology* 40(4): 473–99.

Fletcher, Richard. 1997. *The Barbarian Conversion.* New York: Henry Holt.

Folan, William J. 1970. "Architectural Drawings by Gordon and Ann Ketterer. The Open Chapel of Dzibilchaltun, Yucatán." In *Archaeological Studies in Middle America,* 181–99. Middle American Research Institute, no. 26. New Orleans: Middle American Research Institute, Tulane University.

Foor, Charles W. 1994. "Analysis of Late Postclassic Censer Materials from Structure Ii, Negroman-Tipu, Belize." Master's thesis, Department of Anthropology, Southern Illinois University, Carbondale.

Foster, Elizabeth Andres, trans. and ed. 1973. *Motolinía's "History of the Indians of New Spain."* Westport, Conn.: Greenwood Press. Originally published in 1950 as *Documents and Narratives concerning the Discovery and Conquest of Latin America,* new series, no. 4 (Berkeley, Calif.: Cortés Society).

Foster, George M. 1953. "What Is Folk Culture?" pt. 1. *American Anthropologist,* new ser., 55(2): 159–73.

Foucault, Michel, and Gilles Deleuze. 1977. "Intellectuals and Power." In *Language, Counter-Memory, Practice,* edited by Donald Bouchard, translated by Donald Bouchard and Sherry Simon, 205–17. Oxford: Basil Blackwell.

Freedberg, David. 1989. *The Power of Images: Studies in the History and Theory of Response.* Chicago: University of Chicago Press.

Freeman, Charles. 2002. *The Closing of the Western Mind: The Rise of Faith and the Fall of Reason.* London: Pimlico, Random House.

Freidel, David A. 1978. "Maritime Adaptation and the Rise of Maya Civilization: The View from Cerros, Belize." In *Prehistoric Coastal Adaptations,* edited by Barbara L. Stark and Barbara Voorhies, 239–65. New York: Academic Press.

Gallareta Negrón, Tomás, Anthony P. Andrews, and Peter J. Schmidt. 1990. "A 16th Century Church at Xlacah, Panaba, Yucatán." *Mexicon* 12(2): 33–36.

Gann, Thomas W. F. 1926. *Ancient Cities and Modern Tribes*. London: Duckworth.

García Bernal, Manuela Cristina. 1972. *La sociedad de Yucatán, 1700–1750*. Seville: Escuela de Estudios Hispano-Americanos.

García Granados, Rafael. 1935. "Capillas de Indios en Nueva España (1530–1605)." *Archivo Español de Arte y Arqueología* 11(31): 3–24.

García Icazbalceta, Joaquín, ed. 1941. *Cartas de religiosas de Nueva España, 1539–94*, 2nd ed. Mexico City: Editorial Salvador Chávez Hayhoe.

García Targa, Juan, and Alfonso Jordi Gussinyer. 2004. "Primeros templos cristianos en el área Maya: Yucatán y Belice, 1545–1585." *Estudios de Cultura Maya*, no. 25: 95–119.

Geary, Patrick J. 1988. *Before France and Germany: The Creation and Transformation of the Merovingian World*. New York: Oxford University Press.

———. 1994a. "The Uses of Archaeological Sources for Religious and Cultural History." In *Living with the Dead in the Middle Ages*, by Patrick Geary, 30–45. Ithaca, N.Y.: Cornell University.

———. 1994b. "The Ninth-Century Relic Trade—A Response to Popular Piety?" In *Living with the Dead in the Middle Ages*, by Patrick Geary, 177–93. Ithaca, N.Y.: Cornell University.

Geertz, Clifford. 1968. *Islam Observed: Religious Development in Morocco and Indonesia*. New Haven, Conn.: Yale University Press.

———. 1973a. "Religion as a Cultural System." In *The Interpretation of Cultures: Selected Essays by Clifford Geertz*, 87–125. New York: Basic Books.

———. 1973b. "Thick Description: Toward an Interpretive Theory of Culture." In *The Interpretation of Cultures: Selected Essays by Clifford Geertz*, 3–30. New York: Basic Books.

———. 2000. "The Pinch of Destiny: Religion as Experience, Meaning, Identity, Power." In *Available Light: Anthropological Reflections on Philosophical Topics*, by Clifford Geertz, 167–86. Princeton, N.J.: Princeton University Press.

Gell, Alfred. 1998. *Art and Agency: An Anthropological Theory*. Oxford: Clarendon Press.

Gerhard, Peter. 1979. *The Southeast Frontier of New Spain*. Princeton, N.J.: Princeton University Press.

Ghilardi, Agostino. 1969. *The Life and Times of St. Francis*. London: Paul Hamlyn.

Gibbons, Tony, ed. 2001. *The Encyclopedia of Ships*. London: Amber Books.

Giddens, Anthony. 1995. *A Contemporary Critique of Historical Materialism*. 2nd ed. London: MacMillan.

Ginzburg, Carlo. 1979. "Cheese and Worms—The Cosmos of a Sixteenth-Century Miller." In *Religion and the People, 800–1700*, edited by James Obelkevitch, 87–167. Chapel Hill: University of North Carolina Press.

Giorgi, Rosa. 2003. *Saints in Art*. Translated by Thomas Michael Hartmann. Los Angeles: J. Paul Getty Museum.

———. 2005. *Angels and Demons in Art*. Translated by Rosanna M. Giammanco Frongia. Los Angeles: J. Paul Getty Museum.

Goddard, Peter. 2004. "Two Kinds of Conversion ('Medieval' and 'Modern') among the Hurons of New France." In *The Spiritual Conversion of the Americas*, edited by James Muldoon, 57–77. Gainesville: University Press of Florida.

Graham, Elizabeth. 1985. "Facets of Terminal to Post Classic Activity in the Stann Creek District, Belize." In *The Lowland Maya Postclassic*, edited by Arlen F. Chase and Prudence M. Rice, 215–29. Austin: University of Texas Press.

———. 1987. "Terminal Classic to Early Historic Period Vessel Forms from Belize." In

Maya Ceramics: Papers from the 1985 Maya Ceramic Conference, edited by Prudence M. Rice and Robert J. Sharer, 73–98. BAR International Series 345(i). Oxford: BAR.

———. 1989. "Brief Synthesis of Coastal Site Data from Colson Point, Placencia, and Marco Gonzalez, Belize." In *Coastal Maya Trade*, edited by Heather McKillop and Paul F. Healy, 135–54. Occasional Papers in Anthropology, no. 8. Peterborough, Ontario: Trent University.

———. 1991. "Archaeological Insights into Colonial Period Maya Life at Tipu, Belize." In *The Spanish Borderlands in Pan-American Perspective*, edited by David H. Thomas, 319–35. Columbian Consequences, vol. 3. Washington, D.C.: Smithsonian Institution Press.

———. 1994. *The Highlands of the Lowlands: Environment and Archaeology in the Stann Creek District, Belize, Central America*. Monographs in World Archaeology, no. 19. Madison, Wis.: Prehistory Press; Toronto: Royal Ontario Museum.

———. 1996. "Maya Cities and the Character of a Tropical Urbanism." In *The Development of Urbanism from a Global Perspective*, edited by Paul Sinclair. Uppsala: Uppsala University. http://www.arkeologi.uu.se/afr/projects/BOOK/graham.pdf.

———. 1998a. "Mission Archaeology." *Annual Review of Anthropology*, no. 27: 25–62.

———. 1998b. "Metaphor and Metamorphism—Some Thoughts on Environmental Meta-History." In *Advances in Historical Ecology*, edited by William Balée, 119–37. New York: Columbia University Press.

———. 1999. "Stone Cities, Green Cities." In *Complex Polities in the Ancient Tropical World*, edited by Elisabeth A. Bacus and Lisa J. Lucero, 185–94. Archaeological Papers of the American Anthropological Association, no. 9. Arlington, Va.: American Anthropological Association.

———. 2002. "Perspectives on Economy and Theory." In *Ancient Maya Political Economies*, edited by Marilyn A. Masson and David A. Freidel, 398–418. Walnut Creek: Altamira Press.

———. 2004. "Lamanai Reloaded: Alive and Well in the Early Postclassic." In *Archaeological Investigations in the Eastern Maya Lowlands*, edited by Jaime Awe, John Morris, and Sherilyne Jones, 223–41. Research Reports in Belizean Archaeology, vol. 1. Belmopan, Belize: Institute of Archaeology, National Institute of Culture and History.

———. 2006a. "An Ethnicity to Know." In *Maya Ethnicity: The Construction of Ethnic Identity from Preclassic to Modern Times*, edited by Frauke Sachse, 109–24. Acta MesoAmericana, vol. 19. Markt Schwaben: Verlag Anton Saurwein.

———. 2006b. "A Neotropical Framework for Terra Preta." In *Time and Complexity in Historical Ecology: Studies in the Neotropics*, edited by William Baleé and Clark C. Erickson, 57–86. New York: Columbia University Press.

———. 2007. "Lamanai, Belize from Collapse to Conquest: Radiocarbon Dates from Lamanai." Paper presented at the 106th Meeting of the American Anthropological Association, November 28–December 2, Washington, D.C.

———. 2008a. "Lamanai Historic Monuments Conservation Project: Recording and Consolidation of New Church Architectural Features at Lamanai, Belize." With contributions by Claude Belanger. Foundation for the Advancement of Mesoamerican Studies, Inc. http://www.famsi.org/reports/06110C/index.html.

———. 2008b. "Socially Sanctioned Killing in America, Then and Now." In the session "Socially Embedded Violence in the Ancient Americas: Beyond Sacrifice and Cannibalism," organized by Miguel A. Aguilera and Jane E. Buikstra, at the 73rd Meeting of the Society for American Archaeology, March 26–30, Vancouver, British Columbia.

―――. 2009. "Close Encounters." In *Maya Worldviews at Conquest*, edited by Leslie G. Cecil and Timothy W. Pugh, 17–38. Boulder: University of Colorado Press.

―――. Forthcoming. "Darwin at Copan." In *Ecology, Power, and Religion in Maya Landscapes*, edited Christian Isendahl and Bodil Liljefors Persson. Acta MesoAmericana, vol. n.d. Markt Schwaben: Verlag Anton Saurwein.

Graham, Elizabeth, and Sharon Bennett. 1989. "The 1986–1987 Excavations at Negroman-Tipu, Belize." *Mexicon* 11(6): 114–17.

Graham, Elizabeth, and Nick Golson. 2006. "The Faces of Tribute." Paper presented at the symposium "Interregional Exchange and Its Role in the Sociopolitical Organization of Prehispanic Latin American Cultures: Session in Honor of Warwick Bray," organized by Helen Haines, at the 71st Annual Meeting of the Society for American Archaeology, April 26–30, San Juan, Puerto Rico.

Graham, Elizabeth, Grant D. Jones, and Robert R. Kautz. 1985. "Archaeology and Ethnohistory on a Spanish Colonial Frontier: The Macal-Tipu Project in Western Belize." In *The Lowland Maya Postclassic*, edited by Arlen F. Chase and Prudence M. Rice, 206–14. Austin: University of Texas Press.

Graham, Elizabeth, and David M. Pendergast. 1989. "Excavations at the Marco Gonzalez Site, Ambergris Caye, Belize." *Journal of Field Archaeology* 16(1): 1–6.

Graham, Elizabeth, David M. Pendergast, and Grant D. Jones. 1989. "On the Fringes of Conquest: Maya-Spanish Contact in Early Belize." *Science*, no. 246: 1254–59.

Guderjan, Thomas H. 1993. *Ancient Maya Traders of Ambergris Caye*. Benque Viejo del Carmen, Belize: Cubola Productions.

Guderjan, Thomas H., and James F. Garber, eds. 1995. *Maya Maritime Trade, Settlement, and Populations on Ambergris Caye, Belize*. Lancaster, Calif.: Labyrinthos.

Gussinyer Alfonso, Jordi. 1999. "Arquitectura Paleocristiana de Mesoamérica: Tercera Parte." *Boletín Americanista* (Universidad de Barcelona), 49: 135–73.

Guthrie, Stewart Elliott. 1993. *Faces in the Clouds: A New Theory of Religion*. Oxford: Oxford University Press.

Gutiérrez Estévez, Manuel. 1993. The Christian Era of the Yucatec Maya. In *Southern and Meso-American Native Spirituality: From the Cult of the Feathered Serpent to the Theology of Liberation*, edited by Gary H. Gossen, 252–78. London: SCM Press.

Hamilton, Bernard. 1990. *Religion in the Medieval West*. London: Edward Arnold.

Hammond, Norman. 1976. "Maya Obsidian Trade in Southern Belize." In *Maya Lithic Studies: Papers from the 1976 Belize Field Symposium*, edited by Thomas R. Hester and Norman Hammond, 71–81. Special Report No. 4. San Antonio: Center for Archaeological Research, University of Texas.

Hancock, Ron G. V., and Elizabeth Graham. 2004. "Elemental Analysis of European Glass Beads from Tipu, Belize." Paper presented at the 34th International Symposium on Archaeometry, May 3–7, Zaragoza, Spain.

Hanke, Lewis. 1935. *The First Social Experiments in America: A Study in the Development of Spanish Indian Policy in the Sixteenth Century*. Cambridge, Mass.: Harvard University Press.

Hanks, Willima F. 1990. *Referential Practice: Language and Lived Space among the Maya*. Chicago: University of Chicago Press.

Hanson, Craig A. 1990. "The Spanish Chapel at Xcaret, Quintana Roo, Mexico. A Report on Operation Two and Summary of the 1989 Season." Submitted to Arqlga. María José Con, Directora del Proyecto Xcaret. Centro Regional de Quintana Roo, INAH.

———. 1995. "The Hispanic Horizon in Yucatán: A Model of Franciscan Missionization." *Ancient Mesoamerica* 6(1): 15–28.

Hanson, Norwood Russell. 1971. "The Idea of a Logic of Discovery." In *What I Do Not Believe, and Other Essays*, edited by Stephen Toulmin and Harry Woolf, 288–300. Dordrecht, Neth.: D. Reidel Publishing.

Harding, Sandra. 1987. "The Method Question." *Hypatia* 2(3): 19–35.

———. 1993. "Rethinking Standpoint Philosophy: What is 'Strong Objectivity'?" In *Feminist Epistemologies*, edited by Linda Alcoff and Elizabeth Potter, 49–82. New York: Routledge.

Harries-Jones, Peter. 1995. *A Recursive Vision: Ecological Understanding and Gregory Bateson*. Toronto: University of Toronto Press.

Hart-Davis, Adam. 2000. "What the Romans Did for Us." Documentary presented by Adam Hart-Davis, directed by Inge Samuels, produced by Caroline van den Brul, BBC Two, November 6–December 11. www.bbc.co.uk/history/ancient/romans.

Heisenberg, Werner. 1958. *Physics and Philosophy*. World Perspectives, vol. 19. New York: Harper and Brothers.

Herrin, Judith. 1987. *The Formation of Christendom*. Princeton, N.J.: Princeton University Press.

Hill, Robert M., and John Monaghan. 1987. *Continuities in Highland Maya Social Organization: Ethnohistory in Sacapulas, Guatemala*. Philadelphia: University of Pennsylvania Press.

Hinnebusch, William A. 1973. *The History of the Dominican Order*, vol. 2, *Intellectual and Cultural Life to 1500*. New York: Alba House.

Hitchens, Christopher. 2007. *The Portable Atheist: Essential Readings for the Nonbeliever*. Selected and with an introduction by Christopher Hitchens. Philadelphia: Da Capo Press.

Horton, Robin. 1971. "African Conversion." *Journal of the International African Institute* 41(2): 85–108.

Houston, Stephen D. 1993. *Hieroglyphs and History at Dos Pilas: Dynastic Politics of the Classic Maya*. Austin: University of Texas Press.

Howie, Linda A. 2006. "Ceramic Production and Consumption in the Maya Lowlands during the Classic to Postclassic Transition: A Technological Study of Ceramics at Lamanai, Belize." Ph.D. diss., University of Sheffield.

Hostettler, Ueli. 2004. "Rethinking Maya Identity in Yucatán, 1500–1940." *Journal of Latin American Anthropology* 9(1): 187–98.

Hunt, Marta Espejo-Ponce. 1976. "The Processes of the Development of Yucatán, 1600–1700." In *Provinces of Early Mexico*, edited by Ida Altman and James Lockhart, 33–62. UCLA Latin American Center Publications. Los Angeles: University of California.

Ingham, John M. 1986. *Mary, Michael, and Lucifer: Folk Catholicism in Central Mexico*. Austin: University of Texas Press.

Insoll, Timothy. 2004. *Archaeology, Ritual, Religion*. London: Routledge.

Izquierdo, Ana Luisa. 1988. "Documentos de la División del Beneficio de Yaxcabá: El castigo a una idolatría." *Estudios de Cultura Maya* 17: 159–95.

———. 2006. "Las jurisdicciones en la Chontalpa del siglo XVI." In *Nuevas perspectivas sobre la geografía política de los Mayas*, edited by Tsubasa Okoshi Harada, Lorraine A. Williams-Beck, and Ana Luisa Izquierdo, 159–82. Mexico City: Universidad Nacional Autónoma de México.

Jacobi, Keith. 2000. *Last Rites for the Tipu Maya: Genetic Structuring in a Colonial Cemetery*. Tuscaloosa: University of Alabama Press.

James, Noel P., and Robert N. Ginsburg. 1979. *The Seaward Margin of Belize Barrier and Atoll Reefs*. Special Publication No. 3 of the International Association of Sedimentologists. Oxford: Blackwell Scientific.

James, William. [1902] 1982. *The Varieties of Religious Experience*. New York: Penguin.

Jedin, Hubert. 1946. *Katholische Reformation oder Gegenreformation? Ein Versuch zur Klärung der Begriffe nebst einer Jubiläumsbetrachtung über das Trienter Konzil*. Lucerne: Josef Stocker.

John, Jennifer Ruth. 2008. "Postclassic Maya Ceramic Iconography at Lamanai, Belize, Central America." Ph.D. diss., Institute of Archaeology, University College London.

Johnson, Matthew. 1999. *Archaeological Theory*. Oxford: Blackwell.

Jones, Grant D. 1982. "Agriculture and Trade in the Colonial Period Southern Maya Lowlands." In *Maya Subsistence: Studies in Memory of Dennis E. Puleston*, edited by Kent V. Flannery, 275–93. New York: Academic Press.

———. 1983. "The Last Maya Frontiers of Colonial Yucatán." In *Spaniards and Indians in Southeastern Mesoamerica*, edited by Murdo J. MacLeod and Robert Wasserstrom, 64–91. Lincoln: University of Nebraska Press.

———. 1989. *Maya Resistance to Spanish Rule*. Albuquerque: University of New Mexico Press.

———. 1994. "The Roots of People's Resistance in Colonial Belize, 1508–1733." Second Annual Clifford E. Betson Memorial Lecture, given at the 8th Annual Studies on Belize Conference, October 18th, Bliss Institute, Belize City, Belize.

———. 1998. *The Conquest of the Last Maya Kingdom*. Stanford, Calif.: Stanford University Press.

———. 2005. "Ethnohistorical Knowledge and Interdisciplinary Research: Rethinking Colonial 'Resistance' on the Colonial Frontiers of Yucatán." In *A Catalyst for Ideas: Anthropological Archaeology and the Legacy of Douglas Schwartz*, edited by Vernon L. Scarborough, 287–316. Santa Fe, N.M.: School of American Research Press.

———. 2009. "The Kowoj in Ethnohistorical Perspective." In *The Kowoj: Identity, Migration, and Geopolitics in Late Postclassic Petén, Guatemala*, edited by Prudence M. Rice and Don S. Rice, 55–69. Boulder: University Press of Colorado.

Jones, Grant D., Robert R. Kautz, and Elizabeth Graham. 1986. "Tipu: A Maya Town on the Spanish Colonial Frontier." *Archaeology* 39(1): 40–47.

Jones, Oakah L., Jr. 1994. *Guatemala in the Spanish Colonial Period*. Norman: University of Oklahoma Press.

Kamen, Henry. 2005. *Spain, 1469–1714: A Society of Conflict*. 3rd ed. Harlow, U.K.: Pearson Longman.

Kelly, Henry Ansgar. 2006. *Satan: A Biography*. Cambridge: Cambridge University Press.

Kemp, Peter, ed. 1980. *Encyclopedia of Ships and Seafaring*. London: Stanford Maritime.

Kepecs, Susan. 1997. "Native Yucatán and Spanish Influence: The Archaeology and History of Chikinchel." *Journal of Archaeological Method and Theory* 4(3/4): 307–29.

———. 2003. "Chikinchel." In *The Postclassic Mesoamerican World*, edited Michael E. Smith and Frances F. Berdan, 259–68. Salt Lake City: University of Utah Press.

Kepecs, Susan, and Marilyn Masson. 2003. "Political Organization in Yucatán and Belize." In *The Postclassic Mesoamerican World*, edited Michael E. Smith and Frances F. Berdan, 40–44. Salt Lake City: University of Utah Press.

King, Richard. 1999. *Orientalism and Religion: Postcolonial Theory, India and 'the Mystic East.'* London: Routledge.

Kitcher, Philip. 2001. *Science, Truth, and Democracy.* Oxford: Oxford University Press.

Klor de Alva, Jorge. 1982. "Spiritual Conflict and Accommodation in New Spain: Toward a Typology of Aztec Responses to Christianity." In *The Inca and Aztec States, 1400–1800,* edited by George A. Collier, Renato I. Rosaldo, and John D. Wirth, 345–66. New York: Academic Press.

———. 1989. "European Spirit and Mesoamerican Matter: Sahagún and the 'Crisis of Representation' in Sixteenth-Century Ethnography." In *The Imagination of Matter: Religion and Ecology in Mesoamerican Traditions,* edited by Davíd Carrasco, 17–29. BAR International Series 515. Oxford: British Archaeological Reports.

Koester, Helmut. 1990. *Ancient Christian Gospels.* London: SCM Press.

Korzybski, Alfred. 1994. *Science and Sanity: An Introduction to Non-Aristotelian Systems and General Semantics.* 5th ed. New York: Institute of General Semantics.

Krautheimer, Richard. 1986. *Early Christian and Byzantine Architecture.* New Haven, Conn.: Yale University Press.

Kroeber, Alfred L. 1944. *Configurations of Culture Growth.* Berkeley: University of California Press.

Kubler, George. 1948. *Mexican Architecture of the Sixteenth Century.* 2 vols. New Haven, Conn.: Yale University Press.

Küng, Hans. 2001. *The Catholic Church: A Short History.* Translated by John Bowden. New York: Modern Library.

LaFarge, Oliver. 1947. *Santa Eulalia: The Religion of a Cuchumatán Indian Town.* Chicago: University of Chicago Press.

Lambek, Michael. 2000. "The Anthropology of Religion and the Quarrel between Poetry and Philosophy." *Current Anthropology* 41(3): 309–20.

Lambert, Joseph B., Elizabeth Graham, Marvin T. Smith, and James S. Frye. 1994. "Amber and Jet from Tipu, Belize." *Ancient Mesoamerica,* no. 5: 55–60.

Lara, Jaime. 2004. *City, Temple, Stage: Eschatological Architecture and Liturgical Theatrics in New Spain.* Notre Dame, Ind.: University of Notre Dame Press.

LeGoff, Jacques. 1988. *The Medieval Imagination.* Translated by Arthur Goldhammer. London: University of Chicago Press.

Leonard, Elmore. 1987. *Touch.* New York: Quill, William Morrow.

Leopold, Anita Maria, and Jeppe Sinding Jensen. 2004. "General Introduction." In *Syncretism in Religion: A Reader,* edited by Anita Maria Leopold and Jeppen Sinding Jensen, 2–12. London: Equinox.

Lessa, William A., and Evon Z. Vogt, eds. 1979a. *Reader in Comparative Religion, An Anthropological Approach.* 4th ed. New York: Harper Collins.

———. 1979b. "General Introduction." In *Reader in Comparative Religion, An Anthropological Approach,* edited by William A. Lessa and Evon Z. Vogt, 1–6. 4th ed. New York: Harper Collins.

Lett, James. 1977. "Science, Religion, and Anthropology." In *Anthropology of Religion: A Handbook,* edited by Stephen D. Glazier, 103–20. Westport, Conn.: Greenwood Press.

Lewis, M. Paul, ed. 2009. *Ethnologue: Languages of the World.* 16th ed. Dallas, Texas: SIL International. http://www.ethnologue.com/.

Lindberg, Carter. 2006. *A Brief History of Christianity.* Oxford: Blackwell.

Link, Luther. 1995. *The Devil: The Archfiend in Art from the Sixth to the Sixteenth Century.* New York: Harry N. Abrams.

Lippy, Charles H., Robert Choquette, and Stafford Poole. 1992. *Christianity Comes to the Americas, 1492–1776*. New York: Paragon House.

Livingstone, E. A. 2000. *Oxford Concise Dictionary of the Christian Church*. Oxford: Oxford University Press.

Lockhart, James. 1992. *The Nahuas after the Conquest*. Stanford, Calif.: Stanford University Press.

Longino, Helen. 1990. *Science as Social Knowledge: Values and Objectivity in Scientific Inquiry*. Princeton, N.J.: Princeton University Press.

Loots, John. 1717. *The Fifth Part of the New Great Sea-Mirrour discovering the West-Coasts of Africa with a great deal [dial] of America*. Newly collected and published by John Loots . . . translated into the English Tongue, by Ericus Walten. Amsterdam.

Lopetegui, Leon, and Felix Zubillaga. 1965. *Historia de la Iglesia en la América Española*. Madrid: Biblioteca de Autores Cristianos.

López de Cogolludo, Fr. Diego. (1688) 1971. *Los tres siglos de la dominación española en Yucatán, o sea Historia de esta provincia*. 2 vols. Graz, Austria: Akademische Druck-u. Verlagsanstalt. Reprint of 1842–45 edition: vol. 1 published in Campeche in 1842 by José María Peralta; vol. 2 published in Mérida in 1845 by Castillo y Compañía. First published in 1688 in Madrid.

Lothrop, Samuel K. 1924. *Tulum, An Archaeological Study of the East Coast of Yucatán*. Carnegie Institution of Washington, publication no. 335. Washington, D.C.: Carnegie Institution of Washington.

———. 1927. "The Word 'Maya' and the Fourth Voyage of Columbus." *Indian Notes* (Museum of the American Indian, Heye Foundation, New York) 4(4): 350–63.

Lowden, John. 1997. *Early Christian and Byzantine Art*. London: Phaidon.

MacKie, Euan W. 1963. "Some Maya Pottery from Grand Bogue Point, Turneffe Islands, British Honduras." In *Effects of Hurricane Hattie on the British Honduras Reefs and Cays, October 30–31, 1961*, by David R. Stoddart, 131–35. Atoll Research Bulletin, no. 95. Washington, D.C.: Pacific Science Board, National Academy of Sciences, National Research Council.

MacLeod, Murdo J. 1973. *Spanish Central America: A Socioeconomic History, 1520–1720*. Berkeley: University of California Press.

———. 1982. "An Outline of Central American Colonial Demographics: Sources, Yields, and Possibilities." In *The Historical Demography of Highland Guatemala*, edited by Robert M. Carmack, J. Early, and Christopher Lutz, 3–18. Albany: Institute for Mesoamerican Studies, State University of New York at Albany.

Marnell, William H. 1978. *Light from the West: The Irish Mission and the Emergence of Modern Europe*. New York: Seabury Press.

Martin, Simon, and Nikolai Grube. 2008. *Chronicle of the Maya Kings and Queens*. London: Thames and Hudson.

Martinón-Torres, Marcos, Roberto V. Rojas, Jago Cooper, and Thilo Rehren. 2007. "Metals, Microanalysis, and Meaning: A Study of Metal Objects Excavated from the Indigenous Cemetery of El Chorro de Maita, Cuba." *Journal of Archaeological Science* 34(2): 194–204.

Marzal, Manuel M. 1993. "Transplanted Spanish Catholicism." In *Southern and Meso-American Native Spirituality: From the Cult of the Feathered Serpent to the Theology of Liberation*, edited by Gary H. Gossen in collaboration with Miguel León-Portilla, 140–69. London: SCM Press.

Masson, Marilyn A. 2000. *In the Realm of Nachan Kan*. Boulder: University of Colorado Press.

———. 2002. "Community Economy and the Mercantile Transformation in Postclassic Northeastern Belize." In *Ancient Maya Political Economies*, edited by Marilyn A. Masson and David A. Freidel, 335–64. Walnut Creek, Calif.: Altamira Press.

Mathews, Thomas M. 1993. *The Clash of Gods: A Reinterpretation of Early Christian Art*. Princeton, N.J.: Princeton University Press.

Matos Moctezuma, Eduardo, and Felipe Solís Holguín. 2002. *Aztecs*. London: Royal Academy of Arts.

Maudslay, Alfred P. 1956. "Commentary by the Translator." In *The Discovery and Conquest of Mexico, 1517–1521*, by Bernal Díaz del Castillo, translated by A. P. Maudslay. New York: Farrar, Straus and Cudahy.

Maurer Avalos, Eugenio. 1993. The Tzeltal Maya-Christian Synthesis." In *Southern and Meso-American Native Spirituality: From the Cult of the Feathered Serpent to the Theology of Liberation*, edited by Gary H. Gossen, 228–50. London: SCM Press.

Mayfield, Tracie Diane. 2009. "Ceramics, Landscape, and Colonialism: Archaeological Analysis of the British Settlement at Lamanai, Belize, 1837 to 1868." Master's thesis, Department of Sociology and Anthropology, Illinois State University.

Mayr-Harting, Henry. 2001. "The Early Middle Ages." In *Christianity: Two Thousand Years*, edited by Richard Harries and Henry Mayr-Harting, 44–64. Oxford: Oxford University Press.

McAnany, Patricia A. 1995. *Living with the Ancestors: Kinship and Kingship in Ancient Maya Society*. Austin: University of Texas Press.

McAndrew, John. 1965. *The Open-Air Churches of Sixteenth-Century Mexico*. Cambridge, Mass.: Harvard University Press.

McCaa, Robert. 1955. "Spanish and Nahuatl Views on Smallpox and Demographic Catastrophe in Mexico." *Journal of Interdisciplinary History* 23(3): 397–431.

McClure, Judith, and Roger Collins, eds. 1969. *The Ecclesiastical History of the English People*, by Saint Bede, the Venerable. Oxford: Oxford University Press.

McClymont, James Roxburgh. 1916. *Vicente Añes Pinçon*. London: Bernard Quaritch. ["McClymont" also catalogued as "MacClymont."]

McGee, R. Jon. 1990. *Life, Ritual, and Religion among the Lacandon Maya*. Belmont, Calif.: Wadsworth.

———. 1998. "The Lacandon Incense Burner Renewal Ceremony: Termination and Dedication Ritual among the Contemporary Maya." In *The Sowing and the Dawning*, edited by Shirley Boteler Mock, 41–46. Albuquerque: University of New Mexico Press.

McKillop, Heather. 1996. "Ancient Maya Trading Ports and the Integration of Long-Distance and Regional Economies: Wild Cane Cay in South-Coastal Belize." *Ancient Mesoamerica* 7(1): 49–62.

———. 2002. *Salt: White Gold of the Ancient Maya*. Gainesville: University Press of Florida.

———. 2005. *In Search of Maya Sea Traders*. College Station: Texas A&M University Press.

M'Closkey, Kathy. 2002. *Swept under the Rug: A Hidden History of Navajo Weaving*. Albuquerque: University of New Mexico Press.

McLuhan, Marshall, and Quentin Fiore. 1967. *The Medium Is the Massage*. Co-ordinated by Jerome Agel. London: Allen Lane, Penguin Press.

Megged, Amos. 1995. "'Right from the Heart': Indians' Idolatry in Mendicant Preachings in Sixteenth-Century Mesoamerica." In "Mesoamerican Religions: A Special Issue on the Occasion of the Seventeenth International Congress on the History of Religions, Mexico City, August 5–12, 1995." *History of Religions* 35(1): 61–82.

Melville, Elinor G. K. 1994. *A Plague of Sheep*. Cambridge: Cambridge University Press.

Mendieta, Geronimo de. 1945. *Historia eclesiástica indiana*. 4 vols. Mexico City: Editorial Salvador Chávez Hayhoe.

Michelet, Jules. 1973. *Satanism and Witchcraft*. New York: Citadel Press.

Milbrath, Susan, and Carlos Peraza Lope. 2003. "Revisiting Mayapan: Mexico's Last Maya Capital." *Ancient Mesoamerica* 14(1): 1–46.

Mock, Shirley B. 1994. "The Northern River Lagoon Site (NRL): Late to Terminal Classic Maya Settlement, Saltmaking, and Survival on the Northern Belize Coast." Ph.D. diss., Department of Anthropology, University of Texas, Austin.

Montanus, Arnoldus. 1671. *De Nieuwe en Onbekende Weereld, of, Beschryving van America en 't Zuid-land*. Amsterdam: Jacob Meurs.

Morales, Francisco, O.F.M. 1991. "Fray Pedro de Gante." In *Misioneros de la primera hora: Grandes evangelizadores del Nuevo Mundo*, edited by R. Ballán, 75–81. In *Enciclopedia Franciscana*, http://www.franciscanos.org/enciclopedia/pgante.html.

Mortimer, Ian. 2008. *The Time Traveller's Guide to Medieval England: A Handbook for Visitors to the Fourteenth Century*. London: The Bodley Head.

Molina, Alonso de. (1546) 1941. "Doctrina Christiana breve traduzida en lengua Mexicana por el padre fray Alonso de Molina de la Orden de los Minores, y examinada por el Reverendo padre Joan Gonçalez, Canónigo de la Iglesia Cathedral de la ciudad de México, por mandado del Rmo. Señor Don Fray Juan de Çumarraga, obispo de la dicha ciudad (1546)." In *Códice Franciscano, Siglo XVI, Informe de la Provincia del Santo Evangelio al Visitador Lic. Juan de Ovando, Informe de la Provincia de Guadalajara al Mismo, Cartas de Religiosos, 1533–1569*. Mexico City: Editorial Salvador Chávez Hayhoe.

———. 1565a. *Confessionario breve, en lengua Mexicana y Castellana: Compuesto por el muy reveréndo padre fray Alonso de Molina, de la ordén del seraphico padre San Francisco*. México: Antonio Espinosa.

———. 1565b. *Confessionario mayor, Instrucción y Doctrina, para el que se quiere bien confessar: Compuesto por el reverendo padre fray Alónso de Molina de la orden de señor San Francisco: Traduzido y vuelto en la lengua de los nauas, por el mismo autor*. México: Antonio Espinosa.

———. 1744. *Doctrina Christiana, y Cathecismo en lengua Mexicana. Compuesta, por el P. Fr. Alonso de Molina, de la Orden del Glorioso Seraphico Padre San Francisco*. México: Viuda de Francisco de Rivera Calderon, Calle de S. Agustin.

Momigliano, Arnaldo. 1963. "Pagan and Christian Historiography in the Fourth Century A.D." In *The Conflict between Paganism and Christianity in the Fourth Century*, edited by Arnaldo Momigliano, 79–99. Oxford: Clarendon Press.

Monaghan, John D. 1995. *The Covenants with Earth and Rain: Exchange, Sacrifice, and Revelation in Mixtec Sociality*. Norman: University of Oklahoma Press.

———. 2000. "Theology and History in the Study of Mesoamerican Religions." In *Ethnology*, edited by John D. Monaghan, 24–49. Supplement to the Handbook of Middle American Indians, vol. 6. Austin: University of Texas Press.

Morison, Samuel Eliot. 1974. *The European Discovery of America: The Southern Voyages, 1492–1616*. New York: Oxford University Press.

Morrison, Kenneth M. 1990. "Baptism and Alliance: The Symbolic Mediations of Religious Syncretism." *Ethnohistory* 37(4): 416–37.

Muchembled, Robert. 2004. *Damned: An Illustrated History of the Devil*. Paris: Éditions du Seuil.

Murray, Roy. 2006. *Family and People all Well—: An account of the Occurrences in the Business of Mahogany and Logwood Cutting in the Bay of Honduras in 1789*. Benque Viejo del Carmen, Belize: Cubola Productions.

Nash, Manning. 1958. *Machine Age Maya: The Industrialization of a Guatemalan Community*. Chicago: University of Chicago Press.

Nees, Lawrence. 1978. "A Fifth-Century Book Cover and the Origin of the Four Evangelist Symbols Page in the Book of Durrow." *Gesta* 17(1): 3–8.

Neff, Hector. 2001. "Production and Distribution of Plumbate Pottery: Evidence from a Provenance Study of the Paste and Slip Clay Used in a Famous Mesoamerican Trade-ware." Grantee Reports, Foundation for the Advancement of Mesoamerican Studies, Inc., http://www.famsi.org/reports/98061/section01.htm.

Neusner, Jacob, and Ernest S. Frerich, eds. 1985. *"To See Ourselves as Others See Us": Christians, Jews, "Others" in Late Antiquity*. Chico, Calif.: Scholars Press.

Newson, Linda. 1981. "Demographic Catastrophe in Sixteenth-Century Honduras." In *Studies in Spanish American Population History*, edited by D. J. Robinson, 217–41. Boulder: Westview Press.

Nock, A. D. 1998. *Conversion: The Old and the New in Religion from Alexander the Great to Augustine of Hippo*. Baltimore: Johns Hopkins University Press. First published 1933.

Oakes, Maud. 1969. *The Two Crosses of Todos Santos*. Princeton, N.J.: Princeton University Press.

Oakley, Ann. 1981. "Interviewing Women: A Contradiction in Terms." In *Doing Feminist Research*, edited by Helen Roberts, 30–61. London: Routledge and Kegan Paul.

Okoshi Harada, Tsubasa. 1994. "Ecab: Una revisión de la geografía política de una provincia Maya Yucateca del período postclásico tardío." In *Memorias del Primer Congreso Internacional de Mayistas*, 280–87. Mexico City: Centro de Estudios Mayas, Instituto de Investigaciones Filológicas, Universidad Autónoma de México.

———. 2006. "Los Canul y Los Canché: Una interpretación del 'Códice de Calkiní.'" In *Nuevas perspectivas sobre la geografía política de los Mayas*, edited by Tsubasa Okoshi Harada, Lorraine A. Williams-Beck, and Ana Luisa Izquierdo, 29–55. Mexico City: Universidad Nacional Autónoma de México, Universidad Autónoma de Campeche, Foundation for the Advancement of Mesoamerican Studies.

———. 2009. *Códice de Calkiní*. Mexico City: Universidad Nacional Autónoma de México.

Okoshi Harada, Tsubasa, Lorraine A. Williams-Beck, and Ana Luisa Izquierdo, eds. 2006. *Nuevas perspectivas sobre la geografía política de los Mayas*. Mexico City: Universidad Nacional Autónoma de México, Universidad Autónoma de Campeche, Foundation for the Advancement of Mesoamerican Studies.

Oland, Maxine H., and Marilyn A. Masson. 2005. "Late Postclassic–Colonial Period Maya Settlement on the West Shore of Progresso Lagoon." In *Archaeological Investigations in the Eastern Maya Lowlands: Papers of the 2004 Belize Archaeology Symposium*, edited by Jaime Awe, John Morris, Sherilyne Jones, and Christophe Helmke, 223–30. Research Reports in Belizean Archaeology, vol. 2. Belmopan, Belize: Institute of Archaeology, National Institute of Culture and History (NICH).

Oliver, José R. 2009. *Caciques and Cemí Idols: The Web Spun by Taíno Rulers between Hispaniola and Puerto Rico*. Tuscaloosa: University of Alabama Press.

O'Malley, John W. 2000. *Trent and All That*. Cambridge, Mass.: Harvard University Press.

Ortiz de Montellano, Bernard R. 1990. *Aztec Medicine, Health, and Nutrition*. New Brunswick, N.J.: Rutgers University Press.

Oulvey, Fray Bill, S.J. 2004. "Jesuit Service in Belize." http://www.catholicchurch.bz/About%20Belize.htm.

Oviedo y Valdéz, Gonzalo Fernández de. 1851–55. *Historia general y natural de las Indias, islas y tierra-firme del Mar Océano*. 4 vols. Madrid.

Pagden, Anthony. 1982. *The Fall of Natural Man: The American Indian and the Origins of Comparative Ethnology*. Cambridge: Cambridge University Press.

———, trans. and ed. 1986. *Letters from Mexico*, by Hernán Cortés. New Haven, Conn.: Yale University Press.

Pagels, Elaine. (1979) 2006. *The Gnostic Gospels*. London: Orion Books, 2006.

———. (1995) 1996. *The Origin of Satan*. New York: Vintage Books.

Paine, Crispin. 2008. "The Portable Altar in Christian Tradition and Practice." Ms. on file, Institute of Archaeology, University College, London.

Palka, Joel W. 2005. *Unconquered Lacandon Maya*. Gainesville: University Press of Florida.

Pelikan, Jaroslav. 1971. *The Emergence of the Catholic Tradition (100–600)*. The Christian Tradition, A History of the Development of Doctrine, pt. 1. Chicago: University of Chicago Press.

Pendergast, David M. 1975. "The Church in the Jungle: The ROM's First Season at Lamanai." *Rotunda* 8(2): 32–40.

———. 1981. "Lamanai, Belize: Summary of Excavation Results, 1974–1980." *Journal of Field Archaeology* 8(1): 29–53.

———. 1982a. "Lamanai, Belice, durante el Post-Clásico." *Estudios de Cultura Maya*, no. 14: 19–58.

———. 1982b. "The 19th-Century Sugar Mill at Indian Church, Belize." *Industrial Archaeology* 8(1): 57–66.

———. 1985. "Stop Me Before I Dig Again." *Archaeological Newsletter* (Royal Ontario Museum, Toronto), Series II, no. 11.

———. 1986a. "Stability through Change: Lamanai, Belize, from the Ninth to the Seventeenth Century." In *Late Lowland Maya Civilization: Classic to Postclassic*, edited by Jeremy A. Sabloff and E. Wyllys Andrews V, 223–49. Albuquerque: University of New Mexico Press.

———. 1986b. "Under Spanish Rule: The Final Chapter in Lamanai's Maya History." *Belcast Journal of Belizean Affairs* 3(1–2): 1–7.

———. 1988a. "The Historical Content of Oral Tradition: A Case from Belize." *Journal of American Folklore* 101(401): 321–24.

———. 1988b. "What's In a Name? Lamanai and Early Maps of Mayaland." *Rotunda* 20(4): 38–42.

———. 1988c. "Lamanai Stela 9: The Archaeological Context." Research Reports on Ancient Maya Writing, no. 20. Washington, D.C.: Center for Maya Research.

———. 1990. "Up from the Dust: The Central Lowlands Postclassic as Seen from Lamanai and Marco Gonzalez." In *Vision and Revision in Maya Studies*, edited by Flora

S. Clancy and Peter D. Harrison, 169–77. Albuquerque: University of New Mexico Press.

———. 1991. "The Southern Maya Lowlands Contact Experience: The View from Lamanai, Belize." In *The Spanish Borderlands in Pan-American Perspective*, edited by David Hurst Thomas, 336–54. Columbian Consequences, vol. 3. Washington, D.C.: Smithsonian Institution.

———. 1993. "Worlds in Collision: The Maya-Spanish Encounter in Sixteenth and Seventeenth Century Belize." In *The Meeting of Two Worlds: Europe and the Americas, 1492–1650*, edited by Warwick Bray, 105–43. Proceedings of The British Academy, no. 81. Oxford: Oxford University Press.

Pendergast, David M., and Elizabeth Graham. 1991. "The Town beneath the Town: Excavations at San Pedro, Belize." *Archaeological Newsletter* (Royal Ontario Museum, Toronto), Series II, no. 45.

Pendergast, David M., Grant D. Jones, and Elizabeth Graham. 1993. "Locating Spanish Colonial Towns in the Maya Lowlands: A Case Study from Belize." *Latin American Antiquity*, no. 4: 59–73.

Peñalosa, J. A. 1969. *La práctica religiosa en México: Siglo XVI*. Mexico City: Editorial Juan.

Pharo, Lars Kirkhusmo. 2007. "The Concept of 'Religion' in Mesoamerican Languages." *Numen*, no. 54: 28–70.

Phelan, John L. 1970. *The Millennial Kingdom of the Franciscans in the New World*. Berkeley: University of California Press.

Picart, Bernard. 1723. *Ceremonies et coutumes religieuses des peuples idolatres*. Amsterdam: J. F. Bernard.

Pieris, Aloysius, S.J. 1988. *An Asian Theology of Liberation*. Edinburgh: T & T Clark.

Pinney, Christopher 2001. "Piercing the Skin of the Idol." In *Beyond Aesthetics: Art and the Technologies of Enchantment*, edited by Christopher Pinney and Nicholas Thomas, 157–79. Oxford: Berg.

Pinto, Marina. 1998. "Reflecting on the Grave and the Bones Within: A Locus for Individual Will, Action, and Identity." Ph.D. diss., Department of Anthropology, Tulane University, New Orleans.

Pollard, Helen Perlstein. 2005. "From Core to Colonial Periphery: The Lake Pátzcuaro Basin, 1400–1800." In *The Postclassic to Spanish-Era Transition in Mesoamerica: Archaeological Perspectives*, edited by Susan Kepecs and Rani T. Alexander, 65–76. Albuquerque: University of New Mexico Press.

Poole, Stafford. 1992. "Iberian Catholicism Comes to the Americas." In *Christianity Comes to the Americas, 1492–1776*, by Charles H. Lippy, Robert Choquette, and Stafford Poole, 1–129. New York: Paragon House.

Popper, Karl. 1972. *Objective Knowledge*. Oxford: Clarendon Press.

Pugh, Timothy W. 2001. "Architecture, Ritual, and Social Identity at Late Postclassic Zacpetén, Guatemala: Identification of the Kowoj." Ph.D. diss., Department of Anthropology, Southern Illinois University, Carbondale.

Quezada, Sergio. 1993. *Pueblos y caciques yucatecos, 1550–1580*. Mexico City: El Colegio de México.

Rabasa, José. 1993. "Writing and Evangelization in Sixteenth-Century Mexico." In *Early Images of the Americas*, edited by Jerry M. Williams and Robert E. Lewis, 65–92. Tucson: University of Arizona Press.

Redfield, Robert. 1941. *The Folk Culture of Yucatán*. Chicago: University of Chicago Press.

Redfield, Robert, and Alfonso Villa Rojas. 1934. *Chan Kom: A Maya Village*. Carnegie Institution of Washington, publication no. 448. Washington, D.C.: Carnegie Institution of Washington.

Reents-Budet, Dorie. 1994. *Painting the Maya Universe*. Durham, N.C.: Duke University Press.

Reff, Daniel T. 2004. "'Making the Land Holy': The Mission Frontier in Early Medieval Europe and Colonial Mexico." In *The Spiritual Conversion of the Americas*, edited by James Muldoon, 17–35. Gainesville: University Press of Florida.

Reina, Ruben E. 1966. *The Law of the Saints: A Pokomam Pueblo and Its Community Culture*. Indianapolis, Ind.: Bobbs-Merrill.

Restall, Matthew. 1997. *The Maya World: Yucatec Culture and Society, 1550–1850*. Stanford, Calif.: Stanford University Press.

———. 1998. *Maya Conquistador*. Boston: Beacon Press.

———. 2003. *Seven Myths of the Spanish Conquest*. Oxford: Oxford University Press.

———. 2004. "Maya Ethnogenesis." *Journal of Latin American Anthropology* 9(1): 64–89.

Restall, Matthew, and John F. Chuchiak IV. 2002. "A Reevaluation of the Authenticity of Fray Diego de Landa's *Relación de las cosas de Yucatán*." *Ethnohistory* 49(3): 651–69.

Restall, Matthew, and Ueli Hostettler. 2001. "Introduction: The Meaning and Mechanics of Maya Survivalism." In *Maya Survivalism*, edited by Ueli Hostettler and Matthew Restall, ix–xiv. Acta MesoAmericana, vol. 12. Markt Schwaben, Germany: Verlag Anton Saurwein.

Reynolds, Susan E. 1985. The Excavations of Two Historic Maya Structures at Negroman-Tipu, Cayo District, Belize. Master's thesis, Department of Anthropology, Trent University, Peterborough, Ontario.

Ricard, Robert. 1966. *The Spiritual Conquest of Mexico*. Translated by Lesley Byrd Simpson. Berkeley: University of California Press.

Rice, Don S. 1986. "The Peten Postclassic: A Settlement Perspective." In *Late Lowland Maya Civilization: Classic to Postclassic*, edited by Jeremy A. Sabloff and E. Wyllys Andrews V, 301–44. Albuquerque: University of New Mexico Press.

Rice, Don S., Prudence M. Rice, and Timothy Pugh. 1998. "Settlement Continuity and Change in the Central Peten Lakes Region: The Case of Zacpeten." In *Anatomía de una civilización: Aproximaciones interdisciplinárias a la cultura Maya*, edited by Andrés Ciudad Ruiz, Yolanda Fernández Marquínez, José Miguel García Campillo, María Josefa Iglesias Ponce de León, Alfonso Lacadeno García-Gallo, and Luis T. Sanz Castro, 207–51. Madrid: Sociedad Española de Estudios Mayas.

Rice, Prudence M. 1987. *Macanché Island, El Petén, Guatemala: Excavations, Pottery, and Artifacts*. Gainesville: University of Florida Press.

———. 1996a. "Postclassic Censers around Lake Peten Itza, Guatemala." In *Arqueología mesoamericana, homenaje a William T. Sanders*, vol. 2, edited by Alba Guadalupe Mastache, Jeffrey R. Parsons, Robert S. Santley, and Mari Carmen Serra Puche, 123–35. Mexico City: Instituto Nacional de Antropología e Historia.

———. 1996b. "La cerámica del proyecto Maya-Colonial." In *Proyecto Maya-Colonial: Geografía política del siglo XVII en el céntro del Petén, Guatemala, Informe preliminar al Instituto de Antropología e Historia de Guatemala sobre investigacíons del campo en los años 1994 y 1995*, by Don S. Rice, Prudence M. Rice, Rómulo Sánchez

Polo, and Grant D. Jones, 247–318. Carbondale: Center for Archaeological Investigations and Department of Anthropology, Southern Illinois University.

Rice, Prudence M., and Don S. Rice. 2004. "Late Classic to Postclassic Transformations in the Petén Lakes Region, Guatemala." In *The Terminal Classic in the Maya Lowlands: Collapse, Transition, and Transformation*, edited by Arthur A. Demarest, Prudence M. Rice, and Don S. Rice, 125–39. Boulder: University Press of Colorado.

———. 2005. "The Final Frontier of the Maya: Central Petén, Guatemala, 1450–1700 CE." In *Untaming the Frontier in Anthropology, Archaeology, and History*, edited by Bradley J. Parker and Lars Rodseth, 147–73. Tucson: University of Arizona Press.

———. 2009a. "Introduction to the Kowoj and Their Petén Neighbors." In *The Kowoj: Identity, Migration, and Geopolitics in Late Postclassic Petén, Guatemala*, edited by Prudence M. Rice and Don S. Rice, 3–15. Boulder: University Press of Colorado.

———, eds. 2009b. *The Kowoj: Identity, Migration, and Geopolitics in Late Postclassic Petén, Guatemala*. Boulder: University Press of Colorado.

Richardson, Miles. 2003. *Being-in Christ and Putting Death in Its Place: An Anthropologist's Account of Christian Performance in Spanish America and the American South*. Baton Rouge: Louisiana State University Press.

Ringle, William M. 1999. "Pre-Classic Cityscapes: Ritual Politics among the Early Lowland Maya." In *Social Patterns in Pre-Classic Mesoamerica*, edited by David C. Grove and Rosemary A. Joyce, 183–223. Washington, D.C.: Dumbarton Oaks Research Library and Collection.

Rodríguez-Alegría, Enrique. 2005. "Eating Like an Indian: Negotiating Social Relations in the Spanish Colonies." *Current Anthropology* 46(4): 551–73.

Rodríguez Becerra, Salvador. 1977. *Encomienda y conquista—Los inicios de la colonización en Guatemala*. Publicaciones del Seminario de Antropología Americana, vol. 14. Seville: Universidad de Sevilla.

Rodseth, Lars, and Bradley J. Parker. 2005. "Introduction: Theoretical Considerations in the Study of Frontiers." In *Untaming the Frontier in Anthropology, Archaeology, and History*, edited by Bradley J. Parker and Lars Rodseth, 3–21. Tucson: University of Arizona Press.

Roys, Ralph L., ed. 1939. *The Titles of Ebtun*. Carnegie Institution of Washington, publication no. 505. Washington, D.C.: Carnegie Institution of Washington.

———. 1943. *The Indian Background of Colonial Yucatan*. Carnegie Institution of Washington, publication no. 548. Washington, D.C.: Carnegie Institution of Washington.

———. 1952. *Conquest Sites and the Subsequent Destruction of Maya Architecture in the Interior of Yucatán*. Carnegie Institution of Washington, publication no. 596. Washington, D.C.: Carnegie Institution of Washington.

———. 1957. *The Political Geography of the Yucatan Maya*. Carnegie Institution of Washington, publication no. 613. Washington, D.C.: Carnegie Institution of Washington.

———. 1962. "Literary Sources for the History of Mayapan." In *Mayapan, Yucatan, Mexico*, edited by H. E. D. Pollock, Ralph L. Roys, Tatiana Proskouriakoff, and A. Ledyard Smith, 25–86. Carnegie Institution of Washington, publication no. 619. Washington, D.C.: Carnegie Institution of Washington.

———. 1967. *The Book of Chilam Bayam of Chumayel*. Norman: University of Oklahoma Press. First published by the Carnegie Institution of Washington, publication no. 438, 1933.

Rubial García, Antonio. 1978–79. "Evangelismo y evangelización: Los primitivos franciscanos en la Nueva España y el ideal del cristianismo primitivo." *Anuario de Historia*, no. 10: 95–124.

Ruesch, J., and G. Bateson. 1951. *Communication: The Social Matrix of Psychiatry*. New York: Norton.

Russell, James C. 1994. *The Germanization of Early Medieval Christianity*. Oxford: Oxford University Press.

Russell, Jeffrey Burton. 1977. *The Devil: Perceptions of Evil from Antiquity to Primitive Christianity*. Ithaca, N.Y.: Cornell University Press.

Sabloff, Jeremy A., and William L. Rathje. 1975. "Cozumel's Place in Yucatecan Culture History." In *Changing Pre-Columbian Commercial Systems*, edited by Jeremy A. Sabloff and William L. Rathje, 21–28. Peabody Museum of Archaeology and Ethnology Monographs, no. 3. Cambridge, Mass.: Peabody Museum, Harvard University.

Saliba, John A. 1976. *"Homo Religiosus" in Mircea Eliade: An Anthropological Evaluation*. Leiden: Brill.

Sanders, William T. 1960. *Prehistoric Ceramics and Settlement Patterns in Quintana Roo, Mexico*. Carnegie Institution of Washington, publication no. 606. Washington, D.C.: Carnegie Institution of Washington.

———. 1970. "The Population of the Teotihuacan Valley, the Basin of Mexico, and the Central Mexican Symbiotic Region in the 16th Century." In *The Natural Environment, Contemporary Occupation, and 16th Century Population of the Valley*, by Anton Kovar, Thomas H. Charlton, Richard A Diehl, and William T. Sanders. Teotihuacan Valley Project Final Report, vol. 1, 385–452. Occasional Papers in Anthropology, no. 3. Department of Anthropology, Pennsylvania State University, University Park.

Sanmark, Alexandra. 2004. "Power and Conversion: A Comparative Study of Christianization in Scandinavia." Occasional Papers in Archaeology, no. 34. Department of Archaeology and Ancient History, Uppsala University, Uppsala, Sweden.

Sandstrom, Alan R. 1991. *Corn Is Our Blood: Culture and Ethnic Identity in a Contemporary Aztec Indian Village*. Norman: University of Oklahoma Press.

Sanson d'Abbeville, N. 1650. *Mexicque, ou Nouvelle Espagne, Nouvelle Gallice, Iucatan etc. et autres Provinces jusques a L'Isthme de Panama; au font Les Audiences de Mexico, de Guadalaiara, et de Guatimala*. Paris: Chez Pierre Mariette.

———. 1670. *Cartes generales de toutes les parties du monde, ou les empires, monarchies, republiques, estats, peuples, etc. . . .* Vol. 1. Paris: Chez Pierre Mariette.

Sapper, Karl. 1985. *The Verapaz in the Sixteenth and Seventeenth Centuries: A Contribution to the Historical Geography and Ethnography of Northeastern Guatemala*. Translated by Theodore E. Gutman. Institute of Archaeology Occasional Paper 13. Los Angeles: University of California, Los Angeles.

Sauer, Carl O. 1966. *The Early Spanish Main*. Berkeley: University of California Press.

Sawyer, Birgit, and Peter Sawyer. 1993. *Medieval Scandinavia: From Conversion to Reformation, circa 800–1500*. Nordic Series, vol. 17. Minneapolis: University of Minnesota Press.

Schackt, Jon. 2001. "The Emerging Maya: A Case of Ethnogenesis." In *Maya Survivalism*, edited by Ueli Hostettler and Matthew Restall, 3–14. Markt Schwaben, Germany: Verlag Anton Saurwein.

Scholes, France V., and Eleanor B. Adams. 1938. *Don Diego Quijada, Alcalde Mayor de Yucatán, 1561–1565*. Documentos sacados de los archivos de España y publicados por F. V. Scholes y E. B. Adams. 2 vols. Mexico City: Antigua Librería Robredo, de J. Porrúa e Hijos.

Scholes, France V., and Ralph L. Roys. 1938. *Fray Diego de Landa and the Problem of Idolatry in Yucatan*. Division of Historical Research, Carnegie Institution of Washington, publication no. 501, 585–620. Washington, D.C.: Carnegie Institution of Washington.

———. 1948. *The Maya Chontal Indians of Acalan-Tixchel*. 2nd ed. Norman: University of Oklahoma Press.

Scholes, France V., and J. Eric S. Thompson. 1977. "The Francisco Pérez *Probanza* and the *Matrícula* of Tipu." In *Anthropology and History in Yucatán*, edited by Grant D. Jones, 43–68. Austin: University of Texas Press.

Scholes, France V., Carlos R. Menéndez, J. Ignacio Rubio Mañe, and Eleanor B. Adams, eds. 1936–38. *Documentos para la historia de Yucatán*. 3 vols. Mérida: Compañía Tipográfica Yucateca.

———. 1938. *Documentos para la historia de Yucatán*, vol. 2, *La iglesia en Yucatán, 1560–1610*. Mérida, Yucatán.

Schroeder, H. J. 1978. *Canons and Decrees of the Council of Trent*. English translation by Rev. H. J. Schroeder, O.P. Rockford, Ill.: TAN Books and Publishers.

Schwaller, John Frederick. 1987. *The Church and Clergy in Sixteenth-Century Mexico*. Albuquerque: University of New Mexico Press.

Scotchmer, David G. 1993. "Life of the Heart: A Maya Protestant Spirituality." In *Southern and Meso-American Native Spirituality: From the Cult of the Feathered Serpent to the Theology of Liberation*, edited by Gary H. Gossen in collaboration with Miguel León Portilla, 496–525. London: SCM Press.

Scott, J. G. M. 2004. *St. Martin's Church, Exeter, Devon*. London: Churches Conservation Trust.

Seznec, Jean. 1981. *The Survival of the Pagan Gods*. Translated from the French by Barbara F. Sessions. Princeton, N.J.: Princeton University Press.

Sharer, Robert J. 2006. *The Ancient Maya*. 6th ed. Stanford, Calif.: Stanford University Press.

Shoman, Assad. 2000. *13 Chapters of a History of Belize*. Belize City: Angelus Press.

Sierra, Vicente D. 1944. *El sentido misional de conquista de América*. 3rd ed. Buenos Aires: Editorial Huarpes.

Silverblatt, Irene. 1987. *Moon, Sun, and Witches: Gender Ideologies and Class in Inca and Colonial Peru*. Princeton, N.J.: Princeton University Press.

Siegel, Morris. 1941. "Religion in Western Guatemala: A Product of Acculturation." *American Anthropologist*, n.s., 43(1): 62–76.

Simmons, Scott E. 1991. "Arrows of Consequence: Contact Period Maya Tool Technology at Tipu, Belize." Master's thesis, Department of Anthropology, University of Massachusetts at Boston.

———. 1995. "Maya Resistance, Maya Resolve: The Tools of Autonomy from Tipu, Belize." *Ancient Mesoamerica* 6(2): 2: 135–46.

Simmons, Scott E., David M. Pendergast, and Elizabeth Graham. 2009. "The Context and Significance of Copper Artifacts in Postclassic and Early Historic Lamanai, Belize." *Journal of Field Archaeology* 34(1): 57–75.

Smart, Ninian. 1983. *Worldviews: Cross-Cultural Explorations of Human Beliefs*. New York: Scribner's.

———. 1997a. "Preface: Reflections in the Mirror of Religion." In *Reflections in the Mirror of Religion*, edited by John P. Burris, ix–xi. Houndmills, Basingstoke, Hampshire: Macmillan.

———. 1997b. *Reflections in the Mirror of Religion: Ninian Smart*. Edited with an introduction by John P. Burris. Houndmills, Basingstoke, Hampshire: Macmillan.

———. 1999. *Atlas of the World's Religions*. Edited by Ninian Smart. Oxford: Oxford University Press.

Smith, Jonathan Z. 1985. "What a Difference a Difference Makes." In *"To See Ourselves as Others See Us": Christians, Jews, "Others" in Late Antiquity*, edited by Jacob Neusner and Ernest S. Frerichs, 3–48. Chico, Calif.: Scholars Press.

———. 1998. "Religion, Religions, Religious." In *Critical Terms for Religious Studies*, edited by Mark C. Taylor, 269–84. Chicago: University of Chicago Press.

Smith, Marvin T., Elizabeth Graham, and David M. Pendergast. 1994. "European Beads from Spanish Colonial Lamanai and Tipu, Belize." *Beads: Journal of the Society of Bead Researchers*, no. 6: 27–49.

Smith, Michael E. 1986. "The Role of Social Stratification in the Aztec Empire: A View from the Provinces." *American Anthropologist* 88(1): 70–91.

———. 2003a. *The Aztecs*. 2nd ed. Oxford: Blackwell.

———. 2003b. "Small Polities in Mesoamerica." In *The Postclassic Mesoamerican World*, edited by Michael E. Smith and Frances F. Berdan, 35–39. Salt Lake City: University of Utah Press.

Smith, Michael E., and Frances F. Berdan. 2003. "Spatial Structure of the Mesoamerican World System." In *The Postclassic Mesoamerican World*, edited by Michael E. Smith and Frances F. Berdan, 21–31. Salt Lake City: University of Utah Press.

Smith, Robert E. 1971. *The Pottery of Mayapan*. Peabody Museum of Archaeology and Ethnology, Papers 66. Cambridge, Mass.: Harvard University.

Sotelo Santos, Laura Elena. 1988. *Las ideas cosmológicas Mayas en el siglo XVI*. Mexico City: Universidad Nacional Autónoma de México.

Stoudemire, Sterling A. 1970. *Pedro de Córdoba's "Christian Doctrine For the Instruction and Information of the Indians."* Introduction and translation by Sterling A. Stoudemire. Coral Gables: University of Miami Press.

Stravinskas, Reverend Peter M. J., ed. 1998. *Our Sunday Visitor's Catholic Encyclopedia*. Rev. ed. Huntington, Ind.: Our Sunday Visitor.

Stuart, David, and Stephen D. Houston. 1993. *Classic Maya Place Names*. Washington, D.C.: Dumbarton Oaks Research Library and Collection.

Tambiah, Stanley J. 1990. *Magic, Science, Religion, and the Scope of Rationality*. Cambridge: Cambridge University Press.

Taube, Karl A. 1992. *The Major Gods of Ancient Yucatán*. Washington, D.C.: Dumbarton Oaks Research Library and Collection.

Taylor, Richard. 2003. *How to Read a Church*. London: Rider. Illustrated edition published 2004.

Tedlock, Barbara. 1982. *Time and the Highland Maya*. Albuquerque: University of New Mexico Press.

Tedlock, Dennis. 1993. "Torture in the Archives: Mayans Meet Europeans." *American Anthropologist*, new ser., 95(1): 139–52.

Terraciano, Kevin. 2007. "People of Two Hearts and the One God from Castile: Ambivalent Responses to Christianity in Early Colonial Oaxaca." In *Religion in New Spain*, edited by Susan Schroeder and Stafford Poole, 16–32. Albuquerque: University of New Mexico Press.

Thomas, Charles. 1981. *Christianity in Roman Britain to* A.D. *500*. London: Batsford.

Thompson, Charles D., Jr. 2001. *Maya Identities and the Violence of Place: Borders Bleed.* Aldershot, U.K.: Ashgate Publishing.

Thompson, Donald E. 1960. "Maya Paganism and Christianity." In *Nativism and Syncretism*, by Munro S. Edmonson, Gustavo Correa, Donald E. Thompson, and William Madsen, 1–34. Middle American Research Institute, no. 19. New Orleans: Middle American Research Institute, Tulane University.

Thompson, J. Eric S. 1938. "Sixteenth and Seventeenth Century Reports on the Chol Mayas." *American Anthropologist* 40(4): 603.

———. 1966. *The Rise and Fall of Maya Civilization*. 2nd ed. Norman: University of Oklahoma Press.

———. 1970. *Maya History and Religion*. Norman: University of Oklahoma Press.

———. 1972. *The Maya of Belize*. Belmopan, Belize: Benex Press.

———. 1977. "A Proposal for Constituting a Maya Subgroup, Cultural and Linguistic, in the Peten and Adjacent Regions." In *Anthropology and History in Yucatán*, edited by Grant D. Jones, 3–42. Austin: University of Texas Press.

Thompson, Philip C. 1999. *Tekanto, A Maya Town in Colonial Yucatán*. Middle American Research Institute, no. 67. New Orleans: Middle American Research Institute, Tulane University.

Thomson, Peter. 2004. *Belize: A Concise History*. Basingstoke, Hampshire, U.K.: Palgave Macmillan.

Todorov, Tzvetan. 1984. *The Conquest of America*. Translated by Richard Howard. New York: Harper and Row.

Tokovinine, Alex. 2006. "People from a Place: Re-examining Classic Maya 'Emblem Glyphs.'" Paper presented at the 11th European Maya Conference "Ecology, Power, and Religion in Maya Landscapes," December 4–9, Malmö, Sweden.

Toussaint, Manuel. 1927. "La arquitectura religiosa en la Nueva España durante el siglo XVI." In *Iglesias de México*, vol. 6, *1525–1925*, by Manuel Toussaint and Ing. J. R. Benitez, 7–73. Textos y dibujos del Dr. Atl. Mexico City: Secretaría de Hacienda.

Tozzer, Alfred M., trans. and ed. 1941. *Landa's relación de las cosas de Yucatán*. Papers of the Peabody Museum of American Archaeology and Ethnology, vol. 18. Cambridge, Mass.: Harvard University.

Trevor-Roper, Hugh R. 1970. "The European Witch-Craze." In *Witchcraft and Sorcery*, edited by Max Marwick, 121–50. Harmondsworth, U.K.: Penguin.

Turner, Victor W. 1986. "Dewey, Dilthey, and Drama: An Essay in the Anthropology of Experience." In *The Anthropology of Experience*, edited by Victor W. Turner and Edward M. Bruner, 33–43. Urbana: University of Illinois Press.

Valenzuela Márquez, Jaime. 2004. "Confessing the Indians Guilt: Discourse and Acculturation in Early Spanish America." In *The Spiritual Conversion of the Americas*, edited by James Muldoon, 169–91. Gainesville: University Press of Florida.

Vander Aa, Pierre. [1761?]. "Nouvelle Espagne, Novelle Galice, et Guatimala dans l'Amerique Septentrionale. . . ." Part of *Atlas nouveau, contenant toutes les parties du monde: Où sont exactement remarquées les empires, monarchies, royaumes, états, républiques &c.* Amsterdam: Covens and Mortier.

van Keulen, Johannes 1681–96. *De Nieuwe Groote Lichtende Zee-Fackel*. Vol. 2, map 32. [Amsterdam(?): Johannes van Keulen]

Vargas Pacheco, Ernesto. 1997. *Tulum: Organización político-territorial de la costa oriental de Quintana Roo*. Mexico City: Instituto de Investigaciones Antropológicas, Universidad Nacional Autónoma de México.

Varner, John G., and Jeannette J. Varner. 1983. *Dogs of the Conquest*. Norman: University of Oklahoma Press.

Vega, Agustín de. (1744) 1974. "Noticia del principio y progresos del establecimiento de las Missiones de Gentiles en el Rio Orinoco, por la Compañia de Jesus, con la continuación, y oposiciones que hicieron los Carives hasta el año de [1]744 en que se les aterro, y atemorizo, con la venida de unos Cabres traydos, que se havencindaron en Cabruta. Lo que para mejor inteligencia iremos contando por los años, en que se establecieron dichas Missiones, y lo que en cada uno passó, cómo passó, la qual relacion haze un testigo de vista que lo ha andado todo por si mismo muchas vezes, Religioso de la Misma Compañia." In *Documentos jesuíticos relativos a la historia de la Compañía de Jesús de Venezuela*, vol. 2. Edición e introducción por José del Rey Fajardo, S. J. Biblioteca de la Academia Nacional de la Historia, vol. 118, pp. 3–149. Caracas: Italgráfica.

Vicaire, M.-H. 1964. *St. Dominic and His Times*. Translated by Kathleen Pond. London: Darton, Longman and Todd.

Vico, Giambattista. 1984. *The New Science of Giambattista Vico*. Translated by Thomas Goddard Bergin and Max Harold Fisch. Unabridged translation of the 3rd ed. (1744) with addition of "Practic of the New Science." Ithaca, N.Y.: Cornell University Press.

Villacorta Calderón, José Antonio. 1942. *Historia de la Capitanía General de Guatemala*. Guatemala City.

Visscher, Nicolas. 1717. "Atlas Minor sive Geographia Compendiosa qua Orbis Terrarum. . . ." Part of *Atlas complet contenant toutes les cartes geographiques du monde.* . . . Amsterdam: Chez la Veve de Nicolas Visscher avec privilege des N.S. Les Etats Generaux.

Vogt, Evon Z. 1976. *Tortillas for the Gods: A Symbolic Analysis of Zinacanteco Rituals*. Cambridge, Mass.: Harvard University Press.

Voragine, Jacobus de. 1993. *The Golden Legend: Readings on the Saints*, vol. 2. Translated by William Granger Ryan. Princeton, N.J.: Princeton University Press.

Wagley, Charles. 1949. *The Social and Religious Life of a Guatemalan Village*. Memoirs of the American Anthropological Association, no. 71. [Menasha, Wis.]: American Anthropological Association.

Walker, William H. 1995. "Ceremonial Trash?" In *Expanding Archaeology*, edited by James M. Skibo, William H. Walker, and Axel E. Nielsen, 67–79. Salt Lake City: University of Utah Press.

Ward, Benedicta. 1987. *Miracles and the Medieval Mind: Theory, Record, and Event, 1000–1215*. Aldershot, U.K.: Scolar.

Warren, J. Benedict. 1985. *The Conquest of Michoacán: The Spanish Domination of the Tarascan Kingdom in Western Mexico, 1521–1530*. Norman: University of Oklahoma Press.

Warren, Kay. 1978. *The Symbolism of Subordination: Indian Identity in a Guatemalan Town*. Austin: University of Texas Press.

Wasserstrom, Robert. 1983. *Class and Society in Central Chiapas*. Berkeley: University of California Press.

Watanabe, John M. 1989. "Elusive Essences: Souls and Social Identity in Two Highland Maya Communities." In *Ethnographic Encounters in Mesoamerica: Essays in Honor of*

Evon Zartman Vogt, Jr., edited by Victoria R. Bricker and Gary H. Gossen, 263–74. Institute for Mesoamerican Studies, Studies on Culture and Society, vol. 3. Albany: Institute for Mesoamerican Studies, University at Albany, State University of New York.

———. 1992. *Maya Saints and Souls in a Changing World.* Austin: University of Texas Press.

Watts, Dorothy. 1998. *Religion in Late Roman Britain.* London: Routledge.

Weeks, John M., and Nancy J. Black. 1991. "Mercedarian Missionaries and the Transformation of Lenca Indian Society in Western Honduras, 1550–1700." In *The Spanish Borderlands in Pan-American Perspective*, edited by David Hurst Thomas, 245–61. Columbian Consequences, vol. 3. Washington, D.C.: Smithsonian Institution Press.

Welsh, Thomas Jerome. 1950. *The Use of the Portable Altar: A Historical Synopsis and a Commentary.* Washington, D.C.: Catholic University Press.

White, Christine D., and Henry P. Schwarcz. 1989. "Ancient Maya Diet: As Inferred from Isotopic and Elemental Analysis of Human Bone." *Journal of Archaeological Science*, no. 16: 451–74.

White, Christine D., Lori E. Wright, and David M. Pendergast. 1994. "Biological Disruption in the Early Colonial Period at Lamanai." In *In the Wake of Contact: Biological Responses to Conquest*, edited by Clark Spencer Larsen and George R. Milner, 135–45. New York: Wiley-Liss.

Whitehouse, Ruth D., and John B. Wilkins. 1986. *The Making of Civilization: History Discovered through Archaeology.* New York: Alfred A. Knopf.

Wiewall, Darcy L. 2009. "Identifying the Impact of the Spanish Colonial Regime on Maya Household Production at Lamanai, Belize, during the Terminal Postclassic to Early Colonial Transition." Ph.D. diss., University of California at Riverside.

Wilk, Richard. 2006. *Home Cooking in the Global Village: Caribbean Food from Buccaneers to Ecotourists.* Oxford: Berg.

Williams, Jay. 1976. *Everyone Knows What a Dragon Looks Like.* Illustrated by Mercer Mayer. New York: Four Winds Press, Scholastic Magazines.

Williams-Beck, Lorraine A. "Patrones de asentamiento y organización comunitaria previos a la formación de una jurisdicción política: Una evaluación arqueológica del *Códice de Calkiní.*" In *Nuevas perspectivas sobre la geografía política de los Mayas*, edited by Tsubasa Okoshi Harada, Lorraine A. Williams-Beck, and Ana Luisa Izquierdo, 291–338. Mexico City: Universidad Nacional Autónoma de México, Universidad Autónoma de Campeche, Foundation for the Advancement of Mesoamerican Studies.

Wilson, Amelia. 2002. *The Devil.* London: PRC Publishing.

Wilson, Eden W. 1991. "Classification of Postclassic Redware Pottery from Negroman-Tipu, Belize." Master's thesis, Department of Anthropology, University of Florida, Gainesville.

Wilson, David Sloan. 2002. *Darwin's Cathedral: Evolution, Religion, and the Nature of Society.* Chicago: University of Chicago Press.

Wilson, Richard. 1995. *Maya Resurgence in Guatemala: Q'eqchi' Experiences.* Norman: University of Oklahoma Press.

Winzerling, E. O. 1946. *The Beginning of British Honduras.* New York: North River Press.

Wood, Ian. 2001. *The Missionary Life: Saints and the Evangelisation of Europe, 400–1050.* Harlow, Essex, U.K.: Pearson Education.

Woodward, Ralph Lee, Jr. 1999. *Central America: A Nation Divided.* 3rd ed. Oxford: Oxford University Press.

Wrobel, Gabriel D., Marie E. Danforth, and Carl Armstrong. 2002. "Estimating Sex of Maya Skeletons by Discriminant Function Analysis of Long-Bone Measurements from the Protohistoric Maya Site of Tipu, Belize." *Ancient Mesoamerica*, no. 13: 255–63.

Wylie, Alison. 1994. "Reasoning about Ourselves: Feminist Methodology in the Social Sciences." In *Readings in the Philosophy of Social Science*, edited by Michael Martin and Lee C. McIntyre. Cambridge, Mass.: MIT Press.

———. 2003. "Why Standpoint Matters." In *Science and Other Cultures: Issues in Philosophies of Science and Technology*, edited by Robert Figueroa and Sandra Harding, 26–48. London: Routledge.

Wyschogrod, Edith. 1998. "Value." In *Critical Terms for Religious Studies*, edited by Mark C. Taylor, 365–82. Chicago: University of Chicago Press.

Wytfliet Louaniensis, Cornely. 1597. *Descriptionis Ptolemaicae Augmentum*. Lovanii: Typis Iohannis Bogardi.

Yaeger, Jason, Minette C. Church, Jennifer Dornan, and Richard M. Leventhal. 2005. "Investigating Historic Households: The 2003 Season of the San Pedro Maya Project." In *Archaeological Investigations in the Eastern Maya Lowlands: Papers of the 2004 Belize Archaeology Symposium*, edited by Jaime Awe, John Morris, Sherilyne Jones, and Christophe Helmke, 257–67. Research Reports in Belizean Archaeology, vol. 2. Belmopan, Belize: Institute of Archaeology, National Institute of Culture and History (NICH).

Zavala, Silvio Arturo. 1955. *Sir Thomas More in New Spain*. London: Hispanic and Luso-Brazilian Councils.

———. 1973. *La encomienda indiana*. 2nd ed. Mexico City: Editorial Porrúa.

Index

Page numbers with *t* refer to tables; page numbers with *i* refer to illustrations.

Acalan, 32*i*, 47, 127, 130

Acolhua, 145, 147, 352–53n70

Agriculture: agrarian collectivism, 145; annatto production, 307; coastal, 123, 138; Lamanai, 212, 327n37; soil, 37–38, 123, 199, 346n98; spiritual being Chac, 81; swidden farming, 329–30n22

—crops: cacao, 157, 197, 203, 238, 244, 274, 307; cotton, 197, 238; maize, 197, 327n37; papaya, 189; sorghum, 327n37; sugar, 212, 254

Aguilar, Gerónimo de, 121, 122, 125, 345n77, 346–47n101

Aguilar, Gregorio, 223, 244, 247, 367n54

Aguilar, Juan de, 204, 362n87

Ah Canul, 31*i*, 32*i*, 38

Ah Kin Chel, 32*i*, 38

Ah Kin Pol (AjK'in P'ol), 245

Ajaw Kan Ek', 157

Alacranes, 346–47n102

Altun Ha, 43, 118, 119

Alvarado, Pedro de, 112, 134, 344n51, 349n165

Ambassador's Fund for Cultural Preservation, 363n111

Ambergris Caye, 118, 119, 120, 130

Animals: diversity, 235; as food, 235; invasive species, 16; role in Christian and Maya beliefs, 26*i*, 291–95, 292*i*, 293*i*

Anthropology of religion, 66–67, 75–76

Apocalypto (2006), 331n54

Aragon, 152, 334n13

Arawak (language), 332n80

Archaeology: disjunction with ethno-history in Belize, 12–13, 18–19, 194, 236, 289; documents (*see* Historical documents); effects of sea-level rise, 118; relationship with magic and religion, 309–11, 313, 373–74n12 (*see also* Religion, academic research). *See also specific sites*

—academic considerations: author's research philosophy, 14–15, 25–28, 310–11, 327n33, 328n55–56, 374n14; discovery process and knowledge building, 27–28, 62, 328n55–56, 335n16; importance of contextualizing, 11–12; importance of intellectual flexibility, 11, 12, 15, 326n11, 327n29; interpretation of behavior, 76–78; interpretation of "material culture," 10–11, 25–26; interpretation of negative evidence as absence, 187; interpretation of "resistance," 289–90; what scholars make of the sources, 288–91

Architecture: influence of trade on style, 47; Kowoj, 54; Paleochristian, 172

—church: single-nave with blind sanctuaries, 158, 159*i*, 355n159; Spanish and Mexican influence, 57, 230, 232, 237; terms and typologies, 167–87; *See also* Lamanai church *headings*; Tipu church

Arellano, Bishop Domingo Villa-Escusa Ramírez de, 324*t*

Aristotle, 67

Arriaga, Bishop Antonio, 324*t*

Arrowheads and spearheads, 252, 253*i*

Art: aesthetic expression *vs.* social/cultural context, 9–12, 263–72, 325n1; anthropomorph emerging from a shell, 265, 267, 268*i*, 269*i*; depiction of angels, 292, 301–4, 302–4*i*; depiction of

Art (*continued*)
the devil, 266*i*, 267, 269, 270*i*, 271–72, 293, 302*i*, 303; emotional response to, 9, 325n2; imagery and sacred space, 305–6; open mouth as symbol, 214*i*, 216*i*, 220*i*, 265, 266*i*; religion as, 70, 75–76; religious paintings, 23, 240; *vs.* idolatry, 9–10, 25, 161, 273–74

Art history, 11, 325n2

Astronomy, 73–74

Atrio, 17, 172, 173*i*, 180–87, 205*i*, 210*i*, 221, 222*i*

Augustine of Hippo, 92–93

Avendaño y Loyola, Fr. Andrés, 251, 321*t*

Aztecs: beliefs, 276; conquest, 134, 139, 352–53n70; destruction of antiquities, 10; health and medicine, 338n121; impact on Christianity, 147; misperceptions by the Spanish, 145; Templo Mayor, 146*i*; trade, 45; tribute system, 36, 331n59; use of term, 6, 352–53n70; warfare, 41, 125–26

Azuaga, Pedroi de, 152

Bacalar: secular mission, 158, 160, 161, 162, 240, 251; villa of (hamlet), 195, 199, 249
—province: flight and population loss, 203, 207, 239; military post in, 368n82; during Pacheco conquest, 142; Pérez interim governor, 250; population, 204
—town: church, 187; under jurisdiction of Yucatan, 121; maps, 53*i*, 108*i*; move to Xamanha, 127; pirate attacks, 249; secular clergy and parishes, 142, 151; settlement in 1527, 125
—Villa de Salamanca de Bacalar: as a governing center, 111, 133, 157, 246–47; Melchor and Alonso Pacheco in, 203; modern-day location, 111; remoteness, 163; secular priest in, 142; settlement, 133

Bajlaj Chan K'awil, 331n62

Barrientos, Fr. Martín de, 160, 314*t*

Batab/batabob (governor), 38, 46, 64, 241

Bay of Honduras, 13*i*, 108*i*, 112, 113*i*, 122–24, 346n87, 347–48n116. *See also* Gulf of Honduras

Beads: amber, 233; bone rosary, 233, 235*i*; gifts from Franciscans to the Maya, 240; jade, 214*i*, 215*i*, 218; shell, 216*i*, 218
—glass: jewelry from, 22, 23*i*, 24*i*, 233, 327n50; Lamanai, 50, 224, 233; Tipu, 50, 230, 237

Becerril, Fr. Bartolomé, 161, 248, 249, 317*t*, 319*t*

Bede, 86, 106, 343n16

Belize: as a British Crown Colony, 2*t*, 223; British logging, 252, 255; British sugar production, 212, 254; chronology, 2*t*; climate, 118, 135, 138, 162, 174, 188; coastal areas (*see* Coast); colonial period communities, 241*i*; "colonial," use of term, 5–6; conquest of Yucatan and, 112, 124–33, 153, 196, 199; *encomiendas* (*see Encomiendas*, Belize); entradas, 249–52, 368n69; first European contact, 79, 105, 342n1; first Spanish contact, 122–23, 156, 346nn88–90; maps, 13*i*, 108*i*, 113–15*i*, 241*i*; missions, 130, 142–43, 156–63, 194–96; population estimates, 203–4; then and now, 195–96; use of term, 110–11
—geopolitics: environment of early contact, 135–36; on the eve of Conquest, 37–38, 46–51; as part of the Kingdom of Guatemala, 134; as a safe haven from Spanish authority, 131, 196
—lack of sustained Spanish motivation to conquer: dense vegetation, 198, 258; hot and humid climate, 135, 138, 162, 198, 258; inability to grow Spanish crops, 138, 162; insects, 198; lack of resources, 134, 135, 162, 342–43n4; lack of safe port/navigation for large ships, 105, 107, 124, 129; remoteness, 128–29, 161, 196–98, 342–43n4; threat from pirates (*see* Pirates, privateers, and buccaneers); timeframe, 342n3; very few settlers, 195, 360–61n36
—Maya resistance and rebellion: Chanlacan, 204, 236, 362n87; Colmotz, 249; Lamanai, 212, 239, 248; overview, 164, 246–49, 289–90; Tipu, 246–47, 249
—relative lack of information on: on the eve of Conquest, 46; few *encomenderos* with authority over, 330n33; few

geographic names, 111–13, 112*i*; lack of name by the Spanish, 135; Spanish archaeological evidence, 195–96, 256; tribute system and economics, 39, 134–35; *See also* Belize, lack of sustained Spanish motivation to conquer

—religious conversion: context for, 137–38, 153–54, 161, 164; founding of Christian communities, 136; as part of Franciscan province of St. Joseph, 328n63; *See also* Bienvenida, Fr. Lorenzo de; Missionaries

Belize. Tourism Development Project, 223

Belize Estate and Produce Company, 199, 259

Belize Institute of Archaeology, 208, 363n111

Belize River and Belize River Valley, 51, 52, 53*i*, 129, 333n111

Bells, 216*i*, 246, 248, 274, 366n13

Benavides, Fr. Francisco de, 160, 314*t*

Bernardone, Giovanni di, 148

Betanzos, Domingo de, 152

Bible: devils and demons, 83, 272, 339–40n184; Eve, 272, 274–75; as gifts for the Maya, 366n13; Old Testament, 83, 90, 272, 273, 274–75, 339–40n184; Polyglot, 150, 152; sole right of the church to interpret, 150; story of the golden calf, 273; translations, 63, 335n24

Bienvenida, Fr. Lorenzo de: background, 158, 159–60; chronology, 314*t*; condemnation of Spanish conquest techniques, 133, 158, 286; first European contact, possible, 79, 111; Lamanai church construction, possible, 204; long-term perspective on conversion, 282; population estimates by, 203–4

Boats and ships: brigantine, 126, 127, 347n116; canoe, 119, 128, 129, 199, 238, 249; caravel, 346nn87,90; 347n116; carrack, 346n90, 347n116; galleass, 347n116; Spanish theft of Maya, 129; war frigate, 255

Books of Chilam Balam, 330n50

British Honduras, 112

Buenaventura, Fr. Juan de, 252, 321*t*

Burial practices: archaeological

interpretation of, 62; Christian, 18, 62, 207, 233, 299; coffins, 233; importance of consecrated ground, 259; reverence for ancestors, 297

—Maya: dental modification, 300; if grave was disturbed, 208; Kowoj, 54; with a needle, 23, 25*i*, 233, 234*i*; post-European contact changes, 121; post-Spanish rule, 18, 20*i*; in sitting position, 254; with a thurible as sign of honor, 154, 154*i*; underneath church or building, 168, 254, 296, 300

Burial sites, 297–98, 299–300, 308. *See also* Lamanai, cemeteries; Tipu, cemetery

Cabacera system, 329n11

Cacao, 157, 197, 203, 238, 244, 274, 307

Cache, 214, 219, 219*i*, 242–43, 269*i*, 308, 360n26

Cacique (Maya lord), 45–46, 125, 332n80

Cah (community-home), 37–38, 163–64, 333n125, 356n191

Calkini, 31*i*, 46, 186

Camal, Gov. Don Fernando, 245

Campeche (ecclesiastical province): Belize under jurisdiction of, 135; Chontal Maya, 116; maps, 13*i*, 113*i*; Maya resistance, 130, 240; missionaries in, 142, 151, 328n63

Campeche (modern Mexican state), 110, 195

Campin, 249, 317*t*, 318*t*, 319*t*

Can Ek, 243, 244, 251, 321*t*

Cano, Fr. Agustín, 320–21*t*

Canpech, 32*i*

Canul, 31*i*, 38, 46

Caracol, 331n78

Caraveo, Juan Rodríguez de, 126, 131

Cárdenas, Gov. Diego de, 244, 246

Caribbean basin, 110*i*, 130, 133–35

Casas, Bartolomé de las, 152, 263

Castile, 61, 152, 334n13

Catholicism. *See* Roman Catholicism or Catholicism

Cattle, 189, 258, 327n37

Caye Coco, 58

Cehach, 33*i*, 108*i*, 205, 246

Ceh Pech, 32*i*, 38, 242
Cemeteries. *See* Lamanai, cemeteries;
    Tipu, cemetery
Censer: Chen Mul Modeled, 368n93;
    effigy, sites found, 130; Lamanai, 210,
    211*i*, 254; Tipu Lacandon-type, 257,
    257*i*, 306; Tipu thurible, 154*i*, 234*i*,
    365n182; Yucatec words for, 277
Central America, 133–35
Ceramics: Augustine orange-red,
    333n110; British colonial, 130, 223,
    254; coastal, 129–30; Columbia Plain,
    364n151; continuity in use of local re-
    sources, 50, 331n51; influences on style,
    47, 57; Kowoj, 54; Peten Itza orange-
    paste, 55; plumbate, 116; polychrome,
    119–20; Santa Rita Corozal, 56, 57; slips
    and washes, 56; Spanish majolica, 130,
    210, 224, 229; thurible, 154, 154*i*; trade,
    47, 118, 119–20, 129–30; Tulum Red
    Ware, 57, 130
—Lamanai: anthropomorph emerging
    from shell, 269*i*; Cib Phase, 57; distinct
    from Tipu ceramics, 58; Postclassic,
    56–58; post-1641 in pre-Columbian
    style, 254; Preclassic, 232; seventh cen-
    tury, 269*i*; Yglesias-style, 50, 51*i*, 56–57,
    129–30, 241–42, 242*i*; zoomorph
    effigies, 57, 213, 214–16*i*, 218, 219, 220*i*,
    221, 223*i*, 243, 363–64n130
—Tipu: consistency in style, 50; distinct
    from Lamanai, 58; found only at co-
    lonial site center, 200–201; maskette,
    237*i*, 242–43; orange-red slip Augus-
    tine, 333n110; from Peten, 55; Spanish,
    237
—vessels: anthropomorph emerging
    from shell, 268*i*, 269*i*; Maya effigy,
    214*i*, 215*i*, 223*i*; olive jars, 50, 221, 230,
    242, 242*i*; water, 119; Yglesias-style, 51*i*,
    241–42, 242*i*
Chac (spiritual being), 81, 301
Chactemal, 32*i*, 47
Chakan, 32*i*
Chalca, 145
Champotón, 127, 128, 131, 132, 239,
    366n13
Chanchanha, 250

Chanlacan, 53*i*, 133, 199, 203, 204, 236,
    250, 362n87
Chanputun, 32*i*
Charles V, King of Spain, 16, 140, 142, 144,
    149–50
"Cheese and Worms" (Ginzburg), 63
Chel Maya, 130
Chests, 226, 227, 230, 233, 364n159
Chetumal (province): conquest, 133, 153,
    199; geopolitics on the eve of Conquest,
    47, 58; language and culture areas, 108*i*;
    maps, 32*i*, 33*i*, 48*i*; resistance, 132, 133;
    Santa Rita Corozal as possible capital,
    58; second stage of conquest, 107, 128
Chetumal (town), 126, 128, 199
Chi, Gaspar Antonio, 34, 329n17
Chiapas, 110, 112, 112*i*, 134, 164, 349n165
Chibal (lineage or patronym group), 38,
    46, 330n41, 333n125
Chichen Itza. *See* Itza, Chichen Itza
Chikinchel, 32*i*, 121, 126, 332n84, 347n109
Children: beads buried with, 233; guard-
    ian angel and, 304*i*; jewelry buried
    with, 22–23, 24*i*, 327n50; religious
    training or conversion, 15, 198, 221, 286,
    290
Chol-speaking peoples, 147, 157
Cholti-speaking peoples, 251
Chonta (language), 121
Chontal (Maya peoples), 116, 147
Christianity: altars, 175–76, 299, 364n154,
    366n13; Anabaptists, 274, 278; angels
    (*see* Religion, angels); animal world
    of, 26*i*, 291–95, 292*i*, 293*i*; Apostles,
    328n63, 372n43; apostolic reform in
    Mesoamerica, 144, 146, 148–49, 155–56,
    157–58; Articles of Faith, 97; authori-
    tarian, 2, 281–82; Bible (*see* Bible);
    Catholicism (*see* Roman Catholicism or
    Catholicism); chalice, 366n13; Chris-
    tians as "enrolled soldiers," 89; context
    of early, 155, 279–81, 309; conversion
    to (*see* Religious conversion); Council
    of Trent, 2, 63–64, 94, 99, 147, 150–51,
    353n82; cross and crucifix, 240, 243,
    275, 305, 306, 366n13; debate, 94,
    96–97; devils and demons (*see* Religion,
    devils and demons); doctrine of the

Church and, 86–102, 370n56; effigies, 81–82, 276; Europe, medieval, 75, 102, 144, 271, 295 (*see also* Europe, Christianization); God (*see* Religion, God); heaven, 20, 83, 294, 299; hell, 265, 266*i*, 267, 271*i*, 303; Holy Spirit, 94, 97, 100, 372n43; indigenous, 106–9, 258–59; Latin, cult of saints, 78; Lutheran movement, 150; martyrs, 244–45, 295, 300, 310; Mary, 372n43; material culture of, 126; Maya (*see under* Religious conversion); miracles (*see* Religion, miracles); monastic system, 106, 280, 343nn10,16; monotheism and, 74–75, 84; offerings (*see* Religion, offerings); Opus Dei, 101; orthodoxy, 78–79, 100–101; pagan roots, 78, 82, 89–92, 106, 143, 156, 271, 278, 283; parallels with Maya beliefs, 275, 291–98; prayer (*see* Religion, prayer); "praying towns," 327n39; Protestantism, 2, 78, 82, 147, 150, 273, 291, 309; reform movement, 2, 96, 139, 147, 309, 353n82 (*see also* Christianity, Protestantism); relationship with native religion, 16–17, 75, 258–59, 287–88; relics, 295–97, 299, 309–10; rituals (*see* Rituals, Christian); role of doctrine and dogma, 92–97, 101–2; Scriptures, 100, 309, 900; sin (*see* Religion, sin); spirit world, 291; Ten Commandments (*see* Religion, Ten Commandments); as a veneer over pre-Columbian beliefs, 16–17, 18, 78–80, 198, 290; vestments and raiments, 240; Virgin of Guadalupe, 275

—individual variations or experiences: author's family, 101–2; Bienvenida, 286; and the formation of the Magisterium, 94–95; and the Maya, 78, 80, 95, 102, 109, 154–56, 258–59, 289–91; Menocchio, 62–63, 95; overview, 77–78, 79–80, 155; St. Francis, 355n135; Valentinus, 94

—Jesus Christ: crèche scenes, 295; in the Deposit of Faith, 99, 100; driving out an unclean spirit, 267; hierarchy of church authority not evident in message of, 281; redemption through the suffering

and death of, 88, 92; rescuing souls, 266*i*

Chronologies, 2*t*, 5–6, 49*t*

Chunukum, 250

Churches: altars, 175–76, 364n154, 366n13; architecture (*see* Architecture, church); author's childhood (*see* Church of St. Michael the Archangel; St. Bonaventure's); Belize (*see* Lamanai church, first; Lamanai church, second; Tipu church); built over burial sites or holy ground, 297; construction process, 177, 181, 224, 229, 231; institutional framework in conversion to Christianity, 106–7; Jeronymite single-nave, 159*i*; missions established in Belize (*see* Missionaries; Missions, Belize); pre-Columbian rituals performed in, 16; presbytery or sanctuary, 171, 176, 178–79, 178*i*, 358n48; temples, 42, 43, 146*i*; *vs.* chapels, 179–86, 187; Western, 176, 177*i*; Yucatan, 182, 183

—terms: "chapel" or *capilla*, 167, 170, 171, 175, 178, 182–85, 187–88; "choir" and "chancel," 171, 176, 178*i*, 211*i*, 357n23; "corner chapel" or *posa*, 173*i*, 180; Indian chapel or *capilla de indios*, 167, 175, 182, 186–87, 237, 359n85; monastery church or *iglesia*, 167, 168, 180, 181, 182–83, 185, 186; "open chapel" or *capilla abierta*, 167, 170–75, 173*i*, 174*i*, 180, 182, 184–88; "ramada," 170, 173, 182, 185, 187–88, 230–31; and typologies, 167–87; *visita*, 5

Church of St. Michael the Archangel, 20–22, 21*i*, 22*i*

Cifuentes y Satomayor, Bishop Luis de, 324*t*

Cisneros, Archbishop/Cardinal Jiménez de, 151–52, 363n95

Ciudad Rodrigo, Fr. Antonio, 349n159

Climate, 118, 135, 138, 162, 174, 188, 195, 358n38

Coast: agriculture and soil, 123, 346n98; climate, 118–19, 135, 138, 162, 174; cultural influence and trade, 56, 108, 120–22; English contact, 109; European perspective, 113, 122–24, 346n90;

Coast: (*continued*)

historical reference to, 111–16, 344n32; maps, 113–14*i*, 117*i*; Maya perspective, 116–22, 127, 129, 137; most vulnerable to Europeans, 45, 121, 123–24; pirates (*see* Pirates, privateers, and buccaneers); raids (*see* Slavery); towns and villages, 118–19, 128–30, 135, 343n23; trade (*see* Trade and commerce, coastal)

—characteristics: barrier reef, 1, 124, 127, 347–48n116; cayes, 1, 105, 108, 124; mangrove, 118–19; shallow coastal shelf, 1, 107, 124; swamps, inlets, and lagoons, 107, 128

Cochuah, 32*i*, 133, 203, 349n151

Cockscombs (Maya Mountains), 113, 116, 123, 129, 346n90

Cocom, 333n124

Cogolludo, Fr. Lopez de, 60, 160, 229, 240, 316*t*, 317*t*

Colha, 118, 119

Colmotz, 53*i*, 199, 248, 249

Colson Point, 118, 120, 130

Columbus, Christopher, 116, 122, 125, 337n102, 346n89

Contact Period: Maya-English in Belize, 109, 255–56; Maya exposure to multiple doctrines, 102, 108–9; Maya-Spanish (*see* Contact Period, Maya-Spanish; Spanish Conquest); Contact Period, Maya-Spanish: disease, 16, 45, 109, 123, 343n25; end of Spanish colonial influence, 255–56; Yucatan, 124. *See also* Spanish Conquest

—Belize: colonial history in perspective, 256–57; date of arrival in Belize, 79; effects of earlier colonizations, 124–35, 196; first contact by Bienvenida, 79, 111; first contact evidence, 122

—environment of early contact: coastal perspective, 116–24, 125, 137; effects of Mexico, Yucatan, Central Amer. colonization, 124–35, 144–47; geographic names in documents, 109–16; overview, 105–9, 135–36

Conversion. *See* Religious conversion

Copilco area, 117, 121, 344n50, 345n79

Córdoba, Hernández de, 124, 140, 348n129

Córdoba, Pedro de, 20, 328n63

Cortés: coastal expedition of 1519, 122, 124–25, 347n106; conquest of the Aztecs, 134, 139, 145; horse left in Peten, 243; influence over missionary selection, 140, 146, 157; negotiation of release of captive Spaniard, 121; religious conversion as justification for conquest, 16

Costa Rica, 110, 110*i*, 134

Cotton, 197, 238

Council of Nicaea II, 310

Council of the Indies, 240, 256, 344n51

Council of Trent, 2, 63–64, 94, 99, 147, 150–51, 353n82

Couoh. *See* Kowoj

Cozumel, 121, 122, 125, 140, 142

Cuautitlan, 180

Cuchcabal (jurisdiction), 30, 34, 46, 58, 329n13, 332n87

Cuchteel (division for tribute), 164

Culhua-Mexica (Aztec peoples), 36, 145, 147, 352–53n70

Cultural issues: coastal culture and trade, 56, 108, 120–22; as context for religion, 66–69, 76, 145, 156, 263, 283–84, 336n49; cross-cultural sacred place, 259–60, 287–88, 371n9; cultural outsider, 36, 71, 80, 330n31; culture areas of Spain, 152; culture areas of Yucatan/ Bay of Honduras, 108*i*; landscape, 258, 287–88; loss of native culture, 145, 207; nature of change, 62, 79, 289–90; powerlessness and absorption, 10, 150, 325n5; shared culture of the pre-Columbian foreigners, 36; trans-local and the local, 285–86, 287–88, 296–97, 299; urbanization, 283, 288

—"the Other": anthropological use of term, 10, 12–13, 325n4, 370n38; the author and, 14–15, 27; as barrier to seeing or observing, 14, 27, 71, 145; in interpretation of beliefs/religions, 71, 76, 80–82, 84–85, 263–65, 274–76, 275*i*, 284; in interpretation of political behavior, 125–26; in interpretation of "resistance," 289–90

Cumux, Don Francisco, 205

Cupul (Maya peoples), 349n151
Cupul (province), 32*i*, 347n109
Currency, 274

Dávila, 127–29, 131, 135, 204
Delgado, Fr. Diego, 154, 160, 244, 315*t*
Delgado, Fr. Joseph, 161, 319–20*t*
Díaz, Juan, 140, 320*t*
Diet and health: Aztecs, 338n121; famine
  of 1628, 246; Lamanai and Tipu, 233–36
—disease or sickness: anemia, 234; mira-
  cle healing, 271; of Spanish soldiers, 125;
  spread by European contact, 16, 45, 109,
  123, 343n25
Documents. *See* Historical documents
Dwellings, 20*i*, 223–24, 228, 229–30, 237,
  241
Dzibilchaltun, 173, 174*i*, 177, 188
Dzilan, 130, 349n151
Dzuluinicob (province), 33*i*, 47, 198–99,
  203, 334n136
Dzuluinicob (river), 49, 56, 198. *See also*
  New River

Ecab: church, 171*i*, 177, 178*i*, 186, 187; early
  Spanish contact, 126, 347n109; geopolitics on the eve of Conquest, 47; map,
  32*i*; resistance to Spanish rule, 349n151
Ecological issues: animal diversity, 235;
  "bush" or *monte*, 361n56; forests as
  shelter for Maya refugees, 258, 276; invasive species, 16; sea-level rise, 118–19,
  345n67; thin soil and access to large
  community-home areas, 37–38
Economics: Belize coast, advantages
  through trade, 5, 44–45, 52, 116, 120,
  308, 333n111; Belize riverine towns, 196;
  competition after the fall of Chichen
  Itza, 47; misinterpretation by the Spanish, 126; nature of hierarchy, 45–46;
  outside the tribute system, 43–45; religious conversion and, 40, 142, 307–8;
  tax or subsidy on traded goods, 44–45;
  warfare and the transfer of wealth,
  40–43, 331n59
Education: Franciscan schools for Maya
  elites, 158, 205, 287; of *maestros cantores*, 49, 82, 156, 175, 332n104, 358n44

Effigies: Christian saints, 75, 81–82, 276,
  278, 295–97, 338n133
—Maya: maskette, 237*i*, 242–43; possible
  uses, 277; of a Spanish horse, 243, 246;
  zoomorph, 57, 213, 214–16*i*, 218, 219,
  220*i*, 221, 223*i*, 243, 363–64n130; *See
  also* Idolatry, perception of adherence
  to
Ek Chuah (spiritual being), 81
El Salvador, 111, 134, 221, 349n164
Encomenderos, 140, 157, 162–63, 240,
  328n17, 330n33. See also *Encomiendas*
Encomiendas (grants of Maya labor and
  tribute): Central America, 134; Guatemala, 355n133; Mendicant missionaries
  and, 141–42; Mexico, 163; overview, 5,
  35, 37, 163–64; restructuring in 1922,
  240; rights dispute, 344n51; slaves, 42;
  Yucatan, 163
—Belize: connections between Tipu and
  Lamanai, 49–50; established by the
  Pachecos, 156–57, 203, 362n76; first
  in 1544, 125, 138, 156, 197, 203; lacking
  permanency, 162–63, 330n33; Lamanai,
  56, 109, 199, 203, 204, 238; overview,
  163–64, 197, 207; Tipu, 109, 203, 205,
  224, 239, 244, 361n60
Entrepreneurs, 44
Epistemology, 27, 373–74n12
Erasmus, 147, 149
Espat family, 189
Estrada, Fr. Juan de, 161, 226, 248, 315–16*t*,
  316–17*t*
Ethnicity, contextualizing the concept, 11
Ethnohistory: disjunction with archaeology in Belize, 12–13, 18–19, 194, 236,
  289; relationship with archaeology,
  309–11. *See also* Historical documents,
  Maya; Historical documents, Spanish
Europe: apostolic reform, 148–49; Chris-
  tianity in the Middle Ages, 147, 271,
  295; church layout, typical, 176, 177*i*;
  Denmark, 61; depiction of the devil
  in art, 266*i*, 267, 269, 270*i*, 271–72;
  Flanders, 61, 82; France, 1, 61, 144, 146,
  148, 346n87; Icelandic sagas, 90; Ireland, 37, 87, 106, 284; Italy, 61, 148, 280;
  The Netherlands, 1, 82, 346n87; pagan

Europe (*continued*)

deities, 78, 84, 89–91, 106, 341n34; Portugal, 61, 149, 334n13; Scotland, 61, 339n184; Spain, 95, 148–49, 150, 152, 255, 256

—Britain: Christianity in the Middle Ages, 105–6, 343nn9–10,13; England, 34, 179*i*; justification for colonialism, 255; knowledge of Belize coastline, 1, 346n87; relationship with Spain, and Belize, 255, 256; slavery of Maya by, 109, 252, 255–56; sugar production in Lamanai, 212, 254; timber extraction in Belize, 252, 255; Wales, Cornwall, and Cumbria, 87

—Christianization: Anglo Saxons, 106, 143, 287; Britons, 106–7; Celts, 143; eastern Europe, 264; Frankish tribes, 280, 297, 300; Frisians, 297; German tribes, 78, 90, 280, 283, 284, 297, 300; globalization and, 143–44, 284; overview, 75, 102, 106, 279–82; Scandinavia, 87, 264; timeframe, 282, 287; urbanization and, 283; Vandals, 143; *vs.* process in Belize, 143, 283–84

Everyone Knows What a Dragon Looks Like (Williams), 307, 311–13, 311*i*, 312*i*

Family issues: *chibal* and, 38, 330n40; links with the deceased, 299, 300; Maya marriage alliances, 39, 55–56, 197; Maya selection of marriage partner, 38; Spanish-Maya intermarriage, 233, 278

Famine of 1628, 246

Fernández, Pedro, 126

Fish and shellfish, 52, 118, 120, 123, 197

Flanders, 61, 82

Food: animal use for, 235; for European ship crew, 123, 124, 129; famine of 1628, 246; fish and shellfish trade, 52, 118, 120, 123; as material culture, 52, 326n10; processing, 121; spoilage in the tropics, 138

"Foreigners," pre-Columbian, 36

Foundation for the Advancement of Mesoamerican Studies, Inc. (FAMSI), 363n111

Fourth Lateran Council, 370n56

Friars Minor, 353n90

Fuensalida, Fr. Bartolomé de: attacked upon return to Tipu, 247–49; entrada and reductions by, 160, 240; idolatry found in Tipu, 243–44; overview, 315*t*, 316*t*; portable altar, 226; religious perspective, 161–62; Tipu residence, 229; treatment by Ah Kin Pol, 245

Fuente, Dr. Constantino Ponce de la, 150

Gann, Thomas, 213, 214, 363nn115,125–26

Gante, Pedro de, 149

Garcés, Bishop Julián, 323*t*, 324*t*

Garzón, Juan de, 205, 237, 314*t*

Geopolitics: Belize on the eve of Conquest, 46–51; *cabacera* system, 329n11; changing boundaries in colonial era, 111; *cuchcabal*, 30, 34, 46, 58, 329n13, 332n87; effects of Spanish Conquest, 49; governance by the Maya (*see* Governance); hierarchy, 45–46; migration, 131, 133, 246–47, 333n125; modern, 34; Peten on the eve of Conquest, 52–56; pre-Conquest units, 37–38; "province" in Spanish documents (*see* "Province"); relationships *vs.* territory, 34–36, 163–64, 329nn18,22, 330nn31,33,34, 333n125; Santa Rita Corozal, 58; Tipu on the eve of Conquest, 47, 49, 52–56, 57, 58; tribute relationships, 34, 36–37, 134, 196, 329n18. *See also* Trade; Warfare

Glossary, 375–84

Glover's Reef, 123, 130, 346n90, 347–48n116

Glyphs, 44*i*, 329n14

God. *See* Religion, God

Godoy, Lorenzo de, 132

God pots, 306

God Shells, 265–67

Golfo Dulce, 111, 113, 123, 133, 344n32

Gonzalez, Alonso, 140

Governance: economic spheres outside the tribute system, 43–45; nature of hierarchy, 45–46; overview, 38–39; transfer of wealth and resources, 40–43

Graham, Elizabeth: connection with medieval Christians, 13–14, 20–21; family background, 13, 326n20; learning the

catechism, 15, 20–22, 25, 26*i*; research philosophy, 14–15, 25–28, 310–11, 327n33, 328nn55–56, 374n14
—Roman Catholic background: and academic study, 9, 25–26; childhood experiences, 20–22, 101, 271, 296; churches, 21*i*, 22*i*, 296; shared perspective with Maya, 22–23, 92, 102, 305; shared perspective with medieval Spaniards, 13, 65, 74
Grijalva, 124, 140, 347n106
Guadalupe, Friar Juan de, 143, 149
Guanaja, 122
Guatemala: *encomiendas* system, 355n133; Franciscan province of Nombre de Jesús, 328n63; maps, 53*i*, 54*i*; Maya social linkages to, 348n123; modern (Republic of Guatemala), 110, 110*i*; as part of Kingdom of Guatemala, 134; religious conversion, 87, 160; trade, 116, 125, 134
Guerrero, Gonzalo, 122, 125, 126, 127
Gulf Coast Maya, 36, 47
Gulf of Honduras, 114*i*, 115*i*, 347–48n116. *See also* Bay of Honduras
Guyana-Surinam, 332n80
Guzmán, Domingo. *See* St. Dominic

Halach uinic (regional lord), 35, 46, 47
Hariza y Arruyo, Capt. Francisco de, 251
Health. *See* Diet and health
Hernández, Francisco, 131, 140
Historical documents: Maya chronicles, 39, 194, 330–31n50
—Spanish: academic use to uncover pre-Conquest ways of life, 289; background of research on, 194–95; church terms, 167–68, 169–88; disjunction with material remains, 12–13, 18–19, 194, 236; *encomienda* administration, 344n51; ethnocentrism in, 12–13, 18, 30, 37, 41, 59, 329nn10–11; "human sacrifice" in, 40–41, 43; maps and geographic names, 111–16, 127; in the Maya language, 38; *probanza* (record of merits; proof of nobility), 47, 332n100; religious bias, 64, 76, 78, 90–91, 294–95, 298–99, 313; scant attention to material culture in,

19, 85; terminology, 59–62, 167–88; *vs.* archaeological records, 194; what scholars make of the sources, 288–91
Hocaba, 32*i*, 142
Holpachay, 250
Holpatin, 247, 248
Holzuz, 250
Honduras: conquest, 128, 132, 349n164; early European contact, 127, 346–47n102; languages, 121; maps, 110*i*, 113*i*; as part of Kingdom of Guatemala, 134; precious metals and mining, 134; resistance, 349n165; slave raids, 130; then and now, 110; trade, 116, 120, 125, 134, 308
Honduras-Higueras, 112, 113, 132, 134
Honey and beeswax, 197, 238, 307
Hopkins, 119
Horses, 129, 243, 315*t*
Horta, Bishop Lorenzo de, 324*t*
Housing. *See* Dwellings
Hubelna, 248–49
Humanism, 147, 149–50, 151, 152–53

Ichmul, 142
Idolatry: extirpation by the Franciscans, 64, 76, 158, 161–62, 207, 276–77; Itza, 157, 161, 243; Maya persecution, 64, 76, 276–78; our saints, your idols, 75, 81–82, 198, 273–78, 294–97, 305–6, 338n133; perception of adherence to, 16, 17, 205, 242, 243, 263–78, 289, 327n41, 352n55; Spanish depiction of Maya, 275*i*; Tipu, 244; use of term, 277, 296; *vs.* art, 9–10, 25, 161, 273–74
"Idol," use of term, 277, 296
Incense burners, 54, 365n182
Indian Church, 224, 362n106, 364n147. *See also* Lamanai; Lamanai church, second
Indio (Indian), 6, 60, 97, 342n80
"Individualism," use of term, 155, 355n134
Individuals and their impact, 151–56, 286
Ipenza, Bishop Andrés Fernández de, 323*t*
Iraq War, 331n56
Isabella, Queen of Spain, 140, 151, 352n40, 353n95
Itza (dialect), 52

Itza (Maya peoples): arrival, 52; ceramics, 55; Cortés's peaceful encounter, 157; geopolitics on the eve of Conquest, 55, 56, 202; impact on Christianity, 147; at Nohpeten, 243, 244, 245, 250, 251, 252; non-Christian elites, 250; Peten Itza, 17, 52, 55, 236, 251; plans to convert, 162; resistance and rebellion, 17, 50–51, 164, 248–49; use of term, 52
—Chichen Itza: decline in the eleventh century, 44, 52; early Spanish contact, 347n109; economic competition after the fall, 47; occupation, 30, 328n9; political decentralization after the fall, 47; resistance to Spanish rule, 349n151; trade, 120; tribute system, 36, 39
Itza (province), 32*i*, 33*i*, 54*i*, 108*i*
Itzamna, 75, 275
Ix Chel, 275
Ixpimienta, 244
Izquierdo, Bishop Juan (Bishop Diego de Izquierdo), 323*t*, 324*t*

Jalisco, 328n63
Jamaica, 256
Jars. *See* Ceramics, vessels
Jesus Christ. *See* Christianity, Jesus Christ
Jewelry: bracelets, 22, 23*i*, 233; from dog's teeth, 233; earrings, 22, 24*i*, 233, 365n184; from glass beads, 22, 23*i*, 24*i*, 233, 327n50; necklaces or pendants, 22, 24*i*, 233; rings, 230, 233, 365n184; from shell, 216*i*, 218, 233
Jicaque (language), 117
Jones, Grant D., 326n15

K'awiil Chan K'inich, 331n62
Kendal, 130
Killing, socially sanctioned, 40, 42, 275
Kingdom of Guatemala, 109, 111–12, 112*i*, 115*i*, 134, 135
Kowoj (Maya peoples), 52, 54–55, 333nn118,124, 348n129. *See also* Tipu, Complex I
Kowoj (place), 52, 54

Lacandon (Maya peoples), 251, 257, 257*i*, 306

Lacetag, 233, 365n178
Lamanai: abandonment, 236; as an *encomienda*, 56, 109, 199, 203, 204; as an island, 113*i*, 114*i*, 115*i*, 192; background on archaeological research, 192; British colonial period, 223, 254; ceramics (*see* Ceramics, Lamanai); as a Christian community, 236–38; chronology, 49*t*; churches (*see* Lamanai church, first; Lamanai church, second); commerce and trade, 44, 47, 199–200, 238, 343n23; diet and health, 233–36; disjunction between archaeology and ethnohistory, 236, 289; dwellings, 223–24; emblem glyph, 44*i*; at the end of the Postclassic, 56–58; etymology of name, 192, 360n19; geopolitics, 47, 56–58; glyphs, 44*i*; Indian Church, 362n106 (*see also* Lamanai church, second); location, 13*i*, 48*i*, 53*i*, 113–14*i*, 115*i*, 189, 192, 199; Maya resistance and rebellion, 212, 239, 248; Maya return after 1641, 251; modern day, 221, 327n37; no Spanish skeletons found, 195–96, 256; post-Spanish occupation, 256–57, 259–60; rectory, 208, 209*i*, 210, 211, 211*i*, 222–23, 254, 362n105; religious conversion, 153, 160, 222, 263, 282; as Spanish administration center, 192–93; Spanish rule from Bacalar, 133; stelae, 211*i*, 213–18, 248, 254, 363nn116,125; town, 224; transition from Classic to Postclassic, 43–44; transition from late Postclassic to colonial times, 221–22; *vs.* Tipu, 230–36, 365n172
—cemeteries: burial practices, 233, 235*i*; excavation site, 208, 209*i*, 218–19, 233; historical use and the churches, 259–60; total number of individuals in, 196, 208, 233
—excavation: dates, 362n105; funding, 363n111; projects in progress, 223; site, 192, 200*i*, 201*i*, 206*i*, 209*i*, 224, 254–55 (*see also* Lamanai, cemeteries, excavation site)
—regional relationships: Marco Gonzalez, 120; Santa Rita Corozal, 58; Tipu, 49–51, 198

Lamanai church, first (YDL 1): ceramic effigy, 215*i*; construction techniques, 231–32; excavation dates, 362n105; excavation site, 192, 193*i*, 200*i*, 218–24, 218*i*, 222*i*, 259; lack of European artifacts from, 204; perspective reconstruction cutaway, 205*i*; as sacred ground, 259–60, 297; to serve entire Maya community, 180, 187; *vs.* Tipu church, 230–32, 365n172
—architecture and layout: blind sanctuary, 158, 355n159; overview, 178, 205*i*; platform, 226, 365n172; presbytery, 168, 169*i*; ramada, 187, 230–32; single nave, 158; terraces, 219, 221

Lamanai church, second (YDL 2): architecture and layout, 187, 188, 210–12, 218, 236–37; atrio, 205*i*, 210*i*, 221, 222*i*; ceramic effigies, 213, 214–16*i*, 218, 363–64n130; construction date, 204, 206, 237–38; construction techniques, 208, 212, 223, 224, 229; desecration or burning, 212, 236, 242, 248, 254; excavation dates, 362n105; excavation site, 192, 208–18, 209*i*, 210*i*, 211*i*, 212*i*; large community implied, 202, 236; perspective reconstruction cutaway, 206*i*; as a smithy in nineteenth century, 212, 254

Lamanai Historic Monuments Conservation Project (LHMCP), 363n111

Landa, Bishop Diego de: anti-idolatry activities, 158, 276, 282, 297–98; influence in the Yucatan, 286; Inquisition, 352n48; reliability of pre-Conquest facts, 289; religious perspective, 84–85, 90; use of secular clergy to perform ceremonies, 142; years in office, 323*t*; Yucatec language spoken, 85, 121

Landscape, 37–38, 287–88, 330n40, 371n9

Language: assimilation of Spanish words into Maya, 329n18; coastal, 117, 121–22, 345n77; friars who spoke Maya, 85, 121, 140, 150, 160, 161, 248; use of terms, 6; of Yucatan and the Bay of Honduras, 108*i. See also specific languages*

La Pimienta, 33*i*, 108*i*

Latin, 41, 46, 89, 176, 309, 337n81, 339–40n184

Lighthouse Reef, 116, 347–48n116

Livestock, 129, 138, 189, 243, 327n37

Lock or lock plate, iron, 226–27, 227*i*, 230, 233, 365n185

Luján, Alonso, 128, 203

Macal River, 189, 190

Madrid, Bishop Pedro Reyes Ríos de la, 324*t*

Maestros cantores (Maya choirmasters/sacristans): admitted to business end of church, 175; connection between Lamanai and Tipu, 49; needed due to short supply of friars, 82, 207; recruits from Tekax, 240; religious interpretation by, 156, 286; responsibilities, 82, 358n44; use of term, 332n104

Magic, 310–11, 373–74n12

"Maia," use of term, 60, 346–47n102

Maize, 197, 327n37

Manan, 53*i*, 128, 247, 249, 317*t*

Manche Chol (Maya people), 205, 249, 367n64

Mangrove, 118–19

Mani/Tutul Xiu, 32*i*, 47, 349n168

Marchán, Francisco López, 255–56

Marco Gonzalez, 118, 120, 130

Marina, Doña, 157, 345n77

Marine resources, 119

Material culture: academic interpretation of, 10–11, 25–26; of Christianity, 126; food as, 52, 326n10; importance of contextualizing, 10–12; relationship between Tipu and Lamanai, 50, 51; religion and interpretation of, 11–12, 85; scant information, 19, 85; specific to coastal sites, 119–20, 308

Maya (language), 6, 41, 108*i*, 277. *See also specific languages*

Maya (peoples): animal world of, 291–95; astronomy, 73–74; beliefs (*see* Maya pre-Columbian beliefs); Christianity even in absence of Spanish authority, 3, 18–19, 20*i*, 285, 299–309; coastal perspective, 116–22, 127, 129, 137 (*see also* Coast); collapse, 116; contact with Europeans (*see* Contact period, Maya-English; Contact period,

Maya (peoples) (*continued*)

Maya-Spanish); destruction of antiquities, 10, 85, 263; ethnicity, 11; forced relocation to Peten, 252, 256–57; Gulf Coast (*see* Gulf Coast Maya); idolatry trials, 64, 76; individuals and their impact, 154, 286; interaction of political and religious influences, 16–19; interregional communication, 122, 129, 157, 308; killing other Mayas, 244–45, 246; as a labor force, 5, 35, 246 (see also *Encomiendas*; Slavery); language and culture areas, 108*i*; long-distance foot travel, 38, 330n40; maps, 13*i*, 108*i*; pyramids, 168; resistance (*see* Spanish conquest, Maya resistance); segregation, 180, 181–82, 183, 187; southern Maya frontier, 196–98; Spanish imagery and interpretation, 10, 81, 193, 272, 287, 367n64; use of term, 6, 59–62, 352–53n70, 361n48

—on the eve of Conquest: Belize, 46–51; "elite visiting among polities," 29, 35; Lamanai at the end of the Postclassic, 56–58; native states, 29–30, 31–33*i*, 34, 328n8 (*see also* Geopolitics; Governance); Tipu and Peten, 52–56; trade, 29; warfare, 29, 40–43, 329n18

—perception of: adherence to idolatry, 16, 17, 205, 242, 243, 263–78, 289, 327n41, 352n55; as docile subjects, 95, 159; as interlopers, 255; as savages, 145, 153; as spiritual, 152, 153; as without honor, 126, 352n55; *See also* Historical documents, Spanish, ethnocentrism in

Maya (place name), 59–60, 60*i*, 334n3

Mayapan, 30, 55, 60, 328–29n9, 334n3

Maya pre-Columbian beliefs: Christianity as a veneer upon, 16–18, 78–80, 198, 290 (*see also* Religious conversion); Heisenberg Principle and, 76–80; icons as tribute payment, 197; interaction of political and religious influences, 16–19, 258–59; languages have no term for "religion," 68; myth of human sacrifice, 40–43; overview, 18, 71–76, 265, 267, 276, 370n42; paganism, 90–92, 285–306; perception of

(*see* Idolatry, perception of adherence to); rituals (*see* Rituals, pre-Columbian)

—spirits: dual nature of deities, 276; our saints, your idols, 75, 81–82, 198, 273–78, 294–97, 301, 305–6, 338n133; parallels with Christianity, 275, 291–98; spirit or divine essence, 75, 338n132

Maya Resistance to Spanish Rule (Jones), 5

Mayflower, 130

Medicine. *See* Diet and health

Melgarejo, Fr. Pedro, 140

Mendieta, Gerónimo de, 152, 153

Menocchio. *See* Scandella, Domenico "Menocchio"

Mercado, Bishop Diego Vásquez de, 323*t*

Mérida: as administrative center, 36, 135, 160, 194, 239, 244, 247–49, 251; missionaries to, 111, 142, 158, 161; road construction to Peten, 250, 251, 252; settlement, 132; Mestizos, 181; Metal artifacts: bells, 216*i*, 246, 248, 274, 366n13; iron lock or lock plate, 226–27, 227*i*, 230, 233, 365n185; iron nails, 233; jewelry, 24*i*, 230, 233, 365n184; needles, 23, 25*i*, 50, 215*i*, 234*i*, 365n184

Mexica (Azetc peoples), 36, 145, 350n3

Mexico: central, 36, 134, 145, 207, 221; colonial area *vs.* modern area, 109, 110; conquest, 124, 133, 140, 146–47; *encomiendas*, 163; Franciscan missionaries, 144, 145–46, 328n63; influence of Council of Trent, 151; religious conversion, 138, 139, 141, 144–47, 152, 328n63; secular clergy preferred, 141; use of term, 350n3. *See also* New Spain; *specific states*

Michoacan, 145, 328n63, 352–53n70

Middens, artifacts found in: beads, 23, 233; ceramics, 119, 254; fish bones, 52; metal, 365n184; Spanish olive jars, 221; use of term, 327n48

Migration: allegiance and, 333n125; due to famine, 246; to escape Franciscan anti-idolatry punishment, 276; to escape pirates, 135, 199, 246; Kowoj, 52, 54–55; to the Peten area, 52, 54–55, 333n124

—to escape Spanish rule: from Bacalar,

203; from Belize, 195; to Belize, 131, 133, 246–47, 252, 258; from the coast, 258; economic context, 197; encouraged by the Itza, 51; by the Kowoj, 54; from Lamaneros, 51; from Yucatan, 196

Mirones y Lezcano, Capt. Francisco de, 244–45, 315t

Mirrors, 23, 197

Miskito (Nicaraguan peoples), 255, 256

Missionaries: apostolic reform and, 137–38, 144, 146, 148–49, 152, 157–58, 161, 231, 264; Apostolic Twelve, 145, 149; Augustinian, 139, 141, 144, 145, 152–53; Benedictine, 106, 139, 324t; Bethlehemite, 139; Capuchin, 139, 149 (see also Modern day, Capuchins); Carmelite, 126, 139, 140; destruction of Maya or Aztec antiquities, 10, 85; Discalced, 149; first in Britain, 106; first mission expedition from Spain, 140; first to Belize, possible, 79; homelands of, 61, 149, 152, 334–35n14; Hospitaller, 139; Jesuit, 139, 287, 290, 351n14; Maya-Spanish encounter, 79; Mercedarian, 139, 140; non-Franciscan, 131; role on Spanish ships, 140; secular clergy, 139–43, 150–51, 160–61, 229, 238, 248, 251, 352n40; teaching aids, 22, 23, 328n63; training and education, 141; as vector for Spanish imperialism, 49–50, 137, 141, 144–47, 162, 163–64; who learned a native language, 85, 140, 150, 160, 161; worldview, 14, 85, 143–44, 263–72, 283–84, 309; to Yucatán, Tabasco, and Yucatan, 349n159; to Yucatan, 298–99. See also Churches; Religious Conversion; specific missionaries

—Dominican: to Belize, 139, 148, 161, 350n178; to France after 1229, 144; to Mexico, 145, 152; overview, 96, 148

—Franciscan: church doctrine and, 101, 144, 148–49, 240, 298; encomienda system and, 141, 162–63; to France after 1229, 144; gifts for the Maya, 240, 366n13; humanist and reformist, 151, 158–59, 161; idolatry extirpation by, 158, 161–62, 207, 276–77; independence from Spanish authority, 138,

149; indoctrination by Landa, 286; to Mexico, 145–46, 149, 328n63; overview, 138–39, 148–49, 369n12; political context, 138, 141–43, 145–46, 159, 162–63, 352n48, 353n95; to Yucatan, 132, 150–51, 342n3

—Mendicant (regular clergy): in France, 144, 146; overview, 2, 5, 79, 138–39, 230; political context, 141–42, 143, 146, 151; relationship with secular clergy and the colonists, 141, 155, 160, 161, 162, 239, 240, 279

Missions, Belize, 130, 142–43, 156–63, 194–96. See also Lamanai church, first; Lamanai church, second; Tipu church

Modern day: altar placement, 176; canonization of a saint, 14; Capuchins, 353nn90,94; Christian offerings in Spain, 295; evangelical Protestantism, 78; Friars Minor, 353n90; geopolitics, 34; idols, 273–74, 274i; New Agers, 91; pan-Maya movements, 61; shrine in Spain, 295; terrorism, 339n157; Yucatan, 110, 195

—Belize: agriculture and ranching, 189; geography, 116, 117i; Jesuits in, 139, 351n14; Lamanai, 221, 327n37

Molina, Fr. Alonso de, 328n63

Money, 274

Montalvo, Bishop Gregorio, 323t

Montejo (the Nephew), 132, 349n169, 350n172, 362n87

Montejo, Francisco (Adelantado; the Elder): in Campeche, 130, 131; conquest of Yucatan, 109, 112–13, 122, 125–28, 132, 140; in Dzilan with son, 130; range of proposed conquest, 132, 349n164; rights dispute, 344n51; role of Honduras-Higueras, 112, 113, 132, 134, 349n165

Montejo, Francisco (the Younger), 127, 128, 130, 131, 132, 140, 350n172

Montejo Xiu Xiu, Francisco de, 86, 87

Mopan (Maya peoples), 55, 56, 252

Moran, Fr. Francisco de, 161, 316t

Motolinía, Fr. Toribio, 86, 150, 284

Motul, 178i

Mulatto, 194, 360–61n36

Muros, Fr. Marcos de, 320t

Na, Don Cristóbal, 154, 244, 315*t*
Nachan Kan, 47
Nahua (Aztec peoples), 6, 78, 79, 94, 352n70
Nahuatl (language), 6, 41, 117, 145, 150, 328n63, 352–53n70, 361n48
National Institute for Culture and History in Belize, 363n111
National Museum of the American Indian, 213, 214, 363nn116,125–26, 363–64n130
Native religion. *See* Maya pre-Columbian beliefs; Rituals, pre-Columbian
Naturales. See *Indio* (Indian)
Natural resources, 46, 119, 332n84. *See also* Salt
Navajo, 325n5
Navigation, marine, 119
Needles, 23, 25*i*, 50, 215*i*, 234*i*, 365n184
Negroman and Negroman-Tipu, 189–90, 191, 202*i*, 257, 359n1. *See also* Tipu
New France, 139
New River, 47, 48*i*, 53*i*, 56, 129, 189, 198
New Spain, 65, 127, 140, 147, 328n63, 353n78. *See also* Nahuatl (language)
Nicaragua, 110, 110*i*, 111, 134, 135, 255, 256
Nohpeten, 52, 54*i*, 157, 160, 161, 202–3, 243–44, 245, 250–52
Nuun Ujol Chaak, 331n62

Ocón, Bishop Juan Alonso de, 323*t*
Olmedo, Bartolomé de, 139, 140
Orbita, Fr. Juan de: entrada and reductions by, 160, 240; finding idolatry in Tipu, 243–44; overview, 314*t*, 315*t*; religious perspective, 161–62; Tipu residence site, 229; treatment by Ah Kin Pol, 245
Otomí (language), 352–53n70
Our Lady of Cortes, 295

Pacha, 160, 249, 250, 316*t*
Pacheco, Alonso, 133, 153, 157, 203
Pacheco, Francisco, 133
Pacheco, Gaspar, 111, 112–13, 133, 344n32. *See also* Pacheco conquest
Pacheco, Melchor, 47, 133, 153, 157, 203, 362n76. *See also* Pacheco conquest

Pacheco conquest, 79, 142, 361n60
Panama, 112, 134
Pan-Maya movement, modern, 61
Papaya, 189
Pastor, Don, 259–60
Paterson, N. J. *See* Church of St. Michael the Archangel
Payolel (jurisdiction), 345n79
Pech, Doñ Isabel, 241, 242
Pech, Lázaro, 248, 154
Pérez, Capt. Francisco, 249–50, 318*t*
Peru, 131
Peten: collapse, 120, 345n67; conquest, 240, 251, 368n82; forced relocation of Mayas to, 252, 256–57; geopolitics on the eve of Conquest, 52–56, 202; maps, 13*i*, 54*i*; material culture of the elite, 43; Mendicant missionaries, 151; migration to, 52, 54–55, 333n124; military post in, 252, 368n82; Peten Itza, 17, 52, 55, 236, 239, 240; relationship with Tipu, 51, 52, 55, 203; remaining non-Christian, 164; road construction to Mérida, 250, 251, 252; trade, 55, 157, 203
Peto, 142
Philip II, King of Spain, 142, 150, 334n14
Pietro, Fr. Salvatore Di, 351n14
Pinzón, Vicente, 122–23, 135, 346nn89–90
Pirates, privateers, and buccaneers: attacks on Bacalar, 249, 319*t*; on Belize coast to elude the Spanish, 79, 107, 137, 343n21; brigantines as favored boat, 347n116; Christian, 82; coastal towns abandoned due to, 135, 199, 246; slave raids, 75, 109, 124, 255; spread of disease to the Maya by, 109; use of terms, 339n159
Placencia, 119
Plants, 118–19, 190
Pochteca (Aztec merchants and traders), 45, 331n77
Politics: decentralization after the fall of Chichen Itza, 47; feudalism, 280; misinterpretation by the Spanish, 126; missionaries and conversion, 40, 87, 141–42, 145–46; relationship between the church and state, 106, 280, 343n14.

See also Spanish conquest, Maya
   resistance
Pope John XXII, 148
Pope Julius II, 148
Pope Leo X, 149
Pope Pius IV, 151
Portugal, 61, 149, 334n13
Potonchan, 32*i*
Pottery. *See* Ceramics
"Province": Belize and, 39; boundary
   considerations, 34, 35; relationship with
   cabacera system, 329n11; relationship
   with *chibal* system, 37; social hierarchy
   and, 46
—use of term: area of resource-exploi-
   tation rights, 38, 46, 332n84; area of
   single lineage, 46; jurisdiction of an
   archbishop, 354n96; by the Spanish, 30,
   37, 126, 329nn10,18
Puebla, Fr. Juan de la (Blessed John), 149
Puerta, Bishop Juan de la, 323*t*, 324*t*
Purépecha (language), 352–53n70
Pyramids, 168

Quintana Roo (modern Mexican state),
   13*i*, 47, 110, 118, 170, 195
Quiroga, Bishop Vasco de, 145

Race, mixed, 181, 194, 360–61n36
Refugees, 51, 255. *See also* Migration
Religion: African, 47, 73; afterlife, 267, 275,
   297, 299 (*see also* Christianity, heaven;
   Christianity, hell); Albigensians, 96;
   angels, 267, 271, 272*i*, 291–92, 301–4,
   302–4*i*; Assyrian-Babylonian, 291–92;
   a-theism, 65, 69; Aztec, 276; belief and
   the Heisenberg principle, 76–80; belief
   and tradition, 73–76; Christianity (*see*
   Bible; Christianity; Europe, Christianization); creation theme, 63; cults and
   idols, 80–85, 296; deities as cosmic
   symbols, 73, 90, 91; Donatism, 341n55;
   etymology of "religion," 69, 337n81;
   God, 94, 99, 100, 292, 301, 312–13,
   369n12; heaven (*see* Christianity,
   heaven); hell (*see* Christianity, hell); individuals and their impact, 151–56, 286;
   Islam, 74, 89, 93, 143; is there religion?,

   69–71; Judaism, 83, 84, 273, 291, 301,
   309, 339–40n184; magic, 310–11, 373–
   74n12; Manicheism, 341n55; Maya (*see*
   Maya pre-Columbian beliefs); miracles,
   271, 310; New Age, 91; offerings, 75,
   237, 242, 275, 294, 295, 306 (*see also*
   "Sacrifice," human); Pelagianism, 94,
   341n55; pilgrimages, 275, 296; prayer,
   81, 84, 305–6, 327n39; relationship with
   rituals, 66, 69, 75–76, 336n49; role in
   violence, warfare, and politics, 14, 40,
   312–13; sin, 267, 369n14, 370n42; snake-
   worship, 274–75; Ten Commandments,
   273, 369n14; what is religion?, and use
   of term, 9, 12, 64, 66–69, 80, 312–13;
   "world" and "nature," 73–74, 338n122;
   Zoroastrianism, 292
—academic research: bias and objectivity,
   65–66, 71, 76, 80, 183, 289, 296, 312–13;
   cultural influence in, 68–69, 70–71, 72,
   336nn68–69; five scholarly approaches
   to conversion, 288–91; interpretation of
   behavior, 76–78
—devils and demons: devil-worship,
   264, 335n32; etymology of "devil,"
   339–40n184; overview, 82–85, 226*i*,
   302*i*; perception of Maya imagery,
   263–72; pre-Christian remains as, 298;
   Satan with animal characteristics, 293;
   witches, 340n190
—paganism: associated with demons,
   84, 271; being pagan, 285–306; deities,
   78, 84, 106, 258, 301, 341n34; etymology of "pagan," 89; Maya, 90–92,
   285–306; roots of early Christianity, 78,
   82, 89–92, 106, 143, 156, 271, 278, 283;
   worldview, 283
"Religious conflict," 9
Religious conversion: academic research
   (*see* Religion, academic research); book
   burning, 207; context of apostolic
   intensity of the friars, 137–38, 144, 146,
   148–49, 152, 161; economic and political
   aspects, 40, 78, 87; ethnocentric bias
   in Spanish historical documents, 59,
   76, 85, 90–91, 288–91, 313; in Europe
   (*see* Europe, Christianization); gifts
   awarded, 22–23, 23*i*, 24*i*, 240, 327n50,

Religious conversion (*continued*)
366n13; how it was facilitated, 291–98;
as justification for conquest, 16, 84–85,
142, 279, 327n41; as matter of survival,
3, 78, 258–59; Maya maintenance even
in absence of Spanish authority, 3, 285,
299–306, 307; Mexico, 138, 141, 144–47,
328n63; by missionaries (*see* Missionaries); process of Christianization,
86–88, 155, 156, 282 (*see also* Christianity, as a veneer over pre-Columbian
beliefs); reconfigurations which accompany, 3; reinforced with imagery, 10,
81, 193, 272, 287, 290, 294–95, 367n64;
"religious change," 4, 75–76, 289–90;
scholarly approaches to writing about,
288–91; separation of the message
from the medium, 3, 156, 158–59;
syncretism, 72, 77, 80, 198; theaters
of conversion, 263, 369n1; timeframe
considerations, 282, 287; Yucatan, 82,
87, 139, 142, 144
—incomplete: and existing allegiances,
3; insincere, 92, 94, 152, 290–91; Maya
Christianity as a veneer, 16–18, 78–80,
198, 290; overview, 94–95
—Maya encounter and assimilation: Chel
lord, 140; choirmasters/sacristans (see
Maestros cantores); context for Belize,
137–38, 153–54, 164, 250, 283–84; historical connection to lord, 37; Lamanai
as a Christian community, 236–38; local culture and landscape, 156, 287–88,
296, 299; loss of native culture, 145,
207; in Manche Chol, 205, 249, 367n64;
monotheism and, 74–75, 84; overview,
3, 81–82, 198; pagan deities as symbols
or myths, 90–92; perception of Catholic saints, 75, 81–82, 276, 278, 299–301,
338n133; role of the church institution,
107, 298; timeframe, 282, 287; Tipu as
a Christian community, 237; *See also*
Missions, Belize
—Maya resistance or rejection: archaeological interpretation, 289–90; areas
which remained non-Christian, 164;
individual variations or experiences
of Christianity, 62–63, 77, 79–80, 102,

154–56, 258–59, 286–87, 371n9; lack of a
history of church authority, 281–82
Rio Copilco, 117, 344n50
Rituals: relationship with beliefs, 79–80,
306, 373n76; relationship with religion,
66, 69, 75–76, 336n49; warfare, 42
—Christian: baptism, 84, 88, 126, 142, 207,
275, 290; burial, 207; Communion, 153;
confession, 63, 245, 275, 366n13; exor-
cism, 84; Extreme Unction, 153; lighting
of candles, 126; Mass, 126, 142, 172,
179, 181, 183–84, 243; offerings, 75, 237,
242, 275, 294, 295; parallels with Maya
rituals, 275; rosary, 126, 233, 235*i*, 240;
veneration of images, 26*i*, 126, 193, 287,
304–5, 309–10, 367n64
—pre-Columbian: baptism, 275; in Christian churches, 16, 212–13; confession,
275; by Maya elites, 25, 300; offerings, 237, 242, 275, 306; parallels with
Christian rituals, 275; use of landscape,
287–88, 371n9
Roman Catholicism or Catholicism: apostolic reform, 148–49, 152; author's experience (*see* Graham, Elizabeth, Roman
Catholic background); Canon Law, 184,
225; Counter-Reformation, 150; crèche
scenes, 295; Deposit of Faith, 98–99,
100; doctrine and dogma, 94–97, 99,
298; doctrine of the Church, 86–100,
370n56; heresy and heretics, 83, 95, 106,
144, 148, 151, 298; "Holy Picture," 26*i*,
92; Jeronymites, 139, 159*i*, 324*t*, 351n19;
Magisterium, 95, 98, 99–100, 101;
New Spain, 117, 127, 328n63, 353n78;
novenas, 296, 372n43; orders (*see under*
Missionaries); overview, 74; "province"
as administrative district, 354n96; Tradition or Living Tradition, 99, 100, 101;
worldview, 9, 15, 16, 143–44
—bishops: Mendicants as, 146; overview,
323*t*, 324*t*; religious orders, 139, 353n88;
responsibilities, 240, 256; secular, 140,
142; of Yucatan, 139; *See also* Landa,
Bishop Diego de; Quiroga, Bishop
Vasco de; Zumárraga, Bishop Juan de
—catechism: author's experience, 15,
20–22; definitions from, 99–100; on

imagery, 309–10; for Indian use, by Zumárraga, 149–50; justification of Church's authority, 100–101; Lesson First, 86; for Maya children, 15, 243; taught by local Maya, 207, 243; written by Córdoba, 20, 328n63

—imagery: of angels, 291–92 (*see also* Art, depiction of angels); interpretation by the Maya, 10, 81; overview, 287; used in conversion, 193, 290, 367n64; veneration of saints, 14; *vs.* idolatry, 81, 272, 294–95, 304–6

—saints: cult in Latin Christianity, 78; imagery of, 10, 81, 193, 272, 287, 290, 294–95, 304–6, 367n64; Maya appropriation, 90–91, 301; perception by non-Catholics, 75, 81–82, 273, 338n133; role in Christianity, 299, 300; veneration of, 14, 295–97, 299; *See also specific saints*

Roman Empire or Roman period, 143, 155, 263, 280, 282–83, 300, 369n2

Rueda, Bishop Marcos Torres de, 324*t*

Sacalum, 244, 245

Sacpuy, 54*i*

Sacred places: Christian, 297, 300 (*see also* Churches); imagery and, 305–6; pre-Columbian, 16, 287–88, 297, 371n9; temples, 42, 43, 146*i*

"Sacrifice," human, 40–43

Sahcabchen, 250

St. Anthony, 294

St. Augustine, 162

St. Bonaventure's, Paterson, N. J., 296

St. Ciaran, 293

St. Cuthbert, 364n154

St. Dominic (Domingo Guzmán), 96, 148, 264, 293–94, 293*i*

St. Eustace, 294

St. Francis of Assisi: built first crèche scene, 295; monastic reform and, 264; Order of, 148; as a patron saint, 367n64; preaching to the birds, 292*i*, 293, 372n27; Rule of, 148, 155, 355n135, 366n13

St. Gall, 293

St. Giles, 294

St. Jerome, 337n81, 367n64

St. Lazarus, 292*i*, 293

St. Martha, 293*i*, 294

St. Martín de Porres, 26*i*, 294

St. Michael the archangel, 101, 302*i*, 303–4, 319*t*, 367n64

St. Patrick, 105–6, 266*i*

St. Paul, 155, 355n136

St. Paul the Hermit, 294

St. Thomas Aquinas, 264–65, 291, 369n12

Salazar, Bishop Gonzalo de, 323*t*

Salmanca de Bacalar. *See* Bacalar

Salt, 118, 119, 120, 197, 332n84, 345n67

Salvador, 134

Sandoval, Bishop Juan Cano, 324*t*

San Francisco, Bishop Juan de, 323*t*, 324*t*

San Juan, 118

San Juan Extramuros, 247

San Martín, Gregorio de, 126

San Pedro (church patron), 240–41

San Pedro (village), 118, 130

Santa Cruz, 118

Santa María, Fr. Juan de, 366n13

Santa Rita Corozal, 53*i*, 56, 58, 118, 130, 199

Santo Domingo, 20, 125, 126, 347n116

Sarteneja, 119

Scandella, Domenico "Menocchio," 62, 63, 64, 95, 335n24

Señorío (domain of a lord), 30, 33*i*, 34

Shark's teeth, 219, 220*i*

Shells: artifacts, 216*i*, 218, 233, 237, 242; depiction of anthropomorph emerging from, 265, 267, 268*i*, 269*i*; God Shells, 265–67

Sibun River, 129, 246, 368n69

Silk, 366n13

Slavery: anti-slavery Franciscan, 152; by the British, 109, 252, 255–56; by the Spanish, 122, 123, 130, 134, 152, 252

—raids or capture: Belize, 45, 75, 109, 123, 135, 252, 255; Central America, 122, 130, 134; overview, 1; during warfare, 42, 43; Yucatan coast, 130

Smoking, 271

Social issues: *chibal* (lineage or patronym group), 38; church as social hub, 168; as context for religion, 66–67, 74–75, 76,

Social issues (*continued*)
336n49; hierarchy, 45–46, 197, 332n80, 343n23; interaction due to maritime trade, 120–22; Maya social networks, 34, 35, 120–22, 127, 195, 348n123; mercantile class, Postclassic, 343n23; outsiders (*see* Cultural issues, cultural outsider; Cultural issues, "the Other"); religious conversion and, 87–88; segregation during church service, 180, 181–82, 183, 187; socially sanctioned killing, 40, 42, 275; social obligations and territory, 34, 35, 163–64

Soite, 246, 249, 317*t*, 318*t*, 319*t*, 360–61n36, 368n69

Solís, Juan de, 122–23, 135

Sorghum, 327n37

Sotuta, 32*i*, 347n109, 349n151

South America, 123, 139

"Spaniard," use of term, 61–62, 334–35n14

Spanish (language), 6, 328n63

Spanish Conquest: Aztecs (*see* Aztecs, conquest); "conquest" as an archaeological term, 28; Cortés *vs.* the Pachecos, 157; entradas, 160, 240, 249–52, 369n69; forced relocation of Maya, 252, 256–57; grants of Maya labor and tribute (see *Encomiendas*); justification for, 16, 29, 41, 43, 84–85, 142, 279, 327n41; knowledge of the coast, 122–24, 346n87, 347–48n116; lure of precious metals and fortune, 134; Maya coming to terms with Spanish presence, 203–7; Maya interregional communication about, 122, 129, 157; Mexico, 124, 133, 140; Pacheco conquest in 1544, 79, 142, 199; Peru, 131; phases, 132; Spanish documentation of (*see* Historical documents, Spanish); Yucatan, 107, 112, 124–33, 153, 156, 196

—administration: changing boundaries in colonial era, 111; congregations, 192, 205; definition of territorial boundaries, 34, 35–37, 125, 163–64; governing center of Belize (*see* Bacalar); integration of communities, 50; Maya ability to work with, 195; phases, 50–51; in Postclassic

period, 29, 328n5; reductions, 192–93, 205, 207, 224, 239–44

—Belize: end of Spanish colonial influence, 255–56; entrada of 1654 to 1656, 249–50, 368n69; entrada of 1678 to 1707, 250–52; relative autonomy of (*see* Belize, lack of sustained Spanish motivation)

—Maya resistance to: archaeological interpretation, 289–90; Belize, 128, 133, 164, 195, 204; call to gather, 246; in Campeche, 130; Christianity and (*see* Religious conversion, Maya resistance or rejection); by the Cupul, 349n151; Honduras, 349n165; importance of social linkages, 127, 348n123; by the Itza Maya, 17, 50–51, 244–45; rebellions of 1623 to 1624, 244–45; rebellions of 1638 to 1641, 17, 197, 212, 226, 246–49; refugees (*see* Migration, to escape Spanish rule); role of reformist Franciscan friars, 158–59; stalling tactics, 250; Tipu-Lamanai connection, 50; use of misinformation, 127, 128; Yucatan, 128–33, 204, 349n151

Stann Creek area, 119, 120, 123, 129, 130, 347–48n116

Stelae, 211*i*, 213–18, 248, 254, 363nn116,125

Stingray spine, 219, 220*i*

Stone: amber, 233; blades or points, 215*i*, 216*i*, 218, 219, 220*i*; jade, 213, 214*i*; jet, 24*i*, 216*i*, 233; trade in, 118, 120, 197

Sugar, 212, 254

Sututa, 32*i*

Tabasco, 110, 116, 121, 127, 132, 308, 345n77

Tah Itzá, 32*i*, 52, 53*i*, 245, 314*t*, 315*t*, 320*t*, 321*t*. See also Nohpeten

Taino (language), 332n80

Tamalcab, 53*i*, 170, 177, 357n15

Tarascan (peoples), 352–53n70

Tases, 32*i*

Tayasal, 54*i*

Teeth, 219, 220*i*, 233, 234

Tejero, Fr. Martín, 161, 248, 249, 317–19*t*, 367n64

Tekax, 160, 240, 316*t*

Temples, 42, 43, 146*i*

Tenochtitlan, 149, 172

Tepaneca (Aztec peoples), 36, 145, 147

Testera (Tastera), Fr. Jacobo de, 131, 132, 349nn159,166

Thompson, J. Eric S., 326n15

Thurible, 154, 154*i*, 233, 234*i*, 365n182

Tikal, 43, 45, 54*i*

Timber extraction, 252, 255

Tipu: attack by British for slaves, 255; attack by Mopan Maya, 252; background on archaeological research, 190–92; ceramics (*see* Ceramics, Tipu); as a Christian community, 237, 258–59; chronology, 49*t*; church (*see* Tipu church); Complex I, 55, 333n130; diet and health, 233–36; disjunction between archaeology and ethnohistory, 12–13; dwellings, 20*i*, 228, 229–30, 237, 241; excavation site, 189–91, 201–2, 202*i*, 362n71; geopolitics on the eve of Conquest, 47, 49, 52–56, 57, 58, 202–3; location, 12, 13*i*, 52, 53*i*, 54*i*, 189, 199; massacre of Maya Christian martyrs, 244–45, 246; Maya forced relocation from, 252, 256–57; Maya resistance and rebellion, 246–47, 249–50; no Spanish skeletons found, 195–96; overview, 17–18; plaza, 19*i*, 228–30; population, 240; post-1700 settlement, 256–57; rectory, 18, 228, 229; religious conversion, 153, 160, 229, 240–44, 251, 263, 282; Spanish fortification, 251–52; as a Spanish reduction center, 192–93, 198, 205, 207, 239–44; Spanish rule from Bacalar, 133, 240, 250; spelling of "Tipu," 190, 359–60n2; trade, 55, 157, 203; *vs.* Lamanai, 230–36, 365n172

—as an *encomienda*: beginning in 1544, 109, 199, 205, 224, 361n60; less monitored by the Spanish, 203; restructure in 1622, 239, 244

—cemetery: burial practices, 233, 234*i*, 300; excavation site, 232; jewelry artifacts from, 22–23, 23*i*, 24*i*, 327n50; metal artifacts, 365n184; number of individuals in, 196, 232, 327n50; post-Spanish use, 257; timeframe of use, 232

—regional relationships: Ceh Pech area, 242; the Itza, 250; Lamanai, 49–51, 198; Peten and Belize Valley, 51, 52, 333n111

Tipu church: built on unstable mud, 231; burial sites, 20*i*, 191, 327n50; construction techniques, 225, 231; excavation site, 191*i*, 225*i*; local Maya who looked after, 207; overview, 17; perspective reconstruction cutaway, 226*i*; as sacred ground, 297; to serve entire community, 180; stone slab pedestal, 228, 229*i*, 240–41, 365n160; *vs.* first Lamanai church, 230–32, 365n172

—architecture and layout: apsidal ends, 158, 178; blind sanctuary, 158, 179, 335n159; overview, 169*i*, 225–28, 225*i*, 364n152; ramada, 187, 230–32; single nave, 158, 178

Tixchel, 239, 366n13

Tixcocob, 142

Tizimin, 173, 178*i*

Tlaxcalans (Aztec peoples), 145

Tools: machetes and knives, 203, 240; marine resource procurement, 119; post-European contact changes, 121; stone blades or points, 215*i*, 216*i*, 218, 219, 220*i*

Topoxte, 54, 54*i*, 55

Toral, Alonso, 158, 160, 282, 314*t*

Toral, Bishop Francisco, 64, 158, 282, 323*t*, 324*t*

Trade and commerce: Belize-Guatemala, 116; Belize-Honduras, 116, 120, 308; Belize-Tabasco, 308; currency, 274; Honduras-Guatemala, 125; Lamanai, 44, 47, 128, 238, 343n23; networks extended to Yucatan, 22, 129, 195; Peten-Tipu, 55, 157, 203, 308; pre-Conquest Maya, 29; spiritual being Ek Chuah, 81

—coastal: expertise associated with, 119; of marine resources, 52, 119, 308; Maya trading stations, 128–30, 343n23; to Nohpeten, 157; overview, 108, 116–20; routes, 208, 333n111; tax, subsidy, or percentage from, 44–45; and topography, 128

Treaty of Madrid, 255

Triana, Fr. Francisco de, 317*t*, 318*t*

Tribute relationships: cultural interchange through, 58; goods and payments, 58, 197; grants of Maya labor (see *Encomiendas*); Lamanai, 58; Maya interpretation of baptism and, 290; overview, 34–37, 39, 58, 125, 163; post-Conquest shift in overlord, 37, 57, 196–97, 330n34; resource management *vs.* territorial acquisition, 38, 39; role of landscape, 37–38, 330n40; territories and boundaries, 329n18; Tipu, 55, 57, 58; tribute transfer under duress, 41, 42, 290, 331n59

Tulum, 57, 130, 218, 346–47n102

Turcios y Mendoza, Bishop Juan Escalante, 324*t*

Turneffe Atoll, 116, 130, 347–48n116

Tutul Xiu. *See* Mani/Tutul Xiu

Uatibal, 53*i*, 250

Uaymil: conquest, 128, 133, 153, 199; geopolitics on the eve of Conquest, 47; language and culture areas, 108*i*; maps, 32*i*, 33*i*; population, 203; resistance, 132, 133; second stage of conquest, 107

United States, 327n39, 331n56. *See also* Church of St. Michael the Archangel

Ursua, Gov., 250, 251, 321*t*

Valencia, Fr. Martín de, 145

Valentinus, 94–95

Valladolid, 110, 142, 240, 248

Vargas, Juan de, 246

Vera Cruz, Alonso de la, 152

Vessels. *See* Ceramics, vessels

Warfare: acquisition of slaves, 42, 43; arrowheads and spearheads, 252, 253*i*; capture, 40–42, 43, 128, 129, 245, 331n57; defeated rulers, 41–42, 331n62; interpretation of material culture and, 11–12; Iraq War, 331n56; justification, 40 (*see also* Spanish conquest, justification for); Maya on the eve of Conquest, 29, 40–43, 329n18; Maya strategies, 41; 245; ritualized, 42; role of religion, 14, 40; sanctioned killing, 40, 42–43, 275; Spanish strategies, 41, 133, 350n172; Tipu on the eve of Conquest, 55–56; use of dogs to kill Indians, 133, 350n172

Water, fresh, 123, 124, 137

Wildlife, 190

Worldview: effects on interpretation of art or iconography, 9–12, 325n1; effects on interpretation of geopolitical boundaries, 30, 34; intellectual flexibility and adaptable standpoint, 11, 326n11; landscape in the formation of, 258, 287–88; of missionaries, 14, 85, 143–44, 263–65, 283–84, 309; pagan, 283; religion and, 15, 16, 68, 87, 283

"Worship," use of term, 305

Xamanha, 127

Xcaret, 170, 186, 187

Xibum, 246

Xibun, 368n69

Xicalango, 127

Xiu (chibal), 38

Xiu (Maya peoples), 147, 333n124, 349n168

Xochimilca (Aztec peoples), 145

Yalain, 54*i*

Yaxha, 54*i*

Yich'aak Bahlam, 331n62

Yucatan: churches, 182, 183; climate, 195, 358n38; coastal areas (*see* Coast); conquest, 107, 112, 124–33, 153, 156, 196; disease, 109; early European contact, 124–25, 346–47n102, 347n106; *encomiendas*, 163; Franciscan missionaries, 144, 328n63, 150; Franciscan province of St. Joseph, 328n63; geopolitical units, pre-Conquest, 37–38; languages spoken, 121–22, 345n77; maps, 13*i*, 108*i*, 113–15*i*, 116; Maya resistance and rebellion, 128–31, 204, 349n151; modern, 110, 195; religious conversion, 87, 139, 142, 144, 156, 298; as a single empire, 39; trade network to, 22, 129, 195; use of term, 110

Yucatán (modern Mexican state), 6, 110, 195

Yucatán (province of the 1500s), 135

Yucatec (language), 41, 52, 55, 85, 121, 277

Yuknoon the Great, 331n62

Zacatan, 53*i*, 128, 246, 252, 368n69

Zacpeten, 54*i*, 55, 333n126

Zaczuz, 248, 249, 317*t*, 368n69

Zama, 346–47n102

Zumárraga, Bishop Juan de, 146, 149, 151

Elizabeth Graham is Professor of Mesoamerican Archaeology at the Institute of Archaeology, University College London. She has carried out archaeological investigations at Maya sites in Belize since 1973. Her research interests include coastal archaeology, Maya maritime commerce, the Maya collapse, Spanish contact, Neotropical urbanism, and the long-term impact of human activities on soils. She received her BA from the University of Rhode Island and her PhD from Cambridge University. She was born in Paterson, New Jersey, and now lives in London, U.K.

MAYA STUDIES
Edited by Diane Z. Chase and Arlen F. Chase

Salt: White Gold of the Ancient Maya, by Heather McKillop (2002)

Archaeology and Ethnohistory of Iximché, by C. Roger Nance, Stephen L. Whittington, and Barbara E. Borg (2003)

The Ancient Maya of the Belize Valley: Half a Century of Archaeological Research, edited by James F. Garber (2004; first paperback edition, 2011)

Unconquered Lacandon Maya: Ethnohistory and Archaeology of Indigenous Culture Change, by Joel W. Palka (2005)

Chocolate in Mesoamerica: A Cultural History of Cacao, edited by Cameron L. McNeil (2006; first paperback edition, 2009)

Maya Christians and Their Churches in Sixteenth-Century Belize, by Elizabeth Graham (2011; first paperback edition, 2020)

Chan: An Ancient Maya Farming Community, edited by Cynthia Robin (2012; first paperback edition, 2013)

Motul de San José: Politics, History, and Economy in a Classic Maya Polity, edited by Antonia E. Foias and Kitty F. Emery (2012; first paperback edition, 2015)

Ancient Maya Pottery: Classification, Analysis, and Interpretation, edited by James John Aimers (2013; first paperback edition, 2014)

Ancient Maya Political Dynamics, by Antonia E. Foias (2013; first paperback edition, 2014)

Ritual, Violence, and the Fall of the Classic Maya Kings, edited by Gyles Iannone, Brett A. Houk, and Sonja A. Schwake (2016; first paperback edition, 2018)

Perspectives on the Ancient Maya of Chetumal Bay, edited by Debra S. Walker (2016)

Maya E Groups: Calendars, Astronomy, and Urbanism in the Early Lowlands, edited by David A. Freidel, Arlen F. Chase, Anne S. Dowd, and Jerry Murdock (2017; first paperback edition, 2020)

War Owl Falling: Innovation, Creativity, and Culture Change in Ancient Maya Society, by Markus Eberl (2017)

Pathways to Complexity: A View from the Maya Lowlands, edited by M. Kathryn Brown and George J. Bey III (2018)

Water, Cacao, and the Early Maya of Chocolá, by Jonathan Kaplan and Federico Paredes Umaña (2018)

Maya Salt Works, by Heather McKillop (2019)

The Market for Mesoamerica: Reflections on the Sale of Pre-Columbian Antiquities, edited by Cara G. Tremain and Donna Yates (2019)

Migrations in Late Mesoamerica, edited by Christopher S. Beekman (2019)

Approaches to Monumental Landscapes of the Ancient Maya, edited by Brett A. Houk, Barbara Arroyo, and Terry G. Powis (2020)

The Real Business of Ancient Maya Economies: From Farmers' Fields to Rulers' Realms, edited by Marilyn A. Masson, David A. Freidel, and Arthur A. Demarest (2020)